James Martineau

Types Of Ethical Theory

Volume II

James Martineau

Types Of Ethical Theory
Volume II

ISBN/EAN: 9783741103483

Manufactured in Europe, USA, Canada, Australia, Japa

Cover: Foto ©Klaus-Uwe Gerhardt /pixelio.de

Manufactured and distributed by brebook publishing software (www.brebook.com)

James Martineau

Types Of Ethical Theory

Clarendon Press Series

TYPES OF ETHICAL THEORY

BY

JAMES MARTINEAU, D.D., S.T.D., D.C.L., LL.D.

LATE PRINCIPAL OF MANCHESTER NEW COLLEGE, LONDON

Κινεῖ πως πάντα τὸ ἐν ἡμῖν θεῖον. λόγου δ' ἀρχὴ οὐ λόγος, ἀλλά τι
κρεῖττον. τί οὖν ἂν κρεῖττον καὶ ἐπιστήμης εἴποι πλὴν θεός;
ARIST. ETH. EUD. VII xiv.

Third Edition, Revised

VOL. II

Oxford
AT THE CLARENDON PRESS
1898

[*All rights reserved*]

CONTENTS.

PART II. PSYCHOLOGICAL ETHICS.

INTRODUCTION.

	PAGE
I. Transition	1
II. Postulates Discussed	4

BOOK I. IDIOPSYCHOLOGICAL ETHICS.

	PAGE
CHAP. I. Fundamental Ethical Fact	18
i. Its Contents Developed	21
§ 1. Objects of Moral Judgment	21
§ 2. Mode of Moral Judgment	43
ii. Incidental Tests of the Theory of Conscience	59
CHAP. II. Theory of Prudence	70
i. Objects of Prudential Judgment	70
ii. Modifications by coexisting Moral Judgment	75
CHAP. III. Merit and Demerit	80
CHAP. IV. Nature of Moral Authority	99
i. Inadequate Interpretations Considered:	
§ 1. Bentham's	99
§ 2. Paley's	110
§ 3. Other accounts	114
ii. Whether Obligation can be Transcended	120
iii. How Prudence becomes Obligatory	125
CHAP. V. Springs of Action Classified. Psychological Order	129
i. Primary; how Distinguished	135
§ 1. Propensions: Organic Appetites; Animal Spontaneity	140
§ 2. Passions: Antipathy; Fear; Anger	141
§ 3. Affections: Parental; Social; Compassionate	144
§ 4. Sentiments: Wonder; Admiration; Reverence	151

CONTENTS.

Chap. V. Springs of Action, etc *(continued)*.   PAGE
  ii. Secondary Transformations, how Distinguished. . . 167
    § 1. Secondary Propensions: Love of Pleasure, Money, Power 169
    § 2. Secondary Passions: Malice, Vindictiveness; Suspiciousness 172
    § 3. Secondary Affections: Sentimentality . . . 177
    § 4. Secondary Sentiments: Self-culture; Æstheticism; Interest in Religion 177
  iii. Ulterior Compounds 182
  iv. Relation of Prudence and Conscience to Springs of Action 186

CHAP. VI. Springs of Action Classified. Moral Order 189
    § 1. Secondary Passions alone inadmissible . . . 189
    § 2. Appetites, Secondary and Primary. Animal spontaneity 193
    § 3. Love of Gain, relatively to the Primary Passions . 194
    § 4. Secondary Affections, relatively to the Primary Passions 200
    § 5. Place of both, relatively to the Love of Power . 205
    § 6. Love of Culture, relatively to the Love of Power. 211
    § 7. Primary Affections, relatively to Wonder and Admiration 215
    § 8. Primary Affections, *inter se* 218
    § 9 Supreme Place of Reverence 221
    § 10 How to estimate Mixed Incentives . . . 235
    § 11. Relations of Merit: Gratitude; Generosity; Justice 244
    § 12 Veracity 255
    § 13. Table of Springs of Action 265
    § 14. How far a Life must be chosen among these . 266
    § 15. Resulting Rule; compared with Bentham's . . 270

CHAP VII. Objections Considered 277
  INTRODUCTION 277
    § 1. Is the Love of Virtue among the Springs of Action? 279
    § 2. Intuitive Moralists do not agree as to
        A. Benevolence and Moral Sense . . . 285
        B. Self-love 288
        C. Imperative Claims of Justice 289
        D. Relative Claims of Intellectual Desires and Personal Affections 291
        E. Love of Fame and Love of Power . . 293
    § 3. Difficulty of Reading our Motives . . . 294
    § 4. The Rule reducible to that of 'Rational Benevolence' 298

BOOK II. HETERO-PSYCHOLOGICAL THEORIES.

	PAGE
BRANCH I. HEDONIST ETHICS	304
CHAP. I. Utilitarian Hedonism	304
i. Psychologically considered	304
§ 1. Expositions of Principles by Hobbes, Helvetius, Bentham, Mill	305
§ 2. Refinements introduced by Hartley, J S. Mill, and Bain	315
§ 3. Meanings given to the word 'Pleasure'.	319
§ 4. Passage to and from Disinterestedness	323
§ 5. Mill's Gradations of Quality in Pleasure	325
ii. Ethically considered	331
§ 1. From 'Each for Himself' to 'Each for All,'—No Road	331
§ 2. The Moral Sentiments as an Engine of Social Management	344
§ 3. Can General Rules bind against their *Raison d'être?*	353
CHAP. II Hedonism with Evolution	360
§ 1. Psychology, how Affected by the Idea of Evolution	360
§ 2. The Law of Evolution, sec. Darwin; sec. Spencer	367
§ 3. Spencer's Genesis of Ethics, and Conversion into Intuition	373
§ 4. The Theory Considered, as applied to Intellectual Apprehension	376
§ 5. As applied to Moral Judgment	390
§ 6. Hitches in the Evolutionary Deduction	393
§ 7. Conscience Developed into Social Consensus and Religion	401
§ 8. Objections to the Doctrine of Conscience considered	406
§ 9. Darwin's Explanation of Remorse	419
§ 10. Meaning of 'Higher' and 'Lower' in Evolution	422
BRANCH II. DIANOETIC ETHICS	425
CHAP. I. Cudworth	427
§ 1. Life, Personality, and Writings	427
§ 2. Outline of his Philosophy	437
A. Psychology	438
B. Ontology	445
C. Ethical Theory	451

	PAGE
CHAP. II. Clarke	459
§ 1. Life, Personality, and Writings	459
§ 2. Abstract and Estimate of his Doctrine	463
CHAP. III. Price	475
BRANCH III. ÆSTHETIC ETHICS	485
CHAP. I. Shaftesbury	487
§ 1. Life, Personality, and Writings	487
§ 2 Sketch of his Doctrine	492
§ 3. Appreciation of the Doctrine	504
CHAP. II. Hutcheson	514
§ 1. Life, Personality, and Writings	514
§ 2. Contents of his Doctrine	524
A. 'Sense' Defined. External Senses.	524
B Sense of Beauty	528
C. Moral Sense	536
D. Springs of Action	543
E. Optimist Estimate of Virtue	549
§ 3. Appreciation of the Doctrine	554
A. Relation of Benevolence and Self-love	555
B. Relation of Benevolence and Moral Sense	557
C. Want of Moral Gradation	561
D. Determinism	563
Conclusion	565
APPENDIX	569
INDEX	577

PART II.

PSYCHOLOGICAL ETHICS.

INTRODUCTION.

I. TRANSITION.

THE key to the ancient philosophy is found, as we have seen, in a distinction which our language does not enable us accurately to express: viz. between εἶναι and γίγνεσθαι,—Seyn and Werden,—absolute existence and relative phenomena. By unanimous agreement, the whole sphere of things was competed for by these sole claimants, and to adjust their respective rights constituted the great problem of the Hellenic schools. While Zeno and Parmenides put all their faith in the real ontological ground of the universe, and disparaged phenomena except as the manifestation of this, Protagoras made phenomena every thing, and denied that they opened a way to any ulterior region, and Plato and Aristotle vindicated, though in different ways, a place for both, and sought to define the relation between them. But, under every variety of doctrine, this twofold distribution,— into that which *ever is* and that which *transiently appears*,— was assumed as exhaustive and ultimate. It was moreover *omnipresent*, running through the whole realm of space and time, and reappearing in all objects. There was nowhere any separating line, and never any dividing date, on one side of which lay the eternal entities, while on the other were the successive phenomena; but both were blended in every nature, be it our own, or be it external to us. The same Divine element which constituted the beauty, truth, and goodness of the Cosmos, spread into the human mind and established there the conscious recognition of beauty, truth, and goodness. And the same series of phenomena which manifested itself in the sensible qualities of material things turned up in us under the form of the corresponding sensations. Thus, both members of the division crossed over from the world to man, or rather were continuous through all: the human being was but a part and member of the universe, sharing its mixed character, of ground and manifestation, and in no wise standing to it in any antithetic position.

The key to the modern philosophy is found in quite a different distinction, viz. that between the subjective and objective,—between the mind, as constituted seat and principle of thought, and the scene or data assigned it to think. To determine what belongs to the Ego and what to the non-Ego is the great problem of recent times: the answer to which is *idealistic,* or *realistic,* in proportion as it gives ascendency to the former or to the latter as the source of our cognitions. At the one extreme stands the doctrine which reduces our seeming universe to a mere phenomenon of one's self,—an appearance within us turned up by the living laws of our own mind. At the other extreme stands the doctrine which regards the self as a mere phenomenon of the universe,—a pulsation from the tide of reality breaking into consciousness. The former of these doctrines may succeed in completely disbelieving everything beyond the Ego, of which all else may be treated as the dream. but the latter cannot similarly annihilate the Self, and merge all belief of it in the objective world, the very doubt or denial of self being an assertion of self, and involving an act of logical suicide. Both, however, agree in attempting, from one of the poles of our knowledge, to extinguish the other, or at least to depreciate it as merely dependent and derivative, existing only as the reflection of the first. While

the one raises the Ego to autocracy, the other sinks it into
a necessary phenomenon. In this last light, it may be
regarded as determined into existence either from God, or
from Nature, according as we seek our ἀρχή in an ontological principle, or in physical laws If from God, we
take the pantheistic track, never far from Spinoza; if from
Nature, we take the pamphysical, within sight of Comte ·
in neither case leaving any room for the conditions of moral
agency, viz. a well-grounded distinction of better and worse,
a real authority in the former, and a free personality to give
or to refuse its rights. These varieties of unpsychological
theory we now leave behind.

In recent years another theory has come to the front,
with claims of so high an order, both from its internal
coherence and the external authority of great names, that
it is important to find the right place for its adequate discussion. Mr. Darwin in his 'Descent of Man,' Mr. Herbert
Spencer in his 'Data of Ethics,' and Mr. Leslie Stephen in
his 'Science of Ethics,' have successively and at last elaborately applied the doctrine of animal evolution in general,
and 'natural selection' in particular, to explain the genesis
of human Morals out of prior conditions that were *un*moral.
As the process which they describe is, in their view, only
the latest section of a development that indefinitely preceded all conscious life, their theory would seem to fall, no
less than Comte's, under the category of *Physical* systems,
and so to demand our next attention. But it differs from
the unpsychological schemes in this: that, though it links
the moral phenomena to the physical in one unbroken
chain of causality, it allows that we have *internal* cognisance
of the one, and external of the other; so that, while Nature ·
is *monistic*, our knowledge of it is *dualistic*. Hence, our
process of learning may start from either end: from the
cosmical laws of the outward sphere, or from introspective
study of ourselves; and while one expositor of the method
of evolution may work consecutively downward from physiological data, another may work analytically upwards from

psychological experience, laying aside the differences as he goes, till the moral becomes the useful, and the useful the pleasurable, and the pleasurable the necessary, and at last the two advocates meet half way and find that they are saying one and the same thing. We cannot say that a doctrine thus elaborated is 'unpsychological' On the contrary, it usually begins with the psychological preconception that, in the individual, the ethical sentiments are derivative from other feelings and ideas, e.g. of sympathy, of beauty, of self-regard, so as to be resolvable into a generic term; and is then extended, by help of some law of *heredity*, to the inward life of parents and ancestors, and turned out complete in the form of a hypothetical psychology for the race or a catena of races. How are we *to test* this imagined history? One condition is at all events indispensable; we must be sure of the ultimate phenomena, viz. the existing moral consciousness, of which this story undertakes to render account to pronounce upon the adequacy of the cause, we must accurately estimate the effect. Else, the causality, however truly put on record, may give account of the wrong thing. Since, therefore, we must carry with us a clear and correct insight into the contents of our present moral affections and beliefs, I shall not take up the consideration of the evolution doctrine, till we have scrutinised the phenomena to be evolved.

II. POSTULATES DISCUSSED.

1.

It must not, however, be supposed that the ethical conditions are fulfilled by merely crossing over into psychological theory. Egoistic doctrine also misses them, so long as it remains at its own centre, believes in nothing beyond the self, and lies under the disabilities of every system of Monism. Fichte's Idealism reduces moral obligation, as well as everything else, to a mere modification of Self; in making the mind universal lawgiver, makes it also *its own;* and thus dissipates the very essence of imperative authority, which ever implies a law above and beyond the nature summoned to obey it. Without objective conditions, the idea of *Duty* involves a contradiction, and its phraseology passes into an unmeaning figure of speech. Nothing can be *binding* to us that is not higher than we; and to speak of *one part of self imposing obligation on another part*,—of one impulse or affection playing, as it were, *the god* to another, —is to trifle with the real significance of the sentiments that speak within us. Conscience does not *frame* the law, it simply *reveals* the law, that holds us, and to make everything of the *disclosure* and nothing of the *thing disclosed*, is to affirm and to deny the revelation in the same breath. It is an inversion of moral truth to say, for instance, that honour is higher than appetite, *because* we feel it so; we feel it to be so, because it *is* so. This '*is*,' we know to be not contingent on our apprehension, not to arise from our constitution of faculty; but to be a reality irrespective of us, in adaptation to which our nature is constituted, and for recognition of which the faculty is given. A system, therefore, which disowns all reality outside the mind and resolves everything into a subjective dream, is not less inconsistent than the schemes we have examined with the necessary basis of an ethical philosophy. While those fail to provide the *subjective free power*, this excludes the *objective given conditions*, indispensable to the problems of a moral being. It is clear then that, in order to reach a real ground of obligation, it is not enough, though it is essential, to justify a psychological method against an unpsychological. It is further necessary that our psychology should be dualistic in its results, recognising, as in its doctrine of perception, so in its doctrine of conscience, both a *Self* and an *other than Self*. In perception, it is *Self and Nature:* in morals, it is *Self and God*, that stand face to face, in the subjective and objective antithesis. I am deeply persuaded that no monistic scheme, whether its starting-point be *Self*, or *Nature*, or *God*, can ever interpret, without distorting or expunging, the facts on which our nature and life are built; and whoever will take this clue in his hand, and try it patiently while exploring the labyrinth of speculative systems, will save himself, I believe, many a perilous entanglement, and at his very ingress possess a conception of its ground-plan and its paths which not many evince even at their egress.

What then, in accordance with this view, is the essence of a psychological method? (1) It not only assumes reflective self-knowledge to be possible, but gives it precedence, in ethical relations, over other knowledge, and proceeds thence into the scene around: and (2) it not only begins from the self-conscious man, as the better known, and treats the phenomena so found as genuine phenomena; but accepts also whatever these phenomena carry, and if they imply in their very nature certain objective assumptions, these reports, as contained within the known phenomena, it trusts as knowledge · in other words, it believes in the inner experiences not simply as appearances within us, but, where they offer testimony, as witnesses of realities without us. Adopting this method, we deny that in the cognisance of ourselves we are cognisant of nothing but ourselves, and maintain, on the contrary, that self could never be known except in the apprehension of what is not self. On these fundamental positions we must say a few explanatory words.

The possibility of psychological *self*-knowledge we have already sufficiently vindicated against the objections of Comte; and it is the less necessary to adduce any further plea on its behalf, because the objections against psychology cannot be stated except in psychological terms, or understood without appeal to that self-consciousness which they disparage Are we not continually *telling* our own thoughts and feelings and purposes? Then is it not ridiculous to assert that we *cannot know them?* and if we know them, it is assuredly not by outer testimony or any use of eyesight that we discern them, but by the inner vision of reflection. What then is the matter with this sort of apprehension? Are they not real *facts* that it shows us? Is it not *true* that the sense of shame is different from the sound of thunder, and the comparison of triangles unlike the aspiration of prayer? and if such things be true, is it of no consequence to notice them, and to lay out in order the several classes of mental phenomena according to their felt affinities? or would it be better to wipe out the distinctions that separate each affection of mind from all the rest, and blur into an indeterminate mess perception, reasoning, imagination, passion? Unless this be maintained, it must be allowed that *classification* of phenomena is practicable, beneficial, and inevitable, on the basis of self-consciousness. Will it then be contended, that at all events no *Law* can be discovered in this way? A law is simply a rule or ascertained order of succession among phenomena, whereby one becomes the premonitory sign of another. Is there then *no* rule of order among the phenomena of the mind? Can we assort them after their kinds, and yet not read and mark them in their series? Is there no traceable consecution in the process of reasoning? no intellectual method in scientific induction? no ground of expectation in the repetitions of habit? An inner mental order, legible to the same eye that deciphers the mental classes, it is clear there must be. It may or may not be true that it stands in relation to a corresponding outer and physiological order; but even this cannot be ascertained, unless both series are susceptible of separate notice and of mutual comparison. The relations of the inner phenomena *inter se* may or may not be of less importance than their relation, as a system, to another system in the physical world; but they must be open to self-observation, and be at least of *some* moment, secondary if not primary. So that, were psychology destined merely to adorn an ulterior triumph of physiology, and to bleed to death at the altar of materialism, it must at least be possible, and even actually exist. Meanwhile, it cannot be pretended that, to the inner system of relations as hitherto ascertained, any corresponding outer series has at present been discovered: such discovery, if conjecturally possible, is prospected and hypothetical; and we are left to the inner laws of purely mental succession which the psychologist registers, and which others, if they can, may supplement by future related disclosures.

The other position, that we psychologically know *more than ourselves*, may appear at first less modest and harder to sustain. Yet why should it do so? What is the lurking assumption that suggests a doubt of it? No other than this,—which is the standing snare of all philosophies,—that like alone can be known by like, thought by thinking, self-light by the self-eye. In accordance with this prejudice it is continually said that by our consciousness we learn nothing but our own 'ideas,'—that these are at least our only first-hand and secure possession,—that we can never tell how far an external world corresponds with these, or in what way things so dissimilar as the outer and the inner sphere can stand related to each other. So entirely gratuitous is this assumption that it needs only be challenged, to disappear; and the opposite thesis,—that what is known must be something unlike the knower,—would be at least as easy to defend. The first function of intelligence is to construe, not itself, but the scene in which it is placed, and apprehend its various contents; the eye sees, not vision, but light; the ear hears, not auscultation, but vibratory sounds; the mind naturally contemplates, less its own forms than the matter given it to mould; and, even in the effort of introspection, is obliged to stand off at some distance from the phenomenon it views, and impose a difference at least of space or time. Our *self*-knowledge is the secondary accompaniment of *other* knowledge; inseparable indeed from all our mental action, but not the end on which it is directed; proceeding *pari passu* with our advance among the objects and changes of the universe, but rather as the collateral shadow than as the main figure of the movement. That we *seem to ourselves* to have cognisance of external things is undeniable; and the more closely we study the phenomena of perception, the more does every possible plea disappear for distrust of this primary judgment.

INTRODUCTION.

Subjective knowledge and objective are correlative, and necessarily go together: the same act which reveals the Ego reveals no less the non-Ego; with the extinction of the one must vanish the other, and Nihilism ensue, which, like Silence, you break and destroy by affirming it. On the simple testimony of our perceptive faculty, then, we believe in both the perceived object and the perceiving self. This dual conviction rests on the axiom, that we must accept as veracious the immediate depositions of our own faculties, and that the postulates without which the mind cannot exert its activity at all possess the highest certainty. I ask no more than this on behalf of our ethical psychology. To the implicit beliefs secreted within our moral consciousness let precisely so much be conceded as we readily grant to the testimony of perception, and it will appear that, in learning ourselves, we discover also what is beyond and above ourselves. If then we can but state accurately the essence of the moral sentiments, and find the propositions they assume, we reach the last resorts of theoretic truth.

This statement may perhaps be met by a hypothetic difficulty. Suppose that the postulates of one faculty should turn out contradictory to those of another; what becomes of the reliance due to both? If, e.g. external observation should imply or exhibit *succession without causality;* and if the inner exercise of will should enforce belief in causality with or without succession; or, if the one should teach universal necessity, and the other human freedom; which has claim to our assent? I reply, each is to be dictator *in its own sphere*, and no further;—perception, among the objects of sense,—conscience, as to the conditions of duty: and for this plain reason, that neither has any jurisdiction or insight with regard to the realm of the other. Moral objects cannot be tasted, seen, or heard; nor are sapid, visible, audible objects appreciated by the moral sense. And hence it will turn out that the contradictions alleged between two separate faculties are only apparent: the postulates will really be distinct and never meet; the opposition will be merely negative, amounting not to a confutation, but to simple absence of evidence. Thus, the *causality* which volition compels us to believe, outward observation merely *fails to detect;* which is by no means wonderful, since it is not an object of sense at all. If we insist on framing our doctrine of causation out of the resources of external perception, and forcing the result on our internal experience;—if, that is, we derive it from the *negation of evidence*, instead of from its only positive store; we shall naturally obtain a mere empty and sceptical product, which our personal consciousness will really contradict. But the denial in such case is not put on any postulate of nature; it is put upon the privative doctrine, the vacancy which we have invented out of a mere silence of nature. The positive attestation of any faculty is to be held valid against doubts springing from the mere limitation and incompetency of another: as the ear is not qualified to contradict the eye, on the ground that the light is inaudible, neither is the perceptive power entitled to question the depositions of the moral, on the ground that the distinctions of right and wrong, and the essence of binding authority, cannot be conceived and expressed in terms of the senses. If this rule, which surely recommends itself to the common reason, be carefully observed, it will be found that our nature condemns us to no real contradiction; but only leaves us to struggle against that sluggish and sceptical repugnance with which each lower faculty is apt (without the smallest right) to regard the witness of the higher. Against *that* tendency, to invert the order of psychological jurisdiction and carry our doctrinal appeal from an upper court to an inferior,—in other words, to frame a philosophy, not from our insight but from our incapacity,—it is impossible to be too much on our guard. It is humiliating to think how large a proportion of the speculative systems of the world have arisen from no worthier a propension than that which tempts dulness to disbelieve the inspirations of art, ease to see no misery, and the animal faculties to treat as romance the thirst for ideal perfection.

In thus speaking of different 'faculties,' and distributing among them the possessions of the human mind, I have deliberately used the language of the older psychology, without, however, forgetting the criticism it receives from writers of the most recent school. So far as they simply protest against regarding the human mind as an aggregate of compartments or detached chambers in which, as in a government office, different agents exist for the transaction of different business, their criticism may serve a useful purpose, wherever it finds a person who needs it. But the departmental conception of our nature may be discarded in favour of either of two substitutes. The mind may be regarded as a mere sum-total of individual phenomena, to be counted, sorted into parcels, and regimented into series, so as to be in itself a multiplicity, simplified only by the observer. Or, it may be treated as a living unit, putting forth all its phenomena out of an identity of its own. If the older doctrine is rejected on behalf of the former, it is a change for the worse: if in the interest of the latter, I shall not deny that the end is good, though the means adopted are excessive and superfluous. Let us hear what is said, and endeavour to save the truth which it may contain:

'The theory,' says Mr. Leslie Stephen, 'of an autonomous or independent conscience, of a faculty which exists as a primitive and elementary instinct, and which is therefore incapable of further analysis, appears to be equally untenable. I agree, indeed, that here too we have an inaccurate statement of a highly important truth. The theory needs the less discussion because it is part of an obsolete form of speculation. Nothing is easier than to make out a list of separate faculties, and to call it a psychology. The plan had its negative advantages so far as it was in useful antithesis to an easy-going analysis, which was too quickly satisfied with explanations of complex mental phenomena. At the present day no one will deny the propriety of rigidly cross-examining the claims of any instinct to be an ultimate factor in the organisation. The difficulties which apply to all such speculations (as, for example, to the phrenological theory of separate organs) are not diminished in the case of conscience. When we take into account any theory of evolution, they are greatly increased[1].' This supercilious treatment of the principles of mental classification prevalent from the days of Plato to our own is the more remarkable, because its author himself is continually resorting to them with the mere change of the word 'Faculty' into '*Instinct:*' in the very next page he tells us what happens when 'a separate instinct' meets with 'a conflicting impulse;' and says that 'it is supreme within its own province, but has to struggle because it is part of a complex whole which can only act in one way at once, though accessible to a variety of stimuli.' The difference between a list of separate instincts and 'a list of separate faculties,' I am unable to appreciate. If no more is meant than that it must not be *assumed*, without rational warrant for the arrangement, no writer whose credit is worth preserving will be hurt by the imputation. I advert only to the sweeping attack upon the principle of classification. Whether *the conscience in particular* is entitled to rank among the separate faculties is quite another question, which will in due time present itself for consideration.

Meanwhile, what are we to understand by different 'Faculties' in our nature? *Not* any separate *agents*, though we are unavoidably led at times into language of personification, as when we attribute to them 'conflict,' 'struggle,' 'authority.' No one who has treated of the 'understanding,' of 'perception,' of 'imagination,' ever regarded these as distinct efficients shut up in coexistence within one containing being. Nor again, are we to understand merely seats of unlike *Feelings*. If it were only that '*Faculty*' always denotes an *activity*, '*Feeling*' a *passivity*, we should

[1] The Science of Ethics, chap. viii. l. 4, p. 314.

have to resort, in this field, to the word '*susceptibility.*' But, besides this, mere *unlikeness* is not sufficient to refer feelings to distinct heads of *susceptibility*. As felt, the taste of anchovy resembles that of a strawberry as little as it resembles the affection of blue colour; yet the two flavours are both referred to one head, and separated from vision as *another*. Had we to arrange the sensations purely by themselves, as they exist in consciousness, I see no reason to believe that they would fall into their present classes: the *fundamentum divisionis* in virtue of which they are visual, tactile, &c. is their mediation by different *local organs*, not their interior similarity and dissimilarity; and we reckon as many kinds of susceptibility as we have external causes and sensory organs of feeling.

Faculties (if the word be widened so as to cover the susceptibilities too) are distinct *functions* of one and the same organised *Self* or *Person:* *active*, if modes of the undivided personality; *passive*, if modes of the divided sensory organisation: giving us, in the latter case, what I have called *susceptibility;* in the former, *faculty* in the narrower and exacter meaning. But in all instances, the proper *subject*, that which acts or is acted on, is not the faculty or the organ, but the *Unitary Ego*. This Ego *knows;* the Ego *wills;* the Ego *feels:* three functions, of which the last alone is passive. For the distinction of these functions it is not necessary that they should never go together; and they are in fact usually, though not inflexibly, concomitant: thus, in *Perception* (of the external), the first and third are found; we not only *have a sensation*, but *gain a cognition:* not the eye and ear, but the νοῦς ὁρᾷ, νοῦς ἀκούει: in Attention, the first and second are found; for it is an act of *voluntary thinking*, from which is inseparable a cognition *of the object* as distinct from the *thinking subject* to which it is present: in suffering a *sudden hurt*, the second and third are found; for, along with the pain incurred (say from a blow or burn) is the protective act of either resisting the assault or retracting the limb. Were the whole of these concurrences invariable,—did they never shift in their partnerships and their intensities,—we should never disentangle the functions from each other. But their components, though hardly known to us as *solitary*, disengage themselves into view because they do not vary as each other: each in turn may immensely preponderate in some particular experience: I may be affected by a *feeling* so absorbing as virtually to submerge thought and action; or may *think* some arithmetical truth which in effect leaves will and feeling alone; or, under some instinctive impulse, may *act* without thinking, and at least with more or less of feeling through a considerable range. It is because the functions are thus capable both of meeting and of parting, that they come into view before us as different.

Hence it is easy to see what is meant by the *jurisdiction* or *province* of each. In the self-conscious nature of man, the *knowing* function is never absent from either of the other two, as it may be in the inferior animals. There can be, with us, no kind of *willing*, and no kind of *feeling*, that is wholly without cognition. But one kind of feeling,—be it of the senses, of the imagination, of the affections,—and one kind of volition,—be it of appetite, of compassion, of reverence,—may carry with it a certain part of the area of ideas; another may carry a different part. The portion allotted to it is its sphere of cognition, and measures *the range of its jurisdiction*. It is, therefore, quite conceivable that, however closely questioned, it may have nothing to say to the cognitions belonging to another field.

Now a true psychology will assign these several areas correctly; a false psychology will deny or mix them. And the test of correctness can be found only in the heterogeneous or homogeneous character of the ideas. The interpreter who claims a single source for ideas now plainly differentiated, must himself get rid of the differences by showing their genesis, as Mr. Darwin shows his tumbler and carrier and cropper pigeons to be actually sprung from the rock-pigeon; and must not fancy his case proved by a mere hypothetical psychology, asserting that conceptions now irreconcilably contrasted were once in their germ the same.

Whoever weighs these considerations will not be disposed to dismiss as unreliable the cautionary rule, that we are to limit the jurisdiction of each faculty to its own class of cases.

In order to apply this *cautela* with success, and repose a rightly graduated trust in the testimony of our several faculties, we must evidently be able to know them from each other. If we slur their boundaries, we confuse their authority and cannot assign to each its due. Still more, if we *deny* their boundaries, and by analytical legerdemain resolve the separated realms into one, we shall force a provincial law over a whole spiritual world, and at the end of our research find the truth dissipated which we held at the beginning. This is far from being an imaginary danger. There are several ethical systems, whose authors commence from a psychological starting-point, and are willing to accept the answers delivered in to our self-interrogation; but which, by some false turn in the examination, elicit misleading replies, and confound the identity of our mental phenomena. They make out perhaps to their own satisfaction, that the *moral* differences which they are engaged in cross-questioning are only *sensational* differences under skilful disguise; or, it may be, *intellectual* differences in an emotional form; or, again, *æsthetic* differences brought with an *alias* into court. Should such suspicion be well founded, it evidently affects most seriously the weight of the testimony given. With their disguise the witnesses lose also the authority which it lent to them, and descend to the level of the real character detected in them. If the conscience is but the dressed dish of some fine *cuisine*, if you can actually exhibit it simmering in the saucepan of pleasure and pain, the decorous shape into which it sets, ere it appears at table, cannot alter its nature or make it more than its ingredients; its rights drop down to the claims of Sensation, beyond which all is garnish and pretence. If it be, as others insist, only the scientific Understanding in a judicial mask, then, when its features are laid bare, they look at us with the logical persuasiveness of demonstration or probability: the right and wrong becomes simply the true and false, and should be regarded with no dissimilar affection. If,—once more,—it be only the Artist-faculty applied to the voluntary life of men, the imaginative contemplation of ideals,—then are the claims of *Righteousness* simply those of *Beauty;* the difference is abolished between the ἀγαθόν and the καλόν; and we should aspire to a pure and just mind on the same grounds that make us wish for a comely person. If these results fail to satisfy the whole feeling of which they profess to display the contents, it becomes important to show the fallacy of all such delusive equivalents, and, by vindicating the independent character of our moral perceptions, to rescue them from alien control, and justify the sense of higher and even supreme authority which they carry with them.

Thus does ethical theory on all sides involve psychological discrimination. Entering on this process, we might follow either of two methods. We might first review the several attempts to evolve the moral from the unmoral phenomena of our nature; prepared either to rest in any one of them that may really fulfil its promise; or, in case they should all fail, to invite the conscience itself to declare *its own psychology*. Or, we might invert this order: having first defined the inner facts of conscience itself, with the best precision we can attain, we might then compare with the *Idiopsychological Ethics*, so obtained, the several attempts to find the phenomena under *other categories*, by advocates of this or that scheme of *Heteropsychological Ethics*. The latter arrangement has the decisive advantage of compelling us, at the outset, to visit the moral consciousness in its own home, to look it full in the face, and take distinct notes of the story it tells of itself. And not till we have thus gained a definite intimacy with its real contents, can we have any just measure of aberration by which to try the claims of professed equivalents. I propose, therefore, to hear, in the first instance, what the Moral Sentiment has to say of its own experience; and then, to let other faculties advance each its special pretensions to be the original patentee and source of supply. Thus will the Idiopsychological Ethics immediately follow the Unpsychological which we have left behind, and precede the Heteropsychological which remain for notice; with the effect of placing the positive construction of doctrine at the centre, midway between two wings of critical analysis. The theories inviting examination under the final head are fairly reducible to three. The scheme of Epicurus and Bentham, which elicits the moral nature from the sentient; that of Cudworth, Clarke, and Price, which makes it a dependency on the rational; that of Shaftesbury and Hutcheson, which identifies it with the æsthetic, practically exhaust the varieties of doctrine; all others being mixtures or modifications of these leading types. For, besides the sensitive, the cognitive, and the admiring capacities of the mind, there exists no other into which the ethical can be resolved.

BOOK I.

IDIOPSYCHOLOGICAL ETHICS.

CHAPTER I.

FUNDAMENTAL ETHICAL FACT.

THE broad fact, stated in its unanalysed form, of which we have to find the interpretation, is this: that, distinctively as men, we have an irresistible tendency to *approve and disapprove*, to pass judgments of right and wrong. Wherever approbation falls, there we cannot help recognising *merit:* wherever disapprobation, *demerit.* To the former we are impelled to assign honour and such external good as may express our sympathy, and to feel that no less than this is due: to the latter we award disgrace and such external ill as may mark our antipathy, with the consciousness that we are not only entitled but constrained to this infliction. So *habitual* is this manner of thinking, that the very word in which we sum up its contents,—the word *Morals*,—means *habits, customs;* and so does the Greek word *Ethics;* and so the German, *Sitten.* These terms, no doubt, might be accounted for in either of two modes: as expressing simply what has happened to become usage, and merely on that account is valued and insisted on by us; or, as expressing that which, being insisted on by the inner demand of human nature, is exacted from us all and *made into our usage*. Between these opposite orders of interpretation we can have no difficulty in deciding, if we consider: (1) that the *customs* of a race can never be treated as fortuitous data, out of which, as already *there*, the most essential characteristics and affections spring; but must themselves be the outward product and manifestation of the inner life, and give the most accurate determination of its form; and (2) that, as if in protest against any identification of morality with mere *customariness*, the words which begin together part company at the sight of *customs that are immoral;* and as soon as the evil we condemn ceases to be exceptional,—as soon as we encounter the shock of an *established wickedness*,—we refuse to give it the name consecrated to the prior usages, and condemn it as an offence. Nor is it to our feeling anything less than monstrous to maintain, that what we call falsehood or selfishness could, by any multiplication or perpetuity, change its character, and in becoming *usual*, became also *moral*. It is, therefore, because the sentiments of right and wrong are the *characteristics of human nature*, that the system of action which they call up receives the name of *Mores*, or *established ways*.

Language is the great confessional of the human heart, and betrays, by its abiding record, many a natural feeling which would escape our artificial inspection; and it is better worth interrogating than the mixed product of our spontaneous life and conventional opinion. And the fundamental fact to which we are referring receives further light from another class of terms, in which we characterise it from within instead of from without, and speak of it as it is felt in itself, rather than as it looks in its effects. As a spectator of men on a theatre of character, I speak of their *Morals;* as an agent, uttering the corresponding consciousness secreted at my own centre, I speak of *my Duty*. The word, I need not say, expresses that there is something which is *due* from me,—which I *owe*,—which I *ought* to do. Nor perhaps is it insignificant, that the *tenses* of this verb have lost their distinction, and *one* alone, and that the past, is made to serve for all; as if to show that obligation escapes the conditions of time, and is less a phenomenon than an essential and eternal reality, which, however manifested at the moment, is not new to it. In any case, the word expresses the sense we have of a *debt* which others have *a right to demand* from us, and which we are *bound* to pay. And here we have another term, still more expressive of the inward feeling characteristic of a moral being there is, it seems, something that *binds*, —in Latin, *obliges* us,—puts a restraint on the direction of our will, yet not an outward restraint upon its power, but an interior restraint from shame and reverence. The same meaning may be found in all the language of law and ethics: within, a *binding*,—without, a *rule of usage*. I am aware that these subjective words denoting *obligation* might be explained away, by the same process of inversion already applied to the notion of customs. It might be said that men, having set up a usage, enforce it upon each separate agent, and tie him down to its observance; and that this external necessity put upon him is all that the word Duty originally expressed. The question involved in this evasion must be reserved for future treatment. At present I will only remark that it is a mere hypothetical artifice, to explain the individual's sense of inner obligation by the social imposition of an outer constraint; that, to our actual consciousness, the authority of duty *seems* to be independent of what the world may say of us or do to us; and that it is at least as plausible to maintain, that the law we impose on others is the externalisation of that which overawes ourselves, as *vice versâ*. The truth is, I apprehend, that both factors, the felt inner binding on ourselves, and the enacted outer restraint upon our fellows, are parallel and concurrent expressions of the same nature; neither is before or after the other; and so long as we dispute whether it is the individual constitution that makes the world, or the world that makes the individual constitution, the controversy will spin an endless round. The action and reaction are infinite; and the real question is, how is constituted, and with what inspiration is endowed, that *humanity* which has its unity and completeness, not in the lonely mind, but only in the *individuals of a kind*, raised by their whole system of relations into types of the nature which they represent.

i. ITS CONTENTS DEVELOPED.

§ 1. *Objects of Moral Judgment.*

With a view to determine the precise significance of this general fact, let us notice, in the first place, what are the *objects* on which our moral judgment directs itself; and where, on the other hand, its sphere terminates. *What is it that we judge?*

(1) Self-evidently, it is *persons* exclusively, and not *things*, that we approve or condemn. The mere *given objects* of nature, or the *fabricated products* of art,—the rock, the stream, the star; or the house, the ship, the lamp,—are perfectly indifferent to the conscience; and though they may become the centres of various feelings, we recognise the absurdity of applying to them epithets distinctly ethical. If ever we seem to invest them with such predicates, it is because for the moment we look beyond their simply physical aspect, and regard them as the expression of some Mind. If the rock is *stern*, if the stream is *joyous*, if the star is *mild*, it is because the inner heart of nature is felt to speak through them, and hold communion with us; and only in proportion as we lift the external world into this *personal* element, can such language appear justified. Once let utter negation be put upon this personal element, and the universe appear before us as without an inner meaning, as a mere play of fatalistic forces, and this phraseology loses all truth; and poetry, to whose very essence it belongs, becomes as much the indulgence of illusion as the child's dialogue with her dolls. That we give these words to things, and then first feel their true nature struck, only proves how ready we are to refer back all things to a personal Being behind them. It is the same, only yet more

obviously, when we attach terms of moral judgment to the products of art. To *approve* a house, to *condemn* a ship, is to pronounce upon a fitness or unfitness for a given end; and whatever semblance of moral sentiment the words carry is directed on the skill and faithfulness of the human producer or possessor. Even *admiration*, though not a simply moral feeling, always requires the presence, secret or open, of some living mind on which to fasten; and though often addressing itself to the outer face of things, is really moved by the spirit which they seem to manifest. What else means the memorable parody of Comte on the Hebrew hymn, 'The heavens declare the glory of God,'— viz. that the only glory they declare is *that of Newton and Laplace?* i. e. the heavens themselves, as a physical splendour and infinitude, have nothing glorious to say to us: first when brought into contact with *some mind*, have they significance to move us; and if they represent to us *no prior and inner mind* whose eternal thoughts they hang aloft, they must wait for the genius of some *outward observer and interpreter* ere they can mean anything sublime. This ingenuous confession of the great 'High Priest of Humanity' agrees precisely with the principle laid down in the following striking passage of Friedrich Heinrich Jacobi: '*Intending Thought* it is that makes the difference between a true God and Fate. It is inseparable from Reason, and Reason from it. Nay, it is identical with Mind; and only to the expression of Mind do the feelings answer which are its witness in ourselves,—of admiration, reverence, love. We may indeed pronounce an object beautiful or perfect without first knowing how it came about, whether with foresight or not; but the power whereby it came about we cannot admire, if its product has been set up without thought and intending forecast, in virtue of mere laws of necessitating Nature. Even the glory and majesty of the heavens, which bow down the childlike man in kneeling worship, no longer subdue the scientific soul aware of the mechanism that gives and maintains the motion of these bodies, and even moulded them as they are. Whatever wonder he feels is not at the object itself, infinite as it is, but only at the human intellect which, in a Copernicus, Gassendi, Kepler, Newton, Laplace, has been able to plant itself above the object, to kill out wonder by knowledge, to empty heaven of its gods, and disenchant the universe.'

'But even this admiration, the only remnant spared to the scientific intelligence, would disappear, if some future Hartley, Darwin, Condillac, or Bonnet, were to exhibit to us, with any real success, a mechanism of the human mind as comprehensive, reasonable, and luminous as the Newtonian mechanism of the heavens. Art, science however high, virtue of any kind, we could no longer treat with genuine and thoughtful reverence, no longer look up to as sublime, or contemplate with adoring homage.'

'We might still indeed, even then, be sensibly moved, nay, stirred with an emotion amounting to rapture, by the works and deeds of the heroes of mankind,—the life of a Socrates and Epaminondas, the science of a Plato and Leibniz, the poetical and plastic representations of a Homer, Sophocles, and Phidias; just as even the most accomplished pupil of a Newton or Laplace might still possibly be touched and stirred with pleasurable emotion by the sensible aspect of the starry heaven. Only, no question must then be asked about the *rationale* of such emotion; for Reflection could not fail to answer, "You are but befooled like a child; when will you learn that Wonder is only and always a daughter of Ignorance[1]?"'

Of this general principle we need at present but one of the numerous applications. The approbation or disapprobation which we feel towards human actions is directed upon them as *personal phenomena*; and if this condition failed, would disappear, though they might still, as natural causes, be instrumental in producing much good or ill. Their moral character goes forward with them out of the person; and is not reflected back upon them from their

[1] Jacobi's Werke, Vol. II. Vorrede, pp. 51-55.

effects. Benefit and mischief are in themselves wholly characterless; and we neither applaud the gold mine, nor blame the destructive storm.

(2) It follows, that what we judge is always the *inner spring* of an action, as distinguished from its outward operation. For, whatever else may be implied in its being a personal phenomenon, this at least is involved, that it is issued by the mind, and has its dynamic source there; and on that source it is, accordingly, that our verdict is pronounced. This is expressly admitted by Mr. Herbert Spencer, who says: 'Every moment we pass instantly from men's perceived actions to the motives implied by them; and so are led to formulate these actions in mental terms rather than in bodily terms. *Thoughts and feelings* are referred to when we speak of any one's deeds with praise or blame; *not* those outer manifestations which reveal the thoughts and feelings. Hence we become oblivious of the truth that conduct, as actually experienced, consists of changes recognised by touch, sight, hearing [1].'

With not less emphasis does Mr. Leslie Stephen lay down the same rule. 'The clear enunciation of one principle,' he remarks, 'seems to be a characteristic of all great moral revelations. The recognition amounts almost to a discovery, and would seem to mark the point at which the moral code first becomes distinctly separated from other codes. It may be briefly expressed in the phrase that *morality is internal.* The moral law, we may say, has to be expressed in the form, "*Be* this," not in the form, "*Do* this." *The possibility of expressing any rule in this form may be regarded as deciding whether it can or cannot have a distinctly moral character*[2].' Again he says: 'A genuine moral law distinguishes classes of conduct, not according to external circumstances, but according to the motives involved'; and, therefore, when the conformity to the law is only external, it is more proper to say that it is not con-

---

[1] Data of Ethics, chap. v. § 24, p. 64.
[2] Science of Ethics, chap. iv. § 16, p. 155.

formity at all[1].' Yet another pregnant sentence, 'Virtue implies a certain *organisation of the instincts*[2],' assumes, it is evident, the *Ethics of motive*, as distinguished from the *Ethics of action*.

From moralists of a far different school the same witness comes: the Hegelian moralist, Mr. F. H. Bradley, tells us: 'Morality has not to do immediately with the outer results of the Will:' 'acts, so far as they spring from the good will, are good:' 'what issues from a good character must likewise be morally good[3].' And, with equal distinctness, Professor Green insists that 'It is not by the outward form that we know what moral action is. We know it, so to speak, on the inner side. We know what it is in relation to us, the agents; what it is as our expression. Only thus indeed do we know it at all.' And so 'it remains that *self-reflection* is the only possible method of learning what is the inner man or mind that our action expresses; in other words, what that action really is.' 'Without it,' he adds, 'the customary expressions of moral consciousness in use among men,' and 'the institutions in which they have embodied their ideas or ideals of permanent good,' would be unmeaning, and 'have nothing to tell[4].'

That these testimonies, flowing in from various sides, meet upon a real truth is evident from a very simple analysis. The word 'action' is a word of complex meaning, taking in the whole process from the first stir of origination in the agent's mind to the last pulsation of visible effect in the world. James Mill is fond of laying out its elements into three stages: (1) the sentiments whence it springs; (2) the muscular movement in which it visibly consists; (3) the consequences in which it issues. Of these, cut off the first, and the other two lose all their moral quality; the muscular movement becomes a spasm or

---

[1] Science of Ethics, chap. vii. § 13, p. 277.
[2] Ibid. § 36, p. 302.
[3] F. H. Bradley's Ethical Studies, pp. 207, 208.
[4] Prolegomena to Ethics, Book II, chap. i. §§ 93, 94, 95, pp. 97, 98.

sleep-walking; the consequences become natural phenomena, pleasant like fine weather, or terrible like an incursion of wild beasts. But cut off the other two, and in reserving the first alone, you save the moral quality entire: though paralysis should bar the passage into outer realisation, and intercept the consequences at their birth, still the personal record contains a new act, if only the inner mandate has been issued. The moment which completes the mental antecedents touches the character with a clearer purity or a fresh stain; nor can any hindrance, by simply stopping execution, wipe out the light or shade: else would guilt return to innocence by being frustrated, and goodness go for nothing when it strives in vain. This principle carries its own evidence with it, and neither requires nor admits of further proof. Two remarks only will I make respecting it: (1) It is a characteristic of the Christian ethics, and finds its most solemn expression in the Sermon on the Mount, where the eye of lust and the heart of hate are called to account with the adulterer and the murderer; and reappears, though lifted into a region higher than the ethical, in the doctrine of justification by faith, which, by a simple inward affection of the soul, establishes reconciled relations between the broken performances of man and the infinite holiness of God. (2) It is directly opposed to the maxim, that the only value of good affections is for the production of good actions:—a maxim which is a just rebuke to idle and barren good affections as compared with the healthy and fruitful, but which becomes monstrously false when it demands not only inward creative energy, but outward opportunity and success, and treats with slight even an intense fidelity and love, because its field of life is small, and its harvest for the world is scanty. Instead of measuring the worth of goodness by the scale of its external benefits, our rule requires that we attach no *moral value* to these benefits, except as signs and exponents of the goodness whence they spring; and graduate our approval by the purity of the source, not by the magnitude of the result.

Here, therefore, we touch upon an essential distinction between the Christian and the Utilitarian ethics; and confidently claim for the former the verdict of our moral consciousness.

(3) If we have thus far advanced upon safe ground, we are now in a position to answer a question which, more perhaps than any other, divides philosophic opinion. *Whom do we first judge?* ourselves, or others? In what school do our moral sentiments learn their earliest lesson? in that of reflection? or of observation? The great majority of English moralists, with wide differences of theory in other respects, concur in saying that we begin with estimating others, and then transfer the habit to ourselves. They seem to assume that, without something external to look at and to act upon us through our senses, we should be standing in the dark and have nothing to judge. When we have seen in a neighbour how a certain action sits upon the human character, we discover (says Adam Smith) whether it will be becoming in ourselves; and did we not use mankind as a sort of moral clothes-horse, to try on our actor's dress, we should never know how to play our part. Bentham and James Mill rest the same general answer on a different ground. We first apply moral terms, they tell us, to those acts of others which directly benefit us; next, to those which, though benefiting a stranger, we like to encourage for the chance of their being some time repeated upon us; and, last of all, when these habits have furnished us with general rules of praise and blame, to acts of our own, falling under the analogies we have established. Even the moral-sense philosophers incline to represent the objects of moral judgment as present before us, like works of art before the critic's eye; and conceive of the judicial glance as thrown *outward* and engaged upon an image given in perception or imagination. Our living guides repeat the same story. With Mr. Herbert Spencer[1], the 'moral consciousness' is wholly a social product, due to the observed

---
[1] Data of Ethics, chap. vii. § 44, p. 120.

or experienced consequences of executed action; and preeminently, among those consequences, to the *penalties*, of public opinion, of law, of Divine retribution, supposed to follow upon prohibited forms of conduct: and '*since with the restraints thus generated is always joined the thought of external coercion, there arises the notion of Obligation:*'— a notion which he afterwards curiously interprets as equivalent to *the indispensableness of any means towards a given end*,—the means being that which we are *obliged* to employ, if we would secure the end[1]. For instance, if a carnivorous animal is to live, it must eat: if it is to eat, it must kill: if kill, it must catch; if catch, it must chase: and so, it is under an obligation to do each of these things. To this generic idea of obligation, the differentia 'Moral' is added on, when it is concerned with the means of avoiding the political, social, and religious penalties attached to certain conduct. The 'moral consciousness' is thus the self-application of a lesson learned *ab extra*.

The expounders of the evolutionary hypothesis seem indeed (for reasons more conceivable than cogent), to regard this order of derivation as inseparable from their scheme: we are not therefore surprised to find Mr. Stephen saying, 'The Moral Sense is, according to me, a product of the social factor[2]:' and again, 'The conscience is the utterance of the public spirit of the race, ordering us to obey the primary condition of its welfare[3].' And yet I find passages in which his psychological feeling, no longer guarded and restrained by the watchdogs of a theory, breaks bounds and escapes into another field. Accounting, e.g. for the disapproving sentiment with which we visit an observed indulgence of appetite, he remarks that 'the disgust which we feel for the excesses of others is *a direct result of the correlative impulse in ourselves*. We are shocked by the excess of the glutton, because our imagination is revolted

---

[1] Data of Ethics, chap. ix. § 58, pp. 159, 160.
[2] Science of Ethics, chap. ix. § 17, p. 372.
[3] Ibid. chap. viii. § 39, pp. 350, 351.

when we put ourselves in his place, and fancy ourselves consuming the same monstrous masses of food[1].' If this be so, the *self-revolting* is the earlier and the better known, the given rule for any possible judgment of him: it is the inward consciousness that supplies the outward criticism, and not the outward critics that make us a present of our moral consciousness. This lands us precisely on the truth that I am concerned to uphold, in the face, unfortunately, of the general consensus of modern English opinion.

But, unless we have already gone astray in our analysis, the current opinion cannot be correct. That in which we discern the moral quality is, we have found, the *inner spring of action*; and this is not apprehensible by any external observation, but can be known, in the first instance, only by internal self-consciousness. Of other men's actions the visible part, which follows on the mental antecedents, is the first element that comes before our view; all that precedes is beyond the reach of eye and ear, and is read off only by inference from the external sign. That sign would be unmeaning to us, were not the thing signified already familiar to us by our own inner experience. Of the passion which we have felt, especially of our own characteristic affections and admirations, we quickly catch the symptoms in another; and through the medium of word, or look, or gesture we pass into intuitive sympathy with it. But in proportion as the habitual feelings and tastes of the society around us belong to a world other than our own, do the manners which express them become unintelligible or repulsive. Without susceptibility to love, how stupidly should we stare at the kiss of the mother to the child! without openness to sorrow, at the prostrate and sobbing mourner! without sense of religion, at the clasped hands of prayer! Kindred natures alone can interpret one another; obviously, because they have in themselves the living key to the hieroglyphics of emotion. The very mistakes which they

---

[1] Science of Ethics, chap. v. § 28, p. 201.

are most liable to make afford a converse evidence of the rule: for these mistakes are invariably examples of the proverbial maxim, that *men judge others by themselves*. Whoever is prone to suspect underhand dealings in his neighbour, is little likely to be of transparent nature himself; and the sceptical sneer at disinterestedness is not frequent on the countenance of the unselfish. The presumptions which we carry into the phenomena of life, and by which we construe them, are all drawn from within; such as we are, such will our universe be. Criticism then, like charity, 'begins at home,' and finds, in our own consciousness, the prototypes of all the sentiments and springs of action which it re-detects and appreciates abroad. And censoriousness is a secondary artifice by which we suborn a true light to give us a false vision; it is conscience, as it were, turned inside out, and so looking past the flaws in its instrument as to mistake them for shadows on the world.

It is necessary, however, to guard this general doctrine from a misapprehension to which it is easily exposed. In saying that our moral estimates originate in self-reflection, I do not mean to maintain that a solitary human being could have them; or that there are two appreciable stages in our actual experience, first of self-judgment, and then, after an interval, of judgment directed upon others. Doubtless, the presence of others is indispensable to the development of this part of our nature; not less than external physical objects are requisite to the unfolding of our perceptive power. But in neither case does this circumstance entitle the objective factor to any priority, of time, or of causality. In both instances, it is the means of discovering us to ourselves: without material things around us we should not detect the Ego of Sense; nor, without human persons before us, the Ego of Conscience. The transition from consciousness to self-consciousness, the conversion of implicit into explicit experience, always requires the crossing lines of action and reaction between the inner and the outer world. But even in perception, the two discoveries, of *ourselves* and of our *objects*, are simultaneous, and are given with equipoise of assurance; so that there is no ground for disputing the originality of the egoistic term. And in the moral case there is a difference which partially breaks the analogy and gives, instead of equipoise, a clear preponderance to the subjective side. It is this: In perception, the two things known, viz. the sensations of the self and the properties of the body, are *heterogeneous*, and neither cognition owes anything to analogy with the other; there is no common predicate which you can equally affirm of an inch cube and of my consciousness in perceiving it: the affection of my faculty has not dimension, shape, or colour, like the object. The two cognitions are, therefore, independent reciprocals, and not duplicates. It is otherwise when I learn my own moral or human affection in the mirror of a kindred nature, and from the natural language of a brother man read off at once his passion and my own. Here, the very essence of the phenomenon lies in its duplication; my fellow is merely myself over again, and is, simply on that account, understood by me at a glance; though it is also true that, had it not been for this externalisation of my affection in a second personality, it might have passed through me like a dream, without recognition or appreciation. The visible life of my own *double* throws off a light both ways,—on *his* inner nature which it immediately expresses, and on *mine* which it mediately exhibits and repeats; and there is certainly something very wonderful in that sympathetic affinity between one mind and another which makes mutual intelligence a thing of lightning, and interprets natural signs that have never been learned. It seems as if a feeling was never understood till acted out in open day and flung into shape upon the air; but that its manifestation became a common medium, flashing not only mutual exchange but separate intensity into our self-consciousness. In short, our artificial analysis has unduly separated between sign and thing signified, the inner spiritual fact and the outer physical manifestation; and the Greek conception was truer, which made one term,—*Logos*,—serve for both, and treated the silent thought and the spoken word as one organic act of life, two momenta of the same function, not detached, like involuntary impulse from its deliberately chosen tool, but only opposite surfaces of the same spontaneous pulsation. If this holds of *all* language, it is applicable above all to what is called the *natural language* of gesture and expression. And it may remind us how unreal are the questions which we sometimes raise, and are indeed obliged to raise, as to what is due to the capacities of the individual soul, and what is added to us by the influence and tuition of society. It is in vain that Paley and others tax their ingenuity to decipher the psychology of 'wild boys,' and set up such monstrosities as normal types of our essential powers. A 'man of the woods' is not yet 'a man' at all: potentially human, he is not yet actually so; for the distinctive characteristics that earn the name do not belong to that lonely biped, any more than music would belong to a piano at the bottom of the sea; they are relative to conditions non-existent for him. It is sometimes useful for analytical purposes to isolate the individual soul, and name its faculties and phenomena irrespectively of its surroundings. But we should not yield ourselves to the illusion that the individual is fitted up with his essentials all by himself, and that then society is constituted by the aggregation of such single specimens. The 'individual' is, in fact, the *later product;* and disengages himself into his independent wholeness as the ripest fruit of a collective development. *Humanity* first, as a plural organism; and then *personality*, in its singular force;—*that* is the order of Nature and Providence, by reference to which we must be careful to correct our inference from the inverse method of investigation. Still, this realistic view does not in the least contradict, but only more accurately define and interpret, our main position, that the moral consciousness is at its origin engaged in *self-estimation*, and does not circuitously reach this end through a prior critique upon our fellow-men The self-consciousness is elicited by the image we see of ourselves on the theatre of life; but thus awakened, carries with it, of its own inherent essence, the self-judgment in which moral sentiment consists; and the judgment passes on to others, simply as implicated in the same nature with ourselves. Upon this principle I should be inclined to fix, as the most certain test by which to discriminate true from false theories of morals. It is a central principle, determining almost all the subsequent lines of reflection and deduction; and between thinkers who disagree upon it, no approximation can afterwards be expected. Yet usually it is passed by without distinct notice or discussion; and the opposite schools content themselves with tacitly assuming either it or its contradictory, and forthwith proceeding to draw out the respective results. .

(4) It is conceivable, however, that we might be self-conscious of an inner spring of action without ability to judge it. Were it a *mere spontaneity*, wholly occupying us and propelling us upon some activity, we might be made aware of it by its stumbling on some obstacle which interrupted its course; we might have a sense of the difference between its indulgence and its arrest; we might therefore make our own state more or less an object of attention; yet, under these conditions, might pronounce upon it no sentence of estimation. A Force, simply as such, is no moral object at all. Nor does it make the least difference in this respect that it is put *inside* an organism to work from the centre, instead of *outside* to impress motion from the superficies. The dynamics of living beings are as foreign to ethics as the gravitation of the stars. An animal charged with exclusive instincts tearing it away, now hither, now thither, is no more liable to be approved or condemned than a lunatic; and its external activities are only a natural language of manifestation, expressing the passion within, as the shriek expresses horror, and laughter cheerfulness. The remark is as old as the time of Socrates, that the

aptitudes of spontaneous genius do not constitute *Wisdom*, and it is another side of the same truth, that the impulses of spontaneous action do not constitute *Character*. 'I next betook myself,' says Socrates, 'to the poets, tragic, dithyrambic, and the rest, assured that here I should convict myself by positive fact of inferior knowledge. I therefore took up the poems on which they seemed to have bestowed the greatest pains, and used to question them what they meant, that I might learn something from them. I really hesitate to tell you the result; yet I must say it. I might almost assert, that there is scarcely any one here who would not have spoken better than they on the very subjects of their own poetry. So I soon found how it was with these poets, that it was not any wisdom by which they made their poems, but a certain natural gift and enthusiasm, like prophets and diviners, who also utter many fine things, but know nothing of the things they speak. Something of the same kind seemed to be the experience of the poets [1].' And in another dialogue the same denial of νοῦς to spontaneous genius is still more strongly marked: 'All the good Epic poets utter all their fine poems not by methodic skill, but possessed with an inspiration; and so too good musical composers. Nor is the poet able to produce, till he becomes inspired and beside himself (ἔκφρων, out of his wits), and his reason (ὁ νοῦς) is no longer in him; short of this possession (ἕως δ' ἂν τοῦτο ἔχῃ τὸ κτῆμα), he is unable to create and deliver his oracle [2].' It is not less inconsistent with the idea of *goodness* than with that of *intellect*, that we should be merely the organ of a force disposing of us without our will. Accordingly, we never judge our *spontaneities*, but only our *volitions*. This distinction is one of the greatest importance in many relations; but for the present we have to do with it in only one. We need not decide whether Socrates is right in rating the self-possessed and open-eyed faculties of Reason and Conscience as the crowning glory of our nature; or whether Carlyle is justified in setting above them the

[1] Plato, Apol. Socr. 22 B [2] Ion. p 533 E.

workings of 'unconscious' genius Whatever be their relative place, the fact remains, that the *moral life* dwells exclusively in the *voluntary sphere*; and but for that would have no existence. This fact, however, will show at once the significance of the controversy between the doctrines of Socrates and Carlyle. For, according to the latter, there is something *higher than the moral life;* a region in which the authority of the right and good vanishes and ceases to be supreme ; as soon as we meet the Divine, we leave moral distinctions behind.

(5) What then is the difference between a *spontaneity* and a *volition?* for on this difference, it seems, depends the transition from the unmoral to the moral. However else they may differ, one distinction is evident at first sight : in the spontaneous state, a single impulse is present; in the voluntary, not less than two. The conditions of the former are fulfilled by any sort of inner propulsion from behind urging the living being forward on a track of which he has no foresight; and a nature, disposed of by such a power, is swung helplessly like a projectile on an undeflected path. The latter implies undeniably *an end in view ;* and no end can bring itself into view except in relation to some other to set it off into distinctness for our contemplation. We think only *by differencing;* and nothing can lie before us as an object, otherwise than as it is cut out by contrast either from its antecedents in time or from its analogues in place or possibility. *Comparison* then is essential to purpose; and to comparison, plurality. Or, to put the matter in another light, more true perhaps to our self-consciousness: that which we judge is (we have seen) the inner spring of action. But how can we *judge it*, if it be the only thing there, and absolutely fill the field of mental vision? All judgment *is relative, and predicates distinction;* and our mind could attach no attribute to a spring of action, did we not see it side by side with something dissimilar; which is nothing else than some possible substitute, *some other spring of action*, displaying the complementary colours to the moral

eye. Endeavour to do away with this duality; thin off this second object till it melts into the surrounding field; still there remains this *surrounding field itself*, and you at least have before you, as the condition of judgment, your mind *with* the given spring of action, and your mind *without it;* the positive to compare with the negative, the active with the passive, living force with abstinent inertia. But it would be an egregious mistake to represent our judgment, even when reduced thus low, as a mere comparison of *something with nothing*, of a *phenomenon with an empty ground*. Sweep away the supposed impulse, and what do you leave?—the living Mind that feels it; and this can never be a deserted theatre, but has always an alternative phenomenon ready to take the place of each one that you may remove. To stifle the soul's natural language here or there is not to establish the reign of dead silence within it: if you put down one word, there is ever another: if you choke the perennial spring at the fountain, it will turn up in the neighbouring field. It is not necessary, for our present purpose, to decide whether Mr. Locke has made good his thesis that 'Men think not always.' I believe you can never subtract phenomenon after phenomenon from your conception of Mind till you arrive at zero, retaining the conception of a mind or person at all. But at all events in the case now supposed,—viz. of an impulse pressing importunately for free way,—the alternative cannot be provided by mere negation and letting alone; the impulse cannot be cleared away but by a counterforce of the most positive kind, even though used only for *suppression* and prevention; and in pronouncing upon the spring of action a sentence of approval or disapproval, we conceive it in relation to the state of mind that might have been substituted, not in the way of blank, but as an equally positive expression of the agent's personality. Just as the stillness of the body, when a brave man suffers an agony which he will not betray, implies anything rather than the negation of force, and though named an abstinence is really an energy; so, in the mere resistance to an impulse and the maintenance, in spite of it, of the mind's even continuity, there must always be a positive power not less intense than that which it commands and supersedes. Whatever name be given to this power, it constitutes a second term susceptible of comparison with the first; and establishes our rule, that a plurality of inner principles is an indispensable condition of moral judgment.

(6) This plurality of simultaneous tendencies, however, would still present no case for moral judgment, were it not also felt to be a plurality of *simultaneous possibilities*. I must lay a separate stress upon each of these two words: (*a*) the impulses must be simultaneous *inter se;* and (*b*) they must both be possibilities *to us*.

(*a*) Were they not there together, the first to enter would have a clear stage and take effect at once: that it hangs fire is because another claimant tries to seize the match, and nothing can be done till some superior decides *which* piece has the best-directed aim. *Comparison* is impossible, unless the two things compared are *co-present* to the mind: we cannot choose or reject what is absent from thought; for it is the very thing we think of when we choose. Plain as this seems, it is called in question by the psychology now in vogue; which, in explaining the process of choice, disposes its objects not in simultaneous but in *successive* order; and tells us, that in cases of hesitation, a second impulse steps in and arrests the incipient realisation of the first, and threatens to dispossess it; and now one, and now the other, brings up its troops of auxiliary ideas, till the fuller lines invest the fortress and it yields. If the supports be not very unequal, the decision may waver long, and keep the mere on-looker in suspense; but this is only his ignorance, not any real uncertainty; and an observer, capable of noticing and measuring all the phenomenal elements of the scene, would read it from first to last as a linear chain of necessary events. In this way, what we took to be *comparison* of synchronous impulses turns out to be *oscillation* of *successive* ones; either of which would automatically go into action, were not its 'nascent motor changes' stopped by the interference of the other, with force enough to start, instead, its own set of 'nascent motor changes¹.' As they can no more work together than two antagonistic muscles, 'an unstable equilibrium' ensues; a pause, during which the associated ideas and feelings connected with each have time to accumulate, till the preponderant stimulus, which must belong to one of the two, upsets the balance and issues the act. This analysis may very likely give a true account of what happens when a tiger, luxuriating in his joint of flesh, is interrupted by a threat to take it from him: he dashes out of appetite into rage, and for a moment would prefer his enemy to his dinner; but a little remission of the threat, or a fresh sniff at the meat, sets his jaws to work again till the provocation fires him once more: and of such alternations, following simply and unreflectingly the access and recess of stimulus, consist, no doubt, all the encounters of inconsistent instincts in the mere animals. They simply suffer the upset of an 'unstable equilibrium,' and tumble over. But of the self-conscious human process, in the conflict with temptation and the judgment of right, it cannot be true, until the current terms of such experience,—comparison, deliberation, preference, volition,—are emptied of all their meaning. In short, we have here no healthy and independent psychology, permitted to speak for itself and lay down its own laws; but only one which has been sold into slavery to a physiological hypothesis, and flung, half starved, into its *ergastula*, to do and suffer whatever may be needed at the master's hands. In order to moral judgment, then, the plurality of impulses must be *simultaneous.*'

(*b*) And either of them must be *possible to us;* i. e. it must depend *upon us* in relation to them, and not *upon them* in relation to each other, which of them we follow. It is said, 'Yes, it depends *upon ourselves;*' but what do I mean by '*myself*'? Simply *my character as it is*, made up by inheritance, temperament, experience, formed habit, and

¹ See Mr. Herbert Spencer's Psychology, Part IV. chap. ix.

self-discipline: of this aggregate from the past, with the outward motives from the present, every decision must be the result; and if the second factor is treated as the thing *given*, then the casting vote is vested with the other; and it is the *character*, i.e. *the self*, which decides. Now I do not deny that the Self which chooses includes all these things; or that each of them has its influence upon the choice,— the instinctive impulse, such as the brutes obey; the persistency of habits, which runs in the old ruts; the previously formed disposition and cast of thought; nor do I doubt that, by the skilful estimate of these, it may be often possible to foresee how I shall determine a given problem of conduct. But I cannot allow that *these exhaust the Ego*, and give a complete account of all its actual and possible phenomena. Besides the *effects* of which I am the accumulation, I claim also a *personal* causality which is still left over, when my phenomena have told me the tale of what they are and do; thus pleading guilty to the charge of illusion which Mr. Herbert Spencer brings against those who suppose that 'the Ego is something more than the aggregate of feelings and ideas, actual and nascent, momentarily existing[1].' When he tells me, 'you *are* your own phenomena,' and I reply, 'No, I *have* my own phenomena, and so far as they are active, it is I that make them, and not they that make me,' how will he show me that this is 'an illusion?' how strip me of the consciousness that I am the same permanent subject of varying feeling and the single agent of repeated action, and not a shifting product of factors ever new? It is useless to quote the rules for the comparison of momenta, as if the balancing of reasons must conform to them; that is only to *assume* the very point at issue, viz. the identity of mechanics and morals; and something more than assertion is needed to make me believe, that what settles an alternative for a human mind is the same that defines the line of a doubly struck moving body. When I judge my own act, I feel sure that *it is mine;* and *that*, not in the sense that

[1] Op. cit. P. IV. chap. ix.

its necessitating antecedents were in my character, so that nothing could prevent its coming; but in the sense that I might have betaken myself to a different act at the critical moment, when the pleadings were over, and only the verdict remained. 'Certainly,' says our best living psychologist[1], 'in the case of actions in which I have a distinct consciousness of choosing between alternatives of conduct, one of which I conceive as right or reasonable, I find it impossible not to think that I can now choose to do what I so conceive, however strong may be my inclination to act unreasonably, and however uniformly I may have yielded to such inclination in the past.' Moral judgment, then, credits the Ego with a selecting power between two possibilities, and stands or falls with this.

Did we conceive ourselves to be the arena on which these incompatible phenomena of suggestion tried their strength, until one succeeded in expelling the other and setting up its trophy alone, we should certainly take neither praise nor blame to ourselves for the result. We might possibly await the issue of the contest with interest; might wish to go with one master rather than with another; or, at least, *having gone*, might find that there was a less or more ignoble service. But *servitude* it would still be; we should be *victims* in the least favourable case; and might *compassionate* ourselves, but surely not *reproach* or abhor. For *this* it is an indispensable condition, that we invert the relation just supposed between *ourselves* and the *plurality of impulses* soliciting us; that we feel conscious of being their master, not their slave; of having them at *our bar*, not of being brought to theirs; that we assume the causality to lie, not with them, to do with us according to their dynamics, but with us, to execute our trust, and express, by their just subordination, the symmetry and energy of our will. The mere flashing upon us of opposite impulses

---

[1] Sidgwick's Methods of Ethics, chap. v. § 3, p. 64, 3rd ed. See also Ward's Examination of Spencer's Psychology, Part IV. p. 9, reprinted from 'Dublin Review,' April 15th, 1877.

on the right hand and on the left, determining us, like cattle with two drovers flourishing a stick on each side of the road, would involve no sense of obligation, and be compatible with no self-judgment. We evidently feel the solicitations which visit us to be mere *phenomena*, brought before a *personality* that is more than a phenomenon or than any string of phenomena,—a free and judicial Ego, able to deal with the problem offered, and decide between the claimants that have entered our court.

Whether this assumption is in itself true, or whether it is capable of being set aside by evidence more reliable than itself, is not our present question. We cannot pause to pursue through its subtle windings the controversy between Liberty and Necessity. The only position which for the moment we are concerned to make good, is this alternative one,—that either free-will is a fact, or moral judgment a delusion. We could never condemn one turn of act or thought, did we not believe the agent to have command of another; and just in proportion as we perceive, in his temperament or education or circumstances, the certain preponderance of particular suggestions, and the near approach to an inner necessity, do we criticise him rather as a natural object than as a responsible being, and deal with his aberrations as maladies instead of sins. The ordinary rule which, in awarding penalties of wrong, takes into consideration the presence or absence of violent temptation, assumes a personal power of resistance never wholly crushed but sometimes severely strained. Were we, in our moral problem, as much at the mercy of the laws of association as we are in our efforts to remember what we have forgotten or to invent what is wanting in a design, we ought surely to look on the guilty will with the same neutrality as on the failing memory or unfertile imagination. This is indeed prevailingly admitted by those who reduce the human being to the domination of mere natural laws. The application of praise and blame, they acknowledge, is in itself as absurd as to applaud the sunrise or be angry at the rain; and the only difference is, that men are manageable for the future, and are susceptible to the influence of our sentiments regarding them, while the elements are not; so that it may be judicious, with a view to benefits to come, to commit the absurdity of praising what is not praiseworthy, and censuring what is not to blame. Thus to reduce the moral sentiments to a policy providing for the future, instead of a sentence pronounced upon the past, is simply to renounce them; and amounts to a confession that they cannot coexist with a theory of necessary causation.

Hence, much as I admire the habitual justice and absolute immunity from partisan prejudice with which Professor Sidgwick treats all controverted questions, I cannot but feel that he has pushed this virtue to a point of unreasonable generosity, when, in spite of his irresistible consciousness of free volition, he pronounces the point at issue in the determinist problem neutral to the doctrine of Ethics, and of no influence upon their practice. I can understand and intellectually respect the thorough-going determinist, intensely possessed by the conception of causality that rules through all the natural sciences, and never doubting that, as a 'universal postulate,' it must be driven perforce through the most refractory phenomena of human experience. I can understand the emphatic claim of the reflective moralist for the exemption of his territory from a law which admits of no alternative. I can readily forgive either, if he rises to enthusiasm, and contends with the other as for very life. But I cannot understand the intermediate mood, which imagines the chasm of difference reducible to a step, which, for all practical purposes, it is not worth while to bridge over or fill up. I can grant indeed that, in drawing up an objective code of actions to be prohibited and required, the two doctrines would not widely diverge in their results; for, in this work, we have to look, not at the inner life, but at the outward relations and well-being of Society. But when, from constructing the organism as you would have it, you pass to the living power that is to work it, to the motive feelings and beliefs that shall animate it, is it of no consequence that, as Professor Sidgwick allows, the ideas of 'responsibility,' of 'obligation,' of good or ill 'desert,' of 'justice,' and proportionate 'retribution,' of praise and blame, are either banished, or kept for us only in a non-natural sense? Is it conceivable that such a change should make no difference to the dynamics of the moral life? On such a ground, as it seems to me, you may build your mill of social ethics, with all its chambers neat and adequate, and its great wheel expecting to move: but you have turned aside the stream on which it all depends; the waters are elsewhere; and your structure stands dead and silent on the bank.

Moral judgment, then, postulates moral freedom; and by this we mean, not the absence of foreign constraint, but the presence of a personal power of preference in relation to the inner suggestions and springs of action that present their claims.

This account completes what I have to say about the *objects* of our moral judgment. They are, originally, our own inner principles of self-conscious action, as freely preferred or excluded by our will.

§ 2. *Mode of Moral Judgment.*

Next, we may attend to the *mode* of moral judgment, and determine how the mind proceeds in estimating its own impulses and volitions. For, process of some kind there must be: every verdict implies preference; every preference, comparison; every comparison, things compared, and grounds of resemblance and difference between them. To define these is to explain our mode of judgment.

(1) The one great condition which raises the spontaneous into the self-conscious life is this;— the simultaneous presence and collision of the forces which check and exclude each other. Without the encounter of bodies, the dream of mere sensation would not wake into perception. Without the

answering face of other men, the sense of personal existence would remain dim. And without the appearance in us of two incompatible impulses at once, or the interruption of one by the invasion of another, the moral self-consciousness would sleep. It is not *difference only* that suffices to produce the effect; for differences might coexist among objects side by side in the space before us, yet would they never disengage themselves into view, did they not break their stillness and move among themselves; and living impulses might successively occupy us, yet would they never become objects of our attention, did each one spend itself and fade ere the next appeared, so that we were picked up by them one by one, and caught disengaged in every case. From this state we are rescued by perpetual 'breach of the peace' within our nature, and the clamour of impatient propensities disputing for simultaneous admission, or prematurely cutting short the career of the principle in possession. It is only when *difference amounts to strife*, that it completes the passage from spontaneity to self-consciousness. This perhaps is part of the meaning embraced in the celebrated proposition of Heracleitus, that 'strife is the father of all things:' though in his doctrine, that nothing could arise without the collision of opposites, the subjective world was less in view than the objective. Be that as it may, the maxim has a just application to the phenomena of our moral life. It is not till two incompatible impulses appear in our consciousness and contest the field, that we are made aware of their difference and are driven to judge between them. But the moment this condition is realised, we are sensible of a contrast between them other than that of mere intensity or of qualitative variety,—not analogous to the difference between loud and soft, or between red and sour;—but requiring quite a separate phraseology for its expression, such as this: that one is *higher, worthier,* than the other, and, in comparison with it, has the clear *right to us*. This apprehension is no mediate discovery of ours, of which we can give an account; but is immediately inherent in the very experience of the principles themselves,—a revelation inseparable from their appearance side by side. By simply entering the stage together and catching the inner eye, they disclose their respective worth and credentials. A child, for example, not above the seductions of the jam-closet, finding himself alone in that too trying place, makes hurried inroads upon the sweetmeats within tempting reach; but has scarcely sucked the traces from his fingers before he is ready to sink into the earth with compunction, well knowing that the appetite he has indulged is meaner than the integrity he has violated. A passionate boy will vent his impatience on any inanimate object that obstructs his purpose, splitting his unsuccessful peg-tops, or breaking his tangled fishing-line; and will accuse himself of no wrong. But let his paroxysm spend itself on a sister, and send her wounded and crying away; and the instant remorse brings home to him how much higher is the affection he has slighted than the resentment he has allowed. The thirsty traveller in the desert would seize, instinctively and without a thought, the draught from the spring he has found at last; but if he have a companion faint and dying of the fever, he knows that his appetite must give precedence to his compassion, and he holds the cup of cold water first to another's lips. In these cases,—and they appear to me fair representatives of all our moral experience,—the very same impulses which, when sole occupants, would carry us unreflectingly and unreluctantly to their end, instantly appear in their true relative light when their field is disputed by a rival. Nothing more is needed, and nothing less will serve, than their juxtaposition and their incompatibility. There is no analysis or research required; it is a choice of Hercules, only without the reasoning and the rhetoric; the claims are decided by a glance at their face. We cannot follow both; and we cannot doubt the rights and place of either. Their *moral valuation* intuitively results from their *simultaneous appearance*.

Here, however, complaint may be reasonably made of the inexact, even half mystical language, in which the relation between the conflicting springs of action has been described. They have been contrasted as '*higher and lower.*' These terms are *comparatives*, and with this peculiarity, that their *positives*, 'high' and 'low,' do not, like 'red' and 'hard,' introduce us to two heterogeneous predicates, but only to a 'more' or 'less' of the same, so as still to detain us among mere comparatives. '*High*' carries us towards one extremity, '*low*' towards the other, of some one extended and graduated whole. What then is that whole? How are we to name the underlying quantity or quality, on which these degrees are measured off? As they are not physical altitudes, they must stand upon something inherent in our springs of action, which, in its differences, affects us similarly to varieties of elevation. Till this 'something' is specified, the propositions which assert 'more' or 'less' are propositions about Nothing.

I admit at once the justice of this demand, and the difficulty of meeting it at this stage, where nevertheless it naturally arises. To ask after the *quality* of an object is to ask about the way in which it affects us, i.e. about a feeling of our own from its presence or idea. The *springs of action* are here our object: the question therefore is, in virtue of what kind of feeling in us, excited by all of them, with intensity varied in each, do we apply to them the comparative language in the foregoing description? If I follow impulse A, instead of B, my volition will be 'higher,'—in what scale? —of pleasure? Not so, or I should enjoy the stolen sweetmeats without drawback, instead of being ashamed of them. Of beauty? Not so, for I have no such feeling from my pug-nose, though I wish it were straight. I can only say, that, good as these things may be, it is another sort of good whose degrees affect me here; involving, what they do not, a sense of *Duty*, of *Right and Wrong*, of *Moral* worth, and a consciousness that I am *not at liberty*, though perfectly able, to go with the impulse B. The degrees therefore, I should say, are marked on the scale of *dutifulness*, of *rightness*, of *morality;* and in treating as ultimate and essential the attribute which these words designate, I support myself on the judgment of Professor Sidgwick[1], who 'regards it as a clear result of reflection that the notions of right and wrong, as peculiar to moral cognition, are *unique and unanalysable*.' Of the several words available for naming this quality, '*Moral worth*' seems the most eligible (1) as applicable to what presents *gradations* of value; and (2) as exempt from intrusive associations. 'Duty,' and 'Right,' are so habitually used of single problems and concrete cases, where there is *one good* course and *one bad*, that they represent prominently the *dual* antithesis of each separate moral experience, and do not easily lend themselves to the expression of relative intensities of excellence through the whole system of ethical combinations of motive. The word 'Virtue' is very tempting, from its covering an indefinite number of gradations; but it has two disadvantages : (1) its gradations are only on the *upper side* of the neutral level, and, to mark the *minus values* of which we almost always have to speak at the same time, other language must be sought; and (2) an association of *extra merit*, constituting an approach *to the heroic*, clings to the word, and fits it chiefly for special cases where temptation is above the average.

Is it thought strange that a 'unique unanalysable' quality, whether of an action (as Professor Sidgwick would say), or of a spring of action (as I should prefer), should fail to reveal itself so long as the object was isolated, and should first be discovered when brought up by a double object? Even in our physical life, such experiences are not unknown : e.g. of *heat* we should have no suspicion, if the temperature were always the same in our own organism and around it; the loss of its equilibrium discloses its existence. But, besides this, the *moral* quality arises, not barely from the interplay between the object and ourselves, but in the relation of *two*

---

[1] 'Mind,' No. xxviii. pp. 580, 581.

objects to one another; and can no more exist without them, than fraternity can belong to a solitary man, or a convex surface present itself without a concave. In truth, the quality which we get to know does not really belong to *each* object, but is inherent in the pair as a dual object; and not only could not be *cognised*, but would not *exist*, till they fell into combination.

(2) If this be a true account of our elementary self-judgments, it throws great light on the whole method of the moral sentiments. If the first pair of impulses that compete for our will disclose their relative worth by simply assuming that attitude, it is the same with all the rest. Each in turn might be experienced in isolation, without giving us a moral idea; but each in turn, entering with a rival reveals its comparative place and claims, and falls into the line of appointed order. And when the cycle of original experience has completed itself, when all the natural springs of action have had their mutual play, and exhausted the series of moral permutations, there will be resources within us for forming an entire scale of principles, exhibiting the gradations of ethical rank. We have only to collect the scattered results of particular combinations, and dispose them on the ascending steps of authority, and the flying leaves of the oracle, thus sorted out, fall into the systematic code of Divine law. It must no doubt be long before the materials are ready for the integral work: indeed it may be fairly regarded rather as an approximation than as a scheme ever finished. For, in the constitution of the individual man, new natural springs of action continue to arise, or greatly to change their character, through more than one-third of the common term of life. And the maturing of society around the individual also modifies his spiritual demands; producing, with more refined and artificial wants, mixed forms of impulse, complicating the list with interpolations and extensions. Still, the beginning of a scheme of moral estimate may be made, by following the clue which we have indicated, and seeking with it the true hierarchy of human impulses. But, if we once let

slip this means of guidance; if we either delude ourselves into the belief that our nature is not a system of powers, but dominated by some single autocratic propensity, or treat its inner springs of action as a democracy in which there is no hierarchy at all; it will be impossible to give any explanation of the moral sentiments or any justification of their verdicts in detail. The whole ground of ethical procedure consists in this: that we are sensible of a *graduated scale of excellence* among our natural principles, quite distinct from the order of their intensity, and irrespective of the range of their external effects.

With this general conception of moral excellence, as *internal*, and consisting of rightly *ordered* springs of action, Mr. Leslie Stephen concurs [1]. He proceeds on the 'assumption that virtue implies a certain organisation of the instincts;' and lays it down that 'a man is moral because and in so far as his instincts are correlated according to a certain type.' But the mode in which the right order of the instincts discloses and realises itself he describes in terms very different from the foregoing. While man is [2] 'a hierarchy of numerous and conflicting passions, each of which has ends of its own, and each of which, separately considered, would give a different law of conduct,' 'our psychology,' we are told, 'is at present utterly inadequate to decide what are the elementary passions of which the organic federation is composed, or in what sense they can be regarded as distinct.' The federal *unity* or *centralisation* which there must be to integrate these elements Mr. Stephen conceives to be attained *mechanically*, as a *resultant*, under the law of composition of forces, from reciprocal interaction of all these undecipherable impulses; a resultant possibly calculable by 'a superior being who could examine our characters,' but beyond the reach of a psychology which cannot even read and record its factors [3]. Yet it is admitted that what Psychology cannot do 'Reason' can attempt with considerable

---

[1] Science of Ethics, chap. vii. § 36, p. 302; § 43, p. 308.
[2] Ibid. chap. ii. § 29, p. 69.   [3] Ibid. chap. ii. § 31, p. 70.

success; it 'will tend to bring about a certain unity in the result[1]: so far as any instinct, whether simple or complex, is dominant, Reason will tend to proportion means to ends, and so far bring about unity of action and purpose.' There will ensue 'a process of forming a certain hierarchy in which the separate and special instincts are subordinated to the more central and massive,' and 'reason will develop, if not a unity, at least a harmony of action. For, so far as we reason, the action of each separate instinct is controlled by a constant reference to the requirements of the others. We may act like the lower animals under the immediate impulse of hunger; but our hunger is restrained, not only by the foresight of to-morrow's appetite, but by the knowledge that this indulgence may be at the expense of other pleasures. The passion is regulated and restrained by our desire of a more intellectual or emotional enjoyment[1].' Thus 'the character is modified, as the reason acts; because it enables us, after a time, to judge even of our character as a whole, to rehearse not only particular acts but moods, and so become spectators of ourselves, and regard our feelings with disgust or complacency[2].' Now, I ask, what is this 'Reason' but 'Psychology' under another name? for its objects of cognition are our own inward 'instincts;' it is therefore '*self-knowledge*.' Mr. Stephen himself says, that the 'reasoning being' 'is so far more reasonable as his world is more real[3];' and 'the accurate representation of the world *implies an accurate representation of our own feelings;* a reasonable man, we say, knows his own mind[4].' If by 'comparing modes of feeling[5]' he can 'regulate and restrain' one desire by another and develop 'a harmony of action,' this is all the psychology we want: it is the discovery, by self-consciousness, of a scale of values among the internal springs of action. It matters not, for our present

---

[1] Science of Ethics, chap. ii § 31, p. 71.
[2] Ibid. ch ii. § 31, p 72. [3] Ibid. chap. iii. § 25, p. 65.
[4] Ibid. chap. iii. § 26, p. 65. [5] Ibid. chap. iii. § 28, p. 68.

argument, that with Mr. Stephen the relative values express themselves in terms of *pleasure*, and that this is the quality that renders them 'identical in kind,' and 'commensurable.' 'The criterion,' he says, 'is always simple, the balance of gratification in one way or the other[1].' If this is true, it is a *psychological* truth: if it is false, it is *psychologically* false, and the same introspection which admits or rejects this quality as the ground of a common measure must be equally competent to find any other, if it be there. Supposing 'instincts' to be inherently differenced both by sentient and by moral gradations, what can be more arbitrary than to tell me that I can know what I like, but cannot know what I approve? If I can know both, the former knowledge, when extended throughout the 'instincts' which I experience, sets them before me in hedonistic order; the latter sets them in moral order: the one giving the hierarchy of Prudence, the other the hierarchy of Right. We need not object to setting down these cognitions to the credit of '*Reason*,' provided we do not erase them from the account of psychology, instead of recognising them as the rational registration of psychological facts; and provided also we attach to the word 'Reason' a meaning clear and constant. It is perhaps my own fault that I cannot find any exact sense of it applicable, without variation, to the separate sentences in which Mr. Stephen resorts to it. He says, for instance, 'The supposed conflict between Reason and Passion is, as I hold, meaningless if it is taken to imply that the Reason is a faculty separate from the emotions, *and contemplating them as an external spectator*[2].' Our Reason, then, whatever it may be or do, is not qualified to 'contemplate our emotions as an external spectator.' Yet, when he comes to explain how it is that 'the character is modified as the Reason acts,' he tells us it is 'because it enables us after a time to judge even of our own character as a whole, to rehearse not only our particular acts, but moods, and *so*

---

[1] Science of Ethics, chap. iii. § 28, p. 68.
[2] Ibid. chap. ii. § 20, p. 60.

become spectators of ourselves, and *regard our feelings with disgust or complacency.*' The very thing, then, which *reason cannot do*, it somehow '*enables us*' *to do:* does this change of the acting subject save these propositions from contradiction? Mr. Stephen would be the last to put in such a plea; for he himself recognises no agent beyond the resultant of the composite organism of instincts; and cannot suppose any one else to mean by 'Reason' more than *ourselves exercising rational functions*. The second sentence therefore affirms precisely what the first denies.

If we waive the question of phraseology, and accept the term 'Reason' as tantamount to *self-conscious apprehension of compared springs of action*, or including it, Mr. Stephen's description of the mental advance from the appreciation of 'particular acts' to that of general 'moods' or types of feeling, may be easily translated into the terms of our foregoing exposition. We first judge 'our particular acts;' and because we do so from the inner side of them, and this inner side or motive changes its relation from act to act, the judgment widens to a system of judgments on numerous '*moods*' or actuating feelings, which incur, in determinate proportion, our disgust or complacency. The divergencies, however, which may be covered over by resembling language cannot, I fear, be thus reduced to coalescence. The progressive enlargement of ethical view which Mr. Stephen conceives as a generalisation by inference, whereby rules emerge from cases, I regard as rather an extending range of intuitive perception of relative worth. And the equilibrium of instincts which he contemplates is the adjustment obtained by their mutual trial of strength in the effort of each at self-gratification: while that which I seek to define is their disposal in graduated subordination prescribed by their relative worth as acknowledged by our own comparing self-consciousness. The difference will be seen if I place, by the side of a single happy sentence of Mr. Stephen's, the slightly modified form in which I could make it my own. 'Each instinct,' he says, 'has its voice in determining the action of the federal government; but no one is allowed to take the command exclusively, without reference to the wishes of the others.' Rather should I say, 'Each instinct has its voice in determining the action of the supreme executive; but no one is allowed to take the command, except of its subordinates, without defeience to the orders of its superiors.' In other words, I replace the *federal equality* of 'wishes' by the *hierarchical gradations* of authority.

(3) The sensibility of the mind to the gradations of this scale is precisely what we call *Conscience;*—the *knowledge with one's self* of the better and worse; and the more delicate the knowing faculty, the finer are the shades perceived. Whoever feels no difference of worth between one propension and another, and yields himself with equal unreluctance to appetite or affection, to resentment or compassion, and emerges from them with equal cheerfulness, is without conscience. Nor is his case morally improved, if, while he recognises a difference, it is still a difference, not of inherent excellence, but only of agreeableness or external benefit,—a relish in one viand that is not in another. If this be all, he will feel at liberty, *mero arbitrio*, to fling himself in any direction, and will acknowledge no hindrance but that of distaste, in the way of each chance desire. This state of mind constitutes the direct negation of the consciousness of Duty; of whose very essence it is to feel that we have *no right* to dispose of ourselves by caprice, and that we cannot legitimate an autocratic power by any mere willingness to take its risks and bear its penalties. It is only in proportion as a man is alive to *other differences* than those of pleasantness among the several springs of action, that he has an awakened moral sentiment. And hence we see, with some precision, in what consists the peculiarity of an exact as distinguished from a confused or obtuse conscience. The former, like a fine ear for music, magnifies, as it were, the intervals between tone and tone, and is sensitive to intermediaries quite lost to the duller mind: the latter, accustomed only to the discipline of ruder

instruments, passes without notice a thousand things quite out of tune, and requires strong discords in order to feel a jar. Conscience, then, is the critical perception we have of the relative authority of our several principles of action. The sense of that authority is *implicitly* contained in the mere natural strife of these principles within us: when *explicitly* brought into view by reflective self-knowledge, it assumes a systematic character, and asserts its prerogative as the judicial regulator of life. Its proper business is to watch the forces of our nature, and keep everything in its place.

Professor Sidgwick thinks it 'incorrect to regard this comparison of motives as the normal form of our common moral judgments; nor do I see,' he adds, 'any ground for holding it to be the original form. I think that in the normal development of man's moral consciousness, both in the individual and in the race, moral judgments are first passed on outward acts, and that motives do not come to be considered till later; just as external perception of physical objects precedes introspection[1].' Now that we are in the later stage, he agrees that motives sanctioned by the moral consciousness are 'essential to right action;' but contends that they do not adequately define it as right. 'In a certain sense, no doubt, a man who sincerely desires and intends to act rightly does all he can, and completely fulfils duty; but it will hardly be denied that such a man may have a wrong judgment as to his outward duty, and therefore, in another sense, may act wrongly[2].' If asked, which of these two is to be preferred,—'the subjective' or 'the objective rightness,'—in case of their separation, 'the moral sense of mankind,' it is admitted, would 'regard the Subjective rightness of an action as generally more important than the Objective[3].'

After thus allowing the superior 'importance' and the 'essential' rank of 'rightness' in the inward spring of

[1] Methods of Ethics, III. chap. xii. § 1, pp. 365-6, 3rd Ed.
[2] Ibid. III. chap. i. § 2, pp. 203-4.   [3] Ibid. loc. cit. p. 205.

action, no room seems left for doubt as to the native seat of all moral discrimination. It must have its birth *in conscientia*, from feeling differences in our own springs of action; and thence, its application to the corresponding ones betrayed in others by their conduct. That this really is the process seems evident from the familiar fact that, in case of our mistaking their motive and discovering the mistake, our judgment is immediately altered, though the action remains the same: while, on the other hand, should something done against conscience by ourselves turn out so well as to consist with all the conditions of 'objective right,' it makes no difference in our self-condemnation. This simple test seems to me to make the very soil transparent in which the ultimate root of the moral feeling lies, and to show us whence its fibres draw their first nutriment. *Till* we ascribe to others a motive which we approve, they are without moral quality: and *when* we ascribe it to them, we have learned its moral quality in ourselves.

There is however a difference between the 'indispensable' and the 'adequate'; and something more, it is urged, is wanted than pure motive, in order to fill the conception of 'right action.' What then is the missing element which should occupy the gap? It is, we are assured, a correct '*judgment*' as to the outward action in which the pure motive should express itself: not till this is secured, can we credit the agent with 'objective rightness.' Is then this supplementary feature homogeneous with its antecedent? Professor Sidgwick well says that a man who makes no failure *here* is 'right' '*in another sense*' from that in which the epithet was allowed to the simply conscientious man; but seems to me hardly to appreciate the whole difference. Are right and wrong '*judgments*' no less ethical acts than right and wrong intentions? Or are they not, when initiated by the same intention, *intellectual* instead of *moral?* If guilt is incurred by an erroneous computation of conduct, why not by a faulty column of statistics or a mistaken prophecy of market prices? Surely the word right has an obvious ambiguity, and denotes now the ethically *good*, and now the intellectually *true*. In the phrase 'Subjective right' it has the former meaning; in the phrase 'Objective right,' the latter. To treat it as covering the same quality in both is to make it a fruitful source of illusions. To guard against these, the *whole moral essence* of voluntary conduct must be planted in its inner spring, while its outward history must be judged by the canons of *rationality*. The former emerges to us only in self-consciousness.

The argument for Professor Sidgwick's order of derivation, founded on the earlier development of the perceptive than of the reflective faculties, would press with great force against any doctrine which asserted that the first moral feeling must wait till motive and action were analytically separated in consciousness. Only reflection can separate them; and long before such analyses are possible, the primitive moral energies of mankind have certainly done plenty of work. But the theory of an internal moral consciousness demands no such premature psychology; it indulges in no picture of 'the naked savage' seated on a rock and pulling his ideas to pieces, and wondering how they get the management of his huge painted limbs. All that it affirms of him is this: that, though he goes through no process of introspection and self-examination, yet it is quite possible for him, if in a fit of passion he has killed his child, to be afterwards struck with compunction as he looks at the wounded body stretched in death. You may perhaps say, this may well be, though it be simply *the loss* that grieves him. I reply, that, were you to ask him, he could not tell you: the thing he has done, and the rage that has moved him, are all one to him. Yet the state of his mind is *not what it would have been* if the fatal blow had been not from his own hand, or had been from an accidental swerving of his arm. It owes its special character to the inward spring whence the act has come. *He* does not, and need not, analyse the case; but that he is differently affected when nothing but the motive impulse is changed, analyses it for us, and betrays where the moral differentia lies.

Moreover, this argument assumes a more exact antithesis than actually subsists between the 'perceptive' and the 'reflective' faculties; viz. that through the former we know exclusively *external things and phenomena;* through the latter, *internal.* Of these two propositions, the latter alone is true: reflection certainly begins, continues, and ends with introspection; it has no other object than the phenomena of consciousness,—it has no other instruments than the laws and powers of thought; its life elements are those of a purely ideal world. But perception of outward objects is impossible without self-discrimination from them, and therefore self-consciousness; nor can we *know them,* without memories and beliefs and conceptions, and similarities and dissimilarities of feeling and idea, all which we must also know, whether we think about them or not, inasmuch as we can identify them on their recurrence, and hold them fairly apart. The non-Ego and the Ego come into cognisance together, and perception itself is the consciousness of their relation; and though it explicitly attends to one term of that relation, it implicitly postulates the other, and holds it ready to be looked at whenever the mental eye is pleased to turn that way. The moment this occurs, the contents of the *inward* face of the experience spread themselves out, and can be no less compared and reduced to order than their correlatives. The intellectual act which performs this operation, by concentrating itself upon the play of light and shade and the meeting and passing of images and ideas *behind* the screen, is what we call '*reflection.*' It therefore receives from the hands of perception one-half of their gains, and retires to make an inventory of them, systematically disposed. The true account, therefore, seems to be, that through the perceptive faculty we know both worlds in their relation to each other, the outward explicitly, the inward implicitly; and through the reflective, the implicit knowledge of the latter is rendered explicit. Is it needful to say in what exact sense these words 'implicit and explicit' are to be understood? We may put it thus: the relation between the outer and the inner world,—the relation of antithetic duality,—is known to us in perception, known at once as well as it ever is: each of the two related terms is or contains a complex of phenomena, with their sub-relations among themselves: each of these sub-relations (within the sphere of *our* nature and world) is *felt* by us, and, if different, would be differently felt, whether we have made acquaintance with its component terms or not; so long as we have not yet made their acquaintance, yet, in the feeling which is their conjoint relation to us, have the means of doing so, we possess an *implicit knowledge of them:* as soon as we use these means, and direct upon the sub-relation an analytic attention which resolves it into its factors, we see what goes to make our feeling; and the primary relation, instead of being implicitly known merely as distinguished from others, becomes explicitly known, as exposing to view the contents of its tributary sub-relation. Now it is no doubt true that the phenomena of the outward world become explicitly known to us earlier than those of our own mind; but this only proves that *theories of nature* may be expected earlier than *theories of conscience.* For the *action of conscience, implicit knowledge* alone is needed, *a feeling, true to the real relations of duty,* that *this* is worthier than *that*. This condition demands no reflective introspection, no ability to lay the finger on what it is in the action judged which excites the feeling, or even to *ask the question* whether it be the motive or the effect. Yet it may turn out, when the analysis of the fact comes to be made, that, in the absence of the motive, the feeling would not have been there; and, with difference of motive, it would have been different, all else remaining the same: not till the agent himself becomes aware of this, does his moral knowledge become *explicit,* enabling him to think out into system the rules which nevertheless his judgments have always followed. I see therefore nothing, in the early development of the perceptive faculties, which is at all at variance with the account I have given of the source and essence of the moral sentiments.

ii. INCIDENTAL TESTS OF THE THEORY OF CONSCIENCE.

The foregoing interpretation of our modes of moral judgment, and of the nature and origin of Conscience, does no violence, so far as I can see, to any psychological experience; nor does it materially deviate from the description given by most ethical writers of the facts of moral consciousness. It seems susceptible, however, of some instructive applications, on which, as further criteria of its truth, it will be useful to dwell for a few moments.

(1) It seems to justify the popular notion that *conscientiousness* is no security for *energy*, and is even apt to degenerate into a certain *weakness of character*. If it be the sole function of conscience to discern the *intervals* between the several springs of action, it implies nothing whatever as to their separate intensity. The intervals may be equally great, whether the quantities between which they are set are little or large. And where the finest gradations are to be read off, a microscopic provision must be there for magnifying differences indistinguishable by the coarser natural eye. Such an instrument is apt to have a narrow range, and to be too nice for the broad estimates of the working world. The homoeopathic balance, depressed by a fairy globule, and enclosed in a glass case lest it vibrate with the passing breath, is useless for weighing beef and bread; and can never acquire a momentum that a feather will not break. A mind of this structure serves in the moral cosmos the purpose of a cometary nebula in the physical; its exaggerated movements all the more conspicuously exhibiting the forces which it is unfitted to accumulate and transmit. Anxious scrupulosity, the result of critical inspection, we naturally expect less in the passionate and impulsive nature, than in the comparatively cold and quiet, to which pause is never difficult, and

enthusiasm never importunate. The simply ethical temper is related to spiritual productiveness as mere good taste is to creativeness in poetry and art. With so circumspect a step it makes no way; and though it never wanders, never flies. For ever occupied in distinguishing, it acquires the habit of fear instead of love,—nay, above all things, *fears to love.* Its maxims are maxims of avoidance, which shape themselves into negatives, and guard every avenue with the flaming sword of prohibition, 'Thou shalt *not!*' In apprehension of possible evil, it dares not surrender itself to any admiration and fling itself into unrestrained action for any haunting end: the admiration must first be scrutinised, till it has cooled and its force is gone; the end in view is traced through a thicket of comparisons, till it is lost in the wood. Nothing accordingly is more rare than a character at once balanced and powerful, judicial and enthusiastic; and faultless perception is apt to involve feeble inspiration. Nor is the rule apparent only in individual life. On the larger scale of historical experience, it receives its fulfilment in the alternation, remarked by St. Simon, of organic and critical periods; in the first of which great action abounds and great works of genius are produced, and society displays an exuberance of spontaneous energy; while, in the latter, this almost lawless affluence is reduced to rule, and modesty is imposed on its extravagance; its blemishes are noted, its defects rendered sensible; and the curb is put upon its wild career. In literature, in art, even in religion, fresh life is always at the expense of the old limits, and presses into an air never breathed before: the new product awakens a new consciousness which has to be adjusted in its relation to previous experience, and to furnish new canons of judgment; and thus, to the age of origination succeeds an age of connoisseurship, too busy in sorting out the past with orderly appreciation to become the organ of creation for the future. The autumn which gathers and stores the fruits of culture has no longer the prolific vitality of the summer that moulds and paints them; and every time when economic diligence takes stock is a time of declining freshness, when the sap of nature has grown slack. The difficulty, therefore, is not confined to morals, but repeats itself throughout our nature, of reconciling intensity of power with truth of equipoise. The moment when we most feel the positive forces of our inner being is not that in which we best reduce them to comprehensive estimate; nor is the accurate apprehension of their relative worth any guarantee for their vigorous action. This phenomenon ceases to be the paradox of ethics, as soon as conscience is explained as the mere inner sense of *differences* along the scale of impulses, without regard to the absolute force of any.

(2) It is also easy to understand, how, notwithstanding the uniformity of their moral nature, men may remain far from unanimity in their apparent moral judgments. The whole scale of inner principles is open to survey only to the ripest mind; and to be perfect in its appreciation is to have exhausted the permutations of human experience. To all actual men a part only is familiar; often, a deplorably small part. Still, however limited the range of our moral consciousness, it would lead us all to the same verdicts, had we all the same segment of the series under our cognisance. We should have a narrower, but a concurrent sense of right and wrong. That it is otherwise is not surprising, when it is remembered that to different men different parts of the scale of impulses are familiar by the predilections of their nature or the cast of their experience; so that their moral insight does not sweep over courses parallel and equal, but the measure at which one mind stops short is outstripped and overlapped by the standard of another. The effect of this inequality upon our casuistry is obvious at a glance. If all our moral judgments are *preferential*, two terms must always be present as the objects of comparison. They are not both, however, explicitly stated in the form usually given to our moral problems; one only is advanced; the other, held in reserve, and therefore unnoticed. It is in this suppressed

term, which may secretly differ in the mind of different disputants, that the source of apparent divergency lies. Ask two persons the value of B: if one measures it by A as a standard, and the other by C, their answers will not agree. Not that they contain any real contradiction and may not both be true, when fully unfolded; but so long as the measure tacitly employed remains latent and is not even self-confessed, the *relative* nature of the decision is hid under the disguise of an absolute verdict; one voice declares a given thing to be 'right,' another to be 'wrong;' meaning no more than in the first case that it is superior to one substitute,—in the second, that it is inferior to another. Of no moral activity can the worth be determined without conceiving *what would else be there*, and unless this conception be identical in the thoughts of two advocates, they deal with differing problems under semblance of the same name. When, for instance, a discussion arises, whether we ought to approve of the heroes and heroines who, like Howard, Elizabeth Fry, or Florence Nightingale, go into original fields of humane enterprise at the cost of home blessings of great price; those who condemn the course and those who admire it will have different conditions present to their thought: the former will regard it as an abandonment of family affections and nearer claims; the latter will perceive in it the sacrifice of self at the bidding of a pity and love which, in embracing the wider, does not cease to compass the lesser sphere. The former sees in it something *less*, the latter something *more*, than the faithful service of duty close at hand. It is the same in all the great controversies of practical morals. The defender of the laws of honour secretly compares the sensitiveness to character which asserts itself against danger and death, with the pusillanimity which hugs its safety at the expense of a good name. The impugner of the same laws compares this jealous self-vindication with the quiet appeal to a higher tribunal, and reverential willingness to 'judge nothing before the time.' The same type of disposition is placed side by side, in the one case, with the term below it, in the other, with the term above it. When the phenomenon of Christian martyrdom took the Roman magistrates by surprise, it presented to them the aspect of a mere obstinate egotism,—a setting up of self and its whimsies against sanctities dear to the universal heart of man : seen from a higher point of view, it becomes the completest self-surrender, in allegiance to a Divine Person, who is the reality of all that men revere. The significance of the act is not only changed, it is inverted, in these two views : instead of being an example of individual conceit against a general reverence, it is an utter merging of the individual will in devotion to one who is the substance of all shadows of true worship. For the confessor to yield and pay his sacrifice to the emperor would be, in the eyes of Pagan observers, a becoming modesty; in those of his fellow-disciples, an impious betrayal of the Supreme Friend. The conception, therefore, of what else would be there, were the trial declined, is altogether different : hence the different verdicts, which, though apparently pronounced upon the same act, are really directed upon it in dissimilar and even opposite relations. Thus the facts that a part only of the moral scale is present to particular persons, and to different persons not the same part, readily explain the divergencies of ethical judgment, without compromising in the least the uniformity of moral conception throughout the human race.

(3) The process by which the scale thus partially familiar to us extends its range and familiarises us with nobler problems, deserves attention. 'As in water face answereth to face, so the heart of man to man.' It is the objective image of the nature sleeping within us, that wakes it up and startles it into self-knowledge. The living exhibition in another of higher affections than we have known, far from remaining unintelligible to us, is the grand means of spiritual culture,—the quickener of conscience and the opener of new faith. The natural language of every passion of which we are susceptible speaks to us with a marvellous magic,

and calls up fresh islands and provinces of consciousness where there was a blank before. And whoever is the first to give explicit manifestation to our own implicit tendency touches us with admiration and acquires a certain power over us. If the feeling he expresses is nearly *on our level*, if he is only a little beforehand with us in shaping our dumb and formless wants, he becomes our literary interpreter or our party leader,—a chief indeed, but of the same kind with the followers. If the affection he realises is *above us*, strange to our experience but congenial with our capacity,—a more heroic endurance or more conquering love than we had conceived,—he becomes to us an author of faith, prophet and brother at once, even mediator helping us into nearer union with God. Even amid the passions of war, natures hardened by obstinate antipathies will yield and melt before the experience of a nobler type of feeling than they have yet conceived; as may be seen by the well-attested and softening surprise shown by the wounded Egyptians in the late war, when they found themselves treated by their captor with as tender a care as his own soldiers: that victory should thus instantly quench the angry heats and flood the heart with cooling pity, is more than they had ever dreamed, and will make it hardly possible for them, without compunction, to go and do otherwise. On the same principle it is that the true reformer of character seeks the conscience of men, not through methods of reasoning, or appeals to interest, but through scenes in the drama of life, exhibiting the conflict of the better and the worse, within the range of intelligible possibility, yet a little beyond the verge of realised experience; the story of the saint, the hymn of the martyr, the parable of the Samaritan, wielding a persuasion of which the pleader and the philosopher may despair.

The readiness in the human mind to *look up*, to welcome higher spirits and hang on to them, is only the external manifestation of that hierarchy of principles which we have learned to recognise. As each spring of action, in the ascending scale, has diviner right over us, so have the persons that become its embodiment a corresponding command of our reverence and trust. The steps on which the human world without is ranged are in conformity with the ranks of natural impulse within; not only attesting their constancy, but bringing them into consciousness. Were it not for the *inequalities of human character*, repelling us in aversion, subduing us to veneration,—here given us to rule and there to serve and trust,—life would have no sacred discipline, and would never open to us the resources of our moral nature. Nor could its experience do this, even through the presence of higher minds than our own, if the key were not within us by which to lead off their significance and recognise their authority. The lower creatures, often so quick to interpret in us the signs of susceptibilities like their own, present only blank looks towards every expression of the distinctive characteristics of man,—the abstracted gaze of thought, the pallor of remorse, the attitude of prayer The meaning stops, where their nature ends. And so would it be with the action of nobler beings upon us, were we not of the same spiritual kindred, and therefore open to the Divine contagion of their greatness. These two conditions, —a common nature, and an unequal development,—determine the whole grouping of our humanity, creating everywhere a moral interdependence, of like and unlike, of less and greater, of crude weakness and ripe strength, analogous to that of the *family;* in which indeed we see the proper unit of society and a miniature type of the whole organism of the moral world. Thus, the external discipline and education of human character answers exactly to the inner hierarchy of affection and obligation.

(4) The theory of conscience which has been expounded throws, perhaps, some light on a belief otherwise so paradoxical as to perplex us by its prevalence in almost every age; I mean, the belief in a separate heaven and hell, and a corresponding distribution of men into only two classes, of good and bad, friends and enemies of God. At first sight, nothing can well appear more unnatural and defiant of all

fact than this dual classification. The moment you attempt to apply it to actual persons, and to walk through the world parting, as you go, the sheep from the goats, you perceive how little it answers to any apparent reality, and how shocking the effect would be of running it sharply through life. The varieties of character, and the degrees of faithfulness, are infinite, and are discriminated from each other by the finest shades; nor can any perception less perfect than the judicial eye of Omniscience determine the innumerable gradations. How then can eternal Equity be content with only two provisions for the treatment of these complex differences? Even our coarse human justice, in the administration of a family, a school, an army, a nation, has more exactitude than this, neither treating all culprits alike, nor regarding with equal favour all that escape penalty. Yet, strange to say, this doctrine, seemingly so harsh in itself and so impossible to confront with experience, has by no means been a mere favourite with the rude multitude: it has had the most powerful hold of minds capacious, philosophical, harmonious, devout; and has rarely failed to throw its awful shadow across the holiest souls. Evaded and explained away by mediocre men and in rationalistic times, it is gazed at with full face by a Plato, a Dante, a Milton, a Pascal; and surely has no ambiguous expression in the records of our faith, and is referred by them to the Christian's supreme authority. How is this contradiction to be resolved? I reply: by turning from the outward to the inward look of moral evil. It is when we contemplate its external phenomena and manifestations, when we critically sort out the aspects of human character as objects of natural history, that we find ourselves involved in endless intricacies of classification. It is not, however, from the scene around us that we learn the nature of right and wrong; but from our own self-consciousness. Thither we must retreat, if we would consult the true and primitive oracle of God's will upon this matter. And what do we *there* find, when we interrogate the cases of moral probation, taken one by one? We find, if our exposition has been correct, a controversy between two competing impulses, of which, be their relative vehemence what it may, we well know one to be better, the other worse,—the one to express the Divine, the other the Satanic claim to us,—the one to constitute the highest, the other the lowest possibility which the crisis opens to us. Between them the interval is unspeakably great, a gulf infinite and impassable; they are not first and second best, but simply the absolutely right for us to do and the absolutely wrong. The whole problem lies in this alternative; and if, under the temptation, we fall, we perpetrate the very worst that the moment allows, and take the offer of sin unreservedly and on its own terms. What more could we have done in the guilty service than we have done? We have performed all that it asked of us. It matters not that there are other passions viler still, other acts conceivable of deeper turpitude. They had no place in our problem, and were wholly absent from the field; and what alleviation is it, that we did not lapse under a temptation that never tempted us? Ought it to mitigate to the offender the shame of a lie, that he might have told two? Would it dry the tears of Peter's denial, to be told that he had not murdered, but only disowned, his Lord? No: he would protest, as remorse in its agony ever must, that he had done to the uttermost that which Satan had desired him to do, and gone against Him whom he knew to be the holiest. If this be true of one instance of inner conflict, it is true of all: each, in its turn, presents us with the option of two possibilities, between which is no *via media;* but which are for us, now and here, the ultimate limit of good and evil, the very essence of life and death,—allegiance to God or Devil. Hence the *immeasurable* nature of the compunction awakened by wrong-doing,—the total inability to forgive one's self,—the sense of an evil that is irreparable and a sin beyond all gauge. Were our future to be simply determined by that one trial, it could only present a heaven which we miss, and a hell into which we have flung ourselves away;

and this dualistic conception is but the external counterpart of the single combat within every tempted soul; it is the natural faith of conscience believing simply as it feels.

Nor, perhaps, is this natural faith quite so much checked as we might anticipate by the obvious reflection, that the awards of Divine justice must be given, not in consideration of one single act, but on a survey of the life as a whole, lights and shadows being taken together. There are reasons in the very nature of the moral law, when rightly understood, why there can be no such keeping of accounts and discharge of balances between us and God. But we may meet the difficulty from another side. It is perhaps less unreasonable than might at first appear, to appreciate ourselves by a single moral sample, instead of by an extended average. It may be doubted whether the wider range would often reverse the verdict founded on the solitary case. In the earlier period of responsible life there will, no doubt, be some wavering and alternation between defeat and victory; but so rapidly does weakness or force of conscience set in and become habitual, that every lapse is a fearful portent of another, and every faithful achievement a presumption of more; and the volitions of the same mind fast assume a determinate complexion, rarely differing much from the premonitory symptoms of its first probation. Men certainly differ greatly, and A will not yield under B's temptation, nor B under A's; but rarely does a man vary greatly from himself, victor to-day and vanquished to-morrow; and if a solemn suspicion creeps into his heart that, fallen once, he is fallen for ever, its shadow is only so far deeper than the truth of fact, as may be needful to startle him into truth of impression. An incalculable proportion of what are called diversities of character are constitutional rather than moral distinctions, no more the ground of any judicial award than the fact that, when you were tempted, I did not sin. Were this class of differences removed, and men arranged solely by their fidelity or infidelity in dealing with their own problems, who shall say how near the classification would approach the twofold distribution of the ever yielding and the ever firm?

In thus tracing the doctrine of heaven and hell to its psychological origin in the dualism of conscience, I do not mean to offer a plea for its outward form, but a justification of its inner significance. When the *infinite turpitude* which compunction feels to be inherent in its sin is expressed by *endless duration* of punishment, no doubt incommensurable elements are brought together, as if they had a common measure. Quality cannot thus be translated into quantity, intension into extension, complexion of guilt into duration of suffering; and the attempt to do so must be taken simply as expressing, in a mythological way, the sense of transcendent evil and unworthiness in the conscious violation of moral law. It is ever the tendency of the human mind to evade the necessity of 'comparing spiritual things with spiritual' by comparing them rather with temporal and sensible,—to reduce moral and religious notions to terms of time and space,—to substitute images and magnitudes given in perception for the ideas and intensities belonging to the higher affections; and it is in obedience to this tendency that for superlative shame an equivalent is supposed to be found in everlasting suffering. But the moral infinitude is too real to be thus defined, and delegated to an inferior representative.

The several phenomena which thus turn up precisely as our exposition would prepare us to expect, may serve as confirmatory evidence of its correctness. And we may now rest in the conclusion, that the objects of our moral judgment are, primarily, our own inner springs of self-conscious action, as freely preferred or discarded by our will; and that we are enabled to exercise this judgment by a consciousness, inseparable from the presence together of more springs of action than one, that there is among them a relative order of worth, binding us to admit the better and exclude the worse.

CHAPTER II.

THEORY OF PRUDENCE.

The real nature of our moral constitution will come out still more clearly, if, instead of longer looking at what it includes within itself, we now turn to what it excludes, and mark the boundary that separates it from neighbouring provinces of our humanity. To do this fully and systematically would indeed be to anticipate our review of the chief heteropsychological theories of ethics, which are all founded on an attempted identification of the moral sentiments with some other function of our nature. But without serious trespass on ground that yet awaits us, we may sufficiently complete our present exposition, if from *moral* judgment, in its objects and modes, we discriminate *prudential;* and show how the two, so apt to be confusedly mixed up together, stand at once contrasted and related.

i. OBJECTS OF PRUDENTIAL JUDGMENT.

(1) While the objects of *moral* preference are the *springs of action within us*, the objects of *prudential* preference are the *effects of action upon us*. Shall we smart for what we do? or shall we gain by it? shall we suffer less, shall we profit more, by *this* course, or by *that?* These are the questions, and the only ones, that are asked in the counsels of prudence. Happiness, security, content, so far as they are under human command, are there the grand ends in view, decisive of every alternative. We ask not about the affection it is good *to start from*, but about the result it is pleasant to *tend to;* and choose accordingly. In other words, it is *sentient* good, not of course bodily alone, but incident to all our faculties,—

the good of which we are susceptible as beings of pain and pleasure, and of which all animated nature, moral or unmoral, is susceptible,—that here attracts the eye and directs the will. Were we destitute of sensibility, or were all exercises of our activity neutral in this respect, there would be no room for this sort of wisdom: yet differences of moral authority and value might still remain in a nature thus partially benumbed,—as the tones still hold their intervals in muffled bells. True, the moral consciousness, though not *presupposing* any sentient effects of our activity, would soon be *followed by them;* because we cannot imagine the higher authority either obeyed or resisted without entailing its own inner sequel of satisfaction or shame. This, however, is the aftertaste afforded when the prior ethical energy has asserted itself; and is not a condition of its origination. At all events it is plain that, if a moral consciousness is inseparably followed by a prudential, the prudential does not involve a moral; its only condition being a difference among the sentient effects of the will, without of necessity any difference in the felt intrinsic worth of the impelling cause.

(2) From this difference in their object it follows, that prudence is an affair of *foresight;* moral judgment, of *insight.* The one appreciates what *will be;* the other, what immediately *is:* the one decides between future desirable conditions; the other, between present inward solicitations. Hence, the two do not stand in the same relation to *experience.* Prevision is impossible anterior to experience; nor can we tell, till we have tried, whither even our own propensities will lead us, into what thicket of mixed consequences,—thorn-bearing and fruit-bearing,—they may carry us away. But intuition, as we have characterised it, is simply *self*-knowledge; and requires nothing but the presence and fermentation in the mind of the principles which it has to estimate: the inner eye, unless it droops in wilful sleep, is ever open, and is potentially beforehand with the first problem that can arise. For want of experience

we may *blunder*, but not *sin*. That *moral judgment* should thus anticipate action, while prudence has to wait for it, is surely the proper order of endowment for a being really responsible; for one appointed to be, in character, without excuse for his transgressions, but, in understanding, the pupil of his own mistakes. The instant that any contending principles press their invitations on him, *there* too is the consciousness of their respective rights; and if he is betrayed into wrong, he is self-betrayed. His *duty* consists in acting *from the right affection*, about which he is never left in doubt: it is his *wisdom* only that consists in *pursuing the right end*, and this can afford a little time to grow; and will perhaps grow none the less, for the discipline of a few painful but guiltless errors. The different effect of experience on the prudential parts of character, and on the moral, accords but too well with this mode of discriminating them. The later life of most men is the more discerning and well-advised; but the earlier years are nobler and purer; and to find the true instinct of conscience, we may more often go with hope to the child, than to the grand-parents. Unfaithfulness inevitably impairs and corrupts the native insight, which remains only to those who sacredly use and guard it; and then, the substitute to which men turn is always their foresight, which can scarcely fail to become finer as the combinations of life are more numerous, and the years are prolonged. Thus, in the growth of Prudence there is almost a necessity of nature; but in even the continuance of Conscience, a contingency of pure and obedient will. We need not resort to the hypothesis of a pre-existence of souls, and believe that they are entombed in this life as an expiation, in order to explain either the glimpses of 'heaven about us in our infancy,' or the gathering darkness of a worldly maturity. The clear Divine light, by which we recognise the good at first, is not the trail of any departing glory, going home into some foreign sphere; it is inherent in our fresh nature. Nor does any sad fate quench it by mere mists of time: it will not only abide, but spread and brighten, unless with some smoke of covetousness we spoil and hide the promise of its dawn. Indeed, it would be indirectly conceding too much to experience,—only shifting its scene to an antecedent life,—to pronounce our moral consciousness inexplicable, except as an ἀνάμνησις lingering with us from an earlier state, for should we not thus assume that, somewhere or other, it must have been *learned*,— picked up from without,—perceived or read off from an objective scene? Exalt and spiritualise that scene as you may, call it the realm of Divine ideas, or the sphere of eternal Reason, your resort to it is only in order to supply you with a fund of experience, as the possible source of the higher insight, and to evade the necessity of treating that insight as spontaneous. Far truer in feeling (as well as more thoroughgoing in thought) is the modern philosophy, which is content to assert the simple spontaneity of certain elements of our knowledge, and to substitute the doctrine of *à priori* notions for that of *reminiscence*. To the very nature of moral discernment it is essential, that it be spontaneous, ready to meet the first occasion of moral experience, and that it be not therefore itself a product of experience. The more we appreciate what *obligation* means, the more shall we rest in the psychologically indigenous character of its conditions, without any hankering after a process of derivation for them. We shall expect them among our *data;* and shall seek nothing in the inductions of experience, except what belongs to the *unmoral* intelligence. Conscience is given: Prudence is found.

(3) Now the *effects of action*, in the foresight of which Prudence consists, are of two kinds. First, there is the direct gratification of the impulse whence the action proceeds; and, secondly, there are the indirect and collateral consequences reflected back upon us from the world around on which the act is thrown, and where it sets new agencies at work.

The first of these, being the direct fruit of our own nature, is constant and inevitable, repeating itself each time that the same spring of action has its way. It is of necessity also a pleasure, or at least a relief : for there is no propensity which it is not an uneasiness to suspend and a satisfaction to indulge. Of what kind the gratification will be we do not know beforehand: it is the characteristic of impulse to drive us *blindly* forward on what it is commissioned to obtain; and the thirst that first sends us to the draught gives no prescience of the water's taste and feel. But gratification of some kind is inseparable from the restored equilibrium which ensues, when clamorous impulse is paid off and dismissed. Nor can it well be denied that the greater the tension of the previous affection, the more considerable will be the satisfaction attending its exercise; the intenser the thirst, the sweeter the cup of cold water; the deeper your pity for a sufferer, the greater your joy at his deliverance. This rule holds, not only of the several gradations of each single passion, but of the relative strength of all: the covetous man is never so happy as in his gains, or the ambitious as in his honours, or the resentful as in his revenge. So far therefore as this primary order of effects is concerned, we must say, that they reach their most favourable amount in the wake of the strongest impulse, and that the wages of propensity rise with its vehemence. And, till we are corrected by ulterior considerations, we must pronounce it the law of prudence to gratify the tendencies in the order of their eagerness, and live chiefly in the indulgence of the ruling passion, whatever it be. Apart from all considerations of conscience, and from the hazards of other men's opinions, the intensity of a desire recommends it to the economist of pleasure as first claimant on his choice; and *he* is in this sense the discreetest administrator of his life, who never denies himself his uppermost wish, and heeds every solicitation in proportion to its importance! We should thus reach a definition of Prudence which clearly marks its distinction from Duty: Prudence is self-surrender to the strongest impulse; Duty is self-surrender to the highest. And whoever would show that the two principles concur, must prove coincidence between the scale of strength and the scale of excellence.

ii. MODIFICATIONS BY COEXISTING MORAL JUDGMENT.

The fairness, however, of this account of Prudence may very naturally be called in question; for it omits from its reckoning all the elements of pleasure from action except one. The advantage of yielding to a vehement impulse may be dearly purchased at the cost of the second class, of external and ulterior effects,—the consequences entailed by the order of the world and the sentiments of mankind, including our own. This is unquestionably true. But what are these corrective consequences of precipitate action? They turn out, on inspection, to be no mere phenomena of our *natural history*, but creations, direct or indirect, of our *moral constitution:* they are due entirely to the fact that, in the human being, there is a natural order of worth among the springs of action, as well as an order of strength; and accordingly they are not found in the inferior animals, that are disposed of without penalties by their own propensities. You are suffering, we will suppose, the effects of giving way to some uppermost impulse. Does the smart consist in the compunction of your own mind? *That* is an anguish you would never feel, did you not know of a higher principle which you have neglected; the misery of self-contempt flows from some inner reverence insulted. Or does your punishment consist in the indignation of your fellow-men? This also visits you because the spring of your action is not, in their estimation, the highest, and they recognise a more legitimate authority which you might have been expected to obey. They may very likely misread and misinterpret the case; but their sentiments, however misapplied, are expressive of a moral nature, familiar with the notions of right and wrong; and are the social equivalents of your own conscience, only judging imperfectly at one remove or more from the interior facts. Or do you suffer for your folly in fortune and in health? Only in a morally constituted world could such sad experiences arise: they are attached as consequences, not to any part of our nature, in the proportion it would hold in a perfectly *un*moral or a perfectly moral condition of being; but distinctly and exclusively to *excess*. They are the characteristics of a state where *sin* has room to be; to the mind that has degraded itself they come without surprise, and as if in answer to inner forebodings. They embody, in the very framework of the world, the moral affections of its Author, and reflect our own conscience in his works and ways, not less than the disapprobation of men in theirs. The just inference to be drawn from a survey of such consequences is simply this: that Prudence, in a world morally constituted, where sin has to be visited, and a scale of authority to be felt, will be different from what it else would be, and have new elements of pain to deal with; that Duty will modify Prudence by adding fresh terms to her problem; not, that Prudence, out of its own essence, can ever constitute Duty. Mere sentient susceptibility, filtered however fine, gives no moral consciousness; but a moral consciousness, like every other, cannot fail to be attended by joys and sorrows of its own. Where the susceptibility of conscience is already acute, its sufferings or satisfactions will be considerable enough for prudence to consult; and the good man would be a fool, were he other than good. But in proportion as the moral consciousness is obtuse, its pain and pleasure, being fainter, may be neglected with greater impunity; Prudence may make up her accounts, throwing away such inappreciable fractions; and a bad man without conscience, you cannot call a fool for not acting as if he had one. He neglects no elements of happiness about which he cares; and a career which would make better men miserable brings him no distress. Compunction he escapes by his insensibility; the sentiments of others are indifferent to him, so long as he holds his place among companions on his own level, and, short of the physiological penalties of nature and the direct punishments of human law, there is nothing to restrain him, on prudential grounds, from following the bent of his predominant inclinations. Nothing therefore seems vainer than the attempt to work moral appeals by force of self-interest, and to induce a trial of virtue as a discreet investment. To good men your argument is convincing but superfluous; to the bad, who need it, it is unavailing, because false. If you cannot speak home to the conscience at once, condescend to no lower plea: to reach the throne-room of the soul, Divine and holy things must pass by her grand and royal entry, and will refuse to creep up the back stairs of greediness and gain. Notwithstanding all that philosophers have said about the agreement of virtue with rational self-interest, it may be doubted whether their reasonings ever recalled by a single step any wandering will; while it is notorious that the rugged earnestness of many a preacher, assuming a consciousness of sin and speaking to nothing else, has awakened multitudes to a new life, and carried them out of their former nature. In short, it would never have been prudent to do right, had it not been something infinitely more.

Among our springs of action, then, there prevails a moral scale, according to the order of excellence; and a prudential scale, according to the order of strength. Now, of these, the former, from the very nature of the case, is identical and constant for all men; the latter, variable with different persons; the one, universal, like Reason; the other, individual, like Fancy. I say, 'from the very nature of the case;' because the relative *excellence and authority* vindicated for our several principles is, in its whole essence and meaning, no accident of our particular personality, but binding upon us and upon all natures which are the theatre of the same principles. We accordingly apply its rules to others, as well as to ourselves; and so consonant is this to the general feeling of mankind, that no one objects to the recognition of a common moral law, dominant over all idiosyncracies. Obligation claims sway over the personality,—a claim which would be belied, were it a mere subjective phenomenon. As surely, therefore, as our highest faculty does not lie, so certain is it that each same spring of action is constant to the same relative place in the secret reverence of every human being. Were it otherwise, and could it turn up black in one mind and white in another, no mutual understanding and converse on morals could take place. The fact that comparison of ethical ideas is not less practicable to us than comparison of scientific ideas, sufficiently attests that Conscience, like Intellect, is the common property of humanity, the basis of our union, not of our divergencies. On the other hand, nothing can be more strictly an incident of individuality than the *relative force* of any particular passion: nor can any one fail to observe, that the impulse which tyrannises in one man may be imperceptible in another. Often, it is true, we are tempted to fancy that what is most delightful to us must be so no less to every one else, just as the child insists that his favourite dish must be ambrosia to all who taste it. But this little bigotry of expectation is soon found by experience to be an illusion; and the reaction from it is embodied in a maxim equally extravagant on the other side, viz. that what is 'one man's food is another man's poison.' The general fact, however, is conspicuous, that those who are in accord respecting right and wrong, and recognise the same moral law, feel the force of very different temptations; their agreement is human; their deviations are individual: or, to use the Platonic mode of statement,—the good (like the true) is one; the evil (like the false) is manifold. This presents in a new light the distinction between the two rules of life which we are comparing. Whoever lives out of the *universal order*, permitting the impulses that stir him to hold the rank which the voice of humanity assigns them, follows the *Moral* rule. Whoever lives out of his personal deflection from the universal order, and takes up with his egoistic forces of propensity, follows the *Prudential* rule; and *that* none the less, though, on too dangerous a clashing of the two, he makes concessions against himself; for in such interested compromise he only humours the sentiments of others for the sake of gain or security to his own.

Here we alight upon an interpretation of the doctrine characteristic of the Christian mystics,—that *Self* is the centre and essence of all Sin, and the *surrender of self* the one simple condition of union with God. There is indeed in this doctrine a great deal more than our present exposition avails to reach; but among other things it has this meaning: —that the Will, whenever it goes astray, follows the direction of *individual* tendency and wish,—the forces of the Ego unrestrained by reverence for a good that is not ours, and that, only when all regard to these personal interests is merged in devotion to that hierarchy of affections which, in being universal, is Divine, is the mood begun which sets man and God at one. To have *no wish, no claim, no reluctance* to be taken hither or thither, but to yield one's self up as the organ of a higher spirit, which disposes of us as may be fit, constitutes the mystic ideal of perfect life. And how can we more accurately describe the cessation of all resistance to the rightful claims upon us of the several spontaneous affections? how more vividly express the very essence of Duty sublimed into devotion,—which surely is, to let the Divine order pass through us and take possession of us and turn us to this or to that, without being disputed by inclination or retarded by imperfect alacrity? The identification, which this doctrine implies, between the inner consciousness of a sacred order among our springs of action, and the real, eternal, objective Will of God, seems to me to construe very faithfully the sense of *authority* attaching to the revelations of our moral nature · they are *in* us, but not *of* us: not ours, but God's. And just in this feature of the conscience do we find the point of vital connection between morals and religion; where the rule and method given for the life of man is felt to be a communion established with the life of God. But in these remarks I am trespassing on the next reach of my subject.

CHAPTER III.

MERIT AND DEMERIT.

We have seen what the Moral order of impulses means; and what also the Prudential. In different minds, they variously conflict, or approximate to harmony; and the phenomena which thus arise, with the types of conception and language which we employ to mark them, deserve attention.

(1) Where the order of strength among the springs of action is at variance with the order of their excellence (as, more or less, it is in all of us), inclination will often stand in the way of duty. It is evident that, in such cases, the vehemence of the temptation will be proportioned to the extent of discrepancy between the two scales. In the choice between competing impulses, the agent suffers no violent wrench from the right course, unless the lower passion is by far the intenser of the two, if its importunity is faint, its conquest involves no fierce struggle. And for that reason we feel that we have the greater right to expect a victory, and recognise the deeper shame in a defeat and fall. The demerit and disgrace of wrong-doing become greater, as the temptation is less; the evil seems then transferred from the surroundings of the agent to the gratuitous movement of his personality. A murder committed in subservience to a petty theft, like that perpetrated some years ago on a boy for the sake of his pair of boots, is instantly felt to indicate a far deeper pravity than a homicide from passion or revenge; the solicitations of a trivial gain being so much easier to resist, than the turbulent energy of anger or vindictiveness. It may be said indeed that, in minds corrupt as this criminal's, the cupidity is *not easier* to resist than rage: moulded

or trained to a certain coarse greediness, he may have been susceptible of more vehement excitement from the prospect of a little property, than from that of a great retaliation. Possibly; but the moment we take this view of the case, we judge it differently: we suspend the sentence of exceptional severity, and begin to treat the act as rather an insanity than a crime. But, so long as the impression of its extraordinary demerit continues, we assume, as the ground of that opinion, that a faint inducement of pleasure was allowed to set aside an intense shrinking of the moral sense. And the immediate tendency of men to take this view shows, that they do not readily believe in constitutional incapacity for moral responsibility. A *certain* play of variety in the temptations of different men, and a corresponding margin of lenity in judging them, are freely allowed. But the idiosyncracies of the prudential scale are always presumed to have a limit, and not to run out beyond the conditions essential to a real probation; and until special proof is furnished of maniacal distortion of feeling, we suppose ourselves able to estimate approximately the seductive force there may be in a purse of silver or a pair of shoes, when set against the reverence for human life. Whether this presumption is well founded or not, is indifferent to our present purpose; which is simply to interpret our moral sentiments, to show what they imply, and what must stand or fall with them. If there be no such thing as ill-desert at all, and sane and insane are in the same moral category, it is an illusion to discuss its degrees. But if it be a reality, then its measure follows the rule which I have given. Accordingly, all arguments in aggravation of punishment aim to show, how monstrous has been the violation of moral order on slight inducement; while the plea for mitigation invariably is, that, whatever the offence, the temptation to it was a fearful strain on human frailty. When we would picture to ourselves a very prince of wickedness, to take the headship of all evil, we place our Satan on the original vantage-ground of an angelic nature and a heavenly lot, that his fall may be without excuse. And when we would explain away the guilty aspect of some lost creature, and reduce condemnation to pity, we follow him back to a culprit parentage and fortuitous infancy, that repressed the dawnings of any moral order in the conscience, and inflamed a fever of irregular desires.

It follows from this, that the life of widest visible aberration from a Divine standard of perfection is not necessarily the most wicked. The extent of ethical deflection will have a general correspondence with the force of temptation; and the force of temptation operates, not to increase, but to relieve the shade of guilt. Among the sinful crowd, it is intelligible enough how 'many that are last shall be first, and the first, last.' The habits of most conspicuous depravity and license will usually be found where opportunity for better things has been scantiest, and the springs of action have been brought, by evil influence, into a scale of force having no reference to their excellence; where parental guilt has entailed the curse of filial debasement; and some hotbed of decaying morals has covered the whole ground with rank weeds, and dwarfed every modest flower that needs the pure air and will not grow in steams. The children whom we send to our reformatories, children born among the criminal class, exhibit, or bid fair to exhibit, the lowest type of moral degradation. But it is justly felt that they have been more sinned against than sinning, and while they present a spectacle of character most repulsive to our moral feeling, our *condemnation* bears no proportion to our *disgust*. On the other hand, beneath the smooth surface of a decent life, in a mind that not only knows the scale of right, but has no passions vehemently averse to it, there may well be (who can doubt that there often is?) an unnoticed shadow of guilt, deep because wilful and gratuitous. There is no need for sin to be large in action, in order to reach its maximum at heart; and the all-searching eye, in reading the record of our humanity, may totally change the disposition into which our outward classification would throw the groups. We do so ourselves, in proportion as we can look beneath the surface and estimate the inner springs of the great human strife. The measure, in short, of our simple repugnance to low character is far different from the measure of our moral condemnation; we recoil from it, as we should from any deformity, in proportion to its visible departure from our ideal of humanity; we condemn it, in proportion as it has arisen in full sight of what is higher, and taken only paltry bribes from suborning interests or passions. To the expression of this fact some precision is given when we say, Where the discrepancy is greatest between the moral and the prudential order of principles, the guilt is least; and where the discrepancy is least, the sin is greatest

This account of our ideas of good and ill-desert I regret to find seriously at variance with a chapter on 'Merit' by Mr. Leslie Stephen, which abounds with just and fine observations, and, if it misses the exact solution, does so only because the determinist psychology, however ingeniously manipulated, can turn out no idea of *Merit* which is not an illusion; and because the author, instead of frankly so treating it, and driving it out of doors hanging on the skirts of Free-will, tries to keep it in his service, and makes it speak what it cannot articulately say. His account may be summed up as follows:

The organised opinions of society, founded on the experienced conditions of social vitality, constitute, in their aggregate, the moral code; and in proportion as a man is moulded into conformity with these opinions, so that they become the law of his character, is he *virtuous*, and is sure to be *meritorious*. These epithets, however, are not absolutely synonymous. Two distinctions are drawn between them[1]: (1) 'Merit is *proved virtue*,' i.e. tested by concrete instances of conduct; for, as Aristotle observes, virtue is an inherent quality which a man does not part with when he is asleep, but for which no *merit* can be claimed till it *does* something[2]. (2) 'Merit is *the value* set upon virtue,'

---

[1] Science of Ethics, chap. vii. i. 10, p. 273.
[2] Ibid. chap. vii. 1. 7, p. 270; 10, p. 273.

differing from it as, in political economy, *price* differs from *utility*; i.e. it would not exist but for the limited supply of the desirable object, and a consequent difficulty of obtaining it. Merit is never attributed to conduct, however useful, of which we are as sure as of air to breathe and daylight for our work. According to this distinction, *merit* is *what you will give* for virtue: according to the first, it is *the virtue for which* you will give something; in either case, its amount is measured by its *marketable value*, and is dependent on the opinions and wants of others, not on conditions personal to the agent himself. Hence, when we say that a man has merit, what we really mean is, we are assured, that he has virtue, considered as the product of a certain social discipline, shaping him to the needs of his world[1].

Further, it is essential to meritorious conduct that it be *voluntary*. As this is an undisputed proposition, it cannot have place in conflicting doctrines of merit, unless the predicate 'voluntary' is taken in different senses. Mr. Stephen supplies us with two equivalents, in order to define his meaning[2]; for an act to be 'voluntary,' it must '*spring from the character;*' for an act to be voluntary, it must '*arise from a motive;*' else it would not be the agent's conduct at all. To see how far these equivalents help us, we must ask what else, besides 'the character' and 'the motive,' the action, in Mr. Stephen's conception, must spring from, so as to forfeit its voluntary nature. The only answer which I can find to this question is, that an action compelled by superior force, as when a man's hand is seized by a stronger and the knife it holds is plunged in another's breast, is not due to the character or motive of the owner of the hand. Is then every uncompelled action 'voluntary?' Is the will co-extensive with human activity? At times, I should certainly put this construction upon Mr. Stephen's doctrine: for (1) he identifies 'the character' with the total Ego, exactly as Mr. Spencer does; and (2) he identifies 'motive'

[1] Science of Ethics, chap. vii. i. 7, p. 272.
[2] Ibid. chap. vii. i. 8, p. 271.

with *whatever moves us*, including not only the prospective ends at which we aim, but the blind impulse of each instinct that propels us. As every possible spring of action is thus covered by these two words, there is nothing left to be involuntary, except the externally compelled. Mr. Stephen, however, cannot mean this; and saves himself from it by sliding into a distinction among motives, viz. between 'extrinsic motives,' or 'external influences,' or 'temptations,' —e.g. bribes, threats, dangers,—and 'internal motives;' and he instructs us, in order to find 'what comes from the character,' to subtract the total effect of the external set, and then credit the character with the residue, and give the award of merit or demerit accordingly. Need I point out the unreality of this distinction? The 'external conditions' which are here set up in antithesis to the internal affections, cease to be external the moment they become 'motives;' and the internal affections wake up only in response to the appeals of these same conditions: both take their psychological place side by side, as *simultaneous springs of action*, the 'threats' turning into *fears;* the 'bribes' into *covetousness*, and both into temptations, confronted by opposite affections which start up to defy them; compassion, sense of justice, reverence for right. It is not, therefore, a conflict between the inner and the outer causality. It all 'comes from the character,' after once the problem has been delivered there, if by the character you mean the entire personality; and the struggle lies between two functions or elements of that character, viz. the scale of relative intensity and the scale of relative worth among the several springs of action. And the difference between the voluntary and the involuntary lies in this: that the former first comes into existence when the *conditions of choice* are present; i.e. when more springs of action than one are consciously operative and pressing for indulgence; while the latter has place when we are possessed by a single impulse, instinctively wielding our activity for an unselected end.

Far from admitting the measure of merit on which I have

insisted, Mr. Stephen reverses it; declaring that the man is most meritorious who has most virtue; and that consequently, if we assume that a certain task has to be performed, the man who performs it most easily is the most virtuous[1]. Yet he admits that a good action proves merit so far as it implies difficulty to the average man. To reconcile these statements, he falls back upon the distinction between the outward and the inward: if the difficulty be in the severity of the external conjuncture, it heightens the merit of the internal conquest over it. If the difficulty arises from the internal intensity of the passion which obstructs the right, so that a tremendous effort is needed to give virtue the victory, it detracts from the merit. This I cannot admit: it shows, no doubt, that the habit of virtue is at present weak and precarious; but it also shows a vast strength of virtuous will in dealing with the momentary problem of duty; and is precisely the noble element which elevates into heroism the initial stages of every conversion from negligent to devoted life. The confusion arises from the false identification of degrees of merit with degrees of virtue. One who *has the greatest struggle to make* in order to achieve the task of duty is undoubtedly *inferior in virtue* to the man who throws it off with ease; but one who *makes the struggle*, however great, has higher merit in the act than the man to whom it costs nothing. It undoubtedly follows from this method of award that if, in the intensity of the struggle, the will succumbs instead of triumphs, the *demerit* is less than it would have been, under surrender to a less vehement foe; and Mr. Stephen urges this consequence as conclusive against our doctrine: 'We are thus led,' he says, 'to excuse a man for the qualities which make him wicked; "true, he committed a murder; but he was so spiteful that he could not help it:" or, "he was exceedingly kind; but he is so good-natured that it cost him no effort:" obviously such reasoning is absurd[2].' It is absurd, however, only on

---

[1] Science of Ethics, chap. vii. iii. 34, p. 299.
[2] Ibid. chap. vii. iii. 34, p. 300.

the naturalistic assumption, that virtue (like ἀρετή) is *the best state of each spring of action,* and that *merit is identical with virtue, or proportioned to it* · in that case, every deviation from the best state, every want of equilibrium in the desires, though it be purely constitutional, detracts alike from a man's virtue and from his merit, not only impairing the perfection of the character he has, but exposing him to reproach for having it. But if, refusing thus to identify the natural and the moral, we assume that, over and above the character as it now comes from the past, there is a living personal power of victoriously siding with any of the suggestions which it brings, then it is not absurd to say, that that power may be meritoriously exercised from end to end of the ascent of virtue; and that he who still pants in the stifling air and toils through the mire of its low beginnings, may deserve as well as one who, perhaps born upon an Alp, looks down upon him from serener heights, and has no longer dangers to surmount. Does not the education of every family proceed upon this principle? Would you not give more credit to a timid child that told the truth against himself, than to the bold and frank who could conceal nothing if he would? to the lie-a-bed girl who sets herself never to be late, and never is, than to her sister who can no more sleep after six o'clock than the cock after dawn? to the passionate boy, who forces himself, under provocation, to shut his lips and sit still, than to his meek brother who never had a flush upon his cheek, or a hot word upon his tongue?

The simple fact is, that the conceptions of 'merit' and of 'responsibility' are strictly relative to the assumption or consciousness of Free-will; and only in the light of this assumption do they admit of any consistent interpretation. You may certainly invent new meanings for the words which you dispossess of the old ones. You may employ 'merit' to signify 'the human quality which you praise because your praise may enhance it;' and 'responsibility' to denote the fact that 'for such and such acts you will smart;' but, as the terms thus become a fresh coinage with values changed, they will not work in with the currency of which they have hitherto formed a part; and will especially introduce utter confusion into every portion of our literature in which ideas of *Justice* play an important part.

(2) So much for the mixed cases (including the whole actual world) in which the two scales co-exist but disagree. It is, however, quite possible for the disagreement to cease, and the two orders to fall into coincidence. This may happen by either of them surrendering its separate solicitations, and being content to merge into the other. And both these extreme cases, though, like all vanishing ratios, never realised by our empirical approximations, it is instructive to contemplate. Let then, in the first place, the prudential order become paramount and absorb the other. To reach this condition, a man has only to persevere in living simply as he likes, and follow at all times the lead of his uppermost desire. Whatever resistance he may encounter at the outset from his compunctions will rapidly give way; each expostulation will be fainter than its predecessor, and the tendencies that quench it will establish a less disputed sway; till, at last, every murmur of remonstrance dies, and the autocracy of inclination is complete. What is the effect and amount of this change? Simply this: the characteristic *human* element is gone; *the man* has disappeared; and in his place there stands either *brute*, or *devil*. In proportion as the impulses that occupy him by turns and carry him into action retain the character of half-blind spontaneity, on which he flings himself with only the hazy foresight of Sense, he lives the animal life; in proportion as intellectual aims predominate, and the open eye computes some moves before it, this absolutism of Self is diabolical. No other idea at least can we distinctly form of evil spirits than this, —that they relentlessly exercise the resources of an intellectual nature for their own ends, without any hindrance from moral distinctions, or owning any law but that of self-will. Attempts, it is true, are made, in fiction and in theology, to represent the fiendish nature as having a more *positive pre-*

ference for wrong; and Milton's Satan sets it up in words as a substantive end: 'Evil, be thou my good.' But the conception is intrinsically incapable of being carried out, nor can you present to yourself in thought a mind *preferring a thing because it is worse*, preference is not possible except on the ground that, in some aspect or other, and in relation to the mind choosing, the thing is not worse, but better. Be it spite (to defy and disturb a Divine being), or ambition (to gain command of a rival realm), there must be some personal passion to gratify in order to render action intelligible at all; and the wickedness at its acme still consists in the surrender to such passion, without restraint from any considerations of affection and rectitude. The question has in every age been raised whether evil is to be regarded as a positive thing, or as merely the negative of good: the Manichæan doctrine affirming the former, and setting up an active hostility between the two principles; and the system of emanations giving verdict for the latter, and accounting for all guilt and sorrow by the privation of Divine light at a distance from its fountain-head. The problem might remain for ever unresolved, did we contemplate it, like those ancient theosophies, from the purely ontologic side. But if we will submit it to a psychological test, its difficulties are greatly relieved. In our consciousness, the only positive forces are the living springs of activity which, in and by themselves, are neither morally evil nor morally good, but which, having a relative worth *inter se*, present a moral quality for the exercise of our preference upon them. It is quite possible that an impulse may become the object of our preference simply on account of its superior worth, independently of any isolated urgency of its own; and thus moral good is capable of becoming a positive energy, determining into existence what else would not appear. But, while we may adopt an act *because it is good*, the utmost that iniquity can do is to take a course *in spite of its being evil:* when you have abstracted all deterring power, and imagined an entire absence of compunction, and wholly annihilated the force, without blinding the vision, of moral distinctions, you can go no further in your ideal of wickedness; simply because *inferiority, comparative meanness*, can never be a ground of preference, and to suppose that it can, is simply to contradict the very idea of *Will*, to attribute persuasive power to pure dissuasion, and speak of an infirmity as a force. So far, therefore, it seems undoubtedly correct to regard evil as simply negative,—a detention among lower things,—a failure of reverence for the higher,—a withholding of the will from God, and a living in the meanwhile entirely out of the desires and affections of the Self. And thus it is true that, when the moral order is lost in coalescence with the prudential, the characteristic strife of an ethical, i. e. of a human, nature ceases: if deadened to consciousness and apprehension, the descent is towards an animal being: if remaining in clear view but without any motive power, it is an angel's fall into a Satanic state.

(3) But now, let us follow out the other extreme; and suppose the absorption of the prudential scale into the moral, through gradual abrasion of all resisting discrepancies presented by the former. How do we designate the ultimate coalescence which thus ensues? Here also, it is evident, all conflict of a double nature dies away, and is succeeded by the peace of entire simplicity. If, on every occasion of controversy between stronger desire and higher authority, the former is freely sacrificed; if, letting our reluctance fall, we go again and always into willing captivity to each diviner hint, only ashamed that it should seem a captivity at all, who can doubt that the Self, thus habitually mortified, will cease to hang back, and grow tired of a resistance ever vain? The eagerness of every unreduced wish will gradually collapse, till it shrinks within the limits of the scale of reverence; the faint energy of every deficient impulse will acquire tone and firmness by a patient gymnastic of fidelity; till, in the end, a perfect harmony ensues between the order of strength and the gradations of excellence. This seems to give the true conception of an angelic

determination of character, but by necessity of nature: the *negative* element requisite for every ethical conception, the antagonism to something resisted and rejected, would be wanting; and the evangelical and the heathen Theism would be without further essential distinction. But Christianity knows nothing of this 'absolute God,' detached from the living world: it takes Him up (if I may say so) *in mediis rebus*, and finds Him sympathising with the struggles of tempted souls, taking sides with their fidelity to good and hiding His countenance from their inclinations to evil, and so identifying His life with a conflict from which, in His own essence, He might remain aloof. Nor is it possible to recognise this sympathy with human probation, without in some way carrying up the contrasted light and shade of moral distinctions into His own inmost being. The only question is, how to conceive any shadow there, and hold the idea of a contrast at all? Is it not impossible that the faintest evil should be in Him? Perhaps the natural answer of Christian feeling would be, *Morally* impossible most assuredly it is: but *naturally*, or otherwise than by preferential affection, not so: the *idea* of the alternative evil cannot be denied to Him, without limiting His view of possibilities; the power to realise it, were He intent upon it, can still less be questioned; that He rejects it from His personal determination, and throws His living sympathy into the strife of finite minds against it, expresses His active repugnance to it. Only by regarding Him first as bearing holy partnership in the conflicts of our humanity, does the Christian faith carry the ethical colouring into the secret places of His being, and by adhering to the relative view, avoid the blanching effect of cold metaphysic light. And so, of all dependent orders of spiritual beings: however raised above the personal sense of temptations such as ours, they must be conceived by us to feel them, as it were, at second hand, through an appreciative sympathy; else would their nature seem wholly foreign to the moral sphere; and awaken in us a neutral wonder, rather than an aspiring reverence. With mind; it is the true 'saint's rest;' the ultimate reconciliation between our personality and God's, in which the breach between the natural man and the spiritual man is taken away by our integration with the Divine will. This repose at the upper end once established, the peculiar moral emotions, of approbation and disapprobation, can no longer be directed towards the character: they are in place only among the contingencies of conflict, and have no application either to a nature where liberty has not yet begun, or to one where emancipation is complete: organic necessity is beneath them; free sanctity is above them: a creature, to be *applauded*, must be more than a creature; a God, to be (in any strict sense) *praised*, must be less than a God. These sentiments are replaced, at such an elevation, by the several degrees of admiration, love, and worship, towards which the ethical feelings ever aspire and in which they ultimately merge. They would be simply æsthetic sentiments, as if drawn forth merely by the καλόν unqualified by the ἀγαθόν, were they cut off from the path by which they are approached, and left alone at their insulated height: and the Hellenic philosophy exhibits this type of feeling towards heavenly beings, as constitutionally beautiful, as prototypes and abodes of the true and fair and good, rather than as tinctured with any proper *character*. The strong hold which the Christian conception has of *Holiness* and *Righteousness*, as predicates of God, arises from the fact that it approaches Him along the pathway of humanity, and contemplates both the Divine perfection and the saintly rest as if it were the contrast and outcome of a conflict of moral alternatives, and resembled the repose in which a probationary drama issues. Not, of course, that any Christian supposes God to be susceptible of temptation, or to have *attained* His infinite perfection through antecedent steps of inward self-discipline. Did we contemplate Him as Absolute, and present Him to our thought in metaphysical solitude, out of all relation to the spirits of created beings, we should be obliged to conceive of Him as perfect, not by the reservation, however, that we thus save the moral essence in higher beings, it is true that their characteristic, in our conception, is the entire coincidence of the prudential order with the moral, so that the probationary conflict disappears.

On the whole, then, *any* discrepancy between the two scales involves self-variance and trial: the sharpness of temptation is proportioned to the extent of the discrepancy. The discrepancy may vanish and peace be attained, by either term merging in the other. In the one case, the moral nature, as distinguished from the spontaneous, goes out by degradation at the lower end; in the other, by apotheosis at the higher.

Mr. Herbert Spencer arrives at a conclusion so nearly resembling in its terms the statement here presented, that it may serve to illustrate both, if we look at their points of agreement and difference In his 'Data of Ethics' he expounds his theory respecting the origin of the sense of moral obligation; and closes the section with the following inference :—

'This remark implies the tacit conclusion, which will be to most very startling, that the sense of duty or moral obligation is transitory, and will diminish as fast as moralisation increases. Startling though it is, this conclusion may be satisfactorily defended. Even now, progress towards the implied ultimate result is traceable. The observation is not infrequent that persistence in performing a duty ends in making it a pleasure; and this amounts to the admission that while at first the motive contains an element of coercion, at last this element of coercion dies out, and the act is performed without any consciousness of being obliged to perform it. The contrast between the youth on whom diligence is enjoined, and the man of business so absorbed in affairs that he cannot be induced to relax, shows us how the doing of work, originally under the consciousness that it *ought* to be done, may eventually cease to have any such accompanying consciousness. Sometimes, indeed, the relation comes to be reversed; and the man of business persists in work from pure love of it, when told that he ought not. Nor is it thus with self-regarding feelings only. That the maintaining and protecting of wife by husband often result solely from feelings directly gratified by these actions, without any thought of *must;* and that the fostering of children by parents is in many cases made an absorbing occupation without any coercive feeling of *ought;* are obvious truths which show us that even now, with some of the fundamental other-regarding duties, the sense of obligation has retreated into the background of the mind. And it is in some degree so with other-regarding duties of a higher kind. Conscientiousness has in many outgrown that stage in which the sense of a compelling power is joined with rectitude of action. The truly honest man, here and there to be found, is not only without thought of legal, religious, or social compulsion, when he discharges an equitable claim on him; but he is without thought of self-compulsion. He does the right thing with a simple feeling of satisfaction in doing it; and is indeed impatient if anything prevents him from having the satisfaction of doing it.

'Evidently then, with complete adaptation to the social state, that element in the moral consciousness which is expressed by the word obligation will disappear [1].'

At first view this may seem to reaffirm, only in better language, precisely the doctrine of our last few paragraphs. And the impression is thus far correct; that in both instances the change of character described involves a cessation, in the agent, of all ideas of conflict in realising his higher aim, so that his best becomes his easiest; and to live on the lines of least resistance in his own nature is at the same time to live according to the law of universal nature. We are agreed about the fact that from a duty performed at first against the grain the reluctance is removed by steady persistence, and no centrifugal desire any longer tends to deflect us. But in the interpretation of this fact a difference

[1] Data of Ethics, chap. vii. § 46, pp. 127, 128.

arises, which becomes apparent when we ask, 'What are the opposites between which the subsiding conflict takes place?' Mr. Spencer will reply, 'It is between our *wishes* and a sensible coercion *ab extra*, or,' as he expresses it, 'that "*moral compulsion*" which consists in a "*consciousness of subordination to some external agency*." The duel has to be fought out between an inward impulse and an outward constraint.' Instead of this, I have preferred to speak of both the combatants in this strife as among the inward impulses of the mind itself, alike awakened by the external conjuncture, alike co-present in the internal consciousness, and contrasted therefore, not in their seat within and beyond the Ego, but in their qualities as springs of action. Here, then, is one difference in our construction of the admitted facts It is possible, however, to treat this difference as merely verbal; and to get rid of it by saying, that Mr. Spencer's 'moral compulsion' does not mean coercion as actually administered from the non-Ego, but only *our sense* of a certain *coerciveness* in the conduct to which we are disinclined, and *that* is just as much an inward feeling as the opposing desire; so that he could quite agree that the competitors and their strife are altogether in the ideal field. Be it so: then, next, let us visit them there, and see how, as psychological phenomena, they come to be set against each other in so hostile a way: wherein consists their contrariety? what qualitative difference causes their repulsion? Mr. Spencer will reply, and I accept the reply, We like the one, and we relatively dislike the other; we long to yield to the first spring; we shrink from going with the second. Their difference, therefore, is that of more or less pleasantness; it is their contrasted standing in the hedonistic quality that constitutes their variance. But now, this variance is, by the hypothesis, at last overcome; and we have further to consider how this is accomplished. By what process does the 'moral compulsion' come to be replaced by willing spontaneity? Mr. Spencer replies to this effect: 'Experience, whether personal or inherited, produces in us a consciousness that the remoter effects of conduct, which from being more indirect and diffused are less thrust upon our view than the immediate, are in the long run of superior importance; so that the general ideas of them and the feelings towards them are 'more conducive to welfare' than those which want to be forthwith gratified; and this consciousness invests them with an influence which at last countervails the mere blind intensity of momentary appetency. This change Mr. Spencer calls '*moralisation*,' and regards as the defining essence of the ethical life: the sentiment of virtue is the 'abstract idea,' picked out and unified from all the concrete cases of satisfied want through voluntary conduct, and differs from the image of any given satisfaction only as every generalisation differs from its particulars. It is a 'better guide,' then, to what? *To a favourable balance of pleasure;* and this is its *whole superiority;* an appetite and a virtue are contrasted only as two grades on the hedonistic scale; the latter is but a higher *Prudence* than the former; and to become moral is to be set free from impiudence. So long, then, as any inward *conflict* continues, it lies between a smaller and a larger figure on the list of pleasantness, and discloses no other quality in respect of which the springs of action are different. And when the conflict ends, it is simply the award of final advantage to foresight over blindness, as in any other case of baffled ignorance; the crown, labelled as the prize of Conscience, is found to be sitting on the brows of Intellect. This is the point at which, for reasons already plain, I find myself obliged to part from Mr. Spencer; and to affirm that the springs of action contain *two sets of differences*, the hedonistic and the moral, which cannot be psychologically resolved into one; that of the former the measure is in their sequel, of the latter, in their principle; that in the same pair, the member that is first in the one measure may be last in the other; that just in this, and not in the relatively high and low figures on each scale, taken by itself alone, consists the conflict of. temptation; and that in the persistent recognition by the will of the moral precedences, regardless of the pleasurable, arises the inward surrender and pacification in which the conflict dies. The story therefore ends, not in giving the laurel to Prudence, and adorning her with a stolen title to ethical rights she can never vindicate; but, on the contrary, with the advance of her white flag, that she may lay down her arms and tender her unconditional submission.

Is it, then, true that when the conflict, thus interpreted, subsides and temptation is no longer felt, the '*sense of duty*' must disappear? Of course, if you choose artificially to limit the word '*Duty*' to *still unwilling* decision, the question is answered before it is asked; you bargain for conflict as part of the word's meaning. But though the conception is born amid the experiences of inward conflict, it will survive them; simply because it needs no more than the *idea* and *possibility* of lapse which are ineffaceable from the memory and consciousness of a progressive moral nature. A right act does not cease to be my duty because I do it willingly; nor am I unconscious of doing what I ought because I also am doing what I would, my conscience does not perish the moment my wishes are in harmony with it. The mind which is thus at peace with itself is still the seat of the same springs of action, with full consciousness of their respective worths; and is still called, in every case of choice, to give effect to that consciousness and go with the better impulse. Unless, therefore, you are prepared to say that the conditions of choice themselves will cease, and leave only 'a spiritual automaton,' so that perfected mind is tantamount to no mind at all, you must admit that the relative apprehensions of right, i.e. 'the sense of duty,' can never be bereft of exercise. What is really attained to by the finished nature is, an entire parallelism between the relations of the prudential and those of the moral scale. But there is in this nothing to destroy the felt gradations of either; we continue to *like* this, that, and the other, with various intensities; we continue to *revere* this, that, and the other, with various depth of homage: that the two orders of feeling meet upon the same objects does not identify them; and should I come to wish always and only what is right, then, more than ever, shall I know that it is not because I wish it that it is right. The moral differences will stand out for me as enduring realities; the proportionate intervals of desire will remain the precarious adjustment to them of a mutable personality.

For these reasons I cannot admit, either that an extension of the hedonist scale by growing abstractions can ever set up 'moralisation;' or, that 'moralisation,' when consummated, must extinguish the 'sense of Duty[1].'

[1] Cf. infra, pp 228-230.

CHAPTER IV.

NATURE OF MORAL AUTHORITY.

In speaking of the relation among the separate springs of action, as they appear in the eye of Conscience, I have frequently adverted to the *Authority* which we acknowledge in the higher over the lower. It is important to approach a little nearer to this feeling, and find what it contains. Not indeed that it is in itself other than a simple feeling, admitting of little analysis or explanation. But on this very account, the attempt to unfold it and produce its equivalents occasionally results in very inadequate expressions for it, which, if carelessly accepted, may confuse or disguise for us its real nature. These we may at least examine and dismiss; and their removal will leave the genuine phrase clear of bewildering gloss and free to speak in its own tone to our thought.

i. INADEQUATE INTERPRETATIONS CONSIDERED.

§ 1. *Bentham's.*

What then is the nature of that *authority* which, we are well aware, the suggestions of honour, for instance, have over us against the whispers of perfidy? and where is its seat? Is it in any sense simply *subjective;* wielded *by myself over myself?* the impulse of one part of the Ego as against the impulse of another part of the Ego? Or, waiving the consideration of the source whence it comes, we may present the other side of the question, and ask whither it goes. Does it direct its messages exclusively to me in whose consciousness they speak, and say only, 'This is *better for you;* whether for others also, I do not mean to tell you?' In neither of these senses, as originating from self, or as terminating in self, is the authority of which I speak conceivable as a mere 'subjective' affair. If the feeling of it be, as I have endeavoured to show, a constant characteristic of human nature, this alone goes far to establish our position. But some additional strength may perhaps be given to it by other considerations. It is the standing accusation of the Utilitarian philosophers against any doctrine of Conscience, that it lays down an arbitrary personal dogmatism as ground of Duty, or a phantom of pretension which, being but the shadow of one's self, the self may shift away. Bentham denounces all appeals to a moral faculty as sheer '*ipse dixitism*,'—a fraud by which incompetent philosophers would palm their own tastes and fancies upon mankind. And Paley, it is well known, ridicules as futile a moral authority which a man can disregard if he chooses, and which leaves it his own affair to give the obedience or pocket the consequences.

Now, if nothing more were meant by these statements than that the presumed authority is simply felt in the individual consciousness, and is recognised only because it is so felt, we should admit them at once. It is exclusively on this 'subjective' report that we own and assert the moral claim, and if other credentials are demanded, we cannot give them, but must be content to maintain the sufficiency of these. The depositions of consciousness on this matter are all we have; but they are quite adequate to the weight they undertake to bear.

If it be meant, that because the authority first turns up in my own consciousness, it is manufactured there, and carries with it no weight but that of personal whim,—the mere accident of individuality,—I cannot accept the inference. It certainly stands in direct contradiction to the very nature of the consciousness itself, which distinctly announces a law over me not of my own making, and would be quite false, were there nothing present but a controversy between my own caprices. How can that be a mere self-assertion of my own will, to which my own will is the first to bend in homage, if not to move in obedience? Bentham describes the 'moral-sense man' as a sort of bully, intent on browbeating men into accepting the verdict he wants them to pronounce. But it is apparently forgotten that he wields against others no power that has not already prevailed with himself; and how we are to apply to his inner controversies the picture, drawn with such humorous exasperation, of his aggression upon the independence of his fellows, it is embarrassing to imagine. Does he manage himself by putting on domineering airs towards his own inclinations, and approaching them with some spurious baton of police, which is but a painted stick of his own fancy? Does he like to slap his own likings in the face, and amuse himself with despotisms of which he is himself the first victim? And if the moral sentiment be no more than a case of *sic volo, sic jubeo*, how is it that, by repeal of the volition, there is still no escape from the command? The power that creates law is adequate to alter law; and the sense of authority which we set up for ourselves we could assuredly put down for ourselves. Yet, as we are well aware, we can pretend to no such prerogative with respect to the claims of the moral consciousness: try as we may, we cannot turn lower into higher, or by enactment establish the obligations of perfidy. There is something here manifestly beyond the play of opinionative despotism. 'The notion of "rightness,"' says Professor Sidgwick, 'is essentially positive,' and 'in the recognition of conduct as "right" is involved an authoritative prescription to do it[1].'

Perhaps, however, it may be admitted that the sense of authority is an adequate ground of obligation for myself who feel it; but it may be maintained that it must have no further application in the criticism and estimate of

[1] Methods of Ethics, Bk. I. chap. ix. § 1, p. 103.

others. That honour is nobler than fraud *for me* is, in this case, no reason for supposing it to be so with others; this arrangement of the scale may possibly be contingent on some personal peculiarity,—on its being my scale and not yours; and may be altered by removing into another mind. The higher excellence does not then belong to the principle of honour, as such, so as to go with it wherever it goes; but only to the accidental form which it has in one person and has not in another. Probably the simple statement of this interpretation of the 'subjective' doctrine is sufficient refutation of it. It no less contradicts the very nature of the moral feeling than the former view: the authority which reveals itself within us reports itself, not only as underived from our will, but as independent of our idiosyncracies altogether. It is an integral function of the spring of action that wields it against all inferior members of the scale; is inseparable thence even in idea: transplant the impulse whithersoever you will, in no mind can it have conscious presence and free opportunity without its relative authority reappearing with it. That authority is not an outward sceptre that may be dropped from its grasp, or laid aside like the insignia of a monarch travelling in foreign lands; but the natural language and symbol of its very life and meaning, the loss of which would be the death of its identity. No one who feels the authority at all can at the same time believe that it is an egoistic peculiarity, which affords him no rational ground of expectation from others: by one and the same operation it imposes on him a duty, and invests him with a right; and to deny the reciprocity, yet hold him bound, is to retain the ghost of obligation, when you have cut away that postulate of a common human nature, which alone links it to life. In all our dealings with one another, nay, in all our self-knowledge in presence of one another, we necessarily assume an invariable constitution of humanity in our separate personalities, and never relinquish this natural ground, except where we are forced from it by positive evidence of specialty. The burden of proof always lies upon those who would introduce a limit on this primitive assumption, and reduce the rule to an exception. But Bentham proposes to invert this order; and sharply calls to account any man who is so constituted as to imagine his own thoughts and feelings the slightest clue to other people's; you are to consider yourself perfectly unique and universally repellent, till you have evidence of some concordance or approximation of nature. It is clear that such a principle would invert the whole logic of our intellectual procedure in the mutual comparsion of notions and beliefs, and make the demonstrative sciences, with their axiomatic maxims, the last residuary products after working through every topic of difference and debate. And a confusion equally artificial would accrue from a similar reading backwards of our ethical procedure. Now if I am justified in assuming in my neighbours an apprehension like my own of the equality of two vertical angles, can any reason be given why I may not in like manner assume that they feel with me the respective 'authority' of honour and perfidy? The supposition of 'subjective' morals is no less absurd than that of 'subjective' mathematics.

'The notion of "ought" or "moral obligation," as used in our common ethical judgments, does not' (says Professor Sidgwick), 'merely import (1) that there exists in the mind of the person judging a specific emotion (whether complicated or not by sympathetic representation of similar emotions in other minds); nor (2) that certain rules of conduct are supported by penalties which will follow on their violation (whether such penalties result from the general liking or aversion felt for the conduct prescribed or forbidden, or from some other source). What then, it may be asked, does it import? What definition can we give of "ought," "right," and other terms expressing the same fundamental notion? To this it might be answered that the notion is too elementary to admit of any formal definition.'
'In our practical judgments and reasonings, it must, I

conceive, be taken as ultimate and unanalysable.' And though, 'in the narrowest ethical sense I cannot conceive that I ought to do anything which at the same time I judge that I cannot do' (so that the obligation is individual), yet 'normally' I imply that the judgment is objective: that is, that what I judge 'right,' or what 'ought to be' must, unless I am in error, be thought to be so by all rational beings who judge truly of the matter [1].

For my part, however, I would even venture a little further than this impersonal conception in dealing with the egoistic explanation of the belief in Duty; and would put this simple question: whether an insulated nature can be the *seat of authority at all*, and whether, by merely splitting the mental constitution into a plurality of principles or faculties, such a relation can be established between its superior and inferior parts? Suppose the case of one lone man in an atheistic world; could there really exist any 'authority' of higher over lower within the enclosure of his detached personality? I cannot conceive it; and did he, under such conditions, feel such a thing, he would then, I should say, feel a delusion, and have his consciousness adjusted to the wrong universe. For surely, if the sense of authority means anything, it means the discernment of something *higher than we*, having claims on our *self*,— therefore no mere part of it;—hovering over and transcending our personality, though also mingling with our consciousness and manifested through its intimations. If I rightly interpret this sentiment, I cannot therefore stop within my own limits, but am irresistibly carried on to the recognition of another than I. Nor does that 'other' remain without further witness: the predicate 'higher than I' takes me yet a step beyond; for what am I? A *person*: 'higher' than whom no '*thing*' assuredly,—no mere *phenomenon*,—can be; but only *another Person*, greater and higher and of deeper insight. In the absence of society or human companionship, we are thus still held in the

---

[1] Methods of Ethics, Bk. I. chap. iii. § 3, pp. 33, 34.

presence of One having moral affinity with us, yet solemn rights over us : by retiring into ourselves, we find that we are transported out of ourselves, and placed beneath the light of a diviner countenance. If it be true that over a free and living person nothing short of a free and living person can have higher authority, then is it certain that a 'subjective' conscience is impossible. The faculty is more than part and parcel of myself; it is the communion of God's life and guiding love entering and abiding with an apprehensive capacity in myself. Here we encounter an 'objective' authority, without quitting our own centre of consciousness, an authority which at once sweeps into the widest generality without asking a question of our fellow-men; for an excellence and sanctity which *He* recognises and reports has its seat in eternal reality, and is not contingent on our accidental apprehension: it holds its quality wherever found, and the revelation of its authority to one mind is valid for all. Each of us is permitted to learn, in the penetralia of his own consciousness, that which at once bears him out of himself, and raises him to the station of the Father of Spirits; and thence he is enabled to look down over the realm of dependent minds, and apply to them the all-comprehending law which he has reached at the fountain-head. If this pathway is correctly traced, from the moral consciousness to religious apprehension, all possible excuse is taken away for treating the authority of Conscience as merely personal and subjective, or even as that of Reason, 'impersonally conceived;' for that which is real in the universal Archetype of all Mind cannot be either an abstraction or an accidental phenomenon of human individuality.

In startling contradiction to the position here laid down stands the assertion of the late Professor Green that 'It is the very essence of moral duty to be imposed by a man upon himself[1];' and, but for the habit of consulting the context of an author's dicta, it would utterly dishearten me to find so profound and noble a thinker pronouncing essential

[1] Prolegomena to Ethics, Book IV. chap. ii. § 324, p 354.

what I had declared impossible. The Hegelian aptitude, however, for unifying contradictions is not easily baffled; and, to my infinite relief, it here comes into play with such success as to melt opposite predications into identity of truth. A man's own 'Self' is not to be understood here as a detached finite individuality, that could be what it is in presence of its mere numerical repetitions: that he has a *Self* at all, and knows it, is possible simply because the universe has an Absolute Self, or 'self-conditioning and self-distinguishing mind [1],' which communicates itself to the human being,—the infinite to the finite spirit,—and constitutes thereby the knowledge of moral law as the expression, under temporal conditions, of an eternal perfection. A man, therefore, is 'a law unto himself,' not by autonomy of the individual, but by 'self-communication of the infinite spirit to the soul [2];' and the law itself, 'the idea of an absolute *should be* [3],' is authoritative with the conscience, because it is a deliverance of the eternal perfection to a mind that has to grow, and is imposed, therefore, by the infinite upon the finite. The relation in which this doctrine presents the intuitions of the human conscience, and the Divine perfection of which they are partial manifestations in life, is in essential accordance with that to which I have given more direct theological expression. The difference is only such as must always remain between a doctrine developed from the idea of *duty* and one founded on the idea of *good;* and I am not sure that even this is not reduced below its legitimate minimum by a free resort, in the 'Prolegomena,' to the conception and language of *obligation*, more congenial to the author's personality than to his theory [4].

The difficulty which many persons feel in accepting the foregoing conclusion arises, I observe, primarily from a

[1] Prolegomena to Ethics, Book II. chap. i. § 85, p. 90.
[2] Ibid. Book IV chap. ii. § 319. p. 349.
[3] Ibid. Book IV. chap. ii. § 324, p. 355.
[4] For an important critique by Professor Sidgwick on the doctrine of the foregoing paragraphs, see *Mind*, No. XXXIX, pp. 434, 435; and for the author's defence the next No. of the same Review.

scruple about the initial proposition: I will therefore restate it in a form which I have given to it elsewhere[1], and endeavour to clear it of indistinctness and doubt. 'An absolutely solitary individual, if invested with power of various action and disposition, might affect himself for better or worse by what he did, but would be subject to no obligation and incur no guilt. The harm he occasioned would be a blunder and not a sin; the good which he earned would prove his wisdom, not his virtue.' 'Surely,' it is objected, 'if this Robinson Crusoe in a desert world were to sink into the brute, instead of becoming more of a man, he would be doing wrong, as well as foolishly.' Perhaps so, if he be a Robinson Crusoe; because he will bring into his solitude a consciousness of all the springs of action, with their significant differences, which belonged to his previous human and Divine relations. But this is not the case which I put. The hypothesis supposes the total absence from the universe of any personal nature, or even sentient nature, but his own: then I say, if his nature is in correspondence with reality beyond it, he will feel no duty; and *vice versâ*, if he has any consciousness of duty, he suffers under illusion.

To take the simplest case first, let us assume that the happiness of his which he may enhance or impair varies only in quantity, and, though coming from numerous objects, is homogeneous and subject to a common measure. Then, when from two instincts or passions the offer comes of a protracted mild satisfaction or an intense immediate one, with a balance in favour of the former, the *folly* of taking the latter is obvious; but the *guilt* of doing so cannot be affirmed with any intelligible meaning. How is he *bound* to make the other choice? '*Obligation*' is a relative term, implying somewhere a corresponding *claim of right:* i.e. it takes two to establish an obligation. *To whom* then is the alleged obligation upon the agent to take the larger amount of pleasure? For here there are *not two*, except indeed the two springs of action; and these are not two agents, nor are

[1] Relation between Ethics and Religion, p. 5.

they agent and patient, between whom *obligation* can subsist · they are but *two phenomena;* and a phenomenon cannot be subject of duty. You will say, perhaps, 'It is *to himself* that the obligation lies to choose the more fruitful lot. By the hypothesis, however, he is the person that *bears* the obligation; and cannot also be the person whose presence *imposes it:* it is impossible to be at once the upper and the nether millstone. Personality is unitary; and in occupying one side of a given relation is unable to be also in the other. In order to constitute for him an obligation, as between the two impulses, he must have *two selves*, one for each; but the very essence of the problem depends on their both appearing in one and the same self-consciousness, before one and the same Will; a *pair* of phenomena co-present in an identical subject. To speak, therefore, of the self as dual is only an inexact way of describing two conditions of a single personality,—its apperceptions of different feelings; and if you affirm a duty, you again throw us upon the absurdity of a duty-bound phenomenon. Shall we gain anything better, if, by a change of phrase, we say that, in experiencing the preferable impulse, the *true Self* is there; in experiencing the other, a *false Self;* and that the latter is bound to yield to the former? To determine what this really means, consider how we are to know the true Self from the false. There are two tests conceivable. (1) As the individual, divided (*ex hypothesi*) against himself, leaves you in doubt, you may go round and consult other samples of the same nature, and return with the discovery of *its* common essence or *selfhood*. This test, requiring a plurality of members of the same type, is inapplicable to our case of a lonely being. (2) You may consult the *long run* of the individual, and identify him with his more frequent rather than his less frequent state. Here, no doubt, you will find it accord with his nature in the long run to take the more rather than the less of offered pleasure; and so, *the true self* must be that which exercises this preference. Admitting that a sense may thus be found for this phraseology, I must yet observe that it does not help the required conclusion. For, a predominant preference of the greater pleasure over the less is a *Prudential* characteristic, not a *Moral;* and where he misses it, the agent has indeed to regret an error, but not to repent of a sin. The difference, therefore, between the so-called true and false self reaches no further than that between the sound and the mistaken economist of personal satisfactions.

Perhaps, however, the missing moral element may turn up, if we now take into account what is claimed as a *second dimension* of pleasures, viz. their *quality*, as well as their quantity. There may be no obligation to take the *larger lot;* and yet there may be an obligation to take the *higher kind*. Waiving for the moment all objection to this second dimension, let us put this proposition to the test employed with the former one. There is *an obligation*, you say, to take the higher quality of pleasure, in preference to the greater quantity. *To whom* then is this due? Surely, only *to himself,* there is no one else to be wronged; he, and he alone, is the loser; and the article which he loses is *pleasure*. And are not his pleasures his own concern? If he takes the cheapest lot, regardless of their being shoddy instead of whole wool, what more can you charge upon him than imprudence or bad taste? By importing a distinction of finer or more vulgar into human satisfactions, you do not step into the region of morals, but only change the field of extra-moral good. If the Italian with his delicate appetite enjoys his simple maccaroni, while the Welshman cannot relish his dinner without his leeks, or the Bohemian his without his garlick, the first is of finer perception; but the coarser taste of the others violates no obligation, and, if open to challenge, is so not as a guilt, but only as a mistake, which an extended experience will detect. All that you can say to anyone under such conditions is, 'You do not make the best of the resources of your nature:' and he may answer, 'Perhaps not; but I am the only sufferer by the waste, and am therefore a squanderer only, not an offender; I wrong no one but myself; and am simply a poorer economist.'

Thus, relative quality in that which is *purely mine and under my will* (as *pleasure* is) carries in it no *authority*, but remains still in the *optional field*. Only where the relative quality speaks to me also as *over my will*, and the higher term is above, not only the lower term as a phenomenon in myself, but *myself* in which both appear, does *authority* make itself felt; i.e. in the morally higher quality is implicitly involved the presence of communicated preference from a superior mind. If, therefore, you suppose the lonely man still to be affected by *a duty* in relation to his several impulses, it is because you assume them to carry in them still the implication contained in your own, as framed for the relations of a social and Divine world.

I cannot be content to use, even for argument's sake, the assumption of two dimensions of pleasure, without again insisting on its fallaciousness. If there are *sorts* of pleasure, they must be something more than pleasure; each must have its *differentia* added on to what suffices for the genus; and this addition cannot be *pleasurable quality*, else it would not detach anything from the genus: to mark a species at all, it must be an *extra-hedonistic quality*. And each sort must have its own; and so far as one is preferable, as a kind, to another, it is so in virtue of what it has *other than pleasure;* and the comparison of them all *inter se*, considered as different kinds, must turn upon their several extra-hedonistic qualities. All that they have from the genus is *quantitative;* and till you get beyond the pleasurable as such, quality does not exist.

§ 2. *Paley's.*

So much for Bentham's charge of '*ipse-dixitism.*' Paley's challenge of the 'authority' of Conscience is essentially different in principle, though the same in result. His question is not, 'What is the authority of your conscience to me?' but, 'What is the authority of any man's conscience to himself?' 'Given, the faculty and all the sentiments it carries;

why should not I do as I like, in spite of it? Be it a real angel with a flaming sword, or be it a scarecrow dressed up by the moral philosophers, it is anyhow a thing that, with adequate courage, may be faced; and if I choose to defy it, and to think nothing of the worst it can do, what then? Have I not slipped through your fingers, and left you with nothing more to say to me?' What more then, let us ask, would Paley have to say in such a case, to eke out our defect of 'authority?'—He tells us, with his usual distinctness: he would fall back on the proclamation of future punishment and reward. This, however, be its efficacy what it may, is no exclusive advantage of his doctrine; it is a resource equally available for the 'moral-sense man,' whose idea is inseparable, and alone is inseparable, from the belief in a retributory judgment. The controversy lies, not between the momentary ideal sense of right and wrong, and the palpable apprehension of reward and punishment; but between the bare calculation of sentient pleasure and pain on the one hand, and the same prospect seen through solemn lights of conscience, as the fulfilment of secret foreboding, the expression of eternal holiness, the answering outward award to an inward verdict long recorded on the felt merits of the case. Even if we admit the worst that Paley can say, viz. that, after all, you must come in the end to plain heaven and hell, it still does not follow that it is as well to begin with them at once and trouble ourselves with nothing else. It makes all the difference whether, in your conflict with sin, this is your front and sole battalion, or whether it is your concealed reserve. Flourish it before the eyes as a mere menace and bribe proffered by sovereign power, and do you think that those whom it scares and tempts will be the noblest and most generous souls? Is not the controversy between God and man then plainly put upon the footing of a coarse trial of strength, and submitted to the test of relative determination and daring? And if some Satan's will refuses to bend before a threatening God, and had rather 'reign in hell than serve in heaven,' how will the Utilitarians deal with him? 'What more have they to say to him?' What has become of their ultimate 'authority'? But can we doubt that many, who would thus harden their faces as flint against this coercion of interest, are accessible all the while to any loving voice that can interpret their inward misgivings, and stir up their slumbering reverence for a life better than their own? What indeed is Christian conversion, what the Pauline escape from Law into Gospel, what the deliverance by faith from the bondage of fear into the joy of trust and love, but precisely an exchange of the crushing sanctions of mere happiness and misery for the higher spiritual dynamics on which Paley throws contempt,—the sense of a Divine kindred and Divine likeness, and the free self-precipitation into union with all that is revered by the faithful soul and set aloft by God in heaven? For the truth is, the mere sentient pleasure or pain on which we are advised to fall back is precisely what men feel to be their own concern, and, in the absence of any moral sense, think they may deal with as they please; and if they choose to take their chance with it, they exercise a right, interference with which they will resent. But the sufferings of guilt,—its remorse and humiliation, its cowardice and forebodings,—are just what each man knows he has no right to stifle and escape: however able to do so by spasms of self-rallying, or artifices of self-forgetfulness, he feels himself here in the presence of elements which are not placed at his disposal, and which are doubly incurred in the very attempt to shun them. Strip away the moral aspect and complexion of pain and pleasure, and every semblance of 'authority' is gone from them, and they sink to a business affair: the one only thing that lends them an acknowledged majesty and draws the homage from our hearts is the light with which Conscience invests them.

That it is not the '*Sanctions*' of duty that commend it to us *as* our duty is obvious, both from their notorious failure when unsupported by the conscience or disproportioned to the sin, and from many current forms of thought and speech.

If we only tell the intending culprit, as a piece of information, 'You *will* suffer for this if you do it,' we make no moral appeal, but address simply his interests. If he is visited with excessive punishment, the moral sympathy of observers goes over from the punisher to the offender; as when all men applauded J. S. Mill's defiant welcome of a hypothetical Divine wrong,—'to hell I will go!' And in expressing their conception of a Divine moral government of the world, men are not content to say, 'God *will* deal with us according to our works,' but 'God *must needs* deal (i.e. *in virtue of His inherent perfection*) with us according to our works.' This it is which constitutes the idea of *Justice* in God, i.e. an inward rule of Right which directs the action of His power and determines the distribution of good and evil; and which first elevates into 'Authority' what else would operate only as a necessity or a bribe. How completely the dignity and glory of the world depend on our finding this moral colouring in the ultimate background of all being is nobly expressed in the words of Socrates: 'If the rulers of this universe do not prefer the just man to the unjust, it is better to die than to live[1].'

We may, therefore, meet Paley's charge with direct contradiction of both its parts, and say that 'authority' belongs not in the least to any mere happiness and misery; and that it does belong altogether to the indications of the moral sense. In fact, the case imagined by him is simply absurd and self-destructive. He first supposes a man *to have a moral sense* and to fall under its lash; and then supposes him to snap his fingers at the wounds, and put up with them as so much sentient uneasiness,—a thing possible only on condition of his *having no moral sense*. The only truth I can find implied in Paley's statement is this: that if there were *no award* of retributory happiness and suffering, the authority of the moral law would be curtailed of its adequate supports. This is freely admitted; not, however, because right and wrong are revealed, and

[1] Quoted by Sidgwick, p. 504.

even in themselves distinguished, only by their consequences, and, by erasure of these, would be equalised; but because, with our reflective knowledge of the better and the worse are connected secret auguries of joy and anguish, the failure and falsehood of which would throw discredit on the whole announcement of the inner oracle.

Thus it would seem to be a fatal thing for the opponents of a Moral Sense to allow the faculty *to be there*. If there, it is manifestly adequate to its alleged function, of reporting right and wrong to us with an authority revealing their nature, and belonging to no appeal addressed to our self-love. The only resource for the utilitarian who has admitted our statement of psychological experience is to say that, though such may be the contents of the facts, their evidence is false, and there is nothing in the objective universe corresponding to these subjective representations. To this scepticism respecting the veracity of any one human faculty no answer can be given, except by pointing to the absurd consequences of its equally legitimate application to another. There is as much ground, or as little, for trusting to the report of the moral faculty, as for believing our perceptions, in regard to an external world, or our intellect, respecting the relations of number and dimension. Whatever be the 'authority' of Reason respecting the true, the same is the 'authority' of Conscience for the right and good.

§ 3. *Other Accounts.*

On some other forms of conception employed, especially among continental philosophers, to characterise the title of the moral law, I would make a remark or two. It is often spoken of as invested with the authority of the *whole over the part;* sometimes in the sense of *society over the individual;* at others, of *life in its completeness over the momentary interest;* often, of *humanity, as a type with its own ideal, over the particular cases of imperfect approximation.* The first of these accounts finds expression in Goethe's lines:

'Immer strebe zum Ganzen, und kannst du selber kein Ganzes
Werden, als dienendes Glied schliess' an ein Ganzes dich an[1].'

It is essentially the Hegelian view, which, while setting up *self-realisation* as the imperative end, regards the self as unrealised so long and so far as it is detached and fails to find its own functions, not simply in an embracing social organism, but in an infinite whole, with which the personal will becomes identified[2].

The second is represented by Mr. Leslie Stephen, with whom 'moral laws are statements of essential conditions of social welfare;' and their 'authority,' as felt, depends upon the agent having 'certain instincts,' viz. a reverence for social welfare. Without this he may obey extrinsic interest or coercion, but owns no moral authority[3].

The third forms an important part, though not the whole, of Mr. Herbert Spencer's interpretation of 'authority.' By 'the relative authority of motives' he means the comparative influence which they exercise over the conduct of a living being; and he shows that, in the course of human development, the simple animal instincts, with their proximate satisfactions, are discovered to conduce less to self-preservation than the ideas of sensations to come, which again are surpassed by ideas of those ideas, and so on into more complex and ideal conditions; and thus the ultimate and generalised satisfactions continually gain upon the momentary and concrete; and the consciousness of this law of experience gives a presumption in favour of the remoter outlook and the more compound motive as a guide to self-preservation. This prepossession on its behalf is its 'authority.' Mr. Spencer, however, adds to this chief element of moral influence the ideal effects left upon the mind by the coercive enforcement of moral rules, through laws and sentiments human and Divine: but while the former factor perpetually grows, the

---

[1] Vier Jahreszeiten, Herbst. 45, Werke, I. p. 74.
[2] See Bradley's Ethical Studies, Essay II.
[3] Science of Ethics, chap. xi. §§ 9, 10, pp 441, 442.

latter he regards as a tempoiary paitner, sure to retreat and disappear[1].

The fourth phrase expresses the ground of 'authority' on which several ethical schools have taken their stand. When Kant condenses the moral 'imperative' into the rule, 'So act that the principles of your will might serve as a system of universal legislation[2],' he controls the individual by the type of the kind, and insists on the personal will conforming itself to the ideal of the universal. And if he is not a perfect example of the formula as I have stated it, it is only because his 'Universal' is more extensive than *humanity*, and goes out to embrace the whole range of reasonable Will in the universe. This, however, makes no difference in the essence of the doctrine, viz. that the perfection of the kind determines the right for the individual. With Richard Rothe the Law of *Human* Nature steps into the place of this wider conception of *All* rational nature, and prescribes authoritatively the duty of each man: he states it as a postulate of Morals, that 'each single nature must be rectified in conformity with the conception of Man in himself (*an sich*), i.e. with universal Man, or (as we shall henceforth express it) with universal humanity.' 'It is true,' he adds, 'the human individual can do no more than fulfil his human functions under the given conditions of his concrete individuality: nevertheless, he can and must, without prejudice to his particular individuality, fulfil them at the same time under the conditions determined for universal humanity, i.e. fulfil them under the conditions of his particular individuality, *as a Self determined by the universal humanity*[3].'

No one of these forms of expression seems to me to go to the pith of the matter; though I am far from saying that they may not symbolise it to the mind that resorts to some one of them. They all present a relation between two

---

[1] Data of Ethics, chap. vii particularly §§ 42, 43.
[2] Kritik der praktischen Vernunft, L. i. 1, § 4; Lehrsatz III. § 7; Rosenkranz und Schubert, B. VIII. pp 136, 141.
[3] Rothe, Theologische Ethik, §§ 158, 159.

terms, a large and a small, and lodge the 'authority' in the former; and in all of them, the small is not outside the large, but embraced within it. And, these things being supposed, we are told to look for our *quæsitum*, viz. 'authority,' in the large. Is it qualified to yield this result?

In the first phrase,—'whole and part,'—nothing else is supposed than the data just stated; so that the authority ought to come out of the mere largeness of the containing term as compared with the contained; and be felt by any conscious constituent of a *mere mechanical whole, or aggregate*. Yet it is obvious that you might search for ever in the relative *bulk* of such a thing without alighting upon the notion of *authority*; and even if, begging the loan of gravitation, you add the idea of relative *mass*, all that you gain will be, that in the reciprocal attraction of particles, you *dynamically* subordinate the small term, and count it as a *minority*. This may explain why, if it be conscious, it feels itself the *lesser power*, but not why it confesses *inferior right*.

The second phrase, 'Society and the individual,'—though of much wider connotation, has been taken for little more than 'whole and part;' i.e. the individual has been conceived as a given integer, rounded off in his separate personality, and Society as the mere crowd of such figures assembled on a certain area. So long as this conception,—of Society as an aggregate,—is adhered to, the change from the first to the second form of phrase has no value, and relieves no objection. The two related terms differ only in cumulation of force, without any approach to differentiation of authority. If by Society be meant merely an aggregate of separate persons, the power which their concurrent votes possess against a single voice does not at all represent the prerogative of right with regard to wrong. It is not because there may be ten thousand suffrages on one side and only one on the other, that the reluctant will is bound to succumb; for no population of rascals can acquire rights against the goodness of one upright man; clamour as they may (as the Stoics said), he is the king and they the slaves. Mere magnitude has no moral quality; and what is not justified in the individual acquires no plea by multiplying itself into a crowd. Mr. Stephen, however, is free from this mechanical conception, and distinctly treats Society *as an organism*, in which the parts do not become complete, i.e. attain their totality of functions, except in relation to the whole; so that their self-preservation is dependent on the social self-preservation, and must include this as its most essential condition. This doctrine is an immense advance upon the previous one; and if it were carried out to its legitimate teleological implications (which are wrapped up in the conception of *organic* existence), it could be brought very near to what we want. But he only applies it far enough to explain the growth of social affections parallel with the personal instincts of self-conservation, and capable of transcending them; and leaves the question between them, in case of conflict, to be one of *strength alone*,—without *other authority* to decide the alternative between self-preservation and self-sacrifice.

The third form of phrase presents us only with the difference between long and short-sighted prudence, and misses the idea of moral authority altogether. As that difference would still have place in a rational constitution purely *un*moral, it has nothing to do with the ground of *duty*.

A much nearer approach to a defensible meaning is gained by the fourth variety of phrase: and this, it is fair to say, gives the sense prevailingly intended by German writers. It is not absurd to affirm that the individual is bound to respect his nature, and that from his single personality a certain homage is due to the evident idea and essence of humanity at large. The sentiment is not altogether fanciful, which attributes a certain treachery to one who, as we say, *abuses* his nature, and wilfully mars its ideal. Still, if these phrases are to be charged with any definite meaning, it can only be by giving a *realistic* interpretation to that 'humanity' which we speak of as hurt and insulted by sin. Were it nothing but a generalised notion, a figment of thought abstracted from particular men, we could owe it no allegiance: a mere shorthand formula of the epitomising intellect cannot be the object of any duty. But the language becomes intelligible, if we may regard the ideal of human nature as a distinct type of thought in the Divine mind, communicated as a standard of aspiration to ours. Presented thus, not as a private spoil gleaned from the actual, but as a Divine datum revealed from the possible, it stands invested with the personal authority of the Supreme Holiness; and behind the august image of a perfect and harmonious manhood is secretly felt, if not openly seen, the infinite Inspirer of all harmony and good. Whatever power there is in the words 'humanity,' 'society,' 'nation,' to move our reverence and affection, is due to their being not mere abstractions to our minds, but symbols of concrete semi-personal realities, not larger only but higher than ourselves, and containing the hidden presence and authority of the revealer of all law. No other reason can be given why the *whole* should be obeyed by the *part*: for, more comprehensive scope is so far from carrying with it greater moral weight, that the order is usually the reverse: the animal attributes do not give the law to human nature, though found in it and spreading far beyond it: it is the essence found in the fewest that wields Divine superiority over natures wider but less intense. Be it remembered therefore that, when the right of the whole over the part is set up, it is not any relation of *size* that is meant, but the relation between *the ideal of a Kind* and *the actual of an individual*. That ideal, far from being identified with the average mass of the race, may be rarely even approached, and presented only in one or none; but as a potential universality and Divine limit of tendency, it recommends itself to us as a general type, and is called '*the whole*.' In this sense, it falls back into the Divine nature, and its 'authority' coalesces with that which we have already traced. That authority then is not subjective, but objective; not vested in ideas, but residing in *a Person;* not represented by mere numbers against one, but by the perfect type against the imperfect copy.

ii. WHETHER OBLIGATION CAN BE TRANSCENDED.

The foregoing account of Authority determines the measure of God's claim upon us. It is coextensive with the authority revealed to us, i. e. with the range of the moral consciousness. We therefore strictly *owe to Him* conformity with our own ideal. Short of this, we fail of our due, and incur positive demerit. Attaining it with ever such exactitude, we simply fulfil our obligation, and can pretend to no merit before Him. To surpass it, He does not ask us; for it is the limit of our possibility; unless indeed, by past unfaithfulness, we have already lowered our appointed standard, and contracted the boundary to which He had left a nobler sweep. In such case, it certainly is not for us to take advantage of our own wrong, and demand that our guilt shall choose our law. This rule fixes, with precision, the true mid-point between the presumptuous legalism, which allows of meritorious works that may make God our debtor, and the despairing doctrine which denies everything to humanity, because short of the standard of infinite holiness. It is not His personal and absolute ideal, by which we are to be tried; but His communicated and relative ideal, implanted in our humanity, so far as He has permitted it to dawn on each of us. Beyond this, we are at present out of relation to Him, and not less foreigners to His moral rule than we are to His intellectual life in matters transcending even the guess of our reason. But this relative standard is high enough, alas! to justify the deepest humiliation that, like the Christian, is not abject. If not even the vainest can at heart admire themselves, if all men who are truly attracted to a moral life see a better than they do, if that which they secretly revere looks in upon them at times so piercingly as to fill the best with shame, no room, it is evident, is left for self-complacency, or even for tolerable repose of conscience; and there is no difficulty in explaining that profound sense of sin, which, since the true type of humanity was given, has filled the whole air with a plaint of penitence. Besides, the ulterior question at which I have hinted is a very serious one, and furnishes an indefinite supplement to the clear consciousness of our own shortcomings. We have lagged behind our own image of right; but there is a prior question: how far is that image itself what it might have been? Is it the pure and full-proportioned vision which God had rendered possible to us? or is it dwarfed and stained by the self-incurred perversions of our sight, and the specks and films of many an unfaithfulness? The accelerating ratio with which moral light dilutes itself as it recedes from its first Divine moment, till it is felt in only faint and casual waves amid the dark spaces of the soul, is so fearful a thing as to affect a thoughtful mind with a deeper awe than even the sense of positive evil. Thus is all *self-reliance* for moral harmony with God utterly cut away, and for the peace which even the strenuous conscience cannot honestly win, we are thrown upon a free faith and trusting affection in which there is only surrender into the Divine hand.

In our relations to *men*, it is otherwise: there is nothing to prevent the acquisition of merit towards them. The authoritative measure of duty, in every transaction between different persons, is *the mutually understood ideal*. This, in all that is common between us and the Father of spirits, is simply the highest that ever dawns upon our hearts; beyond which we can never go, so as to *earn* anything. But, in our dealings with our fellow-men, it is *their* ideal, as recognised by us, that measures their claim upon us in the eye of social justice; and in so far as our own sense of right may pass beyond this and draw from us more than is contained in the mutual understanding, we perform what *they* had no title to require from us, and we may be truly said *to deserve well* at their hands. It is sometimes said, by humane but inexact moralists, that since all obligation rests at bottom on the same foundation, charity is as much a claim upon us as justice, and that we violate a right not less when we neglect to fly to the relief of distress, than if we were to steal a neighbour's purse[1]. The difference, it is contended, goes no deeper than this: that in the latter case it is found practicable to enforce the right by coercion of law; while in the former it is not: but the absence or presence of positive enactment is a mere affair of external machinery, leaving the inner essence of the two duties still the same. The truth and the falsehood contained in this doctrine easily fall asunder at the touch of the principle just laid down. *As between man and man*, it is not true that the claim to justice and to mercy are of equal validity, discriminated only by the possibility or impossibility of redress in case of default: no right being established without a common moral sense, or having any social measure except that of mutual understanding, there is a vast interval between the obligation which I have openly incurred in the face of my neighbour's conscience and that which is only privately revealed to my own. Over and above the intrinsic guilt in both instances, there is in the first the additional enormity of violated good faith; and though, on the one hand, it is the sign of a mean and grudging nature to limit the measure of duty to the positive and authorised expectations of others from us, it would be, on the other, a monstrous paradox to say, that those expectations make no difference to us, and add no intensity to the claim upon us. Were it so, there would be no means of graduating offences, or deciding between conflicting suggestions of right; and we should relapse into the Stoic fallacy of reducing to one level the most trivial omission and the greatest crime. The effect of mutual understanding varies with the ethical complexion

---

[1] See a Sermon by the late Dr Southwood Smith, entitled, 'The probable effect of the development of the principles of the human mind on its future progress in knowledge and goodness.' (1818), p. 33.

of the act expected from us. Is that act a wrong? the mutual understanding cannot repeal the guilt. Is it a neutral thing? the mutual understanding takes it out of that category and confers upon it a binding force. Is it already a duty? to its intrinsic obligation the mutual understanding adds an extrinsic increment of binding force, and invests it with a double claim. Nor is this all. Thus much the act gains in virtue of another holding our pledge to it: but its ethical measure is also intensified by our having fetched it out of the silent estimate of consciousness and shaped it into distinct expression, whether by the positive word or by premonitory looks and signs of promise. Till it is realised in reflection, the felt obligation may waver between the implicit and explicit state; and the great instrument for fixing it in the latter is language,—the language of definition and record, whether special and exact, as in the case of written compact, or general and indirect, as in the case of mere 'mutual understanding.' Moral law is thus one of those elements of our life which, through language, not only obtain a *sign*, but also acquire *a new significance.*

In proportion then, and only in proportion, as men have come to understood concurrence on matters of right, have they claims *inter se*. This concurrence is far from being limited to relations of propeity and contract, though it is there most definite and complete: it extends over an indeterminate field beyond, of obligation prevailingly acknowledged, but differently construed, and unsusceptible, from its shifting complexity of conditions, of reduction to precise general enactment. The right of my neighbour, measured from the simply human and social point of view, addresses me with every variety of distinctness and force throughout this scale; with unmistakable emphasis in cases of explicit engagement; with clearness perfectly adequate in cases of implicit trust; with evanescent faintness in cases of simply spontaneous whispers within my own conscience, with nothing corresponding in his presumed feeling and expectation. This very whisper, however, which involves no

understanding with others, is itself an understanding between *myself and God*, and constitutes therefore an articulate
obligation in relation to Him, not one whit less religiously
binding on me than the most palpable debt of integrity. Its
simple presence in the soul with its authoritative look is
sufficient to establish it as a Divine claim upon me. In this
aspect, it is quite true that all duty stands upon the same
footing; and that all transgressions are offences against the
same law. But it is not every unfaithfulness to God that
constitutes a violation of the rights of men, and gives them
a title to reproach us. In forgetfulness of this distinction,
the satirist frequently taunts religious persons with confessing before God sins which they would be very angry to have
charged upon them by men; and evidently regards this as
a proof of insincerity or self-deception. But surely there is
here no real, scarcely even any apparent, inconsistency.
The claims of God upon us, coextensive with our own ideal,
go far beyond the claim of men, which is limited, we have
seen, by the range of mutual moral understanding, and
which in turn limits their critical prerogative of censorship
and accusation. And Conscience, in seeking peace with
Him, must needs have a very different tale to tell from any
that transpires in settling the narrower accounts with them;
and should they thrust themselves in to that higher audit,
and demand to have its sorrowful compunctions addressed
to them, it needs no spiritual pride to be hurt by the
impertinence. Human society may punish us for *crimes:*
human monitors reprove us for *vices:* but God alone can
charge upon us the *sin*, which He alone is able to forgive.
Far from believing that religious sincerity and depth would
gain by the erasure of this distinction, I am convinced that
its scrupulous preservation is a prime essential to their
continuance at all, and needs to be enforced rather than
enfeebled. There is a certain morbid and confused Christian humility which is not content with deploring, in the
sight of Heaven, its failure in humane and charitable zeal,
but speaks of it as *a wrong done* to others, as a withholding *of*

a debt due to the unhappy and neglected and depraved, whose forgiveness is almost asked for the slight they have sustained. I would not deal ungently with any recognition of brotherhood among the separated classes of our modern civilisation. But this language is not true, and tends to disturb the incidence of human responsibility, and fill with the notion of claims and rights those who much rather need to be awakened to their duties. To reform the thief and drunkard, to train the abandoned child, to succour the miseries of the improvident, is indeed a duty; not however *to them*, for their claim looks elsewhere, and we do but pick up a *dropped obligation*,—but to God and His moral order of the world. The total loss of this idea from the humanistic school of writers in the present day is the great drawback on the purity of their influence. The defect springs from the preponderance of social geniality over ethical and spiritual conviction: but the infection has been caught by evangelical philanthropy; and the danger is not slight of establishing the worst element of socialistic feeling in the minds of men, viz. the demand that the duties of one class shall be performed for them by another, and that institutional machinery shall be created to supersede the patient toil and sacrifice of all households and all persons, taken one by one. Let but the same ministrations of charity issue from an inspiration higher than compassion, and be rendered to the Divine order instead of to human confusion and wretchedness; and there will be a wholesomeness and dignity in our humanities, rarely traceable in them now. In this higher department of duty, scarcely less than in the minor cares that else would become flat and mean, is it important to the balanced and sustained force of the soul to render our service 'not as unto men, but unto God.'

iii. HOW PRUDENCE BECOMES OBLIGATORY.

One topic more requires attention, before we dismiss the subject of the 'authority' belonging to moral sentiments.

How is it that this 'authority' extends beyond the scale of principles arranged according to their worth, and takes in also the Prudential system? The fact, I suppose, can hardly be called in question, that we look with positive *disapproval* on rashness and recklessness, as not simply foolish and hurtful, but as *wrong*, even where no interests are visibly affected except the offender's own. We are far from admitting that any man has a right to trifle with his own wellbeing, and dash in wild hunt over his ground of opportunity, heedless of every careful track and natural fence, and crushing every green promise into the earth. We feel that, apart from any injury to others, his career is a wanton waste of what is not at his unconditional disposal; and our dissatisfaction addresses itself essentially to this, that he autocratically deals with that which is but a fiduciary deposit with him. Yet we have maintained a position which seems inconsistent with this feeling; viz. that if our nature contained no scale but the prudential, and our only problem were furnished by its controversies of strength, there would be no room for any moral sentiment, or more than a *rational* rule of life. How are we to reconcile these two statements?

This, I apprehend, is one of the many cases in which the interpretations of life and nature which would be legitimate and true upon a lower stage, cease to be so from a higher point of view; and the light opened overhead streams down and shows everything beneath in a new aspect. *Were* this a simply hedonist world; had we only sentient differences among the forces of our nature; did we know of nothing above us, except the dynamically greater; it is perfectly true that we could differ from each other in skill merely, and not in worth. But then this is *not* the constitution of things: we pass into another order of phenomena, and find there a higher law and a Divine rule; and this discovery necessarily alters all our previous reckoning, by setting aside the hypothesis on which it rests. Over and above the force of nature, there is now the free righteousness of God; behind the supreme Cause, there is the supreme Holiness.

And this cannot be simply appended by a *plus* to what we already knew before, leaving it unmodified there, as still a mere tissue of prudential relations. It lies in the very essence of these two that they are not co-ordinate, so as to have their separate realms, each undisturbed by the other; but the last found is the prior and legislative term, and by inherent authority subordinates and interpenetrates the other. The change affects equally our view of the macrocosm and the microcosm; add to the idea of Divine energy that of Divine holiness of will, and we feel at once that the latter must hold the former in hand and wield it as its instrument: add to the idea of human power over the more pleasurable the idea of human obligation to the more excellent, and this new discovery of a *trust* necessarily spreads over the prior realm, deposes its arbitrary will, and insists upon annexing the *whole* of the voluntary life. Neither in God, nor in us, can mere efficient power keep its ground as supreme, in the presence of Moral good: it has to retire into secondary and instrumental rank: as all things may be possible to the hand, yet not all things congenial to the righteousness, of God; so, that which, in a merely sentient world, we might treat as given to us out and out, becomes only *lent* as soon as we discover a good beyond the pleasurable. To borrow a Platonic phrase, the ἀγαθὸν asserts itself as the highest εἶδος, giving to pleasures all the rights they have, and taking nothing from them in return. So far forth as they are restrained and measured by reverence for order and proportion, for pure health of body and clearness of soul, they have even a share of sacredness, and are full of a joy unknown to lower conditions. But, escaping from these limits, they become an insolent defiance of any diviner claim; a setting-up for one's self, quite at variance with the pervading sense of an authoritative law and a holy presence. It is this shamelessness (ἀναίδεια) inseparable from the rash and reckless life that draws forth the grave disapprobation of men, and makes them feel it to be something worse than foolish. They justly regard it as a sign that the higher functions of character are inoperative, and the personal force at the disposal of the wrong influence; so that, if any trying problem were to apply the test, the requisite clearness and heroism would not be there. The whole temper expressed by the question, 'Why may I not do as I like?' is well understood to be quite uncongenial with the reverential and conscientious spirit; is regarded, therefore, as the sure symptom of its absence, and, even when expressing itself in no conspicuous transgression, is condemned as a boundless potential immorality.

CHAPTER V.

SPRINGS OF ACTION CLASSIFIED. PSYCHOLOGICAL ORDER.

The foregoing sketch of the essential bases of our moral constitution prepares the way for an actual scale of principles implied in the judgments of conscience. If it be true that each separate verdict of right and wrong pronounces some one impulse to be of higher worth than a competitor, each must come in turn to have its relative value determined in comparison with the rest; and, by collecting this series of decisions into a system, we must find ourselves in possession of a table of moral obligation, graduated according to the inner excellence of our several tendencies. The extreme complexity of the combinations renders the task of drawing up such a table precarious and difficult. It is not more so, however, than the enterprise taken in hand by many writers on ethics, viz. the production of a code of external duties computed to meet the infinitely varied exigencies of human life: for assuredly the permutations of outward condition far exceed in number the changes that may be rung on the competitions of inward affections. If the problem, therefore, assumes a discouraging aspect, it is rather from its unusual form than from any unexampled intricacy in its matter; and, though well aware that the following draft can at best be merely tentative, I shall not shrink from proposing it, were it only as a test of the theory which it applies

It is difficult to understand the attitude of the modern English writers on Ethics towards the psychological aspect of their subject. They by no means call in question the general principle that moral worth or defect is an affair of *character*, to be estimated by the inward affection or intention whence action flows; and we have already seen in what unqualified language this principle finds expression in the writings of Professor Sidgwick, Mr. Spencer, and Mr. Stephen. From this principle, viz. 'that a man is moral because and in so far as his instincts are correlated according to a certain type,' does it not follow that, in order to give any account of the moralities, you must be able to enumerate the 'instincts'; not only to enumerate them, but to describe the 'type' of their right correlation, and to contrast it with the varieties of wrong correlation? Either this is possible, or Ethics are impossible. And this is wholly a task of introspective classification and comparative estimate. Yet no sooner have these writers admitted the necessity of this work, than they run away from it as unmanageable and superfluous, and institute a hunt after the differences of morality in the field of external effects of action, instead of among the internal correlations of motive. The apology which is set up for this suicidal procedure will be examined further on. At present, I will no further defend the attempt to keep true to the psychological principle, than by saying, that it has been more or less followed by the chiefs of both ancient and modern philosophy, and has fallen into neglect only in recent times, and mainly through the influence of writers who have approached the study of Morals from either the casuist's or the jurist's point of view. Wherever the object contemplated is to lay down a correct legislative code, overt acts alone come into definition, with merely subordinate reference to the invisible state of mind whence they proceed; and the disposition will always prevail to reduce as far as possible this obscure factor, and give the utmost objective distinctness to the law.

Plato, however, though writing of the State, and carrying his inventive imagination into all its external organisation, did not fail to go back into the recesses of the human mind for the springs of private and public life, and the separating lines of right and wrong. I need only recall his threefold distribution of the inward sources of action, ἐπιθυμία, θυμός, and νοῦς, and the relative rank assigned to each, both in the celebrated myth of the chariot, and in the remarkable enlargement of their group in the 'Republic' by the appearance of the controlling δικαιοσύνη. To an arrangement almost identical Aristotle prefixed the general term τὸ ὀρεκτικόν (impulse), and appended a more detailed analysis running down to particular forms of each quality. There was no one of these impulses that might not have its best state, with faulty deviation on either side, towards excess and towards defect; and the *best state of it* was its ἀρετή, e.g. σωφροσύνη for ἐπιθυμία; ἀνδρεία for θυμός. This best state did not belong to the impulses by nature, but must be determined or ratified by Reason (νοῦς); so that even the most happily constituted child, with no tendencies but towards some variety of good, could not on that account be called virtuous, but, in order to become so, must replace the mere drift of nature by the assenting determination of the self-conscious will. In the production of moral character, Aristotle thus recognises two factors, *instinctive impulse* and *rational election*. Of these, the first supplies the power; the second, the regulation. The former, by itself, would leave us unmoral animals; the latter, by itself, would make us unmoral intelligences: and, as between these two,—random activity and bare thought,—it is reasonable to regard the former as the primary starting-point or matter for Ethics, and the latter as the organiser of their form. In these Greek modes of laying out our subject, two points deserve especial notice: (1) That they look for their whole moral world *within*, among the phenomena of the conscious and self-conscious nature; not among the conditions of external action. And (2) that the rational reflection, which, in their view, first converts *instinct into character*, they regard as exercised upon each impulse *taken by itself*, so as to find out and mark its absolutely right degree; not upon the relative worth of two or more impulses pressing their demand together. In the first point they seem to me to have seized, in the second to have missed, a prime condition of true ethical theory.

The founders of the modern philosophy, no less than the ancient schools, sought the whole material of their moral doctrine in the interior of the human mind; and not till they had set in order the motive forces which lie behind all external action, did they step into the field of applied morals and adjust that inward order to the objective conditions and varying limits of possibility which enter into the problems of actual life. Descartes, though giving us no systematised theory of Ethics, has gathered and arranged its preliminaries in his treatise on *Les Passions de l'Ame*, in the relative ascendency and right gradation of which he evidently conceives human perfection to consist. Malebranche, in his *Traité de Morale*, not only passes under review 'the inclinations' and 'the affections,' as his proper subject matter, but insists on their *proportionate perfection*, and even makes 'Love for their law of order' the equivalent of all virtue[1]. Spinoza, in carrying out his conception of the 'Ethica,' worked upon the same line, pretty closely following Descartes in his enumeration and grouping of '*the affections*,' and explicitly finding in their due subordination the secret of perfect character. The essential correctness of the leading idea of these philosophies is not affected by any imperfection that may be found in their classification of the springs of action. When, e.g. both Descartes and Spinoza give, as their list of primary affections—(1) Wonder, (2) Love, (3) Hate, (4) Desire, (5) Mental pleasure (*Lætitia*), (6) Mental Pain (*Mœror* or *Tristitia*), it is evident that they are mixing together with the genuine concrete type of impulse,—e.g. Wonder,—which is the kind of datum we require, mere general qualities gathered by abstraction,—e.g. Love and Hate,— from a number of concrete impulses. To have an impulse *towards* anything is to love it; *from* anything is to hate it: neither of the words introduce us to any fresh impulse

[1] Supra, Vol. I. pp. 231, 232.

which may be added to the list, but only to a feature invariably predicable of half the set, and since these common qualities are irrespective of the ethical values and run across them (the love of turtle and the love of truth both coming under the head of *Amor*), they have no proper place in the moral psychology. We do not want an analysis of the idea of 'natural instinct,' so as to exhibit its contents; but a list of such instincts, as they are and work; and, in constructing this, we cannot afford to overlook their different types of activity; whether they are mere outbursts of inward feeling, or are directed upon objects, the varieties of which may have much to say about their value. A reference to the catalogue of the 'affections,' which I have formerly given from Descartes and Spinoza, will make it clear that it is a medley of real instincts, with abstractions picked out from them, and with virtues and vices sprung from their operation in their several fields, or from their combinations with each other. But for this initial error, it might have become the basis of a Moral doctrine parallel in its development with the growth of physical science.

If we seek help, in our attempt to classify the springs of action, from the eighteenth-century philosophy instead of the seventeenth,—in particular from the school of Hobbes, which hardly assumed importance till the last century, rather than that of Descartes,—our hopes are disappointed from an opposite tendency, to fallacious simplification; carried to its extreme in the reduction of all impelling forces to *self-love*. This short and easy formula, applied in naked shamelessness by such writers as Helvetius, could not but provoke resistance by its paradoxical interpretation of human life. In the hands of Hartley and Condillac, however, it was started upon a course of evolution, which enabled it to yield any number of disinterested affections as the blossom and fruit of primal self-gratification; and in this form it held its ground with those who insisted upon the recognition of unselfish motives, though upon terms which construed them into illusions. But men will not go on for ever believing that they are tricked by their nature into groundless goodness, or be content to love whatever is dearer than themselves on false pretences; and so they now prefer to cut the alleged dependence of the generous affections upon personal self-seeking, and give them their own separate root. This is certainly a gain, taking us back a step nearer to nature. Yet, as it is but the reactionary split of a false unity, it leaves us with only a duality,—viz. 'egoism' and 'altruism,'—as comprising the total springs of human character. The simplification, though not carried so far as before, is still altogether artificial, counting, not by natural distinctions, but by arbitrarily abstracted resemblance. Many instincts do not become one, merely because, when satisfied, they all please *the same ego;* nor are several heterogeneous affections identified by being directed without exception on *something other* than one's self; yet nothing more than this spurious unification is expressed by the words 'egoism' and 'altruism.' The antithesis which they mark exercises, it seems to me, a tyrannical influence on the minds of our recent writers; turning all moral doctrine into either a duel or a negociation between two opposite tendencies of thought, and forcing the variegated phenomena of character to fling off their native movement and costume, and appear on parade in the regimental uniform of this or that philosophic flag.

Perhaps the writers of the Scottish school have best avoided the misleading conceptions on which I have commented. Dr. Reid's distribution, indeed, of active impulses into (1) mechanical, (2) animal, (3) rational, cannot well be rescued from Dugald Stewart's criticism [1]. But Stewart's own classification is based, I think, upon strictly natural distinctions, though needing to be more explicitly wrought out. Under the five heads (1) appetites, (2) desires, (3) affections, (4) self-love, (5) moral faculty, he finds room for all the motive and directing forces of our nature. We

[1] Stewart's Works, Hamilton's Edition, Vol. VI. p. 125.

have here the rudiments of a philosophical arrangement, because he recognises on the one hand the difference between animal impulse and open-eyed desire; and on the other, between the *dynamical* principles enumerated under the first three heads, and the *regulative* action of the two last,—Self-love and Conscience. These distinctions, however, though verbally mentioned, remain practically unused: they are not permitted to have any effect on the classification, which presents the series of five springs of action, consecutively enumerated, as if they were all in the same rank in the predicamental line, and there were no reason for disposing them in principal and dependent groups. The differential marks prevailing among them are quite too important, psychologically and morally, to be so slightly treated; and the following distribution, with other deviations, differs from Stewart's chiefly in the attempt to give these discriminating characters their just rights.

i. PRIMARY; HOW DISTINGUISHED.

Guided by the fact that man is conscious before he is self-conscious, and has active tendencies in both stages, I would begin by distinguishing between two sets of impelling principles: viz those which urge him, in the way of unreflecting instinct, to appropriate objects, or natural expression; and those, on the other hand, which supervene upon self-knowledge and experience, and in which the preconception is present of an end gratifying to some recognised feeling. The former we may call the PRIMARY springs of action; the latter, the SECONDARY. These names are the more appropriate, because serving to mark, not only an order of enumeration, but an order of derivation: the secondary feelings being not something entirely new, but the primary over again, metamorphosed by the operation of self-consciousness; and demanding a category to themselves, because their original features and their moral position are greatly changed by the process.

That we are subject to impulses involving no rational foresight it would be superfluous to insist, were it not for the attempts of ingenious psychologists to resolve all our activity into *desire*, defined as 'the idea of a pleasure.' The question which is raised by this school of philosophers lies in a very small compass. If nothing moves us but 'the idea of a pleasure,' and the pleasure must first be had in order to leave its own idea, there is but one order of nature by which we are stirred out of an original passiveness and neutrality, viz. (1) a pleasure, (2) its idea, (3) action to procure it again. We are driven, therefore, to ask how we catch the first term of this sequence. If we have nothing to carry us to the pleasure, the pleasure must of its own accord arrive at us: it hits upon our sense, or our sense stumbles upon it, without any inner relation by which they find each other out; and our stock of desires and volitions is at the mercy of an accidental sensitive experience. Is this picture a true one,—of man in equilibrium, without forces hither or thither, and of an outer world walking up to him and flinging at him pains and pleasures, to wake him up? Can anything be more perverse than thus to attribute all the stir and activity to the external scene, and all the indifference to him? Is he not introduced as a *living being* among given objects? and is it not just the characteristic of the living being to be stocked with forces that determine his lines of direction in the field on which he is set, and find out what suits him there? The experience-philosophers forget that, without instinctive forces, there would be no experience to be had, in a world where the food does not drop into the mouth and the stream does not leap up at the lips, and no spontaneous blankets fall on and off the shoulders with winter winds and summer heat. In the relation between our nature and the objects that gratify it, it is most evidently the nature that finds the objects and performs the active part; and but for the heat within, the cold matter of the world would be no fuel, and turn into no flame of joy. As food is sweet only to the hungry, so, universally, is propensity the prior condition of pleasure, not pleasure of propensity.

We may assume, therefore, the reality in human nature of the class of primary principles, impelling us to certain objects without prevision or self-consciousness on our part. The mode of action to which they lead is perfectly analogous to that which we attribute to the lower animals, though in our case directed to a greater range of objects than any other creature is fitted to pursue. Unwilling as are philosophers of the prevailing English school to call anything in the human being by the name of 'instinct,'—a name which denotes no process that is known, but covers one that is unknown,—it would be at variance with all the analogies of the animal creation beneath us, if our nature were *not* furnished with tendencies towards ends which we seek blindly, without preconception of their character. The bird, just released from the shell, selects with infallible precision the insect or seeds proper for its food: the butterfly, fresh from the chrysalis state, goes direct to the flowers, of whose nectaries and their contents it can have no previous knowledge. Every order of creature recognises, without experience, the species fitted to be its prey, and those of which it is to be itself the victim, seeking the one, flying from the other. As man has to perform the very same functions to which these instinctive actions are subservient; as his constitution is, in these respects, in complete affinity with that of other animals, in which these functions appear in a form less implicated with supplementary phenomena and more open therefore to careful observation; as there is every appearance of unbroken analogy in the *modus operandi* of these faculties in our race and in the inferior tribes, we have every reason for concluding that a portion of human action is due to instinctive impulses, putting us in the right way for gaining natural but unexperienced ends. At all events, if any one thinks he can explain the seeming indications of such impulses in man, and by special analysis applied to his case can break the analogy between him and the rest of the animal creation, the burden of proof lies with such an objector. The presumption is evidently against him; and must prevail till it is upset by direct evidence of a new set of causes operating in man, and yielding the same phenomena by a different instrumentality. All the systems which pretend to supply such evidence have this characteristic, that they make use of the long infancy of man, so obscure from its lying beyond the reach of memory in ourselves, and indicating its consciousness by very imperfect signs in others; and refer to this period a number of hypothetical processes and experiences, sufficient to serve the purpose of explanation; processes which nobody can deny, for the same reason that nobody can assert them, and which the equivocal language of infancy is easily interpreted to indicate. It seems to me that man is distinguished from the lower animals, not by having a different mode of action throughout his whole nature and entire life; but by having a *self* with additional functions which act by laws of their own, and modify, during the maturer periods of his existence, the results of his instinctive powers.

I have said that the word 'instinct' covers a process that is unknown. The conception, however, which it involves may be definitely fixed, and ought not to be left indistinct. Let us hear the account of it given by a great naturalist. Cuvier says, 'We gain a clear notion of instinct by admitting that animals have, in their sensorium, images or constant sensations which determine their actions. It is a species of dream which haunts them constantly, and, as regards their instinct, animals may be regarded as a kind of *somnambulists*[1].' I must confess that what I 'gain' from this is by no means 'a clear notion,' but rather an explanation of an '*obscurum per obscurius;*' for, however little insight I may have into the interior of instinct, I have less into that of somnambulism. Moreover, the condition assigned as clearing up the case, viz. the determining presence in consciousness of

---

[1] Quoted in 'Journal of Speculative Philosophy,' Vol. XVI. ii. p 217.

'images and constant sensations,' does not seem to be peculiar to 'instinctive' or 'somnambulist' action, it is no less indispensable to the most wide-awake acts of the human will: if, for instance, on a cold day I resolve to get warm by a row on the river up to Mortlake, am I not moved by 'constant sensations' of chill, and images of the Thames and the boat, and the exercise, and the bridges and the scenes on the banks? If Cuvier means to restrict the phrase 'images and sensations' to purely internal representations and feelings, as distinguished from external perceptions (as the illustration by 'dreams' would suggest), and therefore to say that the animal is disposed of by its own spontaneous series of sensory and ideal states, undistracted by the impression of outward objects, he does indeed bring the case into analogy with that of the sleep-walker who, without knowing where he is, has his consecutive steps directed by the rule of his own thoughts; but still describes only what takes place in every instance of voluntary action which has become habitual with us. The fundamental difference remains unmentioned, viz. that human habit sets a-going the instrumental links of *an end in view;* while animal instinct institutes and follows out the means to an end which is *out of view*. We may dress in the morning mechanically, thinking of other things, but we *mean* to dress: the winged insect deposits its eggs where alone the new life to come can find its nutriment, and knows not what it is about. In this marking feature, the somnambulist analogy would seem to fail. The sleep-walker's world is other than that in which you see him to be and move; but such as it is to him, it no less constantly and rationally affects his feelings and regulates his steps, than the scene from which you watch him determines yours; there is no ground for doubting that he thinks, and reasons, and wills, upon the data of his dream, with as true a logic and as clear a purpose as the observers who take measures to save him from his perils. Nay, even from these perils he is not unfrequently able, by some marvellous tact, to protect himself: the inward intensity of vision still sparing a faint remnant of perceptive power sufficient to thread a terrible way on the verge of crags and floods.

Instinctive impulse, then, is that which spontaneously institutes means to an end not preconceived. It differs from habit, therefore, in being devoid of all *intention*, though the two are alike in the mechanical consecution of the means. It differs from Will still more, by excluding all *choice*, i.e. preferential judgment between two possibilities.

§ 1. *Propensions: Organic Appetites; Animal Spontaneity.*

Now, of these primary springs of action we may distinguish four classes. First, there are the proper *Propensions*, bearing in the highest degree the character of subjective appetency and mere drift of nature; not indeed unrelated to external objects, but requiring from them the minimum of importunity and reaction to move response. They are the forces of first necessity for the mere physical life in its individual maintenance or successive continuance, and exhibit the lowest terms on which it could hold its footing in the world at all. They are three in number; of which two, having reference respectively to *food* and to *sex*, are often included together under the common name of *Appetites*, and are subservient to the functions of what physiologists call the *organic life*,—the life belonging even to the vegetable world. This circumstance is itself a presumption that they cannot be dependent on sensation; for they spread upwards into our kind from an insentient realm of natural history; and would be required here, as in the plants, though we were as little susceptible of sensation as they. To any individual creature needing nourishment, and belonging to a race needing renewal, they or their equivalents are indispensable. The third propension sustains a relation to the *animal* life similar to that which the appetites sustain to the *organic:* it is the *tendency to physical activity* alternating with repose;—the intermittent springiness and spontaneity of exercise and labour, the vivacious contempt of obstacles and pure triumph of energy, which seem inseparable from the muscular and nervous systems, be the faculties that use them great or small. It is manifest indeed in the sphere of mental spontaneity not less than of bodily, and expresses the enjoyment attending the use of all our powers. This tendency directs itself upon no such special object as the appetites require; yet it is not merely subjective, but measures itself against the inertia and resistance of the outward world, in conquering which it realises its exuberant consciousness of life. It is probably this distributed direction of its force that has occasioned it to be so generally overlooked, yet when attention is once called to it, no observer of life, especially of English life, can well deny its existence.

§ 2. *Passions: Antipathy; Fear; Anger.*

The second class of primary springs of action comprises the *Passions;* called so, because they do not arise as forces from the needs of our own nature, but are rather what we *suffer* at the hands of other objects. Those objects, moreover, are in every case painful and uncongenial,—the several sources of disturbance and injury; so that the emotions towards them are invariably *repulsions*, thrusting away what is hurtful or inharmonious, or else withdrawing us thence. By this common feature they indicate their proper function; they are evidently provisions for entrenching our nature in security amid threatening or invading ills, and removing to a distance whatever jars with its appointed life. These passions are three; distributing themselves according to the three elements of time, and visiting with a distinct feeling what is repugnant to us in the present, in the past, and in the future. Towards an object of natural aversion immediately before us we feel *Antipathy;* towards that which has just hurt us, we experience *Anger;* towards that which menaces us with evil, we look with *Fear.* All these appear to me obviously to *go before* any experimental knowledge of the harmful or disagreeable things, and not to be disciplined into existence by a process of smarting under them: though doubtless the same feelings extend themselves to any new objects that disclose their repulsiveness only after experience. Even *fear*, though susceptible of indefinite extension by knowledge of the signs of ill, is evidently, in its rudimentary stage, a truly prophetic premonition of danger not clearly in view. Both in other creatures and in man (whose nature may be illustrated by theirs, so far as it proceeds in company with them), the instances are numerous, in which the *first notice* of the presence of something formidable is given by the inward flurry of alarm. A cat requires no induction of particulars, in order to show the most evident marks of fear at the approach of a dog; her back rises, her fur stands on end, and every movement expresses circumspection and terror. A flock of sheep, hitherto protected from all knowledge of its dangers, will scud in every direction at the sight of a wolf. And beneath the eye of the distant, almost invisible, bird of prey, the farm-yard is thrown into a tumult of consternation: each mother-bird gathering her brood under her wings, and every creature knowing a terror it has never been taught. And though most of the dangers to which man is exposed are known to him by the forewarning of others, or are postponed till his own reason is able to ascertain and foresee them, so that the conception precedes the dread, there are not wanting instances of properly instinctive fear. An infant tossed in the arms a little too high expresses a fright which no one can mistake, and which it would be absurd to attribute to any imagination of the consequences of a fall. The sight of a fierce and angry countenance, or of a wild animal with brilliant eyes, will terrify a child who cannot have learned to interpret the indications of danger which these things afford; and the rush and dash of waves will produce a shudder for which no experience of the washing-tub will account. Any one who can remember what he felt when he first went out in a boat on a tossing sea, will be able to detect in himself an element of *physical fear*, not dependent on the apprehension of dipping or of death, but rather diminishing and passing away as these rational grounds of alarm are substituted. This feeling would probably have no place in the steady mind of an experienced captain in the hour of shipwreck, though then, after having witnessed the perishing fate of passengers and crew, he must have the distinctest image of drowning and of death. Such experiences are doubtless mixed; but contain elements, I think, which betray in man a properly instinctive fear, like that of other animals, directing him to self-protection without involving self-reflection.

The other emotion to which I have given the name of a '*Passion*' is more readily admitted to possess this non-rational character Anger appears so evidently before any idea is formed of directing its action towards a preconceived end; it displays itself with so little discrimination towards all sources of injury, animate or inanimate; it continues so long to take us by surprise and gives us so much trouble with its suggestions, at an age when better means of self-protection are at our disposal; it is so clearly the business of all reflective knowledge of evil, not to create, but to subdue it; that its instinctive character forces itself irresistibly on our convictions. It is, as Bishop Butler has observed, the sudden rising against opposition and harm of any kind, without originally any idea of *moral injury*, or any reflection on the relation between ourselves and the obstacle that hurts us. And it is of obvious use to enable us, by a spontaneous effort, to defeat the attack of such sudden force, and match our weakness against its strength.

From what has been said, and especially from the illustrations supplied by natural history, it will be evident that, thus far, we have not passed beyond the limits of the simply animal nature into the special characteristics of the human constitution. It follows that not one of the principles hitherto enumerated has any necessary reference to *Persons*, or involves more than a relation to *Things,—living things*, it may be, but nothing more. However true it may be that the chief actual exercise of most of these feelings takes a personal direction, and plays a part in the drama of social life, this is by no means an indispensable condition; and were the beings on whom they fix, nay, were we ourselves that feel them, stripped of the personal attributes, and cut down to the resources of bovine and canine nature, the conditions of their possibility would not be lost. We have reached, however, the point of emergence into the proper human nature; and that, at the half-way stage of our enumeration. Two classes of active principles remain to be mentioned; and though in the first of these we find still some affinity with lower tribes of being, yet the special element of *personality* so predominates in their human manifestation, and even so reacts on them and exalts them in the animals that are companions of man, that in dealing with them we must regard ourselves as crossing the line, and say that, *in a world without persons*, they would fail of their proper idea and identity.

§ 3. *Affections: Parental; Social; Compassionate.*

The third class, then, of primary springs of action comprises the *Affections;* called so, because they take us and form us into a certain frame of mind *towards* other persons, and operate therefore as *attractions*, and not, like the passions, as *repulsions*. They belong to us as surrounded by beings more or less in our own image, and repeating to us our own experience; and the lowest condition of their existence is, the presence of *living creatures*, reminding us of our kind, if not belonging to it. To the passions, it will be observed, not even this was needful; they could be conscious of repulsion from uncongenial *things*, though probably not without momentarily investing them with a quasi-life, and looking at them as if their eyes were on us. As we pass from order to order of our springs of action, we find ourselves in the presence of more determinate and higher objects, the ideal forms of our companions clearing and rising as we go. The propensions are not indeed mere egoisms; but the nature towards which they pass is a vague material somewhat, rather felt out by the appetency than sharply coming up to it and speaking for itself. The outward world is but the respondent to the inward drift. In the passions, on the other hand, this relation is reversed; they wait for the appeal of some assailant coming into sight, and then first dart into reply. The *objectivity*, here amounting to antagonism, is more keenly defined; yet still demands no more special condition than some hostile *thing*. At the same time, the feeling is not only capable of rising to the exigency of attack from higher objects, but even obliged, by involuntary *prosopopeia*, to treat its objects as alive, when they are not so. It is therefore a quasi-animated scene that stands before the passions. The affections are not content with this, but rise to a severer precision of demand. Thrusting aside, not only things of fictitious life, but the miscellaneous herds of natural history, they single out *personal beings* like ourselves as their indispensable objects; or if, at their inferior margin, they extend somewhat further down, it is only to take in living beings regarded by them as quasi-personal and drawn into the human analogy. At a lower level their function is exhibited only in its rudimentary state, as the first hint of a higher economy; and their *true idea* is not realised till we enter the world of persons.

The affections, thus generally characterised, are three. Of these, the first in order, as the least exclusively human, is the *Parental;* the conditions of which are, that the beings on whom it is directed be, independently of us, the *image of our essence*, and, dependently upon us, the *continuation of our existence*. Suppose either of these elements of the case absent; suppose the child to be human, but not ours; or to be ours indeed, but to turn out other than human; and the feeling, in the one instance, fades into general kindliness towards the young; and, in the other, shrinks away, and passes into repugnance or terror. The strictly spontaneous character of this affection is so obvious from its operation in the inferior tribes of creatures, that it is a perverse expenditure of ingenuity to explain its origin from factitious association in man. Even the fact mainly relied on for this purpose, viz. its superior intensity in the mother, who is trained by premonitory hopes into readiness of love, holds but very partially; and, even where it exists, will be found much less related to the experience prior to birth, than to the dependence for sustenance afterwards. Where that dependence is equal on both parents, as in the case of birds, the care for the offspring is, often at least, equal too. Perhaps the distinction in mankind between the two parents is not accurately described by assigning to the one a greater share of the whole affection than to the other; and we should rather say, that, of the two conditions requisite to it, the mother is more affected by the idea of the *dependent continuation of the parental existence*, the father by that of the *independent image of the parental essence*. The differences of expression and action thus given to the affection supplement each other, and determine into due relation the feminine and the manly elements of a home;—the one, keeping close to the inner circle of wants, the other, serving equally, but abroad in a wider sweep; the one, conservative of the child's helplessness, the other, pleased with his growing independence; the one regretting the years of infancy, whilst the life yet soft was indeterminately moulded, the other, impatient for the years of maturity, when the individuality shall be set and the image complete. These differences, far from proving the whole affection derivative, are themselves original; and, in inchoate forms, unmistakably appear in the simply animal tribes. The self-conscious and rational nature of man doubtless modifies and enriches the primitive groundwork of this, as of every spontaneity; but does not supersede the fundamental force.

The second affection is perhaps less conspicuously marked, but equally undeniable: I mean the *Social;* directed not only to our *like*, as the former, but to our equals, as respondent natures, holding up the mirror to our being, and at once taking us out of ourselves and sending us into ourselves. Perhaps, if we were to press the inquiry to the last resort, we might find that between *absolute equals, mere self-repetitions*, this affection would hardly arise; that some differences and inequalities must still mingle with the general identity of type, to touch the secret springs from which society arises; and that as, in the family group, the intermixture of strength and weakness, of beauty and force, of looking up and looking down, is essential to its binding love; so, in the wider circle, the real combining principle is a mutual complementing of defective humanities. Certainly, between man and woman, between the elder and the child, the unlikeness is an important element in the attachment; delivering the heart from the staleness of self-repetition, and setting, opposite to each conscious weakness or inaptitude in one's self, the spectacle of an ideal strength or grace; and I see no reason to doubt that a similar secret necessity of completing some ellipsis of consciousness enters into the more general texture of human ties. There is, however, a difference in the proportion of the two constituents. In the domestic relations, the inequality or difference is prominent and fundamental, flinging a delightful wonder and surprise into the identity of nature: in the social relations, it is the fellowship or resemblance that gives the basis of sympathy and interpenetrates all varieties with a certain unity. The former rest on differentiation; the latter on integration; though neither could subsist without infusion of the other. This very contrast again, between the principle of the family and the principle of the community, forms by its antithesis a new system of mutually complementary parts, in which the poles of opposite function elicit new forces; neither the family nor the community fulfilling its idea, without coexistence of the other; the home never revealing its true meaning or perfecting its constitution, but in society; and society never finding its soul or disclosing its moral essence, till formed into an aggregate of families. While, however, not only admitting this reciprocation, but strongly insisting on it, I see no reason for questioning the distinction, as springs of life, between the two affections. As, in inferior natures, there is no observable dependence of the gregarious tendency on the energy of the parental instinct; so in man, the susceptibility to social feeling can in no way be inferred from any domestic tenderness. Pope's celebrated lines comparing the progressive enlargement of the affections, from self as a centre, through the narrow compass of family love, into the sweep of universal benevolence, with the spreading circles made by a stone falling on smooth water, present, I believe, quite a false image of the real experience of human nature. for neither has self-love the least tendency to create the closer attachments; nor have they again any provision within them for expanding into social disinterestedness. Were there any truth in the doctrine of the simile, we should be no less authorised to conclude, from the intensity of a man's self-love, that he would make a most affectionate member of a family, than from the force of a stone's plunge that its secondary undulations must be considerable; and we might reason from the citizen's fondness for his children to the strength of his public spirit, as we should compute from the distant commotion of water the force of the wave which would strike the shore. Into what variance with fact such modes of inference would lead us, it is needless to point out. Only the rarest natures, it would seem, have affluence enough to spare to the world of equals any copious affection, without lessening the tension of home love; and the numerous instances in which fraternities have been formed, bound by the ties of a common life, in the absence and even with the repudiation of all family relations, sufficiently evinces the independent force of the social impulse. The existence and phenomena of *language*, the instinct for utterance and exchange of the inner thought and feeling, may be regarded as the sign of this common sympathetic consciousness, and as a perpetual experiment how far it goes: precisely in proportion as it succeeds in becoming the medium of mutual understanding, does the social sentiment more powerfully assert itself; a foreign tongue being little less than an estrangement of nature; and even the dialect which discriminates class from class of the same people marking the limits of their social union. It is no arbitrary caprice of taste that gives such power to *words*, whether to draw attachment or to excite disgust, and sets them before us almost as living objects of love and hate; but a true human sympathy and antipathy at second hand,— sympathy with what is at one, antipathy towards what is at variance, with our ideal of humanity. On the whole, the social affection is that which is due to the conscious unity of our nature.

The third affection, drawing us to the beings we interpret by ourselves, is *compassion*, the feeling that springs forth at the spectacle of suffering. The quickness and vehemence of this feeling so forcibly attest its instinctive character, that no one who is not embarrassed by the interests of a theory will be disposed to trace it to a factitious origin. In childhood and in maturity, in savage as in civilised man, nay, even in inferior animals that have caught some infection of human nature, it instantly arises on the mere inspection of misery, and is more passionate at the first moment than at any other. There is no feeling which it is less possible to deduce from any interested source. Say that the suffering we see is only our own at second hand,—since we carry its interpretation within, and our whole idea of another person is but the idea of self externalised;—still, this second and outer self, and not the Number One that dwells at home, is the real and immediate object of the affection, and is pitied on his own account, as truly as if he stood alone; nor can we better express the *fellow-feeling* involved in compassion, than by saying that we bewail another's pain as if it were our own, and forget our actual self in flying to the relief of one who stands before us and suffers in its image[1]. If this

---

[1] Compare Hobbes's account: 'Pity is *the imagination* or *fiction of future* calamity to *ourselves*, proceeding from the sense of another

is all that is meant by those who would trace compassion back to self,—viz. that our ability to appreciate the distress of others is limited by the range of our own experience,—the doctrine might be admitted without compromising the disinterestedness of the affection. Even then, however, the assertion requires considerable qualification. For it is by no means true that the signs of anguish, or indeed of any other emotion, are unintelligible to us and convey nothing to our minds, except in so far as we have had occasion to put them forth in our own case. If only the feeling indicated be one *of which we are susceptible*, it matters not whether it be new to us or old; its natural language will speak for itself and carry its meaning home. It happens probably not less often that we first understand a sorrow through our compassion, than that we feel compassion through prior understanding of the sorrow.

When we compare our sympathy with enjoyment and our sympathy with suffering, the superior promptitude and sharpness of the latter cannot fail to strike us, as a manifest instance of adaptation between our nature and our lot. Our associates who are at ease and happy can afford *to wait* for our affection, or even dispense with it, if needs be: but the wretched *want our help*, and if it were withheld till pity, like friendship, had taken time to grow, they would meanwhile perish with the delay. Misery is an acute disease, requiring instant attention and vigilant treatment; and by the power given to it of exciting pity in the beholder, it is enabled to call its own physician and fetch the needful prescription in an instant. by its continued influence in sustaining uneasy emotions, it is secured against neglect; and, in spite of themselves, keeps its natural nurses awake, to tender still the cup of cold water in the intervals of its fever. As Butler has finely remarked, 'Pain and sorrow have a right to our assistance; compassion puts us in mind of the debt, and that we owe it to ourselves as well as to others.' Nor can

man's calamity.' (Human nature, chap. ix. 10, Molesworth's edition of works, Vol. IV.)

we fail to see, in this adaptation, an impressive proof that 'pain and sorrow' are not mere uncontemplated anomalies, arising by way of disorder outside the idea and scheme of things, but embraced within the plan of human life, and distinctly provided for in human nature. What meaning could Pity have, in a world where suffering was not meant to be? Who would raise the infirmary and train the nurse, in Elysian fields of everlasting health? That our constitution is furnished with this medicine of ill, indicates a system constructed, so to speak, on a theory of sorrow, and assigning to it a deliberate place, as a perpetual element of discipline,— as natural, and not unnatural; and affords the clearest evidence of other ends than happiness, of ends that calculate on its loss and replace it with blessings of a higher tone. This consideration quite removes the horror and hate with which we should look on the various forms of human anguish, were they regarded simply as proofs that life was going wrong, and slipping out of its true idea into a turbid chaos; and tranquillises both sufferer and observer with the consciousness of a place in the Divine order and the shelter of a Divine sympathy.

§ 4. *Sentiments: Wonder; Admiration; Reverence.*

The last set of primary principles seems at first to emerge at the upper end, as much beyond the world of *persons* as at the beginning we fell short of it. It includes the *Sentiments;* which direct themselves upon *ideal relations,* objects of apprehension or thought that are above us, yet potentially ours. As the Propensions carry us simply out of ourselves, we know not whither; and the Passions repel from us our uncongenials, be they things or persons; and the Affections draw us to our congenials, who can be only persons, unequal or equal; so do the Sentiments pass out by aspiration to what is higher than ourselves, whether recognised as personal or not. They divide themselves no otherwise than the faculties and sciences of our nature; and as that nature is intellectual, giving us a science of Logic; and imaginative, affording ground for an Æsthetic; and moral, giving rise to a doctrine of Ethics and Faith: so are there three corresponding sentiments, operating as the mainsprings of the respective faculties, and supplying the tension of all their activity: viz. *Wonder*, asking for Causality; *Admiration*, directed upon Beauty; and *Reverence*, looking up to transcendent Goodness. Each of these claims from us a few words.

That *Wonder* is the primitive intellectual impulse, whence all philosophy springs, is a maxim held in common by Plato and Aristotle; drily stated by the latter[1]; embodied by the former in the graceful saying, that 'it is a happy genealogy which makes *Iris* the daughter of *Thaumas*[2];' i.e. which treats the messenger of the gods, the winged thought that passes to and fro between heaven and earth and brings them into communion, as the child of Wonder. For 'this,' he says, 'is the special sentiment of the philosopher, nor has his pursuit any other source.' In order to vindicate for it this originality of position, we must carefully distinguish it from *surprise*, an emotion with which it is very apt to be confounded. Nothing excites *surprise*, except what is contrary to a prior expectation, and breaks in upon an ideal order already established in the mind: as when we meet in Hyde Park a friend whom we supposed to be in Calcutta, or see a conjuror apparently produce entire the handkerchief he had just torn to shreds. Where there is no anticipation, there can be no such shock; and hence there is no room for this startled feeling in the early mind, in which experience has registered no order of customary succession, and to which no one event is stranger than another. It is no less excluded where all is new than it is where all is old, its very essence consisting in an irruption upon pre-existing rules of thought. To the child, therefore, if we may speak of him in antedate of his experi-

[1] Aristotle, Metaphysics, I. 2.   [2] Theæt 155 D.

the two views is intimately connected with a corresponding difference in the doctrine of causation. Brown, who acknowledges no idea of causation other than that of succession, is precluded from admitting any curiosity about causation, till an order of usual succession has become fixed: without this prior basis of comparison, there is for him nothing on which enquiry can arise. Hence he is obliged to presuppose usage in order to give occasion to wonder. But if causality does not wait for succession ere it can be thought, if it be an axiom of our intelligence that 'every phenomenon is the expression of a power,'—then there is nothing to delay the questionings of wonder beyond the first fall of a phenomenon upon the intelligence.

A question of order anterior to memory is not easily determined by a direct appeal to experience. But it is a matter of common observation that this feeling is especially lively in childhood, when there is the least established experience to be shocked; and that its quickening presence is the chief source of the vivacious charm peculiar to early life. Nor does it fail to assert its strength again, whenever in after life we are borne away into new fields of thought; whether by scientific attraction, tempting us beyond the explored paths of law; or by the fascination of creative genius, touching the familiar with colours we had missed, and opening fresh vistas into life and the world and our own nature. No doubt, inert minds that go to sleep upon their first store of knowledge, and are content when they have learned the parade-exercise of life, forget what it is to wonder, till some lightning cleaves the very path before their feet and arrests their customary step · but this is the torpor of blindness, not the living vision of the soul; and precisely in proportion as we resist this sluggish incapacity, and keep awake to new breakings in the clouds, does the childlike wonder perpetuate itself through all our years; nor is there perhaps anything that more goes to make the difference between a nature early dry, and one on which the dew is ever fresh. It is a function both of poetry and of religion to rebaptise

ence, *surprise* is impossible: whether the same remark applies to *wonder* depends on its relation to surprise; viz. on this, whether it is something ulterior to surprise, formed by addition of further elements, or something short of it and of simpler conditions. According to Dr. Thomas Brown, it first arises when the astonished mind begins to look round for explanation of the event which has startled it, or at least dwells upon the circumstances and surveys the possibilities they contain. If this be so, the feeling arises by intellectual additions to the primary emotion, and is excluded *à fortiori* from the inexperienced consciousness. I do not perceive that wonder thus presupposes surprise. Surely, it is the effect upon us simply of *the new and unexpected*,—i.e. of *every phenomenon* for which no way of custom has yet been paved,—but which enters upon the untrodden grass of a fresh nature. There is no need of *an old experience* in order to constitute *a new*, or of *a given expectation* in order to render possible *an unexpected*; the mere *absence* of experience and expectation, in a mind susceptible of both, satisfies every condition. Instead, therefore, of allowing that, until custom be violated, there can be no wonder, I should say, that until custom be formed, there can be nothing but wonder; and that the whole process of acquiring experience and knowledge is a perpetual exercise of this sentiment. The effect of time, carrying us away from the first years, is to blunt and kill out the feeling with regard to all accustomed successions; and *then*, no doubt, we have passed the stage when common things were fresh, and begin to find novelty only in the exceptional. It is by first taking the matter up at this late point, and fallaciously assuming that there was no measure of the new except the old, that Brown missed all vestiges of wonder except on the heels of surprise, and paradoxically identified the opposite cases where all is familiar and where nothing is familiar. The true order of nature, I apprehend, is this: (1) Wonder at the unknown. (2) Custom and expectation of the known. (3) Surprise at the exceptional. The difference between us, when parched up, in floods of wonder; to revive at once and to assuage the thirst. They set things before us again in their first colours, and wipe away the film of custom that made them dead, and reinvest them with the power they had lost of looking in and finding us. And only in so far as they effect this, have they any title to their name: a poetry that becomes imitative, a religion that can only stereotype historic wonders and not touch the heart-weariness of to-day, have become the artificial tank and ceased to be the running waters of life. It is not then without ground that the Greek philosophy laid such stress upon this sentiment, and set it at the first approaches of all culture. We wondered before we knew; and must ever wonder again, before we can know more.

If the account we have given of wonder be correct, it does not belong to the sensitive or merely recipient part of our nature, but to the apprehensive and cognitive activity. Were it incident to a break forced upon associated sensations, it would be thrust upon us and received by us from without; but springing up as it does on the mere excuse of a phenomenon, it is a spontaneous and transitive act of ours going forth upon the new, and issued as an energy from within. And as the equipoise between sensation and perception,—the receptivity and the spontaneity,—of our nature is more or less disturbed in different minds in favour of one element or the other, this sentiment will be intense in proportion as the spontaneous eagerness prevails over the passive receptivity. How agreeable this is to experience it is needless to observe. The wondering inquisitive child is not the most in danger from the pleasures of sense, or the most shrinking from its pains,—not the creature of most passive delicacy; but, on the contrary, has the greatest fund of resistance to mere sensations from without, the readiest self-forgetfulness in the object of his curiosity, and the most unresting activity of interrogation from within. This alone may convince us that the sentiment is something essentially distinct from the mere startling of custom from its propriety;

and illustrates the difference between the *wonder* of man and the *surprise* of animals.

Often as *Admiration* is confounded with Wonder (as in the use of the Latin *Admiratio* for both), the essential difference between them has only to be stated in order to be immediately recognised. Wonder, in the quest of causality, is directed upon the hidden and unknown, and is the expression of a *want;* admiration,—the sense of beauty,—is directed on what is present to the mind, and is its homage to the given object. What it is that makes us feel and pronounce an object beautiful, what common ground for this epithet there can be in so many and such various claimants, —in forms and colours and movements, in language and music, in action and character, in thought and passion, in nature, literature, and art,—is a question of equal interest and difficulty, which is too purely æsthetic to detain us in the course of our moral enquiry. It is sufficient for us to remark, that the sentiment is specifically different from any other with which it may come into comparison. 'The beautiful,' says Jacobi, 'has this feature in common with all that is original, that there is no *mark* by which we know it. It exists, and is *self-manifest;* you can *show* it, but not *prove* it[1].' No attempts to explain away either its distinction or its originality have obtained any admitted success. They all proceed on the same principle, of resolving the beautiful into the pleasing; and profess to show how a certain stock of primitive sensible pleasures spreads and ramifies by countless associations, and confers a factitious attraction on a thousand things in themselves indifferent. To all such theories natural feeling irresistibly replies, that the objects of admiration are not beautiful because pleasing, but pleasing because beautiful; and the simplest observation will convince us that many things may be the source of agreeable experience without acquiring any character of beauty. To evade these objections, the doctrine has been

---

[1] Es kann *gewiesen*, aber nicht *bewiesen* werden. (Fliegende Blätter, Werke, VI. p. 162.)

sometimes worked with a limitation: the senses of taste and smell have been excluded, and the three higher senses alone retained as a basis; and whatever falls into connection with their pleasures, or, *vice versâ*, whatever pleasurable mental affection falls into union with their neutral perceptions, acquires, it has been said, the character of beauty. Thus amended, the doctrine serves to explain, with useful ingenuity, many accidental wanderings and extensions of the feeling of beauty to what is primitively foreign to it; and especially throws light on the caprices of artificial fashion and the contradictions of taste; but the distinctive essence of the feeling remains at the centre, unresolved into anything else; something *ideal*, not *sensible;* and in its idea different from all else, by no means uniformly concurring with the useful, the true, or the good. The discrepancy in human judgments of beauty, like the contrarieties of the moral sense, have been urged against the assumption of any common principle of feeling. To a great extent, the same mode of answer is applicable in both controversies; and I strongly suspect that the alleged differences of verdict would rapidly thin away on near examination. It has always, for example, been supposed, that each race of mankind necessarily regards its own type of form and colour with exclusive or superlative favour; but we incidentally learn from Dr. Livingstone how far this is from being true[1]. No doubt, the direction of this sentiment is susceptible of wide modification

[1] 'The women have somewhat the same ideas with ourselves of what constitutes comeliness. They came frequently and asked for the looking-glass; and the remarks they made,—while I was engaged in reading and apparently not attending to them,—on first seeing themselves therein, were amusingly ridiculous. "Is that me?" "What a big mouth I have!" "My ears are as big as pumpkin leaves!" "I have no chin at all!" Or, "I should have been pretty, but am spoiled by these high cheek-bones!" "See how my head shoots up in the middle!" laughing vociferously all the time at their own jokes. They readily perceive any defect in each other, and give nicknames accordingly. One man came along to have a quiet gaze at his own features once, when he thought I was asleep: after twisting his mouth about in various directions, he remarked to himself, "People say I am ugly; and how very ugly I am indeed!"'

by accidental or extrinsic associations. Every form of deep sensibility is apt to practice a kind of cheat upon the perception of beauty. Descartes supplies a remarkable instance from his own experience[1]: he says that all his life he was conscious of a partiality for persons who squinted. In endeavouring to account for so whimsical a preference, he recollected that, when a boy, he had been attached to a girl who had that blemish; and the affection for this object of his first love had diffused itself over all others who resembled her. And Jean Paul Richter confesses to a no less extraordinary predilection for faces pitted with the small-pox, arising from a boyish love-fancy for a peasant girl happy in this adornment;—a fact which he thus moralises: 'The Professor, however, considers it his duty to declare to all vaccinated fair readers, that he knows how to value *their* beauty as well and as highly as he did at that time a different fashion of face. But, in connection with this discussion of beauty, he pledges himself that every female face whose so-called ugliness has no moral cause, he can, without cosmetic artifice, without paint or pomatum-box, without snow or soap-water, without night-masks, make in the highest degree charming and enchanting. If she will only sing to him some evening a song composed of heart-words, no one shall be more beautiful than the singer:— but then of course only in *his* eyes; for who can speak for another[2]?'

But when every allowance has been made for the accidents of experience and affection, there remains a central apprehensiveness of beauty, which no less *uses* the outward senses and looks through them as organs of the imagination, than the perceptive activity uses them as organs of the understanding. There is a specific difference between mere good eyesight and the artistic vision which instinctively seizes the harmonies of the scene before it, and frames it into a speaking whole. the one reads its objects piecemeal,

---

[1] Letter to M. Chanut, Cousin, X. p. 53.
[2] Autobiography, I. 64, English translation.

by traversing hither and thither, and putting together the contents of the field; the other catches the whole before it fixes upon anything, and carries the entire idea into the interpretation of every part. And the same difference reappears in the mental conception of an absent scene or history, and in the verbal description by which its impression may be passed from mind to mind. One man will present it to you by a process of statistical or enumerative memory, like the naturalist's list of marks for identifying a plant or an animal; a second will give you its intellectual ground-plan, disposing its parts round some scientific or technical idea, to which its physical elements are quite subordinate; a third, with a few strokes that seem to have no material in them, will set its picture before you better than you could have found it for yourself. Why is it that, in this last case, we always pronounce the description '*natural*'? Assuredly because it reproduces our own feeling, and transposes us into the state of mind which the actual scene would occasion, were it spread before our most awakened thought; and what is this but to say, that we all of us see, not with the optic but with the artist organ, and are not replaced where our nature sets us till our ideal faculty is touched? The great difference between the ordinary and the extraordinary energy of this gift,—for example, between the poet's reader and the poet himself,—is perhaps that, in the former, it is dumb and unconscious, doing its work without disentangling the elements into view; while, in the latter, it is too vivid to remain unconscious and instinctive. The sense of beauty clears itself from every foreign impression, flings down the sediment of neutral matter, and by spontaneous analysis disengages the transparent essentials. It is indeed the tendency of all intense human feeling to quit its indeterminate state and become distinct; for, in proportion to its force, is it unable to sleep within; it thirsts for expression; and expression is first self-clearance, and then self-intelligence.

There is, perhaps, no principle of our nature more

obviously unequal in its distribution among men than the sentiment of beauty; and the maxim, 'poeta nascitur, non fit,' embodies an induction from evidence and unchanging facts. No one who has ever met with a child of imaginative eye, spontaneously apprehensive of the language of beauty, never missing a look or tone or movement of either awkwardness or grace, and in quick sympathy with every happy congruity of thought and feeling, can for a moment doubt the originality of this high gift. And, on the other hand, the prosaic mind no less obviously belongs to a constant type,—of men who believe only in concrete facts and their generalisations; who see the world and life in the light of scientific arrangement, not of artistic look; who judge everything by material or moral uses; who estimate feeling as the means of action, not action as the expression of feeling; who look on the combinations of beauty as fancies of the human mind; and treat the imagination as a sort of holiday embellishment, which, like lace curtains in an engine-house or a satin dress at sea, is much out of place in this working world. So great may this contrast become, that the estimates of reality by the two minds may be completely reversed, and that which is the very substance of life and truth to the one may be but the shadow to the other. In determining between them, there is but one principle to follow: viz that every faculty gives insight, every incapacity entails blindness, so that whatever each of these uncongenial men may deny of the other is false; whatever he may affirm of himself is true. By this rule we know at once the larger nature. 'What mean you,' says Jacobi, 'by a fine soul? You mean a soul that is quick to perceive the better, clear to set it in the light, immovable to hold it[1].'

It remains to notice one other sentiment, viz. *Reverence*, which recognises *transcendent goodness*. To assert its origin-

[1] Was nennst du eine schone Seele? Eine schone Seele nennst du, die das Bessere schnell gewahr wird, rein heraushebt, unbeweglich festhalt. (Fliegende Blatter, 1ste Abtheilung, Werke, VI. p. 134.)

ality may appear at first sight inconsistent with the doctrine that we pass moral judgments on ourselves before we are able to pronounce on others, and learn the scale of goodness within us ere we can apply it to outward beings. That recognition of excellence which Reverence requires would seem, in this view, to be the ultimate result of the moral table, when formed; and not to lie among its elementary constituents. I am willing to admit that we might, without violence, resolve this sentiment back into the primary moral consciousness; and consider it as the same sense of authority with which the hierarchy of principles affects us; with the difference, that here it comes to us from outward beings rather than from inward experience. Indeed, I have already[1] shown how the feeling may be provided for in this way. But, though the connection is most intimate between the moral and the reverential consciousness, and they converge upon the same result, I am not prepared to admit their identity, or the ability of the former to generate the latter in its fulness. The simple *obligation* of one affection as compared with another, the *duty* of following it, might surely be revealed without involving that positive homage of the heart, that joyful humility in its outward presence, of which we now speak. When we look on the moral law in the *downward* direction, when we are aware of it chiefly by what it shuts out, and hear its negative voice, 'Thou shalt *not !*' it seems to wither and repel, and sets free no springs of worship; yet so keen is the *binding* sense involved in this state of mind, that this is usually taken as the exact type of the simple apprehension of Duty. It is only when we invert our gaze, and look from the lower principle *upward*, that any dew of reverence softens the strained will; and even then, if the higher invitation is all within ourselves, if it be only some affection actually present *with us*, it is so humanised by its poor domicile, that, though we own its authority, we cannot dwell upon it with any veneration; for no man can venerate himself; and whatever falls into that company

[1] Supra, chap. I. ii. 3, pp. 63-65.

becomes homely and drops the heavenly air. The upward look, therefore, is not in fact realised except through the attraction of *objective* character above us: other minds beyond our station, minds expressing our possibility but transcending our actuality, first call this sentiment into life; and its title to the originality I have assigned to it depends on this question: whether it can *go before* the subjective moral consciousness; or whether it must *wait upon this and follow it*. This question is, perhaps, sufficiently determined by the remarks formerly made and referred to above. Had we no moral nature, it would certainly be in vain to exhibit before us moral phenomena; and did our moral nature come, at a given point, to a dead stop, manifestations of what lay beyond that limit would be also futile; just as you cannot make a revelation to your dog. But, in order to appreciate a type of character, it is not necessary that we should have personally passed through it; be it only possible to us, the key is within us; on the principle that we intuitively interpret the natural language of every human emotion, though we should see the sign ere we have felt what is signified. Now, mysteriously as the inner self-knowledge and the outer sympathy act and react, it appears certain that the objective exhibition of higher goodness is the most powerful means of developing the latent sense of it; that secret shame and nobler hope for ourselves flow down upon us from the greatness and sanctity of our spiritual superiors; and that our personal ideal stretches wider, like their own shadow, with the stature of the beings we behold. If this be so, then the Reverence which passes outward and looks upward, may have priority to the sense of obligation which springs from inward comparison and self-knowledge.

But we may advance yet a step further, and say, that even independently of actual and visible heroes or saints on whom this sentiment may fix when they are present, it finds for itself the means of exercise; goes forth in faith upon invisible objects, and discerns, behind the veil of the actual, a better and higher before which it humbles itself with cries of dependence and aspiration. The religious sense, it cannot be doubted, is capable of anticipating the moral; and worship may recognise its object, while conscience is yet in its mere rudiments. Nor is this strange, if it be indeed a Divine Person that lives in our humanity and coalesces with all its good: the affection which goes out and feels after His personality may easily precede the inner consciousness of what He loves and wills. In the great mass of the human race this is undoubtedly the predominant order; and when the conscience comes to be unfolded, God is already recognised as there. In that early stage of culture, there is so little moral element in the religious reverence, that it seems hardly proper to speak of it as a feeling directed upon *goodness: power, wisdom*, even *passion*, appear rather to stand before the face of the first rude worship. Still, the incipient moral element,—that which differences a *person* from a physical force and constitutes *character*, is what raises the feeling into *Reverence* and distinguishes it from base *fear*. In the conception which the savage has of human beings, there is the same predominance of unmoral elements as in his notion of the Divine: both are necessarily the reflection of himself; but so long as his faith presents something *above him,*—the human qualities on diviner scale and in greater perfection,—the object transcends him in such ingredients of character as he yet knows, and only on that account is regarded with any reverence. Entirely divorced from a moral nature, planted in a cold thinking mechanism, or a malignant devil, mere power or intelligence could be the object of no veneration; and it is to mark this fact, and show that in an unmoral world its essence would be left out, that I have named *Goodness* as its distinctive object. But if any one insists on the rights of intellectual and physical greatness to some share in the feeling, inasmuch as their co-presence vastly heightens the sentiment, he may widen the definition, and speak of reverence as the sentiment we direct upon transcendent *Life*. No important conclusion would be affected by this change; but the narrower definition seems to me to be a more exact statement of the truth.

The three sentiments we have described are the organs through which we apprehend the ideal essence at once veiled and hinted by the universe and life: the first, finding for us its Causal Thought: the second, its divine Beauty; the third, the transcendent Personality which adds *character* to both. They all meet their objects, therefore, first beyond the realm of mere phenomena, and at once attest and interpret an ulterior sphere of spiritual realities.

When from this point we look back on the springs of action in their serial order, we cannot fail to notice the law of their succession. They are none of them mere egoistic phenomena, scintillating and quenched within our isolated history: they all have their external correlates. In the part they play with us, these correlates rise from a minimum to a maximum of qualitative influence; being, of the propensions, mere Conditions; of the passions, Causes; of the affections, personal Objects; of the sentiments, the perfect realisation. They begin with nutritive things; they culminate in the Divine impersonation of Truth, Beauty, and Goodness; ascending thither through the scale of human persons who have not yet wholly escaped the lingering attributes of things. In claiming something of *a natural character* for this arrangement, I do not mean to deny the possibility, or for specific purposes the merits, of other distributions: much less would I suggest that our springs of action are separate *pieces* of us, so that our nature is put together like the contents of a case of instruments, or the pipes and stops of an organ, mechanically detachable for use. The Ego is not multiple; lay it out as we may, we count only its groups of phenomena or acts, the subjective agent being one and the same. But when, with a view to reach the laws of character, we try to bring together the similars, and distinguish the dissimilars, with which these laws have to do, we seem to get soonest upon the right track by surveying the relations of the human being to the scene of his life, and the consequent varieties of his moral experience, in the order on which we have entered. Be it remembered, however, that all logical division is only an artifice of intellectual convenience; and that its fitness for this purpose is not contradicted by the absence of its sharp demarcations from the field of nature, and the habitual substitution there of graduated shades of difference.

It may well be asked, whether these *Sentiments*, special to man and lying so deep in his reflective nature, are properly classed with the *Primary* principles, whose distinction was said to be their impulsive unconsciousness. To know, to admire, to revere, are impossible acts till the subject has discriminated himself from the things known, admired, revered; and can be affirmed only of one who is already set up in his independent personality. Chronologically, this is perfectly true; but it does not really affect the propriety of the arrangement. For, in the exercise of these sentiments, the Self which had been discovered is again lost; they carry us into self-forgetfulness, though they are posterior to our self-knowledge. They engage the mind wholly upon objects extraneous to itself and its feelings, and draw it forth towards them by the same instinctive attraction which constitutes the method of the affections. In this characteristic they are distinguished from the secondary principles, which aim to reproduce in our self-consciousness the experienced effects of the primary. *All the secondary* must be subsequent to the primary whence they come; but *not all* the primary need be on the field, before the self-conscious stage can in any case begin. The disinterested and intuitive engagement of the sentiments upon objects foreign to the Self suffices to justify the place assigned to them.

The absence of two at least out of the three sentiments from the enumeration of principles given by Stewart, and from most similar lists, renders it proper that I should vindicate their title to a position among the *springs of action*.

look, however, will show that the moral effect of self-consciousness is very different in different parts of the series; and that some of the principles no sooner touch this point than they run out into ulterior forms more important than themselves, and demanding recognition by separate names. These deviations from formal parallelism require that we should pause for a few moments on each of the secondary series.

Wise and benevolent observers, from Socrates to Paley, in working out their teleological view of the world, have not failed to remark the gratuitous gift of pleasure attached by the Creator to most of the functions of life, inducing, and, as these moralists justly contend, *permitting* their exercise beyond the limit of mere correlated use. Food, they say, would not have been made so agreeable, and its different kinds so variously agreeable, were we forbidden to enjoy it and bound to consult exclusively for the necessary repair of wasted strength. It is the mistake of asceticism, to distrust this healthful conclusion, to be more utilitarian than the Creator, to tie down each appetency to its strict object; with the result, not of leaving it in its primary and natural stage, but, on the contrary, of inducing a morbid and intense self-consciousness, fatal to the purity it erroneously seeks. It is very true that this argument of the natural theologian can no longer be urged in the form given to it in the 'Memorabilia' and in Paley. *There*, undoubtedly, we find an anthropological conception of the world far too dominant; man is regarded as the central object of all design; and it is too hastily asserted that ordinances of nature for which no other function has been ascertained can be meant only to please and entertain him. Time is pretty sure to disturb such inferences contingent upon our ignorance. Accordingly, we now know that several sensible pleasures, once treated as a gratuitous generosity to man, play else-

animal natures, it can be attributed to only the most rudimentary humanity;—according to the late Professor Green, to no humanity at all. (Prolegomena to Ethics, Book I. chap. iii. §§ 81-84.)

where an indispensable part in the economy of nature; so that, though we could spare them, protests against their removal would pour in from other provinces of life. For instance, the colours and scents of flowers, so often regarded as a mere garden of sweets for us, are now known to be, through their attraction for winged insects, an essential means for the fructification of plants. Thus they are supplied with an end, and take their place among the *utilities*, instead of the *gratuities*, of the world, so that the ascetic, if he is so disposed, may reply to our teleological plea for a certain margin of luxury: 'Be not deceived; these things are *not meant for you;* keep to the ends of your own being.' It is obvious, however, that he here oversteps the bounds of a legitimate answer; for the new teleology only limits, and does not abolish, the old. The pleasure which before was regarded as *absolutely* gratuitous, i. e. as serving *no purpose* beyond improving our lot, is now found to subserve an ulterior use in another department of nature, to the order of which it is indispensable; and it is only *in relation to us*, that it is gratuitous. Thus qualified, the original position remains undisturbed: *relatively to us*, the pleasures in question are *a free gift;* for no necessity can be shown for making us partners in the attractions which regulate the life of bees and butterflies. So far, therefore, as the ascetic relies for his doctrine on a teleological rule, and says, 'You must consult simply the *intentions* of your nature, and let no function go a step beyond the minimum for realising its end, eating, for example, as little and as severely as will properly nourish you,' he is still adequately met on his own ground by the remark, that *among the intentions* conspicuously impressed upon our nature, is this; that, over and above the bare satisfaction of functional ends, it should experience a certain surplus of unearned and merely ornamental pleasures.

§ 1. *Secondary Propensions: Love of Pleasure, Money, Power.*

The Secondary transformations of the Propensions are more easy to distinguish in thought than in word; for they challenge notice and receive names chiefly when they assume the scale of excess; and, even then, the excess of one is so often the excess of more than one, that, when remarked as a feature of character, it is apt to be denoted by a term too general for any simple desire. Thus, when the pleasures of the organic propensions are spoken of as motives, we have no single-worded names of a neutral kind for either the class or its members; but a very sufficient vocabulary of inculpatory words both for species and genus, regarded as no longer innocent; for the genus, Voluptuousness, or Carnality; for the first species, Gluttony or Daintiness as the substitute for Hunger, Drunkenness or Ebriety for Thirst, Epicurism for both · for the second species, Lust or Licentiousness. The fact, that the moment the appetites pass into the self-conscious state and become *ends* instead of impulses, they draw to themselves terms of censure, is highly significant; betraying our natural feeling that this is not their right and wholesome condition, and that in parting with their primary character and becoming chosen self-indulgences, they change into something odious. Not, of course, that it is possible for us to remain mere creatures of instinct and keep any part of our nature in the dark beneath the floor of self-consciousness. But *the attention* conceded to it may vary from zero almost to infinitude: the Will may be directed either to enforce its emergence, or to lay it to sleep into forgetfulness again; and the language in which we speak of character on this side marks our healthy repugnance to see the appetites made the subject of reflective hedonistic elaboration. The nearest approach to a neutral designation of this order of motives is the phrase '*Love of pleasure,*' which may be accepted as naming the secondary spring of action furnished by the organic propensions; for, although it is susceptible of a wider range, being often applied to the pursuit of amusement and other *agréments* apparently unrelated to appetite, yet it is here that the phrase gets its first meaning, and it is hither that the disposition it marks never ceases to tend. Where there is a general weakness towards self-gratification, it will remain true to its origin, and will not be proof against the fascinations of Sense.

The third or Animal propension, of spontaneous activity, gives rise, by its pleasures of energy, to a Secondary motive, the athlete's desire of gymnastic achievement (perhaps what the poet Spencer marks by '*lustihood*'), which in its elementary form seems of no very serious import. Even thus, however, it is the natural opposite to *laziness*, the counterpoise to the *love of ease* induced by the secondary play of the organic propensions; and, by establishing a willing *culture of fatigue*, it disperses the passive love of pleasure, and sets its captive free. But it is at an ulterior stage of its history that this motive assumes its chief importance The pursuit of the pleasures of energy becomes the *Love of Power*, whether shown in the conquest of physical nature, or in mastery over the wills of men. Everybody has a troublesome acquaintance with its rudimentary form in what is called 'the love of mischief' in boys, i. e. the desire of venting force in producing effects of any kind, the more surprising, the better. There are doubtless many tributaries added to this great incentive in its maturest state: the appeals of beings dependent on us for protection, the desires of social benevolence, the watchfulness and previsions of fear, flow into it and modify its stimulus; and the mere earnestness and intensity of any particular aim that possesses us may put on its semblance for a time. But the essence of the feeling as a distinctive feature of character is, I am disposed to think, in *the consciousness of faculty*, brought home and attested by the submission of obstacles against which it is measured. This then is the secondary stage of the propension to Causal activity. *The Love of Money* is nothing but an ulterior development of these two principles combined,—the love of pleasure and the love of power,— usually with a great preponderance of the latter. Its factitious character is evident from its being directed upon an object wholly artificial and representative; upon which it can only be transferred from the things represented. The value of money consists in the command it gives over conveniences and luxuries, and its efficacy as an instrument of ambition: it is under these aspects that it first becomes an object of desire; and though it afterwards assumes the aspect of an end in itself, and in an avaricious mind apparently constitutes a separate passion, it may be doubted whether, even there, money does not charm the imagination as a symbol of security and power, and wield its influence by being indispensable to the consciousness of these. When we see the miser foregoing all the advantages of his wealth, and dooming himself to a life of privation, we are apt to suppose him indifferent to all purchasable things. The habitual pictures of his fancy would probably undeceive us, and would show that the ease and ambition he declined still played off their fascinations on him within; dreams of *potential* splendour and consideration, perhaps of posthumous astonishment at the greatness of his heir, engaging his thought; or at least an anxiety oppressing him to bar out the opposite evils, and win still further security against the haunting terrors of destitution and helplessness. In this last form the feeling undergoes a modification equally observable in many cases of the direct love of power; which often exhibits itself as an *intense dislike of fear*, and an impatience to make excess of provision against it, by sweeping out of sight every formidable possibility and building fortresses against the mere shadow of a foe. The proverb that none is so great a tyrant as the coward, illustrates this repulsive phase of the love of power; and when ambition takes a financial turn and runs into accumulation of capital, the same degrading taint may be observed in the love of money.

§ 2. *Secondary Passions: Malice; Vindictiveness; Suspiciousness.*

None of the other primary principles undergo, at their secondary stage, such disguising transformations as the propensions. The passions, growing self-conscious, produce well marked and familiar forms of disposition. As the original impulses are anything but delightful, it appears strange that a taste for indulging them should be possible at all; yet nothing is more certain than that a man may contract a sort of relish for them, and never be at ease without an antipathy, a resentment, or a fear. There is, in truth, no spring of action, whether repulsive or attractive, which does not win a certain relief and satisfaction in attaining its end: even a mind haunted by the passions rids itself of a burden in letting the lightning slip; and as in the tears at a tragedy, so in the outpouring of even uneasy emotion, there is a secret charm. The fondness for *antipathy*, or *pleasure in hating*, we call, as a feeling, *Ill-will* or *Malice*, and in its expression *Censoriousness:* the cherishing of *resentment*, *Vindictiveness:* of *fear*, *Suspiciousness, or Mistrust*. That all these exist, not merely as illusions or exaggerations, incident to this or that excitement of the primary passion, but as habitual dispositions and set tendencies, is matter of common observation. A censorious man will actually get up antipathies as a congenial excitement. In approaching others, he carries with him a selecting vision which throws into the background whatever they have in common with himself, and draws to the front every alienating feature, and feels towards them as a Suffolk peasant would feel towards a Frenchman, or a Scotch Covenanter towards a Papist. All that can produce sympathy he misses; all that is repellent he intensifies; all that is novel and neutral he misconstrues and derides. He picks up scandals *con amore;* he tells you confidentially the weaknesses he has found out in your friend; and if you set him right and stop his mouth by conclusive proof, is chagrined that his occupation is gone. Half the gossips of the world consist of such traffickers in ill-will; and are numerous enough in our time to have created a literature of their own; for it is in great measure to their vitiated cravings that what are called the 'Society Journals' are addressed. The original antipathy whose indulgence matures into this type of malice may have only the most trivial excuse; yet be none the less bitter for beginning with dislike of some petty personal peculiarity of physiognomy or speech or manner,—a curve in the nose, a colour of the hair, a sniffle in the voice, a smile too much, or an address too curt. The subject of such aversions becomes the slave of his own prejudices. He enjoys the idea of the objectionable person in ridiculous positions or caught in contemptible actions; and is ready to seize this enjoyment on the faintest hint of an hypothesis, so as to pass without scruple from supposition to belief, and from belief to assertion. This is probably the natural history of the great majority of slanders. They are born of the malice of prejudice, more often than from the deliberate purpose of supplanting a rival or avenging a defeat.

Similarly, a vindictive man will look out for occasions of resentment, which will set him on his favourite pursuit, of levying damages for real or imaginary injuries; not always through judge and jury (though every court is familiar with such litigants), but by public complaint, or social exile, or private reproaches and demands for reparation. Few of us can have been so happy as never to come across one who is always being wronged, and tells nothing with so much gusto as his griefs from the conspiracies of this wicked world; and who therefore becomes the ready victim of every talebearer interested in making friends into enemies and preventing alliances founded on natural sympathies. And so he is never long without a quarrel, and a resolve to pay off somebody for taking an unfair advantage. Even if he is withheld by prudential constraint from actively avenging himself, he watches with keen satisfaction the retribution which, without agency of his, events may seem to bring upon his foe. To see the pitch of intensity which this passion may reach, we must turn to Oriental history and literature; nor need we go further than the Hebrew Psalms, where so often the very atmosphere of the sweetest and sublimest piety is darkened by sudden storms and streaked with flashes of relentless rage: 'Break their teeth, O God, in their mouth;

break out the great teeth of the young lions, O Lord. Let them melt away as waters which run continually: when he bendeth his bow to shoot his arrows, let them be as cut in pieces:' 'The righteous shall rejoice when he seeth the vengeance: he shall wash his feet in the blood of the wicked [1].' Indeed, when we wish to emphasise the eager energy with which an act is done, this passion supplies us with the most expressive image: we say, 'He did it *with a vengeance!*'

Again, a *suspicious* man *invents fears* for himself in the mere exercise of his temper. He lives as if every last post had brought him a threatening letter, requiring an instant provision of protective force; and unless a whole posse of precautions mount guard around him, he will be a lost man. Nature and mankind seem to be in league against him; if he catches a cold, he must make his will; if his children have the measles, he cannot expect them all to recover; he will not have a new suit of clothes, lest they should be made by a tailor with scarlet-fever in the house; he removes his account from the bank that has served him well, not liking the look of the new managing director; he warns his wife against her best friend as 'a designing woman,' and snubs the parish curate lest he should be planning to win his daughter. He wonders what bribe it was that induced their opposition member to give a ministerial vote, and says, 'depend upon it, he will be gazetted for an under-secretaryship next week.' His chief intellectual excitement is in constructing hypotheses of mistrust: if he be literary, he finds the historians liars, the poets plagiarists, the moralists and theologians insincere: if political, he expects no public policy but such as may be indicated by spite of a rival or the interests of a party. Like the Eastern prince, secured by tasters against the poison that may lurk in each dish or cup, he treats his life as a perpetual defensive warfare, and pledges all his faculties to the baffling of stratagems and the escape from illusion. However pitiable may seem

[1] Psalm lviii. 6, 7, 10.

to be this incessant dodging of the flying shadows of evil, it is not without the sustaining interest of every game in which the resolve remains possible and strong *never to be beaten.*

In each of these cases it is doubtless some disproportioned strength in the primary passion which at first leads to the tyrannous influence of the secondary: for the intenser any spring of our nature is, the keener is the satisfaction of its indulgence; and the more likely is a taste for this satisfaction to constitute itself. The abuse in this case is obvious. The passions are our planted sentinels at points of danger, permitting the real business of life to go on with disembarrassed cheerfulness within. Leave them at their silent outposts and forget them, and they set you free for all you have to do. But if, instead of letting them alone, you fancy they can never do enough for you, and insist on turning out all the ferment of wholesome work from within the circle to reinforce the circumference, you corrupt the mere negative protection into the positive office of life, and make an inner barrenness bristle with outer repulsions. Intellectual skill lends itself with some facility and promptitude to the passions, whose very nature demands a certain quickness of resource; and the consciousness of this renders their stimulus acceptable to minds not otherwise roused to the same power. Criticism, sarcasm, exclusion, contradiction, are easier exercises of mind than any form of creation; so that intellectual action enters on lower terms with the ungenial than with the genial; and many a sharp cynic and polemic has there been who, apart from his antipathies and rejections, has scarcely shown any force of intellect at all. How greatly this cause may tend to foster the secondary passions is self-evident. To yield to the temptation is to turn the medicine of life into its food, and under a depraved taste for its bitter draughts to lose the thirst for its pure waters.

§ 3. *Secondary Affections: Sentimentality.*

When the affections become self-conscious, and give rise to voluntary attempts to renew their experiences, the condition of mind is produced to which we specifically give the name Sentimental. If, instead of family affection, freely spent on the members of a home, there is a self-regarding play with them, as instruments of sympathetic interest; if, instead of social affection, flowing out upon companions and equals, there is the mere love of society as a means of tasting the fruits of such affection; if, instead of Compassion, there grows up a taste for exciting and indulging Pity; this change is accurately described by saying, that it is a transition from natural health to sentimental disease. The objects themselves are desired for the sake of the feelings they excite; and the very guides given us in order to carry us out of ourselves are treacherously suborned to bring us back and shut us more closely in. The subtlety of this malady is so great, that it often spreads by the very means taken to prevent it; and it is more likely to be increased than diminished by all simply *moral methods* of dealing with the affections. The tendency of all exhortations to love as a duty, of all praise of sympathetic pleasures, of all persuasion to cultivate this side of life, is simply to hinder the primary by substituting the secondary affections, and to render self-forgetfulness impossible through the very din of the chorus that celebrates it. Here emphatically it is that *a redemption* is needed which is beyond the reach of the personal will, and which ethical teaching intercepts rather than invokes.

§ 4. *Secondary Sentiments: Self-culture; Æstheticism; Interest in Religion.*

The Sentiments also have their secondary stage; still bearing the same character, that they are indulged for the sake of the experiences which they bring. They lose their disinterestedness by the change, and are consciously resorted to as personal exercises. The scientific man who, coming down from the deathbed of his wife, locked himself into his library and, as the most tasking diversion he could give to his thoughts, set himself to solve the problem why a top spins, was not yielding to the impulse of wonder, but using it in his own service; and wherever the intellect is exercised by way of gymnastic discipline, wherever the knowledge is absorbed as nutriment to the faculty, instead of the faculty following in the trail of knowledge, the natural impulse is replaced by the secondary desire of self-culture. As the whole process of education is for the sake of mental discipline, and only when the intellect is mature does it place itself at the service of further research, it may seem as if the usual order were here inverted, and the primary impulse entered the field after the secondary. But the process of education is conducted for us, not by us; the object present to the mind of the educator is the pupil's culture; but this does not hinder the pupil from having another object, viz. the knowledge set before him; and no training can be applauded that robs him of this, and substitutes for it the dominant purpose of self-improvement. The perfect method is not attained till the two different incentives coexist without interference in the teacher and the taught; and by the disciplinary skill of the one the curiosity of the other is directed, without loss of its primitive force and simplicity, to such objects as will exercise and balance the whole nature. It is only at a later period, or through the intrusion of foreign motives, that the thirst for truth is exchanged for the desire for accomplishment;—a far inferior inspiration, than which the scholar's life has no more beguiling seduction, and which not a few have attempted, under the name of self-formation, to systematise and make supreme.

Admiration, at the secondary stage, becomes the *love of Art*, or *devotion to the pleasures of Taste*. Its tendency is to lose the simple emotions awakened by beauty, through deliberately seeking them; to pass, by analysis and self-comparison, into fastidious connoisseurship; to bring everything to the test of æsthetic sympathy; and invert the order of mind from the attitude of submission to the object admired to that of judicial superiority to it. It is one of the great evils incident to the pursuit of art as a profession, that it almost necessarily substitutes this state of mind, to a very undesirable extent, for the primitive impulse; and wears out the fresh instinct by the friction of too much speech and the repeated beat of technical formulas; nor can anything, except the corresponding dialect of theology, be more painful to a pure-minded believer in the reality and significance of beauty, than the slang of hardened criticism, and the profane conceit of professional arbiters. It needs a strong and deep basis of the original inspiration to maintain itself in power under the artificial accumulation of self-consciousness thus produced, and secure the happy balance of discriminative perception and creative life. Goethe's epigrammatic couplet notes the fact, and hints the reason :

> Warum will Geschmack und Genie sich so selten vereinen?
> Jener furchtet die Kraft, diese furchtet den Zaum.

Genius, in short, is legislative; taste is judicial; and the power which, finding new beauty, makes new laws, clashes not unnaturally with the conservative habit of mere interpretation, founded on the study of past models. There is an inevitable penalty, I believe, attached to every attempt to live upon a particular order of feelings, and detach them from their place as mere functions of an integral life. Not only do they fritter themselves away into artificial fineness and feebleness, but they lose all healthy reality, become more and more conventional, and, like Chinese cabinet painting, at some tenth remove take leave of nature altogether. Under the torture of analysis,—the great engine of *logical* power,—Beauty gives up the ghost and flies; and for *poetic* power, in all the spontaneous products of genius, man, remaining whole, must commune with life and the universe remaining whole no less, and speaking with him eye to eye. So far as civilisation, through division of employment, creates also division of consciousness, and makes us only *too knowing* respecting some one class of feelings and experiences, it incurs the danger of a barren self-concentration; which is never perhaps more dreary and hopeless than where the pursuits of taste and the language of culture give facilities for varnishing over the lifelessness within. The distinction in morals between primary and secondary admiration corresponds with that between productive Imagination and regulative Taste.

The same characteristic differences mark the change from the primary to the secondary stage in the sentiment of *Reverence*. Strange as it may appear, it is one of the undoubted subtleties of our nature, that *a taste* may be formed for gratifying the feelings of reverence, and *self-seeking* may acquire a turn for *self-escape* in higher objects. When 'interest in religion' takes the place of the love of God; when not Himself, but thoughts and sentiments about Him, are what is present to the consciousness; when instead of our being held, as it were, in His hand and ceasing there to be our own, He simply furnishes an engagement to our mind and belongs to us as an occasion of solemn and tender feeling; the first-hand life of faith is exchanged for its drama: its reality serves only to be worked up into its representation; and Reverence is detected looking in the glass. It is greatly to be feared that in our days this secondary principle, of concern for religion, usurps the place of simple reverence to an incalculable extent. Of systematic and scientific theology it is the essential source; nor perhaps can the much-disputed relation between religion and theology be more accurately determined than by recourse to the distinction on which I am dwelling, and saying that the one is the expression of the primary, the other of the secondary stage of reverence. The division of worships and coexistence of sects within the nominal embrace of the same system, are the grand stimulus to theology; not only in the academic schools, but in the popular mind: curiosity about the faith of neighbours, comparison and criticism of creeds, the sympathies and antipathies of party, all tending to sharpen the lines of conscious distinction and to lay out doctrine in sections, instead of taking up men into higher unity. Nor can it be denied that the separation of a particular sacred profession acts in the same direction: pledged speech at stated times, with a vast ecclesiastical literature at its back, descends almost inevitably into a critical exercise of Review, too busy with exclusion of the false, and with winding its way through the doubtful, to forget itself in the supremely real and true. And even where a reaction takes place from this sterile criticism of others' thoughts, men seem unable to escape except into similar criticism of their own feelings; only exchanging objective analysis for subjective, keenly watching the spiritual weather in the mind, gauging the affections, refining on the temperature, describing the clouds, but spellbound in the personal atmosphere, and never carried out into the Light of lights. Hence the weakness and inefficacy of the so-called 'spiritualist' recoil from the old dogmatic theology: with this critical demon not cast out, it is afflicted still with the mortal curse, and is but the inner side of the same evil: the hectic of consumption, instead of the paralysis of age. It is most difficult for those whose whole life is steeped in the influences of such a time, to find an adequate redemption; consultation on the disease does but fix it deeper; we do not want to discuss it, but to escape it; and the pulse will flutter, till you cease to feel it. Perhaps when human ingenuity and will have spent themselves and worn out their pride, some Divine method will redress the balance of our nature; will convince the secondary sentiments that they cannot set up for themselves; and carry off the love of knowledge, of art, of religion, in a flood-tide of fresh wonder, admiration, and reverence.

iii. ULTERIOR COMPOUNDS.

If this survey embraces all the radical impulses of human nature, the resulting list ought to give an adequate conspectus of the whole system of action and passion. But, as might be expected, it will not do so without some complication. The several principles achieve among themselves numerous combinations; and in some instances not only form transient and accidental partnerships for the production of particular acts, but so habitually run together as to *set* into coalescence. In these cases, the appearance and the name of *one* spring of action will be presented by a union of two or more; indeed the fusion in the mind is real, and the unity of phrase has nothing deceptive in it in its present application. Thus, we have not hitherto mentioned the *love of Praise; Emulation* has no place in our list; and other examples of the same kind will readily occur. To resolve these back into their elements, and retrace them up into their maturity, is an admirable exercise of psychological skill; but the task would detain us too long. The roots of the derivative feelings are usually obvious enough; the love of Praise, for example,—or fondness for *being admired,*—implies some susceptibility for *admiring*, since it transposes the self into the position of an *object admired;* and some *social affection*, to give value to the sentiments of others; and some *self-distrust*, pleased to lean upon any external judgment to give what it rather hopes than claims: and this self-distrust again is not a simple feeling, but due to a certain tempering together of the constitutional springs. It is the frustrated attempt, as pride is the gratified attempt, to feel one's own relative merits. Again, *Emulation* is evidently not independent of the *love of Power;* it is the aim at superiority or ascendency; and a great part of its intensity depends on the prospect of power over two things at once,—viz. over the object contended for, and over the contending competitor,—the companionship in the race keeping both conceptions alive all the while, and furnishing a measure of gradation and comparison throughout. Further, the *love of Praise*, with its contents, is present too; for in the absence of spectators, or under indifference to their sentiments, Emulation is inconceivable. Emulation implies the pursuit by two or more persons of a good which only one can gain . it is a motive that operates during the contemplation and process of pursuit. When the race has been run and the prize awarded, new feelings take its place; then it is that the victor may be thrown into *Exultation*, the vanquished into *Jealousy;* the former being the joy of power won over a coveted good, and of ascendency won over one who might have proved superior, the latter, the disappointment of a coveted good, and aversion to the winner who carries off the trophy of his superiority. This involves *Envy;* which, however, is not limited to the case of competition for a prize which only one can hold, but may be directed towards any persons whose superior advantages we think might as well be ours: it is therefore the grudging sense of relative inferiority.

The laws in conformity with which such complex derivatives arise have been, I think, correctly laid down by the empirical psychologists, though often forced by them beyond the limits of their range. The *law of transference*, the *law of sympathy*, the *law of distance*, are in themselves indisputable, and at least go very far towards explaining all the operative feelings beyond the series which we have reviewed. The law of transference is this: the repulsion from a contemplated pain, the attraction towards a contemplated pleasure, transfer themselves by extension to indifferent things associated with them respectively, and therefore pre-eminently to their invariable associates, viz. their *causes;* and, at a second stage, to the *cause of their causes*, &c. This transferred feeling, in the case of pain, is dislike: in the case of pleasure, liking. For example, the suffering you have experienced in a surgical operation makes you dislike the sight of the instrument which inflicted it, perhaps of the operator who applied it, or even of his carriage or his house; and the charm of a piece of happy news extends for the future to the hand-writing or the voice that told it. Hence the frequent definition, '*Love* is the idea of a pleasure together with the idea of its cause:' '*Hate* is the idea of a pain together with the idea of its cause:' definitions which may be accepted, when duly limited to factitious love and hate.

The law of Sympathy is this: Witnessing or conceiving any human feeling in another, we tend to become ourselves affected by it. The generalised fact is expressed in the words *Mitgefühl* and *fellow-feeling;* and examples of it are numerous enough to constitute the greater part of our social experience. The emotion that stirs a multitude in presence or in hearing of a pathetic incident is intense, through the reverberated reflection of the feeling of each in the hearts of all. When you are thrown into the company even of a stranger, his cheerfulness affects you as the sunshine, his gloom as a chilling cloud. Without art or effort, by mere involuntary assimilation, you take your cue from your associates at the moment: with children you are a child; with the cautious, you are reserved; with the giddy, you laugh; with the afflicted, you are sorrowful. That this habit of borrowing the feelings of others may largely divert and modify our own, is evident. If each has a tendency to adopt the praise and censure which others manifest, the suppression of individual judgment in a general consensus becomes intelligible: if the fact that my neighbours desire a given object makes me desire it too, it is plain that our very sympathy may contribute an element of emulous or even envious feeling to our relations together. The operation of this law has been traced with fascinating ingenuity and subtlety by Adam Smith in his 'Theory of the Moral Sentiments:' only, he has done such execution, on all sides of human life, with his borrowed feelings, as apparently to dispense with the originals, and, unlike a king of political economists, to set up his psychological bank on paper without gold. It is no less impossible in Ethics to resolve moral sentiment into sympathy, than in Optics to treat of reflection of light without any incidence. But when once the primary element has been taken into account, the phenomena that arise upon its encounter with various objects and media are doubtless of wonderful variety.

The law of Distance is this: The attraction of pleasure, the repulsion of pain, diminish with the distance at which they are contemplated. As the moment of realisation approaches, Hope brightens into assurance, Fear darkens into despair. Hence the dangerous influence of every motive in the immediate foreground as compared with reasons no less weighty in themselves, but, from their remoteness, faint and ill-defined. This illusion of mental vision is largely due to the connection which our ignorance establishes between futurity and uncertainty; no calculations of ours being secure except those whose data are fully delivered into our hand, and are no longer liable to disturbance from the irruption of elements omitted or invisible. The experience of baffled expectations is apt to confuse our whole outlook and create a vague distance for all that we seem to see beyond the zone at our very feet; and thus we are tempted to many a shortsighted plunge, in disregard to warnings from afar. The true corrective is found in exact and careful attention to the lines of established causality, that, whatever else may be dim, they may carry their clear tracks into the future on which we gaze, and take with them, unbroken, the same certainty which they possess for us close at hand. We shall then discover that it is more often the fool than the wise who acts upon the maxim that 'a bird in the hand is worth two in the bush.'

These psychological laws supply an apparatus of method by which the composite forms of motive are easily resolved into their elements. Pursuing these analyses no further, I pass on, after one more psychological preliminary, to the moral order of the springs of action.

iv RELATION OF PRUDENCE AND CONSCIENCE TO SPRINGS OF ACTION.

Enough has been said respecting the nature of Prudence and of Conscience to remove all obscurity from their relation to the springs of action. Neither of them is in itself a positive force, so as to range in the series of impulses; each exercises simply a judicial function, and, on grounds peculiar to itself, arbitrates among their pretensions, and sets free some one of them from the hesitation imposed by the importunity of others. In this intermediary office of judgment, Prudence is evidently confined altogether to the secondary principles; while Conscience has a discriminating voice over the whole. For, by its definition, Prudence is simply the act of the understanding in measuring and comparing the pleasurable effects on one's self of this or that mode of activity; and implies a *foresight* which can only come after experience and memory of what our impulses do with us. To suppose a suffrage given in favour of any *primary instinct* on the ground of its superior advantage to us, is to strip it of its primary character, and for its natural object to substitute the self which is to win it. Conscience, on the other hand, is concerned with quite another order of differences;—differences of inherent excellence and authority, which by their very nature must be cognisable *prior* to action, and are accordingly not learned by experiment, but read off by *insight*, presenting themselves to consciousness as premonitions, not as the sequel, of conduct. These differences have their range throughout the entire system, and open to the conscience everywhere the right and power of entrance.

To this assignment of a purely *judicial*, without an *active*, function to Prudence and Conscience it is natural to object, that we continually speak of a person *acting from prudence* and *acting from conscience*, and seem to attach a clear sense to the phrases. I admit the fact, and do not wish to banish the expressions. Postponing for a short time the consideration of their exact meaning, I will only observe meanwhile, that the first phrase more fitly takes the form 'acting *with* prudence;' and that 'acting *from* conscience,' accurately interpreted, describes a process perfectly compatible with the principles we have laid down.

The whole class of secondary springs of action, consisting of some form of conscious aim at our own pleasure, might seem, by its very nature, to sink *en masse* to the bottom of the scale. If we could be made up of these alone, with their common postulate that nothing is eligible but pleasure, there would be no room for preference among them other than *prudential*, by the application of a hedonistic calculus. And it appears at first view strange that our special distinction, of *Self-consciousness*, should thus have the effect of excluding *moral* differences, and equalising all incentives except *in quantity*. But we get rid of this impression by giving their corrective weight to the following considerations: (1) Our self-consciousness does not begin or end with reflecting our own pleasures; but pervades our whole nature, and is the condition of all experience, comparison, and intelligent judgment, rendering prudential selection itself possible in place of random impulsions. We owe to it, therefore, whatever intellectual rule enters to give direction to our life. (2) Even if it did no more than introduce *regulated self-regard*, its office would be amply vindicated; for Egoism has, after all, its legitimate place in the system of right character; and it is not to be left to play the fool even upon its own ground. (3) In thus fixing our attention on the secondary springs, as if they stood alone, we are working out a mere fiction, intrinsically self-contradictory. They know themselves in presence of their parents the primaries, and are well aware of their relative worth in the system to which both belong. This is as much a part of their self-consciousness as their hedonistic memory. It is far from being true, therefore, that the only thing our self-consciousness does on this field is, to turn disinterested instinct into self-seeking: it certainly makes this possible; not, however, without due warning of the character of the change, and clear measure of the moral difference. (4) Our self-consciousness of what the primary springs do with us does not oblige us to go into captivity to their effects; it empowers us no less to turn attention away from their pleasures than to dwell upon them. It does not repeat the story of Adam, and make 'the knowledge of good and evil' tantamount to an enfeebling fall.

CHAPTER VI.

SPRINGS OF ACTION CLASSIFIED: MORAL ORDER.

§ 1. *Secondary Passions alone inadmissible.*

Of all the springs of action on our list one set only requires to be cast out *in limine*, as not simply relatively but absolutely evil, and incapable of ever entering upon the positive scale of admissible principles at all;—I mean the secondary *Passions*,—expressing themselves in Censoriousness, Vindictiveness, and Suspiciousness. Not merely is there nothing to which these are not inferior (for that must hold good of *any lowest term*), but even standing alone, i.e. compared only with zero, or the negation of all living action, they can be allowed no place. We therefore discard them *ab initio*, as mere corruptions of the passions, constituting a truly diabolical element that goes down into infinite depths and evades all the measurements of right. They present a case of repulsions given for our necessary protection turned into attractions indulged for our entertainment; a capacity in which they have no function, and pass into pure malignity. In this judgment I am strengthened by the weighty support of Professor Sidgwick. In the course of a criticism which I shall have to consider hereafter, on the doctrine of moral estimate of motives, he makes two important concessions which involve a near approach to the method he rejects: viz. (1) that springs of action do not naturally divide into *absolutely good and bad*, but only into *better and worse;* yet (2) that the 'malevolent affections,' i.e. the tendency 'to inflict pain on others however aroused,' constitute a solitary exception and never quit the category of the bad. At the same time he qualifies this sentence against them by intimating a doubt whether, in certain cases, they may not have a legitimate function; being unwilling to suppose that an order of affections no less natural than the benevolent feelings should be without an admissible function in the human constitution. 'The first point to notice in considering the ethical result of a comprehensive comparison of motives is, that the issue in any internal conflict is not usually thought to be between positively good and bad, but between better and less good, more or less estimable or elevated motives. The only kind of motive which we commonly judge to be *intrinsically* bad, apart from the circumstances under which it operates, is malevolent affection: that is, the desire, however aroused, to inflict pain on some other sentient being. And it is perhaps doubtful (as we saw in Chap. 8) whether even this impulse ought to be pronounced absolutely bad. Butler allows it to be legitimate in the forms of Instinctive Resentment: and a more sustained and deliberate malevolence is commonly approved as Righteous Indignation: and if it be said that this indignation ought to be directed against the act and not the agent, it may be fairly questioned whether it is within the capacity of human nature to maintain this distinction clearly. At any rate there is no other motive except deliberate malevolence which Common Sense condemns as absolutely bad. The other motives that are commonly spoken of in "dyslogistic" terms seem to be most properly called (in Bentham's language) "Seductive" rather than bad. That is, they prompt to forbidden conduct with conspicuous force and frequency; but when we consider them carefully we find that there are certain limits, however narrow, within which their operation is legitimate[1].'

'It seems that the malevolent affections are as natural and normal to man as the benevolent: not indeed in the same sense normal, that is not at all times and towards all men (for man seems to have naturally some kindly feeling

[1] *Methods of Ethics*, Book III. chap. xii. § 1, pp. 363, 364.

for any fellow-man, when there is no special cause operating to make him love or hate. though this is obscured and counteracted in the lower stages of social development by the habitual hostility between strange tribes and races) but still as arising from causes that continually occur, and, in the main, exemplifying a psychological law analogous to that by which the growth of benevolent feelings is explained. For just as we are apt to love those who are the cause of pleasure to us whether by voluntary benefits or otherwise: so by strict analogy we naturally dislike those who have done us harm, either consciously from malevolence or mere selfishness, or even unconsciously, as when another man is an obstacle to our attainment of a much-desired end Thus, we naturally feel ill-will to a rival who deprives us of an object of competition. and so in persons in whom the desire of superiority is strong, a certain dislike of any one who is more successful or prosperous than themselves is easily aroused; and however repulsive to our moral sense, seems as natural as any other malevolent emotion. And it is to be observed that each of the elements into which we can analyse malevolent affection finds its exact counterpart in the analysis of the benevolent: as the former includes a dislike of the presence of its object and a desire to inflict pain on it, and also a capacity of deriving pleasure from the pain thus inflicted.

'If we now ask how far indulgence of malevolent emotions is right and proper, the answer of Common Sense is not easy to formulate. For some would say broadly that they ought to be repressed altogether, or as far as possible. And no doubt we blame all envy (though sometimes to exclude it altogether requires a magnanimity which we praise): and we regard as virtues or natural excellences the *good-humour* which prevents one from feeling even pain to a material extent, much less resentment, from trifling annoyances inflicted by others, the *meekness* which does not resent even graver injuries, the *mildness* and *gentleness* which refrain from retaliating them, the *placability* which accords forgiveness rapidly and easily, and the *mercy* which spares even deserved punishment. And yet most moralists have allowed instinctive resentment for wrong to be legitimate and proper: and we all think that punishment ought to be inflicted for offences, and also that there is a righteous anger and a virtuous indignation[1].'

The hesitation which these passages betray in covering the whole of 'the malevolent affections' with one common condemnation is well founded; for, in Professor Sidgwick's phraseology, the class embraces the entire group of *Passions, primary* as well as *secondary;* and, having once thrown them all together without noticing this difference, he may well be doubtful whether the same verdict can be justly passed on all, and feel unable to break the force of Bishop Butler's plea in favour of '*resentment*.' The doubt attaches exclusively to the *primary* passions; and the moment they are recognised as of a distinct type, and are withdrawn from the self-conscious sequels, two confusions disappear: (1) exceptions vanish, and the rule of condemnation settles undisturbed on a definite group of incentives; and (2) what is saved from condemnation and allowed to be admissible is the primitive order of passions, as nature provides it: so that we have not to suppose ourselves endowed with energies always and necessarily bad. It is remarkable that Professor Sidgwick had reached the very verge of this distinction, without formulating it or working it into his exposition: for, as if by way of afterthought, a footnote hints at it in one of its applications,—'Perhaps we may distinguish between the impulse to inflict pain and the desire of the antipathetic pleasure which the agent will reap from this infliction, and approve the former in certain circumstances, but condemn the latter absolutely[2].'

[1] Methods of Ethics, Bk. III. chap. viii. § 1, pp. 321, 322.
[2] Ibid. Bk. III. ch. xii. § 1, p. 364.

§ 2. *Appetites, Secondary and Primary. Animal Spontaneity.*

Even the lowest of the remaining principles,— viz. the love of ease and pleasure,—is not in this condition. For though every competitor shames it, it may sometimes escape competition, and present itself at a time when the field is fairly disengaged, and then, it may have innocent way; for even recreation is not without its place in life. Still, it must yield the palm to even the primary organic propensions; for it is surely meaner to eat for the palate's sake than to appease the simple hunger; and there is a conscious degradation in making the pleasures of appetite an artificial object, in which its healthy function is merged. To determine the right limits between instinct and indulgence, in the case of the sensual appetites, is the business of another department of Ethics, viz. that which, after settlement of the rank of motives, estimates the consequences of action. But the *standard* by which, in this case, that estimate must be made is necessarily taken from the primary instincts, the function of which is to maintain human life, personal and social, in the most complete and balanced vigour. There can be no doubt from what side that vigour is chiefly threatened. It is sapped mainly by indulgence; not merely in well marked and revolting degrees for which even lenient moralists have names; but in measures sanctioned by general habit, though too well understood by every wise physician, and inwardly recognised by the shame of many a private conscience. Were every unobserved excess on this side of our nature to cease, life, bodily and mental, would reach an energy at present hardly conceivable, and maintain it with increase, though the medical profession disbanded half its force. That in the sphere of these propensions the love of ease and pleasure, notwithstanding its refinements, is really of lower rank than the primaries, in spite of their being not special to man, is obvious from the fact, that it is *they* that supply the authoritative rule of restraint upon it; the parent says to the child, the conscience says to every one, 'Do not eat till you are hungry, and stop when you are hungry no more; and beware of fancying that you *want*, because you *like*.' Indulgence, indeed, consists in anticipating and exceeding instinctive needs. In them, therefore, the regulative right, relatively to their secondaries, is clearly vested.

The third propension, to active energy, changes its rank, more perhaps than any other impulse, in the course of its history. Even in its first form, of mere vital spontaneity, it stands as much above the appetites as the functions of the animal life are above those of the organic. But being then quite rude and blind, a paroxysm of unselecting movement, it gains by passing under intellectual direction and assuming a regulated aim: i.e. by emerging into the voluntary state. In the order of psychological time, it takes that state first as *the love of power;* but, in the ascending gradations of moral worth, the later principle, of *love of money*, bringing in it as it does a certain gravitation towards ease and pleasure, comes on for earlier and lower estimate. Even in the service of this mediocre desire, the human energy acquires a higher character, in proportion as organised industry is better than the mere frolic of faculty seeking vent; for its function clearly is, to be yoked to the car of some intelligent purpose, and not to spend itself in a wild scamper over the unreclaimed prairies of fancy; and the pursuit of gain puts it to a use which tames and subdues it.

§ 3. *Love of Gain, relatively to the Primary Passions.*

The gainful desire has no more frequent and disturbing rivals than the *Passions;* nor is there perhaps any part of our task more difficult than to determine the controversy of their claims. On the one hand, economic interest, being never perfect unless passionless, is often regarded as the great exorcist of hate and resentment, the security for peace, the preventive of all preventible dangers; so that, under its sway, the elements of anger and terror in our nature might almost be expected to die out. On the other hand, it is urged that even wealth and peace may be bought too dear, at the cost of self-respect, personal or national, and are better dispensed with, if ever they require us to suppress all disgust at what is odious, and all resistance to what is wrong. These general estimates rest, of course, not exclusively on the relative place of the two incentives in the felt scale of worth, but even more upon their prudential consequences in their average application to affairs. For our present purpose, we set aside this latter consideration, and compare the motives purely as objects of moral psychology.

In measuring the *love of gain* against *antipathy or hatred*, we take the latter in its *instinctive* form of *primary passion*, and assume it as a warranted factor of our being, a natural movement of self-protection, interposing a distance between us and harm; and must not confound it with acquired prejudice and groundless ill-will. And further, in settling which we should follow when they are both bidding for our will, we have to determine only their relative claims *at the moment of their joint presence;* altogether apart from the ulterior question, whether perhaps by persistent watering down of aversion through infusions of interest, the repulsion might not in the end be dissolved and die away. Any feeling, habitually discouraged, may be worn out and disappear; and the value of two cannot be fairly compared, if evanescence is assumed for one and permanence for the other. You ask me, let us suppose, to try the case of antipathy against gain by such an example as the following · 'A man who has (what is very common) an intense horror of blood, receives an offer of an abattoir with a good butcher's business attached: should he accept it or not?' Before I can allow this to stand as a testing instance, I must stipulate for one of two conditions: viz. that you either (1) banish from the reckoning the element of continuous time, and concentrate attention upon the moment of volition; or

(2) if you keep it, keep also the present attitude and proportions of feeling unchanged all through; and therefore do not permit him to calculate on the gradual disappearance of his repugnance through the persuasive charm of his profits. Reduced to its simplest terms it is the problem of an instant, whether he should swallow his disgust for the sake of twenty shillings. In practice, the answer which we want is sure to be complicated by intrusive considerations: whether his need is very great: whether he has to provide for others than himself, &c.; but from the pure psychological comparison of quality these accessories, of special intensity and external relations, must be struck out. I purposely begin with an example as near as possible to the mere instinctive antipathy of the animal nature, directed not even upon a living creature, that we may go beneath all the varieties of hatred between enemies. And to me it appears certain that we should look with contempt upon the suppression of even such aversion by hire. When the repulsion is felt towards *persons* instead of things, the meanness of surrendering it *to money* is still clearer; however desirable and possible it may be to remove it, *this* is not the influence to which it should yield. So long as an antipathy exists in one race of men towards another of inferior type or alien culture,—as on the part of the Arab towards the Negro, and the English towards the Hindu or Chinese,—the public opinion of the ascendant race invariably despises all interested alliance involving personal reciprocity with the other. When a European adventurer, for example, tempted by the prize of a great fortune, marries an Indian princess or heiress, his outward elevation is secretly regarded as a real fall, and reveals, even to those who court him, the low moral stature of the man. And it is distinctly the motive, and not the mere external *mésalliance*, which moves their scorn; for if, instead of the presumed uncongeniality, there had been a known engagement of heart, there would have been no condemnation, however strange might appear the romance of such a love; and the breach of conventional rule would

have been readily forgiven. For the setting aside, then, of such natural types of antipathy or hate, we must wait for higher springs of action : the love of money has no authority over them.

Has it any more over the next passion, viz. that of *Fear?* Here again we are concerned only with the feeling so far as it is a true instinct; 1. e. arises from some real evil apparently impending. When thus kept clear from all illusory complications, Fear is in itself a legitimate motive for self-protection; and, in the absence of any higher call, we blame one who fails to act upon it. If a ship captain, caught in a fog off a lee shore, neglects, through indolence and love of ease, to slacken speed and take continuous soundings and open his steam-whistle, we call him to account for all that he imperils, and should still condemn him, though nothing were at stake but his own life. When historians tell us of the plague-tainted city, in which panic-stricken men and women herd together to drive away terror by drunken carouse and ribald song, we are appalled to think of appealing to so low a pleasure against so august a fear. On the other hand, when in the same scene the personal dread is all surmounted, if not forgot, in devotion to the sick, precautions for the healthy, and ministrations to the dying, we look with reverence on the sacred calm that can allay so wild a passion. There are incentives then which have *no right* to quench the terror : there are others which may command it to lie still and be as though it were not. Against the carousers we take sides with the fear; with the apostles of mercy we triumph in its conquest. Where then, between these two extremes, must we place such an intermediate motive as the *love of gain?* It is perhaps possible to put cases which we should naturally answer in opposite ways. Suppose that an Alpine explorer determines to attempt a highly perilous ascent; and that, though aware of its risks, he is too stingy to incur the expense of two or three guides; and therefore keeps his counsel and his money, and goes alone, satisfied either to save his life or lose it, provided it be economically. I presume nobody would pity him, if he perished, or think he deserved it, if he escaped. He would be set down as having acted from the meaner motive. Suppose, again, that a landsman has the kind of dread of the sea that prevails in some tribes; but that, being in need, he is offered good wages as a sailor; and, in the absence of other resource, resolves to face his threatening element and go. He would surely not incur the condemnation passed upon the Alpine man: he might possibly be deemed to have followed the better motive; and, at the very least, would be held quite warranted in his choice, and exempt from blame. The motives, I should say, are here quite upon a level; so that, in the absence of any moral superiority of one over the other, the agent is thrown upon the principles of *prudential* choice, and is at liberty to take the course which, on the whole, *he likes* the best. Nor can we perhaps in the other cases, or in any case, assign to Fear, simply as such, a uniform moral value relatively to other springs of action. Fears cannot be appraised without reference to the worth of the objects feared; just as Hope rises to the noble or sinks to the base, and Love may be a grace or a degradation, according to the object that fixes the eye or wins the heart. The egoist will have fears only for himself; the benevolent, largely for others; and the moral quality of these fears will be imported simply from the affections that inspire them. This passion, therefore, though it could not be omitted from a psychological enumeration of the springs of action, cannot claim a definite and invariable place in their moral hierarchy. Its value is, *per se*, indeterminate; depending in each concrete case, *ethically*, on the affection which is thrown into alarm; and, *rationally*, on the magnitude of the good which is menaced with injury, and the probability of its loss.

With the third passion, Resentment, we recover the power of comparison with the love of gain; still with the same proviso, that it retains its primary form of legitimate instinct, without added taint of artificial malignity. A distinctly illustrative case occurs to my memory: viz. of a boy of remarkable capacity and great intensity of nature, who was about equally passionate under provocation, and greedy of money; so that by cooler heads he could be moved at will on predetermined lines by an insult or a bribe. If, to tame him, the less turbulent of these desires had been played off against the other, and he had been promised five shillings for every instance in which he compelled the cloud of anger to hold fast its thunder and its flash, and sweep silently away, there is little doubt that he might thus have been externally broken into decent form. But would the inward improvement have been real? Is the motive which is nursed into a practised power any nobler than that which is kept under the loaded valve? Surely not. Is its constant encouragement and growth any inward counteraction of its rival's excess, so as to convert the wrathful heart into the forgiving, and the impatient into the serene? or does it merely prevent the boiling deep from rising to the light? It must be admitted, I think, that even the cure of irascibility, still more its mere concealment, is too dearly bought by the creation of selfish avarice. *Politic meekness* offends us as a hypocrisy: and if we observe a man behaving smoothly to one who treats him with hauteur, and then, after obtaining what he wants, cursing him behind his back, we are inclined to think 'the publican and the sinner' nearer to the kingdom of heaven than he. The proposition, so far as I can see, may be made general. Whenever resentment is *bought off* by mere interest, whenever a man with just anger in his heart remains placid only because *he cannot afford* to let his indignation appear, we cannot help despising such self-control as sordid. The two motives also come into comparison, as both of them possible sources of the same type of crime; and a deed of violence perpetrated for gain we invariably regard as more heinous than when prompted by resentment. On the whole, therefore, this passion must rank higher than the love of money. The evil repute into which it has fallen is largely due to the loose habit of confounding it with vindictiveness, but partly also to the currency among Utilitarians of an imperfect theory of punishment; and partly to the habit naturally prevalent with Christian moralists, of comparing the passion less with impulses beneath it than with affections above it which, in transcending, virtually absorb and supersede it. But, if we are to find its true place, we must look along the whole line, from the animal rudiments to the spiritual consummation of our nature.

§ 4. *Secondary Affections, relatively to the Primary Passions.*

Now let a new order of impulses come upon the scene, viz. the Secondary Affections, and place themselves for estimate face to face with these same Primary Passions. In one view, the taste for sympathetic pleasures, and antipathy or hatred towards what offends, will enter into no rivalry, but work in concurrence. For they both impel to the same conduct, viz. self-removal from the hated object; only, in the one case, by keeping out of its way, in the other, by driving it off; the resulting distance being measured by the *sum* of the two forces. In order to find their *difference*, we must look out for an instance of their collision : i.e. a case in which opportunity is offered for social and sympathetic pleasures, saddled with the condition that some hated object is also to be present. As La Fontaine perhaps would put it, trying the human problem on a humbler stage: how would a generous dog decide, if invited to a canine dinner at a West-end club, with the intimation that a fox would be at the head of the table and a cat at the bottom? Would you respect him more for accepting the jollity, or for declining the jar? If he were yours, you would think better of his honesty, and give him a pat of approbation, if he sent a dignified refusal. Here, it is plain, the antipathy must rule; inasmuch as true sympathy is spoiled by it and cannot coexist with it, and the bitter drop is poison in the cup of social joy. To violate this limit, and, under the influence of sentimental effusiveness, to snatch at all exchanges of the circulating coin of pretended sympathy, without heeding whether it be counterfeit or genuine, leads inevitably to acquiescence in low company, and loss of sterling sincerity of affection.

The same superior right must be assigned to legitimate *Fear*, in its occasional collision with the secondary affections. Under the conditions of danger which must then subsist,—in the storm at sea, in the pestilence or the siege on land,—the dictates of fear, i.e. measures of protection, are authoritative as against all conflicting tastes and desires; and the suggestions of social pleasure-seeking are intrusive and usurping. Not only is it a guilty and degrading thing to drown the terrors of a crisis in ghastly festivities, that are little less than a dance of death; but even surrender to the indulgence of compassionate feeling in clinging to the bedside of the wounded may well become a selfish distortion of duty, in a siege which demands all hands to repair the widening breach, and ward off capture from the garrison. The claims of self-sacrifice in the dread emergencies of our common life are sternly impartial, and cannot listen to pleas of exception from sensibilities however refined. Again, therefore, the secondary affections must be silent and withdraw.

Just as little can they assert any claim against well-grounded *resentment*. This feeling, we have seen, is a defensive rising of effort to turn back a hurt of any kind; and it first comes into conflict with sympathetic affections, when the hurt proceeds from a voluntary human act; i.e. when regarded as a *wrong*. Towards the author of that wrong it suspends all *attraction*, and substitutes the attitude and movements of *repulsion;* i.e. it cancels sympathetic relations and puts an end to the possibility of their sincere enjoyment. This forfeiture of good-will by the wrong-doer is the natural defence of Right among men; and to tamper with it is to imperil an essential security of the moral life.

It is, however, a painful security; and though seldom wanting, even in the meekest dispositions, at the moment of injury, becomes so immediately unwelcome to easy-tempered and sociable natures, especially in their sentimental moods, that it often lapses from their loose hold, not from any change of judgment, but from mere soft reversion to a more habitual and pleasanter state of mind. In such cases, inducements soon present themselves, as it is said, 'to let bygones be bygones,' and to cultivate again the social pleasures together, without taking any notice of the past, or caring whether or not any serious guilt was incurred in the temporary breach of relation. This mere *masking* of a grave moral disturbance, this lax shuffling away of all its meaning, simply because it is disagreeable and it is pleasanter to be 'all jolly fellows together,' is a hedonistic offence against reason and right, and can be excused only through utter confusion of mind. It must be admitted, however, that the secondary affections often realise imperfectly their sentimental state, and are saved from the taint of selfish indulgence of feeling by considerable remaining vestiges of their primaries. In proportion as this disinterested element survives, and the shrinking is truly from *giving* pain and not from *taking* it, that mixed state of mind arises which we call an amiable temper, and which leads its possessor, from an undefined repugnance to ill-will, rather to put up with a hurt and make no noise about it, than insist upon its utmost rights. And where the hurt is limited to himself, and springs from no malignity that calls for protest, such a mood may easily rise above the moral level of natural resentment. But when the evil inflicted is a *wrong* distinctly intended, no willingness to bear it, no preference of peace to conflict, can be accepted as an adequate ground for quietude. It needs a higher claim than that of love for sympathetic peace to supersede the authority of resentment.

What then becomes, I shall be asked, of the maxim, '*forgive and forget?*' In strictness, simply this; that as yet it must stand aside, and wait for its credentials from some principle of higher rank than we have at present reached. But not even then, it is well to add, can we expect it to hold good in its absolute form. Placability, if the name is to stand for a virtue, cannot mean the unconditional *ignoring* of all injuries, and treating them, in the mind and out of the mind, as though they were not; for this would be to canonise a lie The lips that gave the precept pronounced also the qualification; and prefaced both by justifying an antecedent indignation: 'If thy brother sin, *rebuke* him; and *if he repent*, forgive him; and if he sin against thee seven times in the day, and seven times turn again to thee, saying, *I repent;* thou shalt forgive him[1].' The change in your feeling is to be the response to a change in his mind: in the life of the spirit, face is to answer to face, and love to love · as the sorrow steals upon the injurer, the soreness is to vanish from the injured. This is to preserve, and not to violate, the inward truth of the relation. Observe too, that here there is no injunction to '*forget:*' it is the rude popular maxim that unites in the same command an involuntary and a voluntary act,—an impossibility and a virtue. Our temper is our own; our memory is not: we can reverse an affection, when its object is reversed; but an experience, once past, we cannot erase. And every fact, though gone and dwelt upon in thought no more, still makes the present other than it would else have been; and one who has surprised us by a deed of wrong we cannot replace in our estimate precisely where he stood before. The feeling of personal alienation is swept away in our forgiveness; but the reciprocal esteem is resumed from a somewhat lower point and has some ground to recover; and this, precisely because we cannot cause that which has happened not to have been. But though the language of the common maxim will not bear any close pressure, it may convey, by a loose interpretation, either of two sound lessons; one, applying to the case in

[1] Luke xvii. 3, 4.

which repentance has been expressed; the other, to the case in which it has made no sign. (1) In regard to the former, the rule virtually says, 'Having forgiven the offender, cease to dwell upon the offence, and let its memory sleep' (2) In regard to the latter, it may be taken to mean, 'Even to one who has not humbled himself before you, *limit the time* of your resentment, and nurse it not for ever; it is the provision of nature *for a crisis or a mood* of injury, which may be presumed to wear out; let the anger take this for granted, and die away too; new conditions bring new possibilities of sympathy.'

There is yet another case of conflict between resentment and the secondary affections, which throws light upon their relation. The anger awakened by wrong-doing is the feeling which prompts to its punishment. When the offence is committed by one who is the object of our love and care, or by a dependent over whom we have virtually a penal power, the execution of punishment encounters serious resistance from feelings that plead for remission. No sooner has the shock of displeasure been felt than, before it can pass into the word of rebuke or the act of repression, the pang of reluctance strikes upon the heart, and with many a false palliative pleads with us to make light of the sin and evade a duty too stern for our weak mood. Have we not heard that Pity rather than Wrath is due to the offender?—a welcome doctrine to one who finds the tenderness of Mercy easier to him than the firm and piercing gaze of Justice. And so, though both alike would give expression to our love, we are tempted to rest in that which is most indulgent to ourselves, dissolving us for a moment in the luxury of commiserative tears, and instantly reinstating the scarce interrupted joy of sympathy. With parents thus disposed many a child is shrewd enough to discover that, as the sunshine is never brighter than after a shower, so he basks in a warmer light after each transgression, and is cherished the more, the more he sins; and he learns the imitative lesson of self-excuse, self-forgiveness, and self-love.

So frequent is this domestic phenomenon, that it is perhaps the strongest reason assigned why parents are unfit to conduct the education of their own children; and should hand over the duty to some more impartial guardian, in whom the vision of justice is undisturbed, and the love of right is proof against the bribes and cowardice of sympathetic self-indulgence. In this kind of experience, the main conflict, it is evident, lies between sentimental compassion and retributive resentment against wrong; and I suppose it cannot be doubted that, unless the latter prevails, the victory remains with the inferior principle.

From the *ensemble* of these psychological comparisons the rule results, that the *Secondary Affections* must yield the higher place to the *Primary Passions*.

§ 5. *Place of both, relatively to the Love of Power.*

We must submit these passions to yet another experiment. The last competitor with which they might dispute the palm of superiority is that *causal energy* which is best known under the unsatisfactory name of the *Love of Power;* and with this they must be compared.

There is plainly a very significant difference between the two. It is as objects operated on from without, that we are subject to the Passions; it is as operative ourselves, that we rejoice in Power. In the one case, we are *Patients;* in the other, *Agents:* the movement of causality is in opposite directions; and *our* part in it is but our response to the world in the one case, our challenge to it in the other. In the former, passive weakness wakes up to its defence; in the latter, exuberant strength makes aggression upon something that will yield; so that the passions are a protest against an incipient *decrement* of life; while the causal energy claims a positive *increment* of life. On the assumption (the necessity of which even the pessimist admits, for it is the blackest clause in his indictment against our nature and our lot), that life is felt to be a good, this difference in itself indicates the subordinate position of the passions, as a resistance on retreat instead of a conquest moving on. The prevention of loss can result at best only in holding what we have; the earning of gains encloses within our lines what we had not. Still, it may be said, this is only a *physical or dynamical*, and not an *ethical* difference, marking the extent of function, but not its *quality*. Energy is, *per se*, morally neutral; and more or less of causality is by no means equivalent to more or less of *virtue*. Yes; that is true of energy, present or absent, in the world of the mechanical and chemical enquirer; whether it is kinetic or latent there, is a fact which has no more *character* in it than heat or cold. And in the human being, it is no *virtue* to have a large range of faculty, and no sin to want it. But, wherever faculty is present, who will tell us that the greater or less putting forth of its energy by the will constitutes no moral difference? Is it not precisely what is typified respectively by the profitable and the unprofitable servant? by the talent earning interest and the talent folded in the napkin? Does not facultative energy contain, does not facultative passiveness exclude, the possibility of all human attainable good? and when we admire the creativeness of the one, in comparison with the laziness of the other, is there no ethical element in our preference? and nothing else than this is the difference which we have indicated between the causal energy and the passions. In the latter, the will lies asleep till it is goaded from its ease by the inroad or approach of some foe to its peace which cannot be ignored: if there were no evil, they would do no good; and the only good they do is to give some check to evil. But the former, springing earlier into the field, anticipates and prevents the evils for which the others wait; not simply combating them better when they come up, but even withholding them from existence at all: for by far the greater part of them are themselves the product of laziness, and grow out of the rot of negligent life: they are the poison-weeds that fructify and run to seed, because the watcher's eye was drowsy and other minds by touching their springs of sympathy, it deserves this description. And perhaps in the Christian reaction from the spirit of the Classical literature, and during the rise and growth of the new type of excellence realised by the *saint* instead of the *hero*, the estimate of this incentive by moralists has become somewhat too disparaging; as it certainly has overshot the sincere feeling of the secular world. Whatever preachers may say, in commending the graces of the meek and modest life, nothing is more readily forgiven by the common conscience, than the exercise and love of power by those whose capacity and energy have marked them out as natural 'kings of men.'

At the same time, the taint which lurks in the very names of this spring of action would not be there, were it not for certain qualifying elements in it which render it liable to corruption. Being essentially facultative energy, it would still exist, though our nature were curtailed in its present scope, and from the hierarchy of springs of action the upper members were lifted off and discharged; so that they are not presupposed in it, and their control over it might be absent. If it conspicuously appeared in a race so constituted, it would be only the more masterful self-assertion of the propensions and passions, bidding high for influence and pushing their way to ascendency in the competitions of gregarious life; and it would simply determine the victor in 'the struggle for existence,' and give to his conquest the character of mere repression,—of a triumph over baffled foes. And this appears to be actually the form which the impulse assumes in several of the animal tribes, especially such as are least touched by affections which qualify the bitterness of inferiority and make even the servile lot congenial. It is also quite possible that among mankind pre-eminent energy may at times declare itself in individuals nearly destitute, through defect of inherited nature or social development, of the higher springs of action; and may carry its possessors far over the heads of contemporaries of vastly larger but less concentrated faculty. In this case there will arise the

the hand of industry was slack. Hence we have reason to say, that the causal energy substitutes a better provision against the encroachments of evil than is supplied by the passions which snatch up arms against it. Nor is this its only claim to superior efficacy. The passions, we have seen, are purely repellent and antagonistic: against human offenders they act as a body-guard of police; and they afford no guarantee for any but hostile relations between the persons whom they set face to face with each other. But if what is commonly taken for the *love of power* be, as I suppose, mainly a high pitch of energy throughout the faculties, it is the expression of a strong and capacious nature, that comprises more than the ordinary human experiences, and condenses in itself the scattered contents of several weaker lives. And with this breadth and intensity are connected a prompt understanding of men, and a versatile sympathy with them in their aims and achievements; a sympathy, no doubt, deficient in equal respect and perhaps directed upon them as upon children, yet considerate and humane. It is impossible to exercise the gift of ruling other wills without living largely in their life, knowing their conflicts, and having the touch of their enthusiasms; and, for the most part, it is only the men *endowed with the gift* that, in the natural joy of its use, have the look and the repute of aspiring to the power. Hence, their causal energy, instead of being simply antagonistic to evil, is essentially sympathetic with good; instead of repelling, and saving for itself a clear space around, is eager with human attractions, and flings itself into the crush of affairs, reducing its cries to articulate speech and its scramble to helpful order. In this view, it is not wholly without reason that Ambition (which is but the depreciatory name for the same fundamental tendency) has been called 'a splendid passion,' and 'the last infirmity of noble minds.' So far as it involves a yearning to conquer difficulties and confusion, to carry the organising force of truth and right into some unreclaimed elements of life, and elicit the resources of deplorable phenomenon of the rule of the worse over the better,—the success of egotistic self-assertion against nobler wills,—that enthronement of the genuine τύραννος on the ruins of trampled rights and reason which, to the free genius of Athens, appeared the ultimate degradation of human society. Even under these conditions, the domination could not be grasped or maintained by mere antagonistic force; there must be in the subjected people some element of admiration mingled with the fear, some sympathy as the price of acquiescence; but it is the sympathy of the lower mind, of propension, envy, greed, and hate, securing a temporary carnival of shame. It is no wonder that, from the glaring aspect of such examples, they should be selected by the moralist as his stock illustrations of the love of power, and should thus have brought on it the stigma of unconditional guilt. They are, however, abuses (and, in comparison with its whole range, very rare ones, I believe) of a motive which, duly subordinated, has a legitimate sphere, neither narrow nor ignoble. And, among the evils of its abuse, not the least are to be found in the bad name which it has thence got among the good, and the grossly selfish conception of it among the lower minds who cannot resist its fascinations. It is less by becoming the scourge of his own generation and the desolator of Europe, than by disorganising and corrupting the moral admirations of mankind, that the first Napoleon forfeited the respectful compassion normally due to a suffering exile, and merits the enduring reprobation of history. But against such instances, in which the incentive is worked out to self-idolatry, we must set those in which it has been compatible with self-sacrifice, if it has not even inspired it. Aristides, and Marcus Aurelius, and Alfred the Great, among statesmen; Socrates, St. Francis, and Savonarola, among reformers; Dante, Michael Angelo, Milton, among poets and artists; are among the host of gifted men too high not to know their power and deeply care for it, yet only stimulated by it to profounder prayer for light and more absolute consecration to the supreme ends of life. It leads, in all such men, to an escape from petty interests and personal limitation; to a larger grasp of sympathy with the contents and destination of humanity, a superiority to pleasure, gain, and passion, and a devotion to ideal rather than material ends, so that their inward longing for a living place in the thought and future of mankind is little else than self-identification with the recognised purposes of God. Nothing can be more foolishly cynical than to mistake for vanity and self-exaltation the consciousness of power inseparable from the insight, and not less from the veracity, of such minds: their genius forbids them to be blind, even to their own relative gifts; but if they seem to hold them proudly as against pretentious rivals, they hold them humbly, and as a sacred trust, beneath the eye of their great Taskmaster; and apply them with no less severe an awe to the most hidden stones in the temple of their life, than to its most conspicuous surface.

If the place assigned to the spring of action now under estimate should appear too high, let it be further considered that the *Love of Liberty*, which has enriched history with its most thrilling episodes, is simply, or at least essentially, the *love of power*. It is a resistance to power *that is* in the name of power *that ought to be*,—the self-assertion of living faculty against inert habit, the claim of competent intelligence and manly character to direct its own steps, and groan no more under the yoke and lash of an effete control. It aims avowedly at a *transfer of power* from hands that *have* it to hands that *want* it; on the ground that the existing distribution of it awards it where it is forfeited and withholds it where it is earned, and that the false balance must be redressed. What is this, but the advance of fullgrown energy to take possession of its inheritance, and by the very motto of its banner,—'La carrière aux talens,'—serve its sleepy trustees with notice to quit? Our sympathy with it concedes the inherent right of faculty against incapacity, and implies that power claimed by the former may, in our belief, be justly and generously pursued. The dispossessed, when flung from their seats, accuse their assailants of being moved by '*Envy*.' And if we take the word to mean, as before defined, 'the grudging sense of relative inferiority[1],' the imputation is no doubt true, without, however, including anything to be ashamed of; for if the 'relative inferiority' be undeserved, an inversion of the order of nature, it may innocently be viewed with a 'grudging' eye. But since, in the vast majority of cases, the relative inferiority of position which gives rise to this feeling is the natural expression of a real inferiority, as when the slower foot inevitably loses the race, the word 'envy' is apt to contract its meaning, and to imply that whoever feels it is *a real inferior*, wanting to take from others what is theirs by better right. In this connotation lies the sting of the charge: which is therefore ineffectual, as boastfully assuming the superiority which is in dispute between the competitors for power.

This incentive, then, I take to be indubitably assignable to a position higher than the passions. It will perhaps be generally acknowledged that the man and the nation that can hold their resentful feelings under control of their sense of power, are less to be condemned than those who bring them under no rational restraint.

§ 6. *Love of Culture, relatively to the Love of Power.*

The next step of ascent brings us to the *Secondary Sentiments*, which, though including three interests, viz. intellectual, æsthetic, and religious ideas, may, for our present purpose, be classed together, as *the Love of Culture*, a zealous care for the higher types of human thought and feeling.

The common characteristics of these three sentiments are due to their all being secondary, concerned, not with the real objects of the primaries, but with the ideas and feelings which these objects excite in the human mind; ideas and feelings which, confessed* by men *inter se*, compared

[1] Supra, chap. v. iii. p. 183.

together, and embodied in language or symbol, dispose themselves into theories, build up sciences, constitute literature and other products of art, create different systems of religious doctrine and observance, and finally institute an intellectual survey of all these, and fix their series and relations in a collective history. Here we have a study, not of things and beings as they are, so far as they tell us what they are, but of what men have thought and said about them;—a study, therefore, at first hand of the human mind, and only at second hand of Nature and God, as reflected in the mirror of its consciousness. It might seem proper, therefore, to treat this whole study as a mere chapter of anthropology, a survey of the psychological phenomena which are comprised in the logic of the sciences, the rules of æsthetic, and the emotions of religion. In this mode of treatment, however, the attitude of the student would be that of an external observer, dealing with the manifested experiences of other minds, with an interest in them purely intellectual; just as several writers on the 'Science of Religions,' or on the 'Religious Consciousness,' have treated with great skill, on the evidence of others, a subject confessedly foreign to the history of their own mind. This kind of simply inquisitive interest, without personal sympathy, in human ideas, does not constitute what I understand by the Secondary Sentiments. They cannot coexist with disbelief of the objects themselves, and conversion of them into ideas which may be fictitious; but must be backed up by the support, however indistinctly felt from moment to moment, of the Primaries, with their real faith and immediate apprehension. No familiarity with processes and methods of investigation, or analysis of inductive logic, or command of the calculus of quantitative relations, or other skill that may be exercised without quitting the student's desk, can ever make the true adept in science, unless it is possible to know without coming into presence of the thing known, or having living contact with the nature that moves and changes according to this code of laws. Between the tones which the beauty of the world and human life draws from the answering soul, and the most delicate criticism of learned *litterateurs*, there is as great a difference as between the lyre of Sappho and the prosody of Alexandria. And a handling of Religion, however ingeniously presented, to which it is indifferent whether Divine things are but clouds, evolved during one season and melting in another within the atmosphere of human thought, or are, in very truth, the real presence within the finite of infinite and eternal Mind, is much too 'impartial' for the 'interest in Religion' which I wish to mark. Without departing so far from the firsthand inspirations of wonder, admiration, and reverence as to forget their objects in what they have contributed to human civilisation, without quite treating it all as capital for the critic and material for the examination room, there is an intermediate state of mind, in which the first impulse to read the order and feel the beauty of the world, and commune with the Divine Spirit that is more than both, is still assumed to be true, but so overlaid by a tangle of thought and apparatus of discovery, and treasures of art, and piles of literature, and monuments of superstition, as to be almost stifled beneath the weight, and rarely draw a free and quickening breath. It is difficult for the mind which has to assume the judicial office of sifting opinions and exposing fallacies and correcting usages and rules, from the high seat of critical superiority, not to lose the inverse habit of submissive learning from the objects of so much thought, as transcending and embracing it. Yet, without any conscious impairing of this habit, it may be gradually replaced by mere mental interest in the thoughts and emotions concerned in it, and have its most conspicuous vestige in a type of culture which is loved and sought. A spring of action is thus supplied which plants in the conscience a new grade of authority.

It evidently carries in it an appreciation of all the ideal side of human life, and aims at the perfecting of the reason, the imagination, and the moral affections. Its zeal is spent upon the highest elements and finest fruits of civilisation,—the increase of knowledge, the refinement and sincerity of art, the purification of religion. It secures, therefore, a genuine liberality of mind, a sympathy with whatever makes man intelligent, gracious, and noble, and a delight in rendering this, as far as possible, common to all. To the causal energy, or love of power, I have assigned, as its usual accompaniment, a certain breadth of sympathy; perhaps a wider than we have here; for there is this difference: that the instinct of power is an undistinguishing intensity of the *whole nature*, understanding and responding to whatever impulse happens to be there: whereas the love of culture is selective; and he in whom it is represented is an epitome of the higher faculties and influences of our life; with sympathy less diffused over men as they are, than concentrated on what they might be and are to be. Hence it is easy to understand how a conflict may arise between these two springs of action: it is the very case which Plato more than once describes as the contrast between the practical statesman of Athens and the philosopher: the former, retaining the helm by indulging the average citizens in all that they like; the latter, left in the shade because he would make them better, and they listen only to those who will leave them as they are; and so the philosopher, if true to himself, must retire into private life, and rather teach the right and the real to a few disciples in a corner, than harangue in the agora the multitude that must be wielded by their uppermost passions. Nothing can be more happily distinctive of the liberal-minded man who impersonates our spring of action, than this feature, that he would rather *teach* his fellow-men than *rule* them. It correctly plants the love of culture above the love of power.

§ 7. *Primary Affections, relatively to Wonder and Admiration.*

There now remain to be placed only the *Primary Affections* and *Primary Sentiments*. In support of my first step, I will avail myself of a remark of Spinoza's, which seems to me curiously significant as coming from a rigid determinist. He says that, towards a being *supposed to be free*, affection is always far more intense and complete, than towards *one under necessity*[1]. A being supposed to be free is what I should designate as *a person;* and the fact before the mind of Spinoza is certainly the familiar one, that we love persons more than things, and indeed, in order to *love* things (as distinguished from merely *liking* them), have to personify them and fancy them returning our look. Of course Spinoza, as a determinist, was obliged to regard all the love which the idea of freedom added, as wasted upon an illusion; so that Man had his heart overstocked with affection, which there was nothing in the universe to claim. The phenomenon, however, admits of being turned round, to face the other way; and we may say, 'Since all our perfect love assumes its objects free, wherever it falls we may look for freedom to be.' In other words, personality is essential to affection. Now, since personality is beyond doubt the culminating fact of the world, at once crowning the universe and transcending it, the affection which culminates with it must be supreme among the springs of action, and be reserved for the last step of our ascent. The sentiments, therefore, must first present themselves for estimate; except that the third of them converts itself, as we contemplate it, into affection of the most perfect kind; so as to leave only its two companions, Wonder and Admiration, still standing outside the golden bar of Love. Not that even they are always forbidden to slip through; for they too can direct a fascinated eye upon persons;·only not, like Affection, upon

[1] Ethica III. xlix. and Schol.

them exclusively: they have their range through all the contents and incidents of the world.

That familiar experience confirms the claim of higher authority for Affection will hardly be denied; though the cases of testing conflict are not perhaps of very frequent occurrence. The student or the artist who, in the pursuit of knowledge or the exercise of imagination, should give no heed to the pleadings of parental affection, and let his children starve in body and mind, would be universally condemned for disregard of the more imperative obligation. He was not bound to assume that obligation: he might blamelessly have declined the engagements of domestic life, and surrendered himself to search for scientific truth, or the service of beauty in form or song; but, once assumed, the home duties admit of no evasion. And had they even been absent, no call of genius could free him from the other forms of affectional claim, to friends, to country, to the unhappy. If, for example, he lavishes all his resources on his library and observatory, or his gallery of pictures, or museum of antiquities, so as to have no succour for a friend in distress, no rescue of misery from death; or if, at some crisis of public calamity and instant want, he hugs all these costly treasures with heartless devotion, and will part with none of them to the fund of the commonwealth, no voice but his own will be raised in excuse. His æsthetic sense itself, however fine in other provinces, has not extended to the moral field, but, with all its fastidiousness, can strangely live complacently in the presence of a hideous deformity of character close at hand.

In case the question should be raised whether there is any difference of rank between the incentives of Wonder and Admiration, it may be well to look a little more closely at their relation. In their psychological germ as felt, they are perhaps indistinguishable, and first diverge by alighting upon dissimilar points. As *wonder*, the feeling is directed upon *a phenomenon that happens:* as *admiration,* upon *a thing or person that is.* In conformity with this distinction, each starts a different question: viz. the former, the question of causality, 'Whence comes it, and whither goes it?'—the latter, the question of essence and significance, 'What does it say to me? what is it like?'—the one therefore instituting the search for origin and consequence; the other, the effort of imitative expression, in language or other mode of reproduction. Of these two, the former, it is evident, is the more *intellectually fruitful;* it has always been a marked characteristic of minds pre-eminently scientific; and I notice a fresh example in Professor Lewis Campbell's interesting life of the late James Clerk Maxwell, of whom it is said: 'Throughout his childhood his constant question was, "What's *the go of that?* what does it do?" nor was he content with a vague answer, but would reiterate, "But what's the *particular* go of it?" And, supported by such evidence, I may hope to win belief for a reminiscence which I might else have shrunk from mentioning. I distinctly remember his telling me, during his early manhood, that his first recollection was that of lying on the grass before his father's house, and looking at the sun, and *wondering*.' The second form of the same feeling approaches much more nearly to *affection*, even when awakened by unconscious objects, as the flowers of the field, and the glory of the sunset sky: and greatly *deepens* affection, when directed upon a person otherwise endeared, and, at least in finer natures, preserves it from degeneracy through the wastes of time and weariness. For it must be admitted that, in minds less happily attuned, there is often found a certain opposition between wonder and affection; the former demanding for its excitement what is new and strange, and quitting the objects of constant custom; the latter, deepening with intimacy, and clinging with tender tenacity to the familiars of constant experience. The one requires to set things at a distance; the other folds them to the heart. But where the springs of our life are rightly adjusted, this contrariety will cease: they will find it possible to act not in succession only, but together; not on contrasted objects, but on the very same: the nearest things to human love will not lose their halo of marvellous colour to the soul: no usage will dry up the freshness of what is dear and faithful: but the daily task, the tried friend, the customary scene, will keep to the end their consecrating charm, and lie in the gentle light of secret wonder. I believe, however, that it is scarcely possible for this fusion to take place by the mere influence of intellectual and imaginative sentiment, or even by their interplay with the level human affections. rather is it reserved for the achievement of Reverence, short of which, as the blending power of all, the affections and sentiments are apt to stand apart, and oblige us to range them in distinctive rank.

If the discriminating feature of wonder and admiration has been rightly indicated, there seems no reason for assigning to either impulse an authority superior to the other. If the one has more movement, the other has more depth; what we learn under guidance of the one is this or that finite series; of the other, an ideal meaning, permanent and infinite. Genius receives a call equally imperative, whether it be to Science or to Art. The relative value of the two to mankind is quite another question, to be settled by a comparison of their external fruits. It belongs to the ulterior department of ethics, which, after dealing with the fundamental morality of *motives*, proceeds to establish the rationale of *Conduct*.

§ 8. *Primary Affections inter se.*

We pass on to the *Affections;* and, with a view to their relative estimate, must first notice some special features distinguishing *parental love*. (1) It does not press its claims upon us without consent. We have ourselves *voluntarily subjected our life to them;* and to evade them is therefore not only to disregard the authority of nature, but to convict ourselves. (2) Its obligations are *pre-eminently inalienable*, so inherent in our personality, that, failing this, no one else can pick them up and as effectually discharge them. Not, of course, that there is anything to prevent the charge of a child being taken by another than the parent; but, if taken, it must be without the inward qualifications divinely prepared in the heart to make the toil a refreshment and the care a joy, and the happy twining of two lives together itself an education for both. This feature is not found, in at all the same degree, in other affections. The misery which I encounter with cold curiosity and pass by on the other side, some good Samaritan may overtake with his compassion, and heal with a gentler hand. And if I be forgetful of my attached friend, though I disappoint, I do not, it is probable, desolate his heart: he has others who are more faithful to him: but the little child has but one father and one mother; the relation is unique, and all in all to him. (3) In its most essential claims, this affection is *limited in time*, as we see in the lower animal tribes, where it totally vanishes as soon as it has carried the young through their period of dependence. With men, it has indeed a function still through the joint lives of the parent and the children; but not without losing its early instinctive force, and merging into equal *attachment*, enriched by longer memories than those which contemporary elders usually form. So too, in the inverse order of the relation, *filial* affection becomes, in the maturity of life, friendship of a high type, often qualified at last, when the parent's turn for *dependence* is reached, by a mingling of the compassion which infirmity invites. But, in both these aspects, the relation outlives its instinctive stage; and the continuous love which emerges and survives belongs to the other heads of affection specially human. These features of the parental feeling,—its voluntary assumption, its inalienability, its limited duration, cannot but affect materially its relative obligation: the third, removing it from competition with its companions during a great part of life; and the other two vastly intensifying its authority so long as it lasts.

Hence, in its presence, *Attachment*, when conflicting with

it, must yield and take the lower place. A mother, for example, who is nursing her infant and therefore inseparable from him, must refuse to undertake the charge of a friend prostrated by scarlet fever, however ready she would else be to serve, night and day, in the isolated sick-room. Or, suppose that the papers from Italy report a capture by brigands of an English traveller, whose life can be bought off only at some enormous price; and that I find it is my friend who has fallen into their clutches. For my love of him, I would ransom him at any cost I could command; but if I am a father, I have no right, for his sake, to beggar my children and deprive them of their education and outfit for the battle of life. Nor can we hesitate to postpone the claims of simple Friendship to the sharp appeal of urgent Pity. If, for example, I am helping my friend in some important undertaking,—a literary work, or a series of scientific experiments; and, while we are at work together, we are interrupted by an accident in the street at the very crisis of our problem; and an injured man will probably die, unless I, summoned as a surgeon on the spot, hasten to take the direction of the case; it cannot be doubted that I must go to the sufferer and quit my friend. Of the three affections, therefore, attachment is the least imperative; and though holding its ground against the love of culture and of power and their predecessors in this review, is often bound to retreat before parental affection and compassion.

In adjusting the relations between the other two, the difference must be noted, that compassion is a sudden impulse rushing upon the moment, while parental affection is continuous during its term, though as cause of action necessarily intermittent. The instants for giving effect to the constant feeling we can, to a great extent, choose for ourselves: but those which subject us to the stroke of pity are determined by events beyond control. Hence, the flash of the latter is an *opportunity given:* the advance of the former is a movement of its own selection; a difference which materially affects the problem of their relative claims at points of apparent conflict. The enduring disposition of the parent is not necessarily impaired by being suspended in expression and made to wait for its occasion; it may even be rendered more effectual by being held in abeyance in deference to the surprise of an exceptional and higher claim; for the spirit of a child may fall asleep upon too constant an expectation of devoted love, and it is not amiss that he should have to exercise, and the parent to demand, a quiet trust in the return home of an affection snatched away for the hour into another field. Although, therefore, what would else be due to the dictate of domestic tenderness may be pushed aside by the shock of some intruding pity, there need be no real variance between the two Only, the impulse which for the moment is supreme must not commit us, when we are in its hands, to any act inconsistent with the permanent obligation to the child, any sacrifice, for example, of needful tutelage for him. Else will he, in his turn, become an object of compassion; and, after having lost us through pity, through pity he will draw us to him again: with the difference, however, that we went in the spirit of duty: we return in the mood of repentance. The advantage which the family affection has, in the nearness and small compass of the relation over which it presides, is balanced by a *keenness* in compassion not less piercing than that of resentment. With this significant intensity, take into account the *universal scope* of the affection, knowing no bounds but those of suffering, and its duration through the whole of our life, and these three features sufficiently pronounce its superior authority to the *provisional instinct* of parental love, though the latter, *during its season*, must sometimes be the more imperative.

§ 9. *Supreme Place of Reverence.*

It remains only to vindicate the supreme place of *Reverence towards goodness*, which, when adequately interpreted, proves to be identical with devotion to God. I am aware that this identity is far from clear to many persons whose fulness of ethical experience gives them every title to judge; and that into these penetralia of ultimate analysis no one should pass with bold and noisy step, but at the threshold should take off the shoes from his feet, and leave his dogmatic haste, and move with listening silence and wakeful eye. Even then perhaps defining words may fail him, if he tries to tell what are the tones that floated to him through that still air, and what recesses the entering lights revealed when they pierced the perspective of shade. But under the profound impression of these cautions, I must endeavour to say how I understand this apex and crown of human character.

When we look back upon the gradations of motive which we have surveyed, and shape into distinctness the feeling with which we contemplate their intervals, it seems to carry two or three varying aspects, each of which is marked by some characteristic expression. This spring of action is noble, and I admire it: it is binding, and I obey it: it is the dictate of perfect Mind, and I revere it. When I reflect upon the second and third of these predicates, I observe a difference between them, which often becomes conspicuous in real life. If, in a case of conflict, we see the binding motive prevail, we *approve* the preference: we do not hesitate *to praise it;* i.e. we stand towards it in the attitude of a critical and judicial onlooker, entitled to distribute verdicts according to deserts, and to *patronise* the trustworthy. This is the characteristic feeling towards *Morality*: it visits whatever is obeyed as *Right* between man and man. It preserves the same aspect, whether the right thing on which it is directed be another's or our own: we approve ourselves in a similar spirit of complacency, realising the Proverb's assurance, 'a good man shall be satisfied from himself[1].' The idea of *right*, crystallised in this form, may be of great efficacy, and produce a morally righteous life; belonging, however, to the type of *dry*

[1] Prov. xiv. 14.

conscientiousness, firmly trusted by others, like the steady climate where the very sunshine and the cloud become mechanical, but not animating to them, or lifting them above their level. It operates, moreover, in the details of conduct, in concrete instances of moral decision, taken one by one, as they arise. Life, under its influence, is taken piecemeal, and is nothing but an aggregate of actions: if each is cared for as it comes, the whole will take care of itself: its real transactions are all in small change. In this way, all the inward affections, whether of others or of ourselves, are out of view, except as a machinery for turning out a sound action, as it is wanted: as elements in the history of a soul, as functions of a permanent inner life, invested with other relations than with the home, the market, and the state, they have no place in thought, and are neither loved nor hated, except in what they have *done*. It is not that the simply conscientious man is indifferent to motives, and wants only to secure the right act, come whence it may: he scorns hollow pretence, however beneficent, and turns away from false excuses, however harmless. But he stops with the instance, and is not diverted by it from his habit of estimating life by its catalogue of external contents.

Now the posture of mind which I describe as Reverence contemplates these things in just the inverse order. It cares for right actions, not simply as good phenomena, but chiefly as the expression of *right affection*, as functions of pure, of faithful, of self-devoted, of lofty *character*. Not content to rest with the fruits, it presses on to the lovely or stately nature that bore them. And in thus passing from them to their producing source, the feeling itself undergoes a change. In place of an approbation which looks with complacency *down*, it becomes a homage which looks reverently *up;* and finds itself in presence, not of a definite thing done, but of the living doer, the cause of it and of indefinite other possibilities of nobleness; and so is transferred from the level of ethical satisfaction to the plane of personal affection and aspiration. Till this change takes place there is hardly any *sacred* element in the ideas of right. The moralities of conduct occupy the human and civic platform; but even in our relations with each other, some other light,—call it poetic or call it Divine,—dawns upon the heart, when the revelations of some pathetic experience, or the disclosures of some rare biography, have opened to us the interior of a tender and strenuous soul, and kindled the heights above us with a fresh glory.

Yet, though the contemplation of *character* and *disposition*, as contrasted with particular instances and problems of conduct, is the proper occasion of reverence, and it is therefore directed specifically upon *persons*, it is not obliged to apply itself to the *whole personality*, for it never quits the presence, and never escapes the restrictions of the conscience; it is rigorously tied down to the *range* of moral approvals, while (within that range) completely transfiguring their *character* Reverence can never go where approval stays away; and must, therefore, always be given to the personages of our human stage with reserves that blend many shadows with the light. The imperfections of venerated men, the mingling in them of littleness and greatness, the alternation of sweetest affection with peevish jealousy, of sublime intelligence and trifling vanity, bring to us some of our saddest experiences, and dash our highest enthusiasms with humiliation. In the very moments of purest homage, they extort from us the sigh for a *perfect spirit*, where our trust and love may be for ever safe.

I have spoken thus far of Reverence in its direction upon other persons, distinguishing it from simple approbation in this; that in approbation we look to the particular act, with praise of its inward spring as compared with its tempting rival; while reverence looks through and past the act to the type of character which it expresses, as compared with the relative weakness of our own. In order to take this outward direction upon objective goodness, the sentiment must, however, have had a prior stage of experience. For that inward disposition and character in another upon which it now fixes, is nothing that can be seen or heard or touched: its presence before us is learned by inference,—by outward signs, of language, look, and act, which, we are aware, have but one interpretation. We read him by the key of sympathy; and what we attribute to him is known to us by its gleams and movements within ourselves. *There* it is that we have learned the feeling that is due to it; that it has looked upon us from above; that it has spoken to us in tones that lift us towards it, and that leave us, if we fall heavily back, abashed and humbled in the dust. In other words, the relation between two springs of action in cases of temptation does not complete its history with mere self-criticism, complacent or disappointed,—with the simply *moral* idea, that in *our own court* we are approved or condemned. It is not *our own face* that could ever put us thus to shame. Nor is it the face of our fellow-men; for they are on the same plane with us, and no claims incurred with them can be other than level and reciprocal, whereas here, the call at once carries our eye *up* · thence the authority descends; and, instead of passing, like coins of exchange between men that make them and men that take them, it lies upon both, it lies upon all; it has the grasp of a moral unity, the range of a moral universality; it is the overflow of infinite perfection into the finite mind. Even without following the history of conscience to this final revelation (which I believe to be the issue of its full development) it is clear that *Reverence* must be given within it, before finding any resting-place without: that its language is more to us than simply *imperative*, that often we do not *like* the mandate, and yet obey it from something quite other than necessity or fear, nay, with deep consent and a severe love. And though the problems of duty are innumerable, and the springs of action which they bring into collision are variously paired, there is no change in the authority, which rests on one as against the other: it repeats itself, with identity of aspect, in every case: it is not therefore an inherent element of this incentive or that, as a phenomenon taken by itself, but a uniform relation hovering over their combinations, and constituting them a hierarchy, into which, as phenomena, they could never construct themselves. Thus, within our own consciousness, we find the same difference which was observable in the appreciation of others, between the simply moral approbation and the feeling of Reverence. The latter cannot express itself without resorting, in the notice of affection and character, to language more than ethical, and plainly crossing the boundary into the field of religion. It lives in the presence of souls that are holy, of dispositions that are heavenly, of tempers that are saintly, of Love that is Divine; and will not bear to have these objects of its thought flattened and disfigured by being labelled as simply *Right* or even *Virtuous*. It insists on investing them with a light of *sacredness*. In virtue of this sentiment, therefore, the whole scale of impulses assumes a new aspect: its intervals are not merely different degrees of emphasis or loudness given to a stern and invariable 'You *must!*' but rather stages of emergence from all the reluctance of necessity into the harmony of a perfected will; and the consciousness of them, no longer the naked enforcement of Law, invites to what we most deeply love, and draws us to the supreme and only freedom. The force of moral restraint gets wings, and, with a last spring of the toiling feet, is borne through the air with the swiftness of devout enthusiasm.

But this account, pondered by some keensighted Aristotle, can hardly fail to start an ἀπορία. For it seems to distribute the sentiment of reverence all along the gradations of worth, and make it a function of them: to say, that wherever *they* go, *it* goes: being but the transcendent form of their relative *righteousness*. Yet we have counted it as *one of them*, though at the summit of their series. How can it be both a member of the set, and at the same time present throughout as a modifier of all its relations? The difficulty seems curiously like that which Plato has left us, in treating his

'*Idea of the Good*,' at one time as the highest term of his εἴδη, at another as lifted above them all, yet concerned with them all, and virtually identified with God, at whose disposal they are. It is perhaps essentially the same difficulty as Plato's; only, from its occurring, not in a great scheme of constructive metaphysic, but in the limited field of moral experience, it may be more accessible to solution. When we take into account the genesis and growth and maturity of that experience, there is no inconsistency between the two positions assigned to Reverence, nor need we indeed, in any case, be surprised that a *feeling*,—unlike a localised physical object,—may be in two *psychological places* at once. In the incipient stage of the ethical life, I have assumed no more than the co-presence of some two competing impulses, with a simple consciousness of one as better than the other: and not till these cases, repeated with variation of the terms compared, gather together fresh judgments in adequate number, do they organise themselves into a *conscience*, able to reflect upon moral relations as a system under the one idea of obligation or right. Because, in each instance as it occurs, and also in riper and more reflective comparisons further on, the act of the mind in pronouncing 'this is the superior claimant,' is a *judgment* as between two suitors, we have said that the function of conscience is *judicial*, not *dynamic*, not *executive:* to find the *motive* you must go to the impulses on which the conscience pronounces: to find the determining agent, you must go to the subsequent will. The act is carried out by the energy of its own spring, just as much as if there had been no competitor and no pause; and to this the external observer would unhesitatingly refer as its motive. There is, however, besides, hidden perhaps from the bystander, the prior internal act of choice between the possibilities present and now judged; and if it select the better, this is certainly an example of the mind's preference for the good, and may, in an intelligible sense, be referred to the *love of right* or of *virtue*. These phrases, however, are hardly justified, so long as the conception of '*right*' and of '*virtue*' are not yet formed in thought or embodied in language, although the agent *feels*, in elementary instances, the differences which these words will afterwards gather up and crystallise, and present as possible objects of contemplation and emotion. When that time has come, he will not only *have*, again and again, a sense of right, but will *think of it*, will compare it with the interfering tendency, will watch the part it plays in human character, will ponder its meaning and its source; till, through reflection upon its contents and relations, he renders it an august power in his life; its vocabulary becomes to him solemn and affecting: its representatives in history, sublime; and, if the experience runs to completion, its mysterious authority supremely venerable and sacred. That is, he is lifted into *Reverence;* and henceforward, his nature is enriched by a new affection and paramount motive, which, in the strictest sense, may be called the love of virtue, the devotion to right. Before, he had the feeling without the conception; now, he has the conception, as the centre and object of a deeper and larger feeling.

The position and play of this final sentiment may perhaps be rendered more distinct, if we recur to our former hypothetical cases of varying and vanishing divergence from each other of the two scales of impulse, viz. as arranged according to strength and according to worth. One in whom the two scales coalesced, point with point, would always act from the right spring; but as, in doing so, he would be simply yielding to his nature, he would be unconscious of alternative, and therefore of any merit in what he did. If he were surrounded by a society of beings similarly constituted, all would be for ever doing right without knowing it, for though, as an onlooker from a different world, you may say that in each of their motive springs there were two operative qualities, viz. intensity and worth, yet with them the rule will apply that what is never separated can never be discriminated. In a society which had existed, *ab initio*, under these conditions there could therefore be no *moral consciousness*, no choice between right and wrong, no ascription of merit, no shame at guilt. As the individual mind could be the scene of no competition between co-present springs of action, the conditions of *Will* would be absent; and life, whatever might be its component ideas and emotions, would be an automatic flow of involuntary phenomena.

But if, here and there, an individual appeared in whom the two scales were not coincident, and at times the inferior spring prevailed, the contrast between the usual order and this exceptional fact would disagreeably strike all observers, and compel them to feel that, in such instances, there was something wrong in his proceeding as compared with theirs; and, for the first time, the *rightness* of what they did, as distinguished from its coming uppermost by nature, would dawn upon them. The deviation from coincidence between the two qualities, still foreign to their own experience, they would learn by witnessing it in another. The previously latent moral attribute would now become patent, and henceforward enter as a conscious partner into the motive; and the more often this occurred, in the face of the opposite phenomenon in others, the more distinctly would this newly discovered element disengage itself to view, and add itself on as a reinforcement to the natural energy of the operative spring. This is the only way in which it is conceivable that sinless natures should become capable of moral consciousness and awake to the influence of right as such: they must be placed in a world where they encounter beings out of tune with themselves: except upon a scene of inward conflict, the phenomena of *conscience* do not come to the birth. Nor could they ever enter largely, as energetic facts into the structure of character, in such a world as we have supposed, part angels and part men; for it is in the personal experience of strife between the natural power of one impulse and the moral appeal of another, that the meaning of temptation, of will, of duty, of rightness, are fully realised; and he who merely watches it in another from his own point of internal harmony, may learn indeed, but hardly *measure*, their difference from himself. We have seen that the gradations of merit depend on the magnitude of the temptation overcome; i.e. on the extent of variance between the scales of intensity and of worth at the point of trial, the more faithful will resisting the larger bribe; and it needs a mind inwardly familiar with the conflict, and an experience of some range through its varieties, to give the true award of approbation or reproach, and reflect in sympathy the glory or the shame. The love of right, therefore, can reach its development in all dimensions only among beings that go wrong.

But how can a sentiment, thus contingent on the existence of sin, form the very apex of human motives, lifting us clear above it? For *Reverence*, which we have assigned to this position, is but the supreme form of the *love of right*. If it could not be felt in a state of unbroken moral harmony, what title can it have to the sacred elevation assigned to it? Must it not be transcended by such affections as we conceive to animate spirits of heavenly type, not to say the Most Holy Himself? The answer is very simple. True; the native place and whole area of service for the love of right, is on the field of moral conflict; its work there is to reduce and neutralise the discrepancy between the relative energy and the relative worth of the springs of action; and the heart-tribute which we pay to it deepens in proportion as its achievements in this work rise nearer to completion; till at length, when the discord seems to have utterly died away, and the soul to be brought into tune with all its chords, the end of the long inward conflict is felt to be attained, and our homage, far exceeding spoken praise, is transfigured into silent Reverence. This sentiment, therefore, belongs neither to the scene of battle, nor to any world where battle could not be; but to the last stage of emergence from the one to the other, to the passing of the peerless hero to the saint's rest. It anticipates the ultimate tendency of our nature's advance along the unswerving lines of conscience; and shoots forward to the distance, infinite, alas! for us, where the interval between the curve of the natural and the asymptote of the spiritual life is evanescent. It is truly intent, therefore, upon the perfected aim and final beatification of our moral nature, in its assimilation to God.

The conception of such a culmination of character, the homage of heart towards it, still more the faith in its reality as the living Spirit of the universe and Soul of our souls, is unparalleled and supreme as a motive. In the personal conscience, it forbids self-gratulation or any mere escape from external fall, so long as the internal leaning to the wrong renders the equilibrium precarious; and keeps us abashed and vigilant, till temptation, tired of its baffled game, is exhausted and retreats. In the selection of our human guides and models, it determines our homage to the summit-levels of character, where nothing intercepts the moral landscape on this side or that, but the panorama of excellence is entire. For want of this help, many a susceptible mind is carried captive by partial admirations mistaken for complete, and led blindfold by indiscriminate imitation into dangerous tracks. But no one whose perceptions have been trained by the great masters of spiritual harmony can ever be fascinated by erratic tentatives, in which snatches of beauty rise to the surface only to be lost again in confusion. The wild enthusiasms of a generation that has lost its guide, and gropes in the dark for some hand to lead it; that tries all competitors for worship,— now science, now art, now order, now progress, arbitrary equality or an equally arbitrary hierarchy, force of intellect or force of dynamite; nay, that sinks so low as to bend the knee to the passing *Zeitgeist*, while turning the back to the consensus of all ages; sufficiently show the helplessness of minds whose Reverence is set afloat without a compass and with the eternal stars shut out. Above all, this last affection has a decisive supremacy because, having reached the crowning ideal in which all excellence is summed up, it steps across the line of the real and finds it *there*, as the inner meaning and secret of the universe, the law of all its laws, the end of all its ends; so that he who trusts himself to it, however lonely his path, lives and breathes in the strength and joy of the Divine sympathy, and moves on the lines of the universal order.

It is not uncommon to hear the power of this motive readily admitted, at the same time that its claim to elevated worth is denied. The present social crusade against religion in France is no doubt animated by a sincere conviction that the removal of its influence is indispensable to any further step of moral advancement. This conviction has reference so much more to the general character of clerical sway over the minds of men than to the particular aspect of religion on which I have dwelt, that its contact with our subject is by no means intimate. Yet questions of this kind may be asked: 'You say that Reverence is the highest of motives. Is it then never to be postponed to compassion? and is the pious persecutor, in his reverence for the Divine truth committed to the Church, bound, as he pretends, to stifle the compassion which he feels for his victim? And are the heretics wrong, in denouncing persecution as a crime?' Concrete examples, like this, must first be resolved into the two aspects which they always mix up together: viz. 'What, in point of motive, is right relatively to the agent in his given position?' and 'What, in point of social effect, is the right mode of action to be instituted under the supposed conditions?' In settling whether or not persecution is a crime to be prohibited by the statute-book, we answer the second of these questions. In settling whether, in a community which legalises it without any suspicion of its being a crime, a person officially engaged in it does his duty in following the motive impelling to it or in following that which withholds from it, we answer the first. With this alone we have here to do: the other belongs to the objective ethics, which have to select the reasonable action for carrying out the moral motive.

In this view, persecution presents only a particular case of the punishments appointed by law; in any one of which the same conflict of feeling might take place in the mind of the judge: between the sense of justice which it is his function to impersonate, and the relenting mood which makes the sentence hard to pronounce. In obeying the former (a composite principle, not yet placed in our list), he undoubtedly follows the higher; and not only so, but when his reflections go out beyond the moment and his court, he realises the wrong on which the penalty is visited, and enters into sympathy with the sufferer from it: so that compassion pleads on both sides, and justice only upon one. It is the same in the instance of the persecutor. However sorry for the heretic's doom, he commiserates also the heretic's victims; who may be saved, or limited in number, by his death, while they might become a formidable host if he were spared. In yielding, therefore, to what with him plays the part of reverence for Divine truth and right, the persecutor has no contention with his own compassion, the balance of which is overwhelming on his side. But, were it even otherwise, he would no less be true to the higher motive, than the judge who sorrowfully condemns the youthful offender he fain would save. If you doubt this, it is because you judge the case by your own affections and not by his; you sympathise with his pity for the sufferings of the rack and the temporal death; but not with that for the quenchless fire or eternal death of the false prophet's deluded followers; and instead of giving him his feelings as conditions of the problem, you keep the one set as facts and dismiss the other as nonsense. It is very true that, in our view, his compassion is, on both sides, directed on imaginary ills,—on the lost state of the heretic's soul, and on the position of his victims, trembling on the verge of the abyss; and that his piety also goes astray to fix on elements not really present in the Divine nature. But this affects only the relations of his character to *facts*, not the relations of its own parts to one another. If things were as he imagines, he would be at one both with nature and with himself; as they are not so, his act is wrong : why? not in its principle but in its application; because it is a blunder, not because it is a sin.

The supreme place among the springs of action which has been assigned to Reverence may perhaps remind the student of ethical literature of a doctrine which has played a considerable part in discussions concerning the criterion of virtue: viz. that the rule of right *is the will of God.* Is the position which I have defended only a reproduction of this? By no means: the apparent resemblance (if such there be) is cancelled by two fundamental differences. Whoever affirms the will of God to be the rule of right means that, to ascertain our duty, we must consult the will of God; which, therefore, we must have some prior and independent resource for knowing. Originally, no doubt, that resource was assumed to be the Scriptures, regarded as 'the oracles of God;' which could be studied to find the heads and contents of duty, just as a code is searched to determine the problems of civil law. Increasing knowledge of the Scriptures rendering it evident that they contain a good deal that is not the will of God and pay slight heed to a good deal that is, the moralist of this school was driven to seek another test as supplement or substitute; naming now one thing, now another, but, with most acceptance, the conduciveness of acts to the happiness of men. By Paley, for example, this feature is taken, not as in itself *constituting right*, but as the *mark*, where Revelation is silent, the *external index*, of the will of God. In this theory we are treated as morally *blank* by nature, but created with power separately to learn the will of God, and through this happy capacity conducted, by a didactic circuit, to an acquaintance with ethical law. The doctrine of the present treatise is found by taking the contradictories of both these propositions, and then inverting their order. Our nature is *not* morally blank, but pervaded with an ethical consciousness throughout; and we have *no unmoral means* of learning the will of God: but, in knowing our inward springs as better and worse, we know his will. This last proposition, indeed, is not quite correctly described as an *inversion* of Paley's order; for the relation, in its two clauses, between the moral consciousness and the Divine authority, is one, not so much of *inference*, as of identification, the ideas overlapping and being entwined together as functions of the same conception; whereas the relation, in the other doctrine, between the two knowledges,—of duty and of the will of God,—is strictly that of conclusion and premiss. The second difference is, that what Paley supposes to be revealed through the Divine will, is the right system of objective conduct; whilst the moral insight, which I conceive to be taken up and transfigured into personal religious relations, has reference only to the contents of the *inward character;* still needing an ulterior process of rational comparison of consequences, before the rules of fitting conduct can be determined.

§ 10. *How to estimate Mixed Incentives.*

It is necessary to supplement the classification we have given of our elementary springs of action by some notice of others no less familiar, which have to be assigned to their place. These are all of them formed by the confluence of two or more of the elementaries, which they transform and modify in value, after the manner already observed in such cases as the love of money, of power, of liberty, and the impulses of emulation, envy, and jealousy. Many other of these derivative compounds yet remain; and a few samples of them we must examine, not only in order to account for their presence, but also that we may weigh a serious difficulty with which they seem to burden the doctrine of an intuitive consciousness of the relative claims of rival incentives. Composite impulses can owe their moral worth and rank to nothing else than the constituents of their formation, and that worth must be proportioned to the aggregate value of those constituents; which can hardly be reckoned, it would seem, without first a refined analysis to assemble and measure the elements, and then an intricate computation to combine and bring out their resultant. Of such process we can hardly be affirmed to have any consciousness; and yet to dispense with it, and keep our moral perception in these cases still upon the line of intuition, is to carry that term beyond the boundary of those simple apprehensions to which alone it is usually applied. In answer to this difficulty I can only fall back upon Aristotle's principle, that you must not ask for mathematical exactitude in matters which do not admit of it, but be content with the best practical approximation to be had[1]. Psychological proportions may really exist and may tell upon our experience, without being measurable; and, what is more, we may feel their synthesis and have a good guess at their shares, without being required or able to spread them out in quantitative analysis. And it needs no exceptional self-knowledge to be aware, that where we have acted from mixed motives, some approvable, others selfish and unworthy, we are by no means unconscious of the spoiling combination, and cannot accept the word of mistaken praise without secret shame. I care not whether this instantaneous judgment be called intuitive, or be regarded as the outcome of a process too rapid to be traced. I only know it is as ready as if it were intuitive, and comes to the surface as soon. For our purpose, this is sufficient. But I admit that, in these complex cases, our first estimate is subject to reflective correction, in a way which is not observable with the simpler impulses. There is no secret of the conscience which the old writers on personal piety more searchingly exposed, than the alloy of impure motive that is apt to taint even our best moments and our least imperfect acts; and in the subtlety of their detective scrutiny they are unsurpassed by the keenest of professed psychologists. But it would be a mistake to suppose that, in thus laying bare the component atoms of a spoiled duty, they give it any unsus-

[1] Eth. Nik. I. iii. 4.

pected character in our eyes, or materially change the complexion of our previous moral consciousness respecting it. They do but make *explicit* the self-estimate which, as *implicit*, is already there, and by its presence enables us to recognise or to reject the truth of their account. And it may be doubted whether, in itself, and until tricks of self-excuse have tampered with its simplicity, this implicit estimate, wrapped up in the feeling, is not more effective as an integer, than when crumbled into its fractional equivalents, positive and negative. It is chiefly for falsifiers that these analytical refinements are needed as correctives: the healthy and honest mind has a short cut to the truth; and through this experience it is, that we have abated our esteem for the literature of spiritual introspection, and should now prescribe it as a discipline even to the ailing conscience, with as much reserve- as books on pathology to the sick. Without any microscopic self-dissection, there is then a quasi-intuitive consciousness, attending even the compound springs, of their greater or less worth as compared with some other that might take their place.

One of the most familiar of these is found in that copious source of human action which, with a slight change of mask, appears under the several names of *Vanity*, *Love of Praise*, *Love of Fame* (or *Glory*). The common root of these varieties is obviously the sentiment of *admiration*, in its secondary form, of a thirst for *the pleasures of admiring*. In the normal state, this feeling would go forth into the scene around, on the look-out for things or persons to meet and gratify it. But here, the characteristic is that this direction is inverted, and the mind stops at home, turns in upon itself, and sits before the glass in pleased admiration. It is at once subject and object of the desired emotion. So little can it bear to part with the pleasant vision, that it devises for itself a beautifying mirror, which sets off the personal features to the best advantage; and, on the other hand, avoids bringing them into comparison with any but inferior or distorted images of the same traits elsewhere; and thus shelters itself from the pains of humility and the possibility of aspiration. A man in whom such estimate of his own relative merits has become assured, finds adequate satisfaction in self-applause, and makes no bid for the suffrages of others · if they do not recognise his perfections, so much the worse for them: their blindness does not dim his light This isolated self-esteem is *Pride*,—involving more or less contemptuous indifference to the sentiments of others. More often, the self-admirer is less confident about his own attractions; has in fact a slight suspicion of his own tricks, and wonders whether anybody could say that he had painted himself up: he is not, therefore, quite self-sufficing, and feels a something counterfeit in his own complacency. At the same time, his social affection is perhaps warm, and, at least in its secondary stage, makes him dependent on the sympathy of his fellows; and if so, the first question to which he will seek a response from them will be, 'Do they sustain him in his ruling desire? Do they echo his self-laudation? or, horrible thought! do they "write him down an ass?"' This dependent and sympathetic type of self-esteem is what we mean by *Vanity:* beginning with self-praise, but uneasy till confirmed by other voices; unable, therefore, to refrain from *inviting* their applause, either by display of what is to win it, or by flattery which cannot pass without reply. To one who is in this state of mind, the impelling desire is *immediate* and *thirsty:* the praise which he wants is nothing to him, except to be enjoyed: if he is not to hear it, he might as well go without it: it serves its end, only while the appetite is there. Just in this feature it is, that the variety called *the Love of Fame* deviates from the other types of the same fundamental tendency. The resolve of the man who is swayed by it is, not to *enjoy* the public praise, but to *earn* it, even though it may never fall upon his ear, but only wake and render his name musical to later generations. He declines to pay the price of the popularity now in the market, viz. conformity, against his own better insight, with the humours of the hour, and the storing up of sickness to the State by their indulgence. He sees, in the history of nations, how many reputations, splendid when full-blown, have fallen to pieces in a night, and, like double flowers, have been barren of all fruit; and how names, that once passed daily from lip to lip in every civilised language, are mentioned now only to raise the question, '*Who was he?*' and he prefers the durable place in the gratitude of men, to the precarious, however ready and however large. That he will himself be absent from the theatre which rings with his name, and deaf to the sound, hardly makes it less welcome to his thought, nay, carries in it a certain pathetic disinterestedness which deepens its charm for his imagination. The world will be wiser then; and there is true dignity in waiting for its approval till it knows its benefactor.

From these varieties it is evident that the composite feeling of *Love of Praise* has a great latitude, according as it is more or less qualified by social affection, and more or less select in regard to the spectators whose praise is coveted. Scarcely can it be recognised as the same feeling in the æsthetic fop who hawks about his graces or his verses in exchange for the adulation of his clique; and in the saintly recluse who has turned his back on the favour of men to breathe a life-long sigh for the approbation of God. In passing through all grades from one of these extremes to the other, it cannot but assume as many values; and ere it can be estimated, its specific type must be clearly stated and conceived. In its broadest and more familiar forms, however, it readily discloses its place relatively to the motives which press for comparison with it.

It is in aid of the *educator's work* that appeals to the love of Praise are most systematically invoked: the whole apparatus of prizes, certificates, degrees, and honours, deriving its leverage from this principle. It may be admitted that in this field, open as it necessarily is to the constant observation of superiors whose good opinion is of great importance to pupils, it is better to recognise and reduce to rule a motive which in any case would have its play, than to allow its limits to be self-determined; and also that, so far as its stimulus wakens faculties and industry which else would lazily sleep, it secures an inward improvement as well as an outward gain. At the same time it should be remembered, that this incentive achieves nothing except what *ought to be accomplished* by a higher, viz. by the native Wonder and quest for light, whence all knowledge springs· and were the minds of the teacher and the taught in the best state, their relations to each other would need no other power than this. In everyone, therefore, with whom the competition lies between the love of praise and the love of ease, the former is entitled to the victory and constitutes a moral gain in the battle of life. In everyone with whom the competition lies between the love of praise and the hunger for knowledge, it is an impertinence in the former to intrude upon the paramount rights of the latter. In framing a system of education, it is a question of moral maxima and minima to determine the point at which the pure intellectual curiosity will reach its utmost efficiency, and the craving for distinction sink most nearly to its zero. Unfortunately, this problem seems to have dropped out of the view of our recent organisers of education, elementary or advanced: the extravagant trust reposed upon the system of examinations and rewards implies a cynical disregard of the natural craving of Reason for enlargement and lucidity of thought, and mischievously forces to the front motives intellectually cramping and morally inferior. Virtual reduction of all study to a graduating drill, and of what is called 'successful' teaching to a forecast of examination questions by the sum of the chances divided by the names of the examiners, might well excite the indignation of such a master of mental training as the late Professor De Morgan; who well knew, from the personal memory of his youth and the long experience of his class-room, how stifling is such a method to all freshness and originality of thought, how superfluous is its competitive stimulus to the better class of minds, and how likely, with the rest, to bring their education to a dead stop with their professional degree[1].

As in academic life the *Love of Praise*, so in political the *Love of Fame*, seems always the poor substitute of something which ought rather to be there, and the absence of which constitutes its sole apology. It is perhaps impossible for private persons to make adequate allowance for the intense regard of public men for the approving sentiments of a miscellaneous multitude vastly inferior to themselves; so that, upon their theatre of action, the very idea of referring problems to the individual conviction and conscience seems to have died out, and the rule to be admitted that, in any case, you have to satisfy some body of opinion other than your own; and that the only question is, whether you will follow the humour of your constituents and of the hour; or whether you will seek approval from a selecter and remoter audience, when the foolish voices shall be silenced, and there remains only the august sentence of the wise. The unblushing avowal on the part of eminent statesmen, of this motive, even in its most farsighted form, has always affected me with grief and shame. We expect it in a Cicero; but when it appears in modern parliaments after eighteen centuries of Christian experience, it is a deplorable evidence how long is the survival of unregenerate morals. Of course it must be granted that the appeal from the clamour of the present to the sifted suffrages of posterity, sets the motive on a higher level. But if it is better to court historic fame than to thirst for momentary praise, it is better still to forget both in simple truth of conviction and faithful service to the state and to mankind. Though, therefore, these motives have their immediate inferiors, which it is well for them to beat out of the field, this opprobrium still adheres to them, that the work they do ought to be put forth by a superior whose place they take.

If we follow these motives from the field surrendered to them and notice their play in the mixed affairs of life, we

[1] Memoir of Augustus De Morgan, by his Wife, pp. 169 184.

find them responsible, if for much serviceable production of industry and art and regulation of manners, yet also for many a ruinous temptation. Rather than forfeit the favour of companions or superiors, how many a lie is told! To escape the jeers and scorn of associates, how often is the false pretence assumed or the guilty compliance made! To keep the goodwill of light-minded associates, in what cowardly silence is the impure innuendo or the hinted calumny allowed to pass! Wherever, indeed, the average social standard of *avowed* ethical sentiment is below the level of the individual's conscience, it is always pressing upon him with a tension which allows him no moral sleep. And this must be the prevailing case; for it is rare indeed for the private mind to have no sacred recesses, no cherished affections, that transcend the conventional tone of miscellaneous men. In childhood, indeed, while the conscience is still rudimentary and has to take much on trust from elders, and also among adults whose moral sense is similarly immature, the eagerness for approval may rather elevate than deteriorate the character; and these are in fact the conditions which define its appropriate field. It is essentially a *puerile* incentive, needful to elicit the energies and sustain the courage of school-boys, soldiers and sailors; but its survival beyond that stage, the flinging of it broadcast as the seed-grain of all social fruits, and the pompous profession of its historic variety by grave seniors before applauding senates, are humiliating indications how far we still are from the moral manhood of the human race. For a vast proportion of its computed gains from this source, society pays too dear in the degradation of minds capable of action from better springs.

Besides the class of feelings towards our appreciation by others, *Generosity* is entitled to a place among mixed incentives. It is, however, rather a certain intensity in the primary social affection,—Attachment,—evinced in selected modes of application, than a compound of many elements. It marks the working of this affection *in giving and forgiving*, when it overflows with sufficient profusion to soften the seals of possession and water down the heats of resentment Provided it does these two things, i.e. bursts the two chief bounds from which the affection suffers check, it earns its name; so that it is essentially a *measureless* impulse, tending to great latitude, and justly bearing the repute of being *free*. This idea attaches to it in all its examples, and occasions its antithesis to *Justice*, which involves exactitude of action in quantitative proportion. Whoever has bound himself by definite engagements to others,—for example, to his servant for stipulated wages,—and in discharging them forgets no extra work and notices every special want, and gives, unasked, more than can be claimed, is regarded as generous And, similarly, if in any game which has two sides, with rights imperfectly determined by rule, he foregoes an advantage that no temper may be disturbed, he earns the epithet again. It is therefore in the indefinite play of social affection beyond the limits of what could be demanded from it as a *right*, that generosity has its field What then are the competitors with which it may conflict, and which may try to restrain its eagerness? Its immediate opposites, it is evident, are *the love of money*, which would check its *giving*, and *resentment*, which would prevent its *forgiving;* and, less directly, protests might also come from the other affections, lest the opened hand should lavish at a single throw the resources needed for the parental duties and the succour of helpless misery. To the indefinite *love of money* the indefinite *generosity* stands related as the superior. But as the resistance of the others addresses itself, or may address itself, only to the *degree*, insisting on *a limit* to what in itself contains none, it is quite possible for the right to be with them Even forgiveness, as we have seen, is not *unconditionally* approvable, and may cast away a discipline needful alike for the offender and the spectator. And the father who, through random liberality to strangers' wants, becomes a niggard to his home, and turns out upon the world a family of beggars, corrupts a possible virtue into an actual guilt We cannot, therefore, insert generosity at an invariable place in our list. Whenever we come upon these questions of *quantity*, we are carried beyond the resources of morality proper, i e. the doctrine of motives, and referred for completion of the answer to the canon of consequences.

§ 11. *Relations of Merit; Gratitude; Generosity, Justice.*

There is no more copious source of derivative moral conceptions, and thence of new springs of action, than the idea of *Merit*. The exposition of this idea already given will prepare us to see that it must itself admit of several variations. For it is wholly a *relative* idea, all merit being comparative, or predicated only in reference to some other term, and assuming a modified aspect according as that term is changed. A given volition, for example, may vary in its merits, when occurring twice over in the same person; and as put forth by two persons; and again, as objectively concerning two persons. At one time it may encounter heavy temptation and cost the agent a severe effort, and at another may nearly accord with his inclination; and in saying 'Well done!' to the former, we bear in mind the latter. Or, the favouring conditions may be found in one agent, and the hindering in another; and then the faint praise which we give to the first will grow emphatic to the second. Or again, the sacrifice which, when made to meet a debt, is accepted without thanks by the creditor, will not fail, if volunteered to ransom a captive stranger, to give the liberator a lofty merit in his eyes; and, in the same way, as we have before shown, the human goodness which can never rise into merit before God, may yet be truly said to have earned it in regard to men. Towards the Infinite Righteousness, the Archetype and Prompter of all our highest possibilities, we can but say, 'We are unprofitable servants; we have done that which it was our duty to do.'

This sentence draws a distinction which often requires to be marked, yet is not easily supplied with adequate expression. It disclaims all *merit* for *the doing of duty*, and evidently reserves it for conduct which goes beyond the bounds of obligation and transcends the equilibrium of rectitude. Such a case, possible only in our relations with each other, arises whenever definite engagements are entered into, the conditions of which are reduced to rule, if not by law or contract, at least by determinate types of usage which exclude mistake. But if we banish merit from the whole field of duties binding among men, and give it its first start outside these confines, we must recall and correct our former statement, that we attribute merit to whatever we approve, and demerit to whatever we disapprove; for we approve *every* right choice, and precisely for the reason (viz. that it is *duty*) which is said to disqualify it for *merit*. Yet how can we help thinking and saying, that it '*merits approval?*' And still more, of an act of bad faith, that it '*merits disapproval?*' It is evident, therefore, that these two words are used at one time as coextensive in their range, at another as unequal, 'approval' keeping the whole field, 'merit' driven to the outlying zone beyond the enclosure of stipulated obligation. It is this narrower sense which has led Mr. Stephen to link it to *virtue* as its 'value;' for 'virtue' also carries the same connotation, of character that volunteers more than the discharge of its definite engagements. It so happens that the word '*desert*,' though supposed to be synonymous with '*merit*,' is free from this limiting idea; perhaps because it has no opposite, like '*demerit*,' which, by taking charge of all the negatives, leaves its companion at large to soar into the higher positives; whereas 'desert' covers every case in which anything, bad or good, is felt to be due, i.e. all the range of approval and disapproval. We might, therefore, obtain appropriate terms for the distinction which we have to mark, by using the word '*desert*' (qualified, if needful, by the epithets 'good' or 'bad') when including what lies within the sphere of pledged duty, and reserving the word '*merit*' for what lies beyond it.

According to this distinction, if there subsist a contract

or mutual understanding between two persons, each of them, in punctually fulfilling the prescribed conditions, deserves approval; but neither can have any claim of *merit* upon the other, or regard an observer's eulogy of his *virtue* as anything but misapplied flattery. All that can be said of such exact conformity with stipulation is, that it is blameless and avoids *demerit;* it is neither positive nor negative, but stands at zero, affording an example of that mere *Truth*, *Good Faith*, or, in matters of property, *Honesty*, which constitutes the *postulated level* of all our transactions together. These are all *duties* which our fellows have a *right* to demand from us, and *less than which* we cannot render without sinking to position below them. Yet this equal balance of relations may be disturbed by intrusion into the problem of one of the other conditions of merit. If we happen to know that, in order to keep his engagement with B, A has had to make some terrible sacrifice, far exceeding the visible benefits of his integrity, we cannot but feel that the conquered temptation imparts something of an heroic character to his fidelity and lifts it into the region of the meritorious. This element of merit, however, being a part of the private history of his mind, and not visible to B or indigenous to the contract, is not towards *him:* it exists, not by overpassing his claims, but by comparison with an almost venial surrender to the strain of a less faithful impulse. In order to introduce merit towards B, A must take upon himself the burden of some conditions not embraced in the agreement, and favourable to his companion; if, for example, he was to pay him £1,000 in December, and, believing him to be hard pressed, pays it in the previous June: or, having to receive something from him at an oppressive date, grants him time to recover; he carries the transaction into an altitude above the ground-line of business, and wins recognition as something more than *true*.

The feeling which constitutes this recognition, and, in its turn, transcends the experience of simple contract fulfilled, is *Gratitude*, a new and conspicuous spring of action, the claims of which have been a favourite subject of discussion with the moralists of all literary ages. Its disputable problems, however, refer almost entirely to the modes and measures of its external expression, and belong therefore to the ethics of objective conduct rather than of inward character. The impulse itself is very nearly simple: viz. personal attachment awakened specifically by receipt of benefits, and therefore answered specifically by the desire of requital. It is the very nature of all love to assimilate, to reproduce the feeling from the contemplation of which it springs, i.e. to respond to love *in kind;* for admiration to return admiration, for sympathy, sympathy: for high example, imitation not less high; and so, for benefits, corresponding benefits. There is, therefore, nothing exceptional in gratitude, obliging us to reserve an unshared place for it: it is a variety of *generosity,* with its indefinite profusion, however, brought to some approximate measure by the extent of the favour conferred; for, though it repudiates all nice calculations and insists on an *ad libitum* range, yet it spends itself and rests in natural equilibrium, when the requital seems in correspondence with the gift. How this correspondence is to be reached, it may be difficult to decide; whether by estimating the effort of the giver, or the service to the receiver, or by framing a compound ratio of the two; or by leaving the whole adjustment to the invisible intensity of the affection. But, in any case, the affection, however expressed, will be owned as a debt on the one side without being held as a claim on the other. As it lies in the very essence of the affection to accept this paradox of love, it is defective in anyone who cannot rest in so generous a relation, but is uneasy till he rids himself of the debt, and obtains his discharge. Such a rebellious haste to escape from an obliged position will not incur our censure, if the benefits received have been heaped upon him by some unworthy giver, or even some stranger with whom he can have no intimate ties. But else, it betrays to us a heart too proud for friendship, and unfitted for generous relations; for, however liberal a giver may be, he is not *generous*, if he bargains always to occupy the *superior* side of the relation, and looks down on the *inferior* whom he has made so by his own act. To the reciprocity of affection it is essential that an exchange of positions should be always welcome; and that the common love should cover with an equal charm the passive and the active part, the humility of dependence and the joy of succour. The sullen receiver is at least as heartless as the grudging giver.

When the moral equilibrium between myself and another is disturbed in just the opposite direction, and instead of his emerging into merits towards me, I sink myself into demerits towards him, there arises in me an impulse, the counterpart of gratitude, *the desire of reparation*. It addresses itself not, like repentance, to the *moral guilt* incurred, but to *the harm done*, and especially to the *affection which has been hurt*. Till this wound has been healed, and its wrong undone, not only am I upbraided by the outward witnesses of my sin, but know that I have violated the conditions of personal and social peace; and whatever sacrifice is needed from me to ·reinstate these must be freely offered, as the first pledge of a sincere penitence. As in the case of gratitude its genuineness was tested by its *ability* patiently to bear its inferior position, so, in the case of the *desire of reparation*, the test is found in the *inability* to bear it. the wrong must not stay upon the field a needless hour: the word of confession must be spoken at once. not a plea must I hint in excuse, but take on me all my reproach, and spare neither toil nor goods that may rebuild the ruined temple of Faith, and open it once more for a true homage. Unless the loss of reciprocal trust is intolerable to me, and I make haste to repair it at any cost, I cannot even begin the hope of *moral* restoration.

From the foregoing exposition it will be easily seen, that *gratitude*, as a spring of action, is subject to the same approvals and the same restrictions as generosity; of which, in truth, it is a modified example, under the limitation of being directed towards a given person and excited by a given kind of act.

The conception of merit lies at the root of another idea, vast in range and importance, and answerable for a corresponding spring of action: viz. the idea of *Justice*,—thus determined in the Pandects,—' Justitia est constans et perpetua voluntas suum cuique tribuendi.' It is indeed impossible to cover with one exact definition all the current applications of this term; for from its nucleus it has radiated far in several directions of somewhat loose analogy, and when its several ulterior usages are brought together, they prove too divergent to be embraced within any formula. Nor can we pretend to trace the history of these spreading lines, pursuing their way now through this language, now through that, till in our modern composite tongues they cease to constitute a coherent system at all. But, without attempting either logical or historical deduction, we may perhaps set up an approximate central meaning, around which may be compendiously gathered the few variations which need detain our attention.

Justice, therefore, let us say, is *the treatment of persons according to their deserts*. And in this two things are involved: viz. (1) that there is *somebody to treat them;* (2) that in treating them he has the disposal of something which they care for, in quantities divisible and proportionable, so as to correspond with the ratios of their deserts. These conditions at once bring before us the image of a *Judge*, presiding over the trial of some charged offence or some disputable claim between two applicants for his decision: on him their treatment depends: and it consists in his award of penalty or of partition, in conformity with their estimated wrongs and rights: these consequences, as well as his own graduated words of condemnation or acquittal, are the common matter which he can distribute, in measures accurately representing the relative values he has determined. If we start from this point, it is plain that, to constitute justice, there must be a triad of persons at the least: viz A and B, whose shares in some common matter of good or ill are in doubt, and a dikast, who solves the doubt; and that it is of the dikast, in his award, that we predicate justice or injustice, and not of A or B in their relation to each other. And this, I am persuaded, gives us the idea of justice at its fountain-head, and is our securest guide to the derivative modifications which appear in its lower currents. That in the early speech of so many peoples the words '*just*' and '*equal*' were interchangeable ('are not my ways equal, saith the Lord'), instead of implying a claim that all men should be on a par, does but throw into the simplest form the conception of *fair play*, wherein each is dealt with 'according to his works:'—a conception which expressed itself by the word '*equal*,' only because, in the development of quantitative ideas, the relations of equality were apprehended and named considerably earlier than those of ratio and proportion, and were alone available for metaphorical transference to exactly correct relations in human life. The phrase is simply tantamount to 'impartial.' It does not follow, therefore, that because 'equality,' which may subsist between two, supplied a synonym for 'justice,' we wrongly resort to a triple relation as essential to the fundamental idea. *He* only is 'just,' in the proper meaning of the word, who, in a case of relative desert, distributes some divisible stock of recompense in the proportion of their several earnings.

This type of relation is not always discernible in our present use of the word. For the word turns up when we are speaking merely of a *dual* relation, whether of determinate contract or of indeterminate obligation. An employer, we say, may 'unjustly' withhold the stipulated wages of a servant; a parent may 'justly' punish laziness or cruelty in his child; an anxious man may 'unjustly' suspect the motives of his friend. Such examples, taken by themselves, might tempt us to identify the *just* with the *right*, as subsisting between two, and to forego the requirement of a third person; and Professor Sidgwick, accordingly, considers the meaning of the word satisfied, by any conduct which fulfils the warranted expectations of another[1]. But it is easy to see how this application of the idea would arise as an extension, or, I might rather say, as a shorthand contraction, of the other. In all these seemingly dual instances, there is a *subauditur* of a third party, either through duplication of one of the pair by playing two characters at once, or by the implicit presence of a suppressed term of comparison. In every case, the person of whom justice or injustice is predicated, occupies the place of *judge;* and the difficulty is to find in the other the *plurality* of suitors for his verdict. The employer, in the first example, acts as judge *in his own case*, i.e. he pleads as a suitor in the court where he sits on the bench, and between himself and his servant, as contracting parties, he decides against the latter: under such conditions, impartiality is impossible; and every one else must see that his decision is unjust; and, to obtain it, he has committed the further wrong of usurping the function which neither plaintiff nor defendant can exercise. In the second example, the punishment awarded by the parent is pronounced 'just,' if it be *proportioned to the fault*, i.e. in keeping with the scale of recompense, which measures out to the child the fitting treatment of each gradation of conduct; and if also it be *impartially given*, i.e. without favour or disfavour to him, as compared with the other children of the family. Here, therefore, the invisible third party is found, either in the culprit himself under other conditions of behaviour, or in the brothers and sisters with whose experience his treatment has to be harmonised. In the third example, the wrongly suspected friend is treated, in the absence of evidence against him, just as an accused person would be, after being clearly convicted: the judge, therefore, does not know the difference between the

[1] Methods of Ethics, III. chap v. § 2. p. 267.

innocent and the guilty, and is unjust. Similar implications lurk in our estimates of judicial sentences upon single prisoners in criminal trials. Though the whole relation seems to subsist between the bench and the dock, the judge has his mind full of analogous and alternative cases, which he brings into comparison with this; and, in pronouncing judgment, his care is to let it be in character with the scale of penalties intended by public law, and registered in the approved precedents of the courts. The justice, therefore, still consists in truth of proportionate distribution. This is the reason why we do not apply the epithets 'just' and 'unjust' to cases of conduct which afford no room for this idea,—to the behaviour, for example, of two persons to one another, each in a single capacity. A mistress does not accuse her maid of 'injustice' for omitting to clean the drawing-room with the stipulated frequency; nor does the maid praise the 'justice' of her mistress for paying her wages at the appointed quarter-day. We should never think of quoting the simple observance of contract, and the keeping of a promise, as examples of justice: though in a judge it would be just to acquit either party, in case of doubt, of any wrong to the other. Fulfilment of engagement is *fidelity*, but not necessarily *justice*: non-fulfilment is *a wrong*, but not necessarily an *injustice*.

The idea of justice undergoes another extension into cases not originally embraced in it. The judge, in his award, deals distributively with some common matter of good or ill, admitting of accurate apportionment, such as fines, damages, terms of imprisonment, forfeitures, &c. His function is limited to cases which, from the definite nature of their relations, allow of such precise assignment of recompense, and in which the good and ill available for his award are measurable quantities out of which nameable proportions can be constructed. The province of Law, which is *his* province, can go no further; for it is bounded by the possibility of definition and the resources of language for marking *degrees* of criminality. But this inevitable limit is mechanical, not moral; and were it to be removed by the invention of some more exact notation and reckoning of right and wrong, his jurisdiction might be widened correspondingly. No new principle would have to be invoked. the same rule,—that men are to be treated according to their deserts,—would still apply, and be susceptible of application out of the store of divisible good and ill at his disposal. In point of fact, however, he cannot push back his boundary: his tools fail him beyond, though his principle does not; and he has to surrender it to the self-administration and spontaneous adjustments of society outside. When we, privates and inexpert, take up his dropped function, we are unarmed with any terrors of the law, and have nothing to distribute which can be doled out in determinate proportions to each according to his worth; but only an indefinite store of affection and sentiment, of approval and abhorrence, of love, of wrath, of reverence. Nor are the cases that come before us and invite their share of these feelings, any longer determinate in their conditions and obligations, they, too, break bounds, and present, not simple *deserts*, but *merits;* and these are what we have now to estimate, as nearly as we can, by extension of the same rule; so as, in principle, to be just, even in our field of free affection. In other words, we ought to treat others according to their *merits;* taking into account all the dimensions of merit, not omitting due respect to the *moral effort* put forth in order to be faithful, and to the spontaneous overflow of disinterested service. Thus it is that, in spite of the strict limits of the realm of Justice, its central idea spreads widely over the indefinite life beyond, and carries its controlling presence into generosity and love themselves. It is in the estimate of character and conduct in this indeterminate field, that what we call *Fairness* of mind is shown; and also in the interpretation given, by one of the partners in a common but vague understanding, to the tacit conditions which afford play to the selfish or the liberal temper. It is the *spirit* of justice, reigning in the zone beyond the borders of its land.

In this form it supplies a new spring of action Justice, pure and simple, is a habit or exercise of moral skill: but when the aptitude, becoming a disposition, quits its own area, and makes its power felt in the embracing territory of life, it takes its place among the incentives, and starts the enquiry, where it is to stand. What, then, is this *love of Justice?* The love of *proportionate treatment* of men and their character according to their worth, i.e. of giving more favourable regards to the more worthy, less to the less. But, to do this is simply to introduce *degrees* into a process already instituted and in operation without them; for each spring of action is secure of *some* approbation from us as compared with one rival, and some disapprobation as compared with another If in the former relation it be the right incentive, and approvable, simply as there at all, it must be *more right*, or right *à fortiori*, if, being susceptible of graduated superiority, it is there *in higher degree;* and the intuitive approval awarded to it at first cannot but receive a corresponding increment of intensity. The same provision of our nature, therefore, which directs a moral welcome upon *this* affection as against *that*, cannot but secure a welcome proportionately deeper to *more of this* as compared with less of it. The love of justice, accordingly, is only a higher figure of the original sense of right. it is the *preference for worth.* Or it might be called the *enthusiasm of conscience for its own estimation of character;* and, so far as it assumes a missionary energy, for a conformable adjustment of social life. Here, however, it is immediately thrown upon problems encumbered with conditions from the *unmoral* side of nature, and unmanageable without the calculus of possibilities and of results, so that the realisation of its ideal cannot be seized at a bound, but must be controlled, in its time and its degree, by natural laws, which need first to be studied and defined. Endless has been the waste of noble energy upon illusory schemes of perfected justice in the affairs of men, for want of clearly determining the relative shares of natural causes and of the human will in shaping both the constituent facts and the successive history of societies and states.

§ 12. *Veracity.*

The last moral quality which needs to be adjusted to our scale is *Veracity* How and where does its obligation enter? Does it, as *Truth*, come in under the wing of *Wonder*, and insist on things being set forth as they are? or does it, as altruistic, belong to *social affection*, and refuse to violate expectations warrantably formed? Obviously, it is not in itself *a spring of action*, coming under any of the heads, propension, passion, affection, sentiment; though, when it has been constituted and recognised, a love of it may ensue, which, like the love of justice, may find a place in the system of moral dynamics. Instead of a propulsion, it is a restraint or limit imposed upon speech, barring us out from innumerable things which else we might say. It is regulative, not initiative: the impulse to say something must be sought elsewhere. We speak, not *in order to be truthful*, but in order to tell some experience, or to elicit such from another, or to stir some sympathetic or antipathetic emotion, or to influence the will of our companion. In all cases, the incentive is supplied out of the familiar list,—be it Wonder in quest of information, or Passion in an explosion of anger, or Affection in the tender of sympathy. Moreover, the impulse, whatever it be, does not spend itself on speech *as an end*, but merely wields it as an instrument for reaching its real object, viz. a certain effect upon another's mind. What is it that we want to do there? We want (let us say, for example) to create a certain belief, or to kindle a certain feeling. In almost all cases, the belief which we wish to impart is *our* belief· the feeling which we wish to kindle is *our* feeling: for, the very act in which we are engaged is an act of sympathy and communion; and our own states of mind are just what we long to transfuse into the mind of our fellow. It is but the inverse reading of this experience that, whenever he tries, by oral address, to create in me a belief or to waken a feeling, I cannot but assume it to be his: his act places it on the line, and impels it with the force, running direct from mind to mind. Thus, the primary impulses to speech carry with them of necessity the postulate of veracity, viz. that what is affirmed is thought, and what overflows as emotion is felt; nor do they contain any provision or opening for deviation; so long as they alone are with us, there can be only *truth* · the very meaning of which word will be unknown to us for want of any insincerity to show it off by contrast. This is what we mean when we say that veracity is *strictly natural*, i.e. it is implied in the very nature which leads us to intercommunion by speech. When regarded as present in duplicate in the two interlocutors, and operative as a tacit postulate with both, it may be taken as tantamount to a 'mutual understanding' between them. But the phrase is apt to mislead, by suggesting the conscious adoption by each of a rule against swerving from simplicity, which by hypothesis is thus far unconceived.

But, along with the impulses which incite us to open our minds to others through the vehicle of speech, we are subject to others which conflict with them, and require that our fellows should *not know* our belief and feeling, in regard to some matter of concern at once to them and us. Are we conscious of recent guilt? Shame urges us to hide our own sin. Are we grieving over the moral fall of a friend? Compassion impels us to hide his. Are we jealous of a rival who threatens to outstrip us? We must keep secret from him some advantageous information. Are we intent on realising a fortune by a happy stroke of speculation? An opportunity occurs of doing it by floating a misleading rumour upon 'change, or even perhaps by an equally misleading reticence. When such deflecting inducements prevail, they clear their way, not by any arms of their own, but by seizing the weapons of their defeated competitor they wield the instrument of speech and all the simple trust which leaves an open path before it, to gain the ends which they conceal; thus turning its postulate to its own ruin, and compelling it to lend confidence to their lies It is, perhaps, the peculiar *treachery* of this process which fixes upon falsehood a stamp of *meanness* quite exceptional, and renders it impossible, I think, to yield to its inducements, even in cases supposed to be venial, without a disgust little distinguishable from compunction. This must have been Kant's feeling when he said, 'A lie is the abandonment, or, as it were, annihilation of the dignity of man.'

The enquirer into the ground of this feeling naturally refers first to the violation of *good faith* involved in all unveracity. He points out that the social union itself rests on mutual trust, and falls to pieces on its failure: that we could not live together but by establishing and respecting the *rights of expectation;* and that no temporary gain, individual or public, can compensate for the irreparable injury of their violation. Such reasoning from the survey of general consequences has, no doubt, legitimate weight as a vindication of the admitted estimate of veracity; but, employing as it does a reflective public spirit of late origin, it is an anachronism as an explanation of that estimate in its birth. Concrete experience is the nursery lesson of ethical and philosophical conviction; and long before we have any idea of society and its conditions and needs, we hate to be cheated, and despise the liar whose victim we are. The feeling, in its social factors, is simply, on the one hand, *resentment for injury*, and, on the other, *hurt affection*, when the offender is in any sense an ally; and under the same aspects will sympathy reproduce it, when another is duped instead of ourselves. If an account so simple seems below the measure of so strong a feeling, it may well be that the bitterness of betrayed expectation passes with increased

VOL. II.   S

intensity from generation to generation, just as we see in countries where the Vendetta prevails, that the inherited feuds between families often become less appeasable as the sanguinary legacy descends The doctrine of heredity, in the sense of cumulative habit of thought and feeling, stored in the tendencies of the cerebral organism itself, has a fair application to mere growth of a homogeneous scale of power, so long as it does not attempt to *create* as well as *enlarge*, and undertake metamorphoses as great as would be needed to make the eye hear and the tongue see, and the hyæna acquire a conscience.

But, when we have given every advantage to the social factor of our feeling towards unveracity, there seems still to be something in its complexion which looks towards another source. Beyond our obligation to do each other no mischief, beyond the claims of reciprocal affection, it touches other relations, not so much within, as beyond our life. Whoever commits a breach of veracity belies two things: primarily, *his own beliefs and feelings;* but also, *the beliefs and feelings which are authorised by reality*, as accordant with the nature of things and the course of the world. He might persuade himself that with his own thoughts and emotions he had a right to do as he pleased, and that it was his concern to tell them or hide them or send them forth in disguise,—that they were a property and not a trust; that, at all events, if he had given his neighbour an interest in them, his management was an affair to be settled between the two and done with. But then, besides the agreement between thoughts and words, there is the agreement between thoughts and things; and into this relation too he has broken with spoiling and burglarious hands: he has tampered with the order of facts which God has made true · he wants us to think of them, not as they are, but as it suits him that we should imagine. He declines to accept the consequences of truth, and quarrels with the realised order of the world, as soon as he is hard pressed by it and it threatens to baffle his designs;

so, he rebels against it, and takes to the crooked ways of his own cunning. This, I conceive, is the element, other and more than simply social, which is felt to be involved in every lie, and which makes it not only a human delinquency, but *an impiety*,—a bold affront against the seat of all truth, the *source* and centre of all beauty and goodness. The exclamation of the Apostle Peter, 'Thou hast not lied unto men only, but unto God,' holds good of every lie; and it is the secret consciousness of this which mingles a certain religious shrinking with the shame and repugnance of all purposed falsehood. Veracity, therefore, wields the authority, not of social affection only, but of *Reverence* also: supported by the kindred sentiments that draw us to all intellectual light and spiritual beauty. Even in men without distinct theological belief, the high-minded rectitude which scorns pretence and loves a pure sincerity has not, I am persuaded, its foundation in the social benevolences, but is equivalent to an *unconscious religion*, a homage paid to a perfection that has rightful hold of the universe and is the inward reality of all appearance. In its explicit form, this image of Moral Right no longer represents itself as a collective conscience of mankind, or as an abstract law and order, but *lives* in the will and personality of God. Were veracity commended to men only by social affection and pressure of opinion, it would rest within the limits of human relations, and cast no look beyond. Yet in all ages and nations it has sought the temples for shelter, and ratified the contracts of the market by the prayer at the shrine, and under the form of vows and oaths betrayed the consciousness that other eyes than those of human kind kept watch over simplicity of word and the purity of truth. The superstitions which have clustered around such usages and perverted their meaning and operation may demand their revision, or their removal from some particular applications; but cannot cancel their testimony to the psychological origin of the estimate of veracity in something more than the social relations.

Here, however, a question may naturally be suggested which our exposition must not evade. If veracity is put under the protection of the *highest* spring of action, it would seem to be *unconditionally* obligatory; for no inferior must be permitted to supplant it; and superior it has none Are we then precluded from even considering such pleas of exception as moralists have held to justify the practice of deception in extreme cases, where nothing else can save life, or its best contents, for ourselves or for our friend? Must the enemy, the murderer, the madman, be enabled to wreak his will upon his victim by our agency in putting him on the right track? Must the physician not mind killing his patient to-day by telling him that his malady will take him off within a year? These exceptions are usually and easily vindicated on utilitarian principles, when the balance of social advantage has alone to be considered; but are supposed to be excluded *à priori* by every doctrine of intuitive morality. Whether room can be found for them within such doctrine depends, however, upon the exact scope of the assumed intuition; we must ask, 'What is it precisely that it authorises and bids us take on trust?' Let us, then, carry this question to each of the two sources in our nature for the felt authority of veracity, the one for relative truth, the other for reality, viz the common postulate of language, and the claims upon us of the objective order of the world.

The postulate or 'common understanding' (as it is called) involved in speech is certainly coextensive, in the obligation which it carries, with the social organism of which language is the instrument, and the ends of which it is an effort to subserve. But what is the extent of that organism? Does it include all who can speak and construe speech? Is there no other qualification for membership than command of the vernacular tongue? Not so; for many who exercise this function every society cuts off from itself, and holds in durance, or drives away as outlaws whose rights are forfeited. If the protection of law ceases to represent them as they are not. the obligation it involves appears to place us face to face with nature and its facts alone, and to have no dependence on the absence or intrusive presence of external witnesses of that relation. It is not so, however; for the relation, so conceived, would be complete *if we were silent;* our reverence for the Divine order of reality and inward conformity with it are satisfied, if only our thought agrees with the attitude of things. The additional act of *speech* has reference to a foreign presence, —of one who wants to make the relation break silence, that he may know what we think; and thereby a second relation is introduced, not between nature and ourselves as *studious of nature*, but between ourselves and him as *studious of us;* and the question, how we should behave under this second relation, is by no means unconditioned by the character and claims of the person who would draw our thought from us. If he be within the pale of the 'common understanding,'—a real member of the social organism which it serves,—to him I am certainly bound to bear witness of fact as I conceive it, and so to put him and nature into right relations. But if, beneath a mask which I detect, I see the features of a 'false brother,' and know that he seeks access to the truth in order to desecrate it, and that the more I give him command of the right relations with things, so much the more will he plunge into the wrong ones, then I am not disloyal to the real order of affairs in the world if I keep it from him, even by telling him something else: on the contrary, I uphold the inmost spirit of that order, by preventing its being turned into an accomplice of crime; and I should be a traitor to it, if I delivered its loaded arms into a villain's hands. Nay, he himself might thank me, if he were not blind; for the ignorance or misconception in which I leave him saves him from far worse ill: I keep him nearer to nature than if I had taken sides with his aberrations and forwarded him on his lost way. Whoever has no care for reality except as a fulcrum in action against its law, is at enmity with nature for him who sets at defiance the ends of law, no less may the protection of the 'common understanding' cease for him who sets at defiance the co-operative ends of that common understanding : if in the one case the courts of judicature, in the other the court of morals, may remove him from 'the body politic' as not a member but a parasite. After incurring banishment beyond the pale of the social organism, he can no longer claim the shelter of its obligations ; for these cease at the confines of the moral commonwealth which they guard. On the area of every human society, and mixed with its throngs, there are always some who are thus *in* it, but not *of* it, who are there, not to serve it, but to prey upon it, to use its order for the impunity of disorder, and wrest its rights into opportunities of wrong. Assassins, robbers, enemies with arms in their hands, madmen, are beyond the pale; and the same principle applies to those who try to turn the postulate of speech to the defeat of its own ends, and through its fidelity compel it to play the traitor. Such persons, we surely may say, can no more claim the benefit of 'the common understanding,' than could a spy who, by stealing the password eludes the sentry's vigilance and makes his notes of the disposition of the lines, expect to be treated as a comrade, if he be found out. The immunity and protection of the camp are not for him; he has nothing in reserve but a short shrift and a high gallows. If then, there are persons to whom, on this principle, we are not bound to tell the truth, it is not that the intuitive rule of veracity is broken down by the admission of *exceptions:* we have not put these people into the rule, and then taken them out again: they have never been within its scope at all ; for its defined range was that of a social organism, in which indeed they may be present, but to which they do not belong.

The other factor in the authority of veracity presents at first view a more inflexible aspect. Reverence for things as they are seems hopelessly incompatible with all liberty no less than with man; and her secrets are not for him. Reverence itself, therefore, seems to authorise concealment of fact from such as he; nor is the religious regard for truth one whit less intuitive for refusing to lose sight of the ground and meaning of its sanctity, and to be tricked by verbal semblances into apostacy from it. No one imagines that the range of its normal obligations extends to the insane, so far as they are insane. They too are human: they too can ask and answer in forms of speech; but, from the condition of their mind, they are not of the community of whose fellowship in faculty and life the postulates of language and the homage to truth are the expression and the guardians; and so they are left out, and necessarily treated by other rules, framed with large concessions to their humours. We do but follow, therefore, a recognised precedent, if we contract the boundary line still further, and say that without a certain *moral consensus* the commonwealth of truth cannot be constituted, and cannot be entered.

The exact limits of this moral consensus it is impossible to define *à priori;* the phenomena of character are so variously mixed that they will be perpetually slipping through all our hard verbal lines; and a sympathetic tact will read the natural classification more truly than the most accurate analysis. Nor can the permissible cases of resort to falsehood be determined without careful attention to the canon of consequences. It is thus that we must settle whether, for example, they go no further than the criminal in open defiance of the law, or include also persons who thrust themselves into unwelcome intercourse with us to worm out our secret. Such persons cannot be regarded as external to the social organism, like its predatory enemies; yet, so far as they overstrain the rights which it confers and seize them without compliance with their conditions, they commit temporary inroads of hostility which, during their occurrence, may be held to forfeit its usual protection. If then they press me with an unwarrantable question which I can neither answer truly, nor refuse to answer, without betraying a confidence accepted as sacred, can I tell a guiltless lie? Problems like this, which terminate in establishing working rules of conduct fitted to the exigencies of life, must find their solution in the rational estimate of results. Among those results, it is usual to deprecate as dangerous any such weakening of an absolute rule as must ensue, if once we admit a limit to its application. But surely, in all applied theory, i.e. in all arts, where the cases differ in their data, the rules of practice must differ too. Nor is it clear that anything but benefit could arise from the establishment of a *no-confidence rule* against the spies and intriguers of society, so as to frustrate their skill in capturing truth by ambuscade or wringing it out by torture On this point, Professor Sidgwick justly remarks 'It is not necessarily an evil that men's confidence in each other's assertions should, *under certain peculiar circumstances*, be impaired or destroyed: it may even be the very result which we should most desire to produce: (*e.g.*) it is obviously a most effective protection for legitimate secrets that it should be universally understood and expected that those who ask questions which they have no right to ask will have lies told to them: nor again, should we be restrained from pronouncing it lawful to meet deceit with deceit, merely by the fear of impairing the security which rogues now derive from the veracity of honest men[1].'

Yet, after all, there is something in this problem which refuses to be thus laid to rest; and in treating it, it is hardly possible to escape the uneasiness of a certain moral inconsequence. If we consult the casuist of Common Sense, he usually tells us that, in theory, Veracity can have no exceptions; but that, in practice, he is brought face to face with at least a few; and he cheerfully accepts a dispensation, when required, at the hands of Necessity. I confess rather to an inverse experience. The theoretic

[1] Methods of Ethics, III. chap. vii. § 3, p. 319.

reasons for certain limits to the rule of veracity appear to me unanswerable; nor can I condemn anyone who acts in accordance with them. Yet, when I place myself in a like position, at one of the crises demanding a deliberate lie, an unutterable repugnance returns upon me, and makes the theory seem shameful. If brought to the test, I should probably act rather as I think than as I feel; without, however, being able to escape the stab of an instant compunction and the secret wound of a long humiliation. Is this the mere weakness of superstition? It may be so. But may it not also spring from an ineradicable sense of a common humanity, still leaving social ties to even social aliens, and, in the presence of an imperishable fraternal unity, forbidding to the individual of the moment the proud right of spiritual ostracism? Is it permissible to feel that outlawry, though a political necessity, is not an institute of the Divine Commonwealth, at the disposal of every citizen in the kingdom of heaven? How could I ever face the soul I had deceived, when perhaps our relations are reversed, and he meets my sins, not with self-protective repulse, but with winning love? And if with thoughts like these there also blends that inward reverence for reality which clings to the very essence of human reason and renders it incredible, *à priori*, that falsehood should become an implement of good, it is perhaps intelligible how there may be an irremediable discrepancy between the dioptric certainty of the understanding and the immediate insight of the conscience: not all the rays of spiritual truth are refrangible; some there are beyond the intellectual spectrum, that wake invisible response and tremble in the dark.

§ 13. *Table of Springs of Action.*

It may be useful to collect the results of our survey of the springs of action into a tabular form. The following list presents the series in the ascending order of worth: the chief composite springs being inserted in their approximate place, subject to the variations of which their composition renders them susceptible.

LOWEST.

1. Secondary Passions;—Censoriousness, Vindictiveness, Suspiciousness.
2. Secondary Organic Propensions;—Love of Ease and Sensual Pleasure.
3. Primary Organic Propensions;—Appetites.
4. Primary Animal Propension;—Spontaneous Activity (unselective).
5. Love of Gain (reflective derivative from Appetite).
6. Secondary Affections (sentimental indulgence of sympathetic feelings).
7. Primary Passions;—Antipathy, Fear, Resentment.
8. Causal Energy;—Love of Power, or Ambition, Love of Liberty.
9. Secondary Sentiments;—Love of Culture.
10. Primary Sentiments of Wonder and Admiration.
11. Primary Affections, Parental and Social;—with (approximately) Generosity and Gratitude.
12. Primary Affection of Compassion.
13. Primary Sentiment of Reverence.

HIGHEST.

§ 14. *How far a Life must be chosen among these.*

This scale of relations aims at exhibiting the duty of the moral agent in each crisis of competitive impulse, as it is given him; but it does not profess to measure the comparative value of the several springs of action in human life as a whole. To determine *this*, another factor, besides that of *Quality*, must be taken into account, viz. that of *frequency*. It is quite possible that the superior springs may have rarer opportunities of putting in their claims upon the will and directing their inferiors to retire; and then the nobler scenes which they mingle with the drama will be but brief heroic episodes in a piece of many level acts. And though even humble and unenvied lives are never without occasions for the play of conscience in its higher strain, yet the temptations recurring day by day bring on the battle further down; for example, against *the love of ease and pleasure* the resistance is more often set up by the *love of gain*, than by the intellectual impulses of *wonder and admiration;* and *resentment* is more commonly subdued, or at least smothered, by the fear of censure (i.e. the love of praise) than melted away by generous affection. It will not surprise us, therefore, if, in many a life that works an upward way, the part of πρωταγωνιστής is taken by some of the middle terms; and if, in the history of civilisation, they seem to fill the page through volumes, while for their superiors a chapter suffices here and there.

But though this may be a true account of the facts as they are, is it compatible with the foregoing doctrine of the moral consciousness to leave them so? Ought we to content ourselves with treating the springs of action as *our data*, with which we have nothing to do but to wait till they are flung upon us by circumstances, and then to follow the best that turns up? However needful it might be for us, as mere children of nature, thus to make what we could of them, as gifts of surprise, have we not, now that we are aware of their relative ranks, an earlier voice in their disposal, determining whether, and in what amount, this or that among them should come at all? Is all our care to be for the comparative *quality* of our incentives, and none for their *quantity*, i.e. the *proportion of our life and action which they control?* If compassion is always of higher obligation than the *love of gain* or *family affection*, how can a man ever be justified in quitting his charities for his business or his home? Ought he not, conformably with the rule, to live at the top of the climax and never descend? Or at any rate is there not *some* measure wanted, in order to determine how far the lower impulses are admissible without unfaithfulness? These are fair questions; and to meet them we must slightly qualify the hypothesis on which we have proceeded, viz. that we are to accept our rival incentives at the hands of circumstance and consider that our duty begins with their arrival. It is from this point that the portion of our moral experience commences which I wished to illustrate; but if there be at the command of our will, not only the selection of the better side of an alternative, but also a predetermination of what kind the alternative shall be, the range of our duty will undoubtedly be extended to the creation of a higher plane of circumstance, in addition to the higher preference within it. No parent is justified in placing his child, no youth in placing himself, in a position or occasion which is sure to abound in low temptations and to blunt and enfeeble the springs of action that would rally the will against them. And so far is this anxiety to mould the external conditions to the moral wants of life sometimes carried, that a profession reached through a costly training is abandoned, because it is not pure enough and disappoints the best affections; and some work is chosen which, it is supposed, will exercise only the supreme forms of love and reverence.

The limits, however, within which the higher moral altitudes can be secured by voluntary command of favouring circumstance are extremely narrow. Go where we may, we carry the most considerable portion of our environment with us in our own constitution; from whose propensions, passions, affections, it is a vain attempt to fly. The attempt to wither them up and suppress them by contradiction has ever been disastrous; they can be counteracted and disarmed and taught obedience only by preoccupation of mind and heart in other directions. Nothing but the enthusiasm of a new affection can silence the clamours of one already there. And though, by selection of employment, I may certainly keep myself out of contact with this or that type of temptation (for example, from love of gain by joining the Brotherhood of Communists), and immure myself for ever in the service of some one or two affections (for example, of compassion and devotion by taking the vows of an Order of Charity), yet experience shows that the total effect will be disappointing, and that the character will not reach the elevation to which I aspire. The sterility of one part of the nature is no security for the fruitfulness of the rest; and so intimate are its reciprocal relations, that it is impossible to live upon any one order of feelings: no sooner am I left alone with them to do only what they bid, than they begin to desert the very occupation they have prescribed, and turn it into a routine, or at best a skill and tact without inspiration. The true discipline of character lies in the various clashing of the involuntary and the voluntary, and the management of the surprises which it brings; and it is morally a fatal thing to be scared by the former element, and try to make it all into *self-discipline:* if we insist on commanding both the data and the quæsita of our problem, we turn the problem into a sham and introduce a dry rot into life. *Necessity is the best school of Free-will.* But it must be a *real*, and not a *self-imposed* necessity, or we shall be victims of a delusion and a snare. Let me support this judgment by a few sentences from a letter of the late James Clerk Maxwell (written at the age of twenty): 'There are advantages in *subordination*, besides good direction; for it supplies an *end* to each man, *external to himself.* Activity requires objectivity. Do you ever read books written by women about women? I mean fictitious tales, illustrating moral anatomy, by disclosing all thoughts, motives, and secret sins, as if the authoress were a perjured confessor? There you find all the "good" thinking about themselves, and plotting self-improvement from a sincere regard to their own interest; while the *bad* are most disinterestedly plotting against or for others, as the case may be: but all are caged-in and compelled to criticise one another till nothing is left, and you exclaim, "Madam!—if I know your sex,—By the fashion of your bones—." No wonder people get hypochondriac if their souls are made to go through manœuvres before a mirror. Objectivity alone is favourable to the free circulation of the soul. But let the object be real, and not an image of the mind's own creating; for idolatry is subjectivity with respect to gods. Let a man feel that he is wide awake,—that he has something to do, which he has authority, power, and will to do, and is doing: but let him not cherish a consciousness of these things as if he had them at his command, but receive them thankfully and use them strenuously, and exchange them freely for other objects. He has then a happiness which may be increased in degree, but cannot be altered in kind¹.'

It suffices, then, for us to admit to our questioner, that a man ought not to become so absorbed in his business or his studies as to leave no scope for the free movement of his higher affections and no time for the duties they enjoin. But this very obligation I would rather rest on the objective claims of the relations, human and Divine, which he is in danger of guiltily setting aside, than on the subjective need, in his self-formation, of being less a stranger to the upper storeys of his spiritual experience. Let him accept his lot, and work its resources with willing conscience: and he will emerge with no half-formed and crippled character.

§ 15. *Resulting Rule; compared with Bentham's.*

. We are now prepared for an exact definition of Right and Wrong; which will assume this form . *Every action is* RIGHT, *which, in presence of a lower principle, follows a higher: every action is* WRONG, *which, in presence of a higher principle, follows a lower.* Thus, the act attributed to Regulus, in returning back to death at Carthage, was right, because the reverence for veracity whence it sprung is a higher principle than any fear or personal affection which might have suggested a different course, and of which we tacitly conceive as competing with the former. And the act of St. Peter in denying Christ was wrong, because the fear to which he yielded was lower than the personal affection and reverence for truth which he disobeyed. The act of the missionaries of mercy,—whether of a Florence Nightingale to the stricken bodies, or of a Columban, a Boniface, a Livingstone, to the imperilled souls of men,—is right, because the compassion

¹ Campbell's Life of Maxwell, p. 177.

which inspires it is nobler than any love of ease or of self-culture which would resist it. The act of the manufacturer of adulterated or falsely-labelled goods is wrong, because done in compliance with an inferior incentive, the love of gain, against the protest of superiors, good faith and reverence for truth. This definition appears to me to have the advantage of simply stating what passes in all men's minds when they use the words whose meaning it seeks to unfold. I will not say that, in his judgment on such cases, *no one* ever thought, with Paley, of his 'everlasting happiness:' or, with Bentham, consulted the arithmetic of pleasures and pains and struck their balance; or, with Butler, took the question for solution to the autocratic oracle of conscience for an absolute 'Yea' or 'Nay.' But, for the most part, these accounts of our reasons seem to me artificially invented, and in very imperfect correspondence with the real history of our minds: particularly the first and third as ignoring the sense of *proportionate worth* among right things, and *proportionate heinousness* in wrong. No constant aim, no one royal faculty, no contemplated preponderance of happy effects, can really be found in all good action. More scope for variety is felt to be needed: and this is gained as soon as we quit the casuists' attempt to draw an *absolute dividing line* between good and bad, and recognise the relative and preferential conditions of every moral problem. This has been remarked as a requisite of any true moral theory by Hooker: 'In goodness,' he says, 'there is a latitude or extent, whereby it cometh to pass that even of good actions some are better than other some; whereas otherwise one man could not excel another, but all should be either absolutely good, as hitting jump that indivisible point or centre wherein goodness consisteth: or else missing it, they should be excluded out of the number of well-doers[1].' The exigencies of this truth are met at once by the fundamental principle of the foregoing doctrine, viz. that, our nature comprising a graduated scale of principles

[1] Eccles. Polity, I. p. 14 (folio edition).

of action, of which a plurality presents itself at the crisis of every problem, our moral estimates are always comparative.

In the practical use of this definition for the settlement of moral problems, difficulties, I am well aware, will often arise. The conditions of these problems are liable to be so complex, and so mixed with unmoral elements, that their exact determination is beyond the reach of any criterion. Hence it is not unusual for ethical writers,—as is the case with Paley,—to lay down their definition, and immediately run away from it, and call it into no active service. With Bentham this is not the case: he sets up his theory, not as a philosophical invention to be put by under a glass case, but as a working machinery to be thrown into gear with the facts of human life. And by compelling our rule to take its stand side by side with his, and give in its answer to the same cases, its method will be illustrated and its position tried by the severest test of comparison.

Bentham, we must premise, draws a distinction, which it is of prime importance to note, between the *Motive* and the *Intention* of a voluntary act. The *Intention* comprises the whole contemplated operations of the act, both those for the sake of which, and those in spite of which, we do it. The *Motive* comprises only the former. Now as these can be nothing but some pleasures or advantages intrinsically worth having, and allowable, where there is no set-off on the other side, there can be no such thing as *a bad motive*: the thief and the honest trader both have the same spring to their industry, the love of gain; and if that were all, both would be equally respectable. The difference lies in the residuary part of the intention; viz. the privation and injury to others, which fails to restrain the thief and does restrain the merchant. To judge, therefore, of the morality of an act we must look, Bentham insists, not at its motive in particular, but at its *whole intention;* and we must pronounce every act right (relatively to the agent) which is performed with intention of consequences predominantly pleasurable.

To bring this account into closer comparison with our own definition, we may conveniently divide the whole intention into three parts, viz. the *persuasives*, the *dissuasives*, and the neutral consequences. The last we may throw out of consideration, as inoperative. The *persuasives*, or *motive*, will then agree with what we have called the principle or spring of action to which we yield. If the rest are felt as dissuasives, it is because they are repugnant to some affection or other natural impulse: which, as its pleading is in vain, is thrust aside and excluded by the importunity of the successful principle. Here, therefore, in the dissuasive part of the intention, we have our baffled competitor of the victorious spring of action.

With these substitutions and correspondences, the two rules may be exhibited in very near concurrence. In casting up your account, says Bentham, you must take in the whole of the intention, and strike the balance of its good and evil: i.e. you must weigh the *good included in the motive* against the *good excluded by the rest of the intention*. This is only to say, that you must compare the principle on which the agent does act with that on which, as he is aware, he might act; and must pronounce him moral or immoral according as the one or the other is higher in the scale.

Take an instance or two. A man who is trustee for a minor swindles his ward out of £10,000. Bentham says, *his motive* is not bad, viz. to gain £10,000,—the very same that may actuate the upright merchant: but *the rest of the intention* is bad, viz. to occasion loss and suffering to others preponderant over the benefit to himself; therefore the act is wrong. Our rule would present the case thus: the principle of action admitted (i.e. the motive) is the *love of money;* the principle of action excluded (i.e. the residue of the intention) is the *sense of justice and good faith:* of the two, the former stands lower in the scale: therefore the act is wrong. Again: a man sacrifices a fortune of £10,000 to pay his father's debts. Motive, to do justice: additional intention, to endure privations, overbalanced by benefit to others: act good. Or, as we should state it: principle of action admitted, *sense of justice:* principle of action rejected, *love of riches and their enjoyment:* the former being higher than the other, the act is virtuous.

So far the two rules are not practically at variance, and may seem to have no important difference. But now, introduce a new element into the last case which we have put: let the son who pays his father's debts, all other persuasives and dissuasives remaining as before, have a lively sense of the applause which his act will win, and reckon on it with eager relish. What is the effect of this modification, according to Bentham's method of estimate? The praise contemplated from the act is a new pleasure thrown in, and, when we take our valuation of the whole intention, helps to swell the favourable side of the account. The act, therefore, would appear to be better than before, and to be open to further improvement in proportion as the privations encountered by the agent's self-denial can be reduced. I need hardly say how completely such a judgment runs counter to the natural verdict of mankind. Try the case by the other rule. The principle of action *rejected* remains the same as before: the principle of action *admitted*, partially the same, is qualified by the accession of the *love of praise;* which, being lower than the incentive on which it is superinduced, can have no effect but to deteriorate it. The interval which separates the competing principles being thus reduced, the act receives a less positive approbation. Here, therefore is a case of direct discrepancy between the two rules; and it evidently represents a very large class, viz. all instances in which good to others is reached at the cost of sacrifice to oneself. The sacrifice abates by the one rule, and enhances by the other, the excellence of the act.

It must be further observed that Bentham's rule applies only to actions performed with deliberate *intention* or *end-in-view;* and does not provide any method of estimate for *impulsive* expression in character, unless by excluding it from the sphere of morals altogether. Yet assuredly this is a prevalent type of human conduct, and more or less mixes itself with the steadiest execution of preconceived aims: nor do we ever hesitate to judge men by the natural language it puts forth, and to regulate by it the direction and intensity of our appreciation of them. The mere unintentional overflow of good affections, the unconscious tact of a pure and gentle heart, the scorn of temptation which makes no reckoning with the future but simply flings aside a present solicitation, are regarded with spontaneous respect and approbation by all observers. It is only by fixing attention on the conscious principle instead of the contemplated tendency of action, that interpretation and defence can be found of this natural sentiment.

Finally, before dismissing our comparison of the two rules, it may be well to point out the true function and place of Bentham's. 'Is there *no room*,' I may be asked, 'in morals for the computation of pleasurable and painful consequences at all?' Undoubtedly there is: in two ways First, the computation is already more or less involved in the preference of this or that spring of action; for in proportion as the springs of action are self-conscious, they contemplate their own effects, and judgment upon them is included in our judgment on the disposition. Secondly: when the principle of action has been selected, to the exclusion of all competitors, the problem may still be indeterminate; because, under the given external conditions, the very same principle may express and satisfy itself in various methods: the benevolence, for example, which in one man is foolish and defeats itself, in another is wise and accomplishes its ends. The choice of *means* by which to carry out the workings of a spring of conduct can be made only by consideration of consequences. This subsidiary rule, however, must be regarded as rather of an intellectual than of a moral nature, for if a man err in its application, he will be mistaken only, and will not be a proper object of disapprobation. Thus, in the solution of all ethical problems, we have successive recourse to two distinct rules: viz. the *Canon of Principles*, which gives the true *Moral criterion* for determining the *right* of the case; and then, the *Canon of Consequences*, which gives the *Rational criterion* for determining its *wisdom*. The former suffices for the estimate of *Character;* but, for the estimate of *Conduct*, must be supplemented by the latter.

CHAPTER VII.

OBJECTIONS CONSIDERED.

INTRODUCTION.

In sketching the outline of a scheme of psychological ethics, I have not disguised the intricacy of the task, or regarded it as more than a mere tentative in the direction which, I am persuaded, affords the only hope of a doctrine true at once to the inward and the outward experience of mankind. It is most desirable that the difficulties with which it is encumbered should be placed in the strongest light, and set off against any pleas which it can urge on its own behalf; and I regard myself as singularly fortunate in finding so eminent and so fair a critic to state them as Professor Sidgwick; who has devoted to this purpose the twelfth chapter of Book III. of his 'Methods of Ethics.' His remarks, though suggested by a few paragraphs only in a Review slightly hinting the doctrine in its first conception, apply so well to its more developed form that I cannot excuse myself from estimating them. Though unwillingly deviating from exposition into self-defence, I have too profound a respect for my critic to pass his strictures without careful appreciation.

This appreciation would be more easy, if I could clearly see the exact limits of Professor Sidgwick's deference to an intuitive apprehension. A reasoner who unconditionally denies the existence, or at least the authority, of any such thing, necessarily builds up all human belief and sentiment out of objective experience, and, in the treatment of ethics, evolves all feeling from sensible elements, and carries all questions to Utilitarian standards. A reasoner who distinguishes from derivative beliefs and incentives certain primary ones which, being beyond the reach of external test, are to be taken on trust, accepts whatever is authenticated by these subjective criteria, and conceives himself to have, besides the data of perception, data also of intuition. He is bound, however, both to specify distinctly the range and contents of these necessary assumptions, and to behave towards them with unwavering consistency; and this it is which I seem to miss in Professor Sidgwick's treatment. He does not relinquish the intuitive doctrine, or dispense with it in laying the foundation of morals. He accepts from it the idea of *Right*, pronouncing it to be 'ultimate and unanalysable[1],' and thus allows it to put the essential meaning into all moral propositions. He further recognises in our nature a number of given impulses or instinctive tendencies towards appropriate objects. He attaches the sense of duty to the inward experience of these, saying distinctly, 'Conflict seems also to be implied in the terms "ought," "duty," "moral obligation," as used in ordinary moral discourse: and hence these terms cannot be applied to the actions of rational beings to whom we cannot attribute impulses conflicting with reason[2].' And again, 'The question of duty is never raised except when we are conscious of a conflict of impulses, and wish to know which to follow[3].' He admits that, of these impulses only one (and that doubtfully) can occupy the dark side of a dual classification into good and bad, and that all the rest have, as motives, different grades of worth[4]. He thinks that the admiration felt for particular virtues, as bravery, justice, &c. had not its origin in any perception of consequent advantages from them, and that the further back we trace this admiration, the less shall we find any tincture in it of Utilitarian considerations[5]. Yet the intuitive sense of right leaves us in the dark as to *what is right*, not in conduct only, but in feeling. And the several impulses, though revealing a gradation, cannot report their degrees. And the moral admirations, though born of other parentage,

[1] Methods of Ethics, Third Edition, I. chap. iii. § 3, p. 33.
[2] Ibid. I. iii. § 3, last par. p. 35.
[3] Ibid. I. vi. § 2, p. 75.
[4] Ibid. III. chap. xii. § 1, p. 364.
[5] Ibid. IV. chap. iii. § 7, pp. 453, 454.

have no *raison d'être* but in the reckoning of utility. I confess to a certain uneasiness in following this see-saw procedure. Too much is conceded in it to intuitive moral consciousness to begin with, to be afterwards nullified or handed over for estimate to the Actuaries of social insurance. If there be a provision in our nature, other than reflection upon experienced effects, for the recognition of *moral distinctions of character*, and if, at the same time, it proves inadequate to the exact determining of problems of *applied morals*, the probability indicated by this posture of facts surely is, that Ethics have two sides,—a Rationale within the mind, and a Criterion out of it: the one, a law of character, the other, of conduct; and that, for their full exhibition, there needs a double construction, viz a subjective *Moral* canon, and an objective *Rational* one. It is possible enough to show that, if with the first alone we attack the problems of the second, we find ourselves in 'a nest of paradoxes:' but since we are no better off with the second in dealing with the questions of the first, it seems arbitrary to make the one abdicate for its defects, and enthrone the other in spite of them. Whatever be the flaw in either limb of a pair of scissors, it is a poor reason for taking out the screw and throwing away one of them Professor Sidgwick does not absolutely do this, because he retains as intuitive the one *idea of Right:* but, in order to learn *what is right*, he resorts to a source,—Utility,—which could not give the idea itself. He thus seems open to the same question which he presses against our doctrine: 'What avails it to recognise the superiority of the impulse to do justice, if we do not know what it is just to do¹?' May I not reply, 'What avails it to recognise the authority of Right, if it does not tell us what it is right to do?'

§ 1. *Is the Love of Virtue among the Springs of Action?*

The first criticism is couched in the form of a question: among the springs of action are 'the moral motives,' or

¹ Methods of Ethics, III. chap. xii. § 2, pp. 366, 367.

'impulses towards different kinds of virtuous conduct,' to be included? Professor Sidgwick is led to ask this question, because Hutcheson answers it in the affirmative, and I in the negative; and he has an answer ready for both. If the love of truth, the love of justice, the love of virtue, are reckoned in, then an impulse to realise them will be an impulse to do what is true, what is just, what is virtuous. But the contents of these conceptions are in their extension indeterminate, i.e. the actions to which they apply are indefinitely various, and are not indicated by the conceptions themselves, but have to be selected by external, i.e. utilitarian considerations; so that the impulse only sends you at last to the umpire that you might as well consult at first. Or, if the case should be so limited as to tie down the conception to a single action, then there will be a dispute between the impulses themselves; veracity, e.g. will have its advocates against benevolence; and benevolence against veracity; and it will be found that the debate will continue till brought before utility as its judge.

If, on the other hand, the loves of the virtues are *not* reckoned in among the impulses compared, these perplexities, it is true, are escaped; but at the cost of an inexcusable paradox; since in a well-trained mind the love of virtue certainly plays the part of a distinct impulse with its own peculiar satisfaction. Nay, such stress does Kant (in common with other moralists of Stoical tendency) lay upon this impulse, that he allows no acts to be moral except such as are done purely from it. Hutcheson makes common cause with Kant against its exclusion; but parts from him to set benevolence on an equal footing with it and commit the moral constitution, like Sparta, to two kings. Nor are these the only divergencies to which the method gives rise. The place of *self-love* is variously assigned: by Kant, excluded from all community with the moral reason: by Butler, admitted to an authority parallel with that of conscience; and by others, allowed, under the name of *prudence*, to rank, though not very high, among virtuous impulses.

For Hutcheson's answer to the question, 'Are we to include the moral motives?' I am not responsible; and it will not escape an attentive reader that Professor Sidgwick's objections to it do but express in other terms the remark with which I have closed almost every analysis of a composite spring of action involving general conceptions; viz. that its best concrete application cannot be determined without consulting the canon of consequences. This only will I add. While agreeing that the mere felt superiority of justice will not in itself secure our doing what is just, I cannot admit the inference that it is *unavailing*. When I am tempted to accept an advantage over a rival by letting some known calumny against him circulate uncontradicted in my presence, is it of no avail to me that I honour his claim upon me and feel the relative shame of silence? Blot out at that moment my sense of the superiority of justice, and would it make no difference in my volition? and even where the particular act which will realise justice is not clear to me, the impulse towards it is no more unavailing than, on the intellectual side of my nature, *the impulse to apprehend truth* is unavailing, during my ignorance of what is true. As in this case we are incited to find the true, so, in the other, we are incited to discover, that we may realise, the just.

My own answer to the same question might well appear to be paradoxical, if understood to deny that any one is ever influenced by an anxiety to do right, or not to fail in this or that particular type of duty,—be it 'candour, veracity, or fortitude.' That no such denial is involved in it will be evident on reference to the doctrine of prudence and conscience, and to the reasons assigned for not placing these among the given 'springs of action,' but treating them as two different modes of relating these springs of action *inter se*. But I will endeavour to make these reasons clearer, without repeating what has already been said.

By 'springs of action' (in the exact sense required for theory), I mean an impulse towards any *unselected form of activity*, i.e. any which might instinctively arise, though there were no other possible to the same nature, or at all events present at the same time. Under such instigation, the nature is *propelled* forward by a want towards it knows not what: the relief of that want imparts a pleasure which, if there be memory, adds itself on as an idea to the spring of action, and increases its intensity when it recurs What before was a movement of mere *need*, now becomes a movement *of desire;* but, if the scope of the living being goes no further, this is all the increment he will receive; and he will be absolutely disposed of by this datum. Give him a second spring, and the same tale comes over again; and if the two take possession of him on different days, his life will simply be made up of a double set of phenomena of similar type, though of differing contents. Throw the two springs together upon the same point of time they cannot both have him; and if he be a mere animal, surrendered to instincts, the intenser will carry the day; but if he have self-conscious reason and will, he will not let the case settle itself without comparison of the two incentives; and, if all differences of value are to him hedonistic, he will go with the impulse of pleasantest promise. Here then steps in a new factor, which gets rid of suspense and gives the act its determinate direction: what are we to call this intruder? Is it a third 'spring?' Does it earn that name by possessing the defining characteristics of the other two? Not so; for each of them is unconditioned by the presence of the other, whereas here is something impossible without them both they have no selective function: it has nothing else: they are blind to their own resulting experiences: it consists in seeing and measuring them. It is, therefore, not a fresh impulse, but a preference between two given ones. The more springs of action are crowded into the nature, the more numerous these instances of choice, sometimes correctly made, sometimes missing their aim: but as they are (by hypothesis) all made on the same differentiating ground, viz. pleasure, we generalise this idea and make a class of them, under

Chap VII.] IDIOPSYCHOLOGICAL ETHICS. 283

the name of pursuit of pleasure or advantage, and set up *self-love* as an imaginary newcomer upon the list of natural springs, though it is nothing but the abstract sum of all the likings already reckoned in the original springs themselves. Choice made upon these data is *prudential:* the habit of making it without mistake is *Prudence* · which therefore might exist under conditions anterior to the existence of moral relations at all; and cannot carry in its essence the characteristics of a virtue, though as little able as any other neutral element to escape the consecrating light of an all-embracing moral atmosphere.

For this end we must enlarge our intelligent Agent's world. When the two springs of action meet within him, he knows them to have a difference other than hedonistic, which speaks to something else than his likings: there is a second scale on which they stand, the one higher than the other, in a new order of values, defining their relative claims upon his will. If, concentrating himself upon this new order, he gives himself to the higher authority and lets the other go, he again gets rid of his suspense by the same third factor as before, viz a volition, only dealing this time with differences unknown before. Is this volition, then, a third 'spring,' any more than the former one? Not so; for it has all the same disqualifications, and, like its predecessor, is a choice between two compared springs; the comparison turning, in the two cases, upon different qualities. In the one case, he wills in a certain way, *because it is pleasant:* in the other, *because it is right*. But this feeling of the right, which is expressed in his volition, is as yet an *unnamed feeling*, which he has but does not know. As repeated instances occur of conflict similarly surmounted, the elements and the story of temptation become familiar and clear to the self-consciousness, and the feeling of right disengages itself by repetition into pretty distinct view as a generalised *conception*[1]; which may then become

[1] This word is open to objection; but cannot well be mended here, without going into interrupting refinements.

an object of thought and interest irrespective of concrete examples of its presence, and enable us to speak of moral phenomena collectively, and to direct emotions upon them as a class. This brings us to the state of mind which we call the '*love of right.*' In its self-application, it is a desire *for right preference under temptation*, i.e. to follow the higher of two or more solicitations to the will. Let us consider, then, in what sense this can be called a separate and independent impulse. When once I have been furnished with this generalisation, I shall go into every particular moral trial with the conception in my mind, and with the desire that, among the competitors about to appeal to my will, I may accept the highest. But this forecasting interpretation of my coming experience, bringing it under a general rule, does but reduplicate my sense of superiority in the higher principle, and exhibit it to me as a particular instance of an authority of wider scope. If I am now said to will in a certain way *because it is right*, the phrase has a changed meaning; denoting conformity not simply with an *unnamed feeling*, but with *a named conception of it as well*. But the superiority to which I yield myself is the same as before; and this is no more a new spring of action than the law of gravitation, when defined, supplies a new force added on to that by which the rain falls. If it were a new impulse, it could be compared with the old one, and even, in virtue of its difference, come into collision with it; but the *preference for right is* the preference for the superior of the competing springs of action in each case, and therefore in this case, and does but designate the same volition under another name. Hence I cannot admit either the *loves of virtues*,—of 'candour, veracity, fortitude,'—or the virtues themselves, as so many additional impulses over and above those from the conflict of which they are formed. I do not confess my fault *in order to be candid*, or encounter danger *in order to be brave*, or resist temptation *in order to be virtuous*, and give a sample of what virtue is. Unless I am a prig, I never think of candour, or virtue, as predicable, or going to be predicable, of me at all; but, *having to act*, I simply take the nearest thing that comes commended to me in the form of duty. So far as these qualities influence my volition, it is not as new impulses, but as old habits, predisposing me to repeat a familiar mode of choice, and concede to my will the mechanical advantage of its acquired momentum. But the fact that formed dispositions tend to self-continuance, and abate the precariousness of volitions under surprise, is very inaccurately expressed by calling these instances of inertia 'in well-trained minds' so many 'distinct and independent impulses[1].' For these reasons I think it inadmissible, after arranging the hierarchy of impulses, and discovering their common difference, to treat this as an omitted term, and foist it in among the series. It is true that in the tabulated list of springs of action which I have given, a few appear which are not primitive, but, like the love of this or that virtue, formed by cumulative experience and abstraction. They are allowed to be there, however, not in virtue of any difference between a general conception and a concrete instance; but because they are composite, borrowing elements from a plurality of springs occupying different positions on the scale, and therefore having a value not identical with that of any member of the list.

§ 2. *Intuitive Moralists do not agree, as to*

A. BENEVOLENCE AND MORAL SENSE.—Professor Sidgwick's next objection to the method which he criticises I cannot feel to be a very serious reproach, since it associates me with such powerful protectors as Butler, Kant, and Hutcheson. He says that we do not agree among ourselves: that one of the incentives which I ignore,—Self-love,—is invested by Butler with half the authority of morals; and another, 'the desire to do right as right,' by Kant with the whole of it: while Hutcheson will not accept Kant's principle unless he may install benevolence

[1] Methods of Ethics, III. chap. xii. § 2, p. 366.

into equal partnership with it. These differences, even when placed in the strongest light, do not appear greater than are found in the writings of eminent Utilitarians, or than must be expected in all early attempts at exact psychological analysis: and, when traced back, behind the phrases which emphasise them, to their position and meaning in the author's mind, they seem to be by no means hopelessly irreconcilable. One common feature strikes us at a glance; viz. that with all these writers an intuitive apprehension of duty stands on the highest level of authority,—under the name of 'conscience' with Butler, of 'pure regard for the moral law' with Kant, and of 'the moral sense' with Hutcheson. All these phrases do but sum up, in generalised terms, the *pervading consciousness of higher authority* which I have described as running through the whole scale of impulses, and as constituting the conscience as soon as its component experiences are collected. In each instance of rejected temptation, the ground of the volition is nothing else than this consciousness of imperative authority in the incentive; and the Kantian condition is fulfilled in our experiences, taken one by one, though it may be long before we know by name the feeling we obey, and can formulate our way of choice as a verbal rule. The same remark applies to Hutcheson's 'moral sense;' what the 'moral sense' feels, or what we feel *quâ moral*, is the element of binding superiority distinguishing impulse from impulse throughout. And when he co-ordinates *benevolence* with the moral sense, he takes benevolence, not in the sense of the bare social affection, as it might exist in an unmoral world, but as devotion to the total good of others having a common moral life with ourselves; and then the meaning of his dual or rather alternative headship is simply this: that the same work may be wrought out either by *love* or by *duty*, and that what is *right for each of us* will be found to *make up the good of all*. To this I have nothing in principle to object. As no one could contribute more to the well-being of others than he who should never fall short in any virtue, it would not matter to a perfectly clear thinker at which end he began to reason out his perfect type of life,—whether from the standard of personal conscience to benevolence towards others; or, *vice versa*, from benevolence towards others to personal duty: the product either way would be the same. It is not so much the essence as *the form* of this doctrine that is unsatisfactory. If it assumes benevolence to be *obligatory*, and reasons from it as such, till it covers the whole ground of conscientious life, it provides for the obligation of duty twice over, viz. once in the shape of benevolence, and again in the shape of 'the moral sense.' If it does not assume this, but takes benevolence simply as altruistic *affection*, no reasoning from it can ever pick up the *idea of duty* by the way, and if the same things are reached which lie within the area of the moral sense, their *meaning* will not be there, for their *obligation* is not provided for at all. Nor can I believe that, in a world not consisting of 'angelic doctors,' the altruistic affection could be substituted for the sense of duty distributed through the hierarchy of impulses, with any chance of practically producing the same result. There are numerous inconspicuous particulars of personal feeling and habit, by no means insignificant as elements of character, which are so private and apparently absorbed into the air of solitude, as to be overtaken, if at all, only by the most remote and subtle inferences from social benevolence. Nor could any progress towards such inference be made without stepping at once from the moral canon to the rational, and working along the lines of utility. This is a legitimate process, if kept within limits, and employed to determine the best objective application of springs of action intuitively approved; and if there be many of these springs of given worth, the appendix of *applied ethics* will not be of long range for each, or of unmanageable scope for all. But if one alone is taken as the germ which is to yield the whole universe of *applied ethics*, the moral canon is almost idle, and the rational is overworked; and hence, as

Professor Sidgwick remarks, the difference is not very great between Hutcheson and the modern Utilitarians[1].

B. SELF-LOVE.—The divergent estimates of *Self-love* among intuitive moralists are less easily resolved; and I cannot plead unconditionally for either Kant's position or Butler's, much less for both. Still, the interval between them is greatly reduced, when we closely observe what exactly it is that each denotes by the word '*self-love*:' for it is by no means one and the same quality that by Kant is opposed to the moral sense and by Butler co-ordinated with it. Under this name the former has in view the mere desire of happiness which belongs to us as sentient beings, and would exist and operate if our constitution went no further than this. Its end, therefore, is one which could be gained in the total absence of a moral nature, and cannot be the object of that nature. Thus understood, the opposition in which Kant places Self-love and Conscience is essentially just, and does but mark the contrast which I tried to bring out in the analysis of Prudence. The *Self*, on the other hand, which Butler supposes to be loved, is *the total human being*, not only with a conscience added to his sentient capabilities, but with knowledge of its place, its rights, its meaning in his nature, and, further, with the whole tissue of his relations towards his fellows complete around him, and under the known Divine moral government of the world. He also assumes the *Love* which is directed upon this complete being to be so 'cool,' 'deliberate,' and wise, as to embrace in its view *all the elements of his welfare*, including every eligible quality of character, and all harmonious relations with men and God. Against *such* self-love, supposing it to exist and operate successfully as an impulse, it may well be difficult to name a motive which could require us to act. As it includes the whole moral nature, it becomes contractor for all its work, and gives security for every duty; and conscience can ask no more. Unfortunately, it labours under one

[1] Methods of Ethics, III. chap. xii. § 2, p. 367.

irremovable disability: that the greater part of the excellence for which it makes itself answerable is in its very essence *disinterested*, and is reached only in *self-forgetfulness*. And self-love cannot undertake to win it, without resolving on an impossible suicide. The real Self-love with which we have to do differs from both these hypothetical conceptions; and this difference accounts for the admission, by general consent, of *Prudence* to a humble place among the duties, if not among the virtues. It recognises the fact that we are not merely sentient, to do as we like; but that certain additional elements of happiness or misery have been imported into life by the presence of a moral order of feelings, both in ourselves and in others; and that hence two consequences follow: (1) that Prudence must not leave out of account this fresh factor of well-being, but must economise it with the rest; and (2) that, inversely, the moral judgment claiming, by its very nature, jurisdiction over all the voluntary life, covers Prudence itself with its authority, forbids us to trifle with our own happiness, and turns the administration of it into a duty. Thus, instead of inflating Prudence till it fills and supersedes the sphere of Conscience, we cancel its independence and adopt it into the service of Conscience. As soon as we look behind the *words*, we find that the alleged diversity of estimate resolves itself into a diversity of meanings.

C. IMPERATIVE CLAIMS OF JUSTICE.—But it is not only with regard to moral motives and self-love that divergent judgments are formed: they are equally conspicuous, it is said, all through the list of incentives: except that, by general admission, the appetites stand below the affections and intellectual desires; and the self-preserving impulses below the disinterested. It is obvious to remark that these 'exceptions' themselves stretch over so large a part of our scale, as to supply at least the outlines of its rule; they touch its terms at leading points from end to end, and leave little range for doubt beyond the sub-classes which they contain. The instances adduced to enforce the objection admit of a construction under which it completely disappears. They belong, if I mistake not, to two classes: (1) that in which a spring of action seems to modify its relative worth with *outward circumstances:* (2) that in which its place is apparently changed by its *special intensity*. As an example of the first, take the natural resentment at wrong, even when brought into the form of love of justice, or desire to treat men according to their deserts. The maxim '*Fiat justitia, ruat cœlum*,' attests the almost supreme place assigned to this motive by the general sentiment. Yet, no sooner do the social conditions become dangerously exceptional, as in times of conspiracy and successful crime, than the best administrators unhesitatingly offer not only immunity to a confessing criminal, but a huge bribe to break his oath of secrecy and betray his accomplices. No treatment can be more at variance with his deserts. A motive principle which can thus be deposed by circumstances is not judge but judged: the estimate of it changes from person to person, and from time to time; and as it is public utility that shifts the value assigned to it, *that* is certainly the criterion on which it depends. I answer, that there is here no change whatever in the estimate of the principle of justice; but merely a sacrifice of its application to one person in order to secure its application to several, instead of acquiescing in its frustration for all. In offering the reward for Queen's evidence, it is always assumed that the promise to participate in the crime and keep it secret is itself a criminal act, and not binding; so that the wages are tendered, not for a new iniquity, but for retreat from an old one; and the departure from justice is limited to the grant of impunity; a grant reluctantly made, with no other desire than to gain the best terms possible for the total justice of the case. The spring of action is therefore still in its dominant place, and is not really dislodged by outward circumstances. And, even if it were pronounced expedient to remit punishment altogether for a particular crime, that so-called 'expediency' would consist in some better security obtainable by the momentary sacrifice for the permanent preservation of just conduct in the society; so that, in any case, the modification is only from smaller justice to larger.

D. RELATIVE CLAIMS OF INTELLECTUAL DESIRES AND PERSONAL AFFECTIONS.—The difference of opinion, however, which is most in Professor Sidgwick's mind,—viz. between the relative claims of the intellectual desires and the personal affections,—comes under the second head; for it is only where the ideal tendencies have more than the average intensity that they ever dispute the palm of superiority with the enthusiasms of human love. But wherever this exceptional intensity of Wonder and Admiration really does exist, it undoubtedly starts the question, whether it invests these intellectual impulses with relative rights not assigned to them upon the scale. Where there is a drift of genius, overwhelmingly strong, towards ideal creation or the search for scientific truth, it is often accepted as an excuse for some carelessness of the claims of the parental and social affections, which nevertheless stand higher in authority. Is this plea to be recognised by the moralist? and, if it is, must it be extended to every impulse that can assert the same title? In that case, the whole doctrine collapses, and *worth* can no longer hold up its head against strength, but fairly falls into its arms. Or, is it only in extreme cases, of great intellectual gifts, that the rule of relative obligation is relaxed, and the negligent private life becomes venial, in consideration of the public gain from rare additions to the treasures of art and knowledge? In that case, we are referred *to utility* to find the point where, with the smallest sacrifice of private claim, the public advantage will be at its greatest; and the inward scale is deserted for the outward. To this I answer: If you admit the plea of special intensity *so far only as the public good requires*, you stipulate that the genius of the individual shall be held in trust for the general advantage, and shall not follow its own impulses beyond that line. In doing so, you do but acknowledge the *superior obligation of social affection*, which is precisely what is asserted in our scale. This affection, therefore, instead of being set aside by the ideal incentive, is *added* to that impulse when intense, with the effect of lifting it into a higher position. Accordingly, the actual feeling of all the greatest workers in the pursuit of knowledge and the creations of art has more or less distinctly been one of self-identification with the well-being of men, and dedication to a sacred trust on their behalf. Thus, these typical cases of seeming divergence from the intuitive series of ranks, are entirely brought back into the line, not without fresh confirmation of its truth.

Even within the compass of Love itself Professor Sidgwick finds two elements which, in the hands of the intuitive moralist, are sure, he thinks, to quarrel for precedence. On the one hand, there is the desire of good to the object of love: on the other, the desire for intimate communion with him; and which of these holds the higher rank in the benevolent affections may be reasonably doubted; the former appearing to be the most purely disinterested; the latter, the only element lofty enough to survive in the love of God, the supreme of all affections. This difficulty arises entirely from treating the confused word Love as the name of a single affection, and as interchangeable with benevolence. We speak certainly of the 'love of man' and of the 'love of God;' but on that account to search in the latter for some test of the elements of the former is no more reasonable than to look for it in the love of money, of power, of knowledge, the fact being, that it is only in the *benevolent affections* that the two elements in question are found combined. Nor does it follow, from the presence in human piety of *a desire of union*, that this must be the superior element in human love; for it may not be, and assuredly is not, the superior element in the religious feeling: in itself, and apart from the decisive question 'union *with what?*' it has no moral quality whatsoever: it may belong to the confidant of a favourite Dæmon, or the worshipper of infinite Holiness. Many a time has there prevailed, in particular crises of religious experience, a highly-wrought and passionate love of God, in which this clinging tendency of emotion has been attended with deplorable degradation of character[1]: it sinks or lifts the worshipper entirely according to the conception which he has of the object of his trust. In order to keep clear of the illusory subsumption of devotion towards God under the *benevolent affections*, I have distinguished them by different names; intending, by the use of the word '*Reverence*,' to lay stress on that subduing sense of *Moral perfection* which is implied in neither of the two elements discriminated in human love. When we look below the film of hazy language into real differences of thought which it hides or blurs, the alleged discrepancy appears to me entirely to vanish.

E. LOVE OF FAME AND LOVE OF POWER.—The last instance of divergent estimate among intuitive moralists Professor Sidgwick finds in their treatment of the Love of Fame and the Love of Power. Again, I see no evidence that the discrepancy is more than apparent. For I find the same phrase employed to cover different things, on which it is quite natural and right that different judgments should be passed. When 'some,' as Professor Sidgwick tells us, 'think it degrading to depend for one's happiness on the breath of popular favour,' they certainly have in view what we have named, and have estimated, as the love of *Praise*. The poet, on the other hand, who eulogises 'the spur which the clear spirit doth raise,' is thinking of what is more strictly called the love of *Fame;* and the differing

---

[1] There is a painful illustration of this danger in an edition of the Hymns of the United Brethren (Moravian); the second, I believe, out of three which have appeared in this country. I refrain from more particular reference, out of respect for the permanent feeling of the Brotherhood. Their leaders became ashamed of the too amorous tone that pervaded the volume, and withdrew it in favour of a collection breathing a far purer and higher devotion.

estimates are but the shadows of the different meanings. He who ranks the love of Fame 'among the most elevated impulses *after the moral sentiments*,' does but express in other words what I intended in saying, that the love of Fame can never be more *than second-best*, but always occupies the place of a higher impulse which *ought* to do the work instead. As for the *love of Power*, it is true, as Professor Sidgwick says, that it produces effects 'of nearly all degrees of goodness and badness:' but that 'we are inclined to praise or blame it accordingly,' I cannot for a moment admit, if by praise and blame be meant moral approval and condemnation, and not mere pleasure and displeasure at what we like and dislike. Regarded as a feature of the individual character, it is invariably recognised as guilty, when it is known to do what a higher impulse,—e.g. love of social welfare,—forbids to be done; as innocent, when it does what the higher impulse, if it had ascendency, would insist on being done; as laudable, when it rescues the life from the thraldom of appetite and passion, and quickens the energy of thought, affection, and will. But no amount of 'good effects' purchased by it for the world can ever elicit towards it, as it seems to me, the faintest movement of moral homage; or even prevent a certain sigh of humiliation at the disproportion between the largeness of the product and the unheroic nature of its spring. I cannot but think that Professor Sidgwick has confounded together the possible value of a spring of action for society, and its moral worth in the individual character.

§ 3. *Difficulty of Reading our Motives.*

A difficulty still remains to be considered, which certainly must be fatal to our whole doctrine, if it cannot be relieved. Is it possible to read our own motives with an accuracy sufficient for their estimate? Struck with the fact that Hobbes resolves the benevolent impulse into the *love of power*, and that Dugald Stewart detects the same insidious incentive in the love of knowledge, of property, and of liberty, Professor Sidgwick shrinks with a kind of despair from the puzzling complexity of our motives, and suggests that we are not competent to decipher them[1]. I cannot but think that he puts the difficulty, whatever it be, in the wrong place. From the different accounts of this or that motive given by different philosophers we are entitled to infer, that it is not easy to compare its exemplifications in separate persons; but not, that each person is in the dark about it in his own case. It is difficult enough to make language available for the exact comparison, by several observers, of even perceptions through the senses, where the presence of an external object secures at least a concurrent direction of attention; and that difficulty is enormously increased where the phenomena compared are wholly internal, and identities and differences can be indicated only by words, whose indeterminate comprehension cannot be fixed but by others that are also indeterminate, and so on to an indefinite distance. On matters of purely psychological experience, to reach general propositions which will equally content a multitude of thinkers requires a precision of analysis, and a tact in the manipulation of language, by no means common even in the philosophic schools. But it does not follow from this that *accurate self-knowledge is unattainable;* and it is within this sphere, in the consciousness of relations between one state and another of the same mind, that the hierarchy of motive-springs constructs itself. It is very true that, in order to serve more than a private purpose, in order to have any *scientific value*, it is indispensable to raise this result of self-knowledge from an individual to a general fact. But no one probably who has sufficient faith in psychology to accept such report on the attestation of personal self-knowledge, will despair of bringing its descriptive language to an exactitude sufficient for gathering up the laws of comparative experience.

That a psychologist of the first rank should have so timid

[1] Methods of Ethics, III. chap. xii. § 3, pp 369, 370.

a faith in the method of which he is a master, as to dwell distrustfully on the 'obscurity of introspective analysis,' and deem it impossible to tell the value of a mixed motive, is certainly discouraging. What am I to do, he asks, if I am driven in one direction by a chain-shot of high and low motives, and in the opposite by a single impulse of intermediate worth? e.g. to punish my injurer by love of justice plus vindictiveness, and to spare him by compassion. It has been agreed on both sides to treat vindictiveness, as not only relatively but absolutely bad, and to place it, as purely malevolent, altogether outside the admissible parts of the graduated scale. The active presence of such a feeling implies much more, I should say, than the mere lowering of a coexisting superior impulse; it so conflicts with it, that any blending of the two in a common function is no less impossible, than the co-operation of aliment that feeds the life and poison that destroys it. Were I conscious of vindictive desire, I should know my love of justice to be vitiated and turned into pretence, and be well aware that the only approvable incentive pleading with me was my compassion. If the lower factor of the compound motive, as well as the higher, lies within the scale, they will together constitute an intermediate incentive; the moral quality of which it would indeed be difficult to know, if for that purpose it were requisite to give the atomic weights of each, and their combining proportions, with the new properties emerging at each stage. But in psychological states there are no quantitative parts and wholes; and the language and analogies of mechanical aggregation or chemical composition are altogether misleading, if pressed upon what we call the analysis of thought. Changes of feeling are not got, and are not estimated, by addition and subtraction, and do not constitute multiples and quotients; so that to show how difficult woud be the problem they present, if they had to be worked a sums in arithmetic, affords no proof that we cannot solve them. However paradoxical the confession may seem, I must own that I find what is called a compound spring of action quite as easy to estimate as the simplest: it carries with it implicitly a report of its relative moral rank to the consciousness, and it is not till I begin to lay it out explicitly, and reckon it up by particles, that doubts and puzzles about it crowd upon me, with the imminent risk of turning my self-knowledge into self-delusion. Such better knowledge of a reputed whole than of its reckoned parts is by no means strange to our experience in other fields. I may have, e. g. a feeling, practically infallible, of the duration of an hour, or of five or six hours, so that its lapse shall not escape me even in sleep, and I can be sure of punctuality without a watch; yet so far is this from depending on my counting the component minutes or quarter hours, that were I to try such calculative method, I should be certain to go wrong. The hour is just as much a unitary object of knowledge, as any shorter time, although it is true that it would not have elapsed, unless also sixty minutes had elapsed; and similarly each impulse is strictly one appreciable state of consciousness, although it may happen only to a mind that has passed through certain nameable prior conditions. Without, therefore, 'estimating the relative proportions' of the so-called components of a motive, we intuitively decide exactly as if we could; or, exactly as if nothing were present but incentives of the simple type. The absence of one of them from our graduated list makes no difference; for that list is not the prior condition, but only the posterior record, of our moral psychology; the history flows on in its own way without looking at our programs; and our best knowledge can do no more than follow with lame steps, and lay out its natural wholes into the nearest artificial equivalents that can enable us to speak together of their quality. All the difficulties charged upon the composition of motives appear to me a mere nightmare of unreal psychology. Practically, everyone knows at first-hand his own incentive, and, unless he has learned the tricks of a cheat, need be at no loss about its relative worth

§ 4. *The Rule reducible to that of 'Rational Benevolence.'*

In a passage which long perplexed me, and which perhaps I still fail to understand, Professor Sidgwick seems to draw a singular conclusion from our rule that, in every conflict of impulses, the highest has the rightful claim upon our will. If so (he seems in effect to say), you practically give up your doctrine and come over to our side; for the highest motive is the Utilitarian's pursuit of universal happiness, or, what is the same thing, 'Rational Benevolence,' or, if you take it more distributively, the several virtues which secure that happiness; and if *that* is what we are to go by, the inferior motives are thrust out of the game, unless they can hang on to the skirts of this superior and pass as its servitors. in the presence of all the virtues and universal good they can have nothing to say for themselves, if they cannot show that they have an instrumental place in the attainment of these ends. Their vindication, therefore, lies in their relation, not to each other, but to one principle set up as supreme. Since to this principle the appeal has to be carried, the pleadings may as well be opened in its court at once. Do I, in this version, rightly apprehend the purport of the following sentences?—

'If it be said that the highest motive present, however feeble compared with others, should always prevail, and that we need only attend to that: then this mode of determining right conduct seems practically to pass over and resolve itself into some other method. For if several virtuous impulses, prompting to realise particular rules or qualities of conduct, are admitted as distinct and independent, these will naturally occupy the highest rank; and if not, then Rational Benevolence, or some similar principle, within the range of which all actions may be comprehended. And thus, when a conflict occurs between motives inferior to these, the inferior will naturally carry up the case, so to say, into the court of the higher motive; so that the practical issue will, after all, depend upon the determination of the object of the higher motive, whether it be conformity to moral rules or universal happiness and the means to this. And, in fact, such a reference seems continually to occur in our psychical experience: our lower impulses, bodily appetites, &c. when they conflict with some higher principle, continually impel us to justify them by considerations of their tendency to promote individual or general good. And thus our estimate of the value of all motives below the highest turns out to have little practical application, as the final decision as to the rightness of conduct will depend, after all, upon some quite different consideration[1].'

The reasoning of this passage, if I do not misconstrue it, addresses itself to some doctrine wholly unlike any which I can undertake to defend. It assumes that in the scale of springs of action will be found a special class distinguished from the rest by being '*virtuous motives*,' possibly all fused *into one* in the shape of 'Rational Benevolence,' or desire for 'universal happiness.' I have already said enough in correction of this misapprehension. It is also assumed, that there can never be a conflict of incentives without one of these 'virtuous motives' (i.e. love of this, that, or all virtues) being present, so that not only is one inferior motive higher than another, but both are eclipsed by a superlative third, and dispensed from further attendance. With the removal of the class of 'virtuous motives,' this assumption also disappears: there is no absolute and constant 'highest,' appearing over the heads of all conflicting incentives; but the 'highest' which claims us is simply the relatively superior of the contending two, and the duty, the moral quality, the call to virtue, consist simply in that felt superiority; so that our rule, 'Go with the highest,' is just as applicable to the humbler as to the loftier steps of the scale, and involves no leap up to the summit before it can be obeyed. It is in vain to urge upon us that from the authority of our hierarchy we are necessarily driven to an infallible Head.

[1] Methods of Ethics, III. chap. xii. § 3, pp. 370, 371.

The same misuse of the word 'highest' in an absolute sense, instead of relatively to the other incitements in each act of choice, leads to Professor Sidgwick's final argument: viz. that it is against common sense to affirm that the higher motive ought always to prevail over the lower: inasmuch as this would require us to banish 'all natural impulse in favour of reason,' and fetch in the supreme spring of action to work the most insignificant problems: in other words, never to descend from the top of the scale. This objection has already been under consideration; and I have nothing to add to the reasons before assigned for treating the natural impulses as the *data* of our moral problem, and not (except within certain narrow specified limits) turning them out among the *quæsita;* i. e. for not meddling with the *relative quantity* of our motives, if only their *quality* receives its due. As I do not admit 'Reason' to be a spring of action at all, it would indeed be strange in me to 'suppress the natural impulses in its favour:' the only effect would be to stop the clock altogether.

Throughout his criticism Professor Sidgwick has lost sight of the place which I expressly reserve for his utilitarian *canon of consequences,* and has argued as if I proposed to work out a *code of morals* from intuitive data. He does not notice the fact that I only give *priority* to the *canon of obligation proper,* and contend that consequences to the general happiness can carry no obligation, *unless the altruistic affections are in their nature invested with authority over impulses that conflict with them;* so that we must go to the scale of impulses before we proceed to the reckoning of consequences. In reading so bare an outline of doctrine as the Essay presents on which he is commenting, this feature might perhaps easily escape attention. Yet the definition of right and wrong with which his quotation closes is immediately followed by these qualifying words: 'this [definition], however, though of very wide application, will not serve for the solution of every problem. There are cases in which one and the same principle has the choice of several possible actions; and among these the election must be made by the balance of pleasurable and painful effects. There is no question of duty which will not find its place under one or other of these two rules, of which the first might be called the canon of principles, and the other the canon of consequences; the former being the true ethical criterion, determining the morality of an act; the latter, the rational criterion, determining its wisdom[1].'

[1] Essays, Philosophical and Theological, Vol. II p. 20.

BOOK II.

HETERO-PSYCHOLOGICAL THEORIES.

In the account which has been given of the psychological basis of Ethics, nothing more has been attempted than an accurate description of the facts of our moral consciousness, and of the beliefs which they implicitly contain. A meaning has been given for the leading terms which enter into our current language of character,—merit and demerit, praise and blame, temptation, compunction, duty and virtue, obligation and authority, right and wrong; and the conceptions thus laid out have brought us (so far as I am aware) across no incoherence among themselves, or inconsistency with necessary beliefs belonging to other departments of human thought. The general result therefore is, that the contents and implications of the moral sentiments stand fast for us as sound, and no less worthy of trust than any other organism of ideas that is found elsewhere within the total sphere of our knowledge. We end, as we began, by believing what they tell us.

So simple a result does not, however, always satisfy the ingenuity of psychologists. It leaves us with an order of thinking and a group of convictions distinct from any that can be got out of the physical and physiological sciences, or from the principles of the fine arts; and philosophers do not like to be encumbered, in their survey of the world, with bundles of first truths as numerous as the elements of a lady's luggage: they cannot move freely till their outfit will all go into a Gladstone bag. So they try to find some one of their packages of thought capacious or elastic enough to hold all that cannot be proved superfluous; and as, in any case, room enough must be left for the senses, which are solid affairs, it is usually the moral sentiments that are apt to get squeezed, and to come out at the end hardly recognisable. Some of these contrivances for reducing the manifold furnishing of our nature to a single all-embracing type, i.e. for *enveloping* the phenomena which are then to be *developed*, it is incumbent upon us to examine, for they undoubtedly alter the aspect, if they do not endanger the existence, of the *authority* under which we seem to live. This indeed it was customary for the older empirical analysts to deny[1]. But in the present day it is no longer possible to treat this question, of the genesis of the ethical experiences, as morally indifferent: the anxiety which has widely spread, since the principle of evolution came to be applied to morals, sufficiently attests the prevalent belief that the reverent estimate of them rests, not upon their useful issues only, but also upon their sacred source. If moral obligation turns out, on cross-questioning, to be *Self-*seeking, or *Fear* of man, or *Assent* to truth, presenting itself under an *alias*, it cannot be denied that the detection of this fact shows it to be, or to contain, *an illusion;* inasmuch as to our consciousness it presents itself under quite a different character from this, and, in virtue of such difference, influences us quite otherwise. The exposure of an habitual hallucination may not, it is true, prevent its recurrence; but if, in recurring, it brings with it its own refutation, we shall no longer go with it as our guide, but bear it as our malady. It is therefore absurd to pretend that no practical interest is affected by the idea we may form of the genesis of the moral sentiments.

[1] See, e.g. James Mill's Fragment on Mackintosh, pp. 51, 52.

BRANCH I.

HEDONIST ETHICS.

CHAPTER I.

UTILITARIAN HEDONISM.

The theory upon this subject which in this country has played, and still plays, the leading part against every doctrine of intuitive morals is that which, started by Hobbes, and descending with various enrichments and some qualifications through Hartley, Bentham, the two Mills, and Austin, reappears in Bain, and in its ethical aspect is popularly known as *Utilitarianism:* while, in its psychological, it is generally (though not necessarily) identified in the schools with *Hedonism*. In reviewing this scheme of doctrine, I shall not select any single writer as its exclusive representative, but avail myself of such statements, wherever found, as may serve to bring out the important features of the doctrine most distinctly; and shall hope to do so, without making any author responsible for positions which, though laid down by another, he would not himself accept.

i. PSYCHOLOGICALLY CONSIDERED.

The common feature of this ethical school under all varieties is the conception of morality or virtue as a *means* to an ulterior end, therefore as subordinate in worth to something which it purchases. The 'Utility' in which its value consists is of course relative to this prize: useful, *for what?* Is it for *truth?* or for *order?* or for *life?* or for something undefined under the name *good?* or, finally, for *happiness*, in the sense of *pleasure?* As the mere word *Utility* makes no selection among these, I have said that it is not pledged to one of them in particular. But, in point of fact, the last is the only one which finds favour with the great masters of the school, and which it is needful for us to notice. The assertion that pleasure is the supreme end of human as of all sentient life, which traces to itself the pathway of all rules, and determines the direction of all effort, is the postulate on which their whole reasoning proceeds, and on the soundness of which depends its security from collapse. A few brief quotations will suffice to substantiate this statement.

§ 1. *Expositions by Hobbes, Helvetius, Bentham, Mill.*

'Nature,' says Bentham[1], 'has placed mankind under the governance of two sovereign masters, pain and pleasure. It is for them alone to point out what we ought to do, as well as to determine what we shall do. On the one hand the standard of right and wrong, on the other the chain of cause and effect, are fastened to their throne. They govern us in all we do, in all we say, in all we think; every effort we can make to throw off our subjection, will serve but to demonstrate and confirm it. In words a man may pretend to abjure their empire; but in reality he will remain subject to it all the while. The principle of *utility* recognises this subjection, and assumes it for the foundation of that system, the object of which is to rear the fabric of felicity by the hands of reason and of law.'

The unflinching way in which Bentham carried out this fundamental principle may be seen by a few extracts from subsequent sections of the same work, and from his

[1] Principles of Morals and Legislation: opening paragraph.

Deontology,—a treatise less authentic indeed, and possibly tinctured by the rhetorical manner of its Editor, Sir J. Bowring, yet probably exhibiting not unfairly the outpourings of the philosopher's unguarded hours. 'In the moral field the end is happiness. The subjects on which prudence is to be exercised are ourselves, and all besides; ourselves as instruments, and all besides as instrumental to our own felicity. To obtain the greatest portion of happiness for himself is the object of every rational being. Every man is nearer to himself than he can be to any other man; and no other man can weigh for him his pains and pleasures. Himself must necessarily be his own first concern. His interest must, to himself, be the primary interest[1].' Accordingly, Bentham cautions us against expecting any disinterested action from others: 'Dream not that men will move their little finger to serve you, unless their advantage in so doing be obvious to them. Men never did so, and never will, while human nature is made of its present materials. But they will desire to serve you, when by so doing they can serve themselves; and the occasions on which they can serve themselves by serving you are multitudinous[2].'

The great hindrance to the recognition of the supremacy of pleasure and pain Bentham finds in the phrases which the moralist has invented for the expression of his imperious and tyrannical ideas: 'His tone is the tone of the pedagogue or the magistrate: he is strong and wise, and knowing and virtuous. his readers are weak and foolish, and ignorant and vicious: his voice is the voice of power; and it is from the superiority of his wisdom that his power is derived.' 'The talisman of arrogancy, indolence, and ignorance, is to be found in a single word, an authoritative impostor, which in these pages it will be frequently necessary to unveil. It is the word "ought"—"ought," or "ought not," as circumstances may be. In deciding "You ought to do this,—you ought not to do it,"—is not every question

[1] Deontology, I. pp. 17, 18.   [2] Ibid. II. p. 133.

of morals set at rest? If the use of the word be admissible at all, it "*ought*" to be banished from the vocabulary of morals[1].'

Similarly he attacks other essential words of the same vocabulary: e.g. 'Men have written great books wherein, from beginning to end, they are employed in saying this and nothing else,—"It is as I say, because I say it is so." What these books have to depend on for their efficacy, and for their being thought to have proved anything is, the stock of self-sufficiency in the writer, and of implicit deference in the reader: by the help of a proper dose of which, one thing may be made to go down as well as another. Out of this assumption of authority has grown the word *Obligation*, from the Latin verb *obligo*, to bind,— while such a cloud of misty obscurity has gathered round the term, that whole volumes have been written to disperse it.' 'It is, in fact, very idle to talk about *duties*: the word itself has in it something disagreeable and repulsive; and talk about it as we may, the word will not become a rule of conduct. A man, a moralist, gets into an elbow chair, and pours forth pompous dogmatisms about *duty* and *duties* Why is he not listened to? because every man is thinking about *interests*. It is a part of his very nature to think about interests; and with these the well-judging moralist will find it for *his* interest to begin. Let him say what he pleases,—to interest, duty must and will be made subservient[2].' It is singular that a philosopher who finds the English word 'duty' so disagreeable should select for his own treatise on the subject a title including its Greek equivalent. He cannot help, however, now and then making up his quarrel with these terms; as when he says, 'Take away pleasure and pain, not only happiness, but justice, and duty, and obligation, and virtue, all of which have been so elaborately held up to view as independent of them, are so many empty sounds[3].'

James Mill says: 'A man acts for the sake of something

[1] Deontology, I. pp. 31, 32.   [2] Ibid. I. pp. 9, 10.
[3] Springs of Action, I. § 15.

agreeable to him, either proximately or remotely. But agreeable to, and pleasant to,—agreeableness and pleasantness,—are only different names for the same thing: the pleasantness of a thing is the pleasure it gives. So that pleasure, in a general way, or speaking generically, i.e. in a way to include all the species of pleasures, and also the abatement of pains, is the end of action. A motive is that which moves to action. But that which moves to action is the end of the action, that which is sought by it: that for the sake of which it is performed. Now that, generically speaking, is the pleasure of the agent[1].'

Again, J. S. Mill says: 'The creed which accepts as the foundation of morals *Utility* or *the greatest happiness principle*, holds that actions are right in proportion as they tend to promote happiness, wrong as they tend to produce the reverse of happiness. By happiness is intended pleasure, and the absence of pain: by unhappiness, pain, and the privation of pleasure. To give a clear view of the moral standard set up by the theory, much more requires to be said,—in particular, what things it includes in the ideas of pain and pleasure; and to what extent this is left an open question. But these supplementary explanations do not affect the theory of life on which this theory of morality is grounded, viz. that pleasure, and freedom from pain, are the only things desirable as ends; and that all desirable things (which are as numerous in the Utilitarian as in any other scheme) are desirable either for the pleasure inherent in themselves, or as means to the promotion of pleasure, and the prevention of pain[2].' These propositions are rendered still more distinct by a subsequent exposition of Desire: 'Desiring a thing and finding it pleasant, aversion to it and thinking of it as painful, are phenomena entirely inseparable, or rather two parts of the same phenomenon: in strictness of language, two different modes of naming the same psychological fact: to think of an object as desirable

---

[1] Fragment on Mackintosh, p. 389.
[2] Utilitarianism, pp 9, 10.

(unless for the sake of its consequences) and to think of it as pleasant, are one and the same thing; and to desire anything, except in proportion as the idea of it is pleasant, is a physical and metaphysical impossibility[1].'

These citations sufficiently exhibit the fundamental principle of the theory. Its emphatic reduction of all springs of conduct to one cannot but strike even its defenders, as apparently not in harmony with the common feeling of mankind, and with the language framed for its expression. Most persons would be affected with some surprise and amusement on being told that in their friendships, their family affections, their public spirit, their admiration for noble character, their religious trust, they had a single eye to their own interests, and were only *using* their fellows, their children, their country, their heroes, their God, as instruments of their personal pleasure. The writers of this school, accordingly, find their ingenuity severely taxed to deduce states of mind which have an aspect so disinterested from the one invariable principle of self-seeking; and the history of their psychology affords examples of expository contortion of natural processes numerous enough to stock the largest museum of pathological curiosities. In Hobbes, the *love of power* is the favourite form of self-interest, which is taken in hand and taught to wear now this mask, and now that, of unselfish feeling. His adoption of this particular key to the passions and affections he justifies as follows: '*Conception of the future* is but a supposition of the same, proceeding from the remembrance of what is past; and we so far conceive that anything *will be hereafter*, as we know there *is something at the present* that hath power to produce it; and that anything hath power now to produce another thing hereafter we cannot conceive, but by remembrance that it hath produced the like heretofore. Wherefore, all conception of the future is conception of power able to produce something. Whosoever, therefore, expecteth pleasure to come, must conceive withal some power in himself

[1] Utilitarianism, p. 57.

by which the same may be attained. And because the passions, whereof I am to speak next, consist in conception of the future, that is to say, in conception of power past and the act to come: before I go further, I must in the next place speak somewhat concerning this power[1].'

Among his applications of this 'conception of power' comes his definition of *Reverence*, as 'the conception we have concerning another, that he hath the power to do unto us both good and hurt, but not the will to do us hurt[2].' With this definition of Reverence we may combine his account of *Religion:* '*Fear* of power invisible, feigned by the mind, or imagined from tales publicly allowed, is *religion: not* allowed, *superstition.* And when the power imagined is truly such as we imagine, *true religion*[3].' It must be confessed that Christian divines have afforded but too much excuse for this identification of religion with self-interest: thus Waterland says that 'It is with reference to ourselves, and for our own sakes, that we love even God Himself.' 'Man may love himself in this instance as highly and tenderly as he pleases. There can be no excess of fondness or self-indulgence in respect of eternal happiness. This is loving himself in the best manner and to the best purposes. All virtue and piety are thus resolvable into a principle of self-love.' 'In this sense it may be truly said that there is no such thing as disinterested virtue[4].' In this view Religion culminates in infinite self-seeking.

The sense or imagination of our own power or want of power Hobbes finds lurking in the most unexpected places: e.g. 'Laughter is nothing else but *sudden glory* from some sudden *conception* of some *eminency* in ourselves by comparison with the *infirmity* of others, or with our own formerly; for men laugh at the follies of themselves past, when they come suddenly to remembrance, except they

---
[1] Human Nature, chap. viii. § 3; Molesworth, Vol. IV. p. 57.
[2] Ibid. chap viii. § 7.
[3] Leviathan, Part I. chap. vi.; Molesworth, Vol. III. p. 45.
[4] The English Preacher, 1773, Vol. I. Waterland's Sermon on Self-love, p. 102.

bring with them present dishonour[1].' 'To fall on the sudden' (in the race of life) 'is disposition to weep: to see another fall, is disposition to laugh[2].' Again: '*Pity* is the *imagination* or *fiction* of future calamity to ourselves, proceeding from the sense of *another* man's calamity. But when it lighteth on such as we think have not deserved the same, the compassion is greater, because then there appeareth more probability that the same may happen to us; for the evil that happeneth to an innocent man may happen to every man[3].'

Not less paradoxical is his account of 'Charity:' 'There is yet another passion sometimes called love, but more properly *good-will* or *charity*. There can be no greater argument to a man, of his own power, than to find himself able, not only to accomplish his own desires, but also to *assist* other men in theirs; and this is that conception wherein consisteth charity[4].' He raises the question, 'From what passion proceedeth it that men take *pleasure* to *behold* from the shore the *danger* of them that are at sea in a tempest, or in fight, or from a safe castle to behold two armies charge one another in the field? It is certainly, in the whole sum, *joy;* else men would never flock to such a spectacle. Nevertheless there is in it both *joy* and *grief;* for as there is novelty and remembrance of our own security present, which is *delight;* so there is also *pity*, which is *grief;* but the delight is so far predominant, that men usually are content in such a case to be spectators of the misery of their friends[5].'

The influence of Hobbes has been considerable upon the writers who are usually classed together as the disciples of Bentham. But upon Bentham himself, it seems, *Helvetius* produced a much deeper impression. To his book *De l'Esprit*, published in 1758, 'Mr. Bentham,' says Sir J.

---
[1] Human Nature, chap. ix. § 13 (Vol. IV. p. 46).
[2] Ibid. Vol. IV. chap. ix. § 21, p. 53.
[3] Ibid. Vol. IV. chap. ix. § 10, p. 44.
[4] Ibid. Vol. IV. chap. ix. § 17, p. 49.
[5] Ibid. Vol. IV. chap. ix. § 19, p. 52.

Bowring, 'has often been heard to say that he stood indebted for no small proportion of the zeal and ardour with which he advocated his happiness-producing theory. It was from thence he took encouragement, flattering his efforts with the assurance that they would not be useless. It was there he learned to persevere, in the conviction that his power would strengthen, and his field of usefulness extend. Not that Helvetius had done the work which remained to do. He had not marshalled pains and pleasures, nor classified them according to their value; but he had brought prominently into view the influence of interest on opinion, and this was a point overflowing with important consequences. He laid bare many of those springs of action, the knowledge of which is absolutely essential to anything like a right estimate of conduct or character. And in showing the subserviency of opinion to interest, he demonstrated not only that the opinions publicly advocated were subservient, but those privately and even clandestinely formed. His list of the causes of misconduct, especially in public men, is as profoundly philosophical as it is sagaciously observant. Sinister interest, interest-begotten prejudice, authority-begotten prejudice, and primeval or inbred weakness,—in these he saw, and in these all men may see, the sources of human infirmity[1].'

It is due to an author so deeply concerned as Helvetius in the genesis of English Utilitarianism, to hear one or two of his expositions of the motives which he is said to have detected under their disguise in human life. His fundamental idea he presents in a form in which we seem to see the germ not of Benthamism only, but of the more recent conception of evolution: 'If we receive at our birth only wants, in these wants and in our first desires we must seek the origin of the artificial passions, which can be nothing more than the unfolding of the faculty of *Sensation*. Perhaps both in the moral and natural world God originally implanted only one principle in all He created, and that

[1] Deontology, I. p. 296.

what is and what is to be is only the necessary unfolding of this principle. He said to Matter, "I endow thee with power." Immediately the elements subject to the laws of motion, but wandering and confused in the deserts of space, formed a thousand monstrous assemblages, and produced a thousand different chaoses, till they at last placed themselves in that equilibrium and natural order in which the Universe is now supposed to be arranged. He seems to have said to man, "I endow thee with sensation, the blind instrument of my will, that, being incapable of penetrating into the depth of my views, thou mayst accomplish all my designs. I place thee under the guardianship of pleasure and pain: both shall watch over thy thoughts and thy actions: they shall produce thy passions, excite thy friendship, thy tenderness, thine aversion, thy rage: they shall kindle thy desires, thy fears, thy hopes: they shall take off the veil of truth: they shall plunge thee into error, and, after having made thee conceive a thousand absurd and different systems of morality and government, shall some day discover to thee the simple principles on the unfolding of which depends the order and happiness of the moral world[1]." He then proceeds to show how, 'man being by nature sensible of no other pleasures than those of the senses, these pleasures are consequently the only object of his desires and passions, viz. avarice, ambition, pride, and friendship[2].' It is a mistake to attribute to the ambitious man any real care 'for the respect and homage of mankind. He does indeed desire it; but why? It is not the respectful gesture that pleases: if that were of itself agreeable, there is no rich man who would not procure himself such happiness without going out of his house to seek for greatness. To please himself, he would hire twelve porters, clothe them in magnificent habits, adorn them with all the ribbons in Europe, and make them wait every morning in his antechamber, to come daily to pay his vanity a tribute of adulation and

---

[1] De l'Esprit, Ess. II. chap. ix. Engl. transl. p. 248.
[2] Ibid. Ess. II. chap. ix. ap fin.; and x. 2nd par, Engl. transl. p. 251.

respect.' No; he likes honours, because 'they inform the people of his power to render, at his pleasure, several of them happy or miserable, and that it is for the interest of them all to merit his favour, which is always proportioned to the pleasure they procure for him[1].' 'The desire of greatness is always produced by the fear of pain or love of sensual pleasure, to which all the other pleasures must necessarily be reduced[2].' 'If there be only two sorts of pleasures, the one the pleasures of sense, and the other the means of acquiring them (for these means are ranked in the class of pleasures, because the hope of obtaining them is the beginning of pleasure, but of a pleasure that has no real existence till this hope is realised), then natural sensibility is the seed that produces pride, and all the other passions, among which I include friendship[3].' This curious version of friendship he thus carries out: 'Love implies want, without which there is no friendship; for this would be an effect without a cause. Not all men have the same wants; and therefore the friendship which subsists between them is founded on different motives: some want pleasure or money, others credit; these conversation, those a confidant to whom they may disburthen their hearts. There are consequently friends of money, of intrigue, of wit, and of misfortune.' 'The power of friendship is in proportion, not to the honesty of two friends, but to the interest by which they are united.' 'People have repeated to one another *ad nauseam*, that we ought not to reckon among friends those who love us only for our money. This kind of friendship is certainly not the most flattering; but nevertheless it is a real friendship. Men, e.g. love in a comptroller-general the power he has of obliging them; and in most of them the love of the person is incorporated with the love of the money. Why is the name of friendship refused to this feeling? Men do not love us for ourselves, but always on

---

[1] De l'Esprit, Ess II. chap. xi. Engl. transl. p. 256.
[2] Ibid. Ess. II. chap. xi Engl. transl. p 258.
[3] Ibid. Ess. II. chap. xiii. Engl transl. p. 268.

some other account, and the abovementioned is as good as any other.' 'If a comptroller-general falls into disgrace, we no longer love him, for this reason, that he is the friend who has suddenly become blind, deaf, and dumb.' But 'Whoever has a want of money, is the born friend of the post of comptroller-general, and of him who possesses it. His love is inscribed in the inventory of his moveables and utensils belonging to his office[1].'

What is true of Friendship is no less true of Justice, and of all virtue: 'Our love of equity is always subordinate to our love of power: Man, solely anxious for himself, seeks nothing but his own happiness: if he respects equity, it is want that compels him to it[2].' 'It is the love of consideration that man takes to be in him the love of virtue; each one pretends to love it for itself: this phrase is in every one's mouth, but in no one's heart.' 'Whatever disinterested love we may affect to have, *without interest to love virtue, there is no virtue*[3].' 'Power is the only object of my desire: he who had the choice of the strength of Enceladus and the virtues of Aristides, would give the preference to the former[4].'

§ 2. *Refinements introduced by Hartley, J. S. Mill, and Bain.*

Such, in its earlier form, was the Hedonism of the Utilitarian school. And let it not be supposed that the foregoing citations have been selected as exceptionally cynical and paradoxical. On the contrary, it is only the more moderate and least characteristic passages of Helvetius that it is possible to quote; for, brilliant and polished as his genius is, it presents the mirror to a most dissolute and ignoble state of society, constantly throwing to the front examples, of the shamelessness of which he seems insensible. The modern representatives, while faithful to the original postulates of

---
[1] De l'Esprit, Ess. II. chap. xiv. Engl. transl., p. 269.
[2] Treatise on Man, Sec. III. chap. x.
[3] Ibid. Sec. III. chap. xii.   [4] Ibid. Sec. III chap. xiii.

the doctrine, place it before us in much more presentable garb; and are distinguished especially by the stress they lay upon two considerable modifications, which may be thus briefly explained:—

(1) Though giving to the pleasures of Sense (or relief from its pains) the *initiative* of all desire and affection, the Hartleyan (as I will call the psychologist of the Mill and Bain class) does not on that account adopt them as *his standard of value*, and, with Helvetius, treat all their derivatives as mere neutral *means* towards these,—a paper '*promise to pay*,' worthless until honoured at the bank and in the coin of the corporeal life. On the contrary, he maintains that any object which comes before us as a standing cause of numerous agreeable states gathers upon itself, by association of ideas, the interest of them all, and, though not able to give more than one at a time, affects our imagination as an equivalent of its whole group of possibilities; and thus its presence, or the conception of it, has a greater charm for us than any particular experience it can give. By a further extension of this 'Law of transference' we are carried back to the cause of this cause, with similar enhancement of attraction; so that, as we retreat from the starting-point of sensation, the fascination and fervour of interplay between ourselves and the scene on which we are placed increase. The ideal worth of objects soon and far transcends the sensational: that which at no moment is good for more than one thing becomes for always a priceless treasure; and what originally was indifferent to us draws towards it a truly disinterested affection. In this way, not only the personal attachments, but the love of country, of justice, of truth, of virtue, are cleared of the imputation of hollowness and hypocrisy, and take their place as honest facts in our nature, which no sophist need trouble himself to explain away. And though the hedonist principle be still applied to these derivative affections, and they be appraised, like their sensory germs, by *their pleasure value* to ourselves, yet they must be counted, not as simply *representatives* of

unrealised advantage, but as *dependent additions* to the primitive stock, growing out indeed as a runner from the parent plant, but now rooted for itself and severed from its source. And hence, when, in estimating the right, we apply our criterion of the pleasurable, these new elements must all come in for measurement; and as, by their own formation, they are quantities of higher power, they will generally quite outnumber the sensational reckoning, instead of leaving the answer to it alone.

(2) But not only does the modern Hartleyan throw in a vast *quantity* of mental pleasure previously treated as illusory; he also insists that pleasures, being heterogeneous, are by no means on the same level of *quality*, but, quite independently of their amount, are some of them intrinsically more eligible than others. In determining their comparative value, therefore, both elements must be taken into account; and if they are not, we shall be liable to deliver in the verdict of a pig rather than of a man. This modification is not universally approved by the new Utilitarians: Mr. John Morley declines to adopt it, and considers J. S. Mill, to whom chiefly it is due, as having materially weakened the defences of the doctrine by introducing it. The merits of this difference of opinion we shall have to weigh hereafter: at present I limit myself to the simple expression of its contents. J. S. Mill says: 'It is quite compatible with the principle of utility to recognise the fact, that some *kinds* of pleasure are more desirable and more valuable than others[1];' and when asked for a test or measure of this specific value, he selects, as umpire between different kinds, the judgment of persons who have experience of both or all, and who give their verdict 'irrespective of any feeling of moral obligation[2].' Such persons 'give a most marked preference to the manner of existence which employs their higher faculties. Few human creatures would consent to be changed into any of the lower animals, for the promise of the fullest allowance of a beast's pleasures: no intelligent human being would

[1] Utilitarianism, II. p. 11.   [2] Ibid II. p. 12.

consent to be a fool, no instructed person would be an ignoramus, no person of feeling and conscience would be selfish and base, even though they should be persuaded that the fool, the dunce, or the rascal is better satisfied with his lot than they are with theirs. They would not resign what they possess more than he, for the most complete satisfaction of all the desires which they have in common with him[1].' 'From this verdict of the only competent judges,' he adds, 'I apprehend there can be no appeal[2].' 'According to the greatest happiness principle, as thus explained, the ultimate end, with reference to and for the sake of which all other things are desirable (whether we are considering our own good or that of other people) is an existence exempt as far as possible from pain, and as rich as possible in enjoyment, both in point of quantity and quality: the test of quality, and the rule for measuring it against quantity, being the preference felt by those who, in their opportunities of experience, to which must be added their habits of self-consciousness and self-observation, are best furnished with the means of comparison[3].'

Since Mill brought the hedonist doctrine into this more refined form, it has undergone one further change, which, without any alteration of base, has introduced a different mode of stating and proportioning its deductions. In the school of Hobbes, the individual was taken as the fundamental unit, which society only multiplied, and whose essence determined the nature of the whole. With the growing belief in Sociological laws, the exigencies of *the kind* pushed the individual into the background, and became the ruling principle in shaping the habits and even the nature of all particular beings. In Ethics the result was, that the rules of conduct which worked themselves out in the struggle for *race-existence* had for their end the *self-preservation of the kind*, rather than *the pleasure of the agent or his contemporaries*. And hence, in the newest school, we

---

[1] Utilitarianism, II. pp. 12, 13 [2] Ibid. II. p. 15.
[3] Ibid. II. p. 17.

hear much less than from their predecessors of balances of personal interest and the happiness of numbers, and much more of the conduciveness of this or that mode of conduct to the *healthy life of associated men*. But though this is what comes to the front, the Epicurean axiom only hides itself a little in the shadow behind. As Mr. Herbert Spencer remarks, *life-conservation* cannot be made the ethical end without assuming that 'life is worth living:' if it be *not*, then *life-riddance* should become the end and supply the rules. The optimist is in actual possession of the field: the pessimist may claim to dispossess him; but the pleas of both bring the question at issue to the same test, viz. whether the gift of life is on the whole a gain of enjoyment or an infliction of suffering. Differ as they may in their estimate of the facts of the case, they cannot even discuss them but on the basis of the irrefragable assumption that without pleasure there is no good in life [1]. Here we have the link of connection between the hedonist and the evolutionary ethics. I content myself at present with simply pointing it out, in order to complete the story of the former; reserving the separate development of the latter for the specific treatment which its importance demands. Meanwhile, I will only remark in passing, that if both optimist and pessimist should happen to be rather wiseacres than otherwise, their agreement in a common postulate might not be a final authority for the reason of mankind.

§ 3. *Meanings given to the word 'Pleasure.'*

If we are to avoid being tripped up by mere verbal entanglements, our first care, in estimating this theory, must be to determine what the word *pleasure*, with its opposite, *pain*, is to mean. Shall we accept J. S. Mill's account, viz. that 'desiring a thing and finding it pleasant' are 'two modes of expressing the same psychological fact [2]?' that *to be more pleasurable* means *to be preferred* [3]? If so, *actum est*,

---

[1] See Data of Ethics, chap. ii §§ 3-10.   [2] Utilitarianism, p. 57.
[3] Ibid. p. 12.

the controversy dies in its birth: if pleasure equals 'what you desire or prefer,' certainly what you desire or prefer equals pleasure: the two psychological experiences which we were intending to compare coalesce in the definer's stereoscope, and are identified in one reality. The hedonist principle that preference goes with the greater pleasure, cannot certainly, in this sense, be denied without contradiction; but neither can it be affirmed without tautology. Mr. Leslie Stephen endeavours to escape from this verbal juggle by throwing the required proposition into another form. 'The true sentiment,' he says, 'is that one emotion may be overcome, not by a something which is altogether disparate from emotion, but by an emotion of a different kind; and this is of course indisputable. It does not traverse the proposition that emotion can be limited by nothing but emotion[1]:' i. e. I suppose, the proposition that the suasion of one pleasure or pain can be counteracted only by that of another. Mr. Stephen, therefore, uses the word 'emotion' simply to cover the alternative of 'pleasure or pain,' and save the trouble of mentioning the pair. Does this substitution, however, really satisfy the meaning of the word 'emotion?' Is it nothing more and nothing less than an abbreviation of the disjunctive phrase 'pleasure or pain,' inasmuch as it is equally applicable to either state? On the one hand, does toothache contain all that is required to constitute an emotion? on the other, does the emotion of love or of reverence contain no more than is needful to constitute pleasure or pain? Till you tamper with the word, no one will deny that 'emotion can be limited by nothing but emotion;' but this proposition is not identical with the hedonist principle, unless 'emotion' *contains nothing but pleasure and pain;* for, if it contains more, the 'limiting' power may reside precisely in this 'something more;' and it is just this which makes the happiness doctrine impossible to the conscience-stricken man, when he exclaims in his remorse, 'If the pain were all, it might be borne: nay, it is

[1] Science of Ethics, II. ii. 4, p. 43.

justly mine, and I welcome it; but to have played the traitor to my best friend prostrates me with a shame, of which the anguish is the smallest part.' It is easy, but ineffectual, to call the shrinking from wrong a shrinking from a sort of pain; and this is the whole magic of the author's case: he virtually defines pleasure and pain as '*whatever moves us;*' and then it is pretty plain that 'pleasure and pain' are our only motives.

Pleasure is a change of feeling in a sentient being which he likes. It is a phenomenon, therefore, of himself; but is brought about by some altered relation between himself and the scene in which he is. In that alteration he may have no part: it may be simply administered to him, while he sits still; as when, his body being cold on a chill and cloudy day, the sun comes out and bathes him in its warmth; or when, being heated, he stands to face a cooling breeze. Here, the initiative of the modified relation is with the outer world; and he is the passive recipient of its sensible effects. Suppose him to have memory, and its functions to be awakened by a recurrence of the same relative conditions; then, undoubtedly, the idea of his former experience will present itself to him, and, if he can look forward as well as backward, will pass into a *desire* for the former relief over again. And further, if any slight difference in the conditions, some movement of his own, e.g. from shade and shelter to exposure, is needed to favour that desire, he will take action in consequence, and shift his position. In this case, we have a true example of what I will call *motive pleasure;* and so far the hedonist theory works without obstruction.

But in establishing a congruous relation between the living being and the outer world, the initiative is not always taken by the latter. The human organism, as we have before shown, is not a motionless lump of sensitive matter, lying where it is till, in their transit, external phenomena are flung upon it, and make it stretch itself and turn hither and thither; but a composite casket of stirring instincts which carry it in determinate directions towards the supply of its various needs. In each movement thus originated, the man acts before he enjoys; without knowledge, therefore, of what is in store for him, be it of the taste for his palate, if he hungers, or of the refreshing draught if he thirsts. He is guided by an inward prompter to what he would be at: there is a given *end* which regulates the line of his advance: that end is the *outward object*, on which at first he seizes as the thing that suits him; and *is not* the pleasure which the thing will give him, for that is a secret from him still. It is an appendix to the completed work of the instinct, and might, without prejudice to this, be withheld or even reversed; for though the food should be unpalatable and the draught bitter, the story of the appetite would be finished none the less. And further: though the appendix were thus rendered neutral or negative, there would still be a distinct satisfaction in the mere fact of the instinct reaching its end, for in saying 'there is an instinct or impulse' we take only the first half of the phenomenon; the other being found in the subsidence of the tension and fulfilment of the aim. The pleasantness of this state is evidently *consequent* upon the previous instinct, and not *its cause:* the object is thus far pleasant, because we had set our desire upon it; and it is not because it is pleasant that we had desired it. Here, therefore, we come across a pleasure which makes its entrance into our thought, not at the beginning, but at the completion of action; and in contrast with the first type, viz. *motive pleasure*, we may call it '*resultant pleasure.*' The distinction had not escaped the notice of Aristotle; who not only repeatedly observes, that it is the natural impulses of men that determine their pleasures, and not *vice versâ*, but puts an extinguisher upon the whole principle of the hedonist morals in the following significant sentence: 'It is not true of every virtue that the exercise of it is attended with pleasure; except indeed the pleasure of attaining its end[1].'

[1] Οὐ δὴ ἐν ἁπάσαις ταῖς ἀρεταῖς τὸ ἡδέως ἐνεργεῖν ὑπάρχει, πλὴν ἐφ' ὅσον τοῦ τέλους ἐφάπτεται.—Eth. Nic III. ix. 5.

Resultant pleasure, it is obvious, being simply that of successful or realised impulse, will be uniform for all springs of action, and subject to no other variation than in degrees conformable with the intensity of the spring. It may therefore be treated as *quantitative*, and so, as admitting of the comparison, lot with lot, which the doctrine of hedonism assumes to be possible. Since, however, the only differences of amount which can find their way upon this scale are due to the relative *intensity* of the several impulses, the attempt to draw moral conclusions from such measurements could but lead to the result which we before fastened on the prudential rule pure and simple, viz. that the *dominant impulse* should have its way.

Motive pleasure, on the other hand, has *no homogeneity*, but is as various as the forms of sensation and emotion of which our nature is susceptible, and as little admits of comparison in its several instances as a circle and a flavour, or a law and a pump. There is no common measure for the agreeableness of a warm fire, of a smart bonnet, of a fine picture, of the news of a sick friend's recovery, of the memory of a favourite poem. It is simply absurd to speak of reckoning the sum or the difference of such experiences; and yet without it, how are we to arrive at the required *maximum* of happiness which is to be the goal of all our aims? When, therefore, we put in practice our instruction, to compute against each other the pleasures of two balancing impulses, what do we find? One set in which there is no pertinent difference; and another in which there is no common unit. The ethical calculus of this system is impossible.

§ 4. *Passage to and from Disinterestedness.*

The theory, on the other hand, of the growth of disinterested affection which has been matured by this school has a fair claim to be regarded as the permanent establishment of a real psychological law: the only drawback upon its merit being the very pardonable attempt to work it everywhere over the whole field of the affections, so as to supersede in every case any other account of their ground. It has, however, been clearly shown how, from motive pleasure to begin with, i.e. from self-regarding desires, the mind may emerge into genuine altruism in which the conflict ceases between another's happiness and the personal content. That the child's love for the parent, the citizen's for his country, the soldier's for his flag, the worshipper's for the symbol of his faith, are formed chiefly by the chemistry of association operating on data of pleasurable consciousness, seems to me more than a probable hypothesis. And if so, *psychological hedonism* (as distinguished from *ethical*) has freed itself from the charge of making provision for nothing but self-love. It has distinctly traced, step by step, a transition from self-regard, not exactly into self-forgetfulness, but into self-identification with the well-being of others; and has shown that, under healthy conditions, the natural crown of a course commencing in motive pleasure is a real disinterestedness. Let us own then that this process takes place, and let us register it as a fact.

Nor can we deny that just the inverse of this process is often to be read in the history of our instinctive springs of action. At the outset they dart upon their objects with no ulterior aim, but fascinated by them alone, they know not why. It is with a disinterested eagerness, therefore, that they start. But no sooner have we, under their influence, tasted the *resultant pleasure*, than we become affected with a desire of its repetition; so that this, in its turn, becomes converted into a *motive pleasure*, which in future blends more or less with the recurring impulse, and detracts from its disinterestedness. If the modification goes on unchecked, the primary spring is replaced by its secondary, and we lapse into complete self-interest. Thus, of the two types of pleasure, the one may begin, and the other may end, in self-love. And if we were surrendered, without *moral* element of feeling, or under its silence, to our mere natural psychology, this would be the normal result.

But the descent into the self-conscious pursuit of resultant pleasure is arrested by the intervention of the sense of right, or inward deference to the higher claim. In every conflict of concurrent impulses, this knowledge is given, and an attendant feeling is awakened, which powerfully reinforces the affections as against the personal interest, and lifts Love to the pedestal of duty, and sinks self-love into self-contempt. This it is which enables the primary affections and sentiments to keep their disinterested enthusiasm fresh under the fervid and penetrating beams of self-consciousness: it sheds on them a heavenly dew of regeneration, that makes self-knowledge burst its capsule and blossom into self-escape. Without this, we should learn, and we should seek, only the *joy* of love: with this we learn, and we revere, its sanctity as well: in the one case, we lose it in ourselves: in the other, we lose ourselves in it. Thus it is, that the elements which enter into conscience come to the rescue of the disinterested springs of action within the area of personal relations, and save them from the usurping grasp of the hedonistic hunger: the sense of the higher and the lower forbids the tyranny of the pleasant and the unpleasant.

§ 5. *Mill's Gradations of Quality in Pleasure.*

And here comes in the question which doubtless J. S. Mill would press upon us: viz. whether from his higher and lower, in the *quality of pleasure aimed at*, the same effect would not ensue,—the same correction of calculation by mere quantity,—the same reinforcement of extra-regarding as opposed to self-centred aims? To secure this result was unquestionably his hope and intention, in introducing a new function or dimension of pleasures, in virtue of which they ranged themselves in a hierarchy of kinds; and it is incumbent upon us to weigh carefully the claims of this distinction to a permanent place in a reformed or reconstructed utilitarianism.

Whatever be the quality which distinguishes one *kind* of

pleasure from another in Mill's specific scale, it must, in order to be consistent with the doctrine which it is introduced to serve, be something *measurable*. For its whole contention is, that the rightness of actions is '*in proportion as they tend to promote happiness:*' that the choice must be made of '*the greatest happiness ;*' and 'proportions' and 'maxima' cannot be found and known except in the case of measurable quantities. Bentham accordingly devotes a chapter to the 'Value of a lot of pleasure or pain, how to be measured[1],' in which he gives exact rules for determining the items and the aggregates of hedonistic magnitude. He admits, indeed, in each pleasure or pain a combination of several '*elements* or *dimensions*' of value which are factors of its worth; but there is not one of these which is not quantitative, so as to admit even of numerical expression; e.g. its *intensity*, its *duration*, its degree of *probability*, its degree of *distance in time*, its *fecundity*, or chance of entailing further pleasure or pain, its *purity*, or chance of escaping reversal into the opposite, its *extent*, or the number of persons affected by it[2]. How completely the rules for working out these elements to a result in the solution of each problem involve processes of definite computation may be judged by the following paragraph: 'To take an exact account, then, of the general tendency of any act, by which the interests of a community are affected, proceed as follows: Begin with any one person of those whose interests seem most immediately to be affected by it: and take an account,

---

[1] Principles of Morals and Legislation, chap. iv.
[2] As this list is not less fundamental for the young Benthamite than the numeration-table for the young arithmetician, the author has considerately adapted it to feeble memories in the following mnemonic lines:

> Intense, long, certain, speedy, fruitful, pure,
> Such marks in *pleasures* and in *pains* endure.
> Such pleasures seek, if *private* be thy end:
> If it be *public*, wide let them *extend*.
> Such *pains* avoid, whichever be thy view:
> If pains *must* come, let them *extend* to few.
>   Principles of Morals and Legislation, Vol. I. p. 49.

'(1) Of the value of each distinguishable *pleasure* which appears to be produced by it in the *first* instance.

'(2) Of the value of each *pain* which appears to be produced by it in the *first* instance.

'(3) Of the value of each pleasure which appears to be produced by it *after* the first. This constitutes the *fecundity* of the first *pleasure*, and the *impurity* of the first *pain*.

'(4) Of the value of each *pain* which appears to be produced by it after the first. This constitutes the *fecundity* of the first *pain*, and the *impurity* of the first pleasure.

'(5) Sum up all the values of all the *pleasures* on the one side, and those of all the pains on the other. The balance, if it be on the side of pleasure, will give the *good* tendency of the act upon the whole, with respect to the interests of that *individual* person; if on the side of pain, the *bad* tendency of it upon the whole.

'(6) Take an account of the *number* of persons whose interests appear to be concerned; and repeat the above process with respect to each. *Sum up* the numbers expressive of the degrees of *good* tendency, which the act has, with respect to each individual, in regard to whom the tendency of it is *good* upon the whole: do this again with respect to each individual, in regard to whom the tendency of it is *bad* upon the whole. Take the *balance;* which, if on the side of *pleasure*, will give the general *good tendency* of the act, with respect to the total number or community of individuals concerned; if on the side of pain, the general *evil tendency*, with respect to the same community[1].'

Mr. Leslie Stephen also, speaking of our 'independent sensibilities,' insists, that, 'however different the feelings may be in kind, *they must be commensurable:* they have a certain value in terms of each other, and as parts of a single whole they have a single and (by a superior being) definable resultant[2].' If once we part with this assumption, the doctrine becomes not simply unmeaning, but self-contradictory: in

---
[1] Principles of Morals and Legislation, Vol. I. chap. iv. § v. pp. 51, 52.
[2] Science of Ethics, chap. II. III. § 30, p. 70.

the same breath it asserts, and denies, that moral reckoning is an affair of quantity alone. If we hold fast by the assumption, then we abolish Mill's distinction and reabsorb his 'quality' back again into 'quantity.' If there is no *calculus of kinds uniform with that of degrees*, which each of us may apply for himself, how are we ever to set a minus of quality against a plus of quantity? The difficulty is not overcome by referring us to 'a man who knows,' to settle the question for us. Even if we are content to treat him as our Pope on the question of *quality*, the other half of the reckoning has to be made by our own consciousness, for we alone can tell what the quantity of the proposed pleasure will be to us; and unfortunately the terms of the Papal answer and of our own will not combine; and our equation has an unknown term too much.

This incommensurability of Mill's new element with the old follows irresistibly from the language of his exposition. If there are several species of the genus 'Pleasure,' each of them is distinguished from all the rest by some quality *of its own;* and from the genus by *the addition of this quality* to the bare pleasurableness. The differentia, therefore, which constitutes the kind *is not pleasurableness*, but something else, over and above the hedonistic base. And as each kind has for its differentia a property which is repeated in no other, 'quality' changes from kind to kind, and is no common element pervading all and expressible throughout in terms of the same predicable. But when we speak of one thing as more *this* or less *that* than another, we talk nonsense, unless 'this' or 'that' belong to both, as an attribute susceptible of degrees. In order, therefore, that Mill's 'kinds' should be some higher, some lower, their differentiæ must all be comprised in some common predicate, which cannot fail to be producible in the *positive* degree: something not only over and above the generic essence of pleasurableness, but also beyond the specific differences, and carrying up their heterogeneous characteristics to an including quantitative attribute which marshals them on a graduated scale. If, as we are assured, their relative eligibility largely depends on their rank in that scale, and will be misjudged by the hedonist test without it, we may fairly ask, What is the attribute, for the comparative and superlative of which we are to be on the watch? It is mere parrot-talk to repeat that it is 'pleasure:' you have already told us that that alone will not do: that there might be the more or less pleasurable, without its settling the more or less eligible; and we now want to know the *supplementary determinant*, whose degrees traverse and correct the other scale. If knowledge-seeking is 'higher' than gastronomy, and vindictiveness 'lower' than compassion, these comparative adjectives are here figuratively used, and not literally of the *vertical line*, as if one of the springs of action were to be looked for overhead, and the other underground. Remove the figure then, and name the real continuum to the extremities of which this language represents the relative approach.

Now there are but two other scales of degrees, as it seems to me, of which it is possible to think as tendered in answer to this demand: viz. that of the καλόν, supplied by our sense of beauty; and of the ἀγαθόν, in the limited sense of δέον or δίκαιον, supplied by our sense of right. And one of these must certainly be present to anyone's thought who feels the nobleness or loveliness or sanctity of this or that type of conduct and character, and is led by his enthusiasm to set his face towards it. Is it, then, the *Æsthetic scale* which Mill silently introduces and finds sufficient to direct and control the simply hedonistic? Its influence is no doubt there, and is traceable enough in his fervent appreciation of intellectual and benevolent life; but it could not be there, were it not sustained and put forward by its parent and essential support, the scale of Right behind it; for when the sense of beauty spreads from the sensible world to that of *character*, it goes only where the Good has gone before it, and suffuses with its light the patience, the heroism, the incorruptible justice, which already attest by their existence the antecedence of the moral perceptions. Character is not admired, till it is there; and it is there, by the self-knowledge and self-assertion of ethical differences. Its rightness is not conditional on its beauty; but its beauty on its rightness.

Moreover, the higher rank which we attribute to the exercise of some springs of action as compared with others attaches, not to the pleasures which they bring, but to themselves as activities and their ends as aims, worthy of our nature, with or without any personal balance of gain. What the 'martyr of science' wants, is, not to enjoy, but *to know*: what the reformer of wrong wants, is, not victory, but *Justice*; and either of them would rather perish than resign the field. It is easy to say that whoever has in him an intense thirst for knowledge or passion for justice has more satisfaction in unbending adherence to his pursuit, than he sacrifices even in death out of loyalty to it; but, if so, the superior satisfaction is due to his loyalty, and not his loyalty to the superior satisfaction; and that loyalty is simply an inward homage to the rightful claim of the spring of action which he is tempted to desert. And thus, under the disguise of a graduated series of pleasures, we recognise the moral hierarchy as the concealed reality; and must own that, in refining upon the defences of his theory, J. S. Mill has practically cancelled its aggressive power. On this point Mr. Lecky's judgment appears to me perfectly reasonable. 'If it be meant,' he says, 'that we have the power of selecting some pleasures rather than others as superior in kind, irrespective of all consideration of their intensity, their cost, and their consequences, I submit that the admission is by no means (as Mr. Mill maintains) compatible with the Utilitarian theory. It may be added that Mr. Mill elsewhere (Dissert. Vol. I. p. 387), admits that every human action has "its æsthetic aspect, or that of its beauty," which addresses itself to the imagination. It will probably appear to many of my readers that these two concessions,—that we have the power of recognising a distinction of kind in our pleasures, and that we have a perception of beauty in our actions,—make the difference between Mr. Mill and intuitive moralists not very much more than verbal[1].'

ii. ETHICALLY CONSIDERED.

From the psychological features of hedonism, let us now turn to the ethical; with a view especially to determine the adequacy of its base to support a coherent structure of duty. The account which I have given of it from the writings of its leading representatives must have left, I think, two opposite impressions; of its courageous vindication,— nay, in Hobbes and Helvetius, almost *parade*,—of self-love; and, on the other hand, of its emphatic insistence,—especially in the younger Mill (to whom Austin might well be added),—on the merging of all self-preference in the equal claims of every other human being whom our conduct may touch: Bentham, like an ethical Janus, facing both ways, with a sort of grimace of extravagance, both in his selfish and in his benevolent aspect. These two impressions affect us, if I mistake not, as if they came from different systems; and leave us in a certain uneasiness till we can ascertain whether they are really discrepant, or admit of being harmonised. To this question we must seek to reply.

§ 1. *From 'Each for Himself' to 'Each for All,'—no Road.*

It has been already admitted that *Altruistic affection* is just as open to the Hartleyan hedonist, as to any other psychologist. He has no difficulty in accounting for the existence in men of every variety of disinterested feeling, notwithstanding his derivation of it from primitive data of sensible pleasures and pains; so that the psychological connection between self-regarding and extra-regarding states of mind is clear, and presents no perplexity. He can tell you how it is that a being who begins with no pleasure but in

[1] Hist. of Eur. Morals, I. chap. i. p. 92, note.

himself, may in later life devote himself for his friend, his country, or even the least attractive of mankind. But if you start the further question, why *he ought* to do so, the answer will be by no means so ready or so distinct. I do not at present refer to the hedonist's antipathy, so humourously expressed by Bentham, to the notion involved in the word 'ought.' Accepting for the moment the only meaning in which he consents to retain it, let us assume that, of *necessity* and therefore of *right*, I desire, and in every voluntary act seek, my own happiness; then I miss the link which connects with this assumption the further proposition that, in the same sense, I *ought* to seek the 'greatest happiness' of others. So far indeed as the same '*necessity*' which makes the '*ought*' in my own case operates upon me also in theirs, i.e. so far as I can no more help pursuing their happiness than pursuing my own, both aims are right in the same sense and covered by the same rule. But how little way this inevitable benevolence will go towards the range of altruism on which our Utilitarians insist, it is needless to say; and the question is, How can they summon all that remains wanting, to come and stand under the same category? why, in cases where *I can help it*, 'ought' I to take account of others' happiness as of my own?

The usual answer is to this effect: it is 'reasonable' and 'authoritative' for me to seek happiness, as the only good; but my happiness is no more desirable than anybody else's; therefore it is equally reasonable and authoritative to seek the happiness of *quivis*, i.e. of any other 'person concerned.' Accordingly, J. S. Mill lays repeated stress on the position 'that the happiness which forms the utilitarian standard of what is right in conduct, is not the agent's own happiness, but that of all concerned. As between his own happiness and that of others, utilitarianism requires him to be as strictly impartial as a disinterested and benevolent spectator. In the golden rule of Jesus of Nazareth, we read the complete spirit of the ethics of utility. To do as you would be done by, and to love your neighbour as yourself, constitute the ideal perfection of Utilitarian morality[1].' That this is the rule at which the best disciples of this school arrive, and which is already embodied in Bentham's maxim, 'Everybody to count for one, nobody for more than one,' is indisputable: the question is whether, from their assumptions, or consistently with them, they can find their way to any such rule. The reason adduced in proof of it is conspicuously fallacious. When it is laid down as self-evident that the only desirable end is happiness, the meaning surely is, that nothing is desirable for A but the happiness of A; and when it is said that A's happiness is no more desirable than B's, the meaning is, that A's is no more desirable for A than B's is for B; from which it is fair to conclude that B has the same warrant for pursuing his own happiness that A has; but *not* that to either of them the happiness of the other is, or ought to be, as desirable as his own. The word 'desirable' is a *relative word*, and has no definite meaning without reference to the person or persons whose desires it implies; and if in twice using the word you change these persons, the meaning is changed, and you must guard yourself against an ambiguity. In the first premiss of the foregoing reasoning the desirableness of happiness is affirmed *for the individual enjoying it*· in the second, it is affirmed as equal for him and for any or all mere observers, irrespective of its personal incidence; for, else, we do not get the conclusion, that it must be all the same to him, whether the good alights on him or on a stranger. As well might you argue that because, of a hundred men, each one's hunger is satisfied by his dinner, therefore the hunger of all must be satisfied by the dinner of each. The terms employed to conceal this leap, from what is only distributively true to what is generically so, are empty or confused abstracts which cannot be realised in conception; e. g. in order to *discharge all relativity*, happiness is pronounced '*intrinsically desirable.*' What does this mean? If, as I suppose, '*irrespective of anyone's desire,*' i.e.

[1] Utilitarianism, chap. ii. p. 24.

whether or not a nature exists to desire it, the phrase involves a *contradictio in adjecto*, the adverb '*intrinsically*' picking out and throwing away all that is meant by 'desirable.' Whatever is desirable is made so by the wants and wishes of some external being; whatever is intrinsic lies in the essence of its subject and is exempt from such external dependence; and to combine these two words is to manufacture a pretended conception out of an affirmation and denial of the same thing. In no way can you legitimately pass from a relative premiss to an absolute conclusion; and though I grant that my happiness is no more desirable to me than is yours to you, yet it is not made out thereby that mine is to me no more desirable than yours : the equality of all the values relatively to their subjects does not prove their equality when taken apart; it is a system simply of *equivalent ratios*,—a very different thing from *identical magnitude* in the terms.

Not only does the hedonist postulate *fail to establish* the rule of 'impartial' regard for 'the greatest happiness;' it sets up the direct opposite. For it affirms, as we have seen[1], not only that 'to obtain the greatest portion of happiness for himself is the object of every rational being,' but that 'no other man can weigh for him his pains and pleasures,' and that, in weighing them, 'himself must necessarily be his first concern.' But the rule of impartiality forbids him to prefer himself to other people, or to weigh his own pains and pleasures except in a common measure with theirs. The language of the latter says in effect, 'Everybody is to do as he likes best, and not one of the million is to have any voice in the matter;' that of the former, 'Nobody is to do as he likes best, but only to have *one vote* towards it out of the million.' Till these propositions can be reconciled, hedonist benevolence may exist as a fact, but will remain an inconsequence.

It is, then, impossible to effect the transition from the cogency of personal pleasure and pain to that of others'

---

[1] Supra, p. 306.

pleasures and pains; it is but a sophistical slip of thought which carries the Utilitarian from the principle 'Each for his own happiness' to that of 'Each for the happiness of all.' The moment a divergency arises between the interests of the individual and those of other 'persons concerned,' you cannot enforce theirs against what you have told him is his own 'first concern.' The only hope for the theory is to show that there can be no such divergency: that the private and the public welfare are coincident: that the personal motive, therefore, works without check over the whole field of social as well as individual morality Can it then be made out that it is always prudent to be virtuous?, or rather, that the dictates of self-love and of altruism are identical?

In proof of such identity, moralists rely on two principal considerations: (1) the inward constitution of the individual mind; which, out of its own pleasures and pains, weaves the disinterested affections and makes the love of others a personal joy: and (2) the external pressure of social sentiment; which restrains the selfish desires, and by its penalties balances any inordinate interests of theirs. In the present section I will speak only of the first of these.

As to the internal conciliation of egoistic interest and benevolence, it is undeniable that when we have come to love, for its own sake, any object,—be it a pursuit or a person,—which was once of no account but as the instrument of some pleasure to ourselves, its well-being is essentially blended with our own and belongs to the same personal aim. I shall certainly desire and enjoy the happiness of anybody that I am fond of, and try to secure it at some cost of effort: if I am true to the assumed principle of my nature, the limit of that willing effort will be, the point at which its strain over-balances the sympathetic pleasure it would save. This point, it may be urged, is not very easily reached in one whose disinterested affections have had full opportunity of growth: such power may they gain in him, that he will risk all, and accept the dungeon or the scaffold, rather than betray a friend or consent to the ruin of the State. That an Epicurean type of humanity might, in an extreme case, if Hartley had the working out of it, produce such an adjustment of preferences as this martyr would exemplify, I would not absolutely deny. But, if self-love can thus become identical with self-sacrifice, it is only by subjecting the nature in which this happens to a fatal illusion, and dressing up a moment's enthusiasm as worth more to it than the collective possibilities of remaining life. Under the law which bears him off on the line least repugnant to him at the time, he flings himself away, and secures, let us suppose, for others the happiness which he renounces for himself. And who is it that does this? By hypothesis, it is the egoistic hedonist, whose reason tells him that his own pleasure is for him the sole good, and except as tributary to this, that of others has no significance. He is betrayed, therefore, by his disinterested passion into direct contradiction of his own reason, and inversion of its fundamental rule. By substituting others for himself, his rational preferences are turned upside down; and nature, like a cruel nurse, replacing him by a changeling ere he knows himself, exposes him to a fate that is not his own. He thinks, you will say, that the happiness he wins for others is the greatest for himself, though it be the last; so that there is no clashing interest. Yes: he thinks so: but is it true? Can it be shown that his twin brother, who in the same crisis was snatched by no fervours from his far-sighted prudence, but made the compliances needful for escape, and lived in opulence and office through another generation, miscalculated his lot, and enjoyed less of 'the only good' than the dead hero? What metrical standard can demonstrate that the felicity of one supreme moment of self-immolation transcends in amount thirty years of unbroken health, of social favour, and satisfied affections? How will you go to work, in order to convince this comfortable citizen of his mistake in declining to share his brother's martyrdom? You remind him of the lies he told: he thinks them venial, and a cheap ransom from the pangs of death. You appeal to the higher truth of which the martyr's death became a missionary to the world: he perceives no higher and lower in matters where he is sure of no truth at all. You point to the almost Divine honours which the invigorated conscience of mankind pays to their self-sacrificing leaders and reformers: he prefers the daily experience of their homage to his rank, his equipages, and his power. Not only is it true that nothing which you, or which the enthusiast brother himself, could say will convince the self-seeker that he has chosen amiss: but it is no less true that the most impartial estimator of happiness cannot convict him of imprudence. Each took the lot which his character rendered the least intolerable, and would have been more miserable in the other's; but that the one was not the victim of his affections, and the other the gainer by his self-care, it is utterly impossible to prove. It does not follow therefore that, because the individual may come to make the greater good of others his own, so that to his feeling the conflict between them vanishes, there is on that account no real discrepancy, and that he is not carried off blindfold to the sacrifice; and that a self-forgetfulness less perfect, and still agonised by the struggle between personal shrinking and devoted love, does not more faithfully represent the actual relation of things. A wound which, inflicted in hot blood, is scarcely felt, still remains a wound after all, and has to be reckoned with in long privations ere all is healed; and if the question is, of keeping accurate accounts of loss and gain, he cannot be blamed who, untouched by the passions of the fight, reads the whole story of its risks, and determines to keep a whole skin. For my part, I have not the least doubt of the reality of the hedonistic sacrifice required by benevolence of affection and rectitude of choice; and that, if it is hid from the agent who makes it, it is because he has lost his measuring rod of pleasures and learned the gradations of another scale.

Mr. L. Stephen sees clearly through the sophistical

attempts to establish the invariable prudence of virtue: after admirably exposing their principal fallacy, he concludes, 'There is scarcely any man, I believe, at all capable of sympathy or reason, who would not in many cases unhesitatingly sacrifice his own happiness for a sufficient advantage to others. Almost every mother would die, or expose herself to sufferings which can never be repaid, for the good of her infant; and though maternal love affords the most perfect example of devotion to others, and is of course much stronger than most other benevolent feelings, I think that the same principle is illustrated even in those commonplace acts of good-nature of which almost every man is capable[1].'

In giving the Utilitarian postulate the benefit of the Hartleyan 'law of transference,' as a means of identifying individual and social happiness, I have thus far supposed it possible for the egoist to be carried through by it into complete disinterestedness, i. e. to lose the idea of his own pleasure in the absorbing idea of pleasure to others. And, unless and until he reaches this point, it is certain that he must fall short of his all-directing aim; for, so long as he thinks of himself, he is a stranger to the joy of sympathy; and many another form of happiness too he cannot have, till he ceases to seek it. But too much is conceded in allowing this possibility. For the condition of his being what he is, viz. an egoistic hedonist, is, that he always pursues his own greatest pleasure; while the condition of obtaining the greatest pleasure is, that he does *not* pursue it. His very characteristic therefore is suicidal, and precludes him from ever consummating the growth of disinterestedness through the working of the Hartleyan law. He is under a very common illusion, that because 'pleasure exists only as it is felt,' the more he attends to it, the more will he have of it, consciousness being intensified by concentration: whereas what is thereby increased is nothing but *intellectual cognition* of it, which, instead of intensifying

[1] Science of Ethics, chap. x. iv. § 36, pp. 431, 432.

the feeling, immediately arrests its growth and crystallises it into an object of thought. The play of the Hartleyan law requires exactly the opposite condition, viz. the presence of felt, but uncontemplated, pleasure, with attention (so far as there is any) engaged upon the perceptible objects that cause it; so that the feeling is let alone in its free expansion, and allowed to suffuse the objects with colours of added beauty. And hence the law receives its chief illustration in the mental history, not of introspective philosophers, but of children, and persons whose eager impulses prevent their ever losing the attributes of childhood. The pleasures which the Sensation-philosophy needs to detain in the unreflecting state, the egoist insists on bringing into the full blaze of self-consciousness; and by that change at once withers their energy, and stops the widening of their empire over neutral fields. He therefore cancels at the outset the qualification for winning the disinterested affections, and closes against himself the path which we have hypothetically left open to him. The only question for him now is whether, having learned that his conscious self-seeking may be intrusive, he can employ the will which has invoked it to turn it out again; so as voluntarily to forget himself, in order to be landed at last in a more pleasurable result. It seems so little disputable that self-seeking and self-forgetfulness are mutually exclusive, that it would no more have occurred to me to ask the former to eject itself than to resort to Satan to cast out Satan, were it not that Professor Sidgwick apparently regards this as by no means an impracticable feat. He thinks it quite possible for an Epicurean who judges himself deficient in impulses and affections which are important factors in the possible sum of pleasures, to put himself in the way of producing these in himself. And this opinion, he reminds us, has the support of many philosophers and divines who have commended the benevolent and the religious affections, as worthy of being fostered by all who would attain to the happiest kind of life.

'It is true that, as our desires cannot ordinarily be produced by an effort of Will—though they can to some extent be repressed by it—if we started with no impulse except the desire of pleasure, it might seem difficult to execute the practical paradox of attaining pleasure by aiming at something else. Yet even in this hypothetical case the difficulty is less than it appears. For the reaction of our activities upon our emotional nature is such that we may commonly bring ourselves to take an interest in any end by concentrating our efforts upon its attainment. So that, even supposing a man to begin with absolute indifference to everything except his own pleasure, there is no reason to believe that if he were convinced that the possession of other desires and impulses were necessary to the attainment of the greatest possible pleasure, he could not succeed in producing these. But this supposition is never actually realised. Every man, when he commences the task of systematising his conduct, whether on egoistic principles or any other, is conscious of a number of different impulses and tendencies within him, other than the mere desire for pleasure, which urge his will in particular directions, to the attainment of particular results: so that he has only to place himself under certain external influences, and these desires and impulses will begin to operate without any effort of will.

'It is sometimes thought, however, that there is an important class of refined and elevated impulses with which the supremacy of self-love is in a peculiar way incompatible; such as the love of virtue, or personal affection, or the religious impulse to love and obey God. But at any rate in the common view of these impulses, this difficulty does not seem to be recognised. None of the school of moralists that followed Shaftesbury in contending that it is a man's true interest to foster in himself strictly disinterested social affections, has noticed any inherent incompatibility between the existence of these affections and the supremacy of rational self-love. And similarly the Christian preachers before mentioned, who have commended the religious life as really the happiest, have not thought genuine religion irreconcilable with the conviction that each man's own happiness is his most near and intimate concern[1].'

I do not doubt the possibility, on which these paragraphs insist, of cultivating, by a self-appointed discipline, desires and affections which we know to be too weak within us: whoever will persistently compel himself to do the duty which ought to spring from some spontaneous love, will not for ever go to it with heavy steps, but will ere long be won over by its interest, and surprised by the richness of its contents. That a self-inclosed man may throw himself open to sympathise, and a timid man train himself to be brave, is certain; *provided* the effort is stimulated and sustained by an adequate veneration for benevolence and contempt of cowardice, or homage to duty; but *not*, I am persuaded, if its only support be a craving for the personal pleasures of benevolence and courage. Professor Sidgwick appears to think that, if there are indirect means by which the will can set up affections and desires beyond its immediate command, it matters not what motive takes the initiative; so that the missing virtues may as well be fetched up by prudential considerations as by any other. In this tacit assumption he overlooks, as it seems to me, the very hinge of the whole case, and fails to notice the blighting effect of mere self-seeking upon the inward movements of the moral life. Who was ever known to make himself a philanthropist in order to add to his enjoyment? or a martyr to truth in order to taste the pleasures of heroism? Whatever comes from such incentives can only be a miserable counterfeit, a histrionic sham, of any sincere and whole-hearted excellence: you cannot give yourself freely away, while you are casting side glances at what you mean to reserve for your private advantage. Professor Sidgwick, I admit, appeals with good right to the precedents of Shaftesbury and the moralising divines, who recommended the cultivation of disinterested and devout affections as a good investment. They are certainly on his

[1] Methods of Ethics, II. chap. iii. § 3, pp. 133, 134.

side. But I wonder that the notorious inefficacy of their teaching, and the low spiritual level of their own and the succeeding age, did not disincline him to their alliance, and suggest the question, whether the feebleness of their influence was not due to the very feature for which he cites them. They failed to do the awakening work which has been achieved by many a man their intellectual inferior, because they harped upon the wrong chord. Hedonistic advance to any higher love is not less impossible than horizontal movement up hill.

The instances which lend some plausibility to Professor Sidgwick's position, and which he probably had in view, are those in which the self-discipline is conducted under the influence of *mixed motives;* and if, in instituting it, prudential desire plays at all a conspicuous part, it may seem as though the whole process were under its direction; yet the agent, once launched upon his course, is again and again taken out of his own hands by currents of enthusiasm which sweep him away from his self-regards. He thus alternates his egoism with disinterested desires; and in proportion as the latter snatch him from his self-love, they neutralise its incapacity, and carry him on while it is laid to sleep. What he thus achieves in the way of disinterestedness is in spite of his prudential aim, not in consequence of it, and should be cited in illustration, not of its triumph, but of its defeat. He passes to and fro between two lives, now watchful of his pleasures, then torn from them by some lavish love; and it is not the measured steps of the former that conduct him to the latter; but the wings of the latter that lift him off his cautious feet. In principle this is admitted by Professor Sidgwick himself; for where 'a stricter disinterestedness' and an 'absolute self-devotion' is required, he pronounces it to be an attainment beyond the reach of Rational Egoism. 'Other persons, however, seem to carry the religious consciousness and the feeling of human affection to a higher stage of refinement, at which a stricter disinterestedness is exacted. They maintain that the essence of either feeling, in its best form, is absolute self-devotion and self-sacrifice. And certainly these seem incompatible with self-love, however cautiously self-limiting. A man cannot both wish to secure his own happiness and be willing to lose it. And yet how if willingness to lose it is the true means of securing it? Can self-love not merely reduce indirectly its prominence in consciousness, but directly and unreservedly annihilate itself?

'This emotional feat does not seem to me possible: and therefore I must admit that a man who embraces the principle of Rational Egoism cuts himself off from the special pleasure that attends this absolute sacrifice and suppression of self. But, however exquisite this may be, the pitch of emotional exaltation and refinement necessary to attain it is so comparatively rare, that it is scarcely included in men's common estimate of happiness. I do not therefore think that an important objection to Rational Egoism can be based upon its incompatibility with this particular consciousness[1].' The concession here made is all that need be asked: I desire no more. For the very same reasoning which is here applied to the animating spring of life as a whole, holds good no less of every interval of self-devotion that intersects a variable spirit with a bar of light: each of its bright disinterested hours is homogeneous with the all-pervading tone of the mind entirely surrendered, and is equally incompatible with the present sway of Rational Egoism; and the difference lies simply in the intermittency of the one, and the continuity of the other. And as we have to do, not with the see-saw of mixed and inconsistent characters, but with the inward analysis of moral causation and the distinctive types of moral experience, I see no reason for referring to different categories what are merely half-cases and whole-cases of one and the same thing.

The conclusion to which we are thus far brought is obvious: notwithstanding the provision in our nature for the partial conversion of interested into disinterested feeling,

[1] Methods of Ethics, II. chap. iii. § 2, p. 134.

it is impossible to identify the greatest happiness of self with the greatest happiness of all concerned; or, from the necessity of pursuing the former to establish the claim of the latter; or, to extract a scheme of duty from rules of prudence; or, to make the motive of self-love, however rationally worked, suffice for building up a virtuous character. The moral consciousness of the individual mind comprises experiences which are not covered by the data and inferences of rational hedonism.

§ 2. *The Moral Sentiments as an Engine of Social Management.*

Now, open the floodgates, and let in the head-waters of *Society* upon the individual; and see whether, in the new positions to which they bear him and the new necessities by which they surround him, his nature does not gain the needful supplement. The moral inadequacy of self-interest may perhaps be remedied by the presence of social interest and the enormous power of public opinion. The close connection between manners and morals, the obvious origin of the former in social tastes, and provision in the latter for social needs, the apparently equal variation of both with change of time and place, have naturally suggested the idea of their virtual identity, and of the expression in both of them of nothing more than the wishes of the majority. Various forms have been given to this conception, according as the collective life of men has been politically, mechanically, or physiologically conceived, as set up by the sway of a Lawgiver over subjects, or by the subjection of the individual to a homogeneous multitude, or by the growth of a civic organism through confluence and unification of functions. The second of these represents the doctrine of the Hobbes and the Utilitarian school, and alone belongs to our present subject. It proceeds upon the assumption that the individual is the unit of society; that, in the antithesis of his single self to the great aggregate personality over against him, he is helpless and dependent, till he has relinquished every conflicting desire, and become moulded to the shape of the common wish: that the rules and signs which express this common wish constitute for him the standard to which he must conform; and that these are what we really mean by *morals*; which, therefore, are simply the statement of the public wants issued as the orders of a superior force to the individual. *His* moral sentiments are thus simply an adoption of the public wish; his conscience, an appropriation of its pleased or displeased mood; his sense of obligation, a consciousness of a *coercion* with which it is armed against him; and his duty, the contents of its expectation from him. Often as this theory has been presented, I have found it worked out by no Utilitarian writer so lucidly and precisely as by James Mill, in his 'Fragment on Mackintosh[1];' and the few comments which I shall make upon it will address themselves to his exposition of the origin of moral rules, and the formation of moral character.

The problem, as Mill takes it, is to get a maximum of useful actions out of the individual agent. A good many may be expected to come of their own accord, his own desire running on the same line with that of his associates: about these, therefore, we need not trouble ourselves. But there is a large number besides which he has not sufficient inducement in himself to put forth; and some contrivance must be set up for the purpose of extorting these from him. The device which we have hit upon for this end is to *Praise* the actions which we like, and *Blame* those which we dislike, or, in extreme cases, to *reward* the one, and *punish* the other; and the particular variety of like and dislike which thus declares itself is called *approval* and *disapproval*. All these are, therefore, an artificial mechanism of influence invented, as a bribe or threat, to stir a will which would otherwise fail us: as Mill says, 'The production of acts of the useful sort, the prevention of acts of contrary sort,' constitute 'the whole business of the moral sentiments[2].'

---

[1] See especially pp. 246-252.
[2] Fragment on Mackintosh, p. 250.

They are thus *a social creation*, or storage of force, for controlling the individual, and getting service out of him.

Thus far, the ordinances of conduct form merely an external law, enforced by the sanction of public opinion. But the individual agent on whom they press is himself one of the public body, and accustomed, in that capacity, to apply the same rule and the same sanction to other agents, i e. to direct approbation and disapprobation upon analogous acts. When, therefore, an action which he would condemn in another proceeds from himself, he not only foresees what it will bring upon him from its witnesses, but, as one of those witnesses, shares their displeasure, and is self-condemned. Hence, the feeling of compunction and remorse, on the one hand, of self-satisfaction and self-applause on the other, are but a personal loan, for private use, of the public sentiment embodied in the established rule; and by the agent's application of it in his own case it becomes an internal law, by which he can administer the affairs of his own commonwealth of thought and desire.

This ingenious theory avails itself no doubt of some processes that actually do mingle with our moral experience; only, not as its constitutive essentials, but as its subsidiary accidents. It is not necessary to deny their reality, in order to prove their inadequacy as a solution of the problem to which they belong. It is sufficient to show that that problem contains phenomena of which they afford no satisfactory account.

(1) In the analysis of our moral psychology, given in the preceding book, it was made evident, if I mistake not, that we judge ourselves before we judge others. To the reasons there given I must refer, as justifying the assertion that James Mill inverts the only possible order of relation between internal and external judgment. If what we disapproved were the disagreeableness of an outward fact, we should disapprove of noxious animals or even the hurtful behaviour of physical things. It is true, as Mill reminds us, that there would be 'no use' in disapproving these things;

for though both of them may admit of being 'modified,' they are not, like man, amenable to such an influence as our displeasure. What then is it that fits the *human activity alone* for the operation of this modifying power? what, but the fact that it issues from an inward spring which does not necessitate it to take its present form, but admits of an alternative which our suffrage may reinforce? our censure, therefore, it is plain, looks behind the scenes, and pitches upon the hidden spring of action which alone it can hope to modify. And if this be so, what do we know of hidden springs, except from their story in ourselves? How could we read them in another, except as in the mirror of our own experience? If the key of *his* nature and character is in *ours*, there it is that we learn the art of judging our *alter ego*. It follows from this that whatever truth there may be in Mill's hypothetical narrative belongs to some of the later acts of our life-drama, and does not introduce us to the opening scene which he professes to present.

(2) The moral sentiments, unless I completely misconstrue them, by no means correspond with Mill's account of their origin and nature. In his view, they are a prospective artifice for extracting serviceable conduct which needs a bonus to produce it. In mine, they are a retrospective verdict of 'well done!' or 'ill done!' on conduct already put forth. And if we laugh at the definition of *gratitude* as 'a lively sense of favours yet to come,' and dismiss it to the region of cynical satire, I do not see how we can more seriously treat an explanation of moral *Approval* as a patronising bid for future services, and moral censure as equivalent to 'Mind you don't do it again!' Such a theory gives an account of everything in them *except their moral character*, as judgments upon the merits or demerits of a free agent's choice. It describes a certain *disciplinary influence* which they undoubtedly exercise; but this itself they would not exercise with any serious effect, were they hollow in their profession of disinterested ethical affection towards conduct that is past, and were they reduced to an administration of

pleasures and pains as purchasing causes of future benefits. This theory, in short, puts the moral sentiments on the same footing with the arts of the horse-breaker, who manages his stud by the crack of his whip and a feed of oats; and treats them, so far as they deviate from this type and affect to be an award of justice to the past, as an illusion which the initiated escape. Punishment, thrown into the alembic of this new analysis, has all its retributory element dissipated, and comes out in the reduced form of deterrent and reformatory pain; and carries thenceforth the implied rationale, 'Punishment is painful, and punishment amends: therefore, give a measured lot of pain, and you will have the amendment.' As well might you argue: 'Medicine is bitter, and medicine cures; therefore, take a dose of bitters, and you will be cured.' The result is much the same in both cases: your malady remains, because the remedial efficacy lies, not in the bitterness of the medicine, but in the quality which you have failed to secure; and your criminals persist and flourish, because the deterrent and reformatory influence resides, not in the naked pain of punishment, but in its justice; and till the offender gets what, in popular phrase, 'serves him right,' he gets nothing that can do him any good. It is the same throughout; all the characteristic expressions of our moral nature are explained away by this school of interpreters, and replaced by something which they *do not mean:* good and ill desert, sin, resentment, penitence, remorse, righteous indignation, are volatilised as illusions, and their functions made over to the remaining rational and sentient nature. Whether these substitutes will be equal to the work thus laid upon them in some future age of passionless intellect, it would be dangerous to predict; but certainly, at present, there is a vast region of human feeling and experience which, by no stretching and straining, they can be made to cover and command.

(3) The conditions assigned by Mill for the genesis of the moral sentiments are by no means those which experience shows to favour their origin and diffusion. Their apparatus

of praise and blame, and their whole body of influence, he
regards as coming into existence, in order to eke out the
defective crop of beneficent acts, and produce more of them
than would be raised by the spontaneous interest of the
individual agent. The more, therefore, the individual fails
to give, so much the more will the supplementary machinery
of the public will be called into operation, and bid high for
so scarce an article as a useful act. The needful pressure,
rising to the occasion, will increase its tension as the force
of nature becomes remiss in men, taken one by one : so the
moral sentiments, following a law of demand and supply,
will most abound where they are most wanted, i e. under
the greatest lack of individual benevolence. By this rule,
nothing would be so favourable to the growth of altruistic
sentiment as the prevalence of universal egoism ; and these
two opposites would reach their maximum together. It is
hardly necessary to point out, how completely experience
reverses this relation. It is not praise that by its force
elicits the virtues, but the unforced virtues that elicit praise.
And whenever there is a dearth of spontaneous goodness, so
far is it from fetching in the compensation of induced bene-
ficence, that, once commenced, the ebb goes on in accelerating ratio ; nor will the tide turn back, though you fling at
it the loudest promise of your plaudits, or threat of your
anathemas. Selfishness breeds nothing but selfishness, and
benevolence reduplicates benevolence ; and to fill up the
lacunæ of a defective love by a supply of factitious self-
interest, is,—when 'asked for bread, to tender a stone, and
for fish, a serpent.' Where 'beneficent acts' do not come of
their own accord, e. g. in a family where the self-seeking
propensities assert themselves all round, there may no doubt
grow up a sort of public opinion from the watchfulness of
each member against the encroachments of the rest : a kind
of 'committee of vigilance' is in permanent sitting, from
which fierce complaints and loud exactions are brought
to bear, now upon this, and now upon that refractory or
reluctant will ; and for the moment the coercion may gain

its end. But he who is thus controlled *hates* what is extorted from him more than ever, and will never repeat it, unless under stress: far from gaining any moral appreciation for his 'useful acts,' he feels them to be slave-work, only more tolerable than the domestic ostracism from which they alone can save him. What is true of a family, is true of the larger social community. under the mere discipline of hope and fear from others, there will be no emergence from self-seeking into self-devotion to duty or self-sacrifice to love, but an inevitable descent into lower depths of egoistic isolation. Mill's theory proceeds on the tacit assumption, that the stock of beneficent acts requisite for the subsistence of society is a constant quantity, which must, somehow or other, be provided, and that where the native yield falls short, the moral sentiments are set up as an artificial bounty on the importation of supplementary consignments, that else would not flow in. It might have occurred to so good a free-trader that such bribed importers usually manage to pocket their profits and the bounty too; and that it is but a poor look-out, if this be all that keeps us from a famine of the virtues.

(4) The mode also in which moral rules are supposed to be got up and enforced, involves a fundamental fallacy; which it is surprising to find overlooked, by a writer so quick to see the illusions which lurk in abstractions. He presents the whole story as a kind of suit or claim of Society *versus* the Individual, treating each as a unitary personality, differing in interests, and most unequal in scale and power. It is assumed that, in its view of his conduct, Society feels and thinks and acts as one man: that his failure in altruism concerns everybody alike, and secures a consensus of rule against him and that, in any objectionable self-assertion, he is in the position of an *Athanasius contra mundum.* If it were so, if it were a case of Joseph and his brethren, without even a dissentient Reuben, of course they might vote him into the pit or the hands of the Midianites, or dispose of him by any rule they pleased. Such a body of people, all

in sympathy with each other, and none with him, would have nothing to hinder their unanimity in requiring the same things from him and praising them, and in fixing opprobrium on the same things from which they meant to deter him. Mill, accordingly, finds nothing simpler than the general agreement about what is praiseworthy and blameworthy: 'When men began to mark the distinction between acts, and were prompted to praise one class, and blame another, they did so, either because the one sort benefited, the other hurt them; or for some other reason. If for the first reason, the case is perfectly intelligible. The men had a motive which they understood, and which was adequate to the end. If it was not on account of utility that men classed some acts as moral, others as immoral, on what other account was it[1]?'

The 'perfect intelligibility' of this solution depends, however, entirely on the 'men' who are here packed together, as if they made up a single personality, being all benefited by the same acts, and hurt by the same acts. That each human being constituted on Mill's pattern, with no motive but self-love, should praise what benefits him, is intelligible enough; but in these praises there will be no consensus, unless it can be shown that what benefits one benefits all; and this, which Mill has heedlessly taken for granted, cannot, upon his data, be proved at all. His idea evidently is, that we like to see the generous act of a benefactor, and to set up a habit of eulogy on his behalf, because it may be our turn to be benefited next, and it is as well to encourage the chance: we feel sympathy with the joy of the beneficiary, as possibly our own hereafter, and express this by laudatory words. But the phenomenon has another half, which must not be suppressed. The generous act is, by hypothesis, one of those which there is no inducement of self-interest to perform, and which, as involving personal privation to the agent, it needs artificial pressure to elicit: the pleasure gained by the receiver is bought by

[1] Fragment on Mackintosh, pp. 261, 262.

pleasure lost to the giver. How comes it then that the sympathy of the neutral observer goes with the lot of pleasure bestowed, and not with the pleasure forfeited? Does not his hedonistic principle commit him as certainly to pity for the donor, as to congratulation of the receiver? Is it said, 'Oh, but he has an eye to his own chance, if he can only get this sort of sacrifice repeated?' Good: but then, there are two sides to this chance: he may be thrown into the position of the gainer; or, into the position of the loser; and, if he applauds the benefactor, he commits himself not less to 'go and do likewise,' than to lie in wait for favours yet to come. And between the two, it would seem, his hedonism would be at fault; for it does not follow from his *liking to be benefited*, that he would take with equal gusto to *benefiting*. It is forgotten, in this calculation, that in human relations, the active and the passive functions are alternate and numerically equal, so that each one of us performs as many acts as he receives, and cannot make a rule for himself as a possible recipient, which will not catch hold of him as a possible agent. What inducement then have we to become patrons of non-spontaneous 'useful acts?' They are useful to us, only when we get them; and we cannot get them without giving them; and when we give them, it is, by hypothesis, at the cost of sacrifice just as repugnant to our self-love, as the corresponding gain is agreeable to it. For a jury of hedonistic egoists to burst into applause at the sight of a benefactor and call him a hero rather than a fool, would be a renunciation by public vote of the very principle upon which the vote is assumed to be taken.

For these reasons, both the attempts, by appeal to Hartleyan psychology and to the weight of social opinion, to identify the individual and the general happiness, must be pronounced unsatisfactory. The rule framed on behalf of the public well-being is demonstrably not always compatible with the agent's own advantage. The Egoist principle, 'each for his own pleasure,' and the Utilitarian principle, 'each for the pleasure of all,' cannot even be reconciled; much less can the latter be deduced as a corollary from the former. Moreover, were the concurrence between private and public desires unquestionably complete, the result would simply be, that *Prudence* would never separate the interested from the disinterested affections: they could be indulged without mutual interference; but to neither of them would any character of *Duty* attach. The 'Rules' set up by social opinion would not really be '*Moral*' at all, if by that word we denote a statement not simply of what *is*, but of what *ought to be;* for all that they affirm is that such and such behaviour is a means of happiness; they are mere instructions how to reach this end; and have no more ethical authority than the receipts of a cookery book, which also tell you how to prepare certain pleasant results, both personal and social. Had the Utilitarian psychology therefore fulfilled its intention ever so perfectly, it would still have left the whole of the moral characteristics of our nature out in the cold, and finished up its supposed human being as a paragon of prudential wisdom.

§ 3. *Can General Rules bind against their Raison d'être?*

In the absence then of harmonised interests, what is to be done by the hedonist Utilitarian, when he encounters (as he believes) a discrepancy between the advantage of others and his own, or, between the recognised prescription for securing both and some different method of which he has more hope? Is he to prefer the pleasures of other people to his own? Why should he? Has he not been taught that he should care for their happiness, because his own is wrapped up in it? And now that they part company, does not this reason disappear? The claim of the extra-regarding feelings upon his attention being dependent on the indefeasibleness of their self-regarding source, that claim inevitably falls, whenever this link is broken. If he is quite convinced that it will serve him better to tell a lie than to speak truth, to indulge a safe passion than to resist it, by what plea can his instructors stop him? They will urge that the general rule is against him. The general rule, he will reply, is made by the many against the one, and in the interest of the many: it is all very well for them to glorify and uphold it; and it is usually worth while for the one to conform to it at some cost, rather than incur their displeasure. But when they are out of the way, and he has his opportunity without fear, the rule has no application; and why should he pay away his own pleasures for nothing? His advisers will perhaps say, that it is dangerous to break in upon right habits, which serve as a compendious formula for determining each case of conduct, and save the necessity of working out every problem from first principles. He will allow all this, but will deny that a habit is right which, having been computed for one set of conditions, is carried blindly into another, and takes no notice of the disappearance of its data: what should we think, he will ask, of a man who, having made it a rule to take a certain daily walk, persisted in it all the same when the floods were out and covered it breast-high? Mere average rules carry in them no binding force; and to trust to them still, when real causalities come into view to vary, to correct, or to supersede them, is to prefer automatism to intelligence, and turn conduct into a stupid idolatry. Least of all should the Utilitarian, who insists that rules of action have no good in themselves, but are simply the *means* which mankind have devised for securing the sole end, viz. preponderant pleasure, encourage a worship of the means, and warn the agent against any corrective reference to the end which justifies and prescribes them. Hence, it seems to follow irresistibly, that the individual is left at liberty, on this system, to secure to himself any over-balance of advantage which he may feel convinced will accrue to him from an exceptional disregard of any part of the recognised ethical code. It may be true that in ninety-nine cases out of a hundred, the greatest attainable pleasure to others may be the best way to his own; but if in the hundredth his pleasantest path diverges from theirs, how can the hedonist dissuade him from taking it? Would he not be a fool for adhering to the old means when they no longer lead to the end? The commonplace plea, that it is indispensable to have general rules that shall not be called in question, means no more, on this theory, than that, men being creatures of habit, rather than of reason, it is necessary to hoodwink and befool them in order to make them always serve you, whether it suits them or not; else, if they use their private judgment, they will now and then halt, and perhaps upset the public coach. This plea holds good only on behalf of an authoritative law or intuitive datum of our nature, which we have to accept with trust, as universally valid and conditioning all our judgments of experience; and has no legitimate application to mere inductive rules, provisionally framed from a majority of observed instances, and for ever open to exceptions and to revision. Of such empirical rules, the whole value depends on their being *not* blindly accepted and shut up, but kept under the eye of a vigilant criticism, that shifts their boundary as life supplies new and modifying experiments[1].

And if the claim of general happiness cannot be pressed beyond its coincidence with the agent's own, the inroads of exception to ethical rules assuredly have no inconsiderable range. This may be approximately judged by comparing the standards of conduct to which rational men conform, on the one hand, when supposing themselves to have the guidance of an intuitive conscience, and on the other, when avowedly ruled by their own greatest pleasure. When was it ever known that this last motive unfurled the flag of an ideal morality, and led the way to heroic attacks upon the strongholds of wrong? Is it not rather the secret excuse or the open plea for cowardly acquiescence in things as they

[1] Mr. F. H. Bradley has well animadverted on this weak point in the Utilitarian morals, in his 'Ethical Studies,' pp. 96 98.

are? Nor is it obvious how one who is surrendered to its influence can be expected to decline the offer of a furtive and prudent licence to his appetites, which adds, as he thinks, to the agreeableness without increasing the obligations of life. It is assuredly from his armoury that all the weapons of argument are borrowed, which try to beat back the missionaries of moral purity and the redressors of the most shameful of all wrongs. From his point of view, their adoption of the Christian aim at inward sanctity, and their trust in the feasibility of all duty and the victory of all right, are dreams of romance, which can visit no eyes open to the light of day. Even in the affairs of bargain and contract between man and man, the rules of integrity are by no means the measure of private advantage; and the scrupulous tradesman who will keep only genuine goods and honest scales, and promise nothing that he cannot perform, is laughed at as a 'slow-coach,' and outstripped in the competition of the market by the rival who drills and plugs his weights, or exports wooden nutmegs and needles without eyes, or dresses up his flimsy calicoes with heavy mineral and glaze. To the adventurer of this ''cute' type, it is a small thing that he cannot often repeat his tricks; for he operates upon a scale that makes once enough; or, if not, he can at least change the market, and finish his fortune in a trice. The whole history of Statecraft shows how difficult it is for strict veracity and honour to cope with the unprincipled arts of the wily diplomatist; who quickly seizes the crisis when a courageous lie may turn the balance and secure the triumph of a nation's policy. However hurtful these things may be to the moral health of society, their immediate success condones the offence for the individual, and wins his coveted prize of wealth or fame. In order to keep an equilibrium between the social and the personal happiness, and prevent either from disturbing the other, a man must desire nothing that does not accord with the public wish. He must be a thorough conformist to the opinions and methods of his party or his age; if he deviates a doctrine Nine-tenths of the ethical habits and convictions of civilised society have become fixed, and placed beyond the reach of question, before it presents itself and offers its services as their philosophic base; so that it is saved the trouble of inventing them *ab initio* by its own light, and constructing them into a reasoned organism by the resources of its skill. Benefits enough are apparent from them, after they have become familiar to experience, to prevent any challenge of their utility; and they easily pass muster without comparison with any alternative. It is only in view of the remaining tenth of the customary rules, i.e. those which have become questionable and fallen under discussion between the conservative and the reformer, that the forces of the theory are mobilised and got under arms. Its activity is critical only, not creative; it tries its hand at correcting the text of a given law for a new edition; and is not tested by demands upon its original legislative genius. But the moment you put it to this severer test, and ask from it an *à priori* determination of the true code of human life from the data of man's constitution and relations to the world, its helplessness and barrenness become conspicuous. How, for example, would it settle the right course of conduct towards the inferior animals? Do not they also fall within the calculus of pleasure and pain, which is the decisive authority in every problem? Why may they be hunted and slain, while man is spared? Why is he a cannibal if he eats the flesh of his enemy, and not if he eats theirs? When he can subsist on the produce of the earth, may he kill them merely because he likes meat better? Or, if he may butcher them for food, may he destroy them for their skins? and to appropriate the ornament of their feathers? and to make weapons against them from their own beaks and bones and tusks? If the 'whole sentient creation' is to enter into our reckoning, can we be sure that 'the locusts and potato-bug may not enjoy our crops now and then more than we should ourselves?' And, if we ourselves are warranted to act as animals of prey, must we not approve of the from this, he is equally punished, whether he sinks to a lower level or rises to a higher. The cry of the multitude, nay, of the Chief Priests and Pharisees,—'Away with him! Crucify Him!'—is as ready for the Saviours as for the Malefactors of the world; and if the end of life is to make the most of its pleasures and minimise its pains, there is no room for the devotee of compassion, whose heart is irresistibly drawn to the haunts of sin and misery, and takes on it the burthen of countless woes besides its own, and bleeds for every wound it cannot heal. Look only at the countenance of such a one, at the tender depth within the eye, the clear and thoughtful brow, the sensitive and precarious calm upon the features, and say whether you are here in presence of the best economist of happiness. If this be the object of your quest, had you not better go to the resorts of refined and easy life, where there is luxury that hurts no health, and art that adorns the scene without and the mind within, and alternate industry and gaiety that brighten all the hours, and neighbourly offices enough just to keep the reproach of selfishness away, and religious observance enough to mingle a deeper tone and higher sanction with it all? Here surely we must count up more pleasures and fewer pains than fall to the lot of the hero of compassion. True it is that he would not exchange his labour for this rest; not, however, because it is a less happy state; but because it is a state too happy for a soul once pierced by the sorrows of humanity. Were the hedonistic rule psychologically imperative upon him, he would be tempted by the exchange, and quit his vows of service. It is only because it is impossible for him to listen to it without shame, that he toils on beneath his cross[1].

The weakness of the Utilitarian theory is concealed from its supporters by the late date in the development of morals at which it makes its appearance and seeks its application as

---

[1] I cannot refrain from referring the reader who would see these positions strengthened, to some impressive paragraphs in Lecky's 'History of European Morals,' I. pp. 60-63.

wolf and the panther doing the same? If once the pleas of instinct are to be abolished and replaced by a hedonistic arithmetic, the whole realm of animated nature has to be reckoned with in weaving the tissue of moral relations; and the problem becomes infinite and insoluble. Nor is it easier to predetermine the right type of relations simply human by considerations of the hedonistic order. The conjugal and family ties, under such regulation, could never set into the form towards which they have passed as their highest; and which, even now that experience has vindicated and sanctified it, is again and again disputed, on the plea of greater happiness, and assailed by rebellious experiments, never tried but with results, not perhaps of misery, but of degradation and moral decay. There is not a commandment in the decalogue which, when submitted to the newest connoisseurs of utility, is not spurned as a superstition or an imposture:—it is the threatened tyrant, we are told, who forbids murder; the rich, who make a crime of theft; the frugal Puritans, who glorify temperance and chastity; but, for other people, other things are more serviceable. And if we urge the superior interests of the social organism, they reply that the social organism is just what they desire not to conserve, but to destroy; and that till its rulers are made away with, and its property seized, and its restraints relaxed, the world will be detained from 'the greatest happiness of the greatest number.' With persons who fall into this state of mind, what can be hoped from argument conducted on their own principles? When they insist on taking a clean page and going over the whole sum again without looking at the old workings, can you feel sure of grasping all the data and bringing out *de novo* the answers which shall put the daring fallacies to shame? Is it not certain that, before you reach the end of your reckoning, you will have utterly bewildered both yourself and your intended convert; and be glad to appeal to some latent sympathy in him, nobler than his cynical defiance?

CHAPTER II.

HEDONISM WITH EVOLUTION.

§ 1. *Psychology, how Affected by the Idea of Evolution.*

No characteristic of modern intellectual method is more striking, or more fertile in results, than the application of the idea of *Time* to the contents of the cosmos, as well as to the vicissitudes of the human race. Science formerly addressed itself to the world as an ordered system of bodies in space, not indeed without incessant movements, but all repeating themselves as night and day, as life and death, and, since their institution, unaffected through the ages which they count. For the same place, the Ephemeris might differ from year to year; but, after a while, the old figures return to their places, and the stars see each other as before. There was therefore no continuous tale to tell; but only a fixed constitution to define, and a circulating list of changes provided for and predicted from its laws. This scheme of things was indeed once set up; but with that the man of science has nothing to do:' he takes it once for all as he finds it; and it is the same for him, as if it had for ever been. On the other hand, it was the drama of mankind that unfolded itself indefinitely through Time, with new persons and new scenes, now tragic, now brilliant, but never reproducing the same attitudes and events. There was thus the strongest antithesis between the studies of the synchronous order of the external world, and of the successive order of human experience: there was nothing historical in the former; and nothing scientific in the latter. All the theories which we have hitherto noticed have borne on them the marks of this intellectual condition. They have menon of existing living beings which does not or may not require to be run back indefinitely into the past in quest of its explanation. Definite constitution from which you may start, or on which as a fulcrum you may rest, there is none: there is no *datum* that is not a *quæsitum* · the old *constants* are set afloat, and the terms of every problem are turned (unless by provisional assumption) into *variables*. The conception of Nature itself parts with almost all that had been taken for substantive, and is resolved into that of a continual *becoming;* so that nothing ever *is*, but something always *happens;* and to give account of it you must relate the before and after. Hence, the newer methods of science have more and more become *historical*, i.e. have devoted themselves to the successive processes, rather than the synchronous conditions, of phenomena; and with such daring glances into the illimitable past that the *regressus in infinitum*, which was once the absurdity, has almost become the favourite instrument of our philosophers. Natural history, which used to be the name for little else than the classification and description of coexisting forms of life, now enriched by the resources of palæontology, ventures to report on their relative chronology, and to relate the story of their development, from the larvæ of a marine hermaphrodite, through the forms of fish, of reptile, of marsupial, of quadrumanal, to the human end of the zoological series[1]. What becomes, in this enormous prolixity of growth, of our search for the nativity and seat of the moral sentiments? Does the Intuitionist say, they are given to us ready-made? He is silenced by the remark, 'There is nothing ready-made: the present is only from the past.' Does the Hartleyan tell us, their genesis is explained from the distinctive data of the human constitution? He is put out of court by the reply, 'There are no such distinctive data: the lines are wiped out which make man specific, and part him off from the brute.' Whatever history there may be of which the present phenomena of conscience are the latest incidents does not

[1] See Darwin's Descent of Man, Vol. II. chap. xxi. p. 389.

open with the birth of him who feels them, or with the first planting of what he owns as his family tree, but goes back into geologic ages beyond all trees, figurative or literal, to lose itself among the molluscs of fucous slime and waste sea shores. It may well seem that such a doctrine must extinguish the very problem of the ethical psychologist. The only thing which it presents as certain is this: that the moral sense is here *now;* that once it was *not* here; that the later state has been regularly evolved from the earlier; and that the theory therefore is one of those which undertake to fetch the moral out of the unmoral. This is the feature in it which brings it properly under notice among the schemes of Hetero-psychological Ethics.

On a first view it might seem that this doctrine differs from that of Hobbes or any other empirical hedonist, only in its allowance of long time for the evolution. The transition is the same, from the sentient difference between pleasure and pain to the moral difference between right and wrong; but in passing through the interval, consciousness, according to one theory, occupies a generation, according to the other, countless geological æons. And, so far as the greatness of the change from mere sensation to the sanctity of conscience staggers us, it cannot be denied that the difficulty is apparently lessened by dilution; and that if we suppose the barrier of generations removed, and an individual subject to live on through the entire development of life to the present date, our imagination will hardly dare to pronounce any metamorphosis impossible to such an experience. To take a grant of centuries by millions appears therefore at first a pure gain of resources that can fall short of nothing required. Against this advantage of time to move in, a logical and sincere psychologist, like Mill, will notice a very serious set off. It is *not the same* consciousness which continues all through, and which, having remembrance of its early gleam and its sweep through its vast orbit, you can cross-question and record, so as to lay down the curve of its advance, and check your surmises of its law.

assumed for their data certain *constants* which seemed to be secure; e.g. a determinate human individual, such as we now find him: a society of his fellows around him, whose common interests extort from him what they want, and a world to live in, admitting of combination and division of labour, of allotment of property, and of the institution of rule and law. These three constants may be differently defined, and differently worked, by writers who elicit the moral characteristic from them. One may treat it as intuitive from the first, another may expound it as a transfigured self-love; a third may interpret it as a reflection of others' approval and aversion; but they all of them find it in the interplay of these fixed constitutions of persons and things. And though, in reckoning for the influence of predisposition and education, they allow for the presence of a formed body of social sentiment and law, and for favourable or unfavourable parentage, they look on these facts only as elements of the individual's experience, on the same footing with others that may appear in him for the first time. Or, if their curiosity pushes the problem further back, it stops at all events with the resources it can command from the present definition of human nature. The Hartleyan reads the story of the moral nature in the experience of each single person: Hobbes, in the formation of the State: Cudworth, Clarke, and Butler, in the impress of eternal law upon the very make of our humanity.

This mode of treatment was inevitable, so long as man was marked off from all other species of living beings, or even placed outside of them as unique. If they were detached from each other by impassable limits, so that each had its own private section of natural history, much more must he be studied in isolation from them all, and interpreted by internal comparison of text with text of his own oracles. Thus regarded, he contains in himself all the conditions for a science of his nature; and his special endowments present themselves as something wholly new, which derive no light from affinity, and are only caricatured by the mocking resemblance of inferior animals. Great is the change, the moment you take away the boundaries of species; a change of which an illustrative example has already been presented within the limits of inorganic science. So long as the threefold classification of bodies, into solids, liquids, and gases, was accepted as definitive, each class had a science to itself; and mechanics, hydrostatics with hydraulics, and pneumatics, constituted so many independent chapters of Physics, with separate laws and formulas that did not speak to one another. But as soon as these three names were found to denote, not different bodies, but only different states of every body, determined by degrees of heat, there immediately arose a molecular science embracing them all, and an immense enlargement of conception, from the possibility that the solid of one period or one world might be the liquid or the atmosphere of another. So, when, after long difficulty in defining the species of plants and animals, and ever recurrent doubts whether in this instance or that they are more than varieties, the bold step is taken at last, and the supposed impassable limits are thrown away, the different departments of natural history enter into family relations, with pedigree enormously extended · the new science of universal biology comes into existence, and finds a group of laws common to all organised beings. What before were treated as separate creations, coexisting *ab initio*, range themselves as the successive stages and manifold ramifications of one stock. And the centre of wonder is shifted by the change: before, the puzzle was, to explain the close approaches and marvellous resemblances of types supposed to be distinct: now it is, to account for the wide divergence and astounding contrasts in the descendants of the same progenitors. If formerly the book of nature was but a collection of separate tales, it is turned into a continuous epic, unfolding itself from end to end; though it is still difficult to seize the links that weave its distinct scenes and recitals into genuine episodes of one unbroken tissue.

It is obvious that, under this change, there is no pheno-

Psychological processes are rigorously shut up within the limits of the personal identity, and have no evidence but in the memory and expression of the individual subject of them; and, in proportion as they are traced back into the inarticulate story of infancy, they become illegible, and the theories into which they are worked are problematical. The masculine egoistic hedonism of Hobbes and Helvetius, boldly appealed for confirmation to the clear inward experience of men and women, who could confirm or contradict them. To escape their paradoxes, their modern followers take refuge from this strong light in an earlier twilight, where nobody can tell exactly what goes on; and the extreme fondness which they show for tossing about psychological babies, and wringing from them *ambiguas voces* about how they feel, is natural, in proportion as their doctrine is hard to prove. And if the confessional of each single life has this blank prelude, how much more completely hid from view must be the inward autobiography, not of acknowledged ancestors merely, but of pre-existent races, that grin and set their teeth at their descendants from the walls of a museum? By spinning out your process indefinitely, you gain time enough for anything to take place, but too much for anything to be seen: in the very act of creating the evidence, you hide it all away; and the real result is, that you may make the story what you please; and no one can put it to the test. If Hobbes, as often happens, gives us a piece of droll psychology, every one who knows himself can tell whether it is true or false, and lay his finger on any distortion it contains. If Darwin describes the inward conflict of an extinct baboon, he paints a fancy picture of what remains for ever without witness.

The fact is, the evolution theory rests mainly upon the evidence of *organisms;* and when they have been duly disposed in the probable order of their development, their animating instincts and functional actions are obliged, it is supposed, to follow suite; and it is therefore taken for granted rather than shown that, by a parallel internal history, the most rudimentary animal tendencies have transmuted themselves into the attributes of a moral and spiritual nature. But the essential difference between the two cases must not be overlooked. The crust of the earth preserves in its strata the memorials of living structure, in an order which cannot be mistaken, enabling us to associate the types that coexist, and to arrange those which are successive; and, in spite of the missing links of the series, to observe the traces of a clear ascent, the higher forms making their first appearance after the ruder. The archæology of nature is in this respect perfectly analogous to that of history, and supplies a chain of relative dates with as much certainty as the coins disinterred at different depths and of graduated workmanship from the ruins of a buried empire. But just as, in this case, the image and superscription report to you only the place and time of the Cæsar they represent, but tell you nothing of his character and will; so, in the other, the fossil organ is silent about the passion that stirred it, the instinct that directed it, the precise range and kind of consciousness which belonged to its possessor. In other words, you have, and can have, no record of psychological relations, in correspondence with the hierarchy of forms; for you cannot get into the consciousness of other creatures; and if, in order to find room for educing the moral affections from what is unmoral, you begin with our præhuman progenitors, and take their private biography in hand, and catch their first inklings of what is going to be conscience, you are simply fitting a fiction to your own preconception. To a certain extent there is, no doubt, a definite and known relation between structure and function in animals, enabling you, from the presence of the one, to infer the other. The wing, the fin, the legs, reveal the element and the habit of a creature's life: the jaw, the teeth, the condyles for the connected muscles, disclose his food-appetite, and his modes both of pursuit and of self-defence. But, long before we reach the problem which engages us, we come to an end of this line of inference.

There are no bones, or muscles, or feathers appropriated to the exclusive use of self-love; no additional eye or limb set apart for the service of benevolence; no judicial wig adhering to the head that owns a conscience; so that in this field, i. e. through the whole scene of the moral phenomena, no help can be had from the zoological record. Nothing can be more chimerical than præhistorical psychology.

These remarks I have premised, in order to indicate the chief difference between the honestly psychological theories (be they right or wrong) which have engaged us hitherto, and the evolutionary Ethics, which have no psychology of their own, but merely pick up what best suits them of the old material, and fit it in with the purely *physiological* story they have to tell. A brief sketch of the new doctrine will bring out this difference more clearly: it shall be taken chiefly from three authoritative works. Darwin's 'Descent of Man;' Spencer's 'Data of Ethics;' Stephen's 'Science of Ethics.'

§ 2. *Law of Evolution, sec. Darwin; sec. Spencer.*

All living structures *do something*, i. e. have some *function*. In the simplest of them, the structure is approximately homogeneous, and without division of labour does everything that happens in the animal history, being the instrument at once of motion, of nourishment, of growth, of reproduction. There is a tendency, however, in each of such actions to localise itself as the habit of a particular part, the structure of which modifies itself in accommodation to its exclusive work: whence arises an order of beings with a plurality of organs, each with its own separate function; and this change to compound or heterogeneously formed natures constitutes an advance in the scale of life. The same tendency continuing, as a permanent and universal law, a succession of ulterior animal types appears, each more highly 'differentiated' than its predecessor: till man is evolved as the present crown or apex of development: himself still carrying on the same sub-division of functions in the organisation of States and the progress of civilised life. Hence the general formula of evolution presents it, in its application to the whole universe, as 'a change from an indefinite incoherent homogeneity to a definite coherent heterogeneity, through continuous differentiations and integrations[1],'—a formula of which Mr. Goldwin Smith says, that 'the universe may well have heaved a sigh of relief when, through the cerebration of an eminent thinker, it had been delivered of this account of itself[2].'

If, being unable to rest in this law as a mere statement of fact, we press for some adequate *cause* of the kind of change it describes, we receive a twofold answer, fixing our attention separately on the organism and on the function. In the former, considered as a mere material aggregate in more or less unstable equilibrium, there is an inherent tendency to variation in several directions,—variation which Mr. Darwin calls 'accidental;' and among such experiments of slight structural change as are always occurring, if one turns up which, by fitting the conditions of the animal's existence, gives it an advantage over its companions and competitors, it will carry its possessor to the front in the race of life, and establish itself in permanence. But again, without any alteration of organ, the animal may have a considerable margin of variety in carrying out its function; and if he chances upon some adroit stroke of action which is a short cut to the end, it is as good as a prize to him, and he wins the profits of a patentee. Though however the initiative of variation may be taken either in the organ or in its function, there is a difference between the two cases in their operative cause. 'Accident' (i.e a confluence of incalculable forces) has a far larger play in modifying structure than in modifying function. The moulding and build of an animal are dependent not less upon numerous

---

[1] Data of Ethics, chap. v. § 24, p. 65.
[2] Contemporary Review, Feb. 1882; Science and Morality, p. 349.

external opportunities and pressures than upon its internal law of development; and there is as much probability of extraordinary hindrance as of extraordinary help from these; so that organs are as likely to deteriorate through variation as to improve. With the *behaviour* of an animal, and even of a plant, it is otherwise. Unless it be disabled by wrong structure, all its tendency is towards action that favours its life, or that of its kind; and if in any degree it deviates from the average habit of its kind, it is in the direction of some vital gain. In the dark, the roots of a shrub will grow towards the water of a neighbouring well, and its shoots towards the light of a window on the other side. The ptarmigan which you start upon the mountain, shuffles piteously away, dragging a seemingly broken wing, till she has decoyed you far enough from her nestlings, and she can laugh at you and fly off. If we ask for an explanation of this difference, we are supplied in answer with this law, that all life-preserving actions are pleasurable actions, and all pleasurable actions are life-preserving; and as the pleasantest action is always done, the whole energy of a living creature is engaged in adding to its capital and its security. It is evident that this explanation, turning as it does on the stimulus of *pleasure*, applies only to the *sentient* world, and does not account for the exclusively gainful direction of all *vegetable* variations of function. The law of identity between the agreeable and the serviceable, expounded by Bain as the result of observation, is promoted by Spencer to the rank of *à priori* necessity. It must be true; for if the pleasurable were unfavourable to life, it would long ago have put an end to life; and if it were neutral, it would have prevented any evolution of life: but the hierarchy of nature is made up of evolved and evolving forms; the law, therefore, is proved[1]. Suppose, however, that we take away

---

[1] 'In the *Principles of Psychology*, § 124, it was shown that necessarily, throughout the animate world at large, "pains are correlatives of actions injurious to the organism, while pleasures are the correlatives of actions conducive to its welfare;" since "it is an inevitable deduction from the hypothesis of Evolution, that races of sentient creatures could have

the postulate, that 'the pleasantest action is always done,' and substitute the proposition that 'instinctive actions are always done,' then from the same line of reasoning a different law emerges, viz. that instinctive actions are life-conserving and life-evolving; and the question between the two (within the limits of the sentient world) would hinge on this: whether it is more reasonable to assign, in animal action, the prior place to pleasure or to instinct; to say that a creature's pleasure is in the satisfaction of instinct, or that its instinct is the pursuit of pleasure. No doubt, the evolutionist feels averse to the former position, because he cannot start so late in the day as *definite instinct;* he is bound to get before it, and give an account of its origin from an indeterminate state, and finds something tempting for this purpose in the look of this vague term, pleasure. But I would submit that, for his problem, he looks in the wrong place when he trusts to the *sensory and passive susceptibility* come into existence under no other conditions." The argument was as follows.—

'If we substitute for the word Pleasure the equivalent phrase—a feeling which we seek to bring into consciousness and retain there, and if we substitute for the word Pain the equivalent phrase—a feeling which we seek to get out of consciousness and to keep out; we see at once that if the states of consciousness which a creature endeavours to maintain are the correlatives of injurious actions, and if the states of consciousness which it endeavours to expel are the correlatives of beneficial actions, it must quickly disappear through persistence in the injurious and avoidance of the beneficial. In other words, those races of beings only can have survived in which, on the average, agreeable or desired feelings went along with activities conducive to the maintenance of life, while disagreeable and habitually-avoided feelings went along with activities directly or indirectly destructive of life, and there must ever have been, other things equal, the most numerous and long-continued survivals among races in which these adjustments of feelings to actions were the best, tending ever to bring about perfect adjustment.

'Fit connexions between acts and results must establish themselves in living things, even before consciousness arises; and after the rise of consciousness these connexions can change in no other way than to become better established. At the very outset, life is maintained by persistence in acts which conduce to it, and desistance from acts which impede it; and whenever sentiency makes its appearance as an accompaniment, its forms must be such that in the one case the produced feeling is of a kind that will be sought—pleasure, and in the other case is of a kind that will be shunned—pain.' Data of Ethics, chap VI. § 33, p. 79.

of the animal life for the *creation and differentiation* of its *spontaneous activities;* and that the analogies both of the vegetable world, which makes very near approaches to instinct, and of the reflex actions of animals, much more favour the derivation of determinate directions of living energy from insensible stimuli.

The law to which these remarks apply establishes a marked difference between Darwin's and Spencer's conception of evolution. The doctrine of 'natural selection' and 'survival of the fittest' means that, out of innumerable tentatives made at random by animals, the great majority come to nothing, but the exceptionally happy hits, that fall in with the surrounding adjustments, make their footing good, and stand. As this idea is applied not less to what the animal *does* than to what his structure *is* or becomes, it presupposes that he can and will put forth actions hurtful to himself and doomed to have no future, and *that* in number out of all proportion to the few successes. On the other hand, Spencer's law apparently affirms in the last paragraph of the foregoing note, that, prior to the evolution of consciousness in living things, their serviceable activities had already bespoken all its pleasures, and their injurious activities, all its pains: so that the animal, moved only by the pleasantest, was secure of doing always the fittest too, a rule which bars out all failure, and strictly obliges the creature to walk only on the narrow rail of the most useful. In this way, the selection of the fittest is not left to be wrought out as the issue of an indefinite lottery of hedonist trial and error; but, as a congenital condition of emerging sentiency itself, is thrown back for its origin upon the earlier history of unconscious phenomena, where no help is to be had from pleasure and pain. Mr. Spencer finds its counterpart and presage there, in the plant-physiology, whence it is handed over ready-made to the animals, after having been itself formed by the process of 'accidental variation.' He appears to me thus to change his working principle of evolution on crossing the chasm (or, as he would rather say, taking the step) from the insentient to the sentient world. In the former, he relies on the elimination of weakness, in the latter, on the pleasantness of growing vitality. Either, in itself, is intelligible; but not the assumed identity or juncture between them. That among vegetable tendencies to change those which most favour the vigour of the species should make their footing good, brings no surprise. That among conscious actions those which are most agreeable should become habitual, is no less a matter of course. But that, antecedently to experience, the movements which are to be serviceable should also be invariably the pleasantest, is a combination neither self-evidently necessary, nor deducible from the other two. It is allowed to slip in by loosely hanging on to their skirts, but has no visible organic connexion with them. When we ask— 'How comes it that what the animal likes is always best for it, or for its kind?' it is nothing to the purpose to say, 'Were it not so, life would disappear:' the non-disappearance of life may prove the *fact*, but does not find the *cause*, of so pregnant an adjustment; and we are only thrown upon the ulterior question, 'Whence this singular security against the disappearance of life?' Darwin has embarrassed himself with no such unique coincidence. With him the creature, sentient as well as insentient, is fitted up with no principle of unerring selection, but flung among the countless radii of accident, to find only by result the difference between the paths of life and death; so that the theory is burdened with nothing that might not happen in a universe of fortuity[1].

[1] Mr. Spencer disclaims the variance, indicated in the text, of his conception of evolution from Mr. Darwin's, and assures me that I have misinterpreted the language quoted in the preceding note. I regret to have regarded him as responsible for any turn of thought which is not really his; and I thankfully accept for myself, and present to my readers in an Appendix to this volume, the re-statement of his doctrine with which he has favoured me in a private correspondence. If I had seen reason to believe that my construction of his meaning was a mere personal misapprehension, I would have withdrawn altogether this section of my book. But as the exposition on which it comments leaves, I

§ 3. *Spencer's Genesis of Ethics, and Conversion into Intuition.*

The tendency of nature to increasing complexity of organic structure and function, involving more volume of life, is habitually spoken of by Spencer in *teleological* terms. Life, preserved or enlarged, is the *end* of all animal 'conduct,' i.e. of all actions beyond the apparently random movements of the infusoria: first, complete individual life; next, preservation of offspring, which indeed advances *pari passu* with the other; and then, as the altruistic affections of the clan or the community advance, the life of Society. It is only in Man that this last stage is fully reached; and that conduct, finding its final purpose, assumes its *ethical character*. Even in his history, it is long before the self-maintenance and the maintenance of offspring permits the operation of the third end and the connected development of a moral order; for, prior to the arts of industry, the spontaneous supplies of food and safety which nature offers are too scanty for the competitors who want them; so that men do not welcome the presence of each other, but see in it only a 'struggle for existence,' except so far as the weakness of isolation forces them into some partnership of self-defence against encroachment. It is in these little knots of co-operation that the first moral adjustments take place; i.e. that several personal and family lives learn, for the sake of common safety, to maintain themselves side by side without mutual interference, and the original repulsions of universal war are driven away into the field of external relations. Even then, the internal peace of a barbarous tribe is very precarious, and little more than an unstable truce, except when danger imposes silence upon rivalries and dissensions, and singles out the strongest will for obedience by the rest. Such

believe, on most readers the same impression which it left on me, I think it better to put on record what they take to be its logical purport, accompanied by Mr. Spencer's authoritative correction.

crises contribute a further experience of the highest importance: viz. that the ends of each may be secured, not only without clashing with those of neighbours, but in a far superior way by combination with them, and prearrangement of parts into a compound action directed by a chief. Such organisation of functions in subservience to a single social end, once started by military necessity, finds its way by extension into the internal relations of pacific settlements; and, by division of individual labour, so increases the resources of life as to relieve the pressure of numbers and abate the causes of war, and multiply the links of interdependence among producers at home, and exchangers abroad. These new adjustments to widening ends arise spontaneously, one by one, at the suggestion of some immediate interest or convenience, till fresh types of conduct gradually set into form, and give rise to corresponding rules. These rules are the *body of Morals*. 'Ethics,' therefore, Mr. Spencer says, 'has for its subject-matter that form which universal conduct assumes during the last stages of its evolution' in 'the highest type of being, when he is forced, by increase of numbers, to live more and more in the presence of his fellows:' and 'conduct gains ethical sanction in proportion as the activities, becoming less and less militant, and more and more industrial, are such as do not necessitate mutual injury or hindrance, but consist with, and are furthered by, co-operation and mutual aid[1].'

The whole of this course of evolution consists, it is plain, in the discovery of more effective means to the desired end, of undisturbed life; and the improvement hinges upon this, that consideration for the needs of others and for the organic vigour of the social life is found to contribute to the personal security and well-being. This it is that gives the rationale of the moral rule, and commends it to each: the authority which it carries is that of a wise economy which every prudent person is glad to adopt: like a labour-saving machine, it quickens production and saves waste. At

[1] Data of Ethics, chap. ii. p. 20.

the same time, though this is its ultimate objective base, the moral rule soon wins assent and compliance without reference to this feature as a motive: it gathers upon itself many a pleasant feeling, like other means to happy ends, as if it were a good on its own account; and leaves the agent's altruistic sympathies free play at the same moment that his self-maintaining impulse pursues its natural way. He is himself a part of the social structure whose health his own personal sacrifices tend to uphold; and his attachment to it overcompensates him for what he foregoes By such associations do the external rules find response and support from internal affections, which may escape into complete disinterestedness and infuse into the character a strong moral enthusiasm. Nor is this all. The psychological life in man is inseparably conjoined with a physiological: an emotion cannot become intensely and habitually felt without leaving its vestiges, if not upon the structure, at least upon the susceptibilities of the brain: so that it will tend to recur with increasing facility, and to institute spontaneously the related series of thoughts, volitions, and actions. But wherever such personal characteristics become fixed, it is well known that they frequently pass from parent to child: so that much of the character which has been won by self-discipline is transmitted by inheritance, and the son starts from a station in advance of his father. From this cause, it is suggested, the inward experience of past generations may establish a cerebral register of themselves, ever deepening in its trace and quickening in its velocity of movement; and this swift compend of what were once long processes of thought or feeling turns up in us as *Intuition*, and, assuming the airs of a heaven-sent conscience, tempts us to overlook and despise the homely utilities which alone it really represents. This is Mr. Spencer's celebrated doctrine that 'experiences of utility, organised and consolidated during all past generations of the human race, have been producing nervous modifications, which, by continued transmission and accumulation, have become in us certain faculties of moral intuition, certain emotions responding to right and wrong conduct, which have no apparent basis in the individual experience of utility[1].'

The sum and substance of this comprehensive and ingenious theory is this: that pleasure and pain are what we denote, and all that we denote, by good and evil, and supply to each agent the sole end of conduct: that pleasant conduct is an increment, painful a decrement, of life: that whatever is a means of personal pleasure or a part of it, including therefore the pleasure of others, becomes endeared to us on that account: that modes of action and feeling which are found to possess this instrumental utility draw to themselves interest and favour, in which all who are served by them will participate: that this favour (with disfavour to the opposites) powerfully affects the happiness of every one who is the object of it, and becomes intense as a motive: that his sensitiveness to it stereotypes itself in his cerebral organisation, reappears in his children, and taking up their added experience passes down with increase in each generation; till, through fusion of countless elements, almost all prior to the individual's life, its origin is lost from view, and we mistake its innateness in the individual for its immutability in the race, and its emotional depth for superhuman authority.

§ 4. *The Theory Considered, as applied to Intellectual Apprehension.*

In estimating this hypothesis, I must first briefly touch upon the alleged law which identifies pleasure and self-conservation. It assumes that the feeling of pleasure is in itself an augmentation of vital energy, while pain is a depression of it: that consequently the experience of the former always sets a-going or intensifies some action for continuing it, while the experience of the latter excites

[1] Spencer's Letter to Mill, ap. Bain's Mental and Moral Science, p. 721.

a rebellion to get rid of our enemy, but under the
disadvantage of the lessened vigour left by pain. The
evidence of this rule appears to me to be altogether
inadequate, even where it presents a colourable aspect;
and to be encountered by unanswerable facts on the other
side. Bain lays stress on such experiences as the following:
that when we are cold, the first warmth of a fire quickens
our pace till we are in front of it and can spread our hands
before it; and that, at the first taste of a nice morsel in the
mouth, we smack at it smartly, and throw double speed and
energy into our mastication. But surely it will occur to
everyone, that these movements are essentially *prospective*,
instituted for the gain of pleasure suggested as within
reach, and not the mechanical consequence of the portion
of pleasure just past. The only function of the incipient
agreeable state is here to supply the promise of what we
like, and the same effect would ensue from any other
feeling or idea, however neutral, that placed us on the
threshold of the imminent enjoyment. In intense thirst,
for example, the sight of a glass of water, or the hearing of
a trickling stream, will stir us into eager action to reach the
draught. Perhaps it will be said that these perceptions are
in such case by no means indifferent, but in themselves
delightful to us, so as still to exemplify the rule. But they
are so only in the capacity of *good news*, and owe this
character only to our state of *want:* in *this* lies the real
spring of our energy in presence of the near alleviation;
and *this* is not a pleasure but a pain. Dr. Bain can the
less object to this interpretation, because he takes refuge in
it himself, in order to escape from a difficulty threatening
his law in its opposite application to pain. If pain induces
'cessation of energy,' he has 'to explain how pain, in opposition to its nature, initiates and maintains a strenuous
activity for procuring its abolition. In this case, the
operating element may be shown to be, not the pain, but
the *relief from pain*. When in a state of suffering there
comes a moment of remission, that remission has all the

elating and quickening effect of pleasure: as regards the agency of the will, pleasure and the remission of pain are the same thing. *Relief*, in fact or in prospect, *is the real stimulant to labour for vanquishing pain and misery*[1].' According to this, it does not matter whether the condition immediately present be one of pleasure or of pain: the activity will equally ensue in both cases; in the one for continuance, in the other for removal, of the momentary state; and will not betray the difference of their prior condition of sensibility by any enhancement and cessation of energy, respectively Under such an explanation, the alleged law simply vanishes. To set up determinate fruition as the positive, and determinate suffering as the negative extreme, of vital energy, and explain by them the conquests and defeats of human effort, is surely an inversion of the order of nature. Life is a cluster of *wants*, physical, intellectual, affectional, moral, each of which must have, and all of which may miss, the fitting object. Is the object withheld or lost?—there is pain. Is it restored or gained?—there is pleasure. Does it abide and remain constant?—there is content. The two first are cases of disturbed equilibrium; and are so far dynamic, that they will not rest till they reach the third, which is their posture of stability, and their true end. Among the numerous needs of our nature, there are always some that are sufficiently in repose to afford a steady base of habit and level feeling, and secure us, if we will, from feverish heats; and always others, which are in dearth, and, keeping the will on strain, fling an intensity of this or that pursuit into this calm; and hence the keen ferment and undying struggle that constitute the waves of movement, as contrasted with the fundamental order of society, the total life of which depends on the proportion between the two. What is the cause of this extra energy? Where does its tension lie? Must we not seek it in the unanswered wants, and their inevitable pressure towards their ends? When these ends are won, then comes the joy of relief and attain-

[1] Mental and Moral Science, Bk. IV. chap. i. § 8, p. 324.

ment: as the recompence, however, and not the cause, of the efforts spent. And when the pleasure arrives, is the effort redoubled? On the contrary, it subsides: the balance of the nature is reinstated, and the dynamical passes into a statical condition Pleasure, therefore, does not start the heightened activity, but closes it; and is no sooner reached than the strenuous exertion ceases, because required no more. The initiative is taken by a *disturbance*, which puts the spur to us all the same, whether our quickened speed is destined to succeed or to fail, whether we are to quench our need, or our need is to quench us

It is an unwholesome flattery, then, to credit pleasure with either the vigour of action or the conservation of life. If we change the phrase, and ask how it is related to '*health*,' which has of late come into great favour with our psychologists as an ideal end, whether for an organ, an individual, or a society, the answer cannot but share the inexactitude of the conception of 'health' But if we take it to mean the condition of approximate equilibrium between want and supply, excluding severe and protracted tension of suspended instincts (and this seems to come very near to the essence of the conception), then it is coincident with the state which I have called *content*, and is consistent only with slight oscillations on either side of this point; whereas pleasure hardly attracts notice till want suspends the pendulum beyond these limits; and is proportioned to the altitude from which at last it has to sweep. The formula, therefore, which identifies 'pleasure-giving' and 'health-promoting' cannot be admitted as true; for though there is a small central interval where the qualities are found together, they soon begin to vary inversely as each other. And this is in accordance with the common sense and observation of mankind. No people are regarded with more general distrust, or are more sharply scrutinised by the life-assurance offices, than the pleasure-seekers: there are none, I should say, who have less chance of establishing a new species by happy variation: or who, in fact, are more continually dying out and commencing their fossil existence. On the other hand, the favourite objects of Mr. Herbert Spencer's eloquent aversion are the opposite class, grouped by him with 'devil-worshippers,' 'who are led by the tacit assumption, common to Pagan Stoics and Christian Ascetics, that we are so diabolically organised that pleasures are injurious and pains beneficial[1]:' to convince us that they are among the most terrible of offenders, he arrests impressive samples of them, manacles them with the chains of his logic, and conducts them in a march-past before us,—a sufferer with heart disease from sitting in the wet,—an acrobat shrunk with hæmorrhage,—a studious man half paralysed from neglecting his dinner for his books or his sleep for the stars,—a 'cadaverous barrister,'—a sickly seamstress,—a rheumatic peasant,—attended by troops of puny children and the prematurely aged,—camp-followers all in the army of misery. It cannot but strike every observer that Mr. Spencer here brings together a somewhat incoherent assemblage. The common feature which all its instances exemplify is neglect of the conditions of health. But as in some the neglect is voluntary and wilful, while in others it is an involuntary incident of the external lot, he mixes together, in the same ethical invective, persons who, as offenders and as victims, stand in very different relations to it. And in adducing them all to illustrate the belief that *'pleasures are injurious and pains beneficial,'* he certainly assigns a 'non-causa pro causa;' for, at all events, not one of the victim-class,—the seamstress, the peasant, the puny child, the premature old man,—is in the habit of courting privation, and declining such pleasure as can be had : nor are their hardships inflicted on them by anyone possessed of such idea. And just as little does the overworking gymnast, or student, or lawyer, transgress the health laws, because he thinks their pleasures harmful and their penalties beneficial to him ; but because, in the preoccupation of another pursuit, he has no

---

[1] Data of Ethics, chap. vi. § 37, pp. 93, 94.

time to think of their pleasures and pains at all. Even if you give a hedonistic interpretation to his conduct, and say that he *likes better* his gymnasium, his books, his brief, than the ease, the food and relaxation, the walk and sleep, which he foregoes, you do so at the expense of the alleged law of 'connection between pleasure and beneficial action and between pain and detrimental action;' and practically contradict the statement, 'Every pleasure increases utility: every pain decreases utility. Every pleasure raises the tide of life: every pain lowers the tide of life[1].' For it is in following his pleasure that he breaks his blood-vessel, or softens his brain, or gets his ghastly look. Mr. Spencer's insistence on the laws of health, as factors in the determination of right action, would merit unqualified thanks, if he had not confused it by taking pleasure as the index to health, and assuming that the self-denying types of morality spring from a worship of pain, and were the chief source of a morbid and stunted humanity. Of even the regular religious asceticism this is neither the theory nor the result. Its war has never been against pleasure, but against disturbing passion, and artificial wants, and weak dependence upon external and accidental things: its aim has been, not to suffer, but to be free from the entanglements of self, to serve the calls of human pity or Divine love, and conform to the counsels of a Christ-like perfection. Condemn its method as you will, and satirise its extravagances, this was its essential principle, as it still is, for those to whom the garden of Gethsemane is more sacred than the garden of Epicurus. And as for the average effects on health, though they were certainly not such as would figure handsomely in our Registrar-General's reports, yet I fancy they would not look amiss when compared with the statistics of the pleasure-seekers. And if a wager were to be laid between the life-policies of a Carthusian monk, and of an ordinary man of society, the theatre, and the clubs, a betting expert would probably offer three to two upon the former. Nay, if the

[1] Data of Ethics, chap. vi. § 36, p 87.

bills of mortality from self-indulgence and from self-denial could be compared, who can doubt that their numbers would be as of the slain in war to the slain in assassination.

The more you press upon Mr. Spencer's hedonistic base of evolution, the more does it crumble away, and leave no ground for the causal proposition, 'unless pleasure were life-preserving, there could be no evolution,' and the corresponding logical proposition, 'because there is evolution, pleasure is life-preserving.' If anything could convince me of his doctrine that axioms can grow out of chance experiences, it would be his own acceptance of these propositions as axiomatic. I even wonder what rational connection can be supposed to exist between the principle of hedonism and the possibility of evolution. Evolution of *organs*, it is plain, has nothing to do with pleasure and pain; for it takes place in the vegetable world as much as in the animal, through the survival of adjustments which turn the external conditions to best account. It is to the evolution of *instincts* alone that the principle can be supposed to apply, and here it is still superfluous. If an improved organ brought no changed feeling, if, for example, it were in the reflex system, would this prevent its performing of its function better than before? Nay, if, with the advance of the organism, its sensibility to pleasure declined and was discharged as a gratuitous appendage, how would this disqualify the highly differentiated machine from acting as a perfected automaton? And if, irrespective of feeling altogether, organism and function can advance *pari passu*, so, in the presence of feeling, it must be indifferent in what order the increments dispose themselves, of what type they are, and where they come in: in particular, whether impulse before pleasure, or pleasure before impulse; whether better and worse separately from agreeable and disagreeable, or synonymously with them. The parts, I mean, in the development of sensibility, may be differently arranged consistently with evolution.

Whoever thinks that evolution requires us to *educe moral distinctions and feelings from unmoral* contradicts this, and prescribes, as essential, an order which I have affirmed to be non-essential : and the hasty imagination, aghast at the apparition, at the head of the ancestral portrait-gallery, of 'a long-eared hairy quadruped of arboreal habits,' is readily frightened into admission of his illusion. But that it is a false inference from the supposed 'descent of man,' a closer scrutiny will easily show. The rude logic which scares us exclaims, 'Talk of our conscience and all its fine feelings ! it is nothing but a *dressed-up brutality !* for, only look at him ! what else could come of that stock ?' But then, we might say the same of the embryo of each human individual, when indistinguishable from that of the dog, though carrying in it the future of a Socrates, a Marcus Aurelius, a Newton. Instead of being a consequence, it is a contradiction, of the idea of *growth or evolution*, that the derivative should be measured by the source, and the adult should have no characteristic predicates absent from the nature in its germ The very essence of the process is, that it is made up of old and new, the one handed down by *heredity*, the other added on by *differentiation;* and whatever the latter contributes must, from the logical construction of the conception, be something which was *not there before*, and is looked for in vain in the contents of the previous stage. The differentiated features are precisely those of which heredity gives no account, but which, on the contrary, define, as a barrier, the limits of its power. Be the provision for contributing them what it may, it brings the surprise of something fresh and incalculable, of which the antecedent conditions give no hint, and which is over and above the measure of their resources. Apply this principle to the case of an enlarged animal function, or what is called an evolved instinct. If the word 'evolved' is meant to suggest that the major phenomenon arising has no more in it than its minor predecessor, just as a scroll spread out has only the same words which it held when folded up, it tricks the imagination by a false analogy. Yet, when it is contended that the moral sentiments are 'reducible to' hedonistic preference, that the conscience is nothing but a transformed love of happiness and of the means of happiness, that, in its *real* meaning the proposition '*This is right*' is identical with '*This is pleasure-giving*,' and that whatever else it is supposed to carry is only semblance, is it not evident that the contention *does* interpret the word by this false analogy? Its whole object is to expunge from the moral experience every element other than is found in the sentient, and prove that the latter is adequate, without any addition, to give a complete account of the former. The hedonists accordingly show a certain impatience of distinctly ethical language; the more plain-spoken and unflinching, like Bentham, treating it with derision, as a relic of superstition, and proposing to strike such words as '*ought*' from the vocabulary : the more considerate and sympathetic preferring to translate the phraseology of morals into terms of sentient and social well-being; as when Mr. Herbert Spencer construes '*Obligation*' into the *indispensableness of using the means if we would get the end*. This is to strip bare the moral type of thought till you have the naked natural animal, and to say, '*There,* that is the real live truth, when you get the clothes off.' Let us compare this spurious conception of evolution with that of which I have hinted the analysis.

When an animal consciously takes a step of evolution, it emerges from a dull indistinctness into states no longer indissolubly blended. The unity splits into a plurality, the members of which are not alike, and among them are some (or at least one) never present before; else there would be no differentiation. *New* feelings or perceptions, then, have appeared and been added to the creature's history. There is *more* in them, then, than there was in the previous undifferenced consciousness. Has this increment, should you say, the nature of *illusion*, or of emergence from illusion? Suppose, for example that, as a naturalist has suggested, the play of sunbeams upon a mass of jelly on the sea shore has brought together its diffused life-feeling into a more specially tingling point on the surface, and set it up as henceforth responsive to the irritation of light; and that from this moment it commences an education which, carried on in it and in some æons of successors, terminates in the production of an eye; and follow the story of the advance, stage by stage. When, from the dull sense which distinguished the jelly from the water of the shore, the photistic thrill disengages itself as something other than the rest, it will not be denied that this is a *perceptive gain*, i.e. an accession not only to the creature's *sensory store*, but to his *life-relations with reality*. Next, the time will come when the organ thus started on its history finds the unity of its *light-feeling* give way; when examined, millenniums further on, in some amphibian now basking on the grassy sedge, then floundering in the ochrey stream, it is first in a green, then in a yellow bath. Is, then, this dual perception truer or less true than its single predecessor? are the links of the later nature with the real world closer or less close than of the earlier? There can be but one answer. Carry the test yet one step further. It is far from improbable that colour-blind persons, who are far more numerous than is commonly supposed, are the surviving representatives of what was once the normal constitution of the human eye, and that the spectrum of science is a comparatively modern apparition. If, then, our literature went back far enough, we should find, in our oldest libraries, books of *two-coloured optics* to set over against the *three-coloured* doctrine of Young and Helmholtz and Clerk Maxwell. It is not possible to doubt, which would teach the truer lesson · refer the question to the colour-blind themselves; and they will surrender all claim for their own constituents. In every instance, then, the *new* elements contributed by evolution are *true* elements; and the measure of their increment of truth is the extent of their departure, by way of difference, from the datum whence they start.

Take another case of supposed evolution, supplied by Mr. Spencer himself, still in the sphere of perception. 'I believe,' he says, 'the intuition of Space possessed by any living individual, to have arisen from organised and consolidated experiences of all antecedent individuals, who bequeathed to him their slowly developed nervous organisation;' and 'I believe that this intuition, requiring only to be made definite and complete by personal experiences, has practically become a form of thought, apparently quite independent of experience[1].' Compare, then, the first state of this experiential series with the last. It begins, we are assured, with the successive sensations of touch, combined with those of muscular feeling, during the movement of a finger or a hand, from end to end of an edge or surface. The series is now less, now more protracted; its muscular components are different, according as the movement is of lateral, of pushing, or of lifting muscles; and these and other varieties, rendered familiar by frequent recurrence, become distinguished in experience, and, with the advance of language, draw to themselves names. What are these names? We have samples of them in 'long' and 'short,' 'up' and 'down,' 'before' and 'behind,' 'broad' and 'narrow,' 'straight' and 'curved,' 'square' and 'circular.' But are these then really the names of the experiences, which are the only assigned data? Is it the *sensations* that are square or circular, broad or narrow, up or down? Not so: these are terms that cannot be applied to states of consciousness. Perhaps, however, they will fit this or that *set* of them, though no single state? No: this will not help us; for, feelings dispose themselves in one of two possible arrangements, viz. together, or one following another; and both of these are relations in *Time;* whereas our list of names gives no specifications of time. It is useless to tell me that my synchronous feeling of the two ends of a box between my hands, or that my memory of the muscular sensations in passing my finger from end to end, *is the box's*

[1] Spencer's Letter, ap. Bain's Mental and Moral Science, p. 722.

length: these states are in me, and not in it; and when reflected on, as they must be in order to be named, are a part of my *self-knowledge*, and not of *other knowledge*. Where then is, I do not say the *intuition* of space, but even the least inchoate rudiment of any geometrical idea, any inkling of an externality at all, any removal out of the limits of the mere time-order of our own feelings and ideas, i. e. of *Number*, in successive or simultaneous arrangement? But Number is not Space. It matters not how many ages and organisms are expended in grinding down and refining and recompounding these materials: they will never turn out either plenum or vacuum enough for a hat to put your head in. If there is nothing to depend upon but 'accumulation and consolidation' of such 'experiences,' the internal history, however enriched, must remain without external counterpart.

Does it follow from this that Mr. Spencer's speculation is inadmissible? That is not the inference which I wish to draw. Let it stand as a true history of at least the order of development. I only say that if and when, in the course of it, the idea of externality enters, it is a *new* idea, *not contained* in any prior element of the conscious life. The translation of time-trains into space-pictures, of inward feelings into outward sizes, shapes, and distances, can only be accomplished when both languages have been consecutively learned; and the utmost familiarity with the vocabulary of the one, and with all its varieties of shorthand, will advance you not one step towards the preconception of the other. That they now furnish each other with reciprocal measures, that so many touches indicate so much length, and *vice versâ*, no more means that they are identical, than the striking of the clock implies that Time is audible. When, therefore, in the development of nature we gain these additional perceptions, and regard ourselves as spectators of a scene embracing, with ourselves, bodies of various figure, and with our station, an horizon reached through countless perspectives, do we *learn anything* by this vast surprise? Is the field which it spreads around us really there,—'a gate of heaven, though we knew it not?' or is it only a dream, an illusory effect from the mere summing-up of ancestral sensations? If you accept it as an enrichment of our cognitive stores, then you grant the authority of evolution, as the accredited messenger of new truth, and not the mere masked reproducer of old columns of accounts, taken in sum instead of in series.

And when you consider what is involved in this *Space*-belief,—that it cannot be present at all without the idea and the assurance of *Infinitude*, that you cannot look out from your own point, or plant a single body in any other, without enveloping yourself and it in a boundless circumambient field, throughout which all measures must be taken by the same three dimensions which are familiar near at hand,—you cannot but perceive, how far beyond the range of any empirical groping of ours extends the sweep of this added knowledge. If it exemplifies and measures the trustworthiness of what evolution adds to us, there would seem to be no limit to the claims of its revelations. I call them *revelations* in order to fix attention once more upon the fact that they are *new*, and could never be extracted as rational knowledge from the experiences assigned as its occasioning antecedents.

Mr. Spencer illustrates the relation between the terminal intuition to which evolution brings us, and the prior conditions out of which it emerges, by comparing it with that between the deduced predictions of the Newtonian astronomer, and the approximate guesses of the ancient calculators by planetary observation[1]. But the analogy does not bear examination. The law of gravitation is drawn from the facts of plane astronomy, especially from Kepler's laws, not by repetition, familiarity, and fusion of the general experience of men that see the skies; but by reasoned analysis of a single specimen, viz. the orbital motion of Mars; and is then tested by rigorous application to other planets, to the

[1] Spencer's Letter, ap. Bain's Mental and Moral Science, p 722, top.

us, than if they had come to us without growth. 'Demonstrations,' as Spinoza says, 'are the eyes of the mind,' with which it sees the things that are.

§ 5. *As applied to Moral Judgment.*

Change the scene to another chapter of the same story. The inward springs and processes of human action as little resemble their initial stage as those of thought; and the character of an Aristides or a Washington exhibits a good deal that would not be found in their long-eared sylvan original. The evolution of the quadruped's nature into the heroic type of humanity may be variously imagined; and whoever requires a definite picture of it had better consult Mr. Spencer, who perhaps is in the secret. For our purpose it is enough that we fix attention on the difference which he himself affirms between the beginning and the end. At the outset, the life was wholly swayed by immediate pleasure and pain, whether of appetite, of anger, of instinctive affection, each, as it came uppermost, wielding the activity and turning it hither and thither, as a veering wind alters the waveline upon a lake. At the point which we have now reached, such surrender to chance incitements is checked by a consciousness of differences among them other than sentient, 'by certain faculties of *moral intuition, certain emotions responding to right and wrong.*' There must, then, have been a time when, in the midst of the primitive sensory and instinctive phenomena, this consciousness of right emerged and took its place in the life, as something new. Conceivably enough, the occasion might be, some crisis of conflict and necessary choice between two instincts importunate at once,—for example, between the agent's own hunger and the saving of his more endangered wife or child Suppose him, under such conditions, visited by a feeling, not of more vehement liking, but of a superior *Right*, of *authority that demands* the self-neglect. is he to welcome it as an insight into a kind of relation unsuspected before, and to find it the lunar movements, and to the tides; so that no one who admits the first principle of rectilinear and deflected motion can resist his intellectual advance to the demonstrated law. The process from the concrete particulars to the universal formula is throughout one, not of custom, but of severe logical inference, which would be just as convincing to an intelligence near the beginning of the experiences as to us at the 'end of the ages.' Is Mr. Spencer's 'Space-intuition' got at in this way? Can he show us the 'Principia' which establish it, and vindicate it as the comprehending truth for interpreting all the phenomena of the objective senses? On the contrary, there is not a scrap of analytic process or of reasoning adduced on its behalf; it is simply picked up as a present idea, of which it is not very easy to render account, but which may perhaps be a kind of *psychological compend* of all the tactual and muscular feelings that have run through the consciousness of myriads of progenitors. Such a product could have no claim to be used, like the law of gravitation, as a verified calculus of deduction: it would be formed in the same way by which baseless prejudices become fixed, and if this were all, it might as probably be false as true. In order to erect it into knowledge, you must go beyond this account, and provide for its being a real differentiation, i.e. for its containing an *original element*, upon which the cognitive value depends.

So far we have touched only on the relation of the perceptive and intelligent powers. Up to this point, we find that, throughout the history of widening apprehension and thought, each increment introduces us to something more of the reality of things: we learn by degrees the predicates of time, of space, the properties of number and of figure, and more and more of the order of nature in the distribution of its bodies and the relation of its events. Every lesson is a gain; and no step is taken that makes a fool of us. On the intellectual side of our nature, all the axioms and most of the procedure of which were once absent and are now its distinctive characteristics, we no more doubt what they tell threshold of a more sacred compartment of the world than he had yet known? Or, is he to slur it, and water it down, and let it flow away as the mere weakness of his own indecision? To take the latter course would be to arrest the evolution and remain at the stage short of the idea of Duty; to take the former is to follow the rule which has held good throughout the history of perceptive and intellectual evolution: viz. that each increment contributed by fresh differentiation constitutes a discovery, and connects us by an added link of truth with the real scene of our existence.

It is plain from this survey of the process of evolution, that we have just as much reason for trusting the sense of Right, with the postulate of objective authority which it carries, as for believing in the components of the rainbow or the infinitude of Space. These ideas are all acquisitions, in the sense that there was a time when they were not to be found in the creatures from which we descend. They are all evolved, in the sense that, gradually and one by one, they cropped up into consciousness amid the crowd of feelings which they entered as strangers. They are all original, or *sui generis*, in the sense that they are intrinsically dissimilar to the predecessors with which they mingle, so that by no rational scrutiny could you, out of the contents of these predecessors, invent and preconceive them, any more than you can predict the psychology of a million years hence. Whence then the strange anxiety to get rid of this originality, and assimilate again what you had registered as a differentiation? You say that, when you undress the 'moral intuition' and lay aside fold after fold of its disguise, you find nothing at last but naked pleasure and utility: then how is it that no foresight, with largest command of psychologic clothes, would enable you to invert the experiment and dress up these nudities into the august form of Duty? To say that the conscience is but the compressed contents of an inherited calculus of the agreeable and the serviceable, is no better than for one who had been colour-blind to insist, that the red which he has gained is nothing but his familiar green with some queer mask. It cannot be denied that the sense of right has earned its separate name, by appearing to those who have it and speak of it to one another essentially different from the desire of pleasure, from the perception of related means and ends, and from coercive fear. Why not, therefore, frankly leave it its proper place as a new differentiation of voluntary activity? Why pretend, against all fact, that it is homogeneous with self-interest, instead of accepting it as the key to a moral order of cognition and system of relations, supplementing the previous sentient and intellectual and affectional experience? Unless we so accept it, we are driven to the unsatisfactory task of *explaining away* the characteristics of our nature which are admitted to lie on its meridian of culmination; of plucking off the mask of Divine authority from duty, and of human freedom from responsibility: of cancelling obligation except in the vaguer sense, 'If you want to walk, you are "bound" to move your legs:' of interpreting altruistic claims as transfigured self-concern; and of reducing moral law from ultimate to instrumental; so that whatever of higher tone and more ideal aspect is superinduced upon the sentient and instinctive foundation comes to be regarded as a species of rhetorical exaggeration and æsthetic witchery, by which we are *tricked* into serving one another and forgetting our self-love. For my part, I object to be led blindfold, through the cunning of nature, into sham sacrifices and heroisms, even though they should land me in a real heaven; much more, when I find that they replace me among 'appetising' creatures, with only the added knowledge that I am a dupe into the bargain. Better far to trust the veracity of nature; and accept the independent reality of the moral relations it discloses, as loyally as those laid open by the perceptive and intellectual evolution. The idea of *a higher* is as much entitled to be believed, as that of an outer: the *right*, as the true; and both are distinct from the *pleasant*.

§ 6. *Hitches in the Evolutionary Deduction.*

Thus far I have refrained from discussing the truth of the doctrine of evolution, and have limited myself to its interpretation and significance, if true If it is to be *inductively* established, the manipulation of its evidence must be left to the experts in natural history, geology, chemistry, and molecular physics; and being quite incompetent to criticise their interior controversies, I have supposed them to be a happy family, all of one mind, in favour of the modern hypothesis. It is to the *deductions from it*, when thus assumed, that the foregoing argument addresses itself; and this is a matter of simply logical concern, open to judgment for any one who understands the meaning of the terms through which the conclusion is reached. The argument affirms the general proposition, that evolution consists in the perpetual emergence of *something new which is an increment of being* upon its prior term, and therefore more than its equivalent, and entitled to equal confidence and higher rank. This, however, though holding good throughout, has an exceptionally forcible validity at certain stages of the evolution, on which it is desirable to pause. Though all the differences evolved are something new, and may fall upon an observer's mere perception as equally new, yet, when scrutinised by reason, some may retain their character of absolute surprise, for which there was and could be nothing to prepare us, while others may prove to be, like an unsuspected property of a geometrical figure, only a new grouping of data and relations already in hand In this sense, there may be a more new and a less new; and it is the former that brings the force of the foregoing argument to its maximum. It will clear our conception of evolution, if we notice one or two of the points where these newest of the new come in. We may find examples without going back to any date anterior to the existence of life. At that time the primitive data, of atoms and motion, have hustled and danced themselves into the shape of solar systems, have practised their first experiments in morphology, and worked up their patent organic cell into seaweed, ferns, and forests. And let us suppose ourselves in possession of the scientific key to all the contents of this richly clad mineral and vegetable world; able to read the molecular differences which constitute the solid, liquid, and gaseous form of bodies: to measure the velocities of atoms and their currents to number the undulations and resistances that make up the history of heat and electricity, of light and its polarisation: to follow the chemical elements through their cycles of combination and dissolution, whether depositing the crystal, or weaving the tissue of the plant, or storing up a future for it in its seed. It is perhaps conceivable that the whole of this knowledge may form a catena, along which our reason can pass from link to link; and that its later equations may be really in terms of the earlier, only compressed into a more generalised notation. For, in all its problems, from first to last, we have dealt with nothing but matter and motion, with their presuppositions of space, and time, and force. If you fix attention on any individual object, imagined to pass, as a sample of what happens, through this entire reach of evolution, and ask how its complication comes about, you will find it not spontaneous, from the contents of the isolated thing, but due to changed conditions in the scene of its existence, modifying its external relations, and through these its internal nature. With an accurate knowledge of these relative conditions and their laws of change, its history could be all foreseen.

We cannot doubt that from this point the next step in the ascent of being was to *Feeling;* and here first we encounter a change, to the understanding of which all that has gone before is absolutely irrelevant. There is certainly, along with the new phenomenon, also some new organic structure or affection, the destined rudiment of the future human being. But though we take up this also, and in its completest form, into our body of scientific knowledge, we get nothing into view but molecular arrangements and movements. If we could observe the whole interior of the cerebral and nervous history, and make pictures of the arrangements and registers of the velocities of transmission, for every sensation, we should be no nearer to any insight into the connection between these phenomena and consciousness. We should see one movement producing another, or shut up by its resistance; and whatever form the energy assumed which ceased to be kinetic, we could follow it and account for it all, had we but perceptions fine enough. But with that cycle of material changes our observing and computing resources are at an end if at any moment in it a pleasure occurs, we shall not see it if a pain, we can learn it only from him that has it · if an idea, no detective microscope can draw it from him. To each of these cases there may belong a different concomitant physical phenomenon, which to one who has once learned their companionship, will serve as a sign of what is being felt; but why this figure in the atomic dance means hearing and that means vision, or why any of them means anything in a mental world which they cannot enter, is absolutely hidden from him; nay, must for ever be so; for the sphere of physical knowledge is without contact with the sphere of consciousness, and can deal with no problems but those which can be expressed in terms of matter and motion

Here, then, our evolution ceases to be deductive. Its next step is dependent, not on any modified conditions in the environment, so as to be calculable from them; but on an increment quite heterogeneous turning up in the inward nature. It therefore constitutes *a new departure*. When pain and pleasure come upon the scene and mingle with the eddy of molecules, they appear as strangers, for whose entrance the physical elements decline to be responsible; for they can give complete account of all their rotations, percussions, and rebounds, to the minutest fraction, without any emergence of these intruders. And if they had never come at all, the physical history of these very rotations, percussions, and rebounds would infallibly go on exactly the same in conformity with the law of transmission of force:

the automatic procedure of the organism taking no notice of the sentient phenomena of its subject. Those phenomena indeed, when they have once gained their mysterious entrance, set out upon a history of their own: feelings by recurrence running into mental habits, and by their varieties constituting different affections, but, whatever be their complexities and laws of combination, hardening, it may be, the mental habits into permanent instincts, and organising the affections into formed character, the root of the whole growth is in a new and hyperphysical initiative. there cannot be recurrence, without something to recur, or variety without something to be varied; and the datum which undergoes this process, and first renders experience possible and starts its history, is the undeduced and undeducible one of *feeling* or *consciousness*. The reason for specially accentuating it is that it presents itself as a clear addition to the nature of the living being, and not as a mere fresh adjustment of the organism in relation to the external conditions.

Once equipped with this new departure, the evolutionist may resume his continuous course and pursue it far without pause or hitch; only that now he advances along the line not of physical but of mental laws, and transfers himself for guidance from the naturalist to the psychologist. From the base of sentient life to the higher operations of intelligence the gradations of ascent are so little sensible, that there is nothing inconceivable in the passage from each to the next: indeed, so large a portion of the distance is traversed by every infant Humboldt or La Place, that Time alone (of which there is no stint) seems needed to twine the whole into one unbroken thread. By the help of well-known laws, the association of ideas, the process of abstraction, the organisation of language and predication, it becomes possible to show how the raw material of animal sensation and perception may be worked up into intellectual tissue of the finest order. So long as the thinking process is traced onward to more and more elaborated forms, as in a continuous direction, there is nothing to stop the way from the 'long-eared quadruped' to Shakespeare. Nor is it otherwise on the active side of the mental nature, while you treat it as if occupied by now one instinct and now another, you can make it intelligible how each can profit by experience, and become a finished art or a deeper affection. But there is a point where this story of rectilinear advance fails to cover the whole case: the point where two conflicting impulses dispute possession of us, and clamour for our decision of the alternative: where, as I have contended, we know ourselves, not as the *theatre*, but as the *cause* of the decision, not as waiting till the rivals have tried their strength, or one of them has been somehow called away, but as imperatively summoned to judge and strike, and *that* by the new rule of *Right*, which never broke upon us till the alternative came. Here we are introduced to the consciousness of Free-will and the dawn of the Moral idea, of which, I venture to say, the prior psychology can no more give an admissible account than can the laws of matter and motion, in their physiological application, give account of simple consciousness. All that it attempts to do is, in effect, to deny the fact of choice, to get rid of it as a phenomenon in nature, and put it on the discharged list of illusions, and persuade us that, in all our strife of temptation and verdicts of conscience, we are dragged along by the irresistible chain of strongest association. Without repeating the reasons before given for rejecting this unsatisfactory analysis, I content myself with adhering to the natural self-consciousness which it tries to explain away; and affirming that, in this feeling of Moral right and freedom which attends the experience of an alternative, we are brought to another resting-place of evolution, which again gives us a new point of departure. I do not say that, first in the birth of consciousness, and secondly in the birth of duty, we meet with any historical suspension of evolution: we can doubtless pursue our journey on the same road in the same coach; only we shall have to *change horses* (or rather, as I am writing for young travellers, who know nothing about horses, to change *engines*); i. e. there is a breach of reasoned continuity, which no theory can bridge over, and which is an effectual bar to the ambitious attempts at unification of knowledge. We are thus supplied with an important ground for treating as distinct in their base, though variously related in their application, the natural sciences, psychology, and morals.

In thus insisting on consciousness and free-will, as initiating stages of evolution not deducible from the preceding, I do but modify in form an admission universal in modern philosophy: viz. that it is impossible to establish a catena of causality which shall link mind and matter into a single line. One who is convinced of this, and yet feels bound to give some relative account of both, has two modes of conception open to him. He may set the material and the ideal principle in independent parallelism from the first, with their phenomena uniformly synchronous, but on separate lines, from neither of which any action passes to the other; and so present us with a dual universe, with no unity unless in the supernatural source of this eternal bifurcation. Or, he may arbitrarily alter the meaning of one of the two words 'matter' and 'mind,' so as to take into the conception the attributes of both; and then, furnished for his journey with this full portmanteau, he can take them out again at his convenience, and deliver all the predicates that may be demanded of him. It is the same obstinate difficulty that drives him to this device; since he cannot persuade matter to manufacture mind, he makes it a present of mind to begin with. The school of Descartes worked out the first of these modes of conception, and through its influence, especially in France, instituted that keen independent pursuit of the sciences of external nature and of internal thought which characterised the last and early part of the present century in Europe. The second result, which is virtually a revival of the Leibnizian monads (with the Primordial monad deposed), seems to find greater favour with the present representatives of the evolution doctrine. That we must 'radically change our notions of matter,' and 'discern in it' 'the promise and potency of all terrestrial life,' will be remembered as the claim and prophecy of Professor Tyndall's celebrated address [1]. And a far more explicit avowal is given us by Haeckel in these sentences: 'Every atom possesses an inherent sum of force, and in this sense is animate (*beseelt*). Without the assumption of an atomic soul (*Atom-Seele*) the commonest and most general phenomena of chemistry are inexplicable. Pleasure and pain (*Unlust*), desire and aversion, attraction and repulsion, must be common to all atoms of an aggregate (*Massen-Atomen*); for the movements of atoms which must take place in the formation and dissolution of a chemical compound can be explained only by attributing to them *Sensation and Will*. ... If the Will of man and the higher animals appears free in contrast with the determinate (*festen*) of the atoms, this is an illusion due to the extremely complex movements of will in the former case, compared with the extremely simple in the latter[2].' It is impossible to desire a more frank admission of the impassable nature of the interval which I have said no rational procedure can span: 'You must bespeak a soul within your atoms, or you will never get it out of them;' nor can we help admiring the naive avowal that this exigency alone prompts the assertion of sentient and volitional atoms, and not anything of the nature of evidence; they are wanted in the interests of a foregone conclusion; so nature is bound to supply them. In Haeckel too you will observe that the spiritual postulate, which was single in Descartes, is *twofold*; the atom is equipped from the first with *Will* as well as *Consciousness*,—a needless violation of the rule of 'parcimony,' if they could have been thrown into the relation of cause and effect. In

[1] Fragments of Science, pp. 52*, 524.
[2] Die Perigenesis der Plastidule, oder die Wellenzeugung der Lebenstheilchen. Berlin, 1876 Pp. 38, 39, quoted by Du Bois-Reymond. Die sieben Weltrathsel, p. 71.

affirming, therefore, that neither from the unconscious to the conscious, nor from the simply conscious to the voluntary, is there any thoroughfare for thought, we may claim the weighty concurrence of this distinguished evolutionist. It would be easy to call other witnesses whose testimony is to the same effect, partially or wholly. Du Bois-Reymond, perhaps the most philosophical of living interpreters of nature, reckons both the problems on which I have paused, viz. of consciousness and of free-will, as what he calls *Transcendent*, i. e. irresolvable by the methods of natural science, yet of imperishable interest for the human mind. Of the moral problem he says: 'One who goes through life in a sleep-walker's dream, whether as king or wood-cutter; one who, as historian, jurist, poet, deals in one-sided contemplation of human institutes and passions, or, as successful Scientist, carries into nature's laws a glance equally limited;—forgets that dilemma on the piercing horns of which our understanding quivers like the victim of the shiike; just as we forget the phantoms which else would never cease to dizzy and pursue us. So much the more desperate are the efforts to extricate themselves from such torture, which spend the strength of a small band who, with the Rabbi of Amsterdam, contemplate the All *sub specie eternitatis:* unless indeed they are content, like Leibniz, to renounce self-determination. The writings of metaphysicians present a long series of attempts to reconcile free-will and moral law with a mechanical determination of the will. Were it given to anyone,—say Kant,—to achieve this quadrature, the series would surely come to an end. None but unconquerable problems are thus undying[1].' That Du Bois-Reymond himself is not prepared to escape from this dilemma by the sacrifice of free-will is evident from the following remarks on moral alternatives · 'It is on passing over from the physical to the ethical sphere that most natures become sensible of the darkness [besetting this problem]. Anyone will readily

[1] Die sieben Welträthsel, pp 94, 95.

admit himself not free, but determined to action by hidden causes, so long as the action is of an indifferent kind. Whether the right or the left boot comes first into Cæsar's hand makes no difference; in either case, he walks booted out of his tent. Whether he crosses the Rubicon or not, is the hinge on which the course of history turns. So little free are we in certain small decisions, that a skilled observer of human nature predicts with surprising certainty, which card we shall take up from among a number dealt out under particular conditions. But in face of the more serious issues of practical life, even the most resolute Monist cannot easily retain his idea that the whole of human existence is nothing but a *Fable convenue*, in which mechanical necessity assigns to Caius the part of criminal, to Sempronius that of judge : so that Caius is led to execution, while Sempronius goes to breakfast[1].'

The conclusion to which I am brought by this notice of intermediate points of arrest and new departure, may be stated thus: If the evolutionist means no more than that, in point of historic fact, Life first appeared in plant-form on this globe, and was followed by sentient types, passing by innumerable gradations from the most simple in organism and function to the present nature of man, he sets up an hypothesis consistent with the evidence at present within reach of the naturalist. If he means that he has found, or can suggest, an adequate system of causation for working out this process from beginning to end, he overstates the strength of his hypothesis; which, meeting with a chasm in two places, is broken, as a reasoned scheme, into three pieces, empirically successive, but logically detached.

§ 7. *Conscience Developed into Social Consensus and Religion.*

From our last point of new departure, viz. the *idea of Right* started by alternative impulses, the course of

[1] Die sieben Weltrathsel, p. 94

development proceeds intelligibly and expands smoothly to an indefinite extent. So far as it depends on the internal history of the individual, it has been already traced, and need only be recalled to mind. Its form of growth is the simplest possible: every case in which the springs of action solicit us in pairs introduces a fresh consciousness of relative right; and as the instances accumulate, the feeling is deepened, if they are repetitions, and widened, if they are new: with the effect of condensing at last the whole of these experiences, gathered by the sense of relative right, into one large affection of special type, whose love and aversion work only within this relation. We call it *Conscience*: but it need not wait for its name till it has wrought out its generalisation and is complete; for in truth it is never complete; and is the same, whether as feeling or as judgment, in the most elementary instance of conflict between two incentives, and in the maturest self-estimate of the total character. *Any* knowledge with ourselves, large or small, which we may have, of the superior right of one spring of action over another, comes under the category of conscience. But the internal history, which brings fresh instincts into operation and enlarges our psychological view, itself depends upon the play of new influences upon us from the external scene: as the relations of the family, the village, the clan, the State, and at last the *genus humanum*, become included within the circle of cognisance, corresponding affections wake into life and enrich the personality with motive energies unfelt and unappreciated before; and as each prefers its claim upon us for a proportionate loyalty, the ratios of our moral life become organised, and, notwithstanding its growing complexity, it attains a more perfect order. And this process so implicates together the agent and his fellows, that we can scarce divide the causal factors into individual and social, inner and outer: *bodily*, no doubt, he stands there by himself, while his family are grouped separately round him; but *spiritually*, he is not *himself* without them, and the major part of his individuality is relative to them, as theirs is relative to him. He has no *self* that is not reflected in them, and of which they are not reflections; and this reveals itself by a kind of moral amputation, if death should snatch them away, and put his *selfdom* to the test of loneliness. It is the same with the larger groups which enclose him in their sympathetic embrace. His *country* is not external to him: he is woven into it by sensitive fibres that answer to all its good or ill: its life-blood courses through his veins inseparably mingled with his own. The social union is most inadequately represented as a compact or tacit bargain subsisting among separate units, agreeing to combine for specific purposes and for limited times, and then disbanding again to their several isolations. It is no such forensic abstraction, devised as a cement for mechanically conceived components; but a concrete though spiritual form of life, penetrating and partly constituting all persons belonging to it, so that only as fractions of it do they become human integers themselves. What we call a conflict between private and public interest, and treat as a dissension between a man's inner self and an outward society, is not really a wrestling match on the part of two independent organisms or personalities, unless it comes to overt rebellion and war: the inner man is himself the scene of the living strife. the public interest that pleads with him is *his* interest too: the Society that withstands him is *his* Society: it is no foreign and intrusive power that confronts and stops the madness of his pleasure or his passion, but his own share of an altruistic zeal and love that throb in other hearts as well. It is a *self-variance* which he feels, between some appetite that feeds alone and an affection which lives in others, between the unsocial and the social instincts of the same nature; and if he goes with the evil counsel, his shame is no hiding from others' anger, but a shrinking from disapproval which he knows from himself to be also theirs. The complication of human relations and the growth of new forms of human affection proceed *pari passu*, and are reciprocal parts of one and the same history; neither can be set up as prior cause of the other; and every attempt either to evolve Society from the data of the individual constitution, or to account for the individual from the requirements of Society, involves the failure inseparable from the method of mechanical monism. A mere antagonism of personal wishes, settled by the force of superior numbers, might no doubt establish a certain order of joint living under terms of peace; but it would be the precarious order of two allied camps, with as many sentinels towards each other as towards the common foe. Social union constitutes itself, not by equilibration of opposite interests, but by concurrence of moral sympathies · the laws of conduct embodying whatever is approved and admired in common by the natural guides of the general sentiment. They are the expression of what has come out in the intercourses of men, whereby they unconsciously explore each other's feeling and disclose their own, in reference to praiseworthy or blameworthy character; and therefore measure the extent to which experience has paired their springs of action, and carried their moral development. They are the consensus of felt right; and so, the product less of coercion than of enthusiasm,—a form of affection towards the incorporated life of many wills.

The moral evolution, however, is not necessarily arrested, when it has moulded into form the existing average of ethical sympathy. There will always be, through the inequalities of character, a tension above, as there is a gravitation below, the level marked by the institutions and habitual sentiments of a community; and as he who has outstripped the general advance and pushed his experience and insight into springs of action of higher rank, has only brought to explicit life what is implicit and potentially present in all, and even ready to wake in his near neighbourhood, his realised advance appeals to minds prepared to respond and follow: his higher vision spoils their contentment with the type of their social organism as it stands : he quickens their perceptions to see a juster than its just, a purer than its pure, a braver than its courage, a nobler than its honour, a diviner than its worship. And so, beyond and yet within the moral empire that covers the broad level of the common world, there is the promise of a state unrealised, or of a transfer of vitality to a new and unsuspected centre: behind Rome there is Jerusalem : and within Jerusalem an upper chamber, whence voices already escape that neutralise the barriers of race and tongue, and are not silenced by the look of the impossible. There forms itself in the minds of men the conception of an ideal commonwealth, whose pattern, as Plato said, is stored in heaven, never itself to descend, yet visible for perpetual approximation by the wise,—'a kingdom of God,' in which at last wrong shall wear itself out, and the energies of life shall be harmonised and its affections perfected Under this aspect it is, that the moral evolution of Society, unable to rest in the *State*, aspires to transcend it in the *Church;* the function of which is to idealise the conception of human existence, to prevent its settling upon its levels, to unfold the contents of its best thought and aims, and lead on the way to their realisation, both by quickening the faith that power Divine is on their side, and by skilfully assailing the resistances to their accomplishment. The ever-widening conscience of faithful men feels in allegiance bound to nothing short of this : it cannot but pass on from Ethics to Religion. Its moral instinct far transcends mere adaptation, however exact, to existing conditions : it snatches the course of evolution out of the hands of 'accidental variation' and the blind groping of tentative adjustment to things as they are, and leads on the open-eyed march to a preconceived and nobler future, and wins a 'survival of the fittest,' not by opportune accommodation to present data, but by startling creation of unforeseen quæsita. It melts down the old conditions in its fires, and remoulds them with its better art, and then lives into them with purposed and ideal fitness.

Were it not indeed for this last and culminating stage, the evolution even of human conduct would never earn even the name of *moral* at all. So long as it is pushed on from behind, knowing not whither it goes, so long as it only slips more and more happily into the groove of movement and advance, so as to smooth the way and outstrip the stragglers upon rugged paths, it is simply a success without a particle of *character*. Not till this necessary causation is replaced by the free, and for the spontaneous is substituted the voluntary, not till the 'selection' passes from Nature into Thought, and is determined prophetically for an end instead of mechanically from the beginning, does the progressive change in human action and in social law become any more *moral* than, in the pigeon, the acquisition of his tumbling trick, or the growth of his portentous crop. And *when* the transference of the process to the Will has taken place, the theory of evolution is no longer an hypothesis in natural history, but merges in the conception of indefinite possible approach to moral perfection.

§ 8. *Objections to the Doctrine of Conscience Considered.*

Throughout this account of the final stage of development I have freely used the word 'conscience,' to mark the special function, whether of feeling or of cognition, which is here in the ascendant, and to which we owe our apprehension of relative *Right*. It is a word, however, to which the expounders of evolution entertain a strong antipathy; and Mr. Leslie Stephen, in particular, while remarking that it 'needs less discussion because it is part of an obsolete form of speculation,' sharply criticises it on grounds which it is due to him, and to a venerable term which can ill be spared, that we should notice.

He assumes, what may be at once conceded, that the word 'Conscience' carries in its meaning the idea of an 'elementary instinct,' 'incapable of further analysis.' In what sense I accept this account will be clear, I hope, from the preceding exposition: viz. that the knowledge we have of relative 'right' and 'wrong' in the springs of action is a unique and irresolvable kind of knowledge, introducing us to a quality neither given us in perception nor accessible by inference, and therefore requiring a separate word to mark the function of our nature which secures its presence. To the recognition of 'an autonomous and independent' character in conscience, Mr Stephen advances two objections (1) it sets up the conscience as a separate and permanently fixed faculty, 'an ultimate factor' privileged against analytical scrutiny; and such a claim is inconsistent with the conception and with the evidence of evolution[1]. And (2) it requires us to co-ordinate the conscience with the particular instincts; from which, however, it is so different in its object and method, that the co-ordination is impossible.

The first of these objections depends entirely upon an arbitrary interpretation put upon the word 'conscience,' and disappears when that interpretation is renounced. True, it *does* imply a function in our nature so far 'separate' as to leave with us an idea which else we should not have. Whenever you come upon an idea which baffles analysis, I suppose you can say no less than that it is 'an ultimate factor;' and till you can analyse it and resolve it into something else, so it must remain. But, in affirming this, you do not say, either, that the idea was always present in all the possible animal progenitors of the existing race, in the first mollusc as in the last Christian ; or, that it is an idea incapable of growth and ramification, of blossoming and fruit-bearing I cannot indeed point out the moment in the chronology of species or in the history of our own, when the idea of Right entered the consciousness , but the evolutionary expositor is here just as much at fault, and, as we have seen, cannot pretend to have no lacunæ in his story. And as for conscience, supposing it a primitive datum, being thereby precluded from development, I can only appeal to the friendly alliance in which they have worked together in the foregoing

[1] Science of Ethics, chap. viii. § 4, p. 314, already quoted, in a different connection, supra, Part II. Introduction, ii. pp. 10, 11 in this volume.

exposition: the germ being in the first felt difference of claim between two competing instincts; the expansion taking place with each analogous experience, and each emergence of new incentives; till at last the collective judgments organise themselves into a hierarchy of ordered affections, constituting an ideal of character and guarded by the all-pervading sense of Duty. Mr. Stephen, assuming that the moral can come out of the unmoral, dwells upon what he calls 'the broad fact that material morality makes its appearance long before any conscious recognition of a moral law.' I can only say that I know no evidence of this 'broad fact,' and utterly disbelieve it. If I understand the phrase aright, it means that, in any given group of human beings, habits of action are formed and enforced by the corporate spirit of the members, before they are backed up by any attendant feeling of approval. How is this absence of any feeling of approval to be established? Is it enough to change the phrase, and say with Mr. Stephen, that 'the moral rule begins in the external form,'—its mandate '*Do this*' instead of '*Be this:*' and that, so long as it is in this form, we need not attend to the motives of the agent: the conduct is approved simply because it is useful, and it is equally useful, whatever be his motive[1]? Far from it. This fuller statement contains indeed a truth, but with it implies an error. True it is, that what is first insisted on as due from another,—the first object of an imperative directed upon him,—is a *concrete act* (a '*Do* this'), and not a *total character* (a '*Be* this'): judgment and feeling always addressing themselves to the particular before they grasp the general: they take hold of the *Doing* as phenomenal, earlier than the *Being* as permanent. But it is *not*, on this account, true, that the particular act thus demanded is conceived of without its presumed motive, instead of being regarded as its simple outcome and expression, and that to the imperative observer's feeling it will make no difference, whether the act, for example, is extorted by fear or is the natural language of

[1] Science of Ethics, chap. vii. § 4, p. 267.

courage. Not having the intimate acquaintance with the psychology of savages which seems to be accessible to the recent investigators of our prototypes, I am unable to conceive of a tribe that cares nothing for personal qualities in a chief or in a wife, and looks with exactly the same feeling upon two equally useful things, of which one comes by the custom and necessity of nature and the other from the affection and the will of a companion. Rather do I believe that, to the instinctive glance of these untrained people, all action is *alive*, and its 'material morality' glowing to incandescence with the fiery impulse that shoots it forth; so that to suppose a change of impulse is to destroy the identity of the action, and disappoint the imperative altogether. But further; when the genesis of the moral principle is thrown into the form of these two imperatives, supposed to be flung out upon the social scene around, the momentous assumption is made, that judgment passes upon others before it is applied to ourselves. Without repeating what has been already said upon this hinge-point of all moral theory, I will only add that no reasoned discussion of it is to be found in 'The Science of Ethics;' and that, although the work is pervaded by the assumption here made, yet the author's truer feeling occasionally trips up his theory, and inadvertently gives free course to the opposite postulate: as when he says (in a passage already cited), that our disgust at gluttony arises from the idea of *what it would be in ourselves*,—a derivation which certainly starts our moral estimates *from self-knowledge*, and thence gains the power of applying them to others.

The conscience, as we have defined it, is so far from excluding historical development, that it presupposes and expounds it, so that the two doctrines are mutual complements. Mr. Stephen entangles himself with a different and artificial conception of it, as a kind of prophetic legislative faculty, which, *ab initio*, is supposed to have set up a finished code, comprising all the known rules of human conduct and character as they now are, and to which, in new cases, we have only to refer under the proper head for ready-made answers for each problem. If ever such a theory of an ethical Papacy found a philosophic advocate (and I am not aware of any writer upon whom it can be charged), Mr. Stephen is certainly entitled to treat it as 'an obsolete form of speculation;' but no less so must we treat his evolutionary argument against it. His sword is sharp, but it cuts through a cloud.

The second objection to admitting conscience among 'the elementary instincts' insists upon a peculiarity which undoubtedly distinguishes it from the most marked examples of that class Of the appetites and passions, for instance, each directs itself upon some one kind of object, which is the answer to its want; it alone is related to that object (hunger, for example, to food), and has a right to it or supremacy over it. If disappointed of it and put down by the inrush of some interfering solicitations, pain ensues: why? Because its natural sway over its own province is suspended and neutralised by an interloper that preoccupies the executive, which, being able to do only one thing at a time, is distracted by the importunities of two. The suffering, therefore, from a disregarded instinct is due to its co-ordination, in a complex conception, with other instincts, and the synchronous action of wants which are at peace only when successive in their operation. But nothing of this sort can be alleged of conscience. It has no detached province with single and separate functions of its own. It has no co-ordinates, whose different and independent functions can claim to suspend it and push it out of its place, when due. If it had, there would arise disputes of relative rights between them and it, and we should need an ulterior judge to determine which was chargeable with arrogating too much: so that we should have to set a conscience behind a conscience *in infinitum*. Conscience, in short, involves 'a judgment of the whole character;' and *that* we can never get, so long as we make it itself a part of the character, by ranging it with the instincts that are its component factors. Thus at least I interpret the rather obscure paragraph which presents the objection under review. 'Conscience in any case means the pain felt by the wrong-doer, or rather the sensibility implied by that pain. It is exerted when we judge that we have deserved blame, and we deserve blame when we display some moral deficiency. Now a separate instinct,—a physical appetite, for example, such as hunger or lust,—may give us pain when its dictates are suppressed by some conflicting impulse. It corresponds to a particular function of the organism; it is excited by the appropriate stimulus, and is the sole instinct directly interested in a given class of actions. It is supreme within its own province, but it has to struggle because it is a part of a complex whole which can only act in one way at once, though accessible to a variety of stimuli. But it is impossible to conceive of the conscience in accordance with this analogy, as a particular faculty co-ordinate with others, or as possessing a separate province within which alone it is applicable[1].'

If it is necessary to an 'elementary instinct' to have a bodily organ, like the eating and drinking apparatus, to itself, of course conscience must forego the name. If its pursuit or its judgment must be directed upon some special kind of material thing, as hunger upon edibles, conscience is not within the category. If it must be blind and homogeneous, so as to be unconscious of differences and incapable of preferences in its own field, conscience is again shut out. But none of these tests will bear application to admitted samples of elementary impulses. Anger has no *limb* to itself: Pity has no palpable and visible object that you can externally define, but experiences and relations hidden within the consciousness. And the senses that are eager for food and light are not without their favourite flavours and colours, the comparative agreeableness of which they immediately feel. Within the province of vision, the perceptions of red, of green, of violet, are

[1] Science of Ethics, chap. vii. § 5, p. 315.

co-ordinated, in the sense of being all alike primitive data of feeling, yet also *subordinated*, one to another, so far as the eye of the seer is pleased with them in different degrees. Extend this experience, familiar to us in each field of primitive function, to a wider range. Suppose that some common quality permeated the objects of our now separated senses, and that, to meet this addition, we were provided with a corresponding susceptibility to it, the 'provinces' would cease to be wholly distinct: a thread of possible comparison and gradation would run throughout; and with the prior co-ordination would be combined a new subordination opened up to us through the fresh susceptibility. Nor is this a mere imaginary case, as every hedonist must allow. For what is *the pleasurableness* attaching to all the instinctive impulses and perceptions but precisely the supposed common quality pervading them and caused by their objects? And if anything is universally granted to be an original endowment of our nature, it is the capacity for having and for estimating pleasure and pain. With this position on the line of primitive data, the scale of degrees which it establishes among pleasurable things is not held to be inconsistent.

An appreciation, therefore, of a universal quality in objects which affect our consciousness may be immediate and intuitive. It is not necessary to shut up an instinct in this or that back parlour or front bedroom of our nature: it may be very proper for some of its kind to be content with such lodgings; but this need not hinder others from having the range of the whole house; which else, in fact, would hardly be kept as clean and bright as we could wish. The field of conscience is certainly not an enclosed compartment of human character and life, but its whole area and contents. Its objects are no isolated things, or acts, or passions, but a certain quality and system of relations belonging to them all upon their inner side, i. e. especially attaching to the internal springs of our own character and life. · It is the quality of *relative Right*. Being really there, why should it be deemed impossible to perceive it intuitively, and feel it in its gradations as truly as we feel the measures of pleasure and pain? It is but the form of immediate self-knowledge of our own mental phenomena under an aspect first revealed in the conflict of their activities. As there is an intuitive estimate of the relative beauty of colours, and intervals of tone, and intensities of light, why should not there be the same of the relative worth of the several springs of action? It is a mere verbal catch to tell us that, each instinct judging its own object, and the conscience judging them all, it cannot itself rank with them, or else it would have to be at the bar and on the bench at the same moment, and to decide between itself and its own prisoners, conscience the second pronouncing verdict on conscience the first. If it is permissible at all to speak of an appetite 'judging' its own object, it is obvious that the quality in it which is judged is quite other than that which the conscience perceives and estimates in the inward springs of action · in the one case, the affirmation is, 'This is what *I want*,' and the only relation felt is between the *object and the person*, 'This is the thing for me:' the whole matter of judgment lies in the sentient experience, and in one function of it at a time. In the other case, the affirmation is, 'This is *what I ought* to follow,' and the relation perceived is between *simultaneous alternative incentives*, 'This is the right and that the wrong:' the whole matter of judgment lies in the *moral quality*, and, involving comparison and perception of gradation upon a totally different scale, demands a new kind of aptitude, prior to which there had been, in fact, nothing *judicial*. Is it urged that, if an instinct is not to be its own justification, but must have another to which it renders account, then the conscience itself, being instinctive, needs, in its turn, to appear before a higher jurisdiction? The fallacy of the plea is on the surface. No instinct has its judgment ever called in question or interfered with by the conscience; it is allowed to be an oracle in the matter upon which it pronounces, viz. on the sort of object that fits its want. Nor does the conscience dispute the result of comparing several instincts in their sentient effects, or quarrel with any one for saying, 'Music for me is worth more than the best picture gallery in the world.' it never tells him that he is mistaken: it pays unqualified deference to the relative sensibilities of the several functions of our nature; and abstains from all meddling with the hedonistic measurements obtained from the experience of the instincts. But while it keeps aloof from their business, it requires in return that they should not intrude upon its own; which is, to appreciate in them a quality which they do not separately perceive in themselves, and take account of an order of relations in which they are no more experts than is vision in the discrimination of sounds. In claiming judicial supremacy here, in pronouncing on the moral rank of the springs of action, the conscience pretends to no more, as an intuitive instinct, than it concedes to the others: if it is morally autonomous, they are hedonistically so: if it judges their right and wrong, they are all at liberty to measure its pleasures and pains. In both instances alike, the postulate is respected, that an elementary instinct is a final authority in its own field.

All through his criticism, Mr. Stephen has conceived of the conscience in its *formed state*, when it has become a 'judgment of the whole character;' and it is not surprising that, preoccupied by this full-volumed idea, he should see in it such a preponderant amount of growth as to miss the little seed of intuition whence this 'greatest among herbs' in the garden of our nature has sprung and spread its branches. To him it is a difficult question, 'how it comes to pass that the conscientious feeling, which is a function of the whole character and not a specific faculty, comes to have so distinctive a quality as is at least frequently attributed to it[1].' The difficulty surely is imaginary, dependent perhaps upon an ambiguity in the phrase 'a function of the whole cha-

[1] Science of Ethics, chap viii § 21, p. 332.

racter.' If by this be meant that the whole formed character must first be there, as a constituted spiritual organ, before the conscientious feeling presents itself as the mode of its action, then undoubtedly it is not easy to see how this expression of the whole could put on the appearance of a differentiated part. But if we may understand that 'the conscientious feeling is a function of the character' *for the time being*, so as to be its expression all through, in its first beginning and during all its growth, and to measure by its range the breadth and compass which the character has attained, this is an office which may just as well be performed by a feeling strictly new and *sui generis* as by one familiar and derivative. If it is but a twin birth with the character, so that they date together, and is its constant and proportionate concomitant, either can be expressed in terms of the other, and there can never be the whole of one with a part of the other. This is exactly what is provided for by our moral psychology. The first moment of *moral consciousness* is in the conflict of two rival springs of action, which, taken one by one, had never given any idea of right: the first phenomenon of *character* is the choice between them; both are original, in relation to their antecedents: both are elementary in relation to their future; and every increment which experience adds to the one is necessarily an enlargement of the other. The only doubt is, in what terms to express most precisely their relation to each other; whether to regard them as identical, one fact described by two phrases; or, if they are distinguished, *to which* should be assigned the priority of place. Since the character is undeclared till the will has taken its line, and since this line is selected as either more right or more pleasant, it would seem most proper to place the moral feeling first, and reckon it among the conditions of volition; so that the relation would be one, not of identity, but of succession; and in that succession, the moral feeling would be the condition, and the character the consequent. On this ground exception might be taken to Mr. Stephen's description of 'the conscientious feeling as *a function* of character;' for he seems by it to *invert this order* and make character the presupposed term. I do not think the phrase a very happy one: it belongs to a considerable cluster, suggested by physiological analogy, which, though better than the older mechanical ones for illustrating mental processes, are nevertheless quite as liable to be overstrained, and are so, as it seems to me, to an extravagant degree by the most recent school of English psychologists. Yet a true meaning may be embodied in Mr. Stephen's proposition. The action between the feeling of right and the will is not all one way: there is *interaction*, whereby repeated conformity with the higher solicitation, gradually constituting a habit, deepens the susceptibility to the better claim, and the persuasion of this order of motives becomes more and more availing with the will; and the word *character* is especially employed to mark the state of the internal springs when they have set into this fixity of form. A man who has a formed disposition to consult at every crisis the duty rather than the pleasure of the hour, attains, in matters of moral judgment, the fine and quick insight which belongs to every practised faculty; so that it is quite true that 'conscientious feeling' becomes his characteristic, in virtue of the very 'character' to which it supplied the originating germ. In this sense, the feeling may be intelligibly, though somewhat loosely, called 'a function' of 'the character.' But there is nothing in the proposition, thus interpreted and justified, in the least at variance with the claim of the moral consciousness to be 'a specific faculty,' i.e. an insight into an order of relations else inaccessible to us.

One further difficulty Mr. Stephen finds embarrassing to the theory of conscience, viz. the difficulty of deciding whether it is 'a simple emotion,' or 'an intellectual perception.' If the former, 'it is more or less arbitrary;' if the latter, 'it is difficult to see how it can affect conduct[1].'

[1] Science of Ethics, chap. viii § 9, p. 320.

No doubt, he suggests, you may 'evade the difficulty,' by setting it up as 'an independent faculty, invested with both intellectual and emotional attributes,' but this he regards as 'an unjustifiable assumption.' It is curious to pass from Mr Stephen's frequent and for the most part just polemic against 'separate and independent faculties,' to this statement of difficulty, which has no existence and no meaning, unless he regards emotion and understanding as without common function and therefore an example of separate faculties. Of course it is easy enough, by a natural resort to the abstraction indispensable for human intercourse and fixed in human language, to conceive of emotion without adverting to any attendant thought, and *vice versâ*. And in the states of mind wherein both meet, the varieties of proportion in their admixture are almost infinite between their respective zeros, represented, let us say, by the absorbed mathematician and the storming termagant. But, for all that, I must confess my total unacquaintance, in the world of human fact, with either feeling without idea, or idea without feeling. In animal natures of more rudimentary type, there are no doubt sensitive changes which may be called infra-cognitive; and it is therefore legitimate to say that sensation does not *per se* necessarily involve perception. But the moment it is introduced into a self-conscious nature, like ours, it becomes inseparably linked with thought: it is known as a phenomenon of self: it is known as an effect of what is other than self: it gives us an object, and reveals us as subject, so that it is impossible to conceive of a sentient or emotional state that tells us nothing, and lives and dies as feeling, pure and simple. The union of feeling with idea is therefore no unheard of peculiarity in our moral self-consciousness, justifying Mr. Stephen's demand, 'Make your choice between them; you cannot have them both.' The discrimination of beauty is no less a judgment and a feeling too, than the discrimination of right: nay, so, for that matter, is the discrimination of pleasure as well: why then is the moralist alone to be hoist in this cleft stick, till he declares which prong he prefers? In working out his argument, Mr Stephen is himself brought to a virtual admission of its arbitrariness. Before reaching the end of the paragraph he acknowledges that the true doctrine of musical interval and harmony is gathered from comparing and combining into system the perceptions of relative beauty in tones which are involved in the sense of hearing, and *if* there were a similar order of differences felt in regard to the objects of moral estimate, the consciousness of them would direct us to a true ethical doctrine, as surely as the ear conducts us to the science of sound. It turns out therefore, after all, not so impossible for 'simple feeling' and 'intellectual perception' to co-operate for a rational and practical result; and under a certain hypothetical state of things, that result would even be 'a science of Ethics.' This is all that I could desire; we seem at last on the very verge of coincidence. But, alas! Mr. Stephen does not find the hypothetical conditions fulfilled. 'the conscience,' he says, 'is not in this way marked off from all other modes of feeling or reasoning,' and 'the law is given much more distinctly than the feeling by which it is enforced[1].'

To narrow still further the issue thus conveniently reached, we must be allowed to strike out the irrelevant words 'or reasoning,' modes of reasoning are everywhere the same, and need not and cannot be 'marked off:' 'the conscience,' and the sense of hearing, ask for no exemption from logical laws in the treatment of their materials. It is only the 'mode of *feeling*' which asserts itself as *sui generis;* and this assertion is the hinge of the whole controversy. Unfortunately it is an *ultimate* assertion, which can be tested only by self-consciousness. To one who does not find in his feeling of *right* anything unique, incomparable, unanalysable, I can offer no evidence that it is so. If, in order to identify it with some other type of feeling, he presents a psychological theory of its derivation,

[1] Science of Ethics, chap. viii. § 9, p. 321.

I can discuss with him the adequacy of such theory, and state why it does not convince me. But critiques of this kind are only in defence of the approaches to the central stronghold; and when all have been exhausted, I cannot but fall back, for the real strength of the case, on the consciousness of relative right as no less self-evident than the difference between concurrent and discordant notes. From Mr. Stephen's concluding remark that 'the law is given much more distinctly than the feeling by which it is enforced,' I need not repeat my dissent; further than to say, that relative '*distinctness*' has nothing to do with the question of *priority of causation*. In one sense, no doubt, and to most people, everything realised in the objective world is '*more distinct*' than anything in the mind's inward history. the word '*distinct*' being applied to what sits apart in the space of the imagination. As external conduct can be pictured to the mind's eye and internal feeling cannot, a rule for the former must in this sense be 'more distinct' than a rule for the latter. But to infer from this that the conduct gives the rule to the feeling, and not the feeling to the conduct, would be a paralogism as much in logic as in morals.

§ 9. *Darwin's Explanation of Remorse.*

Before I close this review of modern evolutionism, I must notice Mr. Darwin's explanation of one of the characteristic features of conscience, the feeling of self-reproach or remorse. Given, an animal with several instincts, some transient and intermittent, others persistent, so related as to be liable to conflict, and with also intelligence enough to secure memory of the past and reflection upon its images; and the feeling of remorse, Mr. Darwin assures us, is certain to follow. For the most persistent of instincts, in a creature thus far developed, will be the social feeling, of attachment to the community in which he lives; but stronger than this will often be, by fits and starts, some paroxysm of passing want or passion, as of hunger or of rage; so that his will is swept away by the more vehement assault. Afterwards, when the satisfied desire falls to sleep again, and in its absence the durable affection returns and makes him conscious of the hurt it has sustained, he cannot but experience, in this changed mood, regret for his short-sighted conduct. his temporary satisfaction has entailed on him a permanent pain. I am far from denying that the process here described really takes place. the question is, whether the feeling in which it issues is identical with the moral sentiment of which it professes to give an account. The whole stress of the explanation is thrown upon a *time-measure:* a short want is gratified: a long one is disappointed: so, the disappointment survives, and that is all. But surely, these conditions may occur, without a trace of the phenomenon which is the object of our quest. The incidents of outward nature may realise them without any human will at all. A sudden rain at evening may rejoice the heart of an Indian commander whose battalion is faint and pining with drought: by next day it has swollen the watercourses, and penned him in between impassable rivers to almost certain destruction by overwhelming force. Momentary joy is exchanged for irretrievable disappointment, without, however, approaching any feature of the conscience at all. Do you say, 'Of course it is understood that, in order to give rise to the feeling in question, the agent must himself be the cause of the evil deplored?' Very well: then that feeling must be something more than '*regret*,' and be directed upon something more special than the difference between a brief enjoyment and a long suffering; and, instead of using indifferently the words 'remorse' and 'regret,' we must investigate their specific difference. Let, then, the action proceed, not from the external elements, but from myself; and suppose that I regard myself as strictly a part of the organism of nature, a wheel of given function in its mechanism, with movement determined by its contiguous part, and transmitting the permeating energy to the ulterior, only with consciousness of the successive pulses of change as they occupy and use me. If this conscious intelligence of what goes on within me be *all* that differences me from the outward world, will it supply what is wanting to turn regret into remorse? Surely not: if there is no help for me but to go with the short instinct because it is stronger, and then be disappointed with the long one because it has been weaker, my regret will be just as much a *necessitated pain*, as if not one of the causal links had passed my inward consciousness. I am simply a *victim* of the major *vis*, to which my *conscience* has nothing to say And *this*, be it remembered, is the very state of things on which every evolutionist insists as actually existing; for his doctrine involves unqualified determinism, so that, even if the '*regret*' for which Mr. Darwin accounts should have any tinge of *self-reproach*, it could only be by mistake, through failure to understand the inexorable order of events; i.e. the moral feeling would be explained as a fact by proving it an illusion. There is indeed yet an intermediate state of mind between simple regret at disappointment and remorse for wrong. If in momentary eagerness to save time I spring too soon off a railway carriage and get my foot cut off beneath a wheel, I shall blame my own folly as long as I live, yet with a feeling which by no means amounts to remorse. Wherein then lies the difference? In both instances, I regard myself as the determining cause of the action which I regret, in presence of an alternative which was equally open to my choice: and but for this belief, I should in neither case pass beyond the sort of disappointment I might feel from a disabling attack of gout. But if, following no worse impulse, I have only made a worse application of a right one, what I have to deplore is a blunder and not a sin: it is my reckoning and not my motive, that has been amiss; and I charge myself with imprudence rather than with guilt. So long as choice goes astray through error of the understanding, we are still in the unmoral field; and for remorse there is no room till we surrender to a lower spring of action against the remonstrance of a higher,—as when, in the rush of passion, we hurt with bitter words an object of enduring love, or, from cowardice, suffer in silence a calumny against the innocent. Then at last the true *moral* feeling, of *compunction*, emerges, and we suffer, not the disappointment at loss, not the regret for error, but the remorse for wrong. All these alike may come under Mr. Darwin's formula of satisfying a short want at the expense of a long one; but for that very reason, the formula touches nothing that characterises the moral nature, and misses the whole essence of the conscience which it undertakes to explain.

§ 10. *Meaning of 'Higher' and 'Lower' in Evolution.*

Throughout the representative writers of this school we encounter again the difficulty in which J. S. Mill left us, with his qualitative ranks of pleasures. They constantly speak of superior and inferior types of being, of higher and lower instincts and affections, of more or less complete development, &c. Yet, when we ask for the *positive* which is the base of these comparatives and superlatives, and look about for the quality which admits of so many gradations, no definition of it or even name for it can be found. What constitutes one organism or one instinct '*higher*' than another? Must we reply in terms of Mr. Spencer's test, and say, its greater complexity or differentiation? If that were all, the Ptolemaic cosmos would have the advantage over the Newtonian, the eye of the dragonfly over that of man, and the tortuous character of the intriguer over the transparent simplicity of the righteous. I cannot persuade myself that Mr. Spencer himself regards *complexity* as *synonymous* with *rank*, or as more than a concomitant sign, in physiological structure, of a nature ranging over many relations and living therefore upon a larger scale; but, except as an index to greater plenitude of thought, capacity for feeling, and variety of action, plurality of constituent parts confers no promotion of being: the polygon is not entitled to look down upon the circle Shall we try another meaning of this nameless scale, and say that the nature is 'highest' which is most self-conserving? This is not very consistent with the previous test; for the more complex the structure, the less stable is the equilibrium of the nature. But, apart from this, to exalt 'self-conservation' is to declare existence a good. were it otherwise, self-extinction would constitute the step of promotion; and the question therefore lies behind, what makes the difference between good existence and existence not good: mere continuity, irrespective of this, has no preferential quality; it is no praise of a thing that it *can be*, unless it *ought to be*, else it had better *not be*. Nor is the problem cleared up if, for the meaning of the 'higher' in nature, we resort, not to superior self-conservation in the individual, but to greater conduciveness towards *permanence of Kind*,—an end frequently consistent with rapid evanescence of its individuals. For why should we laud and magnify this permanence, unless existence is properly assumed to be a prize? It is evident, therefore, that behind this language of gradation there is hidden some unexpressed idea of *good* which supplies it with all its meaning; and that good it is towards the increase of which all evolution is supposed to tend. No consistent account of this good have I been able to find. Both Mr. Spencer and Mr. Stephen do indeed, in certain sections devoted to the subject, declare it to be *pleasure;* and on this account I have entitled this chapter '*Hedonism with Evolution,*' but this identification does not retain possession of them through their treatises; and other ends, not self-evidently accordant with this, are variously substituted: high organisation, preservation of species, survival of the fittest, health of 'the social tissue,' development of thought, altruistic self-absorption, are all indicated as the inevitable results of evolution, and assumed to be *good*, without being tested by the hedonistic definition, and, in the case of Mr. Stephen, with the frank admission that they are not necessarily compatible with it. The representative writers of this school have in truth,—greatly to their honour,—*theorised* in one language and *felt* in another, and have retained ideal conceptions of a scale of good, and admirations for types of character, for which their doctrine can find no corresponding place. Nor is this an accident of their individual presentations of the theory. So long as it sets itself to find the moral in the unmoral, to identify the *order of right* with the *order of strength*, to repudiate any study of what *ought to be* except in studying what has been, is, and will be, it totally shuts the door in the face of all conception and possibility of Duty, and by *naturalising Ethics* reverses the idealising process which rather *ethicises Nature*. It subjugates character to Science, instead of freeing it into Religion.

BRANCH II.

DIANOETIC ETHICS.

OF assignable extrinsic grounds for the preference involved in every moral decision, we have examined the first and most plausible: we approve the Right, because it is *pleasant* If, as I have tried to show, this theory is untenable, it is not that it fails to lay hold of a *vera causa*, for undoubtedly the prospect of pleasure sets in motion a large part of human activity; but simply that this principle is overworked when required to give account of all our inward preferences, and that its competency ends when they cease to be prudential.

Another ground of preference is tried by those who say 'We approve the Right, because it is *true*, if we did not, we should not be intelligent, but should form judgments discordant with the real relations of things; there is no wrong that is not folly' Here again we have a theory which avails itself of a true cause of human choice; for no one will put up with an illusion when once possessed of the reality. But here also the question is forced upon us, whether the intellectual preference is the same with the moral, so that the right and wrong are species of the true and false. As, in the former theory, nothing more would be needed, in order to make us subjects of Duty, than *Sensibility* behind our active capacity, so in this, the sole requisite would be *Reason;* and to see things as they are would be identical with choosing them as they ought to be. To some eminent examples of this doctrine we must now turn; but, as it makes much nearer approaches than the hedonistic to the intuitive basis, and perhaps even *means* to build upon essentially the same foundation, it will need a less extended exhibition, and a slighter and more sympathetic criticism.

Happily our own literature affords the most expressive representatives of this rational school, in Ralph Cudworth, Samuel Clarke, and Richard Price; and as, in their ethical writings, the first had in view the confutation of Hobbes, the second, that of Spinoza, Collins, and Leibniz as well, the third that of Locke and Priestley, they shape their course by the same aims which have determined the reasonings of the foregoing chapters, and only trace a different path towards their attainment.

CHAPTER I.

CUDWORTH.

§ 1. *Life, Personality, and Writings.*

There is a singular contrast between the calm contemplative philosophy of Cudworth and the fierce contentions of his time. Born at a country Rectory (Aller, Somerset) in 1617, the year of Raleigh's execution, and dying in 1688, the year of James the Second's abdication, he spans, by his term of life, the whole period of the Stuart troubles and the Commonwealth : yet his writings might have been produced in a lonely and silent monastery, instead of amid the rage of factions and the reverberation of the Naseby guns. The hurry and passion of their age are wholly absent from them: with infinite leisure they conduct the reader to the Schools of Athens and Alexandria, and beguile him there with spacious arguments, interrupted often by a series of concentric episodes, till he forgets where he is, and is lost, except to the world of theosophic abstractions. This was not apparently from want of inherited and personal connection with the spiritual conflicts of his generation. His early admission as pensioner (1630) to *Emmanuel College*, Cambridge, indicates his Puritan descent and education, and if his distinguished career, first as a Student up to his M.A. degree in 1639, and then as a Tutor, attests only his personal merits, his appointment in 1644 to the Mastership of Clare Hall, and in the next year to the Professorship of Hebrew, implies that he had borne himself discreetly towards the State authorities, and was trusted by men, like Whitelock, who were hard to please. It is plain indeed, from some of his extant letters, that he was consulted by that statesman (1656–7) about a proposed revision of the English version (King

James's) of the Scriptures, and by Cromwell's Secretary, Thurloe, about suitable and trustworthy men qualified for civil appointments under the Government. This is the more remarkable, because of the two great offences, Popery and Arminianism, against which the fury of the hour and the temper of the ruling powers were most excited, he certainly could not be cleared of the latter; and his whole attitude and expression of thought betokened a catholicity of judgment in affairs of State and of Church very unlike the severe Puritanism of the hour. On March 31, 1647,—just half way between the executions of Laud and of Charles the First,—he preached before the House of Commons (Cromwell being present) at the very crisis when the struggle had become one, not between the nation and the king, but between the Presbyterians and Independents, the former dominant in Parliament, and the latter in the army. The tension of party-spirit was at its height, and every question, theological and national, which divided the factions, assumed an exaggerated bulk in the imaginations of men and intensified their antipathies. This is the moment which he seizes (as he says, in dedicating to his hearers the first edition of the sermon), 'not to contend for this or that opinion, but only to persuade men to the life of Christ, as the pith and kernel of all religion; without which, I may boldly say, all the several forms of religion, though we please ourselves never so much in them, are but so many several dreams; and those many opinions about religion, that are everywhere so largely contended for on all sides, where this doth not lie at the bottom, are but so many shadows fighting with one another.' 'I fear many of us, that pull down idols in churches, may set them up in our hearts; and whilst we quarrel with painted glass, make no scruple at all of entertaining many foul lusts in our souls, and committing continual idolatry with them.' And in the sermon itself he insists, that 'Christ came not into the world to fill our heads with mere speculations, to kindle a fire of wrangling and contentious dispute among us, and to warm our spirits against one another with nothing but angry and peevish debates, whilst in the meantime our hearts remain all ice within towards God, and have not the least spark of true heavenly fire to melt and thaw them.' 'Christ was *vitæ magister*, not *scholæ*, and he is the best Christian, whose heart beats with the purest pulse towards Him; not he whose head spinneth out the finest cobwebs.' 'He that endeavours really to mortify his lusts, and to comply with that truth in his life which his conscience is convinced of, is more a Christian, though he never heard of Christ, than he that believes all the vulgar articles of the Christian faith, and plainly denieth Christ in his life [1].' The freedom of this protest against the prevailing tendency of his audience and of his time may perhaps relieve him from the suspicion of temporising compliance, when we find him, in 1658, wishing to dedicate a book against Judaism to the new Protector, Richard Cromwell; yet, in 1660, celebrating the Restoration in a poetical effusion, which he called the Σῶστρα, or thank-offering for the reinstatement of learning in the University of Cambridge, through the king's return. So long as literature, for want of an adequate public, was dependent on patronage, it was deemed as legitimate to seek a noble name for the head of a dedication, as it now is to secure a great publisher's for the foot of a title-page. And if the joyful expectancy with which Charles was received back to his inheritance was excusable in any part of the nation, it was permissible in the Universities to lift up their heads at the downfall of Puritan ascendency, and set free their checked enthusiasm for the whole contents of human knowledge, thought, and art.

Cudworth's last appointment at Cambridge, to the Mastership of Christ's College, had preceded the Restoration by six years, and appears to have finally fixed his position there; for though he was presented in 1662, by Sheldon, then Bishop of London, afterwards Archbishop of Canterbury, to

[1] Intellectual System of the Universe, &c. 2 Vols Andover, U.S.A., 1838. Vol. II. pp 545, 546, and 554.

the vicarage of Ashwell in Hertfordshire, it does not appear that he was ever in durable residence there. It may be reasonably supposed that clerical duties, already little congenial to his studious habits, were not rendered easier to him by the Act of Uniformity and the reactionary ecclesiastical spirit of the new Caroline era; and that he gladly pleaded the claims of his College upon him as a reason for supplying the service of his parish in the easiest way. His proper calling he evidently felt to be the life of thought rather than of action; and, of the few things reported of him, almost every one is some literary project which has left its vestige either in unprinted manuscripts or in vast unfinished published works. Thus, among his papers preserved in the British Museum, there still exists a dissertation (of about 1658) on the prophecy of the seventy weeks in the Book of Daniel, in which he enters the lists against Joseph Scaliger, with such success that Henry More declares its result to be 'of as much price and worth in theology, as either the circulation of the blood in physic, or the motion of the earth in natural philosophy[1]' And in 1664-5 he had laid out the plan of a treatise on 'Good and Evil, or Natural Ethics,' and freely talked it over with his friends; but being slow in execution, he was annoyed to find that, whilst he still mused upon the scheme, his words had set in motion the nimbler thought of Henry More and matured under his hand a disquisition on the same subject. A word of complaint from Cudworth (which had been better withheld) sufficed with the generous More to suppress his work and leave the field open to his friend. He reserved to himself only the freedom of ulterior publication, should the original design remain unfulfilled. To this we owe More's *Enchiridion Ethicum*, brought out (1667) in Latin, that it might not clash with the projected English work. If the purpose so jealously guarded was ever brought to accomplishment, it did not reach the press, but sleeps to this hour in a manuscript discourse on 'Moral Good and Evil.'

[1] Grand Mystery of Godliness, Pref. p. xvi.

The main work of Cudworth's life, 'The True Intellectual System of the Universe,' on which chiefly his reputation rests, did not appear till 1678, though it had been ready and sanctioned for publication seven years before. Birch, in his meagre biography of the author, hints that the delay was due to some influence from the irreligious and corrupt *entourage* of the royal Court, naturally disaffected towards a book 'wherein all the reason and philosophy of Atheism is confuted.' But it is hardly consistent with the levity of that society, alike empty-hearted and empty-headed, to trouble itself about a production well known to be of the most ponderous learning and stiffest metaphysics, and safe enough to be flung in disgust from the hand of every trifler in their giddy crowd. More probably, the postponement must be referred to the author's own dilatory ways; or possibly, to some hope of giving it more completeness in itself; for it is, after all, but the propylæum, or at least first inner court, of a vaster structure that was to have its penetralia behind. In spite, however, of its missing sequel, and the frequent redundancy of its own parts and *excursus*, it leaves a perfectly distinct and powerful impression of the author's own philosophy, and of its relations, whether of affinity or of contrast, with the chief systems of thought in both ancient and modern times.

Both in its substance and in its form, the book was sure to disturb a whole nest of enemies with or without sting. It conceded too much to the Pagan philosophers, recognising among them the essence of Christian wisdom, to suit the assumptions of either the rising High Churchmen or the retiring Puritans. It placed too little value on the instituted observances of religion for the former, and on its niceties of dogma for the latter. It offended the current cynicism of Society and of the Schools, by finding a Divine element in human nature, which only the obtuse and profane could miss It contradicted the exclusive pretensions of both Church and Scripture, as media of sacred light, by planting in the natural Reason an inward apprehension of

Duty and of God. It laid itself open, here and there, to the rebuke of scholars for reading the author's favourite ideas, without adequate warrant, into the Greek text of Plato, Aristotle, and Plotinus. It disappointed the demand, recently heightened by the vigour and precision of Hobbes, for logical neatness and compactness of structure, by diffuse repetitions and enormous digressions, and the heavy flow of overloaded sentences. From these causes the first reception of his book was mortifying, though perhaps not surprising to him. His rare justice and candour towards the opinions which he controverted exposed him to the insinuation of secret sympathy with them and hypocritical replies to them: he has 'raised,' says Dryden, 'such strong objections against the being of a God and Providence, that many think he has not answered them [1].' The theologians accused him, now of being a Tritheist, and then of being an Arian, a Socinian, a Deist [2]. He was not, however, without defenders against these wrongs. Shaftesbury sets them down to the blindness of the partisan spirit: 'You know the common fate,' he says, 'of those who appear *fair* authors. What was that pious and learned man's case who wrote the "Intellectual System of the Universe?" I confess it was pleasant enough to consider, that though the whole world were no less satisfied with his capacity and learning than with his sincerity in the cause of Deity, yet he was accused of giving the upper hand to the Atheists, for having only stated their reasons, and those of their adversaries, fairly together [3].' And Warburton, in his caustic way, remarked that, though few could appreciate his profound reasonings, yet 'the very slowest were able to unravel his secret purpose,'—'to tell the world that, under pretence of defending Revelation, he wrote in the very manner that an artful infidel might be supposed to use in writing against it; that he had given us all the filthy stuff that he could scrape

[1] Translation of the Æneid, Dedication.
[2] Quoted from Turner's Messiah, in Birch's Life of Cudworth (I. 18).
[3] Characteristics, II p. 262.

together out of the sink of Atheism, as a natural introduction to a demonstration of the truth of Revelation; that with incredible industry and reading he had rummaged all antiquity for atheistical arguments, which he neither knew nor intended to answer; that he was an Atheist in his heart and an Arian in his book!' 'Thus ran the popular clamour against this excellent person. Would the reader know the consequence? Why, the zealots inflamed the bigots:—" 'Twas the time's plague, when madmen led the blind,"—the silly calumny was believed: the much injured author grew disgusted: his ardour slackened: and the rest, and far greatest, part of the defence never appeared[1].'

Though the contemporary movement of English thought, under the powerful impulsion first of Hobbes and then of Locke, was in a direction divergent from Cudworth's, the close logic, the masterly penetration, and large erudition of his work gradually made themselves felt, and encouraged Thomas Wise to publish in 1706 an abridgment which, though still extending to two quarto volumes, rendered the book accessible to a wider circle of readers. On the Continent it found a still earlier appreciation: in 1703, Leclerc began a series of analyses of its arguments and extracts from it in French translations, which were continued, for three or four years, through nine volumes of his *Bibliothèque Choisie*. Some of these, expounding the theory of a 'plastic nature,'—a theory not without resemblance to a principle of Evolution,—brought him into controversy with Bayle; the point at issue being, whether such theory was not, as Bayle contended, essentially atheistic, or, as Leclerc maintained and Cudworth intended, perfectly compatible with Theism and favourable to its highest form. Bayle's part of this controversy is to be found in his *Pensées diverses sur la Comète qui parut en* 1680; *Continuation*, Tom I. § 21, and the *Histoire des Ouvrages des Savans*, Art. 12, p. 380; and Leclerc's, in the sixth, seventh, and ninth

[1] Divine Legation of Moses, Vol. II. Part I. Pref. pp. 10–12.

volumes of the *Bibliothèque Choisie*. In 1773, Mosheim published in Leyden a Latin translation of the 'Intellectual System,' enriched with valuable notes and complete references to the Greek and Latin authors so copiously cited by Cudworth, as well as with many extracts from the unpublished manuscripts already mentioned. His task is so well performed, that this foreign edition has an advantage over the original English.

The 'Intellectual System,' however, does not yet bring us expressly to the author's Ethical doctrine. For that, we naturally turn to the 'Treatise on Immutable Morality,' which follows in all the recent editions of Cudworth. Yet the student cannot afford to take the books apart from each other; still less to disregard the greater, in reliance on the sufficiency of the less. The two are by no means so distinct in subject as their difference of title would seem to imply; and theory specifically moral plays no more prominent part in the second than in the first. They present the same philosophy twice over; and as the 'Treatise' is a fragment, left in manuscript by the author without receiving the last touch from his hand, and published not till 1731, it cannot have the authority of the work selected and issued by himself. It is, however, undoubtedly the later production, and so far serves as a valuable commentary on the parallel doctrines and reasonings of its predecessor. It was edited and prefaced by Dr. Edward Chandler, Bishop of Durham, who regards it as removing the idea of Fate from the moral world, as the previous work had removed it from the material, and replacing it by that of a holy God. Had the treatise been wrought out to the end, it might perhaps have justified this conception of its design; but, as it stands, it cannot be said to push its argument much further into the moral sphere than the larger work whose main argument it reproduces.

The year in which his 'Intellectual System' saw the light gave Cudworth his last ecclesiastical promotion. He was made Prebendary of Gloucester. This involved no change in his position at Cambridge, where he remained, till his death in 1688, at the head of the College whose chapel received his remains and bears the memorial of his interment. Of his widow we obtain a glimpse three years later, in a letter of Sir Isaac Newton's to Locke, in which he sends his 'service' to 'Mrs. Cudworth.' The letter was addressed to the hospitable mansion of Sir Francis Masham, of Oates in Essex, where both Locke and Mrs Cudworth were resident guests, and the former at least had found his last earthly home; for here, as his gravestone in the village church attests, he died, October 28th, 1704. Lady Masham (Sir Francis's second wife) was Cudworth's daughter, and deeply imbued with his philosophical and religious spirit, modified indeed by the newer principles of Locke, of whom she was the faithfullest of admirers, but without declension from either the single eye to truth or the pure inward piety which belonged in common to her father and her friend. A little book which she had anonymously published in 1696, —'A Discourse Concerning the Love of God,'—marks her intermediate position between the spiritual fervour of the Cambridge Platonising school, and the less exigent common sense of Locke's interpretation of duty and religion. In this pamphlet she sets the example, soon to be so largely followed, of deprecating the demand for enthusiasm in devotion, and of discouraging any claim, in the name of God, beyond the one true end, of 'a good life.' Her protest in this sense is delivered against the 'practical discourses' of John Norris of Bemerton; who, in the spirit of the Christian mystics, had insisted on the absolute cancelling of every creaturely desire in the all-absorbing love of God. The unreasonableness and dangers of so high a claim are clearly shown, on the supposition that it means, without explanation, all that at first it seems to say; while, on the other hand, the rule and measure of fitting piety which is set up instead, so merges religion in morality as to drain away the aliment from its vital root, and incur the risk of its dwindling till it dies. At this point of contact between the retiring and the approaching schools, it is interesting to observe in this lady, and indeed in her great philosophical guest, the vain attempt to maintain the balance between the ideal and the material interpretations of the world, the intuitive and the empirical. It is a point of unstable equilibrium, at which thus far human thought refuses to poise itself for long. The Christian philosophy of the Cambridge men had made the inspiration of the former felt by many noble minds, with an apparent promise that the Puritan piety might be saved without its narrowness and invested with the persuasion of beauty and of love. But Hobbes had spoken to the opposite side of human nature, and wakened it up in insurrection against a long repression and neglect; disguising his exaggerated claims for it, and his contempt for whatever resisted its autocracy, under forms of decorum towards religion and copious use of Scripture, he had won response to his principles, not only from a few who saw what they meant, but from far more who were blind to it. He had set in motion a tendency which has no real power to arrest itself without overshooting the boundaries of moral conviction and the conditions of spiritual life; and hence the uncompromising tone of resistance with which he was met by the more far-seeing of his opponents. Sensationalism, however, in psychology, and external utility in rules of conduct, have great attraction for a certain middle class of minds, sensible, moderate, and well ordered, rather than profound; and if they happen to feel their knowledge of duty and of Divine things independently secured to them by supernatural tenure, they are readily tempted into inconsiderate concessions to physiological experience, and the doctrine of the *tabula rasa*. So it was with Locke. Safe with an outwardly given Revelation of morals and religion, he could complete the consistency of his mode of thought by building up his nature also out of empirical data; and, submitting the whole of human life to objective regulation, escape the illusions of abstractions and the dangers of enthusiasm, incurred by those who trust themselves to inward light. And so long as that postulate, of a documentary rule of duty and faith divinely dictated, remained unchallenged, all might be well; for under this lay hid, covered with an unconscious shelter, the secret sense of freedom and responsibility, and an open way for the Divine spirit to enter life, and the human spirit to pass into heaven. But, notwithstanding the happy combination of personal characteristics arising from this state of mind,—the practical good sense softened by reverence, the firm conscience tempered with compassion and tolerance,—it is a precarious truce between incongruous elements which, ere long, will strive together for the mastery. By outward witness, be it of this world or any other, by witness addressed to perception and understanding, no duty can be established and no God be found; and where sensible experience and testimony have become the sheet-anchor of trust, the spiritual life is struck with blight, conscience is disarmed, and the victory is bespoken for Necessity. The uneasy coexistence of the two tendencies is so manifest in Locke's wavering treatment of the problem of free-will, that we wonder how he could leave that 'stone which the builders had rejected' without better shaping it to its place as the 'head stone of the corner.' For Hobbes, who well knew what he was about and meant it all, there was a future in reserve; but not so for Locke, except in so far as he moved in the same direction. Through a series of psychological links, the empirical impulse has been transmitted to its inevitable results in hedonism, determinism, and agnosticism, throwing off, as heterogeneous, the ethics and religion which were so dear to him; and, to reinstate these, recourse is now had once more to the intuitive light and self-revealing order which alone can possess authority within and impart it without, and in which Cudworth had found the meaning of Duty and the communion of God.

§ 2. *Outline of his Philosophy.*

To give anything like an adequate account of Cudworth's two principal works would be to review all the ancient philosophies and estimate his criticisms upon them. Within this enormous range my present purpose requires me only to select a single topic, viz. the origin and nature of our Moral Ideas. His system is essentially a *theory of Knowledge;* it revives and rediscusses the question at issue between Protagoras and Plato; and answers it, not indeed in the exact sense of the doctrine of εἴδη, yet in the same interest, and with as near an approach to it as a distinct Christian Theism would permit. It will be convenient to present his scheme of thought first as a Psychology, i. e. an account of the processes of the human mind: then, as an Ontology, i. e. an account of the extra-human realities which correspond with these processes.

A. PSYCHOLOGY.—In effect, though without express definition, Cudworth recognises only two functions or faculties in our mental nature : *Sense,* or *Perception;* and *Intellection,* or Understanding : adopting the old Greek antithesis of αἴσθησις and νοῦς. In the process of *sensation,* we are not agents, but patients, being simply the seat of certain changes communicated to us and continued within us, contributing to them nothing but the susceptibility of being affected in this way or that. These changes, started by and from some external body, complete themselves in two stages after impinging upon us, first instituting certain corporeal movements, passing from the nerves of the recipient organ to the brain; followed then by a specific feeling which, as a modification of consciousness, is not corporeal but mental. These two stages are invariably consecutive, or, as Cudworth expresses it, '*fatally* (necessarily) connected,' the latter being a '*compassion*' (fellowship in feeling) of the soul 'with the body.' He is careful, in describing this process, to keep his language strictly within the limits of a history in which we are *passive;* it therefore stops short of what we should now call *Perception,* though in his time that word was still in use in this country, and yet more abroad, to denote any state of sensation, down to the very lowest.

To emphasise the bounds assigned by him to the experiences of sense, taken by themselves, he criticises and rejects the Platonists' account of them as παθῶν γνώσεις,—*cognitions* of feeling and of what happens in it; for, whether you look at the bodily or at the mental stage of the story, they may both be there without our being aware of either; of the bodily part of the transaction between the nerve and the brain the soul has no suspicion; and that it may be under the influence of the feeling without thinking of it is obvious from innumerable cases of instinctive or habitual actions, such as the winking of the eyes, and the spontaneous progression and equilibration in walking, where, with attention pre-engaged, we are guided right by unrecognised sensitive changes; and are at the same moment wide awake with thought and purpose in one direction, and somnambulists in another. The function of such feeling Plotinus would describe as πρὸς χρείαν, οὐ πρὸς γνῶσιν; by it the 'soul is secretly instructed to notice some other things that concern the body,' to which '*other things*,' away from the feeling itself, its free and sincere action is turned. It is obvious then that Cudworth would by no means have assented to the assumption of the modern empirical psychology, that 'to have a feeling and to know that you have it are two expressions of the same thing.'

But next, what are those 'other things' which, by occasion of the feeling, we are 'instructed to notice?' for at all events, as soon as they are noticed, we are landed in some sort of knowledge. Certainly we are: the soul, thus wakened in its cognitive activity, apprehends the *particular body* which has administered the feeling; i. e. we pass from sensation to perception. But about that body we thus learn one thing only; not its essence or nature itself, but simply its relation to others in a single particular, viz. its effect upon this or that sense of ours; and this superficial apprehension of phenomena is not knowledge, for it terminates in no constant truth, which would remain though we were not, but merely in a mental picture or appearance, not differing from the phantasms of our dreams, except that these occur when they can have us all to themselves, while our waking images are variously checked by a crowd of rivals and by correcting thought. The spontaneous recurrence of these φαντάσματα, in the absence of the object which they represent, constitutes *Imagination;* which is therefore the surviving mental vestige of past perception, and falls under the same limitation as the sphere of apprehension by sense.

If this type of endowment were all our store, many of the other animal tribes would have the advantage over us; for their original outfit of sensible perception frequently surpasses ours in delicacy and range. We may pretty confidently add that Cudworth would not have altered this judgment, if he had been familiar with the mode in which, out of data of sensation and its vestiges, with their pleasures and pains, the Hartleyan law of '*association*' was applied to build up all else that the mind has and does and is. For, the induction which yields this law could find its materials just as readily in the facts of a dog's life as of a man's, and has its illustration in all animal training; yet this similarity of conditions somehow works out into very dissimilar results. Some missing cause must be found, if you are to explain, e. g. the different influence of fine music and fair scenery upon an artist and upon his horse. They can both see; they can both hear; both can connect their feelings into groups and trains, so as to recognise them again and reach them by suggestion, one from another; yet the interval between their experiences is little short of infinite.

In order to help our conception of what the intellect brings into our experience of outward things, Cudworth supposes some object, e. g. *a watch*, to be presented before (1) a crystal ball, (2) a living eye, (3) a mind; and asks us to take account of the relative results. The two first will similarly reflect an image of the watch's size, shape, colour, and other material aspects; but the eye will be affected with sensations from these which the ball has not, attended, it elementary exercise begin, in the absence of such *à priori* notions for the right disposal of our empirical material. Hence it is not without reason that they are called 'anticipations' (προλήψεις), prepared forms or compartments in the constitution of the understanding itself, furnished, however, with active and appropriative tentacula for distributing to its true place each particular in the ever varying scene of life. Cudworth remarks that, inasmuch as we carry with us into our commerce with things some such performed category to which each, as it emerges to perception, is taken home, a new object appears to us, not wholly as a stranger, but almost as the face of a friend recognised by us in the midst of a foreign crowd. It is impossible to have the essence of a nature in the mind, without a virtual though shadowy prediction of the individual.

From this interpretation of cognition, two important consequences follow. It is *an activity:* for it is mind itself that takes the initiative, and fits its prior notions to the facts it encounters. And as these notions are thus beforehand with the facts, the knowing process does *not begin, but end with the individual.* In both these respects, the function of the Understanding reverses that of the Senses; and both of them indicate the reliance of Cudworth on deductive reason rather than inductive as an instrument for the enlargement of knowledge. This order of dependence, which Cudworth had learned in the Greek Schools, Spinoza also maintained, but as an inheritance from the Mediæval Philosophy.

Cudworth's insistence upon the understanding, as 'an active cognoscitive power' and original source of *à priori* regulative ideas, has induced Dugald Stewart[1] (following the example of Meiners) to hint that Kant may well have been indebted to him for some of his 'leading ideas,' especially for his distinction between the matter of sensible experience, and the factors of thought furnished by the mind itself. The comparison only shows how very superficially even a practised philosophical critic may read and judge the most

[1] Dissertation, pp. 398, 399. Works, Hamilton's edition, Vol. L

may be, with a perception of their source as a single external thing; while the mind will excite within itself, in addition, ideas of cause and effect, of means and end, of priority, symmetry, equality, aptitude, &c. and will turn these ideas to account in comparisons quite unknown to the mere living eye. Suppose each of the subjects of this experience able to tell its own story and hear the others'; when the mind gave in its report, the eye would stare at it as nonsense, and reject its characteristic contents, and would itself receive the same treatment of its own sensations on the part of the ball, priding itself in its modest belief in simple physics. And yet we are certain that the intellectual verdict upon the object is what constitutes *knowledge of it*, and merits the name of wisdom, and has the least liability of all to the charge of being a mere imagination or representative figment; for the watch *really is made up* of its intellectual relations, and is what it is in virtue of them, so that the eye of sense, missing the logical *compages* and restricted to the material, truly does not see it; its constitutive unity being ideal. The truth then lies in what the mind brings in, over and above the contributions of the other witnesses. What is this *something more?*

Take any simple judgment for analysis; and mind or intellection has no other form than judgment. When I say, for example, 'this figure is a perfect square,' I plainly have two things in my thought, viz. an image, or φάντασμα, of one particular figure; and an idea or νόημα, of what constitutes a perfect square, i. e. of the essence of square; and my act of judgment consists in applying this model thought as a test to the individual case of the figure present to perception. In order to perform the act, I must bring with me this standard idea; it is a prior condition of the judgment; without it, I am left alone with the imagination of my figure, and *know* nothing of it. This instance is a faithful sample of all intellection: it consists in the application of a given pattern thought, a ready-made category, to the phenomena and objects presented in experience: nor can its most exact and severe productions in the history of human thought. The supposed resemblance disappears on the mere mention of two marked differences. (1) With Cudworth, the endowment of Sense supplies no *à priori* elements; with Kant, it gives us Space and Time, as its own forms. (2) With Cudworth, the Understanding's 'intelligible ideas' (*νοήματα*) are themselves its *objects of knowledge*, and constitute the essences of things, and therefore introduce us to the nature of things in themselves: with Kant, they are purely subjective, inherent only in the make of our faculty, so that we cannot help thinking under these categories, but have no right to treat them as valid for reality irrespective of us. Thus, the ideality of human cognition, which the two writers hold in common, was used by Cudworth to prove, by Kant to disprove, the absolute validity of our knowledge · with the one, it was the means of reaching, with the other, the excuse for surrendering, eternal and immutable truth · with the former, it carries us to the Infinite Nature, with the latter, it shuts us up in our own. For, with Kant, as I need hardly remind my readers, all that is *objective* in cognition is supplied by the material of Sense, taken into the subjective forms of space and time; and therefore destitute, in both its factors, of anything that is not relative to the Ego.

From his general doctrine of *νοήματα* Cudworth never descends into the assemblage of 'Intelligible Ideas' with any discriminative purpose, so as to dispose them in classes, or assign to them differences of value; nor does he attempt any exhaustive enumeration of them, as bases of distinct orders of knowledge. In his frequent lists of examples, they seem all put upon the same footing, with no other test of their belonging to the noetic family than their being *unpresentable to the imagination*. Thus, he tells us, that among them 'justice, duty, thought, effects, genus and species, nullity, contingency, possibility,' &c. are understood by us, yet are inaccessible to any sense; and that *propositions*, e.g. that 'nothing can at the same time be and not be,' are intuitively accepted, though no term in them has any corresponding representation. He gives us, therefore, nothing like Kant's analytical reduction of the categories of the understanding to twelve originals; but leaves us to regard the intellectual notions as an indefinite multitude of thinking activities fetched from within the understanding itself, and constituting, as he sometimes says, 'the reasons of things,' by which, in conformity with his *deductive* logic, he means the containing genus of the things. In this way the understanding becomes for him a living magazine of all the cognisable Kinds that may face it in the Universe; so that, in knowing its own stores it knows the essential riches of the world. By this light he leads into clearness the wonderful maxim of Aristotle, '*The soul is in a manner all things*[1];' i.e. has in itself, *à priori*, the notional categories that fit all things, the sum total of them giving the intellectual scheme of the world: just as God, the soul's archetype, comprehends Himself, with all the possibilities of His goodness and power.

Cudworth, in holding to this doctrine, was well aware that his 'Intelligible Ideas' were explained away by Nominalist psychologists as illusions of abstraction, formed from φαντάσματα, by dropping their sensible contents, and letting them strip themselves bare to their quantitative, intensive, or logical relations. Nor did he deny the speculative possibility of their being evolved by some such process of mental chemistry. But, as they emerged at last just the same in their nature as if they had been there at first, and constituted the intellectual factor of all knowledge, no less and no lower activity of mind was needed for their gradual formation, than for their equable energy all through; Reason has the same essence, whether it springs ready formed, like Minerva from the head of Jove, or, like a human being, gains its clear and full power from a low initial velocity by accelerated movement towards its

[1] De Anima, III viii. 1; Eternal and Immutable Morality, Bk. IV. i. 5.

perfection. If, to attain the end, you prefer to set up an *intellectus agens*, an active understanding, like a smith or carpenter, with his shop or forge in the brain, furnished with all necessary tools for such a work,' it is plain, at all events, that this *faber* knows what he is about [1]; and therefore has in himself the intelligible idea which includes and induces the end.

B. ONTOLOGY.—The mode of Cudworth's transition from his Psychology to Ontology may be readily conjectured from the foregoing exposition. Theoretic knowledge is stable and immutable, because it has for its objects the essence of things,—an ἀκίνητος οὐσία [2]. Perception is variable, because it has for its object their *phenomena*, which are another name for change. The *à priori* types of thinking,— the νοήματα,—are the *constants* of our knowledge, as opposed to the shifting φαντάσματα; and the constancy of the former in each mind, with their sameness in all, arises from their being, not affections of differing and mutable individuals, but a reflection in the Universal Reason of the νοητά, or intelligible essences of real being [3]. Psychologically, they are consciously in our intellect; objectively, they constitute the natures of things; yet, in neither relation do they share the lot of that which has them: a geometric truth has no dependence on our consciousness, but is eternal, though none should know it; and the equation of the parabola holds by unchangeable necessity, though no such curve were ever traced. Here then are ideal realities which bring back upon us the problem of Plato's εἴδη; neither the concrete object to which they give the name, nor the transient thinker that names it, can claim to be their home:

---

[1] Eternal and Immutable Morality, IV. iii. 14
[2] Aristotle, Met. Bonitz. 1069 a 33
[3] τὸ αὐτό ἐστι τὸ νοοῦν καὶ τὸ νοούμενον Arist. de Anima, III iv. 12; Eternal and Immutable Morality, Bk. IV. i. 4, v 2. This passage of Aristotle Dugald Stewart (Diss. p. 87, n.) 'suspects' to be 'very little known,' while he is actually treating of Cudworth, who not only quotes it, but speaks of it as a 'frequent assertion' of the author's (IV. i. 4).

where are they then? must we say that they have their being apart from both,—χωριστά,—as Aristotle reports was Plato's belief? If this means, not only separate from these two finite individuals, but in absolute isolation, it is impossible. For then they, i.e. the sensible truths, must be either substances, or modifications of substance. The former they cannot be; because they are true *of something*, which 'something' would so play the part of substance to them Nor is the latter supposition admissible; for if they are modifications, it must be either of Matter, or of Mind: not, however, of Matter, because they are immutable and universal, and *that* nothing material can be; therefore of Mind; of which, accordingly, they demonstrate the existence with their own eternity and immutable perfection[1]. They are, in their ultimate seat, the wisdom of the Omniscient God: the archetypal ideas, of which our intellectual intuitions are the ectypal miniatures. Thus, Cudworth adopts the interpretation by which an escape has been so often sought from the enigmas of the είδη, referring them to the Divine Mind as their Subject. He seems unaware of the difficulties of reading this interpretation into Plato's text, and confidently applies it to him, while accepting it for himself.

The 'Intelligible Ideas,' then, are eternal and necessary modes of the Divine Mind; and from that infinite seat they pass into the finite world in two distinct, yet related, ways: by an act of God's *Will*, things are called into existence of which they become the essences: by a lending of *His Spirit* to centres of dependent being, and communication of *His Consciousness*, they become the intuitive lights of Reason and Conscience for all free natures: and thus, they guide us, on one line, to the true reading of the universe; and on the other, to the immediate sympathy of God. Hence it is that all men have the same fundamental ideas, to form the common ground both of intellectual communion and of moral co-operation[2]. And

[1] Eternal and Immutable Morality, Bk. IV. iv. 9.
[2] Ibid. Bk. IV. iv. 12.

hence, too, the intuitive notions having the maximum of self-light, it is precisely in proportion to the intellectual lucidity of thoughts, that they have assured correspondence with reality; and whatever is clearly conceived is thereby identified with truth. Certainty has no test but intelligibility. 'It is only the real that can be clear[1].'

An illusion, however, may easily lurk in our metaphor, when we speak of the 'Intelligible Ideas' as archetypes, from which the Creator formed existing things as copies. We are not to think of them as a gallery of models, with stationary pictures and statues, planted there to be looked at by an external artist who tries to repeat their forms[2]. It is not in this sense that $αἰσθητὰ$ are $τοῦ\ νοητοῦ\ μιμήματα$. The ideal conceptions are not passive shapes, but living movements of thought, energies of a mind which consists of all truth, and in which all truth is causative. It is only in a finite nature, like ours,—a nature in which the intellectual relations are realised in fragments and cannot take many steps without arrest,—that truth can seem to stand still and look at us as with dead eyes, and wait for us to put it to use or adornment as an automaton. But when it is said that the essences of things are eternal, and that God's work gives them individualised being, we are not to think that He 'did nothing else but, as some sarcastically express it, *sartoris instar, rerum essentias vestire existentia*[3].' The reader will remember how Plato guards his doctrine against a similar misapprehension.

From the identification of $νοήματα$ with $νοητὰ$, and of both with $νοῦς$, it directly follows that God's existence, as Infinite and Eternal Mind, is no less certain than are the essential properties of the triangle. The proposition is of the order of necessary truth, 'clearly and mathematically demonstrable[4].'

In the application of his doctrine to Ethics we obtain

---

[1] Eternal and Immutable Morality, Bk. IV. v. 12.
[2] Ibid. Bk. IV iv. 7.   [3] Ibid Bk. IV. vi. 2.
[4] Ibid. Bk. IV. iv. 7. 10

very little help from Cudworth himself. But he indicates with sufficient distinctness the theory which it aims to exclude. First, if the mind were at the outset a *tabula rasa*, good and evil could never get written upon it from without; for they have no existence in external objects, taken by themselves, so as still to remain, though there were no souls; nor do they come to us, like light and sound, through the impressions of sense. They are constituted by the accord or discord of action and disposition (our own or others') with certain inward anticipations (προλήψεις) or demands of the soul itself; and not in its passive part, so that they are at the mercy of whatever influence may be flung upon them by circumstances and opinion; but in its living and active essence, whose functions and principles of apprehension are there before the things it does and apprehends. 'Intellectual beings, as such, have a natural determination in them to do some things and to avoid others; which could not be, if they were mere naked passive things.' This is why he has so insisted that 'the soul is not a mere passive and receptive thing, which hath no innate active principle of its own, because upon this hypothesis there could be no such thing as morality[1].' He has already enumerated 'good and evil' among the intuitive intellectual categories, which correspond with the real distinctions of things. And here he says that, in this case, the ideas convey *more than knowledge*, and are attended by an authoritative pleading with the will to move in a determinate direction. In the presence of this constitution of soul, good and evil are unalterably given, and cannot be modified by either inclination in the agent or opinion in others; the inward record tells the eternal Right, and supplies a true νόμος which is no δόγμα πόλεως (State-ordinance), but a τοῦ ὄντος ἐξεύρεσις,—a discovery of the real Right. Human experience could have in it no *moral* element, did not the mind bring with it into the scene of action a secret standard of preference and approval supplied by the ideal Good.

[1] Eternal and Immutable Morality, Bk. IV. vi. 4.

This is the Divine scintilla which moralises life, and chequers it with its pathetic lights and shadows.

Such is the position which Cudworth takes up against the revival by Hobbes of the ancient derivation of moral distinctions from positive law. Unless there was something just and good φύσει, nothing could become just and good θέσει. But the same principle is valid no less against Descartes' doctrine, that the Will of God creates all moral distinctions, and by arbitrary choice turns into good and bad things that would else be indifferent, so that, by a reversed volition of His, virtue and vice would change places. Thus far the Divine absolutism had been carried by many theologians. It was fortunate for the opponents of the paradox, that Descartes pushed it further to its logical terminus, and maintained that nothing was true or false except by the Will of God, so that it was at his option to make the three angles of a triangle equal to two right angles or to any other number. This unflinching adhesion to their favourite doctrine operated like a caricature upon the worshippers of the 'Omnipotent decrees,' and compelled the more ingenuous spirits to feel that, as there must certainly be some things true in themselves, so might there as well be things right in themselves, and that as God's thought concurred with the former, so would His will identify itself with the latter. Cudworth effectually exposes the absurdities of Descartes' doctrine: that it involves 'the compossibility of contradictions,' e.g. that by Divine command a cube could be spherical: that, by rendering everything arbitrary, it destroys all science and demonstration, and reduces the necessary to the contingent: that it renders it impossible to attribute knowledge, wisdom, or goodness to God Himself, since they are His effects and not His essence, and were nowhere until He willed what there should be. In rejection, therefore, alike of theological and of political absolutism, Cudworth rescues the right and good as well as the true from all dependence upon will, Divine or human, and treats them as eternally valid for God no less than for us, as indeed the very ideas and energies that are the contents of His infinite Reason and perfect character, and the sources of all His volition. God may not unfitly be symbolised, He tells us, by an infinite circle, with goodness for its centre, while innumerable radii mark the lines of a wisdom immutable and all-comprehending, constituting together the interior and absolute essence of His nature; the 'interminate' periphery of which represents the circuit of His voluntary activity, exercised always *extra Deum*, without any *imperium ad intra*, determining thus the *existence of things*, but freely determined by wisdom and goodness in their institution and cosmical order[1].

In the theory of Cudworth there is an exact correspondence, in the relative order of thought and things, between the universe and man; they are strictly macrocosm and microcosm. In the former, as Plato had already insisted, Mind and Soul are prior to Matter, being its mastering and determining power, and supplying the preconceived essences to which all single objects must conform. In the latter, Intellection, instead of following Sense as its effect, is potentially there to receive it and mould it into Knowledge, when it comes; and Morality, far from being a conventional expedient of social experience, is its indispensable condition, and is possible only because there is an Infinite Mind, in whose communicable ideas are the prototypes of all Morals. It is from inattention to this order, and from beginning their enquiries with their own special element (Matter and its phenomena) as if it were absolutely first, as well as relatively to their work, that the physiologists lapse into Atheism. They start, as Plato complained, from corpuscles and their motion as primordial existences that must not be asked to give account of themselves; and then assume that the soul springs up afterwards out of this, as a second thing or shadow of the first; and so they leave no place for God, or for the Just and Right as having any reality, or being more

[1] Eternal and Immutable Morality, Bk. I. iii.

than passive impressions,—it may be at one remove or more, —from corporeal things[1].

C. ETHICAL THEORY.—If the doctrine of Cudworth be tried by the only test which is just to an author's genius, its merits relatively to the prevailing thought of its age, it is entitled to a rank considerably higher than has been usually assigned to it by historians of English philosophy. Embodied as it is in unfinished books, and buried in massive erudition, it has been distantly respected rather than closely studied; and has left upon few readers an adequate impression of the depth of the author's penetration, the comprehensiveness of his grasp, the subtlety of his analysis, and the happy flashes of expression by which he flings light upon real though unsuspected relations. The vastness of his philosophic aim, and the elevation of his moral conception were less congenial to his countrymen, half of them schooled in Calvinistic Divinity, and half breaking loose into unblushing worldliness, than the limited compactness, the scientific precision, and the systematised cynicism of Hobbes. But Cudworth's thought gives evidence of its originality and independence by its freedom from all the strong pressures of his time; and to readers exempt from prepossession can hardly fail to appear the expression of the larger and the nobler mind.

For the purpose of the present enquiry, a different comparison must be instituted; the theory must be contemplated in its relations to our existing psychology, whether to correct it, or to receive correction from it. In the following criticisms I limit myself to a single question: whether the Moral Sentiments can be resolved into modes of *intellectual* apprehension, and deduced from the essentials of *Reason*.

(1) When Cudworth insists that *Sensation* in itself gives us no knowledge, and simply supplies occasion for the mind

[1] Eternal and Immutable Morality, Bk. IV. vi. 6-14. Comp. Intell. System, chap. v. § v. (Vol II pp. 349-360), where he refutes the corresponding doctrine of Hobbes.

to put forth a cognitive activity, he does but draw the distinction, now so familiar, between Sensation and *Perception*. Our reference of a sensation to an object that gives it and to a self that receives it, is a cognitive act over and above the mere sensitive state, and is put forth by a mind charged with the distinction between itself and other than itself,— i.e. with the postulates of cause and externality or space. These ideas we characterise as *à priori*, in order to indicate that they are the conditions whereby the mind is ready to deal with sensitive experience, as soon as it comes. Exactly in the same sense Cudworth calls them προλήψεις or anticipations; and in defending their existence and originality he uses, in part, the same arguments as Kant and others have advanced against the extreme empirical psychologists. So far, he moves upon safe ground. But, advancing further, he steps, as it seems to me, into an insecure position. Without any formal attempt to mark off from each other the primordial and the acquired ideas, he tacitly assumes, as a test of the former, the absence from them of any *image* presented to the 'mind's eye;' and, following this rule, he includes, among his given intelligibles, conceptions of particular virtues, e.g. Justice, and of complex relations, e.g. Symmetry and Aptitude and Art, with many others of which the genesis may readily be traced by a reasonable psychology, and which cannot without absurdity be supposed to precede experience. That Cudworth should be misled by the mere absence of a representative picture is the more remarkable, because he recognises, like Spinoza, a class of unreal universals, formed, after the manner of our common nouns, by extension of the same name to partial similars and the consequent dying out of all unrepeated features;—a process which must end, especially with the names, not of things but of their relations, in a total elimination of imagery and the emerging of a bare abstract. It is a serious defect in these writers, that they supply no definite rule for separating this *à posteriori* class from the 'real universals.' The task remained over for the genius and enterprise of Kant.

(2) The mode in which Cudworth deals with his true *à priori* categories, when he has fairly found them, is not altogether satisfactory He makes them the *objects* of our knowledge: they really are its *conditions*. They are our way of knowing, and not the facts of existence immediately known. As 'intelligible ideas,' i. e. in their universality as functions of cognition, they belong to us as subjects; and, when carried by us into application, what they reveal to us in the object is the property which comes under this universal of ours. When, in perception, I say to myself, in front of a bright lamp, '*the cause* of my dazzle is *there*,' I use the categories of *causation* and of *space;* but what I know in that experience is the lamp's light as an instance of the one, and its position as included in the other ; and I direct no attention to the heads themselves which cover these phenomena. They are the containers, not the contents, of my knowledge. It is perfectly true that, without the universal, the particular could not be recognised for what it is; and that, as in all cases of relation, both terms must mentally coexist; but the phenomenal instance is that explicit occupant of the foreground which we call the object, while the implicit background which definitely shows it to the mind is an unheeded presence. As such categories constitute my way of thinking, they cannot, or they need not, remain permanently hidden from me. I may afterwards reflect upon what I have been about, and read my own methods from end to end; and then these 'intelligibles' become *objects of knowledge* to me: not, however, as ontological genera, but as psychological facts of my own inner history. On my thus becoming acquainted with them, what do I find them to be? the necessary moulds of thought itself, the constitutive essence of my intelligence, which it is impossible for me to disbelieve, inasmuch as the disbelief itself is a mental act which assumes them. Their ontological contents, therefore, though not otherwise known, I accept as their significance ; esteeming nothing more reasonable than to conform my thinking to the law of reason.

This undoubtedly amounts to resting everything at last upon the veracity of our own faculties, and taking on trust their ultimate reports; and security higher than this it is chimerical to seek. Cudworth is far from being content with it, and struggles hard to escape from it on to some absolute and adamantine rock[1]; but to evade it is impossible: the relativity of knowledge can never cease to mean that, if we were cheated by either of its terms, the knowledge would fail.

(3) Let us admit that, among the primordial axioms of the understanding, we may find some fundamental ethical affirmation. Still, though its *certainty* will be thus assured, its *meaning* will be hid from us, so long as it is shown to us by intellectual light alone. That light suffices for *knowledge:* knowledge is the apprehension of *what is:* morality (on its cognitive side) is the apprehension of *what ought to be,*—a very different sphere, by no means involved in the conception of the other. Were moral ideals resolvable into rational, right would be a kind of *truth*, and virtue would be constituted by *assent;* yet it is plain that, though these are present, they are not all or even the chief features of what is there. They miss altogether the very essence of morals, viz. the Sense of *Duty*, which could never belong to a mere thinking being, however perfect an organ he might be for reflecting things as they are and as they must be. It is an inseparable concomitant of the mental apprehension of the right, but rests upon a different base; for Truth, by simply displaying the logical nexus of its links of thought, *necessitates* assent; while Duty, in spite of the clear vision of the right, does not *necessitate obedience;* freedom of choice yet remains, when the knowledge of the right is already complete; so the moral problem begins where the intellectual ends. The understanding works in the sphere of the caused and determinate: the moral nature in that of the yet uncaused and indeterminate. The contents of the

---

[1] Eternal and Immutable Morality, Bk. IV. v. 6-12

latter can never be brought into the categories of the former.

(4) Cudworth's προλήψεις are always represented by him as certain preconceptions which, on being carried into experience, are found to fit now this class of its cases, and now that; just as, when once possessed of the definition of 'triangle,' I see that it answers, here for a right-angled, there for an acute-angled figure of three sides. The relation, then, between the 'intelligible idea' and the particulars to which it is applied, is that of genus to species or of species to individual, and is identical with logical subsumption Hence it is always absolutely true, or absolutely false, that the concrete instances are embraced by the universal; if they have its defining marks, it is true; if they have not, it is false; and it can never happen that of the same object you can be justified in at one time affirming and at another denying it. This law of intellectual judgment does not, however, hold good of moral judgment. If it did, the same spring of action, once found right, would be right for ever; or, once a culprit, would be condemned for life; its goodness or its guilt would be something absolute, as the properties of a sphere or pyramid. Unless our psychology has gone astray, it is far otherwise. The springs of action disposing themselves upon a scale of worth, eve y one of them, lying between a lower and a higher, is right in competition with the former, wrong when resisting the latter, and cannot be judged without reference to its alternative. All moral obligation is *preferential*, and binds us to select the better as against the worse of two possibilities. For this mode of thinking there is no provision in the quantitative logic of the understanding.

(5) Hence it follows that the *order* assigned by Cudworth to the process of knowledge, viz. from the universal to the particular, is *not* that in which we gain our moral wisdom. Our intuitive apprehension of Space gives us the whole Infinitude at a stroke, on occasion of the smallest instance; and that of Cause is for us a universal as soon as it is a

particular; and all that we afterwards do with these 'intelligibles' is to distribute them in all the details and corners of our experience. But our intuitive feeling of right gives us no similar inkling of its range; it not only arises *on occasion of* some individual act of will, but is strictly *a part of it*, a consciousness that the motive we have obeyed is better or worse than that which we might have followed; and there is no implicit forecast of the future extension of the incipient scale. It is not a πρόληψις, but a simple συνείδησις. When other springs of action come into play as competitors for our volition, each instance of choice introduces us to a new relation of superiority and adds a fresh term to the climax of right; so that it is constructed for us *piecemeal*, and only at last, on the exhaustion of all the elements of our alternative experience, is it built up into total conscience, and exhibits the sweep of moral authority from base to summit. Here, therefore, the development of our knowledge is not *downwards* from the ideal essences to the instances, taken one by one; but *upwards* from single cases of alternative to the full contents of Right; inverting Cudworth's rule, 'that knowledge doth not begin in individuals, but ends in them[1].'

(6) One reason more I will mention against crediting the intellect with the parentage of the moral apprehensions. It is evident that though human beings cannot be affected by their several springs of action without some consciousness of their relative worth, yet that this consciousness is not necessarily attached to the instinctive impulses themselves; for in infra-human animals many of them exist and operate, obviously unattended by any ethical self-estimate. The question then arises, at what particular point of the interval between other animals and man does this consciousness find entrance? Is it his advantage in point of *understanding*, that makes the difference? If the instinctive skill of the tribes of earth and air and water were made calculative instead of blind; if the bee-hive were built as

[1] Eternal and Immutable Morality, Bk. IV. iii. 13 (p. 461).

an exercise in solid geometry; if the migratory bird, in order to steer his course, found his latitude by the meridian height of sun or star, and his longitude by lunar method, if the insect knew what she was about in depositing her eggs in the precise receptacle which would nourish the future offspring; would these scientific creatures necessarily become ashamed of any appetite they felt before? would they feel a scruple about fighting for their food, or blame their own hot temper in the last quarrel? There is nothing, so far as I can see, in the mere presence of intelligence, to supply the defect of moral consciousness; nor is there any difficulty in conceiving a nature quite neutral or blind on this side, while on the other it has vast capacities for knowledge. Intellect could live and find its full work in a necessitated order of things; and so long as the impulses of animated nature formed a part of that order, they might subsist in partnership with Intellect and suffer no intrinsic change. Not till we break through the cordon of necessity and annex a zone of *freedom*, does the moral difference between the springs of conduct become momentous as a ground of choice, and at the same instant (as is fitting) perspicuous to the chooser. Here it is that we fix the birth-point of possible morality: when the springs of action are planted in a free mind that has to settle their alternatives, they reveal their relative rank to the consciousness, and only in so doing institute for the agent the Divine law of Duty. By this limitation to a free sphere the moral intuitions differ from the intellectual, and refuse to be enrolled upon the same register with them.

Is it consistent with this view to speak of 'Eternal and Immutable Morality?' Provided you prefix the hypothesis, 'that there eternally exists free Mind, moved by several differenced springs of action,' it is not only consistent but consequential to do so; in that mind the authoritative order neither wastes nor changes. But, in the absence of such mind, in a mere mechanical or empty universe, eternity might still be predicated, but morality could not;

for its essence lies in conditions which are here negatived. It does not depend upon God's *will;* but upon His *existence,* as its infinite home and supreme personal life, it does depend, in any sense which leaves its essential significance unspoiled.

CHAPTER II.

CLARKE.

§ 1. *Life, Personality, and Writings.*

In Cudworth the disposition to intellectualise morals was not inconsistent with a large survival of Puritan enthusiasm and devout fervour. The rights of Reason were asserted by him, not as a check upon faith too unflinching and feeling too intense, but in resistance to the pretensions of Sense and the dogmatism of instituted Law; and with the sincere effect of bringing the human mind into closer affinity and more conscious communion with the Divine than were provided for in the current doctrines either of the Schools or of the Church. The theory, at its next stage, loses much of its early glow, and, in the person of Dr. Samuel Clarke, assumes some of the harder features of what is called Rationalism; the Idealism of Plato being replaced in influence by the Physics of Newton, and more of externality being admitted into the relation between man and God. Religion emerges from the Caroline period not without some sense of humiliation, and a reduction of its aggressive tone to one of self-defence; and is anxious, in the presence of Hobbes and Spinoza, to throw its speculative appeal into the forms of the logical understanding, so as to make its Philosophy indistinguishable from Science. And in England it was the new science of the 'Principia,' that supplied the model, in place of the Cartesian, to which all the methods of higher reasoning were to be conformed. And of this idea Clarke was the special representative: having translated into good Latin, and annotated, the Treatise on Physics then in common use at Cambridge,—by *Jacques Rohault* the Cartesian,—for the express purpose of replacing its conceptions by the Newtonian [1]. He was then but twenty-two years of age. The eminent success of the book did not divert him from his purpose of theological study, and by the devotion of several years he obtained an honourable rank among the Greek and Hebrew scholars of his time. After his ordination he was introduced, through the friendship of Whiston, to the favourable regards of Dr. John Moor, the Bishop of his native city of Norwich, and became in 1698 his resident Chaplain, in succession to Whiston, for about twelve years. The era from which his great reputation dates is the Boyle Lecture of 1704, which was entrusted to him, and gave occasion to his 'Demonstration of the Being and Attributes of God, more particularly in answer to Mr. Hobbes, Spinoza, and their followers,' 'being the substance of eight sermons preached in the Cathedral Church of St. Paul.' The great impression produced by Clarke's argument led to his reappointment to the lectureship for the next year, and the appearance of the second series of sermons in 1706, under the title, 'A Discourse concerning the Unchangeable Obligations of Natural Religion, and the Truth and Certainty of the Christian Revelation.' In 1708, the two volumes were united into one, under the title, 'A Discourse concerning the Being and Attributes of God, the Obligations of Natural Religion, and the Truth and Certainty of the Christian Revelation.' In the editions which appeared after 1714 there is appended a correspondence, consisting of five letters and their replies, between an anonymous critic of the 'Demonstration' and its author; which is interesting in itself, and still more so

---

[1] *La Physique* first appeared in 1671, and, with enlargements, in a second edition, in 1683. A bad Latin translation, by Théophile Bonnet, appeared at Geneva in 1674. Clarke's translation was published in 1697, and reached a third edition in 1710. This Latin edition was itself translated into English by Dr. John Clarke, Dean of Sarum, in 2 vols. 8vo.

from the fact that the critic, a student of twenty-one years of age in a Dissenting Academy, was no other than the future Bishop Butler, and that the fellow-student who concealed the authorship and his locality, by posting the letters at Gloucester instead of Tewkesbury, was Secker, afterwards Archbishop of Canterbury. To the generous appreciation of his opponent which Clarke henceforth felt Butler owed his subsequent appointment to the pulpit of the Rolls' Chapel, from which his celebrated philosophical sermons were delivered.

The Boyle Lectures secured to Clarke a permanent place in metaphysical literature, and a certain measure of immediate ecclesiastical promotion. He was appointed Chaplain to Queen Anne and Rector of St. James's,—an office which he held till his death. He was not without opportunities of further advancement; but his 'Scripture Doctrine of the Trinity' having exposed him to proceedings in Convocation, which were quieted only by a very equivocal retractation, he became so far conscious of his false position, as an Arian in an Athanasian Church, as to decline any removal which involved renewed subscription to the Articles and Creeds. By the favour of the Court he was offered the post of Master of the Mint, vacated by the death of Sir I. Newton, to which an income was attached of from £1,200 to £1,500 a year; but he felt the incongruity between his pastorate and this secular office, and remained content with his rectory. Measured by the moral standard of his profession and his time, this self-denial has no slight claim to respect; but hardly neutralises the reproach of half-hearted compromise brought against him by the outspoken Whiston, who had to the utmost the courage of his opinions.

The two great principles for which Clarke had pleaded at St. Paul's—*Moral Freedom* and *Rational Religion*,—were reasserted at Cambridge in his exercises on taking his Doctor's degree in 1709; the theses being stated thus: 'All religion supposes the freedom of human action:' and,

'The Christian Religion contains nothing contrary to Reason;' and were maintained with such power that 'every creature present was rapt up into silence and astonishment, and thought the performance truly admirable[1].' It was inevitable, however, that a conception of religion so little congenial with either the faith or the scepticism of his time should provoke strenuous resistance. His doctrine of the Natural Immortality of the Soul involved him in controversy with Dodwell; who maintained that the life eternal was conferred in baptism, and depended on the sacramental function of the legitimate priest[2]. Clarke's letter in reply meets the eccentric High-Churchman on scriptural and patristic as well as on philosophic ground. More formidable and persistent was the opposition, on the metaphysical side, to his vindication of Free-will. The year 1715 allowed him no rest upon this subject. Anthony Collins published anonymously 'A Philosophical Enquiry concerning Human Liberty,' than which there is no abler statement of the Necessarian argument; and Leibniz entered on a correspondence with Clarke, which largely turned upon the same problem After five papers had passed between them, Leibniz's death broke off the discussion in the midst; but it was published, by desire of the accomplished Princess of Wales, who had throughout taken the greatest interest in it, and, according to Dr. Clarke's own testimony, 'had understood what answers were to be given to Leibniz's arguments, before he drew up his reply to them, as well as he himself did[3].' Appended to the volume is Clarke's reply to Collins's 'Philosophical Enquiry,' with some letters on the same subject which passed between him and an anonymous 'Gentleman of the University of Cambridge[4].'

[1] Whiston's Historical Memoirs of the Life of Dr. Samuel Clarke, p. 18. London, 1730
[2] Dodwell's Epistolary Discourse, 1706.
[3] Whiston's Historical Memoirs of the Life of Dr. S. Clarke, p. 132.
[4] The book is entitled, 'A Collection of Papers which passed between the late learned Mr. Leibnitz and Dr. Clarke, in the years 1715 and

Of Clarke's other writings it is foreign to my purpose to say more than that he was not alienated by his metaphysics or his theological polemic from either his physical or his classical studies. His 'Natural Religion,' indeed, was intimately connected with his 'Natural Philosophy,' and Newton was hardly less his guide in the former than in the latter; precisely as, on the Continent, the Cartesian modes of thought influenced speculative doctrine quite as much as scientific method. Both Greek and Latin literature retained their attraction for him. In 1712 he edited a splendid folio edition of Cæsar's Commentaries; and in 1729 appeared, under his hand, the first twelve books of Homer's Iliad, with a Latin translation and notes, in quarto. His death immediately followed; but he had left materials which enabled his son to issue the remainder of the Iliad in 1732, and the Odyssey, 1740. If these editions had appeared before the age of Bentley, they might have had some prospect of more durable reputation; but the rapid advance of modern scholarship has left them far behind; and they now remain chiefly as witnesses of the large and liberal culture of a mind more scientific than critical.

§ 2. *Abstract and Estimate of his Doctrine.*

In the case of Clarke, as in that of Cudworth, I pass by the earlier treatise, which deals with the question of Theism, and fix exclusive attention upon the second, which develops his Theory of Ethics. Nor is it needful to notice, in this theory, any features which it has in common with Cudworth's: it will suffice, if its additions and variations are brought out, in order to see how far they protect the doctrine from the difficulties previously attaching to it. At the same time, where he selects, for the expression of a

---

1716, relating to the Principles of Natural Philosophy and Religion.' By Samuel Clarke, D.D., Rector of St. James's, Westminster. London, 1717.

theory fundamentally the same, forms of language characteristically different, he must be allowed to speak for himself, lest he should be made answerable for more than he has distinctly said.

The links of his argument, from end to end, are these: We have necessary knowledge of the Natural attributes of God: they involve the Moral attributes: these entail the acceptance of moral obligation and natural religion: which carry in them the sanctions of a future state: and thence is justified the Christian faith, which has 'brought life and immortality to light.' And, inversely, to reject the last of these propositions involves directly the denial of its immediate antecedent, and, by successive regress, of all the rest. He admits, however, that the nexus which secures the last two terms of the series is less close than that which unites their three predecessors · though we knew nothing of any special revelation of a future life, the immortality of the soul would remain assured to us; and though the retributions of that state were hid, Duty would still hold its place of indefeasible authority. These two links, therefore, are rather reasonable adjuncts attached by strong probabilities, than integral portions of the adamantine chain; but for the other three he claims that they begin with absolute certainty, and hang together by demonstrative necessity, as rigorous as that which the geometrician follows. It is with this part alone that our subject is concerned. His thesis with regard to it is to the following effect:

> There are eternal and necessary differences and relations of things, constituting an original and immutable fitness of them, or unfitness, to each other:
>
> To these, as data, God *necessarily* (i.e. in virtue of His inherent perfection) conforms His Will; and this conformity constitutes His justice, goodness, and truth towards the whole: our *voluntary* conformity to the same data constitutes the corresponding

virtues in us, and is our *Duty*, and this, irrespective of positive command, and of personal reward and punishment.

Under cover of the first of these propositions, Clarke puts upon the same footing mathematical and moral relations, as similarly apprehended in their first principles and similarly worked out in deduction. The human differences are as obvious as the various sizes of physical objects; the fitness of actions and characters, as the proportions of numbers and geometrical figures; and every perceived change in personal relations involves modifications of behaviour, just as an altered diagram loses or acquires some property. Thus, the infinite superiority of God *renders fit* the veneration and obedience of men, since it is *true* that on Him we depend, and that His will is just and His power irresistible; and for Him it is *intrinsically fitter* to rule by law and order than by chance, to secure the good of the universe than its misery, and to deal with men according to their deserts. Similarly, it is *fitter for us* to promote the good rather than the ruin of our fellows, quite apart from all expected recompence. To call in question these differences as eternal and unchangeable is no less absurd than to doubt whether a square is double a triangle of the same base and height. Yet this absurdity Hobbes commits, when he founds all moral distinctions upon a treaty of peace among men, to rescue them from mutual conflict and destruction. What should start such compact, and make it binding, if mutual conflict and destruction were not already wrong? Is it that such a compact is for the public good? Then is the public good eligible to begin with, and is *not indifferent*, but carries an obligation into the engagement. To show that a thing is *really indifferent* is to disqualify it for becoming a subject of law [1].

Understanding is the reporter of reality: else it would be *mis*understanding. Such, therefore, as the eternal differences and relations *are*, such does intelligence perceive them to

[1] Unchangeable Obligations, pp 172-183.

be; and by that perception directs the will, unless some disturbing passion interposes. In the passionless Supreme Mind, the whole activity must be in accord with eternal Right[1].

In our nature, too, it *ought* to be the same: for in our intelligence also the eternal relations stand revealed, and claim our assent as necessarily as any demonstrated truth; and to suspend or withhold it is no less perverse than to say, that a crooked line is as short a path between two points as a straight one. But in our mixed constitution, distorting passion, which has no play upon the geometrical field, is apt to intercept the message of the intellect to the will, and delude us by inferior guidance. But, since we have reason, and are free to follow it, we are without excuse, and are well aware of our obligation to do voluntarily the thing which passion contests: of which we have clear witness in our own *inward assent* to what we outwardly contradict, and our self-condemnation when we choose the wrong. The unreasonableness is just the same as if we refused assent to some demonstrated certainty; it is a vain attempt to make things be what they are not; which is 'absurdity and insolence.' 'So far then,' he says, 'as men are conscious of what is right and wrong, so far they *are* under an obligation to act accordingly:' and 'that eternal rule of right which I have been hitherto describing, 'tis evident, *ought* as indispensably to govern men's actions, as it cannot but necessarily determine their assent[2].' This important passage condenses Clarke's doctrine into its simplest form: that the moral consciousness, when awakened, is *intuitive and self-evidencing;* and carries in it an *inherent imperative authority*.

That there should be latent in the mind, prior to experience, a potential consciousness of essential objective relations, may excite our wonder, but was long ago illustrated as a fact by Plato's memorable method of eliciting geometrical truth from an untaught slave, by simply interrogating

[1] Unchangeable Obligations, p. 184.   [2] Ibid. pp. 184-190.

his native intelligence. Equally ready for the questioning appeal of experience is the response of reason in regard to matters of right and wrong; and equally accordant, however many witnesses you call; for though men will resent your censure of their acts, and from passion may even blind themselves, their judgments become concurrent when passed upon others who are removed from their partialities, like the personages in history or fiction. Not even the wicked, who have done most to paralyse the conscience, can escape moral conviction; which sometimes wrings from them confession of crimes long forgotten by the world. If it be true that tribes of savages are found destitute as yet of moral ideas, this is no more surprising than that they should be destitute of geometrical ideas; they are but rudimentary human beings, in whom the rational consciousness still sleeps[1].

From this theory of eternal moral distinctions Clarke proceeds to deduce in order[2] the duties of men to God, to one another, and to themselves: to show that though these duties do not depend for their existence upon the command of God, they gain an infinite sympathy and a sublime hold upon the affections by their identity with His will; and that, while it is not any future that makes them binding, yet is their impression deeper and their story more complete, when their sequel of immortal issues is laid open. Neither into these applications of his doctrine, nor into his deduction from it of the truths of natural religion[3], is it necessary to follow our author. Nor shall I dwell upon his very effective criticism of Hobbes. All these topics are treated with great firmness of hand, and calm breadth of thought, and in a spirit of fairness far beyond the prevailing controversial temper of his time. I must turn, however, from his conclusions to his principles, in order to find, if possible, his place among the varieties of moral psychology.

The essential question is, whether Clarke succeeds, any

[1] Unchangeable Obligations, pp. 190–196.   [2] Ibid. pp. 197–223.
[3] Ibid. pp. 239–272.   [4] Ibid. pp. 224–238.

better than Cudworth, in reducing Moral perceptions to Intellectual Assent. It is impossible to discuss such a question with advantage, unless we are agreed at the outset upon the characteristic contents, and hence the intended boundary, of the term 'Intellect' or 'Reason;' and this condition is unfortunately not secured by any definition: it is therefore very possible that, where the author fails to convince his reader, it may simply be that the one gives a larger, the other a narrower range to this central conception. In one sense, every experience of our nature might be pronounced intellectual; inasmuch as it is accompanied by self-consciousness and implicit or explicit judgments which are competent to intelligence alone; passion and emotion themselves are, in us, not without thought, and may be always treated as *thought in a glow*. The personal activity is indeed an undivided living unity, issuing from an abiding centre in varying directions, and not a federation of faculties occasionally meeting, but for the most part busy with separate enterprises on their own account. Nothing is more deceptive than psychological classification, when the categories it sets up are treated as component factors of a manifold structure, instead of heads of similarity among the expressions of one nature; and when the claim of a phenomenon to be referred to one rather than to another is turned into a quarrel between entities, instead of being tested by the exigencies of arrangement. To guard in the present instance against illusion from this cause, let us say that by Reason we mean that action of the mind whereby we discriminate between true and false predication, and apprehend some things in the kinds, groups, and sequence to which they really belong. I say '*some*' things, because, wherever this is done at all, the act is rational, and the function vindicates the presence of reason, though there should be other things as yet unapprehended in these respects, and other relations than these, for the apprehension of which a different type of activity is required. No phenomena can be properly claimed for the Reason, which cannot be brought under its essence or definition, i.e. under the minimum required to make it what it is; to ask for more is to confess the need of borrowing from another field. By this rule Clarke fails, as it seems to me, to make good his rationalisation of Morals. The following remarks will explain the grounds of this judgment.

(1) He plants Morals at the outset among '*Eternal relations.*' Eternal relations can be predicated only of *eternal things:* and in the use of this phrase he was doubtless determined by the thought of *mathematical* relations, from which all his illustrations are drawn, and which he treats throughout as homogeneous in necessity with the obligations of rectitude. The mathematical relations are what they are in virtue of their dependence on *Space and Time*, which are eternal, and which carry these attributes into all their dimensions and properties; and even in the absence of a cosmos they would be there, as a condition of its possibility; as Plato thought when he said that, as Creator, *God geometrises*. But, in order to save this class of necessary relations, there is not even need of God to think the eternal truths; the geometry would be there, whether there was geometer or not. With *moral* relations it is otherwise: in the infinite void, in the infinite duration, they are not to be found. They are conditional on the existence of souls: aye, and of souls in which *not all is necessary*, like the properties of figure and of number, but a range is left of Free-will, i.e. of choice, and, to this end, an alternative provided of a better and a worse in the consciousness. It cannot be admitted that *this* condition is 'eternal and necessary' in the sense in which Space and Time are; for though in our thought the latter can be emptied of contents, mind and all, they themselves insist on staying with us as two infinitudes, the naked possibilities of all else. Clarke endeavours to invalidate this objection and to discharge the two necessities,—of *Space and Time* on the one hand and of *Mind* on the other,—from his battery, as chain-shot inseparably linked, by making out that Space and Time, not being

Substances must be *Attributes* of an Infinite self-existing Being, i.e. God; so that these quantities, though in the first instance presentable to the imagination *per se*, immediately conduct the rational faculty to the necessity of the Divine nature as their ground. The untenableness of this doctrine Leibniz's correspondence has so conclusively shown that it would be idle to revive the discussion. It is sufficient for our purpose to say, that a Being known only as a necessary *Substratum* for space and time, would not on that account be a *Mind or Soul*, and would leave us no less destitute than before of the *Free-will in presence of a better and a worse;* which Moral distinctions postulate. It is impossible, therefore, to put Mathematics and Ethics upon the same footing. The former want only the empty conditions of existence; the latter require existences themselves; and whatever *intuitive* character they have is given in the contemplation of phenomena by an elective mind; both of which must accordingly be there before the intuition can be realised.

(2) Let us now waive this objection, and concede to Clarke his hypothesis of the existence of Mind coextensive with Space and Time. Still, the argumentative use which he makes of it gives no satisfactory account of Moral obligation. Its essence lies, with him, in its *cognitive* function: it is as *intelligence or reason* that he contemplates and applies it, and claims its competency to interpret and institute the laws of right; as if it were impossible for Intellect to live where their light was not. But, as I have already remarked in treating of Cudworth, there is no difficulty in finding plenty of exercise for the Understanding in a world *unmoral:* the whole body of the Natural Sciences being actually its achievement in just such a field,—a field claimed by too many of its cultivators as the total compass of the Universe. The intellectual relations do not give us what we want in our ethical enquiries; vainly does Clarke try to borrow from them terms which will adequately speak to the conscience. 'Fitness,' for example, and 'Congruity' are ideas which in

themselves are by no means equivalent to moral conceptions. They are too wide in their extension: they are too narrow in their comprehension. The first enters, wherever there is a relation of means to end; the piston is fitted to slide before the steam and to move the crank: the second enters, where there is a relation of parts to a common result; there is congruity in the limbs of a walking animal, where the legs are equal or conform to an assignable ratio: and so in innumerable instances which would be present in a purely mechanical world. And when these conceptions are predicated of Morality, it is not they that constitute it moral; there is as much 'fitness' in the stroke of a dagger over an intended victim, as in the interposing blow that turns it aside: only the one is fitness to kill, the other, to save. There is also as much 'congruity;' only, in the one case, to the character of the ruffian, in the other, to that of the deliverer. The words presuppose an end or standard of comparison by which you estimate the property they assert; nor can they ever gain an ethical significance till you are already in possession of your idea of *right character*. It is not fitness that makes an act moral: but it is its morality that makes it fit. From some other source, then, we must be preoccupied by a conviction of right and wrong, before we can take up what is here erroneously described as its natural and sufficient language.

Even if the understanding were competent to the revelation assigned to it, it would not be in virtue of the same theoretical function whereby it apprehends the 'eternal relations' of thought. 'Fitness' and 'Congruity' are terms, not of *Science*, but of *Art;* and it is not till *truths* are turned into *rules*, and receive concrete application for the attainment of a given end, that they become invested with these relative qualities. Of demonstrated truths, and of the reasonings which lead to them, we speak as forming a 'coherent' or 'consistent' or 'inseparable' system; but not, surely, as 'fit' or 'congruous:' intelligence has got to its practical work, before its products earn these epithets of praise. This is important, not only as another failure in the analogy alleged between Geometry and Morals, but because, if morals, to gain their 'fitness,' have to wait for practical work, they do not find it in the speculative Reason, which only thinks and proves and does not work: they win it first on the path of immediate conversion of thought into action. The indeterminate state of the psychological boundary between Logic and Ethics is answerable for more than one unsettled dispute left by the 'Rational' School of Moralists to their successors.

(3) *Good and Evil*, in will and character, cannot be reduced to the *True and False;* because the latter are unsusceptible of degrees, which attach to the very essence of the former. Every definite affirmation demands an unqualified *Yea* or *Nay:* there is no *tertium quid* of which it admits. If ever we say, 'There is *some* truth in that,' it is only because the affirmation is as yet *indefinite*, either from the quantity of the subject being unspecified, or from the predicate being ambiguous; the proposition in both cases being an agglutination of two, one true and the other false. But every moral judgment is between *a better and a worse;* and the relatively worse at the moment is not necessarily and for ever the absolutely bad; nor is the relatively better the eternally best: each of these, shifted into another position of comparison, may appear at the other end of the relation. Hence there are shades of excellence in character, emerging at the upper limit into Divine *Perfection;* and this, not because for different persons there are different frequencies of absolute sins mingled with absolutely virtuous acts, so that the statistical averages come out unequal, but because the whole levels of the voluntary life are separated by intervals and exhibit a series of altitudes. The certainty and the interior nature of this fact become at once apparent on referring to the scale of worth that runs through our springs of action. But *truth* has no comparative or superlative: it can never be less than true, and never more: its existence is its perfection. It is only we that, by missing it here and ap-

prehending it there, hold it but in part, and need indefinite increments to be at one with it all.

(4) A similar difference is found when, instead of looking at truth and moral good in their own essence, we follow them into the human mind, and compare their reception there. To Truth we accord *assent:* to Right, we accord *approval:* and approval, I venture to affirm, can neither be identified with assent, nor deduced from it. And when, in order to scrutinise their relation, we lay them side by side and look at their contents, we see at once that the features present in approval and absent from assent are precisely the whole of the *moral* characteristics, whence the judgment derives its ethical quality. In my assent to the proposition that any two radii vectores of an ellipse, meeting at their peripheral extremities, are together equal to the transverse axis, and my dissent from the assertion that they are always equal to one another, I have none of the self-contentment and of the compunction respectively involved in my right and wrong volitions; I assign no *merit* to the truth, no *demerit* to the error, or to the mind that is subject to them, were my belief rewarded, I should be ashamed of the absurdity: were my misbelief punished, I should resent the injustice. But these experiences, which fail to attend the *Yes* and *No* of Reason, are the sum of the moral sentiments which attends the *Yes* and *No* of Conscience. There is nothing, therefore, in common except the naked fact of acceptance or rejection; the thing accepted or rejected, it is plain, is wholly different.

These criticisms need not hide from us the noble source of Clarke's scheme of thought, namely, an anxiety to exhibit Duty as no more arbitrary than Truth, and to establish Righteousness as coeternal and coextensive with Mind. His work upon this thesis was weakened by the attempt to merge the moral relations in the intellectual, instead of allowing the category of right and wrong to be distinct from that of true and false. But, in spite of this, by lines of thought independent of it, he contributed powerful aids to the realisation of his main end, and effectively continued Cudworth's reasoned protest against the cynical theory of Hobbes, with its enthronement over the world of a multitudinous Leviathan.

CHAPTER III.

PRICE.

Did we select always, as chief representative of a Philosophical School, the author of its completest expository work, we should perhaps take as our text-book, for the study of the 'Dianoetic' Ethics, Dr. Richard Price's 'Review of the Principal Questions and Difficulties in Morals,' published in 1758. Some of its distinctive features would commend it to our preference. It is not a fragment, like Cudworth's treatise: it is not a subsidiary chapter of Natural Theology, like Clarke's: it presents an integral ethical theory, standing on its own independent territory, and carefully guarded from threatening border warfare all round: it pretty decisively quits the metaphysical method which, in its predecessors, is always pressing to the front: and though it rests in the same ontological conclusions, it traces a way to them with less departure from the purely psychological path. But, on the other hand, Price cannot, after such predecessors, materially strengthen the foundations of the theory; and when we proceed to test them, we find ourselves measuring a familiar corner stone, only beginning from a different angle. His chief originality and freshness are brought out by the fact that he is writing for a new generation, and that, meanwhile, ethical doctrine has broken bounds and is exploring the possibilities of more exact delimitation. The writings of Shaftesbury and of Hutcheson had touched some springs of *disinterested* feeling, and wakened some conceptions of *beauty* in character, of which the Schools had taken little or no account; and had thus presented the moral phenomena under an aspect to which terms borrowed from cognitive processes did not seem exactly to apply. To meet the needs of a more delicate psychology, words were taken from the vocabulary of art and of emotion; and from the Professor's chair, as well as from men of letters, it was not uncommon to hear of Moral *Taste*, and *Sensibility*, and *Sympathy*. The first tentatives of language in the survey and enclosure of a new field are rarely precise; being necessarily the outstretching of terms of more limited application, they seem to carry with them something which they mean to leave behind, and are easily found objectionable till they have had time to mark and drop what is irrelevant. By just such a crisis the ethical feeling of Price was made uneasy. He did not like the rising talk about a Moral *Sense*. He was accustomed to the long-standing division of human nature, founded on what it had in common with the brutes and what was added on as the speciality of man, into Senses and Reason; and was offended by the proposal to hand over the self-conscious capacity for Duty from the rational to the sensitive province of the soul. Like his two predecessors, therefore, he reclaims for the intellectual faculty what is being snatched from it; only, his polemic is no longer directed, like theirs, mainly against Hobbes, but against the new assailants from the opposite side, who are for consigning the moral nature to æsthetic or benevolent rule.

To enter into the merits of this controversy would be to anticipate the notice of Shaftesbury and Hutcheson. And it is the less needful to do so, because, in conducting it, Price advances no positive doctrine and no body of argument which is not already found in Cudworth or Clarke; only, it is employed to displace a different form of sensitive experience: i.e. not what is given through the external senses and their vestiges, but the *inward* feeling of love or aversion awakened by voluntary actions witnessed or performed. The case against this more refined type of sensibility is still the same: a state of sentiency, be its seat or be its cause what it may,—an emotion, a relish, a disgust,—is something of which I am recipient in virtue of a passive susceptibility; it knows nothing, it does nothing; it is simply *felt:* but a moral apprehension is *a judgment of Right*, and cannot come out of mere administered material; it looks at two things together; it compares them; it reads their predicates; it seizes their relations; and pronounces a preference: all this is energy, and belongs to the work which the mind performs upon what is delivered to it in its exposure to experience; and this active dealing with passive data, so as to think them, distinguish them, and know them, is precisely what is meant by Reason or Understanding. In this power, therefore, we have a separate source of ideas, both in its own primary forms of activity, and in the results of comparison among the materials of its work: the former, simple and intuitive; the latter, sifted out and derivative; and among the simple ideas, applied as categories to the determination of voluntary actions, is that of right or wrong. Now 'the proper objects of the understanding are truth, facts, real existence.' so that in these intuitive ideas we read the very nature of things, and are as sure of it as that space cannot grow and that two times cannot coexist.

Such, in brief, is the construction of Price's argument. 'What I have had chiefly in view,' he says, 'has been, to trace up virtue to *truth* and the nature of things, and these to the Deity[1];' and again, 'I cannot help considering it as some reproach to human reason, that, by the late controversy and the doubt of some of the wisest men, it should be rendered necessary to use many arguments to show, that *right and wrong*, or *moral good and evil*, signify somewhat *really true* of actions, and not merely *sensations*[2].'

It is more easy to share Price's confidence in his conclusion than to accept it on the security of his reasoning. The first step indeed we must take with him, and agree that the conviction of Duty cannot be referred to the passive

[1] Review of Morals, Introduction, p. 7.
[2] Review of Morals, Preface, p v.

susceptibility of our nature, and if the word 'Sense' is to bear only this meaning, it can never, by help of any epithet, name the essence of that conviction. But the next step I find it impossible to take, I cannot say that this exclusion from the category of Sense drives the moral insight into that of the Understanding; for, although doubtless all understanding involves activity, it cannot be admitted that all activity is expended in understanding; the wakened mind may as conceivably seize intuitive *rules* for the will, as intuitive *truths* for the intellect; and if the moral consciousness presents itself to us in the light, not so much of a theoretical disclosure as of a practical imperative, if it says to us, not 'So it *is*,' but 'So it *ought* to be,' there will be good ground for distributing the activity of Mind into two kinds, one of which shall keep the intellectual name, while the other shall appropriate the moral. In determining the essence of morality we are not shut up to the alternative,— Sense or Understanding; when the first term fails us, we have still a choice, the mind's power is not limited to intelligence, but enables us, in one function, to see the true, in another, to create the right. It is impossible to resolve these two functions into one, under cover of a single term significant only of cognitive and thinking processes.

Price must have been on the very verge of perceiving this, though not till it was too late to affect the statement of his doctrine. For towards the end of his treatise he finds it necessary at last to draw a distinction between '*Speculative* Reason' and '*Moral* Reason[1],' which exactly coincides with Kant's antithesis of 'Theoretical and Practical' knowledge[2], and is in both instances set up on purpose to save Ethics from being identified with intellectual apprehension. It is no wonder that the contrast forced itself

---

[1] Review of Morals, p. 393.
[2] Ich begnüge mich hier, die theoretische Erkenntniss durch eine solche zu erklaren, wodurch ich erkenne, was da ist, die praktische aber, dadurch ich mir vorstelle, was da sein soll. Kritik der reinen Vernunft; Elementarlehre, 2te Abtheilung, II. iii. 7. Rosenkranz, Band II. p. 492.

upon him between movements of mind so different; the one, springing into a ready-made scene and reading the relations of its interior contents; the other, glancing forward at impending possibilities and discerning the lights and shades of their relative worth; the one, a vision of facts; the other, a choice of ends; the one, exercised with impersonal tranquillity, swept only with a gleam of satisfied curiosity; the other, with eager impulse or resolute strife, plunging into bitter remorse, or rising to a Divine repose. The marvel is that, after once realising this difference, Price should still have held on to 'Reason' as a comprehending genus of both as species; for between the theoretic apprehension of truth and the moral appeal of right, I know not what common attribute he could name, beyond the fact of their being, both of them, functions of the same active Ego. His motive indeed is plain enough; he is prepossessed with the idea that the security for the eternal obligation of right is, to stretch over it the conception of the true, and thus protect it by identification with τὸ ὄν. But the right can take care of itself, and needs no such guardianship. The relations of *existence in the objective sphere*, i. e. the relations which subsist between things *inter se* irrespective of any minds cognisant of them (and this is what we mean by '*reality*'), are not the only possible eternals. The *relations of possibility in conscious agents*, i. e. relations between alternatives of objective action and the approval of the subject's mind, may equally be eternal; so that if ever, and whenever, the alternative offers itself to a free spirit, the inward answer will be the same. This is the immutability, not of τὸ ὄν, but of τὸ δέον,—a system of enduring relations among contingent things. The reading of reality, and the ranking of possibility, may both start from intuitive acts and be secured in uniformity by permanence in the relations concerned. But they are essentially different operations, irreducible to any steadfast meaning of the word 'truth.'

We may assent, then, to the negative half of Price's doctrine, that our consciousness of Right is no phenomenon of a passive sense; yet dissent from the positive inference, that it is inseparably involved in the act of intelligence; and in doing so, we claim no more than he himself unwittingly concedes, when he separates the moral from the theoretical judgment. In his anxiety to keep 'Sense' at a distance, and reserve the central place for 'Reason,' he habitually speaks of the ethical emotions as *effects* and *appendages* of the judgment of right, just as an intellectual satisfaction may follow the discovery of a geometrical equality. But surely the cases are not parallel; the feeling of obligation, the enthusiasm of approval, are absolutely *integral* to the moral judgment, and not *consecutive* upon it; they constitute its very form, so that we cannot even conceive of its holding any contents without them; take them away, and the intellectual matter of the judgment will go with them. This feature, no doubt, it is which has tempted Hutcheson and others to experiment, in their Ethics, with the vocabulary of sensibility in preference to that of rationality; and Price, in his alarm at the uncertainty of Sensation and Emotion, fails to recognise what is correct in their critical perception.

On one point more in Price's treatise it is incumbent on me to say a few words. He directly calls in question the fundamental principle on which the foregoing book on Idiopsychological Ethics is based, viz that among the springs of action there is a graduated scale of worth, conformity to which constitutes rightness of character; and maintains, in opposition to this, the monarchy of Reason over the whole lot, as its subjects. 'It may be asked,' he says, 'whether a due order and balance of the several inferior powers of our nature, among themselves, ought not to be taken into our idea of a good character, as well as their common subordination to the faculty of reason?' observe his reply: 'This subordination of the lower powers infers and implies likewise their due state, measure, and proportion in respect of one another. Though some of them should be stronger than of right they ought to be in comparison with others; yet, if Reason governs, the irregularity and disorder which would otherwise follow will be prevented, and the right balance will by degrees be restored; the defect on one side will be supplied by a higher principle, and the excess on the other will, by the same principle, be restrained; so that no harm shall ensue to the character, and nothing criminal discover itself in the life and temper [1].' With this answer I can hardly fail to be content, for, when I ask, 'Had we not better marshal the springs of action according to their rank?' it only says, 'No occasion; Reason will see to that!' It seems, then, it is a task competent to Reason; and there really is a rational order of subordination in which they should be arranged. If so, it is difficult to see why the office of Master of the Ceremonies should not be assumed by the psychologist's Reason in the ante-room, instead of leaving the procession, at the mercy of each separate reason, to scramble into a risky order of precedence at the last step of presentation to action. The constant recurrence, in Price's treatise, of the dual division into an absolute good and bad, right and wrong, not without occasional, nay deliberate, yet unreconciled admission of degrees of virtue and of guilt, makes us feel the need of precisely the rule of order and proportion which is relegated to the care of 'Reason.' When once the preferential principle of moral judgment has been worked out, and its hierarchy approximately constructed, what fulness of definite meaning it adds, for instance, to the following noble passage: '"Reason" is essential to direct, as far as its dominion extends, the passions to their proper objects; to confine them to their proper functions and places; to hinder them from disturbing our own peace or that of the world; and, in short, to correct whatever is amiss in the inward man, or inconsistent with its sound and healthy state. It is scarcely possible to avoid reflecting here, on the flourishing and happy state of the person whose temper and life are formed and governed by Reason in the manner I have now described. What

[1] Review of Morals, pp. 396, 397.

tranquillity and bliss must that mind possess, whose oppressors and tyrants lie vanquished and expiring; which has regained its health and liberty; is independent of the world, and conscious of the peculiar care of the Almighty; where no seditious desire shows itself, and the inferior powers are all harmonious and obedient; where every tumult is laid, and hope and love, candour, sincerity, fortitude, temperance, benignity, piety, and the whole train of heavenly virtues and graces, shed their influence, and have taken up their residence! What *beauty*, or what *glory* like that of such a mind? How well has it been compared to a well-regulated and happy State, victorious over every enemy; secure from every invasion and insult; the seat of liberty, righteousness, and peace; where every member keeps his proper station, and faithfully performs his proper duty; where faction and discord never appear; order, tranquillity, and harmony and love prevail, and all unite in cheerful submission to one wise and good legislature! Is there anything that deserves our ambition, besides acquiring such a mind? in what else can the true blessedness and perfection of man consist? with what *contempt*, as well as pity, must we think of those who prefer *shadows* and *tinsel* to this *first and highest good;* who take great care of the order of their *dress*, their *houses* or *lands*, while they suffer their *minds* to lie waste; and anxiously study and pursue *external* elegance, but study not to make *themselves* amiable, to cultivate *inward* order, or to acquire a regular and happy state of the heart and affections[1]!'

This is a fair vision, of which Plato himself might have been the Seer. It leaves us with only one misgiving. whether its realisation is committed to an adequate power. Can Reason, which completes its function in seeing things as they are, transform them into what they had better be? Can its stately and placid neutrality command that wild inward world, and, like Neptune's head emerging from the deep, silence the winds and allay the waves by the look of an eye? As well might you commission an academy of

[1] Review of Morals, pp. 400-402.

sciences to quell a rebellion. Truth has no executive; and to achieve any readjustment of the affections, to expel a traitor, to free a captive, to chain a tyrant *there*, appeal must be made to a faculty that can *cause something*, instead of merely *understanding everything*,—i.e. to conscience-guided will, with all the gradations and harmonies of reverence. Until the solemn feelings of ordered approval and reprobation, which are said to be the appendix of intellect, invert their place and take the initiative, the conflict of the elements within will not subside. No better practical evidence of this can be desired than our author's own words afford: his praise is of Reason; but his pleading is addressed to the Moral Consciousness in all its variety and in its fullest glow; to the confessed humiliation of slavery to low desires, to the free joy of vanquished temptation; to the 'beauty,' the 'glory,' the harmony, of an obedient soul, and its repose in communion with God. With the instinctive tact of a pure and fine nature, he here passes at once away from the logical resources of the mind to the true dynamics of character; and exemplifies the very distinction which in form his theory denies.

Perhaps the defect of the Dianoetic School of Ethics is due to the unanalysed condition in which they left the conception of *voluntary action*, i.e. of the *object* of ethical judgment. They contemplate it, for all the purposes of their theory, as an integral fact, in which, as a single thing, a certain quality, of right or wrong, is perceived. As there is not always agreement in assigning these epithets, and the applications of them admit of being justified by argument, their allotment was naturally attributed to reason. So long as the quality of rightness was left somewhat indeterminate, this account might pass without serious challenge. But as soon as rightness was insisted on as an absolutely simple quality, intuitively apprehended by Reason, it became impossible to understand how its presence in a given act could be affirmed by one person and denied by another; and how, without any complex contents admitting of comparison, it could ever be reasoned about between two opponents. The rational faculty had got the credit of it on precisely the ground that was now taken from it, viz. that it could be the subject of argument among persons seeking the truth about it, but not yet agreed: this was exactly the process of which the *intuitive* reason did not admit. The difficulty which thus arises, of reconciling discrepancies of ethical judgment with intuitive certainty, no writer of the school has been able to overcome. It can never vanish till you fix separate attention upon the springs of action in the mind, and the operation of action when put forth; of the former the (relative) quality is known by intuition; of the latter by calculation. The total character of the action is composed of both, its rectitude depending upon the first, its wisdom upon the second; in the one aspect it is amenable to conscience; in the other, to reason; neither of which can perform the function of the other.

BRANCH III.

ÆSTHETIC ETHICS.

CONDUCT, as an object of contemplation, touches so many varieties of feeling that it is no wonder if each in turn has claimed to be its principal function and to lie closest to its essence. It may commend itself as happy for the agent; as rationally adapted to its scene of things; as useful for the world; as beautiful or majestic; and our sentiment towards it may be supposed to come from interest, from reason, from good will, or from good taste. We have seen how from the first of these the School of Hobbes evolves the moral characteristics, and that of Cudworth from the second; and it might be expected that each of the other two would similarly find its separate champion, one identifying right with benevolent affection, and the other with the χαρίεν and καλόν,—with what is charming and lovely in temper and action. It so happens that both these principles have committed their cause to the same advocates, who plead, with apparent unconsciousness of change, now in terms of the one, and then in those of the other, and seem to blend them in thought, much as the Greeks melted the καλὸν κἀγαθὸν into one conception and almost into one word. Hence it is difficult to designate with precision the writers who remain for review, Shaftesbury and Hutcheson. Whether the term which they emphasise is the *Moral Sense*, or *Disinterested Affection*, they seek their key to the judgments of conscience in some form of inward emotion, and not in the mind's submission to the truth of external things; so that the Right is not, as with the previous School, felt because it is known, but known because it is somehow felt. To this new turn of thought we certainly owe a vast accession of fine psychological observation, and subtle analyses of human manners and character. The change from Hobbes to Hutcheson is little less than from Rabelais to George Eliot.

CHAPTER I.

SHAFTESBURY.

§ 1. *Life, Personality, and Writings.*

The initiative in this new movement of ethical doctrine was taken, not by any professed philosopher, but by a man of letters, who purposely avoided the formal divisions and pedantic manner of the Schools, and sought an audience from the wider public to whom the play of fancy and the ease of style are not indifferent. Anthony Ashley Cooper, born February 26, 1671, at Exeter House, London, was grandson of the first Earl of Shaftesbury, to whom England owes its Habeas Corpus Act, and who atoned for his share in the restoration of Charles II. by his part in excluding James II. The boy, for reasons of family convenience, was thrown upon his grandfather's care, and educated at his house in Dorsetshire under the directions of John Locke; as we learn from an autobiographical letter (February, 1705) to Leclerc, found thirty or forty years ago in the Remonstrant Library at Amsterdam[1]. His acquisition of Latin and Greek was made, as tradition reports, under the tuition of a learned lady, Miss Birch, who, being a fluent speaker in both languages, taught him in great measure through the ear, and with such success that, at eleven years of age, he easily read authors in either tongue. An equal proficiency in French and Italian, which he spoke perfectly, he owed to a miserable episode in his life at Winchester School. Sent thither at twelve years of age, he found himself in the midst of Jacobite school-fellows, imbued with loyal hatred of his grandfather's name (who had just died in

[1] Published in Notes and Queries, Vol. III. p. 97, seqq.

exile in Holland). They so persecuted him that he had to be removed. He was sent with a tutor to travel on the Continent, where he devoted some years to the study of art in the Italian cities, and formed his literary taste upon foreign models. On his return in 1689, the political relations, reversed by the Revolution, favoured his entrance upon public life and the service of William; but though he had strong convictions in favour of the new constitutional order, he declined a seat in Parliament till 1694; and, finding his health giving way under the long sittings of the House, did not seek re-election after the dissolution. A characteristic anecdote is related of an early attempt to address the House. A bill was brought in to allow counsel to persons on trial for high treason. Feeling a lively interest in it, he prepared himself to speak in its support; but had scarcely begun, ere he let slip the thread of thought, and was unable to proceed; and after a fruitless pause, voices all round him called on him to sit down. He obeyed them, but in doing so said, 'If I, who have only to give my opinion on this bill, am disabled by confusion from the feeblest utterance of what I would say, what must be the position of the man who, with none to aid him, has to plead for his life?' This happy turn at once covered his personal retreat, and, for his object, was probably not less persuasive than the lost speech.

Restored to the freedom of private life, he went in 1698 to Holland, attracted apparently by the liberal theology of Leclerc, and even the sceptical tendencies of Bayle; preserving his incognito, in order to cultivate an unembarrassed friendship. His father's death, however, within a year, devolving the earldom on him, revealed his secret; with so seasonable an increase of influence that he was able, before his return home, to prevent the banishment of Bayle from the United Provinces. On his return to London he was annoyed to find published, without his knowledge, an essay, written when he was twenty years of age, and permitted to circulate among a few private friends, under the title 'Enquiry concerning Virtue and Merit.' In a fit of indiscreet zeal, Toland, who admired the essay and the man, had taken this unwarrantable liberty; not only leaving its crudeness of conception and faults of style uncorrected, but adding to them others of his own. It was not till it reappeared in the three volumes of collected writings, published in 1711 under the name 'Characteristics,' that this essay received the author's corrections, and could be fairly quoted in evidence of his opinions. It is by far the most important of his productions, as an exposition of his moral theory.

Though, on his accession to the peerage, he still kept aloof from official life, his advice was often sought by the king, and his vote, on critical occasions, always ready for his ministers. The foreign policy of William, constructed from a continental rather than an English point of view, had involved engagements and expenses which had long made him unpopular, and when, on the eve of the Spanish king's (Charles II.) demise without natural successor, he proposed, in order to adjust by compromise the rival pretensions of the Emperor, of France, and of Bavaria, and twice carried to the point of acceptance, treaties for the partition of the inheritance, the national repugnance was strongly declared; the more so when it appeared that the dying monarch's government had never been consulted, and that, to resent this insult and secure the integrity of his dominions, he had bequeathed them all to the French competitor, the Duke of Anjou, grandson of Louis XIV. This, however, was not known till the death of Charles brought his will to light in November, 1701. Two months before, William had busied himself with forming a triple alliance, of England, Holland, and the Emperor, for enforcement of the recent treaty of partition; and, to give it effect, he needed the sanction of Parliament. This was not easy to obtain; for the election of the previous February had returned a Tory majority, hostile to the measures of the king; and the feeling of the Upper House was increasingly doubtful. Somers, the minister, found it necessary to beat up for support; and he despatched a courier to inform Shaftesbury, then in Somersetshire, of his anxiety. By an extraordinary effort of speed, the earl appeared in the House next day, and took a prominent part in the debate, remaining in town to support the tottering ministry. In November came a new turn of affairs; Louis XIV. on learning his grandson's interest in the Spanish king's will, renounced the partition treaty, and by his attitude justified William's fears, of the virtual union of France and the Peninsula. Shaftesbury advised that, while this impression was fresh, an appeal to the constituencies should be made; and when the new Parliament, which met in December, proved to have a ministerial majority, it was to his efforts chiefly that the king attributed the reversed position of parties. The victory was transient. The accession of Anne, two months later, brought, as is well known, a Tory reaction. Displaced from his Lord Lieutenancy of Dorsetshire, Shaftesbury was set free for his more congenial life of study, which he never again quitted. Early in 1703 he paid another visit of some twenty months to Holland; but, with that exception, remained in his English retirement, till driven to a milder climate by the last failure of his health. Most of his writings were produced in the interval In 1708, the fanatics, called the Prophets of Cevennes, producing popular disturbances by their missionaries in England, an outcry was raised for repressive laws against them. True to his principles of toleration, learned from Locke, Shaftesbury protested against such proposals in a 'Letter on Enthusiasm,' addressed to Somers, the President of the Council; and whilst he urged the graver reasons for letting the missionaries alone, he treated their teachings and pretensions with such happy ridicule, that the whole movement speedily disappeared from the scene. The next year, appeared 'The Moralists, a Philosophical Rhapsody,' called so as an apology for its discursiveness, which, however, in the free movement natural to dialogue, does not seriously disturb the reader; and then, 'Sensus Communis, or Essay on the Freedom of Wit and Humour,' in which he vindicates his celebrated paradox that 'Raillery,' or ridicule, is 'the Test of Truth,' and himself applies it, by way of example, to the philosophy of 'Selfishness' as propounded by Hobbes, and embodied in the writings of Montaigne and Rochefoucauld. In 1710, followed his 'Soliloquy, or Advice to an Author;' the double title denoting that the advice is *to himself.* The essay contains a body of reflections, often very searching and impressive, on the self-deceptions and disguises which deform the truth of things in life, in literature, and in philosophy, and beneath which it is the business of honest authorship to pierce. This closes the series of his more considerable writings; the minor pieces which form the third volume of his collected works need not be separately specified.

Shaftesbury would seem to have laid out for himself too studious a life to be compatible in his estimation with the claims of a married man of rank; and it was with some reluctance that he yielded at last to the remonstrances of friends, and in 1709 wedded his cousin, Jane Ewer, who became the mother of the fourth earl, an only child. The marriage does not appear to have been sufficiently happy to effect the husband's complete conversion. With an exceptional temperament and a contemplative turn of mind, he had probably judged better for himself than his friends for him. In 1711, a serious failure of health drove him once more to Italy: at Naples he rallied sufficiently to busy himself with revising and completing his writings, first issued in that year under their collective title of 'Characteristics of Men, Manners, Opinions, Times,' though in the later editions augmented by some supplementary matter, and reaching their final form in 1732. This, however, he did not live to see. After a year's reprieve since his departure from England, his strength finally collapsed, and he died at Naples, February 4, 1713. Three years after his death appeared some letters of his, addressed in

1707-8 to a divinity student named Ainsworth, under the title 'Letters written by a Nobleman to a Young Man at the University;' and in 1721, some 'Letters to Lord Molesworth' were edited by Toland. He was generally regarded by contemporary critics as an insidious enemy of the Christian religion, and is placed by Leland among the English Deists. Yet his more intellectual opponents could not deny his personal and literary merits; even the unsparing Warburton confessing that he had many excellent qualities as a man and as a writer. 'He was temperate, chaste, honest, and a lover of his country. In his writings he has shown how much he has imbibed the deep sense and how naturally he could copy the gracious manner of Plato.' This Platonic strain in his genius withdrew him into a philosophical direction divergent from that of his mentor, Locke; but never touched his loyalty on the moral side; through life his guiding affections remained, the love of freedom and the love of truth.

§ 2. *Sketch of his Doctrine.*

It might be supposed (Shaftesbury remarks), that in Christendom no room was left for the existence of a Moral Philosophy, all its problems being included and answered in the Divine teachings of the Church. But the interfusion of religion and virtue is not in fact so close as to secure their habitual coexistence. It is by no means uncommon to meet with enthusiastic devotion in persons whose word, whose temper, whose self-control you cannot trust; and, on the other hand, with men of inflexible honour, benevolence, and magnanimity, who seem impenetrable by religious appeal. Hence it is clear, that there must be a distinct provision for *character* in human nature, without passing through the intermediate steps of any theology: and, if so, this provision is an independent object of rational study, which cannot fail to benefit, in the end, the religion from which it detaches itself at the beginning; because it must bring out into clear light the real relation between the two, instead of presuming a false one.

Having thus vindicated the rights of his 'Enquiry,' Shaftesbury approaches it, as might be expected, from the heathen rather than the Christian side; starting, that is, from the conception, not of *Duty*, but of *Good*. Good is entirely relative to *function* and its needs, and could never be predicated of the purely statical conditions of the world. It enters wherever there is a being with a living nature, and denotes that which satisfies the wants of that nature, and enables it to fulfil its *ends*. Whatever does this is the private good of that particular being; but if the result is reached not without balking some other nature of its proper functional achievements, it is only a partial good, and may be a preponderant evil. And conversely, if that which disappoints the function of an individual fulfils thereby that of a larger and embracing nature, the relative evil is an absolute good. Thus explained, good is not identical with pleasure, and, if attended by it, is so because it must be always pleasant for an instinct to succeed: it is the supply of a need, the attainment of an end; and the need and the end are given in the nature, before there is any knowledge of the sensations in which they terminate, before therefore they can be the object of desire. This conception agrees essentially with the Hegelian *summum bonum* of *self-realisation*, the perfect and proportioned accomplishment by each nature of its own ends. The idea conducts Shaftesbury, by an easy extension, to a doctrine of optimism. We are fair judges, he says, of such good as is measured by the constitution of a particular being wherewith we are familiar; and if he were isolated, this would be the total matter for judgment. But each single being belongs to a kind; and each kind to a hierarchy of living natures; and every planet that holds them, to a solar group; serving in turn as a mere member of some constellation, flung as a spurt of spray from the stellar ocean: and throughout this system within system, the tissue of interdependence is so close, that no single function ever fails but by the working out of some other, so that good which sinks away at one point emerges at another, and the whole suffers no abatement by the local defalcation. The comparison of alternative universes is a task entirely transcending our competency; but the unity of nature and the relativity of good, the fact that what is evil here is not evil there, warrants the belief that the world's order is as good on the whole as it could be, and that no real ill has place in it, to mar its perfection.

Good is something that we may *have*. *Goodness* marks something that we may *be :* an attribute, not an adjunct, of ourselves. The former is relative exclusively to our own wants, and would remain to a lonely organism: the latter is prevailingly measured by the wants of others, which our nature is fitted to supply. A man is said to be good, when, instead of being absorbed in self-regarding ends, he is disposed to serve the needs of his fellows, and take his place in the partnership of humanity. It is true we apply the epithet, beyond the limits of our own race, to any object that has an end and answers it: we speak of a good horse, a good pear tree, a good sewing-machine; but these things would hardly earn the term, did they not, in fulfilling their own idea, go out beyond themselves and satisfy some need of ours. A creature, to be good, must have its extra-regarding functions in working order. Moreover, it is not enough, in the case of a being with instincts and dispositions, that he shall minister, by accident or force, to human wants: even a flock of sheep we should hardly call good, merely in contemplation of their making good mutton; we reserve the epithet for the spontaneous action of the nature; and shall not give it unless, instead of extorting what we want by coercion of fear, we can depend for it on the instinctive play of temper and feeling.

This advance, however, does not yet bring us to anything which can be called *virtue*. The 'goodness' of which we have spoken looks indeed very like it, when exemplified in a man whose affections are so harmonised as to be perfect instruments of public good; but were it possible for them to be so by natural temperament alone, without reflection or conscious preference on his part, his goodness would be indistinguishable, except in its higher field of display, from that of the shepherd's dog in performing his marvels of vigilance, energy, and apparent duty. What, then, is still needed to plant us upon *moral* ground? Goodness refers to something that we *are;* *virtue*, to something which we *will;* that is, which issues from us, not as an impulsive spontaneity, but as the expression of *choice*. It is only in a reflective nature that this condition can be fulfilled; for the choice has to be made between alternative wants or soliciting inducements; and it needs a mind self-conscious of its own affections and capable of comparing them, to make election among them according to their claims. These are in truth the only 'moral objects,' and man has *character*, because he can and must think of these as 'foul or fair, harmonious or discordant, sublime and beautiful:' that he cannot help 'taking sides' with or against them is the elementary form of his 'sense of right and wrong.' It is the spring of voluntary action which alone qualifies it for approval or reprobation, and not its effect, be it of unintended benefit or mischief, or of frustrated good. And 'virtue consists of proportionable affection of a rational creature towards moral objects,' so defined.

Shaftesbury's 'Enquiry' is concerning 'Merit' as well as 'Virtue;' and he plainly sees that they are not the same; nay, that there is even a paradoxical contrariety between them, which makes them vary inversely as each other. Virtue culminates in the perfect accord between the strength of the several springs of action and their worth,—a condition under which the right choice is the easiest choice, having no reluctance to overcome. Merit is shown in resolute surrender to the worthier solicitation against the vehement resistance of some lower impulse; it is born of difficulty, and is measured by it; and every increment of that difficulty is an equal decrement of virtue, attesting the disproportion between the intensity and the worth of the inward affections; so that the merit would seem greatest where the virtue is least. I have before explained how Mr. Leslie Stephen avails himself of this consequence to escape, as every determinist must, from the idea of merit, and to make the word mean, if not the very same as virtue, at least its marketable value on the Exchange of human life, that is, what men will give for it; the relation between them being the same as that of '*price* to *utility*.' Shaftesbury sees nothing to frighten him in the alleged paradox, and disenchants it by a very simple exorcism. Virtue is harmony won; Merit is the winning of it: the former is a ratified peace; the latter, the conflict whence it results. Were there no strife of inward propensity, were all the affections in the best order to begin with, virtue would be perfect on the same terms on which a Venus or an Apollo would be beautiful, and would itself be first to feel that it deserved nothing. But it is not given to the human nature to stroll into its perfection on such a quiet track; its springs of action do not spontaneously fall into tune, but have to be reduced into accord by a will that knows the scale of right; and where the discord is loud and strong, the will, in accomplishing its task, will be put to a severer strain, and give evidence of a more resolute intent and power, than where the false intervals are few and small. It is not that the faulty passion confers the merit; but that the high courage of its enemy and conqueror earns it. 'If,' says Shaftesbury, 'there be any part of the temper in which ill passions or affections are seated, whilst in another part the affections towards moral good are such as absolutely to master those attempts of their antagonists; this is the greatest proof imaginable, that a strong principle of virtue lies at the bottom, and has possessed itself of the natural temper. Whereas, if there be no ill passions stirring, a person may be indeed more *cheaply virtuous;* that is to say, he may conform himself to the known rules of virtue, without sharing so much of a virtuous principle as another. Yet if that other person, who has the principle of virtue so strongly implanted, comes at last to lose those contrary impediments supposed in him, he certainly loses nothing in *virtue;* but on the contrary, losing only what is vicious in his temper, is left more entire to virtue, and possesses it in a higher degree[1].'

If we press upon Shaftesbury the psychological question, how we come to be 'proportionably affected' towards our several springs of action, that is, what kind of faculty it is to which we owe this capacity for 'virtue,' we shall not draw from him any very exact reply. That it is by *some* natural insight or intuitive appreciation, he consistently assures us; but the language he applies to it seems at times to bring it under other sorts of judgment, now of *truth,* and then of *beauty;* yet again, to separate it as a *special function,* concerned with the elements of character alone. Thus, he says that, if you add *Reason* to a creature previously the subject of affections only, he will immediately obtain 'the sense of right and wrong,' approving on the instant gratitude, kindness, and pity; and be taken with any show or representation of social passion, and think nothing more amiable than this[2].' Here we could fancy ourselves listening to the voice of Price, expounding his 'Rational' Ethics. Elsewhere, *Beauty* takes the lead: 'What is *beautiful,*' he says, 'is *harmonious and proportionable;* what is harmonious and proportionable is *true;* and what is at once beautiful and true, is, of consequence, agreeable and good[3].' And again he says, 'No sooner are actions viewed, no sooner the human affections and passions discerned (and they are most of them discerned as soon as felt), than straight an inward eye distinguishes, and sees the fair and shapely, the amiable, the admirable, apart from the deformed, the foul, the odious, or the despicable. How is it possible then not to own, that as these distinctions have their foundation in nature, the discernment itself is natural and from nature alone[4]?'

---

[1] Enquiry, pp. 37, 38. [3] Miscellaneous Reflections, Vol. III. p. 183.
[2] Ibid. II. p. 53. [4] The Moralists, II. pp. 414, 415.

'There is no real good beside the enjoyment of beauty[1].' But he emerges from the rational and æsthetic relations of character, into an independent moral sphere, wherever he predicates and measures the *merit* of conduct, and strips its demerits of their false excuses, and insists upon the reality of *Duty*, and the justice of penal suffering. We can only say, therefore, that the three conceptions, the true, the beautiful, the good, were blended in his idea of the right; and that their precise relations to each other are left undetermined. The only approach to a definite distinction among them is found in his separation of a developed moral *Taste* or *Tact*, formed by education and social culture, from the original intuitive feeling of differences in the worth of the affections, which constitutes the natural susceptibility for such culture. The delicacy of the moral sense upon this side admits of no less indefinite increase than the perceptions of excellence in the fine arts. Taking the writings of our author as a whole, we cannot justly affirm that he merges the ἀγαθόν in the καλόν; but the increasing tendency in his later essays to accentuate the æsthetic aspect of morals is very observable.

As no one can help having the apprehension of right and wrong, so as to know the one as praiseworthy, the other as blameworthy; and as that apprehension consists in a 'proportionable' approval or disapproval of the springs of action, how is it that the moral sense is ever suppressed and shows no trace? Shaftesbury bravely replies, it never is destroyed; the secret homage is still in the heart of its most audacious blasphemers; but, under the tyranny of rebellious passions, they have lost their *liking* for what they know to be the better, their *antipathy* for the worse; so they contradict in act their inward thought, till it withdraws and openly remonstrates no more. It waits, however, within call, and will come back at the slightest hint; the most depraved offender cries out for justice, when the wrong falls upon himself; and the dissolute father does not wish his son to be the same.

[1] The Moralists, II. p. 422.

He who sinks the lowest is not wholly evil; some touch of honour or of pity will be found in natures prevailingly corrupt; and if a note or two upon the scale remains true, there is a standard base from which the spoiled proportions may be restored. The chief seductions which triumph over the sense of right come from the instincts referring to private good; their power lies in the illusion that, when we are not seeking something for ourselves, we are losing something, and that for all the love we give to others we are poorer at home; whereas the impulses of the private passions inflict upon our self-interest losses quite as great as are incurred by the sacrifices of benevolence. This fine remark is usually credited to Butler, and may very probably be original with him; but it is interesting to find it already in Shaftesbury's earliest essay.

The perversions of the moral sense through superstition are so revolting to our author, especially the cruelties of persecution, that he cannot extend to them his patience with involuntary ignorance and invincible delusion, but sets them down, under the head of 'monstrous opinions,' as chargeable with inexcusable crimes. He would hardly have formed this judgment, if he had looked at the religion of a people rather as determined by their moral stage of conception, than as determining it, so that what the religion required could not be what the conscience failed to suggest. He took up the problem with the opposite preconception; supposing that the intuitive appreciation of moral differences was already there, so that the mind knew the gradations of its duty; and that then came the assailing superstition to beguile the passions, and drug the reason, and sophisticate the conscience, and play in every way the part of active corruption. He might well say that if an agent, with such a fine outfit of faculty to begin with, did not defy the wretched arts of such a tempter, he had no excuse for his sin. The operation of Atheism and of Theism on character are estimated in the same way, as an influence superinduced on a prior moral constitution. The former doctrine, as a mere blank, might be supposed to be ethically neutral, having nothing to say to the naked human facts In reality, however, it is not without effect; by limiting those moral facts to the small human scale and shutting them up within the mere personal experience, it dwarfs their importance; it teaches that there is no beauty or perfection in the universal system of things, and nothing better to be expected in the future; and in a scheme of thought upon this level it is vain to trust for any enthusiasm of virtue. Theism, on the other hand, involving faith in an order just and good, administered by an ever-living and righteous will, gives powerful support to constancy and patience, and breathes into virtue the inspiration of piety. It is in this sublime justification of the moral affections, the consciousness of an infinite and eternal sympathy with them, that the elevating influence of religion consists; and not in the fears and hopes of recompense, or the indulgence to the love of life through anticipation of its renewal; so far as these conceptions avail with the conscience, it is as essential elements of an ideal righteousness, and not as an appeal to personal interests.

So far Shaftesbury takes pains to frame a theory of right and wrong truly independent, and owing nothing to the reckoning of personal pleasures and pains; and if we went no further, we should suppose the virtue which he has been describing to be binding on its own account, and to need no credentials for its imperative authority. It is not without surprise that, at the opening of his second book, we find him asking, 'What obligation is there to virtue? what reason to embrace it?' and thinking it necessary, by way of answer, to show that to be virtuous is to be happy, to be wicked is to be miserable. Thus to back up obligation by interest, and treat it as holding its commission from the balance of profit, is a downward step from his own level to the platform of hedonism; and I do not see how it can be defended. That the inconsistency escaped his notice is due probably to the distinction which (as explained above) he drew between *pleasure* and *good*; he *meant* perhaps to show that in man virtue was the greatest possible self-realisation; vice, on the other hand, self-contradiction; and this proposition he might have worked out, without identifying the 'self' with its sensitive experience. But, in point of fact, his proof is conducted with constant reference to the test of *enjoyment and suffering;* so that there is little to remind the reader that the line of argument does not proceed from a pure Utilitarian hedonist. He admits, as Stuart Mill does, that wrong-doing to others may often be outwardly gainful to one's self; but insists that, when the inward relations of character are taken into account, it can never be said, of one who has done ill, 'He is none the worse for it.' It is accordingly upon the internal history of the affections themselves that he throws the stress of his proof, that virtue and happiness coincide.

He groups the springs of action in three sets: (1) Natural affections towards the good of others; (2) Natural affections towards one's own good; both of which admit of being either right or wrong; and (3) Unnatural affections towards no good at all; which can never be anything but wrong. The others have all of them a legitimate function, so that in themselves they are right enough; and when any one of them goes wrong, it is by becoming relatively too strong,—a fact which might be equally well expressed by saying that its opposite is too weak; such excess or defect being unnatural, because by nature (that is, the true idea of the human constitution) there is a given right proportion among the several affections; the test of rightness being the economy of social welfare. The mind or character of a man or a society is a composite system for a concordant end, like a musical instrument, which is spoiled for its performance if even one or two of its strings should have a tension too great or too small for the pitch of the rest. Disturbances of character, that is vices, arise from (1) the public affections being too weak; (2) the private being too strong; (3) the presence of unnatural affections that tend to no good at all. To be in the first of these conditions is to forfeit the chief source of enjoyment; to be in the second is to court unhappiness; and to be in the third is utmost misery.

It is needless to recite, at any length, the evidence adduced by Shaftesbury in support of these propositions. Its strength and main feature, so far as the first two are concerned, centres in the simple truth, that the natural affections themselves, especially the disinterested affections, *are* the happiness of life; or else, where not absolutely identical with it, are essential co-partners in its causation. Not even are bodily pleasures, or the enjoyments of possession, worth much, unless redeemed from the shame of lonely appetite by social joy and generous use: unshared prosperity palls and pines, and carries no blessing in it; avarice weighs on the breast as a perpetual load of care; luxury and sloth multiply artificial wants, and cancel the faculties that could satisfy them; and the hopes of emulation and ambition are overbalanced by envious disappointment. On the other hand, in the life of the mind there is no joy that is not born of some enthusiasm which withdraws it from sensible things, or teaches it to see through them to a higher light within. The intellectual delight of the mathematician in the relations he investigates lifts him into a tranquil air above the zone of passionate disturbance. And the impulses that take us out of ourselves,—gratitude, love, generosity,—are doubly blest; being, in their very essence, all that we *mean* by happiness in its own exuberance; and being also the *cause* of pleasure reflected back upon us from the hearts which we brighten, and prolonged in the memory of a conscience innocent of neglect or wrong. In solitude or in society the secret of a sweet and easy temper is in self-forgetfulness and open sympathy; the absence of which soon marks itself by a tinge of harshness and gloom, and by the want of inward elasticity to bear up against bodily ills and external disturbance. Nay, the sustaining power of religion itself lies in the affections of trust and venerating love towards a Guardian infinitely good

In order to yield these results, however, it is indispensable that the springs of action be rightly balanced, so that each may gain its proper object, and usurp no place that is another's due. It is the standing illusion of the self-seeking impulses to believe that they are the best providers for the good of self; and under this hallucination they thrust themselves into innumerable counsels which they bring to ruin. If they only knew it, they are really the very worst caterers for the personal well-being, and, by their eagerness to get the most, reduce life to the verge of bankruptcy in joy. Whatever is sour and gloomy and spiteful and hollow and suspicious in human society, arises from the wrongful ascendency of the self-seeking passions; and how grave and how superfluous is the disturbance it involves, is obvious at once when you stand in presence of one who breathes a different air, and shows the cheerful calm, the patient disengagement, the pure simplicity of a modest, loving, and religious soul. The affections of such a soul are in themselves the perfection of peace; unlike the malevolent passions, whose very satisfaction is nothing but relief to a misery, they have a happy energy in their aims, as well as a crowning exultation in their achievement.

Of Shaftesbury's third class,—'the unnatural affections' (exemplified by 'inhuman delight in beholding torments,' 'wanton mischievousness,' 'misanthropy'),— it is the less necessary to speak, because a remark which he makes respecting two of them, viz. *tyrannous and vindictive arrogance*, and *treachery*, is applicable to the whole; that is, that they are mere exaggerations of the natural passions; and the miseries in which they not only live and move, but absolutely consist, are referable to the violated proportions admitted among the springs of action. Certain it is that to hate, to envy, to despise, to see nothing but the ugly and the evil, and spend life in barricading oneself against them, is a condition as wretched as that of a prisoner left with no choice, but to help himself to poisoned viands or to starve.

Such is the course of argument by which Shaftesbury seeks to reconcile self-interest and social. His treatment of it abounds with fine observation and just reflection. The two points which should be specially watched in their bearing upon his general theory are,—whether his optimist conclusion is fully sustained by the evidence adduced; and what is its logical connection with the existence of moral obligation.

§ 3. *Appreciation of the Doctrine.*

In passing from the representatives of the 'Dianoetic Ethics' to Shaftesbury, the reader soon becomes aware of one pervading change. They are chiefly intent on finding what they want in '*the nature of things:*' he, in '*the nature of man.*' The distinction of right and wrong they will not suffer to be blotted out from reality and relegated to the sphere of phenomena: he will protect it from being slurred in human consciousness and denied its unquestioned place there. Their favourite affirmation is accordingly transcendental, of the eternal and immutable character of moral differences, irrespective of our being and of all worlds: whilst he rarely ventures so far upon the wing, and is content to claim for these differences a fundamental seat in our inward experience. The parallel so frequent in the writings of Cudworth and Clarke, between mathematical and moral relations, in their absolute necessity in themselves and their *à priori* validity for all intelligence, might well have induced us to consider their doctrines among the systems of Metaphysical Ethics; were it not that, from their ontological commencement, they transfer themselves so freely to the faculty in us which apprehends it, and deal so largely with the interior history of its reflection there, that there is more to say of their psychology, secondary though it is, than of its prototypes in real being. Respecting Shaftesbury no such doubt could ever be raised. He lives and moves on the plane of human life: his only question is, what do we think and feel,—all accidental variations aside,—about right and wrong; and what, from this indication, must we suppose they really are? For, be it observed, he did not intend, in looking first at the representation within the mind, to question their reality and treat them as mere subjective affairs: on the contrary, he conceived that such as we apprehend them to be, such they are, i.e. cannot but be to every mind capable of discerning the relations to which they refer. Only, this objective belief he held as an *assumption*, guaranteed simply by the *good faith of our own faculties;* apart from which he did not pretend to verify it, by any independent application of the intellect to the necessary relations of things. The ethical Realism which is Cudworth's starting-point is Shaftesbury's goal: while the psychology which is the sequel with the former, is the antecedent with the latter.

Of his ethical psychology a fair estimate can hardly be formed, without first clearing away some misleading conceptions of it, which have obtained currency through writings better known than his own. For those who know him only at second-hand it is hardly possible to escape the impression, that he explains away the authority of moral conviction, by resolving it into some unauthoritative experience or idea, for this is the common assumption of his principal critics, though they give by no means the same account of the type of unmoral feeling in which he swallows up the independence of conscience.

I have already hinted at the prejudice which his use of the word '*Sense*' in combination with the epithet '*Moral*' excited in the mind of Price; to whom it meant, only and always, some passively received pleasure or pain, leaving behind it a liking or disliking, operative no doubt as a motive for the future, but a motive of mere self-interest. Under the influence of this interpretation, Price protests against degrading the apprehension of Right into a '*relish*,' and reducing the interval between the highest virtue and the deepest depravity to a matter of taste; so that the most shameless criminal would differ from a Marcus Aurelius or an Alfred the Great, only as the carnivorous quadruped that tears his meat raw differs from the fastidious biped who prefers it cooked. It is impossible to carry this narrow conception of the word *Sense* into Shaftesbury's writings, without missing the purport of his whole doctrine. It denotes, no doubt, *feeling* of which we are susceptible: far, however, from a simply passive state, terminating in itself, like the pain of toothache or the pleasure of repletion; on the contrary, carrying in it, under the intuition of right, a relation to the understanding, and, under the special emotion of approval, a mandate to the will. The term is meant to be inclusive of these cognitive and imperative elements, and not exclusive, as Price's criticism assumes; and notice of this inclusion seems sufficiently given by prefixing the epithet *Moral*, which at once lifts the word *Sense* out of the limits of its first animal significance.

Nor can we permit the mere æsthetic interpreters of life to carry off Shaftesbury into their camp, on the plea that he regarded morals as only one of the fine arts, and virtue as no more than the supreme accomplishment. No doubt, it is easy to quote from him many detached sentences which are open to this construction; as when he bids you pursue the beautiful, and then the good will come of itself; and says, that virtue is moral beauty, and that the knowledge of beauty is the discipline of virtue. And it must be admitted that his own high artistic perception and culture blended too closely in himself the distinct though allied feelings of *approbation* and of *admiration*,—one of the many marks of an ethical commencement from the idea, not of Duty, but of Good. But still, these partial indications must accept the limitations which are clearly imposed upon them by other and more exact statements of his doctrine; and when this is done, he will be found to say, that the right indeed is always beautiful, but not that it is the beautiful which constitutes the right.

Freely as Shaftesbury draws upon the vocabulary of the senses and the imagination in speaking of conduct and disposition, his theory plainly saves its distinctively *moral* character by two of its essential features. (1) It asserts the intuitive and universal apprehension of right and wrong, with the inherent knowledge of obligation and warning against guilt; and treats this throughout, not as possibly a freak of sensibility, but as an absolutely trustworthy insight. Of no 'relish' or 'liking,' of no 'grace' or 'beauty,' could any such predicate be affirmed; nor could their disappointment or failure incur the shame and remorse which he recognises as the equally necessary award to wrong. Nay he expressly distinguishes the *inward approval* of the right course from the impulsive 'liking' for it, and makes declension of character consist in a breach between them; the approval remaining ineradicable and constant, while the liking dies away or goes over to the once hated opposite[1]. It is impossible in plainer terms to exempt the moral scale, as binding and steadfast for all minds, from the contingencies and variations of the individual subject. (2) Our author's treatment of the doctrine of *Merit* frankly adopts as veracious the consciousness of personal freedom and responsibility, and establishes rules, for measuring the degrees of ill-desert, which else would have no meaning. He has no non-natural sense to put upon this group of words, that they may keep their place to the eye and ear and seem still to speak of a '*Duty*' which has been struck out from their contents.

As Shaftesbury thus has an undoubted place among genuine Moralists, so does he find support for his theory in some firm points of psychological observation. (1) He perceives that, to reach the moral quality of conduct, you must go behind the overt action to the prompting affection; and that the interior springs are the sole objects of ethical judgment. (2) He discerns among them an order to which a 'proportionable affection' is due. (3) This order he regards as intuitively known, as soon as reflection is turned upon the several springs of action. These points are not indeed brought into strong light, or combined into any connected scheme; but, as detached glimpses of truth, not the less rich in promise from their simplicity, they appear

[1] Enquiry, p. 43.

to me remarkable; especially in their contrast with the artificial equivalents, which the analytical school of Hobbes has largely substituted for the real facts of inward experience.

These truths, however, were not so firmly held and closely followed out as to secure the cohesion of an enduring structure. The idea of *obligation*, in the form of an ultimate authority, intuitively known, after being affirmed and justified, is again lost: the question being raised, 'What underlies this bottom of all?' 'where are the credentials of this power which legitimates itself?' If it is disappointing to find this question asked, it is still more so to hear the answer, viz. that what binds us to the right is the balance of personal happiness it brings us;—an answer at which the independent base of virtue suddenly caves in, and the goodly pile that seemed immovable is shifted on to the sands of hedonism. If, in order to be obligatory, action must be pleasantest, what can be meant by saying that the apprehension of obligation is intuitive? It must mean, either that we prophetically know what will be pleasantest, before trying or reckoning, and so feel bound, as a matter of self-interest, to take it; or, that the first idea of the voluntary act is attained by a feeling *sui generis*, that we have to do it, come what may; and that then this feeling proves, in point of fact, a correct guide to the balance of pleasure, of which we never thought at all, but which is in reality the key to the whole process. The latter of these interpretations keeps the consciousness of obligation, without the reality; the former dismisses both; so that Duty is struck off from life and thought, unless indeed its illusory image is danced before our mind to cheat us for our good, and please us better than our own self-love.

In consequence of this apparent forgetfulness of his own prior positions, Shaftesbury's second part of his 'Enquiry' seems to belong to a different system from the first. It would hardly be out of place as an Appendix to J. S. Mill's 'Utilitarianism,' and would not have been denied by him the praise of a very striking defence of the harmony between individual and social happiness. For the hedonist Utilitarian it is of the utmost moment to prove this harmony: when once he has owned that nothing becomes a duty unless it be on the whole a pleasure, he has staked the entire code of character and life on the coincidence of its requirements with self-interest; and the links of his logic in demonstrating that thesis form his only chain for controlling the impulses of private passion. But the intuitive or independent moralist has no such interest in this theme. However glad he may be to back up his enforcement of duty by subsidiary pleas of prudence, he is not pledged to produce them, still less to find them adequate to his whole case: nor would he feel embarrassed and have to change his voice, if confronted by a plain instance of some higher good demanding from the individual will the utmost price of 'stripes, torture, and death.' Be the world constructed as it may,—so as always to give the advantage to the nobler character, or often to lay it open to the keener anguish,—it makes no difference of Duty to those who trust the insight of Conscience rather than the reckonings of sensibility. And yet, strange to say, the best defence of the invariable eudæmony of virtue proceeds from Shaftesbury, to whom it was superfluous; and the frankest denial of it from Mr. Leslie Stephen, to whom it is essential.

The explanation of this paradoxical fact is to be found outside the limits of these authors' ethical theory. As a support to their ideas of obligation, the promise of a maximum of personal felicity to public virtue is indifferent in the one case, while it is indispensable in the other. But as an element in their conceptions of the general system of the world, this question, of the incidence of happiness with or without regard to character, occupies a very different position. The devotee of Duty, who puts an ultimate trust in his intuitions of right, may say, 'Be the universe governed by God or Satan, I must hold on by the ways of justice and humanity, and keep this little space and time pretty clear of devils, cost me what it may.' Simply as a moral agent, he need not trouble his head about what he cannot alter in the system of things. But if he carries his thought out beyond the law of his own life, and tries whether that law has a wider sweep and fits the great order of the world and the courses of history, he throws himself into a problem to which the issues of conduct, in men and nations, are no longer indifferent; it is left with those issues to establish for him, or to contradict, an unswerving moral agency at the heart of things. And thus it was with Shaftesbury. He longed, and not in vain, to find in the spiritual law of human life the principle of unity, and the key of interpretation, for all nature as the abode of self-conscious minds: he saw universal traces of the rule of righteous order and perfect beauty; in comparison with which the dark lines affected his faith with no deep shadows. It was in the interest of this optimism, which constituted his religion, that he was concerned to show, how favoured by nature was the lot of true goodness. In the school of thinkers, on the other hand, with which Mr. Leslie Stephen has most affinity, there is no more favourite object of attack than this optimism: in their eagerness to correct its extremes, they dwell with a bitter satisfaction, pathetic or cynical, on the blunders of nature and the wrongs of life; and while hasting to prove how badly happiness is allotted, so that goodness suffers and wickedness enjoys, forget that in that case each (according to the theory that happiness alone constitutes obligation) must have missed its way, and strayed from its own track upon the other's. It is in proof of optimism, or in rebuke to it, that each writer has lost for a moment the thread of his moral theory.

In reading Shaftesbury we frequently come across the group of 'particular passions,' which afterwards assumed such importance in the sermons of Butler; and we find them similarly treated as primary instincts, and not as derivative varieties of a sovereign Self-love. In like manner, he recognises a plurality of 'particular affections,' the parental, the filial, &c. directed separately upon others, without being specialised forms of a prior general benevolence. From this true psychological insight he unfortunately relapses, when he comes to classify the springs of action for moral purposes: he then sets them all down as either selfish or social; and so accentuates the opposition between these heads as to leave the impression, that human nature is worked throughout by two given incentives, and that, in case of conflict, all ethical problems lie between egoism and altruism. This is a very rude and inadequate classification of the motives to voluntary action, though doubtless it covers a large and important set of trials of conscience. There are numerous temptations to wrong which involve no struggle between selfishness and benevolence: intellectual conscientiousness, or strict submission of the mind to evidence, has its inspiration in pure love of truth, and would not survive an hour, if entrusted to the keeping of either prudence or social affection. The brave are certainly safest in themselves, and serviceable to the community: but courage never springs from discretion, and not always from love. The self-indulgent assuredly hurt both themselves and others: but it is a precarious temperance and purity which has no guardian angel but care for health and for example. The demand for *justice* which plays so great a part, both terrible and glorious, in the history of nations, is neither selfish nor benevolent; not the former, because intent chiefly on what is due to others; not the latter, because often insisting on punishment alone; and *that* without any reckoning of social advantage, but from mere impulse to treat men as they deserve. And so with the inward attitude of affection towards things Divine; who will say that this is to be kept right, either by self-love or by benevolence? Call it, if you please, with the old divines, 'Duty to God;' there can be no objection; for it is a directing upon Him of the thought of trust and the mood of worship which are *due* to His perfection, and our relation to Him. But this is to acknowledge a dutiful state of mind which contemplates neither our own good nor the good of another; and therefore to break through the limits of Shaftesbury's twofold classification. In fact, we have affections directed upon objects far more various than our own experience and that of our fellows; and no doctrine of character can have harmony and completeness which does not provide the fitting relative place for each and all.

One further defect is observable in Shaftesbury's theory: but it is one which it seems hardly possible for any statement of moral doctrine wholly to escape. Merit, he says, consists in successful resistance to inferior incentives and preference of a superior instead. When we ask him to specify what he has in view under these names of 'inferior' and 'superior' impulses, he replies that by the former he means 'sensible affections,' by the latter, 'rational affections,' both of them seated in 'the natural temper' or constitution, but in different 'parts of it.' These affections then, relatively bad and good, are the data supplied by nature in every conflict of temptation; and in the choice between them, in conquering the lower or in succumbing to it, consists the merit or demerit which accrues. Where then is the umpire,—where the Hercules,—who is to decide between the pleas, and earn the crown or the shame? Without this judicial agent, the scene is set upon the stage; but, for want of its hero, the drama makes no way. This want Shaftesbury does not supply: he invokes no living Ego, no personal subject, over and above the rival affections which turn up as phenomena of his nature; but seems to think the whole story told, when these states within him stand face to face and look fiercely at each other. Nay, he speaks of the whole struggle as completing itself between the two competitors; now the sensible affection 'prevails,' or it 'refrains;' and now the 'rational' 'masters the attempts of its antagonist¹:' they manage it all between themselves, with no one there. But if so, it goes simply by relative strength, and is a mere matter of dynamics; and whether

[1] Enquiry, pp. 36, 37.

the volition that ensues in me is the lower or the higher, is no more a moral question, than whether I remember or forget. The personal temptation, the defiance of difficulty, the intentional effort, the victorious agency, in virtue of which the merit is awarded, disappear, and lapse into passive alternations of suggestion, crossing the theatre of consciousness, till the less vivid and habitual fades away. I am far from thinking that Shaftesbury intended to teach any such complete subjection of the mind to 'nature;' but the fact that his language logically leads to it, and that he did not appreciate the distinction between *spontaneity* and *free-will*, must be taken to indicate a certain immaturity in his psychology.

CHAPTER II.

HUTCHESON.

§ 1. Life, Personality, and Writings.

THE desultory character of Shaftesbury's authorship, and the early age at which he sketched the outline of his ethical doctrine, account for the imperfect organisation of his thought. Had he been charged with the duty of again and again expounding his theory, and meeting the difficulties which it raised in others' minds, he would doubtless have become aware of its weak or missing links, and taken pains to render it firmer and more compact. The task of developing his fruitful hints and constructing from them a systematic psychology, naturally fell to a regular teacher, who was forced to concentrate attention upon every point in turn, and secure each step as he went along; and it may well be doubted whether he does not owe his place as the head of a new school less to himself than to his follower and interpreter, Francis Hutcheson. This interesting man rose to distinction under conditions as opposite as possible to those of Shaftesbury's life. Born in 1694, he was the son of John Hutcheson, a poor Presbyterian Minister of Armagh. For some family reason, not certainly from any defective learning or worth in his father, he was sent at eight years of age, with an older brother, to be educated by his grandfather, Alexander Hutcheson, Presbyterian Minister of Saintfield in the County Down[1]. During his four or

---

[1] He had been for two years, 1690-1692, Minister of Capel Street (afterwards Mary's Abbey) Congregation, Dublin; but the city not suiting his health, he returned to his former congregation.

five years' residence there, his eagerness for knowledge and rapid progress in all his studies, his natural refinement, his winning affectionateness of disposition, made him a universal favourite; a distinction which, by, throwing his brother into the shade, gave him a generous distress which spoiled its natural joy, and made him feel as if guilty of a hateful wrong. Nor was this feeling temporary; for, when it appeared that his grandfather's will had been altered in his favour, he absolutely repudiated the preference, and insisted upon the equal division which had at first been intended. After a year or two of more advanced study in some unknown Irish academy, he entered in 1710 upon a course of six years' study in the University of Glasgow, which was at that time the natural resort of the Ulster Presbyterians for professional education; and was especially so in the case of a family which had only recently crossed over from the County of Ayr. The time had not yet come, —Hutcheson himself was to inaugurate it,—for Scotland to claim its distinguished rank in the history of speculative philosophy; nor, among his instructors at Glasgow does any eminent name survive, except that of Robert Simson, the restorer of the Greek geometry. He applied himself, however, with impartial zeal to the study of classics, mathematics, and metaphysics; and followed up his undergraduate years by the full theological course which qualified him for ordination in his native country. For a short time he exercised his ministry in Ulster, without apparently any regular pastorate; but in 1719 was induced to follow the bent of his natural genius and acquired aptitudes, and establish himself in Dublin as a teacher. The 'Academy' over which he presided is usually described as a private school; and it may probably have passed itself off under this modest guise; but it was in reality a public institution intended, like the Belfast Academy, for the higher education of Nonconformist youths without compliance with the ecclesiastical conditions imposed by law. The Irish Presbyterians were left, up to that date, in a most anomalous legal position, protected only by their numbers, and their social importance in the anti-catholic struggle, against direct persecution from the Anglican side. As the Toleration Act did not apply to Ireland, they lived, till the time of Walpole's administration, under the Act of Uniformity, and exposed to the penalties of the Caroline legislation: their meeting-houses, their worship, their sacraments, their catechisms were illegal: they could hold no office, civil or military, without conforming by partaking of the communion at church; and, by an extension of the Schism Act to Ireland in 1711, they lost control over the education of their children; no one being allowed to keep either a private or a public school, or even to act as tutor, without a licence from the bishop, conditional on his being a communicant at church and engaging to conform to the established liturgy. A single attendance on any other form of worship exposed the possessor of such a licence to its forfeiture for the whole of his life and to three months' immediate imprisonment. It is true that this monstrous legislation was but rarely enforced against allies so powerful as the Presbyterian wing of Irish Protestantism; and was greatly mitigated on the accession of George I.; relief from the penalties of the Test Act being granted by annual resolutions of indemnity. The Schism Act was repealed in 1718, and a Toleration Act resembling the more liberal Scottish law was passed in 1719. The coincidence of date may perhaps imply that this was the conjuncture deemed most favourable for the opening of Hutcheson's 'Academy.' Under his management it had every advantage, except in the very reputation which it gained from his success. The social favour and intellectual respect which were accorded to his personal qualities drew attention from jealous as well as friendly eyes to his educational work; and while, on the one hand, he was urged by powerful persons to secure his career by conformity, on the other, he was threatened with penalties still unrepealed for unauthorised theological teaching. He was not to be turned, however, by hope or fear, from his simple integrity; and was protected by the friendship of Archbishop King and Dr. Synge (afterwards Bishop of Elphin) from the menaced action of his persecutors.

His engagement with pupils who were past the stage of school instruction, and who looked to him for guidance in more advanced studies, enabled him to take up his favourite subjects, and give determinate form to his psychological and moral conceptions. Within a year of his settlement in Dublin, the first result appeared in his 'Enquiry into the Original of our Ideas of Beauty and Virtue.' The volume was at first issued anonymously; but its philosophical and literary merits secured it immediate attention on the part of reading men. Among the patrons of good books one of the most eminent, Lord Granville, was on the spot, as Lord Lieutenant of Ireland: his interest in the treatise was so great that, after vainly attempting otherwise to discover the author, he addressed a letter to him through the publisher, which removed the disguise, and led to relations of intimacy and friendship. A similar sympathy had already procured him not only personal encouragement but critical aid, from the only person who was in the secret of the authorship, Viscount Molesworth, a thoughtful and accomplished man, in whose conversation Hutcheson always found instruction. In the second edition, of 1725, dedicated to Lord Carteret, he no longer conceals his name. The two essays of which the volume consists, the one upon Beauty, the other upon Virtue, are avowedly a development of Shaftesbury's leading conception; and make only the modest claim of presenting it with more completeness and exactitude, and clearing it from the irrelevant anti-christian prejudices which clung to it in the noble author's mind.

One other memorial was left by Hutcheson of his life in Dublin. In 1728 he brought out his 'Essay on the Nature and Conduct of the Passions and Affections, with Illustrations on the Moral Sense,'—a treatise of moral psychology in which he deals with the active rather than the perceptive functions of the consciousness of Right. Both these volumes must be regarded rather as the tentative approaches to his philosophical scheme, than as presenting its finished structure. They are highly interesting as exhibiting the genesis of his thought; but should not be quoted as authorities for any opinions foreign to his later productions. The later work, like the earlier, consists of two essays; the first, classifying and distinguishing the several affections and passions, and defining the limits of our control over them; the second, defending the doctrine of a Moral Sense, as propounded in the previous book, and comparing it with the theories of the dianoetic moralists. The inspiration under which both volumes were written is avowed in their prefaces and is manifest throughout: it was an intense ethical revolt against the attempt of Hobbes and Mandeville to set up self-love as the autocrat of human life, and a corresponding intellectual protest against the artificial simplifications which Locke's psychological analyses had brought into favour. Hutcheson found in the record of nature many a passage which the key of 'sensation and reflection' failed to unlock; and boldly replaced among the primary data of humanity numerous springs of action and modes of feeling which neither interest nor reason could be shown to evolve The enthusiasm of disinterested affection in himself made it impossible, by any ingenious play of ideas, to impose upon him the fallacies of hedonism, and gave a persuasive genuineness to his descriptions of the self-forgetful impulses of mankind; so that his writings brought relief to a kind of cynical anxiety left by the current philosophy, and fetched back into the light of self-evidence many a generous trait of inward experience which had disappeared in the solvents of a disintegrating mental chemistry. Hence, his Dublin treatises obtained an unexpected and a wholesome popularity; producing upon their first readers something of the same effect which they wrought a century afterwards upon the pure and fervent mind of Channing. To him, it would seem, Hutcheson brought the very hour of regeneration. 'It was while reading, one day, some of the various passages in which he asserts man's capacity for disinterested affection, and considers virtue as the sacrifice of private interests, and the bearing of private evils for the public good, or as self-devotion to absolute universal good, that there suddenly burst upon his mind that view of the dignity of human nature, which was ever after to "uphold and cherish" him, and thenceforth to be "the fountain-light of all his day, the master-light of all his seeing." He was, at the time, walking as he read, beneath a clump of willows yet standing in the meadow a little to the north of Judge Dana's house. This was his favourite retreat for study, being then quite undisturbed and private, and offering a most serene and cheerful prospect across green meadows and the glistening river to the Brookline hills The place and the hour were always sacred in his memory, and he frequently referred to them with grateful awe. It seemed to him that he then passed through a new spiritual birth, and entered upon the day of eternal peace and joy. The glory of the Divine disinterestedness, the privilege of existing in a universe of progressive order and beauty, the possibilities of spiritual destiny, the sublimity of devotedness to the Will of infinite Love, penetrated his soul; and he was so borne away that (as he said to a friend in later years) he longed to die, and felt as if heaven alone could give room for the exercise of such emotions[1].'

The acceptance accorded to his books, and the influence gained by his personal character, were not unnoticed by Hutcheson's College friends and instructors; and were doubtless looked upon, with natural pride and without surprise, as continuing in a new scene the impression which he had left behind him in Glasgow. It is no wonder therefore that, on the occurrence of a vacancy in 1729, he was spontaneously appointed to the Chair of Moral Philosophy. It offered neither financial promotion, nor any bribe to ambition: but it promised him the power of

[1] Memoir, in 3 vols. London, 1848. Vol. I. pp. 62, 63; Part I. chap. iii.

concentration upon his favourite pursuits, and the modest security of a permanent office; and he accepted it and returned to the land of his ancestors; taking with him the greater part of the students under his charge. The change realised the best hopes both of his electors and of himself. His first course of lectures, delivered in 1730, at once rekindled the zeal for philosophic studies which had been wearied out by barren scholastic methods, and touched the springs of admiration and affection which few teachers have so beneficently stirred. He entered upon his work with a distinct conception of his proper function. In Scotland, logical and psychical investigations were still dominated by metaphysical assumptions, and conducted on *à priori* lines: the principles of the 'Novum Organum' had carried their conquest no further than the sciences of external nature. In England, the first attempts to push them further, and annex the mental and moral provinces as well, had resulted in the empiricism of Locke and the egoism of Hobbes; and by variously conflicting with both the natural consciousness and the theological prepossessions of the Scottish teachers, had occasioned a disaffection towards the new method. Yet it was plainly impossible to save the old deductive scholasticism. Hutcheson had as little confidence as Locke in the entities of what was called *Psychologia Rationalis*, and was equally convinced that inductive observation afforded the only hope of insight into the laws of the human mind and character. He was for attacking the problems of the inward life of thought and will by the same instruments which had wrung from outward nature so many secrets of its ways; and could not be charged with any half-hearted allegiance to the Baconian revolution. Only, he could not allow that the phenomena, as hitherto analysed and reduced, had been rightly interpreted: many, he thought, had been overlooked; not a few had been misdescribed; and almost all subjected to false and coercive simplification. He therefore set himself to clear his own inward eye and look at the facts anew; and when they were all laid out in their relations, they presented, not only a landscape upon the surface, but a stratification in the interior, essentially different from the scenery of the Leviathan or the structure of the Essay on the Human Understanding. He therefore carried the Inductive reform through its second stage in Scotland, bringing up moral science into parallelism with physical; not by importing the tentative already made, but by independently setting up another, which at least avoided some weaknesses of the former, and rescued from neglect some truths which it disparaged. It is not without reason, therefore, that M. Prévost places him at the head of what is known on the Continent as the Scottish school: of this school, he says, 'the virtual founder was Hutcheson, the master and predecessor of Adam Smith: this philosopher it is who stamped his character on him, and gave him his first repute[1].' This estimate of M. Prévost's is confirmed by a witness who stood in intimate personal relations with A. Smith in his later years: 'The lectures,' says Dugald Stewart, 'of the profound and eloquent Dr. Hutcheson, which he had attended previous to his departure from Glasgow, and of which he always spoke in terms of the warmest admiration, had, it may be reasonably presumed, considerable effect in directing his talents to their proper objects[2].'

These lectures, in the form which gave them their characteristic power, were never known beyond his classroom. Profoundly interested in his duties and in his pupils, he gave himself up to their claims upon him, with the modest resolve to keep awake to all new light on their behalf, and allow himself no single line of slovenly work, and without ambition that looked beyond the University he loved. He published nothing till after fifteen years of service; when he brought out, as a text-book for his class, a Latin manual, with the title, '*Philosophiæ Moralis*

[1] Translation of Smith's Posthumous Works; ap. Stewart's Dissertation; Works, Vol. I. p. 428, note.
[2] Life and Writings of Adam Smith. Smith's Works, Vol. V. p. 408.

Institutio compendiaria libris tribus Ethices et Jurisprudentiæ Naturalis principia continens.' The publication of this book he survived only two years; just before the appearance of an English translation of it (Foulis, Glasgow, 1747) he was carried off by fever, closing a few months of warning weakness, in 1747, at the age of fifty-two. His son, Francis Hutcheson, a physician of repute, the sole heir of his name and crown of a singularly happy married life, gathered together the written materials of his lectures, and, arranging them in three books, published them, under the title 'System of Moral Philosophy,' in two quarto volumes, with a biographical preface by Principal Leechman[1]. The book did not appear till 1755; the delay being probably due to the compendious nature and imperfect literary form of the notes from which he had lectured, and the consequent necessity imposed upon the editor, of filling them up by reference to the reports taken down by his most assiduous students. The volumes themselves contain internal evidence of some such process of mixed fabrication; and justify the following apology of Dugald Stewart for calling Hutcheson's lectures '*eloquent.*' 'Those,' he says, ' who have derived their knowledge of Dr. Hutcheson solely from his publications may perhaps be inclined to dispute the propriety of the epithet " eloquent," when applied to any

[1] William Leechman, though educated at the University of Edinburgh about 1723-8, had lived in Glasgow as private tutor to Mr Mure of Caldwell, and attended Hutcheson's lectures and became his admirer and friend about 1731-3. He was chosen parish minister at Beith in 1736, and must there have acquired, with the strict Presbyterians, the repute of too latitudinarian a theology; for, when proposed in the Senatus Academicus as a candidate for the Professorship of Divinity in 1744, a competitor was strongly supported under ecclesiastical influence by the orthodox party. His election was carried only by the casting vote of the president; and attempts were still made for some time, though overruled at last, to set it aside as illegal. He had not the quick and effusive genius which gave such a charm to the lectures of Hutcheson; but the warmest friendship subsisted between them, and their combined influence gave great strength to the school of rational and moderate theology, which then held a precarious ascendency in the Scottish Universities. The appointment of Leechman was amply vindicated by the range of his learning, the dignity of his character, and the wisdom of his administration.

of his compositions; more particularly when applied to the
"System of Moral Philosophy" which was published after
his death, as the substance of his lectures in the University
of Glasgow. His talents, however, as a public speaker,
must have been of a far higher order than what he has dis-
played as a writer; all his pupils whom I have happened to
meet with (some of them, certainly, very competent judges)
having agreed exactly with each other in their accounts of
the extraordinary impression which they made on the
minds of his hearers. I have mentioned, in the text, Mr.
Smith as one of his warmest admirers; and to *his* name I
shall take this opportunity of adding those of the late Earl
of Selkirk; the late Lord President Miller; the late Dr.
Archibald Maclaine, the very learned and judicious translator of "Mosheim's Ecclesiastical History" My father,
too, who had attended Dr. Hutcheson's lectures, never
spoke of them without much sensibility. On this occasion
we can only say, as Quinctilian has done of the eloquence
of Hortensius, "*Apparet placuisse aliquid eo dicente, quod
legentes non invenimus.*" Dr. Hutcheson's "Enquiry into
our Ideas of Beauty and Virtue," his "Discourse on the
Passions," and his "Illustrations of the Moral Sense," are
much more strongly marked with the characteristic features
of his genius than his posthumous work. His great and
deserved fame, however, in this country rests now chiefly
on the traditionary history of his academical lectures, which
appear to have contributed very powerfully to diffuse in
Scotland that taste for analytical discussion and that spirit
of liberal enquiry, to which the world is indebted for
some of the most valuable productions of the eighteenth
century[1].'

In the contingent which the Schools have furnished to
the advance-guard of human knowledge, there are many
greater figures than Francis Hutcheson's; but few that are
more attractive, more complete in symmetry, more noble

[1] Life and Writings of Adam Smith. Smith's Works, Vol. V. Note B,
pp. 523-525.

in sincerity of nature: what he thought, he loved; what he taught, he was. A generous philosophy became in him a generous personality. With an enthusiasm for truth and goodness, unalloyed by the scholar's fault of jealous property in ideas; with a contempt for nothing but meanness, vice, and wrong; with a transparent unreserve, neither ashamed of an honest admiration, nor afraid to avow a righteous anger; he drew forth what was best in others by simple self-expression; and by the total absence of pretension rendered personal dislike impossible, except with those to whose narrowness of heart and mind his very presence was a rebuke.

§ 2. *Contents of his Doctrine.*

A. 'SENSE' DEFINED. EXTERNAL SENSES.—The chief interest of Hutcheson's philosophy concentrates itself upon two questions, which are so far left in obscurity as to be differently answered on his behalf: (1) Whether he resolves the *sense of right* into the *sense of beauty;* and (2) in what relations he places the *benevolent affections* and the *moral sentiments.* In the brief account which alone I can give of his opinions, I shall select, as most characteristic, the features which bear upon these questions; for, on their correct determination depends the place which must be assigned to him among moral philosophers.

He adopted, avowedly from Shaftesbury, the widened use of the word *Sense*, to denote certain mental feelings other than those incident to known changes in the bodily organs; and it is through his school that the term αἴσθησις, though still kept true to its proper meaning in the stricter nomenclature of Kant, has been made to yield the modern conception of 'Æsthetics.' If we ask what common element induced him to apply to purely ideal states a word previously limited to affections through the instruments of perception, the answer will be that, in both instances, the mind is *passively* recipient, i.e. is put into a certain state of feeling by a given object, be it of sight, or be it of conception. This is the one distinctive mark of *Sense* in our author's writings; that the *initiative* of the phenomenon so denoted is not with the mind, but with the object presented to it.

The new province which, by this shifting of boundaries, is annexed to the word, requires to be discriminated from the old. This is done by designating the latter as *External* Sense; including all feelings or ideas delivered on us by the action of outward things upon our organism. Of these the elementary form is conceived by Hutcheson exactly as by Locke: a 'simple sensation' is the special feeling given us by some single quality of a body, e.g. its shape, or its temperature, or its colour. These simple sensations are very numerous, and need to be parcelled out into lots, if they are to be at the command of thought and language. They arrange themselves in two different orders. They have varieties of likeness and difference: on putting the homogeneous together, and separating the heterogeneous, we find them fall into five groups (to take the ordinary division), each of which we refer to a single sense; the most dissimilar members of each having more affinity than the most similar of any two or three sets. I fear that introspective psychology would hardly stand the test, if it were required to make out a true list of the special senses by pure feeling alone, without the experiments which determine the bodily localisation, in finger, or eye, or ear. Simple sensations also are liable to come together, or to keep apart; those which always keep together are recognised as administered to us by the co-existent qualities of an object; they are a complex lot, unified by companionship, and subscribe to make up our idea of a thing or substance that has them; so that we do not get the conception of an object, till we can add uβ the *sum* of its heterogeneous attributes[1].

Of the sensations thus given to us for classification, some

[1] Enquiry, I. i pp. 1-3.

are limited to a single sense, as cold and heat, colours, sounds and smells; others are furnished by more than one, as extension, figure, motion and rest, duration and number [1]. This is a somewhat careless reproduction of Aristotle's division of αἰσθητὰ into ἴδια and κοινά [2]; to him it was appropriate, for his αἴσθησις was always an active cognition and more than a mere state of feeling into which the subject was put; and there was nothing to prevent a common activity flowing through different data and fetching the same lesson from them. But Hutcheson, in cutting down Sense to mere passive feeling, and making up as many senses as there are parcels of *heterogeneous* feelings, precludes himself from finding anything common to the separated lots. A confused use of the word *Perception* as the equivalent, at one time of *sensation*, at another of *consciousness*, at a third of *objective apprehension*, led him to forget the distinction he had drawn between a sensory πάθος and an act of intelligence. His misapplication of Aristotle's division is even worse than it looks; for when he comes to the 'common percepts,' he drops the vocabulary of *Sense*, and speaks of the '*Ideas*' of extension, duration, number, &c. as derived from two or more of our organs, of feeling, hearing, sight; and we have no difficulty in supposing that, among the materials out of which we elaborate these fruitful ideas, each of these sources of experience may play its part. But, in thinking thus, we take the '*idea*' so reached to be the ultimate result of a mental process, of combination and abstraction, performed upon the sensory data. This, however, is to mistake the author's meaning, which in this case completely identifies 'sensation' and 'idea;' 'those *ideas*,' he says, 'which are raised in the mind upon the presence of external objects, and their acting upon our bodies, are called *sensations*[3].' So that extension, figure, motion and rest, duration and number, are affirmed to be 'passive sensations' of two or more of

[1] System, I. i. 3, p. 46.   [2] De Anima, II. vi.
[3] Enquiry, I. i. p. I.

our senses, just as colour or smell is of one. It must be owned, this is very 'popular psychology.'

The 'simple ideas of sensation,' like the organisms which are their media, are subject to some variation from person to person, and in the same person at different times; especially those which, instead of being neutral, like the ideas of extension and number, are attended, like the colours, tastes, and smells, with pleasure or pain; for they admit of gradations of intensity over a considerable range; and, in virtue of this, are the source of desire or aversion towards the objects which produce them.

Of all these simple ideas, passively received by us, we are not simply the theatre, but the *conscious subjects;* and, in being so, are no longer passive, but set actively to work upon the materials committed to us: contemplating, comparing, compounding, abstracting, measuring them, noting their order and their relations. In these processes the whole of the mind's activity is expended; it creates no new ideas, except so far as the products of its industry are virtually new by transformation of their elements. It deals only with the seed dropped upon the field, and, in maturing it, can deviate into no other growth. The whole contents of the mind are accounted for by these two conditions, of sensation and consciousness, or as Locke calls them, 'sensation and reflexion:' when the acts performed are those of judging and reasoning, they are referred to the *Understanding;* when they are desire, aversion, joy, sorrow, they are referred to the *Will.* But we do not yet escape, under Hutcheson's guidance, the question which perplexes us, viz. how exactly to conceive, and where to find, the agent of all the needed 'Activity.' A sensation is delivered *ab extra* upon a point where there was none before, and where (as it is passively received) there is as yet no activity, and was, till now, no opportunity even for passivity. Of this sensation there follows a consciousness,—'I feel this;' *whose* consciousness? *Quis loquitur?* for the sensation (*ex hypothesi*) was the first thing, besides which there is nothing present; it wants, therefore, an owner to make this claim; unless the sensation is to feel itself. Other sensations succeed, and are seized upon by other activities: they are compared together; the like are put into a parcel, the unlike sifted out; the regular are trained to march in file; and the hundreds to divide into decades. Where is the operator of all these feats? Do the sensations institute comparisons *inter se*? judge of their resemblance or difference? fasten the links of their order? count their own numbers? and know their own organs? All this is against their passivity and their purely objective position, as that of which there is a consciousness. To tell us that it is 'the Mind' which is active, virtually surrenders the whole of the empirical psychology; the object of which is to put together and fabricate the personality; and which cannot therefore set up the personal cause, at the starting-point, to effect the first step. I am far from saying that Hutcheson *meant* to explain away the living, acting *Ego* as the subject of all the mental feelings, processes, and energies, and exhibit it as the mere aggregate of like and unlike phenomena: on the contrary, as he proceeds, he assumes it again and again as a persistent individual being, invested with both definite and alternative powers. But, side by side with this natural view, we notice the influence of Locke's dissolving analysis. First, the activities are broken up and distributed: the *Understanding* does this; the *Will* does that; and then each of these delegates crumbles away into particular facts, single or in trains; Understanding being the *sum* of sensation, consciousness, judgment, and reasoning; Will, of desire, aversion, joy, and sorrow[1]; and so, of the great nature that seemed advancing with so entire a wave, nothing is visible, after encountering the shock of a dispersive philosophy, but an infinite spray of phenomena.

B. SENSE OF BEAUTY.—*Internal* Sense differs from *External* by having to do, not with single qualities of objects,

[1] System, I. 1. 1, pp. 7, 8.

but with a sufficient number to give rise to relations among them. These relations are no sooner presented to us than we are affected by a special feeling, wholly different from the mere seeing, hearing, touching, the separate things related: they dispose themselves in an order; they constitute a harmony, exemplify a proportion, which gives us immediate delight; just as immediate as the 'simple sensation' of the external sense from the fragrance of a rose. It is in virtue of this immediateness, and of its being a feeling that passively befalls us, that Hutcheson places it under the category of *Sense*: had it been derived from any reckoning of design or advantage, it would have fallen under the head of *Thought*. This feeling of *Beauty*, moreover, belongs to the province of sensibility by even a stronger right than the experiences of the eye, the ear, the touch, &c; for of these, there are many that are quite indifferent to us; we do not care whether the postman knocks or rings, whether we jump into a brown cab or a blue; but it is never indifferent to us whether we are exposed to what is beautiful or to what is ugly: neutrality is absent here; it is all pleasure or displeasure. And, finally, this sense is properly called '*internal*,' because it has no dependence on the impressions of outward things upon our organs; but is just as much at home among intellectual relations, the symmetries, the graces, the lucidities of thought, as among the proportions of what is visible and audible. There is beauty in conception, in affection, in character, as truly as in person and in dress; so that the system of objects contemplated, no less than the feeling itself which they awaken, may be apart from sensation and exist only for internal thought[1].

Though beauty may be predicated of single objects, it must be in virtue of a complexity comprised within them, and the proportion and disposition of their parts or attributes. When these conditions are fulfilled, we intuitively feel the charm of the effect, without knowing anything of

[1] Enquiry, I i. pp 7-10.

its cause, the individual thing itself, as an unanalysed unit, gets the credit of the perfection. This case Hutcheson distinguishes, by the not very happy phrase '*Absolute* beauty,' from those in which the feeling depends on a comparison of object with object, such as pictures, statues, and other products of the imitative arts; for which, therefore, as involving a conscious judgment of the bearing towards each other of two or more things, he reserves the term *Relative* beauty. To this it is by no means necessary that the component members of the pair or the system contemplated should be separately beautiful. There is beauty in identity of ratios, or proportion, yet none in the single quantities which compose them, and many a lovely picture has been produced, though among the sitters for it there was neither a Venus nor an Apollo. In his endeavour to define the precise *Relations* which constitute either kind of beauty, our author is largely influenced by Addison's celebrated papers in the 'Spectator' on 'The Pleasures of the Imagination.'

The fundamental condition is *Uniformity amidst Variety*. With a given uniformity, beauty is in proportion to the variety; with a given variety, in proportion to the uniformity; e.g. that of the triangle is less than that of the square; which, in its turn, is less than that of the pentagon, as this again is less than that of the hexagon, &c.; and the beauty of the scalene is less than that of the isosceles, which is less than that of the equilateral. The same is manifest in our judgments of organic nature: in the vegetable world, plants may be too formal, on the one hand, too irregular on the other, to satisfy our taste, which needs a clear type of being, freely modified in its details of ramification and leafage, of height and breadth, of curvature and colour, and finds it perhaps in a noble beech or lime tree. So in the animal tribes, nothing is more fascinating than the vestiges of one structural plan, carried out with variations gradual yet bold, to work the functions of walking, swimming, flying, &c.; nor is there any specific admiration felt by us for living creatures, be it in their form, their movements, their integuments and dress, which will not be found to involve the same principle. Any breach of the required uniformity,—a short leg, a squinting eye, a hump back,—offends us; and as we descend towards the elementary forms of life, æsthetic interest fades away for want of sufficient organic and functional variety.

Another factor in the phenomenon of beauty is *Similarity;* which indeed is, in strictness, only a development of the former, no otherwise entitled to separate mention than as covering a large number of cases. The fact that the fine arts are so largely concerned with *imitation*, not merely of the human figure on its scenes of action, and of the aspects of external nature, but, in the epic and the drama and all *moratæ fabulæ*, of incident, character, and manners, bears emphatic witness to the range of this principle. On a minor scale it appears in the perpetual play of metaphor in literature, and the very movement of language, as it grows, by the suggestions of resemblance Even the beauty of scientific law depends on its linking together, as similars, facts of unsuspected affinity; enabling us to enroll among intellectual friends innumerable phenomena previously dispersed over an indifferent and foreign world.

The considerable part which *proportion* plays in the total effect of beauty is a further application of the same fundamental rule. It might also be brought under the head of similarity; for it is a pleasure in the similarity of ratios. The relations to one another of a circumscribing cylinder, the inscribed sphere, and its inscribed cone, as the figures 3 : 2 : 1, give to every one who is introduced to their evidence a feeling of their beauty. The uniformity, which here lies in geometrical necessity, is sometimes supplied by a teleological idea, the tacit assumption of a regulative *end in view*, as in the case of a machine; and not less so in that of an animal organism. The idea of *Intention* involved in the very nature of such an object is indispensable to its beauty, and defines the perfection to which the parts conspire, and the rule of order which relates them among themselves as a hierarchy of means and ends. By an inverse argument, Hutcheson contends that, as a preconceived design supplies us in such cases with a standard of beauty, so the appearance of regular beauty in a product warrants the inference of design in the cause; that, in the absence of *Selection*, i.e. under the condition of *indifferent forces*, the appearance of *regular forms*, of *numerous similars*, the combination of several shapes which *fit together*, like a tube with a stopper in the orifice, a complexity of parts concurring towards one end, and, *à fortiori*, a law providing at a stroke all the means of numerous heterogeneous services (like those of Heat and of Gravitation) would be to all intents and purposes *impossible;* involving, by the mathematical computation of chances, improbabilities as the *n power of Infinite to One*[1]. This ingenious argument, being really a digression, I must pass with only one remark. It is essentially the same which a few years ago led the late Professor Clerk Maxwell and Sir John Herschel to assert, that the atoms assumed as the starting-point of the physicist's cosmogony had all the marks of 'manufactured articles.'

The 'Internal Sense' of beauty, thus expounded, Hutcheson maintains to be *intuitive and universal* in men; an original source of pleasure added to them, without any antithetic pain. For, *ugliness* he will not allow to be a positive infliction, like a bitter taste or a nauseous smell: it is but the failure of beauty; and displeases us only by disappointing some preconception. However wide may be the legitimate application of this rule, we must surely except from it discords in music; the distress of which seems, in its positive character, quite on a par with the pleasure of harmony, and to be equally independent of factitious associations. But, with regard to the countenances of human beings, which are the chief depositories and epitome of

[1] Enquiry, I. v. pp. 47-69

beauty and deformity, there can be no doubt that, when they do more than fall short of our instinct for beauty, they displease us by their *expression of temper and probable disposition;* we are repelled by *what they signify*. The universality of the taste for regularity amidst variety is evident from features common to human arts in every stage, quite apart from considerations of utility ; e.g. the rudest habitations, as well as structures of finest architecture, are symmetrical in form; if angular, their walls are parallel; if in stones, their floors are horizontal; if lighted from without, their windows are upright and regular: however barbarous the fashions of dress, they recognise the correspondency of the two sides of the body, and arrange their adornments by reference to the medial line. Nor has any tribe been found that, in choosing its king, looked out for a man that squinted or had a goitre. The same instinctive craving for the weaving together of the many into the one is apparent in the earliest intellectual interests of such men : the village chronicler, whose memory goes back to the third generation, may have the useful authority of an almanac; but it is the ballad-singer or ῥαψῳδὸς that will gather an eager and silent crowd, by stringing the loose beads of fact upon a continuous thread of human life, spun from the whirl of passion and the filaments of character; not till the poet's insight reads the unifying plot, does history arise, and gain its meaning and its charm[1].

When Hutcheson wrote, the most skilful attempts had not yet been made to derive the æsthetic conceptions and emotions from associated vestiges of sensation, and the second-hand influence of custom and education, founded on utility. In no direction has the doctrine of association of ideas been worked out with more ingenuity by its exponents, from Hartley to Alison, than on the track of our appreciation of sublimity and beauty. But I hardly think that the position of the main problem has been changed.

[1] Enquiry, I. vi. pp. 72–80.

A thousand aberrations of taste and caprices of fashion, discrepancies of admiration without end, nay, natural extensions as well as artificial modifications, of the perceptions of beauty, have been traced through a very possible history sketched with infinite delicacy. All the morbid excrescences and all the natural expansions of this sensitive and flexible affection have been explained; but the living seed of all this development remains unique, and cannot yet be manufactured out of elementary atoms of sensation and utility. Habit or custom may be a 'second nature;' but it is not a first nature, and a first nature there must be, in order to form it; for through habit we gain only the more nimble emergence of a natural feeling, the quicker execution of a regulated natural act. No apprehension of advantage or disadvantage could ever, by persevering recurrence, convert itself into a sense of sublimity or beauty, any more than the exhilaration of stimulants can make us think them delicious to the taste if we have no taste. And so it is with the influence of education. We cannot borrow, from others' teaching, a feeling for which there is no provision in ourselves. They may, no doubt, mislead us into false taste by their authority and example; but only by availing themselves of the preconceptions we already have of something fair or ugly; by associating disgusting ideas with what is really neutral, or attractive affections with what would else repel, and it is thus that Superstition is brought to misinterpret the expression of things, and read a spiritual beauty or horror into physical objects and phenomena which are empty of both. But even to misjudge beauty, there must be the power to judge it.

At the beginning of this account of Hutcheson's psychology, I have explained the extended meaning which he gives to the word Sense, by appending to it an 'internal' province. His readers, after observing that he leaves the five external senses where they were, naturally desire to know how many of the internal class he adds to these. It is a singular fact that they will nowhere find a definite answer to this question; and that, on closing his volumes, one may assert with good ground, that he allows but two; another, that he provides no less than ten. The latter opinion would seem to be borne out by a chapter of his 'Moral Philosophy[1],' which expressly treats 'of the finer powers of perception,' distinguishing man from other possessors of the five external senses, as well as by the corresponding part of his Latin 'Compendium[2].' In both of these we find enumerated: (1) the sense of beauty; (2) delight in imitation; (3) musical harmony, whether in simple concords, or in the themes of larger compositions; (4) the perception of design and fitness; (5) the sense of grandeur; (6) sense of novelty; (7) sympathy, i.e. the spontaneous assumption of any feeling observed in another,—e.g. in the case of compassion, of congratulation, and of fellow-feeling in action and enterprise of all sorts; (8) the moral sense, directing enthusiasm on benevolent and indignation on selfish and injurious conduct, involving at the same time joy at the prosperity of the faithful and displeasure at the success of the cruel; (9) the sense of honour and shame; (10) the sense of decency and dignity. When, however, the author proceeds to add (11) the conjugal and parental affections, (12) the civic and social, (13) the religious, it becomes obvious that his classification, intentionally or inadvertently, embraces a wider field than the language which introduced it led us to expect. The personal affections, towards beings human or Divine, he cannot have meant to include among 'internal senses.' On the other hand, he has here placed under separate heads several varieties of feeling which he has elsewhere assigned to one and the same 'internal sense;' e. g. in his treatise on the 'Ideas of Beauty' he has covered by that name the pleasure in 'imitation,' in harmony, in design, in grandeur and dignity; yet each of these, in the present list, takes its place beside the sense of beauty, on equal terms. Sympathy, again, sometimes finds its way to its natural kindred, the personal affections; and the susceptibility to shame and

[1] Bk. I. chap. ii. [2] Lib. i. cap. i. §§ 4-14.

honour takes shelter with the moral sense[1]. If, instead of interrogating any of his formal divisions (in which Hutcheson is seldom very happy), we trust to the general purport of his writings, we shall find in them, besides the Sense of Beauty, only one other of the internal class, viz. the *Moral* Sense.

C. MORAL SENSE.—In reporting his doctrine on this point, it is not easy to give it perfect coherence; partly from causes inherent in his first conception of it; but partly, I suspect, from a later modification of that conception through the influence of Bishop Butler's Sermons, published in 1729; for certainly, the posthumous 'Moral Philosophy,' which represents his ultimate teaching, assigns, in language akin to Butler's, some predicates to the Moral Sense which we miss in his original statement of its nature; and it is doubtful whether any complete interfusion of the similar ideas was ever effected in his mind. The difference is marked at the very outset of the two expositions. In the 'Enquiry' he lays down his thesis thus: 'That some actions have to men an *immediate goodness;* or, that by a *superior Sense*, which I call a *Moral one*, we perceive pleasure in the contemplation of such actions in others, and are determined to love the agent (and much more do we perceive pleasure in being conscious of having done such actions ourselves), without any view of further natural advantage from them[2].' In the 'System,' he calls the 'Moral Sense,' in the very heading of the chapter devoted to it, 'the *faculty* of perceiving moral excellence, and its supreme objects[3].' I need not point out that the subjective 'Sense,' or passive susceptibility to a certain 'pleasure' relative 'to men' has here become an objective 'Faculty,' or active apprehension of 'an *independent quality* immediately perceived in certain affections and actions consequent upon them' (as he shortly afterwards

---

[1] In his Treatise on the Nature and Conduct of the Passions, Hutcheson brings the same contents under five heads: (1) external sense; (2) internal sense of beauty; (3) public sense (benevolence); (4) moral sense; (5) sense of honour.
[2] Introduction, p. 116.   [3] System, L. i. 4, p. 53.

expresses it)[1]. From a form of sensibility we are handed over to a cognitive power; and instead of a special 'pleasure' to be received, we have a mental energy to be put forth. Still more marked is this feature, when he says that the 'faculty' carries in its very nature the prerogative of commanding and controlling the other powers, appreciating as it does a quality superior to any with which the others have to do[2]. Here surely we hear a voice in tune with the deep authoritative tones of Butler, rather than with the soft and winning tenor of Shaftesbury.

The side from which Hutcheson approached the study of our ethical nature accounts for this difference, and throws light upon the characteristics of his doctrine. He began his investigations with the scrutiny of our æsthetic judgments and emotions, and came to the conclusion that they were not circuitously derived from any more elementary interest, but immediately given by a special quality apprehended in beautiful objects by a perceptivity in us related to it. In this case, it is a '*Sense*' that is exercised, because the mind is affected by an object from without, which reports its contents to the mental gaze. With this analogy in his thoughts, Hutcheson addresses himself to the moral judgments and emotions, and by following its parallel line was brought to a similar inference; that they too are no offshoots of personal pleasure or advantage, but the intuitive cognisance of a special quality inherent in a certain type of conduct and character; and that it was in virtue of a mental organ of apprehension reserved for the purpose, that this 'goodness' in voluntary action spoke to us at sight. This organ of apprehension, therefore, was in its turn called a 'Sense,' because affected by a contemplated object external to the mind. Under the guidance of this preconception, Hutcheson, in his search for 'goodness,' looks *outward*, and assumes that it is primarily something to be seen in the actions of others, and that all our feelings towards it are but extensions of the joy incident to

[1] System, L. i. 4, p. 58.   [2] Ibid. p. 61.

its first vision. Let us consider some of the consequences involved in this point of departure.

(1) It certainly secures the position which Hutcheson was most anxious to establish, viz. the complete disinterestedness of moral approval and reverence. This is the point on which he was intent, and which most needed defence from the shameless cynicism of Hobbes and Mandeville. And though, for this end, any mode of demolishing the pretended links that hung the enthusiasm for right on to the promptings of self-interest would have sufficed, there was an advantage in selecting one which could first be tried on the quieter case of the æsthetic emotions: for against these there was a less resolute crusade of detraction: they had the men of genius, instead of the clergy, for their bodyguard; and there was no knowing how a railing accusation against them as selfish impostors might get punished. It was not amiss, therefore, to work for a verdict on their behalf, and then repeat the pleadings and quote the precedent in the adjacent court. The arguments by which both classes of sentiments are set free from the taint of sordid origin and left in possession of their intuitive rights, have lost by time little or none of their validity.

(2) In looking for virtue where he looks for it, viz. in the *visible scene*, Hutcheson necessarily fixes his attention upon *action*, in its perceptible features, and fancies the approval which it may win from him due to it as a whole, without distinction of its inward source, its immediate execution, its ulterior consequences. So that all these are mixed up together as moral phenomena, and sharers in epithets of the same praise and blame. Accordingly, if you ask him whether virtue is a quality of the action or of the agent, you gain no steady reply[1]. At one time he is so occupied with

---

[1] Professor Sidgwick characterises this statement as a 'serious misunderstanding' of Hutcheson (Mind, XXXIX. p 442, note) In refutation of it he refers to a passage in the *System* (Bk. II. ch. iii), distinguishing between the happy *consequences* of an action, as constituting its '*material* goodness,' and the right *affection* whence it springs, as constituting its '*formal* goodness.' Does this distinction then concentrate the 'good-

the *objective product*, that the measure of goodness lies entirely in it: thus he commits himself, *totidem verbis*, to the Utilitarian principle, that an 'action's morality is immediately adjusted, when the natural tendency or influence of the action upon the universal natural good of mankind is agreed upon¹;' and supplies us with a regular bit of Benthamite arithmetic when he says, that altruistic virtue is 'in a compound ratio of the quantity of good and the number of enjoyers².' Yet, at other times, unfortunately more rare, he tells us that the moral quality is perceived by us *in the affections*, and only on that account in actions consequent upon them; and the 'primary objects of the Moral Sense are the affections of the will³.' So that he measures the morality, now by the action's spring, and now by its effects. It is not without reason that the Utilitarian asks him, what is the use of his moral intuition, if, after all, he has to compute his morality by the compound ratios of observable quantities; and whether the 'quality of goodness' which it 'immediately' reveals is simply the answer to that sum, which would emerge no less through the medium of calculation. If so, he endows intuition with a function never assigned to it before,—that of merely saving us the trouble of using our instruments of knowledge,—of putting into our hands the printed key to the problems given us to work. Nor are there wanting expressions of his which give some colour to this interpretation of his meaning: he speaks, for example, of the Moral Sense as an '*expeditious* monitor,' an '*importunate* solicitor⁴,' that goes ahead of Reason; as if it

---

ness' upon either the *inward source* or the *outward consequences*? On the contrary, it assigns it to both, and makes them, as I had said, 'sharers in epithets of the same praise and blame;' the adjectives *material* and *formal* marking only varieties in the same category of '*morality*,' and leaving both terms alike 'objects of the *Moral Sense*.' This 'mixing up together as moral phenomena' of two things of which only one is entitled to the rank, is precisely the confusion complained of in the text. Even if the passage had drawn exactly the distinction which I miss, it would not, as a single instance, suffice to meet my only allegation, of the want of a '*steady* reply' to the question involved.

¹ Enquiry, II. iii. p. 165. ² Ibid II. iii. p. 177.
³ System, I. i. 4. pp 58, 62. ⁴ Enquiry, II vii. p. 271.

were only a *quick and impatient* provision for the same end which Reason reaches with more leisurely steps. The pretensions of any such *prophetic* intuition are open to extreme suspicion. 'Immediate' apprehension is apprehension of what *now is*, not of a future train or sum total of consequences to flow out of it; and unless the 'goodness' of an intended act is already present, neither can it be already apprehended: if it be dependent on what is yet to come, it will not be known till the resources of rational prediction have been expended upon it and determined its amount. The moment we depart from the rule that the moral quality of voluntary action lies in its inward spring,—which is a present fact,—we forfeit the right to claim 'immediate' knowledge of it.

(3) To the same *objective outlook* for goodness it is due, that Hutcheson habitually supposes us to get our ideas of it from observation of men, living or historical; and that, only after learning the lesson from the characters of others, do we apply it to our own. He frequently remarks that, in order to reach our real and sincere moral sentiments, we must consult our judgment of others' conduct. I cannot reconcile this with his distinct statement that 'the object of the moral sense is not any external motion or action, but the inward affections and dispositions which by reasoning we infer from the actions observed[1];' for of 'the inward affections and dispositions' we can know nothing but from our own experience of them. But in the see-saw of his doctrine between the two directions, the longer arm of the lever is certainly on the external side, and the tendency is to settle it in preponderance. His dominant conception obtains emphatic expression in a generalised form, when he says that '*the original of moral ideas*' is '*the moral sense*' (*perception*) 'of excellence in every *appearance or evidence of benevolence*[2].' Without recurring to the reasons already assigned for inverting this order of derivation, I will only remark in the present connection, that from Hutcheson's

[1] System, I. i. 5, p. 98.   [2] Enquiry, II. vii. p. 266.

view a doctrine of *Virtue* only can result, not a doctrine of *Duty*, i.e. only a critique of character, as an object of study and preference, but not a rule of authoritative obligation or an organism of relative rights. It is not, therefore, surprising that, when he encounters the term 'obligation,' and has to say something of its meaning, he should find himself thrown back of necessity upon the personal consciousness, yet, even upon this true ground, should alight only upon this awkward definition of obligation, as 'a determination, without regard to our own interest, to approve actions, and to perform them; which determination shall also make us displeased with ourselves, and uneasy, upon having acted contrary to it[1].' From which, and an assumed 'instinct towards benevolence,' he infers that 'No mortal can secure to himself a perpetual serenity, satisfaction, and self-approbation, but by serious *enquiry* into the tendency of his actions, and a *perpetual study of universal good*, according to the justest notions of it[2].' 'Obligation,' then, consists in our own approving satisfaction with an act and uneasiness in its omission, provided we are regardless of this gain or loss from it; the act in question,—thanks to the 'instinct of benevolence,'—is, or involves, 'a perpetual study of universal good;' to which we are encouraged by the promise of a secure serenity and self-content that are to be kept wholly out of view! 'Obligation,' self-imposed by the subject's own satisfaction or uneasiness; to an act immediately known by him as good; yet whose goodness consists in its balance of consequences in relation to the universal system of things; under sanctions, of which he must not think; presents surely a singular combination of contradictions. Still, the incidental admission is important, that for the idea of obligation it is necessary to withdraw the eye from the field of observed character, and retire to the consciousness within.

(4) Hutcheson's treatment of 'goodness,' as a perceptible quality read off at sight in the outward conduct of others,

[1] Enquiry, II. vii. p. 266. [2] Ibid. p. 267.

accounts for his readers' difficulty in distinguishing between his two 'Inner Senses.' Separated in phrase, they are continually running into each other, and exchanging epithets, till their vocabularies seem to have entered into partnership: a temper or disposition is 'fair' and 'lovely:' a building is 'chaste and severe.' This is perfectly natural, if the moral attributes are given to us, like the æsthetic, through objective inspection; *approbation* is then so like *admiration*, and *disapproval* so like *distaste*, that it may well appear a superfluous refinement to keep the two provinces apart. Objective virtue indeed *is* beautiful, and in that capacity belongs to the materials of art, and plays a great part in the literature of fiction, and indeed of history. It is not wonderful, therefore, that Hutcheson mingles the two orders of predicates, as if they meant the same thing, as when he says, 'We have a distinct perception of *beauty or excellence* in the kind affections of rational agents[1];' and again, 'All strict attachments to parties, sects, and factions, have but an imperfect species of *beauty*, unless the good of the *whole* requires a stricter attachment to a part[2].' Sometimes his identification of the conceptions seems absolute; as in the words, 'If there is no *moral sense* which makes rational actions appear *beautiful* or *deformed:* if all *approbation* be from the *interest* of the approver, what's Hecuba to us, or we to Hecuba[3]?' Again and again he speaks of 'the *moral beauty or deformity* of actions[4]' as synonymous with their rightness or wrongness, as in the proposition, 'We have a sense of *goodness* and *moral beauty* in actions, distinct from advantage[5].' It is true that sentences may be quoted in which he expressly distinguishes the two 'Senses,' not only in name, but in specified function. Here is an example: 'As the Author of Nature has determined us to receive, by our *External Senses*, pleasant or disagreeable ideas of objects, according as they are useful or hurtful to our bodies; and to receive from *uniform objects* the pleasures

[1] Enquiry, p. 118.   [2] Ibid. p 180.   [3] Ibid pp. 121, 122.
[4] Ibid. p. 176.   [5] Ibid. p. 190.

of *beauty* and *harmony*, to excite us to the pursuit of knowledge and to reward us for it, or to be an argument to us of His *goodness*, as the *uniformity* itself proves His *existence*, whether we had a *sense* of *beauty* in *uniformity* or not; in the same manner He has given us a *Moral Sense*, to direct our actions and to give us still *nobler pleasures:* so that while we are only intending the good of others, we undesignedly promote our own greatest private good[1].' It will be observed, however, that the three separate places here assigned to the several 'Senses' are in a classification or hierarchy of *Pleasures:* they are so many stages of a homogeneous but ascending scale, and are differenced, as Stuart Mill would say, in the 'quality' of their agreeableness. This is not the distinction which meets the requirements of a true psychology. I am afraid that, in spite of some contrary appearances, we must treat Hutcheson's doctrine, on this side, as one of *moral æsthetics* only, which essentially reduces perfect character simply to a work of high art.

D. SPRINGS OF ACTION.—So much for the passive susceptibilities of our nature,—the Senses, external, internal, moral, with their several types of pleasure and pain. From them we pass to Hutcheson's doctrine respecting the *Springs of action* or powers of the will. The common feature of them all is the preconception and desire of Good; and Good means nothing else than happiness and the means of it: it is therefore purely relative to the nature and sensibilities of the recipient, and must not be sought in any absolute object of the Reason or eternal congruities which would be present in a universe without life; but only in the constitution of the being whom we are studying. Our human good, then, consists in the enjoyments attending on the foregoing senses: they supply *the ends in view* which stir our varieties of activity. But they are not private and exclusive possessions: we see others affected by them, like ourselves; and this is a

[1] Enquiry, pp. 134, 135.

spectacle in which we experience an instinctive and original delight; which might indeed, as a distinct kind of feeling received, be added on to the lists of senses, and actually is so, in our author's treatise on 'The Nature and Conduct of the Passions,' under the name of the 'Public Sense[1].' It is there defined 'Our determination to be pleased with the *happiness* of others, and to be uneasy at their *misery*.' We are moved to action, therefore, wholly by some affection towards rational or at least sensitive beings, whose pleasures and pains make up our good and evil; and, if we confine our attention to *persons*, they must be either ourselves or others; the care we necessarily feel for our own happiness is self-love; that which we feel for the happiness of others is benevolence. Both of them alike supply us with our *ultimate ends;* for, our sympathetic distress or joy in the presence or at the thought of others' suffering or relief is no less an instinct of nature than our self-regards.

To the establishment of our 'Public Sense' or benevolent affection in this position, viz. of an instinct co-ordinate with that of self-love, the most characteristic part of Hutcheson's philosophy is devoted. He takes it up as the sole possible antagonist of the Epicurean principle of personal hedonism, and insists that the whole ground of ethical theory is covered by the reasonings of these two rival claimants[2]. Not that he is unacquainted with the schemes of Cudworth and Clarke; but he denies them a place in moral philosophy at all, on the ground that the relations which they set up, of absolute truth and fitness of things, are objects of contemplative Reason, not of practical volition; so that these systems, however true, can supply only a doctrine of the understanding, not of the will[3]. Having narrowed his problem to a conflict between the dictatorship of Self and its joint consulship with Benevolence, he pronounces against the former as

---

[1] Sect. I. p 5.   [2] Illustrations of the Moral Sense, p. 210.
[3] Ibid. Sect. I. II.

incompatible with the obvious facts of human experience, unless they are distorted and caricatured by cynical interpretations. We are conscious of no secret view to personal advantage in the love we bear to friends and benefactors and country; in the pity that responds to suffering, in the enthusiasm that draws us in heart to the great figures of distant ages and far-off lands; in the effort and the risk involved for the rescue of an innocent victim, or the overthrow of a guilty oppressor If these affections were present with us only as the means of some pleasures of our own, they could be bribed away by any offer that should outbid them; yet we well know how completely inoperative such attempted competition would be. The slow and subtle process of transforming the primitive selfish desires into complex forms of seeming disinterestedness, does not avail to cancel the instinctive look of the generous impulses: for, when occasion arises, they rush to the front and carry off the will of the child, the savage, even the habitual criminal, whose life has afforded little room for such refining processes[1].

By the ordinance of nature, then, we are placed at the disposal of two springs of action, Self-love and Benevolence. Each of these exercises its sway over us in two forms, distributed or concentrated. Our personal desires are numerous as the sources and inlets of pleasure; and each, as it turns up, will run its course, if there be nothing to stop it, and will fulfil its aim. But experience soon shows us a number of mutual interferences among our desires, which make it either impossible or self-defeating to float upon whichever at the moment is on the surface. And hence we are led to take them all into comparative view, and adjust their relations so as to keep the incompatibles from clashing, and admit the rest into the happiest co-operation. Thus arises 'calm, deliberate self-love,' exercised from a central survey of its whole realm. But there still remains

[1] Nature and Conduct of the Passions, I. Art. iii. pp. 13-26; Illustrations of the Moral Sense, pp. 211-213.

some room for the earlier form of the motive, in which the 'particular desires' have nothing to fear from their free play, and need take, or at all events do take, no counsel from the larger Prudence. In point of fact, it is only among the considerate few that the incentive expands into the wiser form. It is the same with the affection for others' good; it may be exclusive to a friend, may stop with the family, or the sect, or the state; may select some special class, the sick, the prisoner, or the slave; and in each case, its unconditional indulgence may run counter to the well-being that falls under some other head: nor will this liability cease till the mind's survey embraces the universe of human good, and the benevolence expands into philanthropy. This is 'universal calm benevolence,' as opposed to the 'particular affections,' beyond which the majority of mankind do not pass.

In case of a quarrel between one of my 'particular desires' and my 'calm self-love,' it is quite conceivable that it may be settled between themselves, without any mediator armed with arbitrating powers: because the impelling motive is the same with both, and the difference is only one of computation, where there is a common measure. With the understanding to step in as accountant, the true balance may easily be found. And so too it is (though somewhat less securely) with the variances of benevolence in its narrower and its wider range: the same affection,—the wish for others' happiness,—is the inspiration of both, and must be open to the persuasion of the larger success: revise the working of the sum, and the double answer will disappear.

But suppose the dissension to arise between the two different motive principles, and that the persuasion of the benevolent instinct is met by dissuasive pleas of self-love: both affections carry the same authority of nature: as heterogeneous, they have no common measure: they are in contradiction, and one of them must go out; and which is to be the victor must be determined, unless some helper appears, by their relative strength,—a mere accident of the individual subject. Here it is, however, that Hutcheson comes to the rescue with his doctrine of the Moral Sense. This faculty, in its pilgrimage among men and notice of their characters, has always 'approved of every kind affection[1],' has pronounced 'morally good' all actions 'which flow from benevolent affection or intention of absolute good to others[2],' nay, has declared 'all virtue' to be 'benevolence[3],' and 'benevolence the universal foundation of the Moral Sense[4].' The very end and function of this third principle implanted in the mind, is to decide between the other two when they clash; and were it not for its interposition as umpire, the controversy between them could never have been legitimately closed. It sides unconditionally with the universal happiness, and identifies all virtue with benevolence[5]. The question may doubtless still be raised, what the benevolent impulse gains by this accession of an umpire converted into an ally; and whether the defeated litigant will own itself crest-fallen at the verdict. This at least, perhaps on Hutcheson's representation this alone, is clear: the sentence is given by the *approving* faculty; and if the benevolent instinct takes effect, it will now entail, besides the satisfaction of its sympathetic aim, the joy of inward self-approval; and will escape the pains of self-reproach which, under an opposite choice, would have subtracted largely from the personal gains.

If this be all, however,—if the Moral Sense only adds the pleasure of self-satisfaction on one side of the scale, and the pain of self-dissatisfaction on the other,—the experiment is still hedonistic, and may still, for all that appears, leave the balance, though reduced, to the selfish arm of the lever. A tempted man may say within himself, 'True, if I refuse this good office, I cannot congratulate

---

[1] Illustrations of the Moral Sense, p. 113.
[2] Nature and Conduct of the Passions, II. p. 38.
[3] Enquiry, II. iii. p. 162.
[4] Ibid. II. iv. p. 196. [5] System, I. iii. pp. 50, 51.

myself on being a fine fellow, and may feel rather like a guest with thick boots and a cutaway coat in a ball-room: but it is not necessary that I should bask in my own admiration; I can dispense with that luxury, and, for the sake of what I like better, put up with a poor opinion of my conduct which I can soon manage to rub off or forget.' To a philosopher who simply trusts to the appeal, 'Do that thing, and you will be uneasy in your mind,' such an impudent reflection would seem to be not without avail. Hence, perhaps, it is that Hutcheson, instead of treating the moral verdict as something more than a prophecy of personal feelings, as something imperative and final, shows the greatest anxiety to corroborate it by proving the invariable coincidence of individual happiness with unswerving devotion to the universal good. Upon this thesis he virtually stakes everything: 'The principal business,' he says, 'of the *moral philosopher* is to show, from solid reasons, that *universal benevolence* tends to the happiness of *the benevolent*, either from the pleasures of *reflection, honour, natural tendency* to engage the good offices of men, upon whose aid we must depend for our happiness in this world; or from the sanctions of *Divine Law*, discovered to us by the constitution of the universe: that so no apparent views of *interest* may counteract this *natural inclination*[1].' To prove this proposition, Hutcheson provides an elaborate valuation of pleasures and pains from the several senses and affections, including the Moral Sense[2]; and sums up the results of its application in these words: 'Thus, upon comparing the several kinds of pleasure and pains, both as to *intention*' (intensity) 'and *duration*, we see that the whole sum of interest lies upon the side of *virtue, public spirit*, and *honour*. To forfeit these pleasures, in whole or in part, for any other *enjoyment*, is the most foolish bargain, and, on the contrary, to secure them with the *sacrifice* of all others, is the truest gain[3].'

[1] Enquiry, II vii p. 269.
[2] Nature and Conduct of the Passions, Sect. V. [3] Ibid. Sect. VI. p. 167.

The reader who has followed with some fervour of assent the proofs of human disinterestedness and of an intuitive Moral Sense, is naturally surprised to see matters brought at last to this bald issue of gain and loss. The Moral Sense then, far from delivering us from hedonism, only contributes an additional item to its reckoning. And though self-interest would poison and destroy the virtue of social actions, taken one by one, it is what constitutes the virtue of them all together; and every impulse of affection becomes right by forgetting the reason which makes it so! Disinterestedness surely is but a painted illusion of excellence, if it is a mere veil to hide the real ground of good, and make that appear an ultimate end which is only a means. In such case, it is on a par with any other pious self-deceit; and a clear-eyed philosopher, whose sole allegiance is to the truth, would more fitly feel shame than pride in proving it to be an inherent element of human affections. We get, I fear, no ethical good from Hutcheson's Moral Sense and disinterestedness: no sooner are we gladdened by the semblance and promise of it, than it is swallowed up again by the omnivorous digestion of the Epicurean monster.

E. OPTIMIST ESTIMATE OF VIRTUE. — The problem, however, of the accordance between happiness and virtue, though not fundamental, is highly important in its subsidiary place; and Hutcheson's treatment of it is both ingenious and large. In order to establish his measures of value he separates homogeneous pleasures from heterogeneous; estimating the former by their *intensity and duration;* the latter, by their *dignity and duration;* and pronouncing that duration is of less account to the higher than to the lower; and that for inferior dignity no compensation can be found in any intensity and duration. He admits the difficulty of establishing an exact scale of amount among pleasures which are necessarily variable with the differing tastes of men; but he avails himself of the rule that, while the narrower and lower nature cannot appreciate the superior experience of the more capacious and higher, the latter is familiar with the whole system, and can compare all its parts : so that, as Aristotle said, 'the good (and complete) man is the judge and standard of all things[1].' The anticipation of J. S. Mill's well-known doctrine respecting the dimensions of pleasure[2] is here very striking, extending almost to the words of the exposition; though Hutcheson follows out the principle more into detailed classification than Mill. Lowest in the scale he places the *Appetites*, which require antecedent wants to make them good for anything, and adventitious attractions, social, æsthetic, and affectionate, to give them their true worth; and which, in their proper place, are not only compatible with virtuous life, but at their best in it. (2) The pleasures of knowledge and taste, which he assigns to the next rank, are more durable as well as higher; and so far as they are sought in a direction and among objects readily accessible, are a precious embellishment to life; but as they are apt to run out into costly indulgence, they need a firm hand of control. (3) A step higher brings us to the sympathetic pleasures, of family, friendship, citizenship, humanity: these it is that furnish us with the chief business of life, and the occasions of deepest joy and sorrow; nor is their durability measured even by that of their objects. Bordering upon them are (4) the moral pleasures, from the consciousness of good affections and actions; which carry, in their very essence, a natural repose and harmony; and put forth energies intrinsically healthy and without misgiving. Should they even fail of their aim, they suffer from disappointment less than the selfish desires; and their satisfactions, inherent in the character, are beyond the power of fortune: in their perfect form they culminate in religious joy. (5) Here we might well suppose ourselves to be at rest upon the summit;

---

[1] System, L iv. p. 121. Cf. Arist. Eth. Nic. II. vi. 15; VI. v. 1.
[2] Utilitarianism, chap. ii. pp. 12–16.

but we are invited on to an ulterior point, apparently in the ascending order, viz. the pleasures of *honour and approbation by others*. Hutcheson guards himself here from expressly assigning them to higher rank, by saying that they are so connected with the pleasures of virtue as to render comparison between them needless. In their union with each other and with the sympathetic affections, crowned by faith in God's approving goodness, they almost realise the 'joy unspeakable and full of glory[1].' It is evident that Hutcheson's affectionate and dependent nature was keenly sensitive to the sympathy and the good opinion of others Of 'true glory' he speaks with enthusiasm: it is more than durable: it survives the life that wins it: it is posthumous in one world, and everlasting in another. To a man so glowing with this fire it is more than an honour, that it seems never to have tempted him to any questionable compliance or dazzled the intentness of his eye on truth and right.

On considering what alone can be really meant by the 'quality' of pleasures, it will be evident that, in its aim and purport, this classification is the equivalent of the 'scale of worth' on which the springs of action are arranged in a former chapter. I own that the differences between them are great enough to be discouraging; but in the comparison of independent tentatives lies the only hope that something better may emerge. I cannot but think that the dominance of the hedonist idea, though under the select aspect of quality, has thrown the system of impulses, in Hutcheson's thought, out of their true moral proportion; and that if he had enthroned the genius of Right in the seat of judgment over them, they would have appeared in different order and with further discrimination. But he was on another track, i. e. on his way to prove the good 'bargain' effected by the virtuous life; and provided he gathered into his account all the constituents of its experience, it was of no essential consequence that they should

[1] System, I. vii. pp. 125-135.

be taken in their correct turn : his reasoning may remain sound, though the order of a subsidiary member of it should be a little loose. To complete his thesis, he similarly appraises the pains incident to the several desires, and shows, in each class as it appears, that the immunities and alleviations prevailingly attach to the lot of the righteous. (1) *Bodily pain*, with which we could ill dispense as an index of disturbance needing attention and arrest, is regarded by weak minds as something to be escaped at any price; so that, by the threat of it, you may make them accomplices in any crime. Yet, when they have bought exemption by falsehood and treachery, and have taken in exchange their burden of shame and remorse, they confess too late that the moral ill is worse than the natural. To judge of the relative place of these, we should compare them at their maximum, i. e. in the case of the *worst crimes* committed as the ransom from the *worst pains:* every sound and brave man would accept or keep the torture and decline the sin. And so would he decide for another, even the dearest to him, and would sooner see a son subject to any malady than lost in guilt and shame. (2) Lighter than bodily pains are those *of Imagination:* such, for example, as arise from the contrast of mean and hard external lot with bright dreams of seemly and handsome conditions of life. They are not only relatively light: they are completely controllable by self-discipline, and therefore vanish from virtuous experience. Where they feel no firm repressive hand, they carry off their victim into reckless expenditure and all the miseries of scrambling indebtedness. (3) To no greater pain can we be subjected than the sympathetic and moral, which may be taken together: to witness the suffering of one dear to us, especially when it admits of no alleviation from efforts and sacrifices of ours, is, or may be, an agony to leave an indelible impression and haunt us with pathetic images for ever. It would hardly seem so indeed, from the pleasure we take in witnessing tragedies. But then, the suffering is only in a subsidiary place : it is but the indispensable means to the manifestation of heroism, and the pleasure we feel is that of admiration and moral sympathy; and this is of so high a character, as to be worth purchasing at the cost of compassionate pains. Take away these experiences of nobleness and justice, and the naked 'pity and terror' of the tragedy would be simply repulsive. Fellow-feeling for suffering, however, is still open to some alleviations which are inaccessible to remorse and guilt This, kept down, it may be, or defied in the heat of passion, rises as soon as we 'come to ourselves,' and poisons life by making the inmost self hateful, and leaving us without retreat; and though it may become blunted by habit, and sleep in intervals of forgetfulness, it wakes again with the touch of sorrow, and haunts us with returning self-abhorrence. (4) The counterpart to the satisfactions of honour is the pain of *Infamy*. If justly incurred, it is but the external corroboration of remorse: if unjustly, it is assuaged by a supporting self-approval and rest in God; but even the human alienation is felt to be more terrible than bodily anguish, and not infrequently leads to suicide [1].

From this survey of the contents of human experience, Hutcheson thinks it evident that the life of greatest virtue is, and must be, that of greatest happiness. Its very element is the social and moral affections, whose pleasures are supreme, and secures it from the moral pains, which are the hardest to endure. And though it is fully exposed to the sufferings of sympathy, it brings them the best relief in the activities of succouring love and the admiration of noble fortitude. And in proportion as the affections widen and take in larger and larger circles of human good, i. e in proportion as they become more virtuous, do they more easily rebound from the stroke of private suffering and recover hope and joy in fellowship with well-being upon a grander scale. And as for the inevitable ills that are the impartial liability of all, none certainly can be more

[1] System, I. vii. pp. 139-148.

ready for them, and less cast down by them, than the temperate, the prudent, the just, and the brave[1].

§ 3. *Appreciation of the Doctrine.*

In looking back on Hutcheson's whole scheme of thought, with a view to store up its gifts and drop its imperfections, I feel how harsh may become the critic's duty in dealing with the doctrines he describes. To appreciate the merits of their authors, he must judge them with relation to their place and time, and tell what enrichments they have added to their past: to appreciate the contents of their theories, he must test them by the standards of the present, and apply the very light which they have helped into existence to detect their flaws and their lacunæ. Again and again, historical feeling and personal admiration make me shrink from the task, as if it were ungenerous. But the quest of truth, like that of right, is simple and severe, and sometimes imposes on the least willing censor the correction of his nearest friend. It is thus that I must point out how Hutcheson, in bravely taking the field against the most insidious and dangerous fallacies of his time, and reclaiming from them no small portion of their momentary gains, occupied some ground which he did not provide the means of permanently holding.

He found the whole world of English philosophy and theology in slavery to the autocracy of self-love; and, what is worse, in unsuspecting and contented slavery to it: it was the accepted lawgiver and interpreter of human life, here and hereafter. He abhorred the tyranny, and raised the standard against it; and, within the circle of his influence, reinstated a faith in human disinterestedness and an enthusiasm for goodness, which scattered the subtleties of the hedonist school. Routed enemies, however, whose ranks are broken by too impetuous a rush, are pretty sure to rally and return; and it is evident enough that the Epicurean host has reappeared in force, and, owning no defeat, still claims the

[1] System, I. viii. xi.

field. Let us first consider whether this conflict was fairly closed for the time, and is reopened on fresh ground.

A. RELATION OF BENEVOLENCE AND SELF-LOVE.—I fear that Hutcheson's distinction between benevolence and self-love is illusory. He understands by benevolence regard for others' good, and claims for it the character of an original instinct, co-ordinate with the impulse towards any personal good. By establishing it in this position, he thinks that he secures it in all the rights which had been previously monopolised by its companion, but which must now become partnership affairs. He admits, however, that the partners do not always agree, but in the exercise of their equal rights will draw different ways: on which line, then, is the movement to take place? The public instinct, he decides, is to prevail over the private. If we ask 'Why?' and what it is that upsets the equality of the partners? he tells us of another instinct that steps in and reports in favour of the public affection. But why should this secondary witness be listened to as an oracle? At best, it is only like a witness to character, who thinks well of one of the litigants. True, it is an instinct: but what makes that conclusive? According to our author, instincts are our true guides, because to disappoint them is painful, and to satisfy them is pleasant. The account, therefore, stands thus: through instinct number one, we like the public good: through instinct number three, we like that liking: through instinct number two, we like the private good: and, however the balance may be settled, the determinants are the agent's pleasures and pains, and nothing else: and if, as is quite possible, the satisfaction of the instinct which is backed up by another, together with that of its patron, are no greater than those of the single competitor, no reason is offered for the repression of the latter. The good of others, by being made the object-matter of an instinct, becomes *our* good, i. e. our pleasure, for with Hutcheson the words are interchangeable; and the preference of benevolence is but the choice of the greater pleasure. He even denies, what appears to me evidently true, that in instinctive action, the motive power lies in the *want*,—it may be the *blind* want,—propelling us from behind towards the appropriate object; and insists that it consists wholly in the expectation of the terminal good or evil[1]: so that pleasure desired, or pain shunned, is the only possible incentive to the will. This is surely inadmissible. The very existence of instincts that provide for they know not what, disproves it. And, even in other cases, the stirring power is in the contrast felt between the consciousness now present and the consciousness conceived, between the actual, and the ideal experience: the effort to enter upon the latter is an effort to escape from the former: the motive is in *the relation* between the two, and cannot be identified with one term to the exclusion of the other. But, if his position were made good, it would simply establish the impossibility of disinterestedness, and identify Hutcheson's psychology with that of the school which he set himself to confute. Once assume as axioms, that good means pleasure, and that pleasure sets up instinct, instead of instinct pleasure; and there is no escape from the whole coherent system of the hedonist and determinist philosophy. Hutcheson's concessions to it appear to me fatal to the object which he had most in view. In what light do these concessions exhibit the disinterestedness which he claims for benevolence? He means it to be its crown of glory; but, on his own showing, it is little else than a mere blindness and imbecility. For the agent addresses himself to the happiness of others, as if it were given him as a good upon its own account, irrespective of its relation to himself; but this, we are told, is precisely what it is *not:* this fancied absoluteness is false; and were it not that with the happi-

---

[1] System, I iii. p. 42. Prof. Sidgwick (Mind, XXXIX. p. 442, note) speaks of Hutcheson as here 'expressly referring to *selfish* desires' The words are, 'In all our desires, benevolent or selfish, there is some motive, some end intended, distinct from the joy of success, or the removal of the pain of desire,'—'the prospect of some other good.'

ness of others nature had wrapped up his own, his benevolence would be without its *raison d'être*. If the instinct is unaware of this, and assumes the contrary, it is in ignorance and error; and it is so far from clearing itself thereby into higher merit, that it sinks into a puerile stupidity. It can never redound to the honour of a rational being to shut the eyes to the real reasons and relations of things. Hutcheson insists that the real reasons are *interest:* the highest honour is *disinterest*. I find, therefore, his distinction between Benevolence and Self-love illusory.

B. RELATION OF BENEVOLENCE AND MORAL SENSE.—
Further: his distinction between *Benevolence and the Moral Sense* is illusory. There are indeed passages in his writings which so describe the moral faculty as satisfactorily to save its essence. When, for example, he tells us that 'Moral goodness' is *not* that which pleases us by sympathy (arts and inventions may do this): or, that which gives us the *pleasure of approbation* (for it is not good because we approve it, but we approve it because it is good). or, that which *is serviceable to the agent or the approver:* or, that which tends to *procure honour:* or, that which *conforms to law,* Divine or human: or, that which *conforms to truth:* or, that which *has fitness and congruity:* or, that which is *sanctioned by education and custom :* but, *an inherent and independent quality immediately perceived in certain affections* with their consequent actions, and perceived by instinctive intuition; and when he adds that this intuitive instinct not only rightly guides each separate affection, but, working in a reflective nature, compares the several affections in respect of their apprehended goodness, and, after practice and cultivation, notices 'many degrees' among the objects of its approbation, and finds 'some much more lovely than others;' he employs language to which no exception can be taken, unless it be to its final lapse from ethical into æsthetic epithets[1]. But a reader who, with this statement

[1] System, I. iv pp 54–60.

in his thoughts, follows him with any vigilant precision through his numerous references to the Moral Sense, is driven, if I mistake not, to say within himself, 'O si sic omnia!' He never clears the 'independent quality of goodness' which the instinct is appointed to discern, and which it finds existing in various degrees: so that it remains cognisable, i e. distinguishable from other qualities, only by its relation to our moral sense, as 'that which we approve,' and in affirming that we approve it because it is good, we say no more than that 'we approve it because it is *approvable.*' The nearest approach to any objective identification of this 'good' quality is in the frequent statement, that what we approve is always '*kind affection,*' or good-will, sometimes towards 'universal happiness,' at others towards that of particular persons. This surely seems to be sufficiently provided for in the benevolent affection itself, unless 'approval' of it is to mean something more (as with Hutcheson it does not) than to have æsthetic pleasure in it: one who loves the happiness of others, *ipso facto* loves the 'good-will' which causes it; and there is no need of a reduplicating instinct to repeat what the first has done. It seems, indeed, plain that all clear difference disappeared, in Hutcheson's feeling, between the affections towards others and the Moral Sense: 'happiness in benevolence' is a phrase used by him as a synonym for the '*Moral Sense*[1];' and 'happiness in benevolence' is benevolence itself. And so, after resolving, as we have seen, all virtue into benevolence, he identifies the Moral Sense with it, and reduces the distinction between them to a verbal illusion. This, no doubt, is partly due to his singular omission, from his conception of virtue, of all human springs of action and feeling that do not come under the head of affections towards persons. The control of appetite and passion, the exercise of courage and presence of mind, the regard for order and beauty, the search for truth, can by no means be brought under the category of benevolences, yet are

[1] Enquiry, II. p. 248.

justly regarded as having place among the attributes of a noble character.

It will be evident, I think, from these remarks that there is a characteristic want of clearness in the following sentence: 'The affections approved as right are either universal good-will, and love of moral excellence, or such particular kind affections as are consistent with these[1].' We ought to be able to add up together the two items here enumerated as jointly constituting the sum total of *Right affections*,—viz. 'universal good-will,' and 'love of moral excellence,' i. e of what is right. But as he has identified 'moral excellence,' or virtue, with 'universal good-will,' this is only to say that right affections consist of 'universal good-will' and the love of it, which surely cannot be added to it, as it is included in it. Or, if for 'moral excellence' we substitute its equivalent, 'what is right,' then it becomes apparent that into the definition is imported the conception defined · 'right affections consist of universal good-will and love of right affection.' In truth, Hutcheson is continually passing to and fro between the 'Moral Sense' and 'universal benevolence,' without ever settling any definite relation between them, or assigning to the former any function to which the latter is not competent. They play the part, apparently (if they are two at all), of parallel and separate determinants of the inwardly right, and simply do the same thing twice over. Benevolence, for example, is represented as in itself intuitively aware that the wider it is the better it is, and that the more extensive type of it is entitled to control the less extensive; so that, if we were merely affectional beings, without any further guidance, our rules would be what they now are. When the moral faculty is let in upon the stage, its business is to deal with the very same relations and dispose them in conformity with the same rules; so that it contributes nothing but a ratification of the instinctive adjustments. This is indeed expressly avowed where he says, 'The course of life pointed out to

[1] System, I. iii. p. 252

us immediately by the *Moral Sense*, and confirmed by all just consideration of our true interest, must be the very same which the *generous calm determination* [i. e. 'universal benevolence'] 'would recommend [1].'

It follows from this parallelism that it is open to our author to carry questions for decision into either of the two co-ordinate courts, of public benevolence or of the Moral Sense: and it is impossible not to notice his preference for the former. Butler, it is well known, draws a distinction between *Justice*, in the sense of treating men *according to their deserts*, and *regard for the public good* in dealing with them; on the ground that, in consulting for the public good, it may be necessary to let off the guilty (for the sake of their evidence), or to inflict suffering on the innocent: you are not sure therefore of being led, by the rule of public good, to treat men as they deserve. Hutcheson replies to this effect, that, though social good may sometimes require you, in the treatment of men, to look at other matters besides the merits or demerits of their past conduct, yet whenever you go by the rule of their deserts, it is because this is required by the public good; Justice, therefore, receives its credentials from social utility [2]. The answer, it is plain, is not ultimate: what makes it useful and ethically efficacious to treat men as they deserve? The universal sense of Justice in human communities, and the inward response and approval given to all behaviour which is rightly adjusted to character, and did not the public law find support in the private conscience of the citizens, it would have neither remedial nor controlling power: its social utility is accredited by its equity. Take away that equity, and there are no scales in which you can weigh out its disciplinary pains or honours: Benevolence itself will be bereft of its calculus, and will work out no answer to its sum, unless by stealing it, through furtive glances, off the slate of its quicker neighbour, Justice. Under failure of the distinction between Benevolence and the

[1] System, I xi p 222.   [2] Ibid. II. iii. p 256.

Moral Sense, it is the affectional element which Hutcheson almost invariably saves, and the dutiful that is left to its fate.

C. WANT OF MORAL GRADATION.—I have already pointed out the temptation under which Hutcheson lay, to fix his attention upon outward action as the seat of moral qualities, and to seek therefore in what *it did* for the marks of what it *was*. And he simply carried out this preconception, when he made the benevolent affection, which he identified with virtue, depend for its worth on the extent of its range over persons. At times, his whole Ethics appear to be comprehended under this objective formula; for example, when he says, 'In governing the Moral sense and desires of virtue, nothing more is necessary than to study the nature and tendency of human actions; and to extend our views to the whole species, or to all sensitive natures, so far as they can be affected by our conduct[1].' When writing in this mood, he might be supposed, nay he actually is, a pure Utilitarian: as indeed everyone must be, who looks for right and wrong in action, instead of in the agent. But, at other times, he finds the proper objects of approval and disapproval in the motive affections only, and distinctly affirms them to be the primary candidates for moral judgment. Nor does he fail to see, when his eye is thus turned inward, that, without waiting for external consequences, the invisible springs of action have in themselves their differences of worth, so that there is an *intensive* order of right, before coming to the *extensive*. He thus prepares the way for the inevitable questions, 'What is the rule of this order?' and 'What is the series contained in it?' To these questions he gives no definite or constant reply. When he says, 'There is a plain graduation in the objects of our approbation and condemnation, from the indifferent actions ascending to the highest virtue, or descending to the lowest vice,' we expect him next to lay before us the

[1] Nature and Conduct of the Passions, Sect. VI. p. 193.

scale of values that is in his thoughts; but the 'graduation' that is so 'plain' is withdrawn into obscurity on this plea,—'It is not easy to settle exactly the several intermediate steps in due order, but the highest and lowest are manifest[1];' and he contents himself with bringing these extremes,—of selfish and of generous desire,—into strong contrast, and intimating that the relative degree of worth in any particular affection depends on its ratio of strength to the total energies of the character[2]. If such a series of ratios, between the character as a constant term and each affection, taken with it in turn, could be defined, it would give us only the component factors in the moral value of the permanent personality; and, what we want to know is not the true estimate of this whole man, and the way in which he is made up, but how to rate each impulse as it stirs the will, and how conflicting affections that beset it together stand ethically to one another. And until this is determined, and the measures of comparative worth are settled among the several springs of action, the ratios which they should respectively bear to the entire character are without the means of expression. No such graduated scale does Hutcheson provide. Again and again he tantalises us, by bringing us to the very spot where it should be found; but nothing is there, except the rude and confused strife and defiance between self-love and benevolence. Every scene in his moral psychology runs into a duel between these two rather tiresome actors. He promises us a well-peopled stage, astir with some intricacy of plot and variety of sympathy; but the forms slip away and pass without doing anything, beyond committing their cause to one or the other of the irremovable combatants, that are for ever fighting and never slain.

In spite, therefore, of much language indicative of a true theoretic tendency,—respecting 'a just proportion of strength in the narrower affections,' their rights against the selfish desires, their subordination to 'more extensive affections,'

[1] System, I iv. p. 64.   [2] Ibid. p. 65.

and the essential dependence of the moral quality of action upon its inward springs, rather than upon the intellectual reckoning of the greater good [1],—Hutcheson appears to me singularly wavering and unsteady in his moral doctrine; inclining now to an external, and then to an internal rule of right, without distinguishing the different parts which they must play; recognising, but leaving undefined, the gradations of worth in the springs of action, and instead of inferring thence the relative and preferential character of all virtue, still regarding it as an absolute quality inherent in an act *per se,* using the conceptions of Duty and Obligation, but, from preoccupation with those of Beauty and Virtue as Gemini, failing to sound the depth of their significance. When he quits the business of theoretical construction, with which alone my subject brings me into contact, and enters upon the treatment of applied morals, his best qualities of intellect and feeling come out in their full strength, and so win upon his readers, that they can hardly close his volumes without the consciousness of having gained a wise and generous friend.

D. Determinism.—Not a word has yet been said or invited, by Hutcheson's scheme of thought, as to his relation to the controversy about Free-will. His reticence on the subject might well be cited in confirmation of Professor Sidgwick's opinion, that it is perfectly possible to construct an ethical system, while maintaining a neutral attitude towards the advocates in this dispute. Notwithstanding this reticence, however, it is neither difficult nor unimportant to define his opinion upon the question at issue. When I affirm that he is a decided Determinist, it is probable that many of my readers may receive the statement with surprise and incredulity; for it is so usual in England for the Necessarian to reject the belief in an instinctive Moral Sense, that it is not easy to conceive of the coexistence of the two beliefs in the same person. Yet there is no inconsistency in their

[1] System, II. xvii. p 118.

combination. The Determinist philosophy regards man as simply a product or effect; the Libertarian, as in part an originating cause, capable of determining what was indeterminate before: in the one case, he is throughout, and has to be, submissive to the play of given causes centring upon his life, that move and mould him as they come and go, and unite and part; in the other, he himself stands in the midst, master of an autonomous reserve, which has a voice and vote to give, ere the drift of things can settle on its lines. Is man the absolute creature of the cosmic powers that set him up? Those powers may be found at work in two different seats,—in the scene around him, in the constitution within him; and it matters not where they are, if between them they completely dispose of him and make him what he is. It was the humour of the empirical psychology introduced by Locke, to minimise the nature within the man and bring it down, as far as possible, to pure receptivity: while making the very most of the surrounding nature, as it beats upon his senses, and 'imprints' its ideal vestiges on him, and accumulates what is called his 'experience.' Hutcheson thought that, out of the whole stock of natural data, too much had been emptied out of the human creature and thrown into the crowd of exterior laws; and resolved to take back an instinct or two, without which it seemed difficult to give account of the phenomena. But the Moral Sense for which he thus provided a constitutional place was no less a function of Nature, than the fabricating processes of '*experience*' which it superseded; and in the ideas, the volitions, the movements which he owed to it, man was as truly shaped by agencies in which he had no voice, as in the trains of his memory and the logic of his understanding. From whatever play, of concurrence or conflict among the instincts, the determinations of his will may issue, they are but the resultants of conditions found or formed for him, and are dependent only on their relative strength. Thus, the proportion between the empirical and the instinctive element in a psychology has nothing to do with its relation to the doctrine of Free-will; and Hutcheson was in no way bound to adopt that doctrine, as a twin-birth with his Moral Sense. The evidence of his determinism, though not very conspicuous, is unmistakable; he says, for example, 'When any event may affect both the *agent* and *others*, if the agent have both *self-love* and *public affections*, he acts according to that affection which is *strongest*, when there is any *opposition* of interests. If there be no opposition, he follows both[1].' And again, to the phrase 'determining ourselves freely' he allows only two possible meanings, between which we may have our choice, viz. '*acting without motive or exciting reason*,' and '*acting from instinct or affection*[2].' The first is the absurdity which he justly excludes: the second is the *spontaneity* which alone he keeps; and this, I need not say, by no means amounts to free-will. To his prepossession upon this question must be attributed the loose and unsatisfactory account which he gives of the central group of words in the Vocabulary of Morals; for example, 'Duty,' 'Ought,' 'Right,' 'Merit,' 'Approbation,' 'Reward,' and their opposites: a set of terms with which, it is plain, he feels himself ill at ease, and can hold no pleasant intercourse, till he has made converts of them, and baptised them into a non-natural sense. For him, perhaps, they may emerge regenerate; to the unconverted, they appear bereft of their wits.

Here we may take our leave of Hutcheson: not without gratitude to him both for what he has achieved, and for what he has failed to achieve: that he has let in a light of so much beauty upon the virtues; and that he has not been able, in the flood of beauty, to dissolve all their moral essence. In parting with him, we stand at the end of our long and winding road: he is the last of many companions, stately or keen, severe or facile, mystic or humane,

---

[1] Illustrations of the Moral Sense, Sect. I. p. 227.
[2] Ibid. Sect. V. p. 292.

with whom we have held by the way a series of dialogues of the dead. Yet not always with the dead; for the problems which have engaged us span the history of thought from end to end, and though they were already speaking in the language of Plato and Aristotle, are still not silent in the literature of to-day. It would have been easy, and in some respects rewarding, to indulge in detours, and make acquaintance with other intellectual chieftains, not less worthy of deference than those with whom we have taken counsel. But, in doing so, we should have wandered beyond the map that was to guide us, and have lost, perhaps, the memory and image of our track. There are but a few possible types of ethical theory: they are best studied in the person and reasoning of some eminent representative; and are most clearly conceived, when the selection stops with the perfect development of the type. Of the three great divisions of method, it is the central one alone in which, instead of teaching by historical example, I have ventured to speak for myself: not that representative instances were wholly out of reach; but because I knew of none that traced the lines of the procedure as far as I believed they might be legitimately carried.

The effect, however, of declining every deflection from the main order of my subject, has been the omission of some great names which, in a history of philosophy, would have stood at the head of its most important chapters; and it is perhaps incumbent on me to present, in regard to two or three of these, an explicit apology for passing them by, and to indicate the place, in the foregoing classification of systems, to which they must be referred.

It is scarcely less a surprise to myself than it can be to my readers, that no pages of this book have been reserved for Kant. The reason, paradoxical as it may seem, is found, not in any slight of his ethical theory, but in an approximate adoption of it; so that if, in working at my subject, my thoughts seldom consciously encountered his, it was from coalescence too near for adequate difference.

In spite of its *a priori* aspect, his moral doctrine is really based on the contents of inward experience, and in particular on the intuitive consciousness of Duty: it is, therefore, idiopsychological; and though its architecture is different in form from that of the construction which I have sketched, it covers the same ground, and rests upon the same foundation. This sanction of the method of reflective self-knowledge is the more impressive, because in Kant it involved a distinct breach with metaphysics, and constituted a refusal to descend into human nature from a prior ontologic sphere, and with an artillery of infinitudes explode and annihilate the meaning and worth of finite personalities. As this feature of Kant's philosophy, on which alone it would have been pertinent to dwell, is usually regarded by his disciples as a weakness and inconsequence, I may hope for indulgence to my silence respecting him[1].

A similar plea,—of essential accordance,—is all that I can offer for giving no express analysis of Butler. He occupies, more nearly perhaps than any other writer, the position of a discoverer in moral theory; nor can its problems ever be accurately discussed without some reference to his thought. But sermons cannot be the depository

[1] Kant attempted to pass from the *Seyn* and *Geschehen* to the *Sollen* by way of the *Pure Reason*, to which, without empirical elements, he referred his first principles—'Act so that you can will your rule as Universal Law for all minds.' This principle, expressible only in abstract terms, I cannot accept either as an *a priori* datum, or as alighting (in the property *Universality*) on the *essence* of *the Moral*. This predicate and the two following, viz. that a 'rational being is an end in himself,' and that 'the Will is autonomous,' are surely not prior forms which, carried into experience and fitting on to it, make it moral; but later products of that experience. Kant himself admits that, after all, 'it is inexplicable how Pure Reason can be also Practical' (Grundl. z. Met. d. Sitten, Rosenk. viii. p. 98). And it is not till his empty 'Categorical Imperative' finds in experience what orders to give, that its ghostly voice utters living words Once on the human side of the Metaphysic chasm, Kant seizes on the true symbolism of Morals,—the terms *Duty*, *Merit*, *Sin*, *Holiness*; and in them detects the Postulates of a Responsible Will, of a Righteous Rule of the world, of a Life beyond Death, of an Infinite Perfection. In effect therefore he draws from the same moral consciousness the same results as are presented in these volumes.

of a philosophy. He left only the first sketch and the unhewn materials of a systematic structure, and receives his best tribute of honour from those who try to fill in the design, and here and there add a sound stone at a weak place.

It is perhaps with an undue disregard of the spirit of the time, that I have shunned all criticism of Hegel. Prudence alone would have withheld me from an attempt for which, in spite of frequent study, I still distrust my competency. But, besides this, Hegel's philosophy does not admit of dismembering: the whole organism must be taken *en masse*, to be understood at all; and though an Hegelian may address to fellow-disciples a separate treatise on Morals or on Logic, it is impossible for the stranger to appreciate its reasons and its results, till he has received his complete initiation: it hangs in the air for him, and he knows not its relation to the solid world. The selection of Hegel, therefore, as the representative of metaphysic method (and he could hold no other place), would have involved an encyclopædia of exposition, before reaching the margin of Ethics at all: with the effect, not only of distorting the treatment out of all proportion, but of giving no conception of the mode in which systems of earlier renown and protracted historical influence operated upon moral doctrine. I would not, however, that my contentment with a less ambitious aim should be mistaken for any insensibility to the great and growing influence exerted by Hegelian conceptions upon the thought and faith and feeling of our time.

APPENDIX.

I. *Mr. Herbert Spencer to the Author.*

38, QUEEN'S GARDENS, BAYSWATER, W.
9 *March*, 1885.

DEAR DR. MARTINEAU,

I am much obliged to you for sending me a copy of your just published *Types of Ethical Theory*, and I join with my thanks my felicitations that you have been able to execute so elaborate a work at so comparatively advanced a period of life.

Of course, it is out of the question for me to enter into a discussion of that part of the work which deals with my own views; but I may in brief space indicate a cardinal error in your criticism. Contrasting Darwin's conception of evolution with mine, you say of Darwin's: 'As this idea is applied not less to what the animal *does* than to what his structure *is* or becomes, it presupposes that he can and will put forth actions hurtful to himself and doomed to have no future, and *that* in number out of all proportion to the few successes. On the other hand Spencer's law affirms that the animal can do nothing but the pleasantest, and that the pleasantest is identical with the fittest;—a rule which bars out all failure, and strictly obliges the creature to walk only on the narrow rail of the most useful.'

This is an entire misapprehension, which would surprise me, but that I am so accustomed to find that statements which I had as I supposed made as clear as possible, are misapprehended even by the most capable readers. If you will turn to p. 79 of the *Data of Ethics*, you will find a quotation from the *Principles of Psychology*, which I should have supposed made it manifest that I assumed no connexion between pleasure-giving acts and life-sustaining acts of any other kind than that which is established by survival of the fittest. I supposed I had clearly implied in the paragraph quoted as well as in the illustration beginning 'A plant which envelops[1],' &c. the belief that organisms may vary not only in respect of their structures, but in respect of their tendencies to do this or the other in all kinds of ways,—many or most of the ways at variance with welfare; and that those, the doings of which are conducive to welfare, alone, in the average of cases, survive, leading to the establishment of an inherited tendency towards such doings. The implication being that, agreeable sensations being the prompters, such of the agreeable sensations as go along with detrimental actions will cause the disappearance of individuals and varieties in which they occur; and those only which go along with beneficial actions will survive; resulting in the establishment of a connexion between pleasure-giving actions and beneficial actions. This view is not at variance with the view of Mr. Darwin, but is the application of that view to pleasure-giving and pain-giving actions as to other incidents of structure and life.

On referring, since writing the above paragraph, to the *Principles of Psychology*, Vol. I. p. 281, I find in continuation of the argument contained in the paragraph quoted in the *Data of Ethics* the following: 'But mis-adjustment invariably sets up re-adjustment. Those individuals in whom the likes and dislikes happen to be most out of harmony with the new circumstances, are the first to disappear. And if the race continues to exist there cannot but arise, by perpetual killing off of the least adapted, a variety having feelings that serve as incentives and deterrents in the modified way required.'

[1] The passage completes itself thus: 'A plant which envelops a buried bone with a plexus of rootlets, or a potato which directs its blanched shoots towards a grating through which light comes into the cellar, shows us that the changes which outer agents themselves set up in its tissues are changes which aid the utilization of these agents. If we ask what would happen if a plant's roots grew not towards the place where there was moisture but away from it, or if its leaves, enabled by light to assimilate, nevertheless bent themselves towards the darkness; we see that death would result in the absence of the existing adjustments. This general relation is still better shown in an insectivorous plant, such as the *Dionæa muscipula*, which keeps its trap closed round animal matter but not round other matter. Here it is manifest that the stimulus arising from the first part of the absorbed substance, itself sets up those actions by which the mass of the substance is utilized for the plant's benefit.' *Data of Ethics*, chap. vi § 33, pp. 79, 80.

APPENDIX. 57ᴉ

You will I think perceive that this initial error, underlying as it does your subsequent criticisms, in large measure invalidates them.

I am, truly yours,
(Signed) HERBERT SPENCER.

II. *The Author's reply to Mr. Herbert Spencer.*

35, GORDON SQUARE, W.C.
March 13, 1885.

DEAR MR. SPENCER,

I am sorry that you find reason to complain of the distinction I have drawn between your presentation of the principle of Evolution and Darwin's; and I need hardly say that I thankfully accept the re-statement of your meaning which your letter affords, and shall take the first opportunity of placing it, as a correction, side by side with the passage in which I seem to have gone wrong.

Let me explain why the passage to which you refer me failed, in connexion with its context, to give me a right conception of your doctrine as now expressed. Your letter says, in regard to the doings of sentient organisms, that 'agreeable sensations being the prompters, such of the agreeable sensations as go along with detrimental actions will cause the disappearance of individuals and varieties in which they occur; and those only which go along with beneficial actions will survive; resulting in the establishment of a connexion between pleasure-giving actions and beneficial actions.' Here it is assumed that, at the outset of animal consciousness, agreeable sensations are concomitants now of detrimental, now of beneficial actions; and that this indiscriminate distribution is only worked off by the gradual disappearance of individuals and varieties: so that the law of coalescence between pleasure-giving and life-promoting actions gets established as the result of the competitive animal experience. This is certainly in complete accordance with Mr. Darwin's view.

But in § 33 (pp. 79–82) of the *Data of Ethics* I understood you to assign an earlier date to this law, and to treat it as coeval with the dawn of sentiency and ready to direct the first act of conscious activity. It appears, in fact, as the mere emergence into feeling of such 'fit connexions between acts and results' as 'must establish themselves in living things, even before consciousness arises.' And accordingly you say '*At the very outset*, life is maintained by persistence in acts which conduce to it and desistance from acts which impede it; and whenever sentiency makes its appearance as an accompaniment, its forms must be such that in the one case the produced feeling is of a kind that will be sought—pleasure, and in the other case is of a kind that will be shunned—pain.' And again, 'It is demonstrable that there exists a *primordial* connexion between pleasure-giving acts and continuance or increase of life, and, by implication, between pain-giving acts and decrease or loss of life.' '*Setting out with the lowest living things*, we see that the beneficial act and the act which there is a tendency to perform are *originally* two sides of the same.' I interpreted this to mean, that the law of connexion on which you insist, instead of establishing itself as a *result* of eliminating experiments with pain and pleasure, was present at the cradle of conscious natures and directed their activities from the first. In this view, the indeterminate character of animal action from which Darwin starts is already precluded when pain and pleasure first enter upon the scene; and the succeeding evolution must be described in different terms from his. He is silent of your law: and it rather surprises me that you are willing to throw away the advantage which in some respects it gives you.

I was not inattentive to the argument, quoted from your *Principles of Psychology*, to show that your law is an inevitable deduction from the hypothesis of Evolution. But I supposed it intended to prove that, unless your law were in operation, evolution would be impossible; and *not*, to prove that, evolution being there, your law was its necessary result. 'The acknowledged fact of *survivals of the fittest*' (I understood you to plead) 'gives evidence, as an effect, of your law as its cause: reverse that law, and no such effect would ensue.' The logical validity of this argument is complete, whether your law is 'primordial' and pleasure and pain enter under it *ab initio*, or whether it clears itself into existence out of a mixed distribution of pleasure and pain. The reasoning therefore did not forbid me to believe that you deemed the law congenital with consciousness.

I learn now, for the first time, that the argument is to be turned round and read as an inference, not from effect to cause, but from cause to effect: i.e. 'the law must be there, because Evolution is sure to produce it.' This certainly throws us back upon Darwin's conception of an indeterminate initiative, and attenuates my contrast between your view and his. But, with the sincerest pains, I find it difficult to read this interpretation into your language respecting the primordial law which was no later than the first sentiency.

I wrote the paragraph on which you comment under the influence of your *Data of Ethics*. After reading (on the suggestion of your letter) the corresponding part of your *Principles of Psychology* in their present form, I perceive that I must withdraw or considerably modify my first remark upon your doctrine, viz. that 'it leaves upon your hands a mystery, i.e. an unexplained relation, which the simpler naturalist escapes, viz. "how comes it that what the animal likes is always best for it or for its kind?"'—for in the anterior and biological stage of the evolutionary history you point to an established connexion between functional acts and life-promoting tendency which, on the emergence of consciousness, passes into your law and plays the part of its explanation. Though, from my point of view, this rather shifts the difficulty than cancels it, yet I see that the terms of my criticism, as it stands, leave a wrong impression which I shall be anxious to remove.

I remain,
Very truly yours,
JAMES MARTINEAU.

III. *Mr. Herbert Spencer to the Author.*

38, QUEEN'S GARDENS, BAYSWATER, W.
17 *March*, 1885.

DEAR DR. MARTINEAU,

I am obliged by your note, and see that you had more reason for putting the interpretation you did than I supposed; though I should still have thought that the general character of the context, joined with my known views at large, would have negatived the interpretation you put.

The word 'primordial' as used in one place is doubtless somewhat misleading. It was used by me to imply a connexion which establishes itself along with the earliest vital activities;

and considering the matter from the point of view which I supposed I had made clear, it did not occur to me that it could be understood as meaning anything like pre-ordained; for of course the notion of any such connexion as pre-ordained is altogether at variance with the doctrine of evolution. I supposed it to be made clear that my conception was that in a developed creature any variation of feeling (as a taste for a new kind of food) which happens to be at variance with welfare, will cause the disappearance of the individual or the diminished prosperity of offspring, and will therefore tend to destroy itself, and maintain the connexion between pleasurable feeling and favourable action; and that just in the same way, such mere physical and præsentient actions as fragments of protoplasm under stimulation, must become adjusted to the maintenance of the species. Similarly when, in a manner we do not understand, there begins to emerge out of this lowest form of vital action the faintest sentiency (the apparent necessary implication being that the raw material of consciousness is pre-existing in the organic matter, if not indeed omnipresent), this also must from the very beginning be subject to the same process of adjustment to the welfare of the type, and must perpetually be undergoing such modifications and such re-adjustments as to make the connexion between pleasure and beneficial action adapted to the changing conditions of life, and adapted every now and then to some modified mode of action leading to a higher life.

Any other view than this would be in diametrical opposition to the whole scheme of evolution as I have set it forth.

Sincerely yours,
(Signed) HERBERT SPENCER.

IV. *The Author's reply to Mr. Herbert Spencer.*

35, GORDON SQUARE, W.C.
March 18, 1885.

DEAR MR. SPENCER,

Do not think me bent on minimizing my misapprehension if, in thanking you for the justice you do me in your note of yesterday, I touch upon one expression in it which shows that I have not yet made myself quite clear.

Your word 'primordial' did not lead me to think of anything

further back than the dawn of sentiency in living things. I understood it simply of that particular date in the indefinite process of evolution, and not of anything like a remoter '*preordination*.' It was precisely because I knew how little compatible was such an idea with your whole doctrine, that I spoke of your having '*a mystery* on your hands,' when you found the connexion between life-promoting action and pleasant sensation to be no later than the initial point of consciousness. The law seemed to crop up suddenly, without explanation. Here (as I have already said) you have quite a right to pull me up and tell me that, if I will only go back to your insentient biology, I shall find the explanation: for there, life-promoting actions have already driven off all competing tendencies and appropriated the vegetal functions to themselves. That, when consciousness steals in, its agreeable pole lies in the life-promoting acts and its disagreeable pole in the detrimental, is only the same biological fact, with a developed predicate, which makes it also psychological.

In this view, pleasure and pain seem to fall into their right places as they arise, the sifting process having been performed behind the screen, ere they emerged as feeling: and a psychologist who supposed any agreeable sensation to be 'at variance with welfare' I should expect you to accuse of playing truant from biology. I had supposed that your history of conscious life began with and from the law of determinate adjustment which Darwin, on the other hand, works out as its ulterior stage, through sentient experiments of elimination and self-definition. But the whole process, in both instances, I conceived to be kept strictly within the limits of the principle of evolution.

Indulge me with this Postscript. I send it only because, as a mere personal explanation, it needs no answer.

I remain,
Yours very sincerely,
JAMES MARTINEAU.

INDEX.

ABSOLUTE notions' not involved in metaphysics, 1. 456, 457.
Action, extrinsic effects of, transformed in a moral nature and world, ii. 75, 76.
—— moralist's concern with, ii. 275, 276.
— intrinsic effects of, vary in pleasure and in strength of spring, ii. 74.
Admiration, distinguished from wonder, ii. 156.
— of equal worth with wonder, ii. 216–218.
'Æquivocal' and 'univocal,' true meaning of, 1 134.
Æsthetic Ethics, coexist with benevolent principle, ii 485.
— contrasted with the Dianoetic, ii. 504, 505.
Affections and intellect, Sidgwick on conflict between, ii. 291, 292.
— common characteristics of, ii. 144, 145.
— compassionate, nature and function of, ii. 149–151.
— derived and classed by Spinoza, i. 343–347.
— do not come of persuasion, ii. 177.
— how far susceptible of purposed culture, ii. 339–343.
— parental, of higher claim than social, ii. 218–220.
—— relatively to compassion, ii 220, 221.
—— varied in father and mother, ii. 145, 146.
— predominant over intellect in Positivism, 1 452.

Affections, Primary, above wonder and admiration, ii 215, 216.
— Secondary, inferior to primary passions, ii. 200–205.
— social, conditions of, ii. 146–149.
Altruism and self-love, not in harmony, ii, 335–338.
—— how reconciled by Hutcheson, ii. 551–553
— Comte identifies with morality, i. 454.
— gain of, upon egoism, unexplained by Comte, i. 499–502.
Ambition, estimate of, ii. 208–210.
Anaxagoras' doctrine of 'formative νοῦς,' 1. 87.
'Animal spirits,' application of, by Descartes, 1. 144
—— Malebranche, 1. 175. 190. 205.
—— Spinoza, i. 326.
— spontaneity, above appetite, ii. 194.
Antipathy, relatively to love of gain, ii. 196, 197.
— superior to secondary affections, ii. 200, 201.
Approval and disapproval, applied to persons only, ii. 21–23,
—— fall only on volition, ii. 33-36
—— given to inner spring, ii. 24–26
—— passed first on ourselves, ii. 27–30.
— intuitively preferential, ii. 43–46.
— not interchangeable with assent, ii. 454. 473.
— thirst for, a puerile motive, ii. 242.

VOL. II. P p

Aquinas' 'preordination' used against Malebranche, ii. 162.
Arago disparaged by Comte, i. 414.
Aristotle criticises Plato's ideas, i 25.
Aristotle's account of Plato's 'ideal numbers,' i. 31, 32. 55-57.
— antithesis to Plato exaggerated, i. 119, 120.
— denial of hedonist ethics, ii. 322.
— factors of moral character, ii. 131.
— 'thought of thought,' i. 87.
Arnauld, Antoine, supports Descartes' doctrine, i. 155.
— controversy of, with Malebranche, i. 161, 162.
Arnott's and Comte's classification of sciences compared, i. 469-472.
Art, love of, genius decomposed, ii. 178-180.
Asceticism, Spencer on, ii. 380, 381.
— teleological base of, ii. 168, 169.
Attachment subordinate to parental affection, ii. 219, 220.
Attribute, Spinoza's definition of, i. 299.
Attributes (Spinoza's) disparate, i. 306
—— Erdmann's interpretation of, i. 310, 311.
—— meaning of, i. 389.
—— parallelism of, untenable, i 306-310 324
Augustine's theology, influence of on Ethics, i. 17-19.
Authority can have no seat in an insulated nature, ii. 104-110.
— (penal) lies in justice, not in pleasure and pain, ii 113.
— of conscience, affected by its psychology, ii. 302, 303.
—— no moralist's 'ipse-dixitism,' ii. 99-103.
— whether in 'ideal of genus' over actual member, ii. 118, 119.
—— 'rational benevolence' alone, ii. 298, 299.

Authority, whether in society over individual, ii. 117, 118.
—— 'whole over part,' ii. 117.

BAD, the absolutely, limited to the secondary passions, ii 189.
Bain, on pleasure as self-conserving, ii. 376, 377.
Beauty, essence and division of, in Hutcheson, ii. 528 530.
— factors of, given by Hutcheson, ii 530-534.
— sense of, how far factitious, ii. 156-158.
— teleological significance of, ii. 531, 532.
Bekker, Balthasar. of Amsterdam, supports Descartes' doctrine, i. 154
Benevolence and moral sense have the same function in Hutcheson, ii. 557-561.
— and self-love, Hutcheson inadequately distinguishes, ii. 555-557.
—— parallel instincts in Hutcheson, ii. 543-546.
Bentham, Jeremy, influenced by Helvetius, ii. 311, 312.
— resolves 'authority of conscience' into dogmatism, ii. 99-103.
— says that we judge others first, ii. 27.
Bentham's mensuration of pleasures and pains, ii. 326, 327.
— rule of conduct, valid place for, ii. 275, 276.
— statement of principle of Utility, ii. 305-307.
Berkeley, Bishop, alleged interview of with Malebranche, i. 163.
Best, the, are not the happiest, ii. 355-357.
Body, idea of the, is (in Spinoza) the mind, i. 321, 322.
Boehmer, E, discovers 'linementa' of Spinoza's 'Short Treatise,' i. 249.
Bossuet, Bishop, disapproves of Malebranche, but reconciled, i. 161, 162.

INDEX. 579

Boursier, Laurent-François, opposes Malebranche's 'immediate Divine action,' i. 162.
Boyle, Robert, intercourse of with Spinoza through Oldenburg, i. 263.
Bradley, F. H., concentrates approval on inner spring, ii. 25
Brandis's, Christian August, interpretation of Plato's 'Ideas,' i. 34.
Bredenburg, John, controverts Spinoza, i. 225
Bressei, John, physician, disciple of Spinoza, i. 260.
Brewster, Sir David, reviews Comte, i. 417.
Bridges, Dr J. H., characterises Comte's 'synthesis' as 'subjective,' i. 437.
Bruno, Giordano, quoted, i. 303, 304.
Butler, Bishop, co-ordinates self-love and conscience, ii. 280.
— criticises Clarke, ii. 460, 461.
— restorer of Psychological Ethics, i. 20
— use of the word 'self-love' by, ii. 288.

CAMERER, Theodor, denial of intellect and will to God, i. 312.
— on Spinoza's Intellectual Love of God, i. 356.
— on Spinoza's eternal part of the mind, i. 373. 381–384.
Campbell's, Professor Lewis, Memoir of Maxwell, quoted, ii. 217.
Carl Ludwig (Elector of Palatinate) offers Spinoza a Professorship, i. 155.
Carlyle's, Thomas, idea of insight, compared with Plato's, i. 76, 77; ii. 34, 35
Caste, Polytheism tends to (Comte), i. 447.
— disappears under Monotheism (Comte), i. 449.
'Causa immanens' and 'transiens,' distinguished, i. 34, 35.
'Causa sui,' definition and use of by Spinoza, i. 296, 297.

'Cause,' applied to two distinct relations, i. 286, 287.
— identified by Spinoza with the common properties of things, i. 320.
— of two kinds in Spinoza, i. 318, 319.
Causes, excluded from knowledge by Comte, i. 428, 429. 458, 459.
— not phenomena, i. 459.
— occasional, scheme of, i. 156–158.
Censoriousness, 'rejoicing in iniquity,' ii. 173, 174
Chalybæus, H. M., Theism of, i. 22.
Chandler, Bishop, edits Cudworth's 'Immutable Morality,' ii. 434.
Character, inequalities of, an education of conscience, ii. 64, 65.
— the adjustment of two necessities (Spinoza), i. 369-371.
Charity, account of, by Hobbes, ii 311.
— obligation of, different from that of Justice, ii. 121–125
Chasdai Kreskas, possible influence of, on Spinoza, i. 252
Christ, Spinoza's language respecting, i. 254. 315.
Christianity, foe to disinterestedness (Comte), i. 451.
— misconstrued by Comte, i. 507, 508
Christina, Queen of Sweden, draws Descartes to Stockholm, i. 156.
Clarke, Dr. Samuel, confounds mathematical and moral necessity, ii 469, 470.
—— truths and rules, ii. 471
— diverts English Science from Descartes to Newton, ii. 459, 460.
— life and writings of, ii. 459–463.
— omits to provide for moral degrees, ii. 472.
Clarke's demonstration of eternal morality, ii 464–467.

INDEX.

Coler, Jean, biographer of Spinoza, i. 248.
Coleridge, S T., on Spinoza's rejection of 'final causes,' i 389, *note.*
Collegiants, Spinoza's sympathy with, i. 253, 254
Compassion, in what sense fellow-feeling, ii 149, 150.
— relatively to parental affection, ii 220, 221.
Comte, Auguste, as Priest of Humanity, i 415 424.
— connection with St. Simon, i. 401, 402 409.
— deprived of office at Polytechnic, and subsidised, i. 412–415
— education and first literary work, i. 399, 400.
— formulates law of mental development, i. 410.
— opens *Philosophie Positive* leçons, i 402
— identifies morality with altruism, i. 454.
— postulates more than his forerunners, i. 395-398
— produces the *Politique Positive*, i. 423, 424.
— regenerated by Mme. de Vaux, i. 418–423.
— rejects sidereal astronomy, i. 416–418.
— reviewed by Herschel and Brewster, i. 416, 417.
— suffers from brain attack, i 411.
Comte's account of 'personality,' i. 464–468.
— antipathy to 'causes,' i. 458–461.
— boundary of possible knowledge, i 428, 429.
— disproof of self-knowledge, i. 461–464.
— hierarchy of sciences, i. 430–434.
— personal ritual and habit, i. 423, 427.
— programme of education, i. 478–480.
— theory, contrasted with that of Diderot, i. 503.

'Conatus,' law of (Spinoza), i. 338–340.
Condé, Prince de, invites Spinoza to French camp, i 274, 275.
Conscience, authority of, reduced by Bentham to dogmatism, ii. 99–103.
— doctrine of, criticised by Mr. L. Stephen, ii 406–408.
— how evolved, ii 401, 402.
— implicit feeling, brought into explicit thought, ii. 53, 54
— judicial, not active, ii. 186, 187.
— the scale of relative worth, thus far, ii. 48, 49.
Conscientiousness, why compatible with feebleness, ii. 59–61.
Consciousness, opens a new stage in evolution, ii. 394–396.
Consequences of action, moralist's concern with, ii. 275, 276.
Cowardice, moral, dangers of, ii. 241, 242.
Cromwell, Oliver, hears Cudworth's Parliamentary sermon, ii. 428, 429.
Cudworth, Dr Ralph, confounds objects and conditions of knowledge, ii. 453
— distinguishes feeling from cognition of feeling, ii. 439.
— identifies virtue with assent, ii. 454
— life and times of, ii. 427-437.
Cudworth's criticism of Descartes, ii. 449.
— doctrine of intellection, ii. 440–445.
— — intelligible essences, ii. 445–447.
— — sensible perception, ii. 440.
— 'Intellectual System,' how received, ii. 432, 433.
— order of knowledge inapplicable to morals, ii. 455, 456.
— priority of mind in macrocosm and microcosm, ii. 450.
— vindication of his προλήψεις, ii. 446, 447.
Culture, love of, explained and estimated, ii 211–214.
Cuvier's account of instinct, ii. 138, 139.

DARWIN, Charles, evolves the moral from the unmoral, ii. 3.
— explanation of remorse by, ii 419-422.
— uses teleological language, i. 154.
Death, Spinoza's treatment of, i 374-385.
Demerit, condition and measure of, ii. 80-88.
Democritus resolves all perception into touch, i. 308, 309.
De Morgan, Augustus, on competitive examinations, ii 240, 241
De Sauzet, H., editor of *Nouvelles Littéraires* (1719), i 248.
Descartes', René, 'attribute' distinguished from 'quality,' i. 136.
— automatism of brutes interpreted, i. 146.
— certainty of Divine existence, i. 130
— *De Homine*, effect of on Malebranche, i. 160.
— evidence of outward things, i. 130, 131.
— first law of motion, i 140.
— list of primary affections, ii. 132.
— 'matter' is 'extension,' without vacuum, i. 137-139.
— — infinitely divisible, i 139.
— — measured by bulk, i. 139.
— reference of truth and right to Divine institution, i 148, 149.
— rejection of final causes, i. 153.
— relation between understanding and will, i. 147.
— residence and death at Stockholm, i. 156.
— scheme, Catholics divided about, i. 155.
— — estimated, i. 150-154
— — factions about, at Utrecht, i. 154, 155.
— — interests the Princess Elizabeth and the Queen of Sweden, i. 155, 156.
— theory and division of sensations, i. 141-143.
— ultimate principle of certainty, i. 127-129.
— — test of truth, i. 133, 134.

Descartes' use and application of the word 'substance,' i 134, 135
— — of 'animal spirits,' i. 144.
Desert, relation of to merit, ii 244, 245
Desire, Hutcheson's exposition of, ii 555.
— J. S. Mill's exposition of, ii. 308.
De Versé, Aubert, controverts Spinoza, i. 224
De Witts, Spinoza's relations with the, i. 273, 274
Dianoetic Ethics, contrasted with the Æsthetic, ii. 504, 505.
Diogenes of Apollonia, doctrine of intelligent atmosphere, i. 87.
Disinterested affections, descent from to interested, ii. 324, 325.
— excluded by Christianity (Comte), i. 451.
— explained by Hartleyans, ii. 316, 317. 323, 324.
— insisted on by Hutcheson, ii. 543-545. 555, 556.
— supreme in Christianity, i. 507, 508.
Distance, law of, in mental perspective, ii. 185
Dryden, John, on Cudworth's 'Intellectual System,' ii 432
Dualism in Catholic Christendom, i 126, 127.
— in Cartesianism, i. 127. 134.
— lost in Malebranche, i 207.
Du Bois-Reymond, Emil, on Freewill, ii. 400, 401.
Du Fresnoy, Abbé Lenglet, editor of book whence addenda to Coler, i. 249.
Duty, Bentham's dislike of the word, ii. 307.
— impossible to an insulated nature, ii 104-110.
— modifies prudence; prudence cannot constitute duty, ii. 75, 76.
— sense and contents of, invariable, ii. 77, 78.
— unprovided for in Spinoza, i. 392, 393.

EDUCATION, limits of emulation in, ii. 239-241.

Education, natural order of, missed by Comte, i. 478-480.
Egoism, conquest of by altruism, unexplained by Comte, i. 499-501.
Elizabeth, Princess (of Palatinate), disciple of Descartes, i. 155, 156.
Emulation, factors of, ii. 182, 183.
Enfantin, Barthelemy Prosper, disciple and interpreter of St. Simon, i. 401.
Envy, origin and range of, ii. 183.
Epicurus, a 'flowing philosopher,' i. 9.
Error, Descartes' theory of, i 148.
'Eternitatis sub specie' knowledge (Spinoza), i. 331.
Eternity, Spinoza's definition of, i. 299
Ethics, defined, i. 1.
— fundamental fact of, stated, ii. 18.
— Greek, based on idea of 'Good,' i. 67.
— psychological and unpsychological, distinguished, i. 3, 4.
— Rational or Dianoetic school of, described, ii. 425, 426.
— theories of, classified, i. 15. 19, 20.
— unpsychological, why disabled, i. 508-512.
— vocabulary of, significant, ii. 18-20.
— ways of studying, i. 2-4.
— what, 'if geometrical?' i. 278-282.
Evil, moral, inconceivable as positive, ii. 88-90.
Evolution, animal, applied to genesis of morals, ii. 4, 5.
— Darwin's account of, ii 368, 369. 371.
— has separated stages, ii. 393, 394.
— how affecting the treatment of morals, ii. 361-364.
— meaning of 'higher' and 'lower' in, ii. 422-424.
— of morals, ii. 373-376.
— Spencer's account of, ii. 367-372. *See Appendix.*

Evolution, whether applicable to psychology, ii. 364-367.

FACT, fundamental ethical, ii. 18.
Faculties, Mr. L. Stephen's criticism on, ii. 11-13.
— need of discriminating, ii. 13-15.
— supposed conflict of, resolved, ii. 9-11.
— what they are and what they are not, ii 11-14.
Fame, love of, defined and estimated, ii. 238, 239. 241.
— differently estimated by moralists, ii. 293, 294.
Fear, bearing of, on avarice, ii. 172.
— claims of, relatively to love or gain, ii. 197, 198.
— superior to secondary affections, ii 201.
Feeling, opens a new stage in evolution, ii. 394-396.
Fetichism, has no priest or temple (Comte), i. 445.
— origin and end of (Comte), i. 441, 442.
— place assigned to, conjectural, i. 494.
Fichte, J. H., Theism of, i. 22.
Finite, defined by Spinoza, i. 298, 299.
— things, how reached by Spinoza, i. 316-318
Fontenelle, Bernard Le Bovier, on Malebranche's literary merits, i 164.
Forgiveness, conditions and meaning of, ii. 202-204
Foucher, Abbé Simon, controverts Malebranche, i 161.
Freedom, belief in, deepens affection (Spinoza), i 346.
— how gained (Spinoza), i 365-367.
— meaning of (Spinoza), i. 346, 347. 365. 370-372
Free-will, Du Bois-Reymond on, ii. 400, 401.
— implied in 'Merit,' 'Guilt,' 'Responsibility,' ii. 37-41. 87, 88.

Free-will, not recognised by Hutcheson, ii. 563-565
— opens a new stage in evolution, ii. 397, 398.
Friendship, account of by Helvetius, ii. 314, 315.

GAIN, love of, how related to fear, ii. 197, 198.
— — inferior to antipathy and resentment, ii 195, 196. 198, 199.
Gall's function of phrenological organ compared with Comte's, i. 466, 467
Generosity, essence and application of, ii. 242-244.
Geometry, why apodeictic, i. 281, 282.
Geulinx, Arnold, propounds his 'Occasional Causes,' i. 156-158.
Glasemaker, Joh. Heinr., probable Latiniser of preface to Spinoza's Op. posth., i 253.
God, Descartes' mode of knowing, i. 129, 130.
— identified by Plato with 'the Good,' i. 85
— 'Nature,' 'Substance,' how far interchangeable in Spinoza, i 293, 294.
— Plato's, whether personal, i. 86-92.
— Spinoza's definition of, i. 297.
— union with, Malebranche's 'perfection,' i. 191, 192.
— will of, whether available as the rule of right, ii. 234, 235.
Good, contents of the, compared with the right, i. 66, 67.
— Plato's account of the, i. 84-86.
— Shaftesbury's account of, ii 493, 494
Goodness, how distinguished by Shaftesbury from good, ii. 494, 495.
Granville, Lord, an attached friend of Hutcheson, ii. 517.
Gratitude, a variety of generosity, ii. 246-248.

Green, Thomas Hill, concentrates approval on inner spring, ii. 25.
— takes 'duty' as imposed by a man on himself, ii. 105, 106.
Guizot, François P.G., disparaged by Comte, i. 413, 414.

HAECKEL, invests atoms with feeling and will, ii. 399, 400
Hamilton, Sir William, on the *object* of perception, i. 308, 309.
Happiness, individual and social, not identical, ii. 335-338.
— principle of the greatest, fails the hedonist, ii 332-335.
Hartleyan account of disinterestedness, ii 316, 317.
Hartmann, Edouard von, admits final causes, i 154.
Heaven and hell, dual classification of, accounted for, ii. 65-69.
Hedonism, how modified by Hartleyans, ii 315-318.
— — by sociology, ii. 318, 319.
— leaves disinterestedness possible, but not obligatory, ii. 331, 332.
— Shaftesbury's apparent lapse into, ii. 500, *seqq*
— utilitarian, chief representatives of, ii 304.
— — psychological principle of, stated, ii. 305-307.
Hegel, G. F. W., contrasts Greek and Christian valuation of the individual, i. 83.
— intellectually related to Spinoza, i. 20, 21.
— why not expounded and reviewed, ii. 567.
Helvetius, Claude Adrien, hedonism of, centres in the senses, ii. 312, 313.
— influence of, on Bentham, ii. 311, 312
Helvetius's version of friendship, ii. 314, 315
— — of justice, ii. 315.
Heracleitus and his doctrine of motion, i. 9. 25.
Heredity, relation of, to differentiation, ii 383.
Herschel, Sir John, confutes Comte on Laplace, i. 416-418.

'Heteropsychological,' meaning of, ii. 16, 302, 303.
Hobbes, Thomas, definition by, of Pity, ii 149, *note*
— definitions by, of Laughter, Pity, Charity, ii. 310, 311
— — of Reverence and Religion, ii 310
— intellectually related to Comte, i. 20
— on Euclid, criticised by Malebranche, i 181.
— on the conception of power, ii. 309, 310.
Hooker, Richard, on gradations of goodness, quoted, ii. 271.
Humanity, deemed progressive before 'Sociology,' i 496, 497.
Hutcheson, Francis, a determinist, ii. 563–565
— appraises the pleasures and pains, ii. 549–554.
— avowedly develops Shaftesbury's doctrine, ii. 524.
— co-ordinates benevolence and love of right, ii. 280, 285, 286.
— derives moral ideas from observed benevolence, ii. 540.
— disappoints the promise of moral gradation, ii. 561–563.
— early education of, ii. 514, 515.
— excellent in his applied morals, ii. 562, 563.
— has no separate function for moral sense and benevolence, ii. 557–561.
— influence of, on Channing, ii. 518, 519.
— position of, in Dublin, ii. 515–518.
— Professorship of, in Glasgow, ii. 519–522.
— publications of, in Dublin, ii. 517, 518.
— reforms philosophy in Scotland, ii. 519–521.
— slips unconsciously into hedonism, ii. 548, 549. 551. 555, 556.
— wavers between intuition and utility, ii. 538, 539.
Hutcheson's classifications, variable and inexact, ii. 535, 536, *note*.
Hutcheson's death, and traditional reputation, ii. 522 524
— 'internal sense' characterised, ii. 528–530.
— Latin Manual of Ethics, ii. 521, 522.
— moral sense arbitrates between self-love and benevolence, ii. 546, 547.
— — how affected by the analogy of beauty, ii 538, 541, 542
— — influenced by Butler, ii. 536, 537.
— sense-doctrine compared with Aristotle's, ii. 525, 526
— 'System of Moral Philosophy,' ii. 522.
Huyghens, Christian, correspondence of, with Spinoza, i. 267. 301.
— on unity of substance, i. 301.

IBN-EZRA'S writings known to Spinoza, i. 252.
Idea and Ideatum, how related in Spinoza, i. 322, 323.
'Idea,' extension of, in 17th century, i. 338.
Idealism renders moral consciousness illusory, ii. 4–6.
Ideals, the Christian, cited in excuse for the 'worship of humanity' (Comte), i. 453.
Ideas, as objects, Malebranche's doctrine of, i. 168–172.
— association of (Spinoza), i. 327
— order of, same as of things (Spinoza), i. 323.
— 'primi generis,' confused and inadequate (Spinoza), i. 328.
'Idiopsychological,' meaning of, ii. 16.
Imagination and memory explained (Spinoza), i. 326.
— errors of, in Malebranche, i. 166, 167.
'Immanens' and 'transiens' distinguished, i. 304.
Imprudence, why immoral, ii. 125–128.

INDEX. 585

Inclination, distinguished by Malebranche from passion, i. 176
Industrial pursuits, despised under Polytheism (Comte), i 447.
— favoured by Monotheism (Comte), i. 449
Instinct, Cuvier's account of, considered, ii. 138, 139.
Instinctive springs of action, vindicated for man, ii 136-138
Intellect and affection, Sidgwick on conflict between, ii. 291, 292.
— and will denied to God (Spinoza), i. 312 390.
— does not secure moral consciousness, ii. 456, 457. 482, 483
— includes 'ratio' and 'intuitus' (Spinoza), i. 336
— 'infinite,' meaning of, in Spinoza, i 311. 337, *note.*
— Spinoza limits to 'natura naturata,' i. 312. 337, *note.*
— subordinate to affection, in Positivism (Comte), i. 452
— takes sides with altruism (Comte), i. 452.
Intention, distinguished from motive, ii 272.
Intuition, not a short cut to the calculable, ii 539.
Intuitions, evolution of, according to Spencer, ii. 374-376.
Intuitive moralists, Sidgwick on disagreements of, ii. 285-294
Intuitus, meaning of, in Spinoza, i. 331-335.

JACOBI, Friedr. Heinr., quoted, ii. 22, 23. 156.
Jelles, Jarigh, wrote (in Dutch) preface for Spinoza's Op. posth., i. 253.
Jowett, Professor B., quoted, i. 46.
Judgment, moral, applied only to persons, ii. 21-23.
— begins upon ourselves, ii. 27-30.
— intuitively preferential, ii. 43-45.
— not deductive, ii. 455.
— not elicited by mere spontaneity, ii. 33, 34.

Judgment, passed on inner spring of action, ii 24-26.
— passed on volition only, ii 35, 36
— why not more visibly uniform among men, ii 61-63.
Justice, account of, by Helvetius, ii. 315.
— essence and ramifications of, ii. 249-254.
— idea and place of, in Plato, i. 71-73. 77.
— implies free-will, ii 87, 88.
— love of, as a spring of action, ii. 254, 255.
— obligation of, different from that of Charity, ii 121-125.
— why admitting of Queen's evidence, ii. 290, 291.

KANT, Immanuel, on self-love, ii. 288.
— on the love of virtue as sole moral motive, ii. 280. 285, 286.
— why not expounded and reviewed, ii 566, 567, *note*
Karkeris, Miriam, sister of Spinoza, i 251.
King, Archbishop, protects Hutcheson, ii. 517
Knowing, Malebranche's four modes of, i 172-174.
Knowledge, constitutes the perfect life (Spinoza), i 350.
— developed in three stages (Comte), i. 438-444.
— limited to facts by Comte, i. 428, 429.
— psychological, impossible (Comte), i. 429.

LABOUR becomes free under Monotheism (Comte), i 449
Lamy, F., imputes 'Quietism' to Malebranche, i. 162
Land, J.P N , editor of completed works of Spinoza, i. 250, *note.*
Laughter, account of, by Hobbes, ii. 310, 311.
Law, Comte's triple, real significance of, i. 490-492
— — tested by historical experience, i. 485-488.

586 INDEX.

Law, Comte's, tested by individual experience, i. 482-485.
— distinguished from morals under Monotheism (Comte), i. 448.
— of succession in the theological stage (Comte), i. 441-443
— of 'transference' explains disinterestedness, ii. 316, 317. 323, 324
— of three intellectual stages (Comte), i. 438-444.
Lecky, on Mill's two dimensions of pleasure, ii. 330, 331.
Leechman, Principal, influence of, in Glasgow, ii. 522, *note*.
Leibniz, Gottfried Wilhelm, controversy of, with Clarke, ii. 462
— Spinoza's relations with, i. 268, 269.
L'Enfant, Abbé, Latin translator of Malebranche, i. 161.
Le Roy, Heinrich, of Utrecht, advocates Descartes' doctrine, i. 154.
Lewes, G. H., defends Psychology against Comte, i. 462.
Liberty, love of, a variety of the love of power, ii. 210, 211.
— (of will), how understood by Malebranche, i. 165.
Littré, E., institutes Comte's 'subside sacerdotal,' i. 415.
— inveighs against 'absolute notions,' i. 457.
Livingstone, Dr., on common feeling of beauty, ii. 157, *note*.
Locke's, John, 'Men think not always' controverts Malebranche, i. 168.
— philosophical position unstable, ii. 436, 437.
Lotsij, M. C. L., on 'the mind's eternal part' (Spinoza), i. 373.
Love, how idealised by Plato, i. 68.
— (Malebranche) 'never bad, but may be of bad things,' i. 178.
Lucas, physician, disciple and biographer of Spinoza, i. 248, 249.

MACKINTOSH, Sir James, criticism of, on Malebranche, i. 230.

Maimonides read by Spinoza, i. 252.
Malebranche, Nicolas, alleged interview of Berkeley with, i. 163.
— condemns Spinoza, unnamed, i. 223, 224.
— criticises Epicurean doctrine, i. 190.
— criticises Stoic doctrine, i. 188.
— disparages Astronomy; and erudition, i. 182.
— effect on, of Descartes' *De Homine*, i 160.
— identifies mind with thinking, i. 167, 168.
— in relation to Descartes, i. 207.
— — to Spinoza, i. 159, 160. 223, 224.
— literary and personal characteristics of, i. 163, 164.
— loses, but regains, Bossuet's goodwill, i. 161, 162.
— on the blindness of the passions, i. 192-196.
— pupil of Richard Simon, i. 160.
— sacrifices personality, i. 208-219.
— wavers between transcendence and immanence, i. 225, 226.
Malebranche's account of God's chief end, i. 177.
— analogy between motion and will, i. 175.
— controversy with Arnauld, i. 161, 162.
— derivation of affections from love and hate, i. 198, 199.
— distinction between inclination and passion, i. 176. 187.
— doctrine of union with God, i. 191, 192.
— errors of misdirected 'inclination,' i. 178-187.
— — of sense and imagination, i. 164-167.
— ethical doctrine stated and criticised, i. 227-246.
— four modes of knowing, i. 172-174.
— 'ideas' in God, as objects in perception, i. 169-172.

Malebranche's 'Love never bad, but may be of bad things,' i. 178.
— *Recherche de la Vérité*, reception of, i. 161.
— sensible helps to clear thought, i. 201-203.
— Theism at variance with his philosophy, i 219-221.
— 'understanding' not a 'mode' of mind, i. 167, 168.
— use of 'animal spirits,' i 175. 189. 205-207.
Malice, the relish for antipathy, ii 173.
Man, 'a spiritual automaton' (Spinoza), i. 392, 393.
Manasseh ben Israel absent at Spinoza's trial, i 257.
Mandeville, Bernard de, Hutcheson's doctrine a revolt against, ii 518. 538.
Manichæism and its opposite, ii 89.
Mansvelt, Professor Regnier à, Utrecht opponent of Spinoza's 'Theol.-Pol. Treatise,' i. 271.
Mariolatry generalised by Positivism (Comte), i 453, 454.
Masham, Lady, daughter of Cudworth, ii. 435.
— discourse by, on the 'Love of God,' ii 435, 436.
'Materialism,' Comte's meaning of, i. 503.
Matter, Descartes' conception of, i 137-140.
Maxwell, J. Clerk, anecdote of, ii 217.
Melchior, Joh., Utrecht opponent of Spinoza's 'Theol.-Pol. Treatise,' i 271.
Memory, explained (Spinoza), i. 326.
Merit, condition and measure of, ii. 80-88.
— how distinguished from 'desert,' ii. 244-246.
— how possible towards men, ii. 121-125.
— Mr. L. Stephen's interpretation of, ii. 83-87.
— Shaftesbury's relation of to virtue, ii. 495-497.

Merit, why impossible towards God, ii 120, 121.
Metaphysical Ethics, characteristic of, i. 12.
— — (1) Transcendent, (2) Immanent, i 21-23. 118, 119.
— stage of mind, reached in Protestantism (Comte), i 443.
Metaphysics and Physics defined, i. 8.
— claim no knowledge of the Absolute, i 456, 457.
— how far stationary, i 492-494.
Meyer, L, editor of Spinoza's Op. posth., i 249 260. 264 277.
Military spirit, becomes defensive under Monotheism (Comte), i. 449
— — fostered by Polytheism (Comte), i 447.
Mill, James, that we judge others first, ii 27.
Mill's, James, account of the moral sentiments examined, ii. 345-353.
— — identification of consciousness and self-consciousness anticipated by Spinoza, i. 324.
— — statement of principle of hedonism, ii 307, 308.
Mill, John Stuart, and friends raise temporary fund for Comte, i. 415.
— — defends Psychology against Comte, i. 462.
— — defines the principle of Utilitarian Hedonism, ii. 308, 309.
Mind, 'eternal part' of the (Spinoza), i. 358, 359. 374-385.
— is (in Spinoza) the idea of the body, i. 321, 322.
'Mode,' defined by Spinoza, i. 304.
Modes, 'eternal,' meaning of, in Spinoza, i. 313-315.
Molesworth, Viscount, friend and confidant of Hutcheson, ii 517.
Money, love of, whence developed, ii. 171, 172.
Monism contradicts moral consciousness, ii 4, 5.
— in ancient philosophy, i. 122, 123.

Monism, vain attempts to save, ii. 398, 399.
Monotheism, Christian, incompatible with disinterested love (Comte), i. 451.
— divides morals from law (Comte), i. 448
— — spiritual from temporal power (Comte), i. 448, 449.
— exemplified in Catholicism (Comte), i. 443.
— favours industry and free labour (Comte), i. 449.
— — Science more than Art (Comte), i. 448.
— makes military spirit defensive (Comte), i. 449.
— transition to (Comte), i. 442.
Moral affections, on what ground ascribed to God, ii. 91, 92
— consciousness, cancelled, leaves *brute* or *devil*, ii. 88–90.
— — intuitive preference between rival springs, ii. 43–45.
— — universal and uniform, ii. 77, 78.
— distinctions, Descartes refers to Divine Will, i. 148, 149.
Morals, identified by Comte with altruism, i. 454
— insecure under the pleasure-test, ii. 357–359.
— practical, merits of Comte's, i. 497, 498.
— separate from law under Monotheism (Comte), i. 448.
More's H., *Enchiridion Ethicum*, origin of, ii. 430.
Morteira, Saul Levi, teacher of Spinoza, i. 251, 252.
Motion, Descartes' first law of, i. 140.
Motive, how distinguished from intention, ii. 272.
Motives, mixed, how estimated, ii. 235–237.
— 'the moral,' as springs of action, ii. 281–285.
— whether and how cognisable, ii. 294–297.
Muller, F., finds and publishes Spinoza's 'Short Treatise,' &c., i. 249, 250.

Musens, Jena, opponent of Spinoza's 'Tractatus Theol. Polit.,' i 271.
Mystics, Christian, aim of at self-surrender interpreted, ii. 79.

NATURA, naturans and naturata distinguished, i. 303, 304.
Nature, God, Substance, how far interchangeable in Spinoza, i. 293–296.
Necessity, all existences determined by (Spinoza), i. 327. 367, 368
— two meanings of, confounded, i. 285–287.
Nominalism, versus two forms of Realism, i. 23.
Norris, John, of Bemerton, criticised by Lady Masham, ii. 435.
Noumena, inseparable from Phenomena, i. 456–458.

OBJECT and Cause confounded, i 308, 309.
Obligation, Bentham's dislike of the word, ii. 306, 307.
— Hutcheson's account of, ii. 541.
— Spencer's definition of, ii. 384.
— *See* 'Authority,' 'Duty,' 'Right.'
Occasional Causes, scheme of, i. 156–158.
Oldenburg, Heinrich, correspondent of Spinoza, i. 263.
Optimism, influence of, on Shaftesbury, ii. 493, 494 509, 510.
'Ought,' Bentham's wish to expunge the word, ii. 306, 307.

PALEY, William, on pleasure conferred 'gratis,' ii. 168.
— on the Will of God as rule of right, ii. 234, 235.
— reduces moral 'authority' to retributory sanctions, ii. 110–113.
Parallelism of attributes (Spinoza) untenable, i. 306–310. 324.
Parmenides, doctrine of, i. 9. 25. 37.
Passion, distinguished by Malebranche from inclination, i. 175, 176.

Passions, function and varieties of, ii 141-144.
Patriotism fostered by Polytheism (Comte), i. 446.
Persecution, ethics of, considered, ii. 232, 233.
Personality, Comte's account of, i 464-468.
— conception of, in Plato, i. 86-92.
— not resolvable into a phenomenal aggregate, ii 40, 41.
— realised in society, ii 32, 33.
— unprovided for in Spinoza, i. 367-372
Persons sole objects of moral judgment, ii. 21, 22.
Phenomena, mind can observe all, except its own (Comte), i. 429
'Phenomena only,' cannot be known, i. 456-458.
Phenomenon and Reality, antithesis of, i. 5-7 ; ii. 1, 2.
Philosophies, ancient and modern, analogous yet inverse, i 8-10.
— — key to each, ii. 2, 3.
Physical Ethics, characteristic of, i. 12, 13.
Physics and Metaphysics, defined, i. 8
Pity defined by Hobbes, ii. 311.
Plato, central problem of, i. 26, 27.
— identifies 'Cause' with 'Mind,' i. 45-47..
— no hedonist, i. 84, 85.
Plato's account of mathematics and dialectic, i. 52-55.
— argument for the soul's immortality, i. 62, 63.
— attitude towards the idea of responsibility, i. 92-95.
— coincidences with Bentham illusory, i. 74-76.
— — with Carlyle illusory, i. 76, 77.
— distinction between 'cause' and 'condition,' i. 61.
— Ethics, anti-affectional, i. 114-116.
— — equalise the moral and the unmoral, i. 112, 113.
— — not a doctrine of Duty, i. 110, 111.

Plato's ethnological characters, i. 66.
— God, whether personal, i. 86-92.
— 'Good,' contents of, i. 66, 67. 85
— grades and analogies of knowledge, i 55-57.
— ideal cosmogony, i. 59-62.
— idealisation of Love, i. 68.
— 'Ideas,' Aristotle's criticism of, i. 35.
— — as eternal patterns, i. 39, 40.
— — culminate in 'the Good,' or 'Mind,' i. 48-50.
— — distribution of, in 'the many,' how described, i 29, 30.
— — for what purpose wanted, i. 30.
— — how affected by test passage, Phileb 23 C., i. 41-44.
— — hypostatised universals, i. 26-28.
— — represented by numbers, i. 31, 32.
— — whether invested with causality, i. 36-39.
— — whether seated in the Divine Mind, i. 33-35.
— myth of Er the Armenian, i. 98-108.
— — of the chariot, i 69-71.
— 'No one is voluntarily bad,' i. 74.
— relation between νοῦς and ψυχή, i. 45-47. 52. 60. 63.
— ruling faculty, 'Reason,' or 'Right?' i 71-73.
— State, an ethical personality, i. 77-79.
— — a social absolutism, i. 79-81.
— — compared with the Catholic Church, i. 82-84.
— transmigration of souls, i. 64. 93. 94. 104-108.
— triads of cognitive and active principles, i. 51, 52.
— use of τὸ μὴ ὄν and its equivalents, i. 58, 59.
Pleasure and pain are (Spinoza) transition to and from more perfect being, i. 343. 347.

Pleasure identified by J.S Mill with 'object of desire,' ii. 319, 320
—— by Spencer with self-conservation, ii. 376, 377. 381
— love of, inferior to appetites, ii. 193, 194.
—— in its origin and range, ii. 169, 170.
— 'motive' is not, like resultant, homogeneous, ii. 323.
— not Plato's ground of Ethics, i. 84, 85
— Plato's double estimate of, i. 67, 68
— 'resultant,' inference from, by Socrates and Paley, ii. 168.
— proportioned to intensity of spring, ii. 73, 74. 321, 322.
— two dimensions of, inadmissible, ii. 109, 110. 317, 318. 325, 326. 328-331.
—— incommensurable, ii. 327, 328.
—— J. S. Mill's, anticipated by Hutcheson, ii. 549-551.
Poetry favoured by Polytheism, i. 446.
Poiret, Peter, controverts Spinoza, i. 224.
Politics tainted by love of praise, ii. 241
Pollock, Professor Frederick, on 'the mind's eternal part' (Spinoza), i. 373.
Polytheism brings priesthood and temples (Comte), i 446.
— favours patriotism and military spirit (Comte), i. 446, 447.
— fosters Art, hinders Science (Comte), i. 446.
— origin and end of (Comte), i. 441, 442.
— tends to *caste* and slavery (Comte), i. 447.
'Positive,' meaning of, in Comte, i. 430.
— stage of mind, since Bacon and Descartes (Comte), i. 444.
Positivism generalises Mariolatry, i. 453, 454.
— subordinates intellect to affection, i. 452.
Power, conception of, deduced and applied by Hobbes, ii. 309, 310.
Power, love of, differently estimated by moralists, ii. 294.
—— in its origin and tributaries, ii 171.
—— ranks above the passions, ii. 205-210.
Praise and blame, account of by James Mill, ii. 345, 346.
— love of, how formed, ii. 182.
—— makes cowards, ii. 241, 242.
— varieties of, ii. 237-239.
Presbyterians, Irish, disabilities of, prior to 1719, ii. 515, 516.
Price, Dr. Richard, thesis and argument of, stated, ii. 476, 477.
— makes, but neglects, Kant's distinction of theoretic and practical Reason, ii. 478, 479.
— questions, yet uses, moral *gradations*, ii. 480, 481.
— upholds Clarke's principle against new opponents, ii. 475.
Pride, distinguished from vanity, ii. 238.
Priesthood comes with Polytheism, (Comte), i. 446.
Primary springs of action, with what self-consciousness compatible, ii. 165.
Progress, of mankind, believed in prior to 'Sociology,' i. 496, 497.
Propensions, characterised and enumerated, ii 140, 141.
— how far and why anonymous in their secondary stage, ii. 169, 170.
Protagoras, doctrine of, i. 9.
Prudence cannot constitute duty, ii. 76, 77.
— judges by foresight, ii. 71-73.
— judicial, not active, ii. 186, 187.
— objects of preference by, ii. 70, 71.
— prefers the strongest impulse, ii. 74
— product of experience, ii. 71, 72.
— rule of, variable with the individual, ii. 77, 78.

Prudence, scale of, if cancelled, removes merit, leaves holiness, ii 90-93.
Psychological Ethics, characteristic of, i 3.
— special to Christendom, i. 15-17
— why lost in Christendom, i. 17-19
Psychology, identified by Comte with cerebral physiology, i. 462, 463.
— the key to objective products of mind, i. 468, 469.
— vindicated, ii 6-8
Pythagoras, why *after* Thales and Anaximander, i. 478.

QUESNEL, PASQUIER, assails Malebranche's doctrine of Grace, i. 161.

. RACE, self-conservation of, replaces simple hedonism, ii 318, 319.
Realism, two forms of, i. 22, 23
Reason, Platonic place of, in the soul, i. 69-71.
— *See* 'Intellect.'
Rebecca, sister of Spinoza, i. 251.
Régis, Pierre Sylvain, assails Malebianche's 'ideas,' i. 161.
Rehault's, Jacques, 'Physics,' Latin translation of, by Clarke, ii. 459, 460.
Reid's, Dr. Thomas, classification of springs of action, ii 134.
Religion, central conditions of, absent in Positivism, i 505, 506.
— definition of, by Hobbes, ii 310.
— development of, not proved to be uniform, i 494.
— social evolution of, ii 404-406.
— true secondary elements of, in Positivism, i. 505.
'Reminiscence,' superseded by *à priori* doctrine, ii. 72, 73.
Remorse, Darwin's explanation of, ii. 419-422.
Reparation, desire of, counterpart to gratitude, ii. 248.
Resentment, superior to love of gain, ii. 198-200.

Resentment, superior to the secondary affections, ii 201-205.
Retribution inefficacious, when unjust, ii. 112, 113
— wields, not makes, the 'authority of Right, ii. 104, 105
Reverence, contingent on conflict, yet directed above it, ii 230.
— definition of, by Hobbes, ii 310
— how far the persecutor's excuse, ii 232-234
— how one of the springs of action, yet pervading the set, ii. 226, 227.
— how related to the moral consciousness, ii. 161-164. 222-226.
— 'secondary,' as 'interest in religion,' ii. 180, 181.
— why supreme, ii. 221, *seqq.*
Richter, Jean Paul, on caprices of admiration, ii 158.
Right and Wrong, definition of, ii 270
— authority of, unaffected by evolution, ii 390-392
— love of, how made a separate motive, ii 227, 228
— name and function of, in Plato, i 72, 73
— notion of, unique, intuitively given in its degrees, ii. 46, 47.
— — universal and uniform, ii. 77, 78.
— rule of, compared with Bentham's, ii. 272-276.

ST. SIMON, Claude Henri de Rouvroy, Comte de, career of, and influence on Comte, i. 402-410.
Schaarschmidt, Professor Carl, edits second MS. of Spinoza's 'Short Treatise,' i. 250.
Schook, Professor Martin, of Groningen, attacks Descartes' doctrine, i 154
Schopenhauer, Arthur, admits final causes, i. 154.
Schuller, Dr. G. H., correspondent of Spinoza, i. 272.
Sciences, favoured more than Art by Monotheism (Comte), i 448.

INDEX.

Sciences, hindered by Polytheism (Comte), i. 446.
— how classed by Arnott and by Comte, i. 469-472.
— order and contents of (Comte), i. 430-435.
Secondary springs of action, why separately and singly treated, ii 167, 168.
Selection, Natural, law of, ii. 371.
Self-consciousness, Platonic estimate of, i. 75-77.
— Spinoza's theory of, i 323, 324
Self-conservation, Spencer's law of, ii. 376-381.
— Spinoza's law of, i. 338-340. 343 347.
Self-culture defined and estimated, ii. 177, 178.
Self-excuse, characteristic of passion (Malebranche), i. 199, 200.
Self-knowledge, involves other knowledge, ii 8, 9.
— parallel, not continuous, with other knowledge, i. 475, 476.
— possible, ii. 6-8.
Self-love, agreement of, with 'altruism,' untenable, ii. 335-338 353-355.
— and benevolence, parallel instincts, in Hutcheson, ii. 543-546.
— differently placed by Butler and Kant, ii. 280.
— how reconciled with social by Hutcheson, ii. 547, 548
— — by Shaftesbury, ii. 502, 503.
Self-reflection, needs the presence of others, ii. 30-33.
Self-seeking instincts, *per se* strongest, yield to 'altruism' (Comte), i 450, 451.
— suppression of, unexplained by Comte, i 499-502.
Self-surrender, why deemed essential to the perfect life, ii. 79
Sensation, Descartes' theory and division of, i. 140-143.
— not denied by Descartes to brutes, i. 145, 146.
Sensational philosophy, Hellenic prototype of, i. 8-10.

Sense, 'internal,' contents of, in Hutcheson, ii. 528, *seqq*
— meaning of, in Hutcheson, ii. 524 527.
— — in Shaftesbury, ii. 505, 506.
Senses and Imagination, errors of, in Malebranche, i. 164 167.
— — supply helps to clear thought (Malebranche), i. 201-203.
Sentimentality, essence of, ii. 177
'Sentiments,' characterised and enumerated, ii. 151, 152.
— interplay of. ii. 166, 167.
Shaftesbury, Earl of, a genuine, though not consistent, Moralist, ii. 500-509.
— anecdote of, in the House of Commons, ii. 488.
— characterised by Warburton, ii. 492.
— life and death of, at Naples, ii. 491.
— Locke's influence on, ii. 487. 490. 492.
— on Cudworth's critics. ii. 432.
— optimism of, ii. 509, 510.
— political influence of, ii 489, 490.
— relations of, with Leclerc and Bayle, ii. 488.
Shaftesbury's account of Good and Goodness, ii. 493, 494.
— — of Virtue and Merit, ii. 495-497.
— apparent lapse into hedonism, ii 500, *seqq*
— classification of springs of action, ii 510, 511.
— defective account of personal agency, ii. 512, 513.
— interpretation of superstition, ii. 499, 500.
— reconciliation of self-love and social, ii. 502, 503.
— variable report of the essence of virtue, ii. 497, 498.
Sidgwick, Henry, attests conscious power of alternative, ii. 40.
— deems Free-will question morally neutral, ii. 42, 43.
— on the 'Moral motives,' ii. 280, 281.
— pronounces 'Right' an idea 'unique and unanalysable,' ii. 47.

INDEX.

Sidgwick, Henry, rejects the inward implication of the word 'Conscience,' ii. 54–58.
— seeks a *via media* in regard to intuition, ii. 277, 278.
— treats malevolent affections as alone absolutely bad, ii. 188.
— treats springs of action as only relatively better and worse, ii 188.
Sidgwick's claim for rational benevolence, ii. 298, 299
— objections to the criterion of motives, ii. 277–297.
Sigwart, Dr. Christoph, on 'the mind's eternal part' (Spinoza), i. 373.
Simon, Richard, teacher of Malebranche, i. 160.
Simplicity, abstract and concrete, vary inversely as each other, i. 477, 478.
Simplicius' comment on Plato's 'ideal numbers,' i. 56.
Slavery, attends on Polytheism (Comte), i. 447.
— discouraged by Monotheism, i. 449.
Smith, Adam, a pupil and admirer of Hutcheson, ii 521. 523.
— develops moral sentiment from 'sympathy,' ii. 184, 185
— says that we judge others first, ii. 27.
Social consensus, advances from State to Church, ii. 405, 406.
— how evolved, ii. 401–404.
Sociology, method of, inverts that of the prior sciences (Comte), i. 435–437.
Socrates, dictum of, interpreted, that 'virtue may be taught,' i. 73, 74.
— on pleasure conferred *gratis*, ii. 168.
Somnambulism and instinct compared, ii 138–140.
Soul, Plato's factors of the, i. 69–73.
— transmigration of, in Plato, i. 64 93, 94. 104–108.
— whether Spinoza's Ethics affirm its immortality, i. 373–385.

Space and Time, conditions, no properties, of things, i. 472–474
— idea of, why fruitful of deduction, i. 282.
— intuition, Spencer's evolution of, ii. 386–389.
Spencer, Herbert, concentrates approval on motive, ii. 24.
— evolves the moral from the unmoral, ii. 3.
— foresees 'Sense of Duty' lost in complete 'moralisation,' ii. 93–98, *Appendix*.
— letters from and to, ii *Appendix*.
— makes 'choice' an oscillation between successive states, ii 37, 38.
— resolves 'Self' into an aggregate of feelings, &c., ii. 39.
— says that we judge others first, ii 27, 28.
Spencer's account of Obligation, ii. 384.
— evolution of intuitions, especially ' Space,' ii. 374–376. 386–389.
— — of morals, ii. 373–376. 390.
— interpretation of asceticism, ii 380, 381.
Spinoza, Benedict, altered estimate of, i. 120, 121.
— condemned, unnamed, by Malebranche, i. 223–225.
— declines Professorship at Heidelberg, i 270
— excommunication of, i. 256–259.
— how far Cartesian, i. 259. 261. 264–266.
— in relation to Malebranche, i. 159, 160.
— in the French camp, i. 274–276.
— parentage of, and teachers, i. 250–252.
— reduces action to understanding, i. 340, 341. 347, 348.
— relations of, with Van den Ende, i. 254–256. 259.
— sources of knowledge about, old and new, i. 248–250.
Spinoza's account of Imagination and Memory, i. 326–3..

Temples enter with Polytheism (Comte), i. 446.
Temporal power separates from spiritual under Monotheism (Comte), i. 448.
Temptation, limit of allowance for, ii. 81.
— measure of, determined, ii. 81–83.
Theism of J. H. Fichte, Chalybæus, and Ulrici, i. 22
Theology, as analysed religion, ii. 180.
Thomasius, Jacob, Leipzig opponent of Spinoza's 'Theol.-Pol. Treatise,' i. 271.
Time and Space, conditions, not properties, of things, i. 472–474.
Transference, law of, ii. 183, 184. 316, 317.
Transmigration of souls, in Plato, i. 64. 93, 94. 104-108.
Trendelenburg, Adolf, classes philosophical systems, i 388, 389.
— on Spinoza's ethical conceptions, i. 372.
Truth and Right, Descartes treats as Divine inventions, i. 148, 149.
Tschirnhausen, Freiherr Ehrenfried Walther von, Spinoza's correspondent, i. 268-270. 272. 284, 285.
Tyndall's, Professor J., potentialities of Matter, ii. 399.

UGLINESS, pronounced negative by Hutcheson, ii 532, 533.
Ulrici, Theism of, i. 22.
Understanding and Will, how related in Descartes, i. 147, 148.
— — in Malebranche, i. 165.
— ideas of the, self-verifying (Spinoza), i. 336.
— in Malebranche, not a 'mode' of mind, i. 167, 168.
— in Spinoza, i. 338. 340, 341.
Universalia *ante res* and *in rebus*, i. 23.
'Univocal' and 'æquivocal,' true meaning of, i. 134, *note*.
Utility, principle of, not pledged to hedonism, ii. 304.

Utility, valid place of, as a test of conduct, ii. 275, 276. 300, 301.

VACUUM denied by Descartes, i. 139.
Van Blyenbergh, Wilhelm, Leyden opponent of Spinoza's 'Theol.-Pol. Treatise,' i. 271.
Van den Hoof's, Jacques, anonymous book on the State, i. 263.
Van der Linde, Dr. A, on 'the mind's eternal part' (Spinoza), i 373.
Van Velthuysen, Lambert, critic of Spinoza's 'Theol.-Pol. Treatise,' i. 271.
Van Vloten, J., editor of Supplement to Spinoza, and coeditor of complete Works, i. 249, 250, *note*.
Van Vries, Simon, devoted to Spinoza, i. 260, 261.
Vanity, distinguished from pride, ii. 238.
Veracity, Divine, use made of, by Descartes, i. 133. 149, 150; ii. 237, 238.
— obligation of, in its source and scope, ii. 255-265.
Vindictiveness, the nursing of resentment, ii. 174, 175.
'Virtue can be taught,' meaning of, i. 73, 74.
— 'intuitive,' is 'intellectual love of God' (Spinoza), i. 354-364.
— not constituted by assent, ii. 454. 473.
— Platonic notion of, i. 69.
— 'rational,' is 'Fortitudo,' i. e. 'Animositas' and 'Generositas' (Spinoza), i. 351-354.
— Shaftesbury's relation of, to Merit, ii. 495-497.
Voetius, Gisbert, denounces Descartes' doctrine, i. 154.
Volition involves choice between co-present possibilities, ii 37-41.
— sole object of moral judgment, ii. 34-37.
— ('Voluntas'), variable meaning of in Spinoza, i. 340, *note*.

INDEX.

Spinoza's 'attributes,' disparate, i. 306.
— — parallelism of, untenable, i. 306-310. 324.
— confused use of the word 'Cause,' i. 286-288.
— correspondence with Huyghens and Tschirnhausen, i. 267-270. 272. 301
— — with Oldenburg, i. 263. 271-273.
— 'De Intellectus emendatione,' i. 265.
— disinterestedness, i. 260, 261.
— doctrine of 'the mind's eternal part,' i. 358, 359. 373-385.
— 'eternal modes,' i. 313-315.
— 'Ethica,' i. 265.
— finites, and their cause, i. 315-317.
— 'Fortitudo,' i. 351-354.
— fundamental definitions considered, i. 296-305
— 'Idea ideæ,' i. 323, 324.
— intellectual love of God, i. 354-364.
— 'Intuitus' explained, i. 331-335.
— last hours, i. 276, 277.
— law of 'Conatus,' i. 338, 339 343.
— meaning of 'freedom,' i. 346, 347. 365. 370-372.
— 'Political Treatise,' i. 267.
— 'Ratio' and 'Notiones communes,' i. 328-331.
— relations with Leibniz, i. 268.
— — with the brothers De Witt, i 274, 275.
— 'Short Treatise on God,' &c., i. 261, 262.
— 'Theologico-Political Treatise,' i. 264. 266. 270-272.
— theory, factors and growth of, i 288-293.
Stallbaum's Gottfried, interpretation of Plato's 'Ideas,' i. 34.
State, Plato's, homologous with the universe and the soul, i. 77. 79.
Static and Dynamic laws distinguished (Comte), i 435.

Stephen, Leslie, admits a heirarchy of springs of action, ii. 49.
— asserts commensurability of feelings, ii. 327, 328.
— concentrates approval on the inner springs of action, ii. 24.
— criticises the doctrine of Conscience, ii. 406-419
— criticism of, 'on 'Faculties,' ii. 11-13.
— evolves the moral from the unmoral, ii 3.
— says that we judge others first, ii. 28.
— settles the hierarchy of motive springs by 'reason,' not by 'psychology,' ii. 49-53.
Stewart, Dugald, blames Paulus for editing Spinoza, i. 120.
— classifies the springs of action, ii. 134, 135. 165.
Stoupe, Colonel, conveys to Spinoza an invitation to the French camp, i. 274.
'Subjective '-' Objective,' as used by Positivists, i. 437, *note*.
'Substance,' cannot unify disparate attributes, i. 306.
— change in Spinoza's meaning of, i. 293, 294.
— idea of, not fruitful, like that of Space, i. 283-285
— meaning of, in Descartes, i. 134, 135.
— 'Nature,' ' God,' how far interchangeable in Spinoza, i. 293-296.
Superstition, Shaftesbury's estimate of, ii. 499, 500.
Surprise, Brown's account of, considered, ii 153, 154.
Suspiciousness, the fascination of fear, ii. 175.
Sweden, Christina, Queen of, draws Descartes to Stockholm, i 156.
Sympathy, law of, ii. 184, 185.
Synge, Dr. (and Bishop), befriends Hutcheson, ii. 517.

TASTE, how related to imagination, ii. 178, 179.

WARBURTON, Bishop, on Cudworth's critics, ii. 432, 433.
Whately, Archbishop, calls Aristotle a Nominalist, i. 119.
— takes 'univocal' and 'æquivocal' as predicates of *words*, i 134, *note*.
Whiston's, William, relations with Clarke, ii. 460–462.
Will and Intellect, denied to God by Spinoza, i. 312. 390.
— how related, according to Descartes, i. 147, 148.
— — to Malebranche, i. 165.
— the power of affirming and denying (Spinoza), i. 340, *note*.
— the source of the true and right (Descartes), i. 148, 149.

Will ('Voluntas'), variable meaning of, in Spinoza, i. 340, *note*.
— *See* 'Volition.'
Wonder, function of, ii. 152.
— *See* ' Plato ' and ' Aristotle.'
— Malebranche's estimate of, i. 194–197.
— relation of, to surprise, ii. 152–154.
Worth, moral, how revealed in its gradations, i. 46–48.

ZELLER'S (Edouard) interpretation of Plato's ' Ideas,' i. 40–47.
Zeno, of Elea, doctrine of, i. 9.

THE END.

www.ingramcontent.com/pod-product-compliance
Lightning Source LLC
Chambersburg PA
CBHW021229300426
44111CB00007B/479